Paul Robeson

Paul Robeson

The Years of Promise and Achievement

SHEILA TULLY BOYLE & ANDREW BUNIE

University of Massachusetts Press : Amherst

Copyright © 2001
by Sheila Tully Boyle and Andrew Bunie
All rights reserved
Printed in the United States of America
LC 2001017155
ISBN 1-55849-149-X
Set in Carter Cone Galliard by Keystone Typesetting, Inc.
Designed by Richard Hendel
Printed and bound by Sheridan Books, Inc.
Library of Congress Cataloging-in-Publication Data
Boyle, Sheila Tully, 1947–
Paul Robeson : the years of promise and achievement /
Sheila Tully Boyle and Andrew Buni.
p. cm.
Includes bibliographical references and index.
ISBN 1-55849-149-X (alk. paper)
1. Robeson, Paul, 1898–1976. 2. Robeson, Paul, 1898–
1976 — Childhood and youth. 3. African Americans —
Biography. 4. Singers — United States — Biography.
5. Actors — United States — Biography. 6. Political activists —
United States — Biography. I. Buni, Andrew. II. Title.
E185.97.R63 B69 2001
782'.0092 — dc21
[B]   2001017155
British Library Cataloguing in Publication data are available.
This book is published with the support and cooperation of
the University of Massachusetts Boston.

Title page: Paul Robeson, c. 1940 (detail). Photo by Alfredo
Valente. (Courtesy of the National Portrait Gallery,
Smithsonian Institution.)

CONTENTS

ACKNOWLEDGMENTS

In addition to the people cited in the notes — especially the friends, relatives, and acquaintances of Robeson's who agreed to be interviewed or who recounted their stories and firsthand remembrances by letter, as well as the owners of privately held manuscripts who shared them with us and, in some cases, gave the material to us — we are deeply grateful to the people mentioned below. What they gave to us in love, help, and support made this book possible.

Sheila Boyle thanks . . . my mother, Anna, and my father, Leo, a Marine and veteran of World War II whose model of tenacity in the face of adversity much more challenging than anything I have ever faced continues to inspire me; Virginia, for encouraging me to write; Eileen, Maryanne, Tom, Peg, and Jim, who in this, as in all things, supported me and were there to help; Jane, for her years of support and for generously sharing her insights with me; Pat, for her friendship and an enthusiasm that never flagged; Anne, Martha, and Kathleen Fraser; Mary Barry, Kathy Flynn, and Kay Walsh; my friends and writing colleagues Frankie Wright and Tammy Zambo; Joanne Wycoff and Chris Kane, whose advice in the early stages of this manuscript proved invaluable; Esme E. Bahan and Joellen Elbashir of the Moorland-Spingarn Library, Howard University; and my husband, Tom, who listened and advised through countless revisions and whose caring made the hardest parts of the project endurable.

Andrew Bunie thanks . . . Ma and Pa, Ukranian immigrants who could neither read nor write in any language but gave it their all as laborers; Mary, Frank, Katie, John, Dottie, and Hazel, who worked to give me the chance they didn't get; the children who became adults as they waited for this book to see the light of day: Jack, Cathi, Jim, and Nick; Pat Sullivan, who was there from the beginning; Tom Knock, for his digging at the Library of Congress and for being a friend; Robert Macieski, a friend, researcher, and scholar who knows where it's at; Joyce Buni; Melinda Ponder; and Charles Blockson of Temple University, who in times of despair urged me on with the maxim, "Put both hands on the plow and hang on."

We both thank the University of Massachusetts Press, in particular Barbara Palmer and Pam Wilkinson, for their thoughtful and insightful edits, and Paul Wright, for his support and willingness to see through to the end a project that took much longer to complete than any of us had anticipated.

S. T. B. and A. B.

Paul Robeson

I

Princeton

1898-1907

In the early summer of 1947 Paul Robeson's friend Miki Fisher and her husband, Saul, invited Robeson to their summer home in Westport, Connecticut, for an informal reception to follow a performance at a local benefit concert. "Westport was a small and quiet town," Miki Fisher remembered, "populated largely by artists and writers. Some lived there year round; others rented places to get away from the hot city. Saul and I and our two-month-old daughter, Rachel, spent the summer there in an old rack-and-ruin 200-year-old farmhouse located in a rural section of town. The friends we invited were all politically liberal, hardly the Madison Avenue set, and we hoped the evening would be a pleasant and relaxing interlude for Paul. As it turned out, he did not sing well (he had a hard time staying on pitch), and from the moment he arrived at the house he was out of sorts. Paul — usually so outgoing and warm — did little even to feign sociability at the party. Later that night, after we had all gone to sleep, we heard a loud crash from his room. His bed, something left over from colonial times, had collapsed — with Paul in it. Under ordinary circumstances Paul would have taken the mishap in stride and probably had a good laugh over it, but not that night. He was annoyed about the whole thing and let us know it. This was not the Paul I knew."[1]

Professionally, Robeson was at his apex. His historic, record-breaking 1943 Broadway run of *Othello* and the two-year nationwide tour of the play that followed had secured him a position rivaled by few white performers and unheard of among American blacks. Nor did the pace slacken over the next few years. Robeson's 1946 and 1947 concert tours were equally spectacular. Never had he been more enthusiastically received. Personally, however, Robeson was angry and unsettled. Lawrence Brown, Robeson's accompanist for over twenty years, was disturbed by the change. "It's ironic that at the peak of his career, the moment when I think he reached his zenith, he was more difficult to work with than during all the years before. He was in a terrible mood. He constantly felt he could not sing another concert."[2]

The drift away from liberal politics that followed the end of World War II upset Robeson. He had expected peace to usher in a period of racial and economic justice at home and goodwill abroad. It did not. Black veterans were welcomed home by riots and racial violence. Labor unrest plagued the fledgling Truman administration. And hostility between the United States and the Soviet Union thickened by the day. The fear that reactionary forces would soon overtake the country preyed on Robeson. Causes that in the past concerned him now obsessed him, and concert-going audiences began to hear less of Robeson singing and more of Robeson crusading. In the beginning they listened patiently: it was a small price to pay to hear that magnificent voice. But, as the cold war intensified, Robeson's pro-Russian stance grew apace, and criticism of him mounted.

In early April 1947, the unthinkable happened. The City Council of Peoria, Illinois, banned Robeson from performing, canceling a concert scheduled six months earlier. Peoria's mayor, supporting the council, accused Robeson of "coming here for a fight" and denied him use of the city hall for a reception that was to have followed the concert.[3] It was a staggering blow; Robeson found it difficult to believe that America would turn against him. But Peoria was just the beginning. At the Fishers' house, weeks later, he was still stunned and angry.

Robeson did not want to chat at the Fishers' gathering any more than he wanted to sing "pretty songs" for audiences unwilling to listen to his political message. The little conversing he did that evening was all about politics, and the more he talked the angrier he became. To one group he bitterly recalled his experiences entertaining for the USO in Germany. It was bad enough that the troops were segregated, but the talk he heard among white officers had appalled him. "We have the bomb," they boasted. "Let's go on to Russia and finish the job."[4]

Moving away from the guests, Robeson sought out Saul Fisher, a psychiatrist, at the time working on Bellevue Hospital's psychiatric ward. Initially Fisher was puzzled as to why Paul would want to talk with him:

I didn't know him well and yet he sought me out. It was not a matter of courtesy. He was deeply troubled about something. We talked for a long time, well after all the guests had left. My sense was that he was frightened about what he was feeling and thought that because of my work I would understand and could perhaps advise him.

He talked a great deal about Africa and told me a story about a West African chieftain who lost face in the community and was deeply humiliated.

For three days the chieftain refused to eat or sleep. Finally, he collapsed and died. The story was very important to Paul, and he told it with great feeling. He talked psychology with me, told me about his own problems: anger he found difficult to control, rage over a lifetime of feeling and being treated as inferior. Paul was a very proud person and unable to tolerate humiliation. He would either react with rage or repress it and turn it inward. Again and again he returned to the story; it had a very personal meaning for him. It reminded him, I think, of a kind of pain he had experienced, a pain so intense he felt it could kill him.[5]

For Robeson the African chieftain's story bespoke a terrifying truth. Respectability, status, and achievement could indeed come to nothing. Professionally, Robeson was at his height. But he had already glimpsed the abyss; he had already experienced the first shudders of the earth slipping out from under him. The story conjured up not only disturbing premonitions but also a feeling of déjà vu. Robeson had himself tasted humiliation and, growing up, had seen it ravage the person he cared most about in the world: his father, William Drew Robeson. Watching his father, literally breathing in William Drew Robeson's shame over losing a position he had worked a lifetime to earn, Paul learned lessons he would remember all his life.

William Drew Robeson was born a slave in 1845 in Martin County, North Carolina. As is true for most slaves, there are no records of his birth; presumably he and his siblings took as their own the name of their slave master.[6] Like so many others who lived through slavery, William Robeson almost never talked about the experience. Whether his silence was due to shame, an unwillingness to bring up a painful past, or natural reticence is not known, but as a result we know little about this crucial and formative period in Paul's father's life.[7]

William's parents, Benjamin and Sabra, were born and died slaves in Martin County. A stained-glass window with the inscription "IN LOVING REMEMBRANCE OF SABRA ROBESON" in the Witherspoon Street Church in Princeton, New Jersey, where William Robeson would later serve as pastor attests to the strong bond between William and his mother.[8] About William's father little is known except his first name, Benjamin. Quite possibly, William knew little more himself, as the slave system tended to make Negro families matriarchal: the slave cabin was usually described as the mother's house; children were considered as belonging to the mother and referred to as such in conversation and on plantation records; owners would often go to great lengths to keep children and their mothers together but thought little of separating a man from his wife and children.[9] William's father may have lived on another plantation; he may have died or been sold into the cotton kingdom as many were during the 1830s, 1840s, and 1850s; or he may have gone from wife to wife, a not uncommon practice because slaves married only with the consent of their masters and their marriages were not recognized legally.

It is likely that William spent his youth working the tobacco fields of one of North Carolina's many small farms. Historically, North Carolina never developed the large plantation systems of neighboring states, primarily because its rugged coastline, lack of good harbors, and poor roads left it dependent on Virginia's and South Carolina's overland trade and ports to move both its slaves and other "commodities."[10] Martin County, where William grew up, had only one large slave owner (Henry Williams of Williamstown, who owned ninety-four slaves); most slaveholders in the area kept only a small number of slaves each.[11]

Whether William learned to read as a slave is not known. Before 1830, slave codes in North Carolina, as well as in many other southern states, were remarkably liberal, but by 1845, the year William Robeson was born, the pre-1830 abolitionist liberality in the state had ended. Nat Turner's 1831 rebellion, in particular, left North Carolina's numerically small but politically powerful slave owners jittery, even those who believed they treated their slaves well.[12] North Carolina's legislature, like that of neighboring states, responded to slave owners' fears by tightening its slave codes, and in 1835 the state took back the right to vote from its free black population (30,463 in 1860, a number exceeded in the South only by Virginia).[13] Even with these added restrictions, however, William may have learned to read, perhaps as part of mastering a trade or through the efforts of local church groups who, to the extent they were able, aided in the education of slaves.

According to family lore, in 1860 at the age of fifteen, William escaped and made his way north.[14] William may have feared that his master was about to sell him "down the river" and into the cotton kingdom in the Deep South.[15] He was, after all, a valuable commodity: young and healthy, with years of productivity potentially ahead of him. He may have sensed the coming conflagration (John Brown's raid on Harpers Ferry, an event that terrified the South and captivated the abolitionist imagination of the North, had occurred only a year before on October 16, 1859) and decided it was time to move. Or, like so many others who attempted escape, William may simply have chosen to shoulder the risk of capture and punishment rather than endure life as a slave any longer.

Whatever his motivation, escape — a venture that required intelligence, courage, resourcefulness, and no small amount of good luck — was not a decision made lightly. Charles Blockson, an authority on the Underground Railroad whose own family had escaped slavery, reasoned that William did not take the overland route north into the Dismal Swamp area of North Carolina and

Virginia.[16] Others had fled to the Dismal Swamp, but because the roads were so bad, few of these escaped slaves ever made their way farther north.[17] Given Martin County's location in northeastern North Carolina and on the banks of the Roanoke River, Blockson conjectured that William took the water route down the Roanoke River, perhaps from Martinsville, out to the bay, then northward to Virginia and the Eastern Shore of Maryland. Aided by black and white agents along the way, with stopovers in the Underground Railroad system, William then made his way up the coast to Philadelphia.[18] If he had been able to forge the proper documents, he may have tried to pass himself off as a free black. It is unlikely, however, that he received assistance from southern free blacks in the area because they seldom took an active role in the Underground Railroad from fear of the severe reprisals that awaited them should they be caught.[19]

Family lore maintains that Harriet Tubman assisted William, and this may well have been the case. Born in Dorchester County, Maryland, Tubman knew the Chesapeake Bay area near Cambridge on the Eastern Shore well. She herself had escaped in 1849 and made her way to Philadelphia. In 1850 she returned to Baltimore and guided her sister and two children to freedom, in 1851 her brother and his family, and a year later another brother. She was known to have made some nineteen trips into Maryland, bringing out from thirty to sixty slaves each trip, working with antislavery persons as she journeyed through Maryland into Delaware, through the towns of Camden, Dover, Odessa, and into Wilmington where her close friend Thomas Garrett would be waiting for her with food and funds, and then to Chester County, Pennsylvania, and into Philadelphia where she was assisted by the Negro leader, William Still.[20]

After managing a successful escape, William Robeson reportedly returned to Martin County at least twice via the Underground Railroad to see his mother. Although Robeson said in interviews that his father served in the Union army, this is unlikely because blacks were not allowed to enlist until 1863. If William served in any capacity, it was probably as a laborer digging trenches.[21] With Emancipation William found himself again just north of the Mason-Dixon line in the pastoral farm area of Chester, Pennsylvania, a locale heavily populated by Quakers and Scotch-Irish Presbyterians and one of the great centers of the prewar Underground Railroad.

William Robeson wanted an education, but newly freed slaves faced two formidable obstacles on this road to self-improvement: most had limited or no previous schooling, and virtually all white educational institutions barred Negroes from admission. Nevertheless, William set his sights on the best of what was available to blacks at the time: Chester County's Lincoln University, the oldest institution of higher learning for blacks in America. In 1866 William began what would be ten years of education at Lincoln, years that would profoundly affect his life. Earning his fees by working on a nearby farm, he completed the three-year preparatory program (grammar, arithmetic, geography, and Latin — equivalent to a basic high school education) in 1869, earned his baccalaureate in 1873, and graduated from Lincoln Seminary an ordained Presbyterian minister in 1876.[22]

Lincoln (originally named Ashmun Institute) was established in 1853 by a white Presbyterian minister and graduate of Princeton's Theological Seminary, James Miller Dickey, to train the elect of black descent for missionary work in Africa.[23] From its inception the college, nestled in the sultry southeastern tip of Pennsylvania and bordering the slave state of Delaware, was intended to be the work of white men for Negroes.[24] Colloquially known through much of its early history as "black Princeton," Lincoln's philosophy reflected the period's most conservative Presbyterian thought.[25] Founded by colonizationists, men who opposed both slavery and abolition and advocated African colonization as the best solution to the vexing problem, it could hardly be otherwise.

Lincoln's white faculty and administration — most, like Dickey, trained in Presbyterian doctrine at Princeton — saw themselves as instruments in a divine plan, called by God to share their gifts and learning with the "less-endowed" black race.[26] Before the Civil War only a small number of students, mostly free blacks from the Philadelphia area, attended the school. Following the war, however, Lincoln was besieged by a vastly increased population of freedmen.[27] Responding to the needs of this new student body, the school relaxed its curriculum, particularly in the preparatory school, but its basic philosophy regarding the education of blacks remained unchanged.

From the moment they arrived at Lincoln, new students were impressed with their special status as God's chosen. A white Presbyterian concept of election permeated virtually all aspects of life at the college. With the Bible the textbook throughout the entire course of study, students maintained a strict regimen of course work and religious observation seven days a week. Midmorning prayers, vespers, and evening services were interrupted only by study and, one of the few permissible forms of relaxation, walking. Lincoln's curriculum included courses in arithmetic, history, and the sciences but placed primary emphasis on theology — church history, moral philosophy, and homiletics — and the classics, with four years of Greek and Latin a requirement.[28] School rules demanded formal attire, and although William, like others, procured his frock coat from barrels of cast-off garments donated by charitable organizations, it was a frock coat he wore nonetheless. Lincoln's "elect" did not sing black spirituals, perhaps because they had never been sung in the Princeton Seminary but more probably because this great black folk art was looked on as reminiscent of the illiterate slave and, as such, out of place at Lincoln. Educational establishments like

Hampton and Tuskegee could train their students in practical skills — manual and industrial arts — but blacks attending Lincoln were to compose "an intellectual elite, a divinely ordained and select upper class, through whom would be exercised . . . the saving grace of God's redemption."[29]

No one more completely embodied the white Presbyterian spirit of the college than Isaac Norton Rendall, president of Lincoln University from 1865 to 1905. Like most of the school's faculty, Rendall had been trained in classical antiquity and Christian teachings at Princeton's Theological Seminary. Affectionately dubbed "Pap," this benevolent autocrat was indeed the school's white patriarch. Six feet tall and handsome, bedecked in his Prince Albert coat and occasionally a silk hat, Rendall carried himself regally and inspired his black protégés to do the same. He believed that every student should own three articles, a Bible, an English dictionary, and spectacles, and saw to it that each was provided them. Those who arrived with curious surnames he did not hesitate to rechristen with a new or altered name. His practice of addressing black students as "Sir" and "Mister" and insisting they enter the president's quarters from the front rather than the back door, confounded many a new arrival. Whatever they may have been before, at Lincoln they were men, chosen by God for a special mission.[30]

Primarily it was paternalism, a Calvinist form of reparation made by "superior" white men to their "less-endowed" black students, that motivated and inspired Lincoln's faculty and administration. When, for example, in 1873, the year of William's graduation, a group of radical black students (most the sons of Philadelphia's black aristocracy) petitioned the school's administration to admit qualified blacks to Lincoln's all-white faculty, President Rendall adamantly opposed the idea, and Dickey, as president of the Board of Trustees, supported him. "It is no fault of yours that you are far back in education," Dickey told the petitioning delegation. "You have had no opportunity . . . you desire the best in instructors. Those who are permeated through and through with 1000 years of advantages and whose very presence with you and daily intercourse . . . will bring you up to their level."[31] And, as Lincoln's administration spelled out in both word and deed, "the best instructors" were invariably white.

Philadelphia's longtime free black families — the Bustills, the Fortens, the Mossells — historically formed the black arm of the abolitionist movement in Philadelphia, and their sons were among Lincoln's earliest graduates.[32] They had strong ties to the school and saw it as their duty to protest Lincoln's exclusionary staffing practices. In 1886 these radical blacks, many active and outspoken members of the school's newly organized alumni, again formally presented their case to the Board of Trustees. Yet another petition demanding the hiring of black faculty was sent in 1888, followed by a final effort in 1893.

Lincoln's administration, however, refused to budge, thus forcing many of these families to withdraw their financial and moral support and fight for their ideals elsewhere.[33]

There is no evidence that William Robeson was among those protesting. Like other newly freed blacks, most of whom had come to Lincoln and its imposing brick buildings from the slave cabins of the South, humble farmhouses, or the tents and barracks of the late Civil War, William was just beginning to fight for the respectability Philadelphia's elite black families had enjoyed for generations. In this context, he would hardly be inclined to question, let alone criticize, Lincoln's helping hand. Indeed, a decade later when the controversy was at its height, northern radicals would speak of the school's southern "loyalists" with undisguised disdain (those "weak-kneed dependent fellow[s]" who have "been so long under the fostering care of some strong arm" that they have "lost all powers of assertion").[34] Lincoln's administration sensed this gap in political sensibilities and in 1883 announced a new admissions policy that would favor candidates from the South and West over those from the Northeast, a measure adopted in part because the educational needs of southern blacks were so pronounced but equally because experience had proven southern-bred blacks more amenable to Lincoln's philosophy than their northern counterparts.[35]

Lincoln commencement services, directed by the school's financial agent, the Reverend Eugene Webb, had over the years become elaborate and gala events designed to promote the school, showcase its accomplishments, and assure benefactors their money was being well spent.[36] The ceremony in 1873, the year of William's graduation, drew as many as 2,500 people — "the best class of white people in the neighborhood" — white notables and political officials and Philadelphia's most prominent black families, as well as local blacks from miles around. From early in the morning until noon, trains from New York, Baltimore, and Philadelphia brought dignitaries, benefactors, and relatives to Chester to join the Lincoln festivities. Following an opening procession headed by the colored band of Oxford, the formal ceremonies began. In a program that included a long line of orations (ten of the eighteen graduates spoke) and offered students ample opportunity to demonstrate their declamatory skills, former slaves represented themselves as eloquently as the sons of Philadelphia's finest black families.[37]

The training in voice and public speaking that William received at Lincoln had enhanced his considerable native gifts (Paul would describe his father's speaking voice as the "greatest" he had ever heard, a "deep sonorous basso, richly melodic and refined"), and the school officially acknowledged his talents by selecting William to deliver the *belles lettres* address.[38] In keeping with Lincoln's basic philosophy, it was a white northern style of speaking William had mastered and would now display. Just as spirituals had no place at Lincoln, so the school shunned southern black speech and saw to it that faculty taught students to speak "correctly." Although there is no copy of William's oration, library records indicate he borrowed a total of twenty-two literary works from Lincoln's predominantly theological library, perhaps in preparation for the event or possibly because he was an avid reader. Among these were six Dickens novels, which, one can conjecture, addressed (from a white perspective) William's own dreams of triumph over adversity.[39]

Immediately following the student presentations, James Miller Dickey took the podium and introduced two visiting missionaries who had brought with them to the ceremony ten native boys from West Africa.[40] Dickey acknowledged the young Africans but added he was loath to introduce them in their "rude state."[41] Isaac Rendall, however, felt no such compunction, and scarcely had Dickey finished his remarks when the ten West Africans, as Rendall had instructed them, came marching across the stage. This demonstration of contrasts — a "before and after" exhibition — proved quite effective. As one reporter noted, "They don't look very bright now, but a few years of culture doubtless will make a vast improvement. The faculty of Lincoln will have a fine opportunity in manifesting their skill in the training of these genuine sons of Africa." (A quarter century later Booker T. Washington would express much the same sentiments concerning Africa. At Tuskegee, Washington encouraged carefully selected graduates to work for colonial developers in Nigeria, the Belgian Congo, and the Sudan. Three such graduates were sent by the American capitalist Leigh Hunt to the Sudan to begin the organizing needed to "prepare the way for a larger colony of American blacks." Before the students left, Washington warned them that "a great many persons going to a warm climate, go to ruin from a moral standpoint" and urged them not to succumb, as it would "do yourself, the school and the race the greatest injustice.")[42]

One can only speculate how this exhibition affected William. Certainly, it reinforced the popular perception of Africans as savages in need of the civilizing influence of Christianity. If such blatant paternalism embarrassed William, it did not show. If anything, his experiences at Lincoln had taught William to equate respectability with distance from the slave experience and, by implication, from Africa. It was a lesson that upper-class blacks as well as the dominant white culture reinforced. To the extent that Lincoln's transformation succeeded, there was virtually nothing save color linking him and his classmates with the "uncivilized" natives displayed on stage.[43]

William Robeson left Lincoln armed with a university degree from a theological seminary, a rarity among black preachers and itself enough of an achievement. The college had also given Robeson a blueprint for achieving that all-important goal of respectability, and William would rigidly adhere to the Lincoln model for most of his life. Decades after completing his studies and even into old age, William Robeson bore witness to his Lincoln training: his head held high, his carriage poised and dignified, his attire the Lincoln frock coat. In exchange for this devotion, William enjoyed in his lifetime a level of achievement and status that under other circumstances might well have taken generations to effect.

While still at Lincoln, William Robeson fell in love with Maria Louisa Bustill, the daughter of one of Philadelphia's most prominent black families. Maria often came to Lincoln to visit her uncle Joseph Bustill, who ran a boardinghouse in the town, and it is likely that on one of these trips she met William Robeson. It is also possible that because the Bustills were active in the abolitionist cause and the Underground Railroad, William may have first met Maria Louisa years earlier, in Chester or Philadelphia, before the outbreak of the Civil War.

Maria Louisa Bustill had all the attributes of class and culture William lacked: lineage, affluence, social status, and a family tradition of political activism and community service. In Philadelphia there were scarcely more than a dozen black families with educational and financial resources comparable to those of the Bustills.[44] They were at the center of Philadelphia's black elite, a tiny group of fair-complexioned, longtime free blacks who claimed a special status by virtue of their family history, education, wealth, and culture. "Old Philadelphians," as they were called, like other similarly situated families in cities throughout the country, outwardly more resembled the "better class of whites" than the rest of the black population: generally they lived in large, well-appointed homes, employed servants, and were well educated and culturally sophisticated.[45] The Bustills boasted an additional distinction that wealthier families, like the Fortens, could not rival: their family history. Measuring age by continuous genealogical records dating back to the first treaty made by William Penn with the Lenni-Lenape Indians, the Bustills claimed themselves the oldest Negro family in the United States.[46]

Philadelphia's black aristocracy inherited a long tradition of leadership from forebears active in educational and religious affairs and in abolitionist, civil rights, and moral reform movements. Cyrus Bustill, Maria Louisa's great-grandfather, was born in Burlington, New Jersey, on February 2, 1732. Having himself experienced slavery (he was sold, inherited as part of an estate, and sold again before being purchased by the Quaker Thomas Pryor Jr., who freed him after seven years of service), Cyrus Bustill succeeded despite the crippling obstacles facing free blacks of his day.[47] After learning the baking trade from his Quaker master, he established his own baking business in New Jersey. He served in the Revolution (baking for soldiers) and at its conclusion received from the hand of George Washington himself a silver piece for his efforts. After the war,

Bustill moved to Philadelphia where his baking business prospered, and along with a handful of other enterprising blacks — James Forten, Absalom Jones, J. M. Douglas, and William Douglas — provided Philadelphia's growing black community something it sorely lacked: sound leadership buttressed by economic substance.[48]

Cyrus Bustill's commitment to community and civic service complemented his business acumen, making him a moral as well as financial community leader. At a young age he became "convinced of the rectitude of [the] Friends' principles" and converted to the Quaker religion. Vowing he "would not perpetuate a race of slaves," he refused to marry until late in life and then chose as his wife a woman of Indian descent, Elizabeth Morely.[49] Acting in concert with the city's most progressive Quakers, Bustill, along with a few other pioneering blacks, helped lay the intellectual framework for the ideas that would later make Philadelphia the center of radical egalitarian thought in America. As a member of several of Philadelphia's benevolent societies and a founder of the African Free Society (1787), Cyrus Bustill labored for the intellectual, social, and moral progress of Philadelphia Negroes. After retiring from business he built a house at Third and Green Streets, where he opened a school. When he died in 1806 the white community extended an uncommon gesture of respect by detailing his life story in the white newspaper. The Society of Friends conducted his burial services.

The Bustill crusading spirit continued with Cyrus's son and Maria Louisa's grandfather, David Bustill, a plasterer by trade, who noted in his diary that God had called him to fight the seizure of runaway slaves. Joseph Cassey Bustill, Maria Louisa's uncle and the youngest of David Bustill's nine children, at the age of seventeen became one of the city's youngest members of the Underground Railroad. An accomplished writer and speaker, he served as secretary of the Philadelphia branch of the state's Equal Rights League, established to gain for blacks the right to vote, and displayed on the wall of his Philadelphia home the banner presented him by the league for his long years of service crusading for black suffrage.[50]

Maria Louisa, born in Philadelphia on November 8, 1853, the eldest daughter of Charles H. Bustill (an active member of the Philadelphia Underground Railroad and Vigilance Committee) and Emily Robinson Bustill, reaped the benefits of her family's economic status and cultural and social prominence. Foremost among these was education. With her sister Gertrude, Maria Louisa attended the Institute for Colored Youth where she was educated by her cousin, Sarah Mapps Douglass, an abolitionist and lifelong friend of Angelina and Sarah Grimké, and upon completing her studies taught at the (all-black) Robert Vaux School in Philadelphia.[51] Founded shortly before the Civil War, Philadelphia's

Institute for Colored Youth (ICY) was unique in many respects. Theoretically managed by a board of white Quakers, the high school was in effect run by its black principal and teachers. Entrance exams were rigorous, the curriculum demanding, and the school's staff exceptional. No other school in the country sent as many black teachers south in the years following the Civil War or as many abroad as diplomats in the decades that followed. Included among ICY's students or staff were the first African American to win a degree from any four-year college, the first to graduate from Harvard, and the first to earn a Ph.D. (from Yale). The school's library boasted several thousand volumes and was open to the community (some 3,000 books were loaned in 1870). An active alumni sponsored speakers, among them Frederick Douglass and the Reverend Henry Highland Garnet, and regular course instruction was supplemented by lectures open to the public. An enormous source of pride to Philadelphia's black community, the Institute for Colored Youth drew nearly 3,000 people to its 1868 commencement ceremonies at Concert Hall, and this for a graduating class numbering only nine students.[52]

A strikingly beautiful woman of mixed Negro, Indian, and white English Quaker ancestry, Maria Louisa was almost six feet tall and slender, with high cheekbones and skin fair enough to pass for white. William was of average height, muscular, broad shouldered, and of pure black stock, his face showing clearly the features of his African ancestors. Their physical contrasts attest eloquently to the vast differences in background and experiences separating the couple. Most of Philadelphia's black aristocracy were, like Maria Louisa, light-skinned; some even bragged about the amount of white blood in their families.[53] Despite their long tradition of activism in civil rights and abolitionist movements, the Bustills and other members of the black elite generally looked down on less-advantaged members of the race. Their position was not dissimilar to that adopted by German American Jews as waves of Yiddish-speaking Eastern European Jews began immigrating to the United States in the 1880s: German American Jews were sympathetic and willing to help out financially; at the same time they did everything they could to distance themselves from these poor, uneducated new arrivals.[54]

With streams of newly emancipated blacks fleeing to the North, the Bustills of Maria Louisa's generation felt keenly the pressure to protect their status and hard-won economic gains. Philadelphia's tiny black aristocracy stood virtually alone in this respect, with no large middle class to look to for either support or potential marriage partners. If the fear of fortunes going to seed haunted established white families, it was a much more imminent danger to the black aristocracy, and never more so than in the years following the Civil War.[55]

Historically, Philadelphia's black elite protected their position by marrying only within their own circle. The Bustills knew precisely where they stood in relation to Philadelphia's black community and the larger white community and made it a point to exclude from their social sphere blacks not of their class and standing. Maria's sister Gertrude would also marry a Lincoln graduate, but a northern black and the son of freeborn parents (Nathan Mossell) who would distinguish himself as the first Negro graduate of the University of Pennsylvania's medical school and later as the founder of Philadelphia's Frederick Douglass Hospital. The marriages of Gertrude and Nathan Mossell's children and grandchildren would, in turn, continue the line by linking the Bustills and Mossells with the Tanners and Alexanders, also prominent Old Philadelphia families.[56]

William shared with Nathan Mossell a Lincoln education, but there the similarities ended. His diploma could not erase his dark coloring, lack of background and lineage, and proximity to the slave experience — all of which branded him lower class. Mossell, like so many of the Bustill forebears, was a crusader, whether battling to gain membership in the Philadelphia County Medical Society or organizing protests against the showing of D. W. Griffith's history-making *Birth of a Nation*. Perhaps because of his own life experiences, direct confrontation was not, nor would it become, part of William Robeson's racial vocabulary — but not because this man, who as a youngster had escaped slavery and then returned to the South at least twice to visit his mother, lacked courage and strength of character. For William Robeson the overriding issue was achieving and maintaining dignity. Thus Robeson kept his feelings and reactions to racial slights in close check, and in most cases appeared inclined not to acknowledge the slight (and thus deny the perpetrator power and maintain his own sense of pride) rather than meet it head-on.

The reactions of Nathan Mossell and William Robeson to the controversy over Lincoln's policy of racial exclusivity in the hiring of faculty illustrate well their differing political sensibilities. Shortly after receiving his medical degree, Dr. Mossell joined the long and ultimately disappointing struggle to change Lincoln's hiring policy. Waged largely on the pages of the newly launched Lincoln *Alumni Quarterly* (a publication for which Gertrude Bustill Mossell was largely responsible), the battle raged for over a decade until finally in 1893 Dr. Mossell gave up in frustration and despair, vowing he would not set foot on Lincoln's campus until Negroes were represented on both the faculty and the Board of Trustees.[57] William Robeson, by contrast, never publicly criticized Lincoln. His eldest son (also William) would graduate from Lincoln in 1902, thirty years before the university hired its first black faculty member and nine years after Nathan Mossell had formally cut himself off from the school; his youngest son (Paul) would coach the university's football team in 1918. If there was any ill feeling toward Lincoln on William's part, there is no evidence of it in his behavior or in that of his children.

Although Maria Louisa and William shared a deep interest in religion, she by virtue of her Quaker roots (throughout her life she used the "thee" and "thou" of her Quaker ancestors),[58] he after long years of training at Lincoln, in the end it was perhaps their differences that most bound this unlikely couple together. Certainly, Maria Louisa did not lack for suitors. Still, she chose idealism and struggle over a stable and financially secure life. William, determined to make something of himself, rightly saw in Maria attributes that even Lincoln could not give him. In marriage Maria would enter into a working relationship with her husband, assisting him with parish duties and the writing of his sermons. And William, in turn, would give Maria the opportunity to live out her own ideals and perhaps recapture the pioneering Bustill spirit.

On July 11, 1878, two years after William's graduation from Lincoln Seminary, the couple married.[59] Among the black elite few events assumed greater significance than weddings, which not only provided an occasion for receptions, parties, and teas but were also considered critical for maintaining proper family connections.[60] In this context, the silence surrounding the marriage of Maria Louisa and William is telling. Whereas the Bustills wrote in their family genealogy with great pride of Gertrude's marriage to Nathan Mossell, they gave scant notice to Maria's marriage and to her partner, William Robeson.

After a short pastorate in Wilkes-Barre, Pennsylvania, the white Presbyterian hierarchy selected William to pastor the (black) Witherspoon Street Presbyterian Church in Princeton, New Jersey.[61] Historically, the Witherspoon Street Church had strong ties with Princeton's (white) First Presbyterian Church as well as with the university's Theological Seminary. Up until 1837 when a fire destroyed the First Presbyterian Church, Princeton's black Presbyterians had worshiped with whites, although the seating was segregated, as were the burial plots. While rebuilding of the church was taking place, black communicants worshiped separately, and when the restoration of the church was complete they were not asked to return (whites worried that "if they do come back they will take up half the gallery"). Thus in 1846 black communicants established their own First Presbyterian Church of Colored Princeton, renamed in 1848 the Witherspoon Street Presbyterian Church of Princeton.[62]

Although by the time of William and Maria Louisa Robeson's arrival the white and colored sections of Princeton's Presbyterian population were totally segregated, the Witherspoon was still theologically and financially tied to its parent white First Presbyterian Church. True to the Calvinist ethic of election, the Witherspoon attracted the elite of Princeton's black population. "Everyone who was anyone," according to local genealogist Anna Bustill, worshiped at the Witherspoon: the Scudder, Simmons, Hoagland, Stockton, and Voeheers families all attended services and generously supported the church.[63] Bound so closely to white Presbyterian Princeton, the Witherspoon congregation reaped the benefits of white philanthropy as well. Of Princeton's three black churches (Mt. Pisgah AME and Bright Hope Baptist were the others), the Witherspoon was the most well endowed.[64]

Nestled in the southern part of the state, Princeton was a quiet town, steeped in history and dominated physically, socially, religiously, and economically by its prestigious university. Although the name "Princeton" evokes many images — rolling hills, ivy-covered university buildings, Palmer Square, and scenic Nassau Street — Princeton is in fact two communities: the first, a smaller one and site of the university, Princeton borough; the other, a largely rural area, Princeton Township. The university and the town took great pride in the role each played in historic events, beginning with the Declaration of Independence, which Princeton College president John Witherspoon and town resident Richard Stockton both signed. The town was the site of a symbolic victory for the colonials in the Revolutionary War, temporary capital of the nation in 1783, and before the Civil War a major stop on the New York–Philadelphia stage and later railway line. Hostelries like the Nassau Inn (where Washington, Jefferson, Adams, and Madison, all in Princeton for the Continental Congress, stayed in 1783) sprang up to service the trade. But the removal of railway tracks to Princeton Junction during the Civil War ended Princeton's days as a transportation hub, whereupon the town settled into the subdued tranquillity of agrarian life, with the university the major employer and social and economic center of Princeton proper.

Historically, Princeton University attracted the elite of southern whites, numbering among its most famous graduates James Madison as well as numerous cabinet appointees, congressmen, and justices of the Supreme Court. There is little evidence that the Virginia-born Thomas Woodrow Wilson, president of Princeton from 1902 to 1910, ever questioned the university's policy of racial exclusion during his tenure (virtually all other large northern colleges by this time were admitting a few blacks), although he did object strenuously to Princeton's eating clubs, which he felt not only undermined the college's "old democratic spirit" but encouraged social activities to the detriment of academic pursuits.[65] The town of Princeton mirrored the attitudes of the university and its genteel student body and more resembled white communities in the upper South than geographically closer cities like New York and Philadelphia. Despite its northern location, the flavor of Princeton was decidedly southern.[66]

Like Princeton's old white families, the town's sizable black community (by the turn of the century numbering 900 of Princeton's 5,136 residents, about 18 percent of the total population) had its own history of military, social, and business achievements.[67] Many of Princeton's blacks were the descendants of slaves who had traveled north with their pupil-masters before Emancipation; others claimed ancestry dating back to colonial times when their forebears labored in the town as servants for rich whites. Black patriots like Oliver Cromwell and Henry Hill fought in the Revolution with the Second New Jersey Regiment, distinguishing themselves in the battles of Princeton, Trenton, Brandywine, Monmouth, and Yorktown. Anthony Simmons, the town's leading caterer, owned a half-dozen properties and was financially secure enough at the end of his life to leave a bequest of $500 to the university. Other black entrepreneurs like Joseph Ten Eyck, Gilbert Scudder, Peter Scudder, and Elias Hort also owned property and ran successful businesses long before Emancipation, thus giving Princeton blacks a reputation as dependable and upstanding citizens.[68]

Reflecting its southern mind-set, Princeton enforced a strict racial etiquette, one that politely but firmly saw to it that the lives of blacks and whites were kept separate. As long as the number of Princeton's black residents remained small, blacks were permitted to purchase real estate where they chose as their means allowed. But as the Negro population increased in the years following the Civil War, residential segregation became an integral part of Princeton's racial etiquette.[69] During William Robeson's time in Princeton, blacks lived almost exclusively in the area of Witherspoon, Green, Hulfish, and Birch Streets (an area nicknamed "African Lane"), where they developed their own separate community and social life.[70]

With the university providing employment for both blacks and whites, there was work. A few blacks were self-employed, but most worked for whites as blacksmiths, bootblacks, hackmen, laborers, painters, carpenters, masons, gardeners, cooks, waiters, maids, dishwashers, dressmakers, pressers, laundresses, and even hot dog vendors.[71] Menial as the jobs were, they represented a step up from laboring as a field hand and provided a measure of status in that they connected blacks with the town's prestigious university.

Princeton was a peaceful town. Blacks and whites knew what was expected of them, and incidents between the races seldom occurred. At a time when recorded lynchings in the South numbered over 200 a year, this relative racial tranquillity was a valuable commodity. But Princeton's peace had its price and hinged completely on adherence to the town's code of racial etiquette. "Those people who worked and had their own business" succeeded because they "knew which side was up, racially," explained James ("Jimmy") Fletcher, a black man whose family had a dairy farm on the outskirts of town. Citing the case of William ("Kid") Green, the black owner of the Witherspoon Cafe, as an example, Fletcher recalled that in the beginning only blacks ate at his cafe, but "the food was so good that Princeton students eventually took it over. Kid Green knew how to run a business in Princeton, and while the colored could still continue to eat there . . . they ate separately. Kid Green set up a special section for them, in the back near the kitchen where they weren't seen."[72] White Princeton seldom had to use violence to enforce its racial codes. Segregation was taken for granted as was southern-style deference in the presence of whites. Blacks knew the rules and abided by them, carefully monitoring behavior within families and methodically weeding out from the community anyone who threatened their hard-won peace.

The Reverend William Robeson played an important role in maintaining the delicate balance on which the town's racial "harmony" depended. On the one hand, black churches were social centers no less than places of worship, stabilizing forces that both healed the community's social wounds and bound it together. As pastor, then, it was William Robeson's duty to encourage and enforce racially correct behavior and act as an intermediary between parishioners and the town's white civic and religious leadership on whom the church depended for financial support.[73] Paul described his father as "a sort of bridge between the Have-nots and the Haves," serving "in many worldly ways — seeking work for the jobless, money for the needy, mercy from the Law," often himself petitioning Princeton's white philanthropists for financial assistance not only for the church but for Princeton's "deserving" black poor as well.[74]

William Robeson earned the respectability he sought in Princeton, but only within proscribed limits. Like other Negro Presbyterian churches, the Witherspoon, even with the assistance of white presbyteries in New Brunswick and Princeton, often could not adequately support a pastor, especially one with a large family.[75] Consequently, William eked out a living and, on occasion, found himself, as notices in the *Princeton Press* testify, forced to depend on the generosity of friends to see him and his family through lean times. (In March 1896 the *Princeton Press* reported that "friends of the pastor 'loaded down with gifts' surprised the Robesons with food and necessities.")[76] Furthermore, despite his status within the black community and his connections to white Presbyterian Princeton, Robeson was still a black preacher and, as such, cut off from the heart of white Princeton life. Standing in front of his parsonage at what is now 110 Witherspoon Street, he had a fine view of elegant Nassau Hall, the oldest building gracing Princeton's pastoral campus,[77] but as far as his children were concerned, the college might as well have been a million miles away. Although his children would grow up in the shadow of the university, and his sons would perhaps earn money working for its white southern students, the worlds of learning within those old ivy-covered buildings would be completely closed to them. Like other blacks in the town, they would be discouraged from aspiring to anything higher than menial labor. They could attend the town's segregated grammar school (the Witherspoon, later known as Douglas Hall) on MacLean Street, but the town's high school admitted no blacks.[78] In Princeton, the very idea of a black attending the university would have been considered ridiculous.

Despite these difficulties, William Robeson labored for over twenty years on behalf of his parishioners, making significant improvements in church properties and over time earning a reputation as an able fund raiser.[79] But in the late 1890s William began to falter. With growing frequency guest preachers appeared in his place for Sunday services, and newspaper notices of the Witherspoon's activities dwindled considerably.[80] To make matters worse, Maria Louisa's health was deteriorating rapidly. In this setting, Paul Leroy Robeson, the youngest of the Robeson children, was born on April 9, 1898.[81] Family members would later describe his birth as an ordeal from which his ailing forty-five-year-old mother never fully recovered.[82] Indeed, by 1898 neither Maria Louisa nor William were the people they had once been. Maria Louisa, who had so ably helped her husband with his parish work and for several years taught in a private school for black children in Princeton, now struggled simply to keep up with household chores.[83] A semi-invalid, incapacitated by chronic asthma and nearly blind with cataracts, she found the task of caring for their five children— Bill (William Drew), age seventeen; Reeve (John Bunyan Reeve), twelve; Ben (Benjamin Congleton), six; Marian (Marguerite), four; and, now, the new baby, Paul Leroy—exhausting.

Maria's declining health was difficulty enough, but in 1900 more hardship struck the Robeson family. After twenty-three years of service William Robeson was forced to give up his position as pastor of the Witherspoon Street Church. The reasons for his departure remain unclear. Paul would later describe his father as the victim of a "factional dispute" within the congregation, with "some of his closest kin part of the ousting faction." Paul's wife, Eslanda Robeson, in her 1930 biography of Paul, describes William as having been forced out by the political chicanery of envious ministers, members of the white Presbyterian leadership that controlled church assignments.[84]

The records of the New Brunswick Presbytery from January 1900 when the controversy first began until nearly a year later in November 1900 when William Robeson finally resigned, reveal few specifics explaining his departure.[85] Initially, complaints focused on the Witherspoon's shaky financial status. An investigating committee appointed by the presbytery, however, found "great carelessness" in keeping records but no evidence of misappropriation of funds.[86] Nonetheless, the commission recommended that the overseeing of the Witherspoon be continued "under the special care of this committee" for a period of three months.[87] Six months later, apparently still dissatisfied with the Witherspoon's financial affairs (appropriations from April 1 through June 30 had been withheld until such time as the church "has complied with the recommendations of the Presbytery regarding accounts"), the commission recommended that pastoral relations between William Robeson and his congregation be immediately severed.[88] William's congregation protested, as did William in a speech delivered before the presbytery in which (according to the local press) he charged that the "feeling against him was because he and his people were colored."[89] Although this line of defense won him few friends among the New Brunswick Presbytery (the chairman of the investigating committee retorted that, had "Mr. Robeson been a white pastor [the] Presbytery would have dissolved the relation long before this"), after hearing evidence of William Robeson's generosity and kindness to his parishioners ("often . . . imperiling his own financial interests and bringing upon himself the very conditions which formed the basis of some complaints made against him") the presbytery elected to recommit the report until the investigating commission had supplied concrete charges.[90]

The commission presented its "supplemental" report to the presbytery in October, with the adamant recommendation that William Robeson be immediately separated from his pastorate. The charges against William remained vague, ranging from a falling-off in church membership and a "disrelish" among some for services "as presently conducted," to the "general unrest and dissatisfaction of others who have been the Church's friends and helpers."[91]

Witherspoon Street Church members were not among those objecting to William Robeson's performance. The church's seventy-two communicants as well as all three of its elders and three of its four trustees protested the initial complaint, and later in November members voted nearly unanimously that Robeson be maintained as pastor.[92] The hearty approval William received from his congregation, however, does not necessarily refute any wrongdoing on his part. It is unlikely, whatever William's transgressions, that fellow blacks would have turned on him, as a blot on the character of the pastor would have sullied their own reputation as well as that of Princeton's entire black community.

Among all the charges leveled against William Robeson, one thing is clear: he had done something to alienate the "[white] friends and helpers" on whom the Witherspoon Street Church depended, something, in the opinion of the investigating commission, that had created such a "lack of sympathy . . . for William Robeson's methods and services . . . that he will never be able to overcome it."[93] Certainly, as a graduate of Lincoln, William knew how to conduct himself with important and philanthropic whites and had done so as part of his pastoral duties at the Witherspoon for over twenty years. The commission itself ruled out misappropriation of funds, a charge sufficient to warrant both the ire of white philanthropists and immediate dismissal. Complaints over the quality of church services (as regular within congregations as the passing of the plate) would not have resulted in as drastic a recommendation as dismissal, nor would such charges have overly concerned either the New Brunswick Presbytery or the church's white friends. More telling than any of the "evidence" cited, is the presbytery's silence (its failure to record any consequential charges) in the matter of William Robeson. Whatever the real complaint, it was weighty enough not only to warrant the formation of a commission to investigate it but also to prevent the New Brunswick Presbytery from setting it down in its official records.

In November 1900 the *Princeton Press* reported that William Robeson had resigned as pastor of the Witherspoon, to take effect on February 1, 1901.[94] His resignation carried an air of scandal. Decades later, many Princeton blacks were reluctant to talk about the incident at all. "Why do you want to go into all that again? Why don't you just leave it alone?" asked one frustrated ninety-year-old resident when questioned on the topic. Robeson's biographer Lloyd Brown suggests a direct link between William Robeson's dismissal and a meeting that Robeson and the principal of the Witherspoon Street School, Abraham P. Denny, helped organize and run a year earlier on November 29, 1899, at the Witherspoon Street Church. The topic under discussion was recent violence in North Carolina (of particular concern to William because he still had relatives living there) and other southern states. Six months later, in June 1900, William's friend and fellow Lincoln graduate Denny was relieved from the position of school principal, a position which he had held for nineteen years. Brown concludes that it was the November meeting and its implied criticism of whites that caused the dismissals of Denny and Robeson.[95] There were rumors of mischief between William and one of the young women in the congregation. According to the theater critic Alexander Woollcott, who conducted his own investigation of the incident in the 1920s, the divinity student who helped circulate this rumor later admitted the story had been fabricated "by someone who wanted to occupy the pulpit himself." Possibly there is substance to what Woollcott unearthed because Princeton Seminary at the time did accept black divinity students (although it was not until 1948 that the institution accepted blacks in any other department) and, according to the *Princeton Press,* Princeton divinity students often served as guests preachers at the Witherspoon, presumably to practice their technique.[96]

James Fletcher, a schoolmate and friend of Paul's and one of the few black Princetonians who would talk about the incident, claimed that excessive drinking and shirking of his duties led to William's downfall. "The fact is, sometimes the Reverend Robeson drank too much, at least that's what my father told me," said Fletcher. "He wasn't a drunkard, but he certainly did overdo it now and then."[97] The Presbyterian church had a long history of opposition to alcohol consumption and in 1871 unequivocally denounced the "sale and use of alcoholic liquors as . . . wholly inconsistent with the claims of Christian duty."[98] Local (white) antiliquor sentiment was strong enough (the Women's Christian Temperance Union [WCTU] was holding meetings almost weekly in Princeton) that, had William let down his guard in this respect, he most certainly would have lost credibility and alienated local white philanthropic support, to say nothing of the white Presbyterian hierarchy.[99]

Whatever the reason, William's fall from grace could hardly have been more complete: an embarrassment not only to black Princeton and his wife's family, but to his beloved alma mater, Lincoln University, as well. According to several sources, "the Bustills, having harbored ill feelings toward William for years for bringing their daughter to this backwater area to begin with, and, more recently, for having put her through the ordeal of birthing a child at the age of forty-five, were furious when word reached them of the scandal and of this no-account black-trash preacher discrediting their family name."[100]

William bore the humiliation with grace and dignity, keeping his own thoughts and feelings to himself. In his final address to the congregation he had served for over twenty years, he never stepped out of his role as minister. Using the Beatitudes as his biblical text, he urged his congregation to refrain from bitterness and recrimination. He admitted that he had "made some mistakes and committed some blunders" but added, "I know my own heart. I have tried to do my work well." Suggesting that perhaps age had been a factor in the ousting, William reminded his listeners "this church sorely needs older men and women of godly lives and praying hearts." Only once in his sermon did he hint at his own sorrow and deep disappointment with church members "who in the hour of its [the church's] darkest need forsook it."[101]

In May 1901 William moved his family from the parsonage to a "shack" close to relatives just around the corner on 13 Green Street, a street littered with run-down homes.[102] For the Robeson family, life in Princeton would never be the same. Unable to find employment, William purchased a horse and wagon and began hiring himself out, hauling ashes for Princeton's rich whites and dumping them in his own backyard.

Paul's earliest boyhood memories were of the dilapidated house on Green Street ("so bad it should have been condemned," Robeson later recalled) "with a great mountain of ashes outside the window" and his father returning home in his frock coat literally caked from head to foot with filth and dried ashes.[103] The Robesons could not make ends meet. Fletcher remembered them as "very poor . . . one of three or four families who had almost nothing."[104] William Robeson tried, working as an ash hauler, an occasional coachman, and an itinerant preacher, but it was not enough.

By February 1903 William, who only a few short years ago as pastor distributed charitable contributions to the town's most needy, found himself listed in the *Princeton Press* as behind in his taxes.[105] Publicly exposed as destitute, William Robeson now had to accept the charity he had once parceled out to others. Several kindhearted ministers, like Dr. D. S. Klugh, at the time pastor of Bright Hope Baptist, recognizing that William was "utterly discouraged . . . made occasions for him to preach" in their churches.[106] According to one resident, Robeson would sometimes be "gone for days at a time on one of his preaching jaunts."[107]

While William traveled from one town to another, Maria Louisa, now almost completely blinded by cataracts, depended on the children, especially Paul and Ben, to lead her about the house.[108] (William Jr. was attending Lincoln University; Reeve, Ben, Marian, and Paul were all at home.) Maria struggled to keep the household together, but Reeve, the second-oldest child, was becoming particularly difficult to manage. In grammar school, in the years before his father's ouster, Reeve had been an outstanding student. His name appeared yearly in the *Princeton Press* honor roll listing, and in the sixth grade he won a scholarship prize for his academic achievements. After graduating from grammar school in 1899, however, Reeve ended his schooling.[109] The Reeve young Paul knew (Reeve was eleven years older than Paul) had little interest in academics. He refused to go to high school and earned money working as a chauffeur for Princeton students.

Maria Louisa appears to have borne these trials without complaint. But in 1904 on a cold morning in January, the Robeson family suffered another crushing loss. The Reverend William Robeson had gone to Trenton, and Maria had asked eleven-year-old Ben (who had stayed home from school to assist his mother) to help her move the carpet from beneath the stove. As they did so, the stove door slipped open, spilling several hot coals onto Maria's long skirts. Because of her poor eyesight, she did not notice her smoldering dress until she felt the heat on her feet and legs. She and Ben frantically tried to stamp out the flames, but within seconds her full skirts were ablaze. Horrified, Ben ran from the house, screaming for help. A passing neighbor heard his cries and rushed inside to find Maria enveloped in flames. By the time the fire was finally put out Maria's torso, legs, feet, and hands were severely burned, and her throat and lungs were scorched from the smoke. A doctor was called, but there was little he could do but give her opiates to relieve the pain until she died hours later.[110]

A horrifying scene awaited five-year-old Paul when he arrived home from school that day: panicked and grief-stricken family and friends watching helplessly as his mother died in excruciating pain. Paul, as one family friend put it, had been his mother's "little guide and inseparable" from her.[111] As an adult, however, Paul could recall little about that day or his mother. "I cannot say that I remember her, though my memory of other things goes back before her tragic death," he wrote in his autobiography. "I remember her lying in the coffin, and the funeral, and the relatives who came, but it must be that the pain and shock of her death blotted out all other personal recollections."[112]

For William Robeson, Maria's death was the final blow. Numbed by grief, he apparently felt he could not handle sole responsibility for the care of his family and so contacted Maria's relatives and asked them if they would take in some of the children. Reportedly, the Bustills refused. Years later Paul confided to Clark Foreman, with whom he campaigned in 1948 for Progressive Party presidential candidate Henry Wallace and others, that his mother's side of the family had always had bad feelings toward his father. "They felt that my mother had not married well and borne more children than her health allowed and that my father didn't care for her properly, especially in her ailing years. I even think that they may have blamed him somehow for her death in that fire. They would not take in any of us because we were too black. They were fair-skinned and considered dark skin a sign of inferior status." (An FBI source in 1942 reported much the same. According to the confidential source, Robeson said his mother's family looked down on his father's people as they were the poor Carolina type that scratched out an existence.)[113] Whether the Bustills' decision was in fact based on color or whether William Robeson only surmised as much from their refusal is a matter of conjecture. Paul grew up believing that such was the case, and the fact remains that, even though they had the means to do so, this philanthropic and civic-minded family did not do anything to help William Robeson through this tragedy. In the end, the boys (Reeve, Ben, and Paul) remained at home with their father, while nine-year-old Marian was sent nearby to live with the family of friend and fellow minister Dr. D. S. Klugh.[114]

Paul, who was always fiercely protective of his father, emphasized in his public recollections of these years in Princeton the nurturing and support he received from his extended family, Princeton's black community. William's brother Benjamin, who had moved from North Carolina to Princeton with his wife and children, lived next door to the parsonage; around the corner, but within the same block, another brother, John, lived with his wife, Hattie. "There must have been moments when I felt the sorrows of a motherless child," Paul wrote in his autobiography, "but what I most remember from my youngest days was an abiding sense of comfort and security. I got plenty of mothering, not only from Pop and my brothers and sister when they were home, but from the whole of our close-knit community. Across the street and down each block were all my aunts and uncles and cousins — including some who were not actual relatives at all. . . . In a way I was 'adopted' by all these good people, and there was always a place at their tables and a place in a bed . . . when my father was away."[115]

Paul's roseate reminiscences notwithstanding, life in Princeton in the years after Maria Louisa's death was difficult. When William was out of town preaching, often for days at a time, the boys stayed at other people's homes — friends or William's relatives from North Carolina. In many respects, the Robeson boys took care of themselves, and Jimmy Fletcher remembered Paul chumming with "a pretty rough gang for a while."[116] Publicly, Robeson never admitted (as he later revealed to a few close friends) the pain of being rejected by the Bustills and then "shifted off among relatives and friends," of having to learn at a young age "to take care of and fend for himself," and of dealing with the feeling that "he had no real home at all."[117] Princeton's black community gave Paul and his brothers emotional support, but it could not erase the feeling that home as it had once been was gone forever. This sense of rootlessness never left Robeson, and long years later when he had the means to purchase a home anywhere in the world, he chose to repeat a pattern that mirrored these childhood experiences: Robeson was most "at home" keeping his things in a small apartment and seeking companionship and emotional warmth in the homes of friends.

The situation with Reeve deteriorated rapidly after Maria Louisa's death, as he made it clear to his father he had no intention of adhering to Princeton's racial codes. Paul remembered many times when Reeve, "resenting some remark by a Southern gentleman-student, would leap down from his coachman's seat, drag out the offender and punish him with his fists. He always carried for protection a bag of small, jagged rocks — a weapon he used with reckless abandon whenever the occasion called for action." As an adult Paul often told the story of being "in the wagon with Reeve in Princeton when some white person insulted Reeve. Reeve took the guy by the neck and straightened him out."[118]

There was no place in black Princeton for an "uppity" black like Reeve. "Colored people did everything they could to keep the rowdy out," one resident explained. "For someone to go to jail was like an execution for the family. Princeton blacks were close knit with solid families and jobs and income. From the start, colored residents saw to it that relatives didn't come up from the South without a job here, and that no hoodlums got in. They kept it quiet."[119] Eventually, there were brushes with the law, and William, forced to don his frock coat and plead with police on Reeve's behalf once too often, finally had to concede he could not make his son behave.[120] So the minister told Reeve he would have to leave Princeton. Paul remembered his father's concern that Reeve's bad influence would rub off on him. "I stood sadly and silently as Pop told Reed he would have to leave," Paul recalled in his autobiography, "because his example was a dangerous one for his young brother Paul." But, in fact, William understood that the issue was larger than that. Reeve's behavior threatened Princeton's black community's hard-won peace: if the minister did not make Reeve leave, community pressure would eventually force him out.[121]

While the evidence indicates a clear and simple line connecting Reeve's anger with Princeton's repressive racial codes, one can also speculate to what extent the real or indirect target may have been his father. Had there been, for example, no racial taboos, would Reeve have found another way to defy his father? Reeve's methodical rejection of education, decorum, dignity, and adherence to racial etiquette represented an assault on some of his father's most deeply held values. Indeed, Reeve's refusal to back down and "behave" threatened not only his continued connection to family but his father's reputation and the family's survival in Princeton as well. Paul, a young child when Reeve was finally forced to leave, saw and remembered only Reeve's hostility toward Princeton's deadening racial structure. In later life, when his own anger and frustration were at the breaking point, Paul would express great admiration for his brother's defiance of convention.[122] But for a seven-year-old youngster, Reeve's expulsion provided a frightening and powerful lesson on the importance of keeping one's place. Failure to conform brought not only disapproval and punishment but, more important, separation from the most basic sources of security and affection: family and community. However much William Robeson drummed into his children that they were as good as anyone else, in this instance they learned with force the inescapable lesson that survival depended on adherence to white rules. Years later Paul's British friend, theater director Herbert Marshall, who with his thick cockney accent had experienced his own share of prejudice, asked Paul, "'How did you put up with it all?' Paul just shook his head, sighed, and said simply, 'You learn, brother. You learn.'"[123]

William Robeson remained in Princeton for six years after losing his pastorate. If in the beginning he had hoped for a second chance, the intervening years convinced him otherwise: never again would he be called to lead a Presbyterian congregation. During this troublesome period it was local Baptist and African Methodist Episcopal Zion (AMEZ) churches that extended both a helping and a forgiving hand, inviting William to preach and easing his financial and family burdens.[124] Despite intense proselytizing in the years following the Civil War, Presbyterians failed to attract any sizable black following. As the denomination's rigid white standards forced William out, so most blacks preferred the less-staid Baptist and AMEZ sects where they at least had control of their own ministries.[125] In 1907 William received a call to pastor a small struggling AMEZ parish in Westfield, New Jersey, a town about thirty miles north of Princeton. He accepted immediately.[126]

Paul was only nine years old when he and Ben left Princeton with their father, but the years there had made a deep impression. He had grown up in poverty and under the shadow of his father's ravaged reputation. Always there were rumors concerning the "real" reasons for his father's resignation. His mother's death provided another occasion for innuendos of wrongdoing and neglect on his father's part, as did Reeve's rebellion and William's inability to bring his son into line. Paul watched helplessly as his father floundered, unable to regain respectability.

Throughout his life Paul would remain passionately loyal to his father, leaving no room in his public statements for anyone to twist the details of his childhood into yet another judgment of this man he loved so dearly. "The glory of my boyhood years was my father," Robeson wrote in his 1958 autobiography. "I loved him like no one in all the world." Paul's recollections paint William as a man without flaw; occasionally they belie the facts of his impoverished and powerless position. "His people, among whom he moved as a patriarch for many years before I was born, loved him too. And the white folks — even the most lordly of aristocratic Princeton — had to respect him."[127]

Robeson's devotion to his father likewise found expression in the bitter feelings he harbored toward the Bustills. "Paul seldom talked about the Bustills but when he did he never forgot the way they mistreated his family, especially his father," said Joseph Andrews, Paul's dresser and confidant for nearly thirty years.[128] To biographer Marie Seton, Paul also spoke candidly about his feelings but asked her not to include that information in her work (a biography of Robeson, published in 1958). "When you deal with the early years and my parents and the Bustills, try not to make it too grim," he said.[129] Still another observer said Paul told him, "I grew up feeling much more at home with my father's relatives than with my mother's who acted as if they were superior," and added that "throughout his life Robeson felt that light-skinned blacks looked down on him because of his dark color, and he in turn, distrusted fair-skinned, upper-class Negroes."[130]

Like his father, who chose to be buried in Princeton with his wife, Paul never resolved his love/hate feelings for this town, the setting of his family's first achievement and catastrophic downfall.[131] In the small New Jersey communities of Westfield and Somerville the Robesons would learn the redeeming value of achievement, as through the success of his children William Robeson regained some of the respectability he had lost. But the ghosts of Princeton would remain with Paul throughout his life.

2

Father & Son

1907-1915

Only once, according to Robeson, did he ever disobey his father, and the result proved so frightening that he never did it again. The incident occurred when Paul was ten, shortly after the family had moved to Westfield, New Jersey.

> My father told me to do something and I didn't do it. "Come here," he said; but I ran away. He ran after me. I darted across the road. He followed, stumbled and fell. I was horrified. I hurried back, helped Pop to his feet. He had knocked out one of his teeth. I have never forgotten the emotions—the sense of horror, shame, ingratitude, selfishness—that overwhelmed me. I adored him, would have given my life for him in a flash—and here I had hurt him, disobeyed him! Never did he have to admonish me again.[1]

Robeson seldom talked about his childhood, but this particular incident he recounted many times. William, an elderly sixty-two-year-old when he began his life anew in Westfield, needed Paul almost as much as Paul needed him. Paul sensed this, as this story so poignantly demonstrates. As children often do when they feel powerless and frightened, Paul ascribed an almost causal connection between his own behavior and his father's well-being. If Reeve's conduct had hurt William, Paul's would protect him and make him proud.

Paul was nine in 1907 when the family moved to Westfield, a small town about thirty miles north of Princeton. Leaving Princeton meant severing ties not only with family and friends but also with Princeton's stultifying southern atmosphere. It meant as well acknowledging that the Robesons would receive no second chance, no reprieve from Princeton's Presbyterians. To this high-minded, sternly principled sect, William's fall from grace was not only unaccept-able but, for all practical purposes, unforgivable. In Westfield, with its more relaxed "northern" racial climate, the Robesons would begin anew the task of earning respectability. For William, the move represented a fresh start; for his children, it was an opportunity to live free of the mantle of shame the family had been unable to shake in Princeton. William Robeson's belief that he and his children were among God's "chosen" remained unshaken, but never again would he look to a Presbyterian elite to confer on him the affirmation he sought. The Robesons would rise above the commonplace by virtue of their own achievements, with or without Presbyterian approval.

Already the Robeson children had begun to demonstrate that theirs was a far from ordinary family. Raised in a town that discouraged blacks from attending high school or aspiring to anything higher than menial or service work, all William Robeson's children with the exception of Reeve earned high school diplomas.[2] William Jr. attended Lincoln University and went on to study medicine at the University of Pennsylvania; Ben would prepare for the ministry at Biddle University (now Johnson C. Smith) in Charlotte, North Carolina, and Marian would become a teacher after completing her schooling at Scotia Seminary in North Carolina and Pennsylvania State Normal School. None of it came easily. Both Geraldine ("Gerry") Neale Bledsoe and Carlton Moss, later friends of Paul's who also grew up in the area, spoke of a "level of aspiration and parental vision. . . . Once that was set in motion, getting an education was no breakthrough, it was the expectation: you just did it."[3]

William Robeson, one of those visionary parents, did everything within his power to see to it that his children received proper and complete schooling including, on more than one occasion, going hat in hand to solicit funds from wealthy philanthropic whites.[4] Princeton's high school did not admit blacks until 1919 and then only after William ("Sport") Moore, one of the town's few well-to-do blacks, threatened to sue if his daughter Bessie was not allowed to attend.[5] Before 1919 Princeton's black families adopted a variety of strategies for dealing with the situation: some sent their children south for schooling; others, like Jimmy Fletcher's family, pieced together a high school education (in Fletcher's case a year of tutoring from the Witherspoon principal and three years at Howard Academy before starting Howard University); and a few, like William Robeson Jr., made the eleven-mile trek to Trenton to earn their high school diploma.[6]

Westfield, an agrarian and working-class town with a moderate-sized black population (approximately 450 out of a total of 6,500), offered a much more racially relaxed setting than Princeton—as Paul put it, one with "more friendly connections between the two groups." But its black community lacked the longevity and size of Princeton's. Paul remembered his father beginning his new ministry with almost nothing: no church, no resources, and a pitifully small congregation, "not more than a dozen members . . . to help him dig the foundation for the Downing Street A.M.E. Zion Church." For a while William worked in a corner grocery store to make ends meet, but in time he established himself as a competent pastor and his congregation grew apace.[7]

Paul, meanwhile, attended a racially mixed grammar school, as the town's black population was too small to warrant a separate school. It was Paul's first experience functioning in a predominantly white setting, and it made a lasting impression on him. One friend later claimed that these early positive encounters kept Paul "from distrusting the white race as most Negroes do."[8] He simply behaved as his father had taught him, with "respectful politeness and courtesy," and was, in turn, received by white classmates as a friend. "I was the respected preacher's son, and then, too, I was popular with the other boys and girls because of my skill at sports and studies, and because I was always ready to share in their larks and fun-making. . . . I wasn't conscious of it at the time, but now I realize that my easy moving between the two racial communities was rather exceptional."[9]

Once Ben began his schooling at Biddle (Marian was already attending Scotia Seminary in North Carolina), Paul was the only one of the Robeson children still at home. William and Paul were family, all that the other had in the world, and during these years the bond between the two solidified. William expected much of Paul, and Paul, in turn, worshiped his father: never would anyone command more loyalty, love, and admiration from him.[10] In later years Paul would recall "winter evenings at home with Pop," sitting "for hours in the parlor, engrossed in our game [of checkers], not speaking much, but wonderfully happy together." But, even in Robeson's most idyllic renderings, one senses the frustration of an only child seeking companionship and warmth with an elderly and emotionally unresponsive man. By Paul's own admission, his father was "[not] demonstrative in his love, nor . . . quick to praise, [but, rather] demanding, and given more to silence than any overt expression of feeling."[11] When Paul succeeded in meeting his father's expectations, as later when he graduated at the head of his eighth grade class, William most often said nothing. "It [academic success] was only what he expected of me," Paul explained, "and his attitude never allowed for feelings of exaggerated self-esteem."[12]

Within three years William had transformed the struggling Downing Street congregation into a fairly well-established one, and in 1910 he received and accepted a call to pastor another indebted (to the sum of $1,600) but larger congregation, St. Thomas AMEZ in Somerville. A growing rural town, Somerville had a population of about 460 blacks out of an estimated 5,000 residents, about the size of Westfield but again a small black population in comparison with Princeton's. Like Westfield and other mid–New Jersey towns, racially Somerville steered a middle path between the extremes of southern and northern modes of racial etiquette, retaining salient aspects of each.

"New Jersey was one of the few northern states that had almost totally segregated grammar schools at the time," remembered Geraldine Neale Bledsoe, who grew up in nearby Freehold. "It all seemed perfectly normal, the school segregation that is. The relationship between blacks and whites was friendly — no hostility. We had our own churches, lodges, and organizations, and most blacks worked in service jobs as janitors, dressmakers, and farm workers. People stayed on as domestics in families for years and years. No one ever talked about being limited by race, and I never felt limited. In fact, it took me forty years to realize that my high school had changed the format of commencement exercises in order to prevent me from being valedictorian. I was not conscious of discrimination. I knew I would go to college and I did. That's all there was to it."[13]

J. Douglas Brown, a white boyhood friend of Paul's, had similar memories. "Mid–New Jersey more or less simply allowed its small black population to be, obsessed neither with keeping them in their place nor with gaining equality for them. Our family maintained black servants and a coachman, even after my father, a successful woolen mill owner, suffered a series of financial setbacks between 1904 and 1906. It was just the way things were done. I had to work as a clerk in a clothing store and as a janitor before and after school, but just the same, every Sunday morning a black shoeshine boy named 'Abe' came to our home, making the rounds, and shined the family's shoes."[14]

It did not take young Paul long to understand Somerville's racial etiquette. Most blacks lived in one of two racially segregated areas: the first from Davenport Street north toward Route 22 (named "Lottery Field," according to residents, because many of the lots were won in a lottery); and the second between Hamilton Street and Franklin Street. William Robeson was one of the few blacks who did not work for whites.[15] In Somerville Paul would be allowed to attend the white high school, but he had to complete the seventh and eighth grades at the town's colored grammar school, the Davenport, located on the corner of West Cliff and Davenport Streets.[16] As in Westfield, the polite and well-behaved minister's son was invited to visit the homes of his white friends, while most blacks in the area entered these houses only as servants. Paul's white friends, however, did not come to his home. Paul was black and lived in a segregated, poor section of town where whites seldom ventured. Paul understood that this just was not done.[17]

Respected by his congregation, William Robeson kept to himself attending to his duties at St. Thomas, but in contrast to his years in Princeton, he maintained little contact with Somerville's white community. Spirited weeklong revivals kept the parish growing and financially solvent (thirty-six new members were added as the result of a 1915 revival), and by 1915 the congregation could afford to have the interior of the church "beautifully and tastefully renovated."[18]

Despite his position in his own black community, on more than one occasion white Somerville residents mistook William for a common laborer like other area blacks. Arthur Van Fleet (later a classmate of Paul's at Somerville High) remembered his mother making such an error. "She was doing her spring cleaning, beating her rugs outdoors. The Reverend Robeson happened to be walking by in his frock coat and all. My mother stopped him and asked him if he wanted to work for her and help her beat the rugs. If he was insulted, he didn't show it. His expression never changed, and he told my mother simply that he would ask at Church whether or not any of the men needed work."[19]

Samuel Woldin, a Jew and recent immigrant from Russia who lived across the street from the Robesons (in the black section of town), was one of the few whites to exchange more than polite hellos with William Robeson. Woldin's son recalled the close friendship between the two. "My father left czarist oppression for free America, so both men, my father and the Reverend Robeson, had escaped oppression. Both also had experienced prejudice in America and in that sense were kindred souls. I remember them sitting evenings on the porch puffing their pipes and discussing the affairs of the world. The Reverend Robeson tended his vegetable garden in our backyard because his own soil was unsuitable for tilling. This was one of the first personal kindnesses Paul ever saw a white person bestow on his father — I don't think Paul ever forgot it."[20]

Paul, in the meantime, increasingly found himself in white settings. He was one of four blacks out of a total enrollment of 250 at Somerville High School. "High school in Somerville was not Jim Crow and there I formed close friendships with a number of white classmates. . . . I was welcomed as a member of the glee club (unlike later at college) and the dramatic club and into the various sports and social activities around the school."[21] J. Douglas Brown, Paul's closest white friend, said that integrating the school's few black students never presented a problem. "Life in Somerville was quiet and simple. The town was so small that the minute you hit the last home on the road you were out in the country. There were few autos and everything was within walking distance, so everyone knew everyone. Since Somerville High drew upon so many outlying areas for its student body — many of the pupils were farmers' kids who came in from the country, stayed in town Monday to Friday, and then went home on the weekends — social activities were always inclusive and general. The school was just too small to have cliques or be bothered with social or racial categories. We needed all the talent we could get."[22]

Robeson always "stood out, but in a good way, at Somerville High," said Brown. Almost all his friends remembered him as big, much bigger than the other students. As a freshman and sophomore, before he stretched out to his full height, he had a large frame but was more plump than muscular. He described himself as "a dumpy-looking thirteen-year-old and not very successful with the girls."[23] "He had such huge feet, you couldn't help but notice his shoes, always scruffy and beat up with the heels worn down to nothing," said one classmate. "He often came to school looking ill kempt—sloppy really—like he had just tumbled out of bed," said another. "Paul sat in front of me and what I remember most is his big feet and long legs sticking out to the middle of the aisle; they were just too huge to stay under the desk. Recitations were given at the front of the classroom, and whenever it was my turn I had to climb over those mountainous legs."[24]

Academically, Robeson stood out as well. He was "among the few (three boys and five girls out of a graduating class of thirty-eight) to take the four-year classical college course of Latin, English, mathematics, and ancient history. Most of the farmers' children did not continue on after high school or, if they did, took 'short courses' in agriculture at Rutgers and then returned to the farm. It was unusual enough in a small town for white kids to prepare for college, but for a black to consider such an undertaking was almost unheard of. Paul's father had plans for him. He was to go to college—and that was unusual."[25]

William Robeson carefully monitored his youngest son's development, and nowhere is the minister's influence more apparent than in the area of education. To the elder Robeson it was one of life's few absolute values: both an end in itself, affording access to worlds of culture long denied blacks, and a means for attaining respectability. If education had opened doors for him, it would do so for his children, and he would tolerate no halfhearted efforts from them in this regard. Trained in the classics at Lincoln and convinced that such study disciplined the mind, William insisted that Paul take four years of Latin in high school (and in college four more years of Latin and two years of Greek) and, as Paul remembered, "was with me page by page through Virgil and Homer."[26] According to Paul, by the time he began high school the expectation was well established that he bring home only perfect report cards. Paul told of one occasion when he brought home a card with six A's and one B. "His father commended him and said mildly, 'But what is the idea of the B?' Paul explained that all the teachers agreed he was doing fine; he was at the head of his class, and most other students were happy to get two or three A's." His father listened patiently but then admonished him for not striving for a perfect grade. Paul replied that nobody ever got 100 percent, to which his father queried, closing the discussion, 'Well, what's the 100 percent for, then?'"[27] To what extent William's rigorously high expectations were driven by his determination to regain the respectability the family had lost, and to what extent they simply mirrored what every black parent knew—that for their children to succeed they would have to be better than "good"—is difficult to say. Paul excelled scholastically, both in grammar school and in high school. "We [Robeson and Brown] were 1–2 academically," Brown recalled. "Technically, there was one girl with a higher average than us, but she was from the commercial class, which offered an easier course."[28]

A small school, Somerville High afforded energetic students like Robeson ample opportunity to participate in any number of school activities, which Paul did with relish. Although William repeatedly cautioned his son to put academics first, he took a keen interest in his son's participation in the school oratory club. "When people talk about my voice," Paul later said, "I wish they could have heard my father preach. . . . The passion of his life was oratory."[29] Biographers who describe Robeson as having had little oratorical training overlook the more than competent "instruction" he received at home and church. In the classroom declamation was treated as a valuable but ancillary skill, but in the home of a black preacher oratory was revered as both an art and a necessity of life. Historically, preaching was the only white-collar trade open to blacks during slavery (when it was a crime in the South to teach blacks to read or to allow them to engage in any activity requiring literacy), and after Emancipation it remained one of the few reliable and marketable skills available to blacks. Preachers and would-be preachers honed their technique as they competed fiercely among themselves for recognition, since within the black community "a reputation for oratory was as good as a diploma and other academic credentials."[30]

William Robeson insisted that all his children learn a refined (white) speaking style, as far removed from the speech of the illiterate southern black as possible. Robeson told one interviewer that his father, convinced that polished speech would open doors for his children as it had for him, began coaching him for public speaking at the age of four.[31] Paul grew up listening to his father's Sunday sermons; later, he watched his brother Ben, then studying for the ministry, practice his speaking technique under his father's watchful eye. "He was my first teacher . . . , and long before my days as a class orator and college debater there were evening recitations at home. . . . Innumerable speeches were given for me to learn. Line by line my father took me through them, dwelling on the choice of a word, the turn of a phrase, or the potency of an inflection. Then, in the evenings I delivered my prepared orations to the family circle and received criticism and encouragement."[32]

R. Anna Miller, one of Paul's English teachers, recognized Paul's oratorical gifts and lost no time working to enhance them. "There were three of us in the school debating team: me, Paul, and Miriam McConaughy, with Paul as anchorman of the group," said Douglas Brown. "In our debating contests we purposely had Paul handle the rebuttal. He was a prodigious speaker." Robeson's ability to convey feeling impressed his classmates: "While I could give a good, sound, logical speech and be a wise economist, Paul . . . had the artistic gift of projection and the flair to move people, the emotion and gift of speaking," said Brown. "Once, the debate centered around the validity of an immigrant literacy test in the United States, and we opposed it. Paul, who spelled his father in preaching sometimes, appealed to the basic fair play of the judges, resorted to histrionics, and just wiped out the opposition. Not by using facts, mind you, but sentiment. We won the sentiment vote. Since Paul did so well in the literacy test debate, the next school we were scheduled to compete with, Bernardsville, made us agree that we would not appeal to sentiment. We lost to them because we had to be staid and solemn and stick to the subject."[33]

Miss Miller also invited Paul to play the role of Othello in the school's "Shakespeare at the Water Cure," a burlesque featuring characters from four Shakespearean plays who meet at a health resort in England.[34] It was Paul's first introduction to Othello, but an Othello stripped of his royalty and working as a waiter at the health resort. Later Miss Miller said she had had misgivings about asking Paul to take the part (Robeson, however, remembered that "the idea seemed eminently right" to her at the time), especially as the production was intended to raise money for a class trip to Washington, D.C., that Paul would most likely not attend as he would be unable to get lodging in any of the capital's hotels.[35]

Along with acting and debating, Paul served as sports editor for the school's monthly newspaper, the *Valkyrie,* and was a member of the glee club as well. Paul enjoyed singing but, like the rest of his family, did not give the matter of his voice much thought. According to Ben Robeson, it was William Jr. who first noticed that Paul had a better than average singing voice. "The family had just finished dinner, the day was hot and sultry. . . . Bill suggested that we strike up a few tunes. We started out with gusto, Bill, Paul and I. 'Down by the Old Mill Stream' was the ballad of the day. . . . We were mulling one of those minor keys known only to home-loving groups; Paul was bearing down on us with boyish glee. . . . Bill yelled: 'Wait a minute, hit that note again Paul.' Paul hit it out of the lot, and Bill said: 'Paul, you can sing.'"[36] Later that evening Bill asked Paul to sing "Annie Laurie" for the rest of the family. "That was," Ben said, "the first time someone actually took time off just to listen to the boy's voice."[37] Still, none of the Robesons—neither the boys nor their father—paid serious attention to Paul's singing. William Robeson appreciated his voice on Sundays when Paul led the Sunday school and junior choir and on weekdays when he sang the solo at church concerts, but as Ben recalled, the family "never thought of singing lessons. Everyone sang; Paul was simply better than most."[38]

Somerville High School's music teacher Miss Vosseller not only noticed Paul's voice but saw to it that he received some rudimentary training. It was she who invited Paul to join the glee club (Brown stressed that it was a serious singing group that one was invited to join), and Brown and Paul made up the entire bass section. In fact, Brown laughingly recalled that "Paul could handle the whole section alone, his voice was that strong. One time we were singing at the Second Reform Church in Somerville the very difficult lines from Haydn's *Creation* beginning with the words 'Despairing, cursing rage,' and Paul could even handle that."[39]

High school evidenced not only Robeson's burgeoning musical, oratorical, and academic talents but his considerable athletic ability as well. As is often the case with great athletes, retrospective accounts of Paul's early athletic achievements often credit him with feats far beyond his youthful abilities. Stories abound like the 1932 *Pittsburgh Courier* report that described Robeson playing "semi-pro baseball" at the age of fifteen against players "who later became members of the New York Giants."[40] The facts of Robeson's high school athletic career are much more prosaic. Playing a variety of high school sports, including basketball and baseball, Robeson showed the most promise in football. He had learned the basics of the game as a youngster from his brother William, a talented athlete in his own right who played for Lincoln University and practiced with Paul on a weed-grown lot in Princeton whenever he was home from college. "He was my first coach, and over and over again . . . he would put me through the paces—how to tackle a man so he stayed tackled, how to run with the ball."[41]

Robeson played high school football as early as the seventh grade, in all likelihood invited by the Davenport's principal, J. L. Jamison, who functioned as a part-time coach at Somerville High. By the time he was in high school Paul had developed the ideal frame for a football player: he was tall, heavy, and physically powerful, with huge hands ("He threw a football the way we throw a baseball—his hands were that big," said one Somerville teammate.)[42] Though in the classroom friends teasingly called him "Chubby," on the gridiron Robeson's size was no joking matter. He almost always managed to intimidate the opposition and on occasion even his own teammates. "I played halfback," Brown said, "but was moved to center when necessary, and the times Paul was in the backfield and carried the ball I was more afraid of Paul running me over than of the opposition charging at me."[43]

The athletic success Robeson experienced at Somerville was small-time, and necessarily so given the size and limited resources of the school, which could not afford even a single paid coach. "We coached ourselves with the help of the manual training teacher and walked five blocks from the locker room to the playing field," said Brown. "Our style of play was rough and unpolished. Paul had big hands, and as much passing as there was, he did it. But the way we played—both offense and defense, a very strenuous game—he was used mainly as a fullback."[44] In short, it was a "learn as you go" game Paul played at Somerville.

Young and inexperienced, Robeson played good football, and in a small town where the Saturday game was a big event in an otherwise routine week, Paul was bound to be a local hero. And he was.

Affable, gregarious, and academically and athletically talented, Robeson was well liked by both teachers and classmates. He worked to live up to his father's and his own demanding expectations, but he had his faults and as a teenager was far from the stereotypical model of perfection portrayed by some of his biographers. Margaret Potter Gibbons, a classmate of Paul's and a lifelong friend of his sister Marian's, lived next door to the Robesons and characterized biographer Shirley Graham's Horatio Alger–like portrayal of Paul's teenage years as "pure fiction." Concerning Graham's claim that Paul rose early each morning to run errands for a local grocer before breakfast, Gibbons quipped: "As a matter of fact he lived a stone's throw from the school and barely made it to class on time as it was. Paul had a habit of oversleeping and was often late."[45]

Miss Miller remembered Paul as exasperatingly lazy, as his wife would later agree. Perhaps it was his unruffled manner that seemed to corroborate the racial stereotype; perhaps because his classwork did come easily, he gave it only half his effort. "His Latin teacher used to say he just made her furious," said Miller. "She declared she knew for certain he hadn't prepared his lesson, but when she called on him to translate he read it off almost perfectly at sight — and she couldn't do a thing. That's how clever he was."[46]

"Paul probably had the problem of being restless or too good for the class academically, and so was a bit on the fooling side," said one classmate. "He could certainly make you laugh."[47] "One of the attributes people so often overlook in Paul is his sense of humor," said J. Douglas Brown. "He could be very funny, but not in a harmful way, all in good fun. He loved to play pranks. Once, hiding outside the window of the biology teacher's home, he made believe he was a hooting owl." On another occasion, playing Marc Antony to Brown's Brutus, Robeson saw to it that humor superseded high drama. Brown recalled, "For this production, in front of the whole school we played a great joke by fixing up a dummy of Caesar and pouring catsup for blood all over it. When Caesar was carried onto the stage, I, as Brutus, gave my speech before the Senate, and Paul exclaimed, 'See where the noble Brutus struck.' Then Paul whipped off the sheet and there were the bloody dagger wounds. Everyone was stunned. Shakespeare would have appreciated it, but Miss Mandell, the drama teacher, sure didn't."[48]

More than once his joking got Paul into trouble. According to a local newspaper account, during his junior year Robeson took part in an unsupervised school variety show filled with coarse songs and jokes, poker playing, and drunken revelries. Audiences were shocked and in the aftermath pressured the

Board of Education to pass a resolution of "severe censure" on all who had participated.[49] Several times Paul's antics landed him in the principal's office. Evans ("Baldy") Ackerman, the stern disciplinarian who replaced student-favorite Anna Miller as principal during Robeson's senior year, failed to see anything funny in Paul's small infractions and punished him accordingly.

Almost everyone found Ackerman difficult to deal with (Brown had his woes in Ackerman's woodworking class, enough so that he transferred out, taking music appreciation instead; Somerville graduates almost universally agreed the principal "had no sense of humor" and "would tell anyone where to go when needed"), but the principal infuriated Paul, and often it took all the discipline Paul could muster to control himself in the principal's presence.[50] "As a boy in high school I tried my best to 'act right,'" Robeson said in 1958. "Certainly I had no idea of challenging the way things were. But courtesy and restraint did not shield me from all hostility: it soon became clear that the high school principal hated me. . . . The better I did, the worse his scorn. . . . He never spoke to me except to administer a reprimand and he seemed constantly to be looking for an excuse to do so." Paul took Ackerman's corrections personally, felt they were racially motivated, and even claimed that when the music teacher made him soloist of the glee club, she did so "against the Principal's furious opposition."[51] Robeson remembered that on those occasions when he was late for school, "like a watchful hawk, Dr. Ackerman would pounce on me, and his sharp words were meant to make me feel as miserably inferior as he thought a Negro was. One time he sent me home for punishment. Usually Pop preferred that the teacher's hand rather than his own should administer the proper penalty, but this time I had something to say about that. 'Listen Pop,' I said. 'I'm bigger now, but if that hateful old principal ever lays a hand on me, I swear, I'll do my best to break his neck!'"[52]

Robeson would always connect Ackerman with blatant racial bigotry, but in almost all other respects his years at Somerville High passed unmarred by overt racial conflict. In contrast to what he would experience playing sports at Rutgers, for example, there were few flagrant racial incidents with neighboring athletic teams. "There was none from our rival, Bound Brook, four miles away, or Plainfield, or New Brunswick," Brown recalled. "There was some trouble in Phillipsburg. With its bare gravel field, we watched out for it there against Paul. Phillipsburg was an industrial town — cement factory, immigrant labor — close to Easton, Pennsylvania. There was a rumor that a prize of a box of cigars would go to the Phillipsburg player who knocked Paul out cold. This was the only town where we worried about race hatred. I saw Paul angry enough times, but never in those settings. He refused to show his feelings when the crowd yelled racial slurs at him, just played hard. He was in every respect much bigger than those who were racially snide with him, and he was not going to let himself be thrown off pace by their remarks."[53]

Still, Paul was always aware that he was black and, therefore, different. "I was always remembering that I must not do this, or that, or I must not hit a boy back because I was colored. . . . In my classes I had to stay up late to prove that Negroes could also measure up in their studies; but every Negro boy and girl knows and accepts these obligations."[54] There were the unavoidable humiliations; some were perhaps so much a fabric of life that one wonders how much of it Robeson experienced as insulting. During his senior year, Paul's class put on a minstrel show in which he sang a solo and his classmates performed in blackface. Although the staging of large-scale professional minstrel shows began to wane in the 1880s, small amateur shows remained popular much longer, and at the turn of the century almost every city, town, and rural community had its own amateur minstrel group. It is possible, with minstrel shows such a staple of small-town entertainment, that Paul did not give much thought to the idea of joining his white classmates as they acted out this caricature of blacks. Or he may have sensed the insult but deliberately chose to overlook it. Or it could be that his own self-confidence and sense that his classmates respected him provided him with a means of disassociating himself from the demeaning stereotype.

To function in a white setting at the turn of the century in America meant negotiating a path through a minefield of such potential racial humiliations. It was a dilemma that Robeson faced repeatedly: how to avoid directly challenging the stereotype and, at the same time, maintain personal dignity and integrity. Like his own father forty-two years earlier, when Lincoln officials paraded young African "savages" across the stage as part of William Robeson's class's commencement services, Paul gave no outward indication as to what he was thinking or feeling or how he managed to reconcile this incident within himself. If he was embarrassed, oblivious, shamed, or angry, Paul sang his solo—"Down by the Old Mill Stream"—without ever letting those feeling show.[55]

In white social settings Robeson felt uncomfortable, even though, as he recalled, several of his teachers (Miss Vandeveer, who taught Latin, as well as Miss Bagg, the chemistry teacher) "made every effort to make me feel welcome and at ease in the school's social life. . . . Miss Bagg urged me to attend the various parties and dances, and when I did so, it was always she who was the first to dance with me."[56] Still, Paul backed away. "There was always the feeling that—well, something unpleasant might happen; for the two worlds of whites and Negroes were nowhere more separate than in social life. Though I might visit the homes of white classmates, I was always conscious that I belonged to the Negro community."[57]

Apprehensive that "something might happen," Paul did not attend the senior class trip to Washington, D.C.[58] Classmate Brown recalled, "There were forty of us in the senior class, and we were the first to take a trip to Washington. We sold chocolates door to door and conducted plays to raise money. Paul, with great sensitivity, decided not to go with us. The Metropolitan Hotel, where we were staying, would not have allowed him inside. Paul's father and older brother must have warned him about segregation in Washington and convinced him to stay home, I don't know. But he didn't come with us."[59] Though most of Paul's white classmates dismissed the incident, observing simply that "Paul knew his place very well," classmate Van Fleet recalled noticing, once the class was in Washington, how blacks were treated in the nation's capital, and understanding, perhaps for the first time, why Paul chose not to make the trip. "There were three rows of seats for blacks in the back of the bus. I had never seen anything like that. And as we were walking through the city, I watched blacks actually going off the sidewalk and walking in the gutter to get out of our way because we were white."[60]

Although Washington, D.C., with a population that was more than 30 percent black, was at the time considered "the undisputed center of American Negro civilization," the racial situation was grim. In 1896 the U.S. Supreme Court's ruling in *Plessy v. Ferguson* legalized the racial segregation of public facilities, and by 1915 equal treatment under the law had all but disappeared in the nation's capital. Racial segregation, already de facto in residential areas, extended to include schools, hospitals, and trade unions. In 1913 the newly elected Woodrow Wilson accelerated the downward spiral by reinstating segregation in federal offices, such as the Post Office and Treasury Department, and by having partitions set up to separate black and white employees. When William Monroe Trotter, editor of the *Boston Guardian*, complained to Wilson that blacks and whites had worked side by side in federal offices for half a century, Wilson told him to leave, admonishing him for his "manner," which the president said "offended" him. After a visit to Washington in 1913, Booker T. Washington wrote, "I have never seen the colored people so discouraged and so bitter as they are at the present time."[61]

Robeson's own social life centered around black Somerville and Princeton. Often he returned to Princeton to play sports for Somerville against old friends like Jimmy Fletcher and others on Princeton's black YMCA teams. It was a friendly but spirited rivalry, duly reported in the local press, as in December 1914 when Princeton beat the "crack team of Somerville" despite "two beautiful forward passes scored by Robeson and Jackson." After the game Robeson spent the day with Fletcher and others, "talking about old times and their plans for the future."[62]

On more than one occasion Paul made the trek to Princeton solely to visit 12 Spring Street, the home of Christine Moore, daughter of one of Princeton's most prominent black businessmen, William ("Sport") Moore.[63] Carlton Moss, a younger black friend of Paul's — also destined to find his life's work in theater and film — lived in the northern New Jersey area. Moss said that "outside of Princeton there was very little social life. I had an 'aunt' he [Robeson] brought home one night from a dance — walked home with her five miles in the snow — and then he had to trudge back by himself. We thought nothing of going twenty miles for a romance."[64] Paul and Christine had a budding romance, possibly even with plans to marry. Geraldine Neale Bledsoe, a friend of Christine's who was herself later (while a student at Howard University) engaged to Paul, said that Paul and Christine may have been engaged just before Paul went off to college. Others, among them Christine's nephew, Donald Moore, insisted they were not. "Engaged or not, Paul was very much in love with her at one time," concluded Bledsoe. "She was beautiful and her family — her parents, sister Bessie, and brothers Arthur and William — just adored Paul."[65]

When Paul was fourteen his brother Ben helped him land his first real job, one that was considered plum employment for young blacks: a summer job at Narragansett Pier in Rhode Island.[66] Boasting "the finest beach in the Northeast: a mile long curving shoreline with sparkling sand, a firm motion and a gentle undertow," Narragansett had for more than half a century attracted a large and faithful following among America's social elite.[67] This luxurious world of dancing, leisurely lunches, polo, music, and sunbathing was a gold mine for young blacks who worked as bellhops, waiters, maids, kitchen boys, and checkroom attendants.[68] Several black women who lived year round in the area amassed modest fortunes running laundries to service the white tourist trade. Hotel management viewed black college students as ideally suited for service positions and used a padrone system to select its hired help, working through its head bellman, a teacher from Augusta, Georgia, whose job it was to ferret out respectable black youngsters. Many black colleges had a long-standing arrangement of this sort with various northeastern resort areas. Booker T. Washington, for example, working through Hampton Institute, secured a job waiting on tables during the summer of 1875 at the prestigious United States Hotel in Saratoga Springs, New York.[69] At the Imperial Hotel, where Paul worked, the area's newest and most elegant hotel, guests always dressed for dinner and children ate in a separate dining room. The Imperial provided patrons with the best and charged them accordingly; a family with children and servants paid $1,500 a week.[70] Despite the hard work and long hours — ten or more hours a day, seven days a week — these jobs were coveted by blacks, not only for the lucrative pay (most earned their tuition after six to seven weeks of work) but also for the status that landing such a position conferred. Only the cream of the young black community — those who had distinguished themselves by family background and education or talent and ambition — won employment in this moneyed resort area.

Paul started out at the bottom as a kitchen boy his first summer. "My work — and I'm sure I never again in all my life worked quite so hard — began at 4:00 a.m. and it was late evening before I emerged from the mountains of pots and pans I scrubbed, the potatoes I peeled, the endless tasks ordered by the chef, the second cooks and helpers, all of whom outranked the kitchen boy and who were finished long before he had mopped up for the last time and put everything away in gleaming splendor."[71] The lessons Paul learned from his father — how to speak and conduct himself in the presence of whites — served him well at Narragansett. It was Paul's first close-up glimpse of a rich white world. In time he would negotiate it with ease, outshining his brother Ben, on whom he so depended that first summer, with his own engaging social graces. By the time he was a senior in high school Paul had worked his way up from, as he himself put it, an "innocent among the other, more worldly-wise, workers" to the enviable position of waiter at the Imperial Hotel.[72]

Almost all the hired help servicing the area's rich white vacationers was black. Like Princeton, then, Narragansett offered Paul a chance to make friends and socialize, whether jogging between shifts down to Narrow River or walking along the beach, singing, spending time together evenings, and attending church events on weekends. At Narragansett Paul met an elite group of young men and women, each "exceptions" in their own right. Whether enrolled in a black college or struggling to achieve in a white setting, these youngsters were bound by common goals, shared dreams, and the sense that they were charting new paths for others to follow.

Perhaps talking with other young blacks working at Narragansett widened Paul's horizons and started him thinking beyond his father's plans for him. William Robeson had always assumed Paul would follow in his and his brother Ben's footsteps, attend a black college, and prepare for the ministry. Paul had second thoughts but was unsure about what else he might do. During his senior year he learned through classmates (one source claims through two Rutgers professors present at a debate in which Paul participated) about a competitive examination, open to all New Jersey students, offering as a prize a four-year scholarship to Rutgers.[73] He told his father about the test, and William encouraged him to take it, as a scholarship would ease financial burdens considerably. "There was," as Paul recalled, "one big hitch: I should have taken the preliminary test the previous year, covering subjects studied in the first three years of high school."[74] Paul's explanation in *Here I Stand* of why he failed to take the preliminary exam, typically, takes on dark tones and suggests a deliberate effort on the part of some Somerville faculty to keep him uninformed. But if such plotting did occur, Robeson kept his knowledge of it a well-guarded secret until 1958. In all other instances, as Paul himself readily admitted, the vast majority of his high school teachers were more than willing to assist him, and it seems unlikely that in this case they suddenly took to malicious conniving to prevent his further academic progress.[75] A more plausible explanation is that Somerville's faculty, aware that Paul's father, brothers, and sister had attended black colleges, assumed Paul would do the same and so saw no reason to mention the exam to him.

Because he had not yet taken the preliminary test, Robeson had to complete both the junior and senior sections in the time span allotted for the senior portion only. This he did on June 5 and 6 at the local courthouse, and on July 15, 1915, the *New York Age* proudly announced that Robeson had won a $650 state scholarship to Rutgers College.[76] "Here was a decisive point in my life," Robeson later recalled. "Deep in my heart from that day on was a conviction which none of the Ackermans of America would ever be able to shake. Equality might be denied, but I knew I was not inferior."[77]

In fact, a gnawing sense of inferiority would plague Robeson for much of his life. It would not be until many years later, when he had to make decisions about his own son's education, that Robeson would begin to acknowledge the extent to which he had been emotionally damaged by his early years in Princeton, Westfield, and Somerville. Although he experienced none of the physical violence of the Deep South, Robeson had indeed been "brought up to believe that the Negro is inferior." It was a subtle but effective indoctrination that even years of success in the white world failed to erase. Thus, in the early thirties Robeson chose to send his own son halfway around the world to the Soviet Union for his schooling rather than hazard his "feeling what I did as a child."[78]

Robeson had proven himself academically and athletically in high school and at graduation ceremonies capped it all by delivering Somerville High School's 1915 commencement address.[79] Nearly six feet, two inches tall, muscular, handsome, and, like his father, very black, he cut a striking figure standing huge behind the podium. His oratorical display, his polished and perfect (white) diction, the product of years of coaching by his father, was no less arresting. In the rich, deep, sonorous voice for which he would one day be world-renowned, Robeson delivered the final message for his class.

Robeson had little idea what awaited him as he prepared himself to begin college. His own approach to racial matters mirrored that of his father, but his decision to attend a white college would confront him with dilemmas far removed from William Robeson's world and experience. Rutgers would offer Robeson opportunities unavailable at Lincoln or other black colleges, but it would also separate him and make him an oddity, one of the few black faces at an all-white institution. Traveling a road few before him had ventured, Robeson would leave for college both armed and weighed down by the legacy of his childhood years: tremendous ambition and drive fettered by shame and a sense of racial inferiority.

3

Robeson of Rutgers

1915–1919

From the day he first arrived at Rutgers on September 15, 1915, with his friend and Somerville classmate Art "Foot" Van Fleet, Paul Robeson stood out. A black face at this small New Jersey school on the outskirts of New Brunswick was enough of an oddity, but Robeson — six feet two, almost 200 pounds, and strikingly black — was impossible to miss.

In the decade before Robeson's arrival, Rutgers had transformed itself from a rural "cow college" specializing in an agricultural-technical curriculum to a serious academic institution offering a variety of liberal arts programs. College president William Demarest began taking steps to effect the change from his first year of tenure in 1906. By 1915 the school's curriculum had been substantially enhanced, admission procedures completely overhauled, and a host of new buildings added on land north of the old Queen's Campus (the Neilson Campus) and at the other end of the city on the Experiment Station Campus. Between 1905 and 1915 enrollments doubled from 250 to 500, and Robeson's freshman class numbered 185, the largest in the college's history.[1]

Despite its growth, Rutgers had not lost its small-school flavor and was still dwarfed by giants like Harvard and Columbia, both enrolling close to 4,000, and neighboring Princeton, which boasted five times Rutgers's student population. Incoming Rutgers freshmen typically hailed from northern areas of New Jersey, most the sons of farmers and ministers, small-town doctors and bankers, many the first in their families to attend college. Forty percent relied on state grants, and others, like Paul, financed their tuition through a combination of college scholarships, work, and benefactor assistance (in Paul's case, Somerville contractor Louis P. Gaston).[2]

Robeson would remember his college years as among the happiest times of his life. At Rutgers he would earn the success he yearned for and more recognition than as a freshman he ever dreamed possible. But this bright, reserved, and earnest seventeen-year-old had significant hurdles to overcome first. By choosing to attend Rutgers, Robeson had elected a course few blacks before him had attempted. (In 1915 fewer than fifty blacks attended white colleges nationwide.) There were no rules and few role models to follow. Racially the situation in America was as repressive as it had ever been. The year Robeson entered Rutgers, D. W. Griffith's spectacular *Birth of a Nation,* the movie version of Thomas Dixon's *The Clansman,* made its debut in theaters throughout the country. A lurid tale of Negro emancipation, the subsequent debauchery of white womanhood, and the South saved from total devastation by heroic Klansmen, *Birth of a Nation* portrayed blacks as stupid, occasionally vicious, brute animals. Off the movie screen, racism was equally oppressive. Jim Crow flourished, sanctioned by law in the South and custom in the North.[3] The sharecropping system and lily-white unions kept blacks economically trapped. In the South, intimidation and ingenious legal devices prevented the vast majority from voting, and lynchings — the ultimate weapon for keeping blacks in their place — remained an accepted fact of life. In such a racial climate even those most impatient with the pace of change thought twice about pushing issues. At Rutgers, then, Robeson would spend much of his time watching, listening, and assessing. He said the "right" things, sang the "right" songs, and assumed the "right" self-effacing attitude toward his own accomplishments. In exchange, he was allowed to succeed in a white environment.

During his college years, Robeson was many things to many people, and he poured tremendous energy into living up to his own and others' expectations. If the inner Robeson, the adolescent with his own thoughts and feelings, appears shadowy and submerged, it is no accident. Paul kept those feelings hidden, to some extent even from himself. For the time being there was the white world of Rutgers to conquer, the challenge of proving himself and his race competent and capable. In that context, attending to his own thoughts and feelings was a luxury Robeson could not afford.

Robeson had come to Rutgers to study, and from the start he devoted himself to his classes. He had his father's respect for learning and was determined to prove himself a scholar. "In the beginning," remembered lifelong friend and Rutgers classmate Malcolm ("Mal") Pitt, "Paul was quiet, almost apprehensive. He was always in the library studying. It was clear right away he was going to be a good student, or die trying."[4] Classmate Steve White agreed: "You never saw Paul as a freshman hanging around the campus. When he wasn't on the football field, he was either in his room poring over the books or trudging to the old Voorhees Library to study there."[5] Mathematics was Paul's favorite subject freshman year, but he applied himself to all his courses: he could not slide by on half efforts as he had in high school. He would earn two A's (algebra and public speaking), three B's (English literature, Greek, and Latin) and one C (English composition) that first semester and work hard for those grades. (Concerning the C in English composition, several of Robeson's friends remarked that although Robeson wrote easily and well, he lacked the patience to revise and rewrite and as a result his writing was often not as good as it might have been had he been willing to give it just a little more attention.)[6]

Robeson shared the universal adjustment difficulties of all college freshmen, but they were compounded and confused by racial factors. With his classmates he went through the traditional initiation rites, but in Robeson's case it was difficult to tell where initiation ended and his special treatment as a black began. A select number of newcomers, arriving with a reputation firmly in hand, would be courted by representatives of school clubs and organizations ranging from fraternities, the Glee Club, and the *Targum* (the Rutgers newspaper) to the school's debating team. Robeson was not among them. Paul endured with patience and good humor the ritual of upperclassmen critically appraising him, wondering what, if anything, the exclusion meant.

But in the area of athletics, and in particular football, the situation was different. Football would provide Robeson his means of winning acceptance at Rutgers. His outstanding play, especially during his junior and senior years, would put Rutgers on the map, transforming the rural cow college into a formidable athletic powerhouse, able to hold its own against the best collegiate teams in the country. Despite the lip service given to education, none of Robeson's academic achievements would even come close to opening the doors that a brilliant college football career opened for him. It would be for his prowess on the gridiron that Robeson would first be recognized and, in many cases, most remembered by sports-infatuated America. Football would introduce Robeson formally to the white world, reinforce for him the importance of modesty and self-effacement as strategies for getting along, and teach him that success — big success — could do much to ameliorate racial prejudices. Playing football would put Robeson's name in the limelight and give him his first real taste of fame. It was an experience he never forgot, and one that changed his life.

Robeson's years at Rutgers coincided with the period during which the game of football, so long denounced for its brutality, would finally come into its own as a sport commanding attention and respect. The road to such acceptance was long and rocky, and the game as we know it today was still in its infancy in 1915. As late as 1910 deaths and serious injuries in the sport were commonplace. (In 1905 eighteen college and secondary school players died and another 159 were injured; in 1909 thirty players, eight of them college men, lost their lives to the game.) Public outrage peaked in 1905 and 1906 as journals like *McClure's, Col-*

lier's, The Nation, and *Outlook* published scathing exposés documenting incidents of premeditated violence (teams often planned to "knock out" opposing players early in the game) and the "insidious" role of money in the game. By 1906 Columbia and the Massachusetts Institute of Technology had abolished the sport altogether, while Stanford and California substituted rugby for football.[7]

Advocates like Coach Walter Camp and "Mr. Athletics" himself, Theodore Roosevelt, ultimately beat down a nationwide crusade to ban the sport. What emerged in the aftermath was essentially a new game, as reforms and rule changes forced the development of new styles of play. Once a simple contest of brute strength, now skill and well-planned maneuvers emerged as equally important considerations in the game. The dramatic upset victory in 1913 of Notre Dame's Fighting Irish over the indomitable West Point eleven heralded the metamorphosis. Brilliant and breathtaking tactical innovations like the Gus Dorais–Knute Rockne forward pass caught the public's eye, and soon colleges and schools throughout the country took a fresh look at the sport.[8] Rutgers was no exception. With increased newspaper coverage and public acceptance of contact sports, by Robeson's junior year football would become the American college sport. And, precisely at the time when the nation was turning itself on to college athletics, Robeson would emerge as one of the game's most gifted players, selected for Walter Camp's elite all-American team to join players of the caliber of Walter Eckersall of the University of Chicago, Carlisle's Jim Thorpe, Eddie Mahan of Harvard, Army's Elmer Oliphant, and Frederick Douglass ("Fritz") Pollard of Brown.

Rutgers had a long football tradition dating back to 1869 when the college played host to Princeton in America's first intercollegiate game. But historically the school's attitude reflected that of the nation as a whole: it tolerated the sport but never promoted it. That picture changed in 1913 when a small but influential group of alumni, led by the head of the Delaware and Hudson Railroad, Leonor F. Loree (class of 1877), decided to put its money and business know-how into building an eastern powerhouse competitive with Yale, Brown, Princeton, and Harvard. President Demarest, anxious to secure increased alumni support of school affairs, encouraged the effort.[9] With the newly launched *Alumni Quarterly* fanning school spirit, Loree easily engaged others to support him in the formation of a "syndicate" to underwrite the improvement of Rutgers's athletic facilities, including erecting stands, building a fieldhouse, and grading and surfacing "the old coppermine field littered with gravel and stone" where the team had played before 1914.[10]

The syndicate wanted the best possible coach and so set its sights on the successful Columbia, West Point, and Yale veteran, Foster ("Sandy") Sanford, an athlete cut from the mold of football greats Walter Camp, "Pop" Warner, and Amos Alonzo Stagg.[11] Loree convinced Sanford to take the job even though as coach he would receive no compensation. Sanford owned a prosperous insurance business in New Haven and, according to player Steve White, "rumors of the day" were that "unofficial payment came from the insurance business he [Sanford] got from Loree's railroad."[12]

Although Sanford agreed only to "come for a few years" to develop a "graduate coaching system" of former players who would eventually take his place, he remained at Rutgers for ten years, earning in that time an impressive record of fifty-six wins, thirty-two losses, and five ties. For a full decade, from 1913 to 1923, Foster Sanford's innovations and trick plays—the hurdle play, the Rutgers formation, and the multiple kick—kept opponents guessing, the Rutgers team scoring, and fans sitting on the edge of their seats.[13]

Rutgers had never known such a personality. Articulate, commanding, colorful, and dynamic, he immediately became an idol to his players and to the vast majority of the student body as well. Without exception, players spoke of Sanford in superlatives and looked to him for advice and encouragement both on and off the football field.[14] Sandy insisted the team be provided proper protective equipment, a training table, and a full-time trainer. He demanded amenities such as undershirts and towels and secured for his men the voluntary services of a team doctor. Fanatic in his devotion to the game, Sandy even had built for himself a high platform from which he could oversee practices and shout orders to players below. "A splendid physical specimen himself, he influenced me more than any man in my life," said player Steve White. "He was like my father. He taught us to achieve beyond our abilities," said all-American Robert ("Nasty") Nash, a veteran senior who later coached at Rutgers and played professionally with Paul in the fledgling National Football League. "Sandy insisted on strict training habits," recalled White. "He did not smoke or drink, nor did he use profanity, but he could talk a very rough English, which everyone understood. He taught us epigrams, written out on posters in the locker room, such as 'When I come out on the field, it's with a stranger's eye' and 'I never judge a man by his yesterday, but always by his tomorrow and his today.'"[15] Many team members, even as old men, could still easily recall the sayings Sanford had drilled into them a lifetime ago.[16]

As Sanford began his third year at Rutgers in 1915, he was well on his way to shaping the "Scarlet Scourge" into a football team to be reckoned with. "Rutgers definitely had its eye on Paul, and the coach knew he was a good player," recalled Somerville High School classmate Douglas Brown.[17] Robeson, however, was not invited to fall camp, and competition to make the team was stiff.[18]

Rutgers had earned a fine record the previous year and could afford to overlook even a talented newcomer. Veteran players quickly made their feelings known. "It was hard enough just making the team," said White, "without having some newcomer like Robeson take over your position."[19]

Robeson understood players would fight to defend their spots and anticipated a rough go of it, some mistreatment even, during tryouts. His initiation, however, proved more trying than even his grimmest expectations. Race, while not the sole cause of his testing, added fire to the fervor with which upperclassmen put him through the paces. The coincidental and widely publicized exploits of the notorious black prizefighter, Jack Johnson, the only black athlete most white Americans had ever heard of, did not make Robeson's task any easier. (Only a very few blacks, a total of fourteen between 1915 and 1919, played on white college teams, and none had the name recognition of Johnson.)[20] Johnson's victories—winning the heavyweight championship in 1908 and successfully defending his title against Jim Jeffries, the "Great White Hope," in 1910—stunned white Americans. His attitude both in the ring (he badgered, taunted, and jeered white opponents) and outside of it (he was a big spender and a flashy dresser with large cars and a white woman always in tow) exacerbated white America's most deeply held racial fears. Most whites were relieved when finally, in 1915, Jess Willard, the giant farmboy from Kansas, "restored the color line" and won back the title, knocking the infamous heavyweight champion out in the twenty-sixth round in Havana, Cuba. Johnson's arrogance and "disrespect" had shaken white America, right down to the small "cow college" in northern New Jersey. Rutgers players did not want to lose their spots—period. But if they did, they most certainly were not about to be sidelined by a Negro.[21]

Sanford's position was that, as far as making the team was concerned, Robeson was on his own: he would not interfere. As coach he understood that if Robeson could not hold his own against his teammates, he would never be able to withstand the assault from opposing teams in a real game situation. "There's a big darky on the field," Sanford announced to the squad in the dressing room before practice. "If you want him OK, if not OK."[22] "I was 17 years old when that happened," Robeson said later. "Rutgers had a great team that year, but the boys—well—they didn't want a Negro on their team, they just didn't want me on it. On the first day of scrimmage they set about making sure I wouldn't get on their team. One boy slugged me in the face and smashed my nose, just smashed it. That's been trouble to me as a singer every day since. And then when I was down, flat on my back, another boy got me with his knee, just came over and fell on me. He managed to dislocate my right shoulder."[23]

Robeson's injuries were serious enough to have him sidelined for ten days.

Discouraged, he wondered whether making the team or even continuing at Rutgers was really worth it. His brother Bill visited him while he was recuperating and urged him not to quit: "Kid, I know what it is. I went through it at Pennsylvania. If you want to quit school, go ahead, but I wouldn't like to think, and our father wouldn't like to think, that our family had a quitter in it!"[24] Paul listened. After ten days in bed and a few days at the training table he was out on the field again.

"Oh yes, he took a terrific beating," recalled Nash, "one of the first colored boys, you know. We gave him a tough time . . . but he took it well." "Remember, Paul was no little boy," Paul's friend Revels Cayton wryly observed. "He was inexperienced, but he had raw physical strength and knew how to use it. He had spent summers working in a brickyard, loading bricks onto a chute all day. 'Believe me,' he told me, 'that was slave labor! And when I finished the day I knew I was tired, but by the time I got to Rutgers I was already as strong as many of these older white fellows.'"[25]

Although Coach Sanford said he wanted "no more monkey business with Robeson on the field," when Robeson returned to practice veteran players continued to muscle in on him. One incident stood out in his mind for years. He had landed on the ground after making a tackle, flat on his back with his arm stretched out, right palm facing down. One of the regulars spotted him and stomped on his unprotected hand. "He meant to break bones," Paul said. "The bones held, but his cleats took every single one of the fingernails off my right hand." Robeson remained in the scrimmage but made up his mind to get revenge. (There were precious few situations in which a black man could safely express anger toward whites, but football was one of them.) On the next play "the whole first string backfield came at me. I swept out my arms . . . and then three men running interference went down. Next came the ball carrier, a back named Kelly, I wanted to kill him, and I meant to kill him. It wasn't a thought, it was just a feeling." Catching up with Kelly, Paul lifted him up over his own head. "I was going to smash him so hard to the ground that I'd break him in two, and I could have done it, but just then the coach yelled the first thing that came to his mind, he yelled 'Robey you're on varsity!' That brought me around."[26]

Some of Paul's teammates later denied that racial considerations played any part in the abuse. William Feitner, himself a 1915 freshman scrub, went as far as to call Robeson's rendition of his tryouts "slanderous." "No one ever stepped on Paul's hand," Feitner insisted, nor was anyone "out to get him because he was colored. Paul was treated no worse than any of us scrubs. All of us were worked hard to see if we were men enough to make the team. It was something we had to live with until we were accepted."[27] Nasty Nash, while less quick to dismiss the racial factor, also took issue with Robeson's "not exactly true" recollections.

"Scrubs got all the poorest equipment—worn pads, shoes two sizes too big, and oversized helmets that spun around your head when you got hit. It was not racial," Nash said, but added with a knowing grin, "Let's just say we didn't exactly greet him with open arms." But, according to several coaches, even as late as 1935 blacks playing on desegregated college teams went through unusually gruelling tryouts, well beyond those endured by their white teammates. To succeed, black players needed not only talent but tremendous self-control and the ability "to take it" as well. Harry Kipke, coach at the University of Michigan, recalled demanding that his veterans pound black candidates "without mercy" during practice. Said Kipke: "If, at the end of the week he doesn't turn in his uniform then I know I have a great player."[28]

All-American Fritz Pollard, a friend of Robeson's who had endured similar experiences at Brown University where he was the only black on the football team, insisted Paul's story was true. Although he was a great ball player and an energetic self-promoter and hustler, Pollard was not a scholar and devoted his energies primarily to playing ball and finding new ways to make money. On the campus at Brown and during summers at Narragansett Pier he ran successful pressing and tailor shops, the first of his many business ventures. His biographer, John Carrol, refers to him as a "tramp athlete" and, indeed, he attended college specifically for the opportunity to play football. He played for Dartmouth and Harvard before enrolling at either school as a student, played for Brown but never graduated, and went on to play professionally.

Pollard knew what playing with an all-white team was like and said that Paul did not exaggerate. "I not only had to practice by myself, separated from the rest of the team, but I was segregated in the locker room as well," he remembered.

My brothers had played football. Leslie played at Dartmouth, and he coached me when I was still in high school. They told me the whites would be out to get me, but by the time I left high school in Chicago and went to Brown I was used to that. In scrimmages I was a scrub and then later in games against opposing teams I had to be especially careful about gang tackles. My brothers taught me to protect myself by keeping my legs and elbows and arms kicking and swinging. That stopped tacklers from piling on. I was a kicking and swinging fool, I'll tell you! At Brown the day the team handed out the uniforms, the athletic department wouldn't give me one. Maybe they thought my color would stain the uniform. That hurt more than any of the other stuff, beatings and all. I went back to my segregated section of the locker room, down in the boiler room—even there they didn't want me—and I hid behind the lockers and cried my eyes out.[29]

Robeson survived his initiation, won a place on the team, and was accepted at the mealtime training table, which, according to Nash, "meant he was really one of us."[30] As a freshman Paul was a solid, rugged ballplayer but still crude and undisciplined. Coach Sanford, who would play such a pivotal role in shaping this raw talent, saw to it that the team helped Robeson improve his play.[31] "Remember, this was long before specialization in football, and you might be called to play a variety of positions—tackle, guard, or end," said Kenneth ("Thug") Rendall. "But Paul was a willing learner. He said very little but listened hard."[32] Player Harry Rockafeller agreed: "Paul's willingness to learn and his desire to be excellent were his major strengths."[33]

Like Pollard, Robeson would be fair game for opposing players out to "kill that nigger," and Coach Sanford personally took charge of teaching him special strategies for protecting himself. At practice Sandy lined up wooden orange crates on each side of Robeson and then had Paul, from a three-point stance, vault upward on signal, flailing away with his elbows and forearms until he had smashed the crates to pieces. "Sandy taught Paul how to use those elbows and forearms as protective weapons. Extremely powerful in the thighs and legs, Paul would get off the mark, bounding up very quickly. As he did so, those elbows and forearms moved with lightning speed. In a game situation he flattened his rival before the opponents or the official even knew what was happening. By the time the victim realized what had hit him, Paul was usually down the field."[34]

The 1915 season put Rutgers in the national limelight as the Scarlet Scourge posted a record of seven wins and only one loss and led the nation in scoring, outdistancing its opposition by a staggering margin of 351 to 33. As the wins mounted, Sandy emptied his bench, allowing freshman Robeson to see action in a number of games. "From the very beginning Paul had a rough defensive assignment," said Steve White. "He was on the left side of the line, opposite the offensive right, and since most of the teams ran right, they came straight at him. You knew he was going to be in on a lot of tackling and it would be rough."[35] Used primarily as defensive tackle or guard, Robeson, with his enormous hands, demonstrated equal talent on offense as a pass receiver. "I remember him backing up the line," said John Wittpenn, "moving around with that excited nervous energy, calling to the lineman 'Give me light, just let me see 'em.'"[36]

Rutgers's only real challenge that season came from the Princeton University team. The rivalry between the two schools was an old one, dating back to 1869 when Rutgers beat Princeton in that historic first intercollegiate match-up. But in twenty-one games from 1870 to 1912 Rutgers had failed to score a single victory against this formidable opponent. "Oh, how we wanted to beat Princeton," player Steve White reminisced with emotion. "They were elite snobs who looked down their noses at us. Rutgers didn't have any of that recognition. They thought we were a small country cow college and we resented their superior airs." Robeson, who remembered well that in Princeton "smart" Negroes kept their place, had his own reasons for wanting to trounce Rutgers's southern rival. But victory eluded them all as Princeton edged Rutgers out by a score of 10 to 0. "Princeton had to fight like hell to beat us ten to nothing," Steve White remembered. "Still, it was a tough loss."[37]

Robeson did not play in the Princeton match-up. According to several of his teammates he was benched, not because the southern team refused to play with a black man in the opposing lineup but because Sanford did not want to play an inexperienced freshman in such a crucial game. Robeson's lack of experience and control did on occasion cause him problems that year. One reporter described Rutgers's 39 to 3 victory over Stevens Tech as "marred a number of times by the unfair tactics used by Robeson." Specifically, the writer detailed a botched play resulting in a fumble and subsequent scramble for the loose football on the Rutgers 22-yard line. A Rutgers man recovered the pigskin but, when a Stevens player tried to tackle him, Robeson "threw his arms around his neck" to prevent him from making the tackle.[38]

Overall, however, Robeson's first season had been a good one. He had listened and learned, and his teammates and Sandy liked him. Often Robeson was seen "walking back to the old gymnasium on Hamilton and George Street after practice on Neilson Field . . . arm-in-arm with Sanford" as the two "raised their voices in a rendition of 'On the Banks of the Raritan'" and Sandy's favorite "Goofa Dust."[39]

Off the football field, in other areas of Rutgers life, Robeson followed a similar strategy for getting along: he watched and listened, kept his feelings to himself, and tried to do the "right" thing. At Rutgers Robeson refined the social etiquette he had learned living in white Westfield and Somerville. Trespassing racial lines in social settings inevitably caused embarrassment, and Robeson did everything he could to avoid such incidents. No one told him to monitor his mingling with Rutgers students, to refrain from joining friends for a sandwich and nickel beer at Hennessey's, the local pub, or to decline meeting them at the drugstore on Eastern Avenue for morning coffee and doughnuts. He understood the social etiquette and had no intention of challenging it.

And, indeed, Robeson had read the unspoken rules correctly. No Rutgers fraternity asked him to join. Paul frequently visited Rendall and Van Fleet's fraternity, "the Queen's," and enjoyed house privileges at several others as well, but because he was not allowed into white fraternities he joined Alpha Phi Alpha, the oldest black fraternity in the country. "I fought in my fraternity, Delta Epsilon, to get Paul in," said Pitt. "But there was a national by-law forbidding the mixture of race. Jews were not allowed in either."[40]

Robeson also was never asked to join the school Glee Club, undoubtedly because of the socializing (with female choruses from other schools with whom Rutgers would sing in joint concerts) that followed performances. There was no question he was qualified; nor was Rutgers unaware of his musical talent. Robeson used his fine singing voice whenever he had the opportunity: in churches and at informal gatherings on campus, accompanied on the piano by Mal Pitt; with his football teammates in between courses at team suppers; and possibly, on occasion, at local Rutgers Glee Club performances. (Robeson did not consider such occasional participation Glee Club membership, nor did *Targum*, which never listed Glee Club as among Robeson's extracurricular activities.)[41] As classmate Andrew F. Eschenfelder explained, "Social functions were all-white, and Robey never forced himself in. As people used to say in those days, he 'knew his place.'"[42]

For the most part Robeson said nothing about these slights. Every now and then, he talked with his friend Fritz Pollard, one of the few people in a position to understand what he was going through, and on a few occasions with family members. But, generally, Paul absorbed the full impact of these experiences himself. Problems that arose traveling with the football team Robeson handled matter-of-factly, as if where he stayed or ate did not matter at all to him. "Never mind making eating arrangements for me. I'll make my own way when I get there," Robeson told the team manager that first year. "The rest of the team didn't want to allow it, but that was the way Paul wanted to approach it," Mal Pitt remembered. "Paul was very sensitive about the race question. Finally, he did agree to eat and stay with the team, but told the manager that if there were any difficulties he would take care of himself."[43]

Often Paul used humor to ease the tension when such incidents occurred. "When he was not allowed into a restaurant with us and had to eat in the kitchen," John Wittpenn remembered, "he kidded us afterwards. 'I feel sorry for you guys. You got such little helpings out there in the restaurant. In the kitchen they fed me royally!'"[44] According to Mal Pitt, on those few occasions when he "did talk about racism he was almost always satiric about it. 'Sure, I can play sports but can't join the Glee Club because that's too *social*! Ha! Ha!'"[45]

Although Paul might have said it was his friends' feelings he wanted to spare, in fact, it was his own sense of self-worth he was trying to maintain in adopting either a humorous or an indifferent attitude toward racial slights. Emotionally, the experience of Jim Crow was so damaging that he would do almost anything to avoid being reminded of the extent to which he was still at the mercy of that social code. Robeson retreated and tried to blend in, but such compliance took its toll on him psychologically. White students saw only a gregarious and easy-going Robeson, singing the old favorite "Goofa Dust" with Sandy and the boys, never the isolated and occasionally despairing young Robeson who on more than one occasion wanted to quit Rutgers altogether.[46]

Robeson was treated with far more tolerance than were the Jewish members of the school's student body. As the only black man on campus his first year and one of three blacks enrolled during his junior and senior years, Robeson's presence constituted no serious threat to the larger student body. The college's Jewish population, however, most the children of recently immigrated eastern European Jews, was substantial, and anti-Semitism at Rutgers, as at other colleges, was not only widespread but tolerated in its most blatant manifestations.[47] A number of Paul's friends recalled jeering the school's "New York Jews," warning them "to go back to CCNY where they belonged."[48] Thug Rendall remembered being "made to sit at the back of the classroom with the Jewish students" as punishment from a chemistry teacher who disliked him because he played football and did poorly in academics.[49] When Leo Frank, a successful Atlanta Jewish businessman convicted of raping Mary Phagan, a white employee, was lynched in 1915 in Marietta, Georgia, a few days after the governor commuted his death sentence, many at Rutgers felt he got exactly what he deserved. None of the school's fraternities would consider accepting Jews, and when Jewish students in 1915 attempted to organize their own fraternity hostilities flared. Three years later, in 1919, after much controversy, the school finally granted the Jewish Phi Epsilon Pi formal permission to exist. The student body, however, pointedly expressed its disapproval by conspicuously ignoring the new fraternity. Similarly, the formation of another Jewish organization, the Campus Club, met with such opposition that members, conceding defeat, bitterly disbanded in 1918.[50]

One can only speculate on how Robeson reacted to Rutgers's anti-Semitism. One thing is clear: he missed none of it. Paul later told friends that he had always felt "a mystical feeling, an almost unexplainable rapport with Jews."[51] Small wonder. There was the shared experience of bigotry, no doubt, but for Paul the ties ran deeper. As a child he had witnessed the easy friendship between his father and his neighbor, the Russian Jewish immigrant Samuel I. Woldin. Woldin was the only white person Paul had ever seen treat his father as both an equal and a friend; it was something Robeson never forgot.[52]

Paul's personal experience with Jews at Rutgers would only solidify the identification. Like Rutgers's Jewish population Paul was expected to room with "his own kind" or by himself. During his first two years at Rutgers Robeson roomed alone in Room 142 in Rutgers's legendary Winant's Hall. (White classmate Steve White conjectured that Robeson preferred this arrangement.[53] Given Paul's temperament, one can safely assume he did not want to make an issue of his rooming arrangements, which is not the same as saying that living alone was what Robeson preferred.) In his junior year Paul was assigned space with two younger black students, Robert Ritter Davenport of Orange, New Jersey (class of 1920) and Leon Harold Smith of Saugerties, New York (class of 1921), but as a senior he roomed with a white Jewish student, Herbert Miskend (class of 1922), apparently without incident.[54] Should anxious parents or alumni protest this apparent breach of racial etiquette, Rutgers officials would have an out: Robeson's roommate may have been white but he was not a Gentile.

Still, Jewish students at Rutgers had each other to lean on whereas Paul was virtually alone. Rutgers would offer Robeson things he wanted badly — status, achievement, a sense of legitimacy — but his need for community, family, and a social life would be met elsewhere: in the black communities of Princeton, Somerville, and New Brunswick (all were within fifteen to twenty miles of each other); during summers at Narragansett; and at gatherings of black college students held periodically throughout the year. Robeson lived two rich but distinct lives: one in the white world and the other in the black community. So separate were these worlds that most Rutgers students had no idea that Robeson had *any* social life. Some, like track manager Harold Higgins, occasionally wondered where Robeson disappeared to when the team traveled. "We had a meet one time, just outside of Princeton, and Robey was nowhere to be found. I finally tracked him down, but he never said a word about where he had been. I assumed he had sneaked off to visit a girlfriend."[55] "I don't recall Paul going to any of the social functions — dances, the Military Ball — things like that," said Mal Pitt. "He never said anything about it one way or the other. I think his father was more of the old school, which meant it was kind of wrong to go to such events and stir racial feelings."[56] Most of Robeson's classmates never gave the matter of his social life much thought. They appreciated his "sensitivity" and would later praise him for knowing enough "never to push himself into social situations."[57] Robeson did not attend Rutgers social functions, and there the matter rested.

On occasion, shuttling back and forth between two worlds created conflicts for Paul. Most Sundays, for example, he returned to Somerville to help his father by singing and reading the Gospel at the various churches where he preached and, during the summer, teaching Sunday school. Paul's accomplishments, large and small, were well known in Somerville, as the *New York Age* and local Somerville papers featured news of Paul and other members of the Robeson family on an average of once a month.[58] (Much of the material was gathered by an itinerant "reporter" in the area, quite possible William Robeson himself.) The emotional, elemental AMEZ church services, with their animated preaching, singing, shouting, and receiving of the spirit were unlike anything Paul saw in the white world of Rutgers. Paul's familial and communal loyalties drew him to church services, but once back at school he felt shame and embarrassment over his participation in what the white world regarded as ignorant emotionalism. More often than not, however, the embarrassment passed. "I'd leave college a little ashamed of my frequent conversions," Robeson recalled, "but if I went to Church, before the service was over I would be singing with the rest of them." Although Robeson would later describe himself to friends as not particularly religious, he admitted that the emotional power of spirituals evoked something very much like a religious experience for him. Later, it would be Robeson's singing of spirituals that would create an experience for secular, worldly audiences that they would remember as religious in its intensity.[59]

At other times the differences between the two worlds were easier to reconcile. Robeson played basketball for Rutgers, but the college placed little emphasis on the sport and in 1915 it even threatened to cancel the entire season unless alumni contributed funds to defray the season's expenses.[60] But Robeson played for better, more competitive teams as well, and these games were social as well as athletic events. During his freshman and sophomore years, for example, Paul often combined visiting his father with playing basketball for the "Manhattan Machine," New Brunswick's all-black YMCA team, against other black teams in Princeton, Freehold, Orange, and Elizabeth. During his junior and senior years he played for the Harlem-based all-black St. Christopher's "Red and Black Machine," a team that played top-notch, high-powered basketball. Win or lose, Manhattan Machine and St. Christopher games always ended with a dance. When the Manhattan Machine, led by "the Rutgers athlete [Robeson] . . . high man for the Manhattans," made the February trek from New Brunswick to Harlem for a match with the Alpha Moguls, the *New York Age*'s Ted Hooks accorded the occasion the attention it deserved and listed by name not only team members ("Lloyd Ivy and C. Ivy, H. Hoagland, Branch, A. Reed, and W. Brokaw") but also the loyal female following and other fans ("Misses Olive Rancher, Isabelle Mason, Estella Stanford, Anna White, Anna Fletcher, Messers Chester and Henry Jennings") who accompanied the team to New York.[61]

Summers at Narragansett put Paul in still another black setting. When he wasn't working, Paul made friends, socialized, gave informal recitals, walked the beaches, and practiced football. Fritz Pollard ("a sort of big brother in a small package," Pollard's own description of his friendship with Robeson) played baseball with Paul and played piano for him when he sang at a small club organized by the summer staff. Pollard knew his way around the area and introduced Paul to people in Narragansett and took him by train "up to Providence to introduce him to the black society there."[62] Paul spent time with Joe Nelson, a Princeton friend attending Howard University who worked with him at the Imperial (Paul got him the job), and together they socialized with Narragansett

Indians and with a few white Jewish girls who lived in the area. "We went to the beach just about every day," Nelson remembered. "Paul brought a football with him and practiced while we watched. It was such a sight to see — that enormous person catching passes on the beach. Among all of us there was an ease and friendliness," remembered Nelson. When asked if anyone complained that he and Paul were socializing with white women, Nelson replied, "It really wasn't dating; we usually did things together, as a group. We didn't pay any mind to it — color that is. Fannie Chopek (her father was a tailor at Narragansett) was white, we were black, and the Indians were red. We were all having a good time, that's all. But then again, I suppose it would have been a different story if we'd been in Jim Crow Washington."[63]

Paul became friends with the Recklings — Ralph and his sisters Louise and Bertha — year-round residents of Narragansett's black community who claimed both black and Narragansett Indian ancestry. Margaret Upshur, another year-round black Narragansett resident whose parents ran a local laundry business, remembered playing piano for Paul at small informal recitals held at a little theater hall on Beach Street. "We even sold tickets to make a little extra money. Some of the white help came and went back and told their employers about Paul's voice, and at the next recital some of the employers came. Paul sang some popular songs, standards, but aside from these, the spirituals were what he sang. Whites thought blacks sang naturally, and Paul — so polite and gentlemanly — sang just what they wanted to hear. At our own get-togethers Paul was great fun. He always liked to sing and loved to dance, too, and was good — very easy on his feet. He was so different from his brother Ben; Paul was the life of it."[64]

When the summer ended, Robeson switched gears and returned to life at Rutgers, which meant another season of football and another year of the grind to keep his grades up. (Robeson's much improved grades, in the second semester after the football season had ended — all A's with the exception of one B — suggest the toll football exacted on his studies.)

The Rutgers football team faced a tougher schedule than in the previous year, but its 1915 showing had been encouraging, and the team was ready for the challenge. The season began magnificently with the team easily downing Villanova 30 to 0, and Robeson, stronger and more disciplined after a year's experience, started and played a full sixty minutes. Players and fans hoped for an especially good showing on Homecoming Weekend against Virginia's Washington and Lee University. Rutgers was celebrating its 150th anniversary, and Homecoming activities promised to be unusually spirited, "*the* big event of 1916, a gala weekend."[65]

More than 200 delegates representing over 150 colleges, universities, and learned societies from around the world and some 900 alumni packed the

Alumni House and New Brunswick hotels that beautiful autumn weekend in October. The cow college had come into its own as a reputable academic institution, and the coming year would see that new identity given formal sanction as the former private Reform Church School was officially designated the State University of New Jersey. That Saturday, after the recognition of delegates and conferring of honorary degrees in Kirkpatrick Chapel, the alumni parade (numbering in its ranks the ten survivors of Rutgers's original 1869 football team) formed on the Queen's Campus and marched through the city and on to Neilson Field for the contest with Washington and Lee.[66] For many, football, now a staple feature of Rutgers life, embodied the school's new winning spirit. Fans expected a good game and the Scarlet Scourge was determined not to disappoint them.

But in the midst of these happy events Robeson faced a painful and humiliating dilemma. Before the game, Coach Sanford gathered the team in the locker room and informed them that Washington and Lee refused to play with a black man in the lineup. "It's up to you fellows," Sanford said. "Does he [Robeson] play or not?"[67] "Paul understood Rutgers would be in an awkward position if no football game were played after thousands had turned out for the big Homecoming contest," player William Feitner remembered. Finally Robeson broke the silence, and "smoothed everything over" by voluntarily benching himself. "'You don't need me,' Paul told the team. 'You can beat them without me.'"[68] Paul's teammates were relieved. As one teammate put it, "The colored boy knew his place and did not butt in or crusade." As they saw it, Paul had done the right thing, apparently taken the incident in stride, and that was the end of it.[69]

Playing without Robeson, Rutgers held Washington and Lee to a 13 to 13 tie and had a great celebration afterward followed by a Sunday morning of festivities, none of which Paul attended. Instead, he went home to talk with his father. William Robeson understood what being on the team meant to Paul and, despite his insistence that Paul put his studies first, had been, from Paul's freshman year on, his son's most avid fan. (By Paul's sophomore year, classmates had grown accustomed to seeing his father, an anachronism in his frock coat, "so long it looked like a six footer's cast-off," at what had become *his* place in the stands. Some even looked upon the "grizzled little pastor" as a "sort of good-luck charm.")[70] Paul was upset about the incident, wanted to leave Rutgers, and told his father as much. "But my father told me he hadn't sent me to college to play football and vetoed my plan to switch colleges [from Rutgers to Dartmouth]."[71] Long before Paul even set foot on the Rutgers campus his father had "drummed it into his head that he would be on display . . . and so would have to bend over backwards to be a good sportsman." In William's mind this case was no exception.[72]

Judging from Robeson's performance during the remainder of the season, his absence cost Rutgers a clear victory on Homecoming Day. For Robeson the disappointment ran deeper than chagrin over a lost game. Like his teammates, Paul looked up to Sanford: although the coach was white, Paul trusted him and regarded him as a friend and father figure. In several instances he went to him with personal problems, and on those occasions when Paul, afraid of injury or holding back for some other reason, failed to work up to his potential, Sandy would call him "into the office and straighten him out."[73] In this case Sanford had let Robeson down. His refusal to come to Paul's defense, or to say anything in Paul's behalf, had, by default, placed all the responsibility on Robeson who, as an unheralded sophomore, had little choice but to save face as best he could by gracefully backing out.

Neither had Paul's teammates, individually or as a group, supported him by refusing to play without him.[74] In later years, when he reminisced about his adolescence, it was Somerville classmate J. Douglas Brown and Mal Pitt from Rutgers—both scholars rather than athletes—that Robeson singled out as friends. He rarely mentioned Sanford or any of his Rutgers football teammates. It is possible that their behavior in the case of Washington and Lee had hurt him deeply, enough so that he would never consider any of them close friends. Or it may be that Paul simply had more in common with someone like Mal Pitt, whose father was also a Methodist minister and whose artistic interests more closely matched his own.[75]

Outwardly, however, Paul "took it" and the next week went back to play before a cheering crowd of 5,000 in Providence, Rhode Island, where Rutgers clashed with Fritz Pollard's formidable Brown University team. Pollard, who talked with Robeson about the Washington and Lee incident at the Rutgers–Brown game, said that Paul "didn't say much, mostly listened while I talked, but he was still mad as anything about what had happened the week before. Even someone as big and physically powerful as Paul had to keep that anger under control. The football field was really the only place where you could do anything that amounted to retaliation—beating up on those white boys. When you got mad about the racial thing it sure made you play all the harder. Yeah, so Paul played a hell of a game defensively against us that day." Rutgers held onto a slim 3 to 0 lead at halftime and bettered Brown well into the third period before Brown moved into high gear and beat Rutgers 21 to 3. "Paul was mad, but he hadn't lost his sense of humor. We actually had some fun together on the field that day," said Pollard. "With two blacks out there, each on opposing teams, they couldn't very well pick on us as 'niggers' that game. There was big Paul staring me down with that smile of his, and joking as he came at me, 'Now Fritz be careful. Look out! Fritz, I don't want to hurt you.'"[76]

Rutgers went on to play West Virginia University to a hard-fought scoreless tie, then rolled over Dickinson, 34 to 0, and beat Washington and Jefferson 12 to 9. Local newspapers had praised Robeson's play all season, but his role in the Washington and Jefferson victory earned him his highest accolades to date. "The strongest man on the [Rutgers] team. . . . Robeson tore great holes in the opposing line," wrote Frank Hathorn, covering the game for the *New York World*. "When given the ball [he] plunged ahead with such power that it often required two or three men to bring him down. . . . His tackling was deadly."[77]

The team was disappointed with its record of three wins, two losses, and two ties. But the season had been a good one for Robeson—he had started every contest (with the exception of Washington and Lee), played a full sixty minutes per game, and earned some glowing press coverage.[78] In short, he had demonstrated his ability and set the stage for what would be two years of uncontested greatness on the gridiron.

Academics and a host of new extracurricular activities—the Philoclean Literary Society, the Rutgers debate team, winter and spring sports—filled the gap left when the football season ended. Paul had his father's love of oratory and at Rutgers demonstrated his prodigious talent by winning every major elocution and debating contest he entered as well as leading the school's debating team to successive victories.[79] In addition, he played basketball, track, and baseball for school teams, and on weekends at home in Somerville he played more sports and took part in local social activities.

The surface picture—the record of academic achievement and a wide array of extracurricular accomplishments—suggests an energetic, enthusiastic, and socially well-adjusted young man who apparently preferred to do many things well rather than a few things perfectly. (Paul's grades in his sophomore year, although still honors ranking and a solid B average, included three C's and a D in physics lab, hardly the flawless performance his father wanted.) Robeson's choices for favorite reading matter (on a form filled out for the school yearbook), however, hint at a darker side to his personality.[80] All of his choices—Tennyson's haunting *Rizpah, Hamlet,* Hardy's *Tess of the D'Urbervilles* and Kipling's poem "If"—feature isolated and lonely protagonists. Each faces the future grimly, with a certain amount of stoicism, and alone. Selected lines from Kipling's "If" illustrate this well:

> If you can wait and not be tired by waiting,
> Or being lied about, don't deal in lies,
> Or being hated, don't give way to hating,
> And yet don't look too good, not talk too wise:

. . . .

If you can force your heart and nerve and sinew
  To serve your turn long after they are gone,
And so hold on when there is nothing in you
  Except the Will which says to them: "Hold on!"
. . . .
If neither foes nor loving friends can hurt you,
  If all men count with you, but none too much;
If you can fill the unforgiving minute
  With sixty seconds' worth of distance run,
Yours is the Earth and everything that's in it,
  And — which is more — you'll be a Man, my son!

Mal Pitt confirmed what Paul's reading preferences suggest: "I think that, for all his gregariousness, Paul was really a solitary and lonesome person. Everyone thought of him as a friend, but with the exception of his brother Ben, he was never really close to anyone. Even though he was a favorite at Rutgers, believe me, Paul was always on guard, always careful about stepping out of line."[81] Robeson's prodigious appetite for activity thus may well have been prompted as much by his need to fill the sense of isolation as ambition to do it all.

In his sophomore year Robeson again listed Mal Pitt as his best friend but added Robert "Davvy" Davenport, who along with Paul composed Rutgers's black student body that year. It was at the end of sophomore year, also, that Paul first met Geraldine ("Gerry") Neale, the pretty, intelligent, and ambitious young black woman with whom he would be romantically involved over the next several years. Gerry Neale lived in nearby Freehold and was just beginning her training at Teachers Normal in Trenton. Like Paul, she had been raised a striver, but a considerably more combative striver than Paul. At Trenton Normal, for example, when she heard that Negroes would not be allowed to join the Shakespeare Club, she decided to confront the situation and find out for herself, something Paul would not have done. And, "Of course," she said matter-of-factly, "I was admitted."[82]

At first Gerry Neale and Paul saw each other intermittently, at parties and occasionally when he visited her in Trenton, but then they began spending time together more regularly. "Paul was not one of those fellows who was everywhere — going to this dance and that dance," remembered Gerry. "Most often I saw him at social affairs, in Trenton and other places where we all came together, those of us blacks attending college. Paul came, and fellows from the University of Pennsylvania, New York College, and other schools all over the East Coast came. I met Marian [Paul's sister] at one of these affairs, and we became lifelong friends. We had a wonderful time. Paul was outgoing but still reserved, almost shy. I first heard him sing at one of our small social gatherings, all very informal, of course." Gerry remembered Paul as thoughtful and sensitive even to small slights and recalled how wonderful it was when that sensitivity was exercised on her behalf. She cited as an example Paul's habit of altering lyrics (something he would do throughout his performing career), "in my case to fit a Negro girl. He was very fond of 'I Love You Truly' and 'Gray Days Are Your Gray Eyes' and he used to change the words because, he said, 'Negro girls have brown eyes.' The song went 'Gray days are your gray eyes / Gold days are your hair / Come storm or sun to me / All days are fair' and he would sing 'Gray Days are your *brown* eyes' and so on. He was thoughtful like that."[83]

Life at Rutgers changed suddenly and dramatically in the spring of 1917: the United States was at war. College sports teams throughout the country were left depleted as older student-athletes enlisted. Harvard, Yale, and Princeton announced they would cancel their football programs entirely and focus instead on military training. Coach Sanford, however, followed a different course. "Heart and soul in back of football as a war preparedness effort," Sanford announced that, rather than drop its football program, Rutgers would make it bigger than ever. With administrative backing, large-scale student support (nearly 100 students tried out for the team), and the largest budget ever allocated for the sport, Sanford substantially enlarged the school's football program.[84]

Rutgers had its problems. Only three of the team's starters were veterans: Rendall, Feitner, and Robeson. But in the season's opener, the team, still "a bit crude, showed signs of power" and beat Ursinus 25 to 0. As the season continued the Scarlet Scourge picked up momentum, mowing down the service team, Fort Washington, 90 to 0. Its first real test, however, came in the contest against Syracuse, a team with both experience and the home field advantage. Players fumbled and penalties abounded on the muddy field that October afternoon in a game described by the *Times* as "about the most bloody battle . . . seen . . . in years." What little punch Rutgers could muster came from Robeson, "the giant colored end from New Brunswick [who] stood head and shoulders above his teammates for all around playing. He was a tower of strength on the Scarlet defense. . . . Practically every forward pass Foster Sanford's men used was built around Robeson. He towered over every man on the field and when he stretched his arms up in the air he pulled down forward passes that an ordinary player would have to use a stepladder to reach."[85] The game ended in a 14 to 0 loss for Rutgers, but not because of any lack in Robeson's play.

Coach Sanford was disappointed. He had hoped for a season with no losses, but he took heart watching Robeson. With Paul on the team Rutgers could still turn the season around. In the weeks that followed, the Scarlet Scourge did just that, pounding in succession Lafayette (33 to 6) and Fordham (28 to 0). Robeson's play again was singled out: "It can hardly be said that one player stood out on the Rutgers aggregation, unless it was Robeson, the giant negro at left end," wrote the *New York Tribune*'s Charles Taylor. "He was a tower of strength on the offense and defense. . . . Twice the big Rutgers negro raced down the field after receiving a perfect toss from Whitehill. . . . On the other occasion Robeson raced twenty-four yards before being brought to earth again close to the Fordham goal line. Each of these passes gave Rutgers a chance to score, and Rutgers did not throw away the opportunity. . . . The dark cloud was omnipresent."[86]

Coach Sanford drilled the team relentlessly in preparation for the contest against the formidable Gilmour Dobie–coached West Virginia Mountaineers, working his men until long after dark on the day before the game. Robeson, touted in the press (albeit often with coon song euphemisms like "dark cloud") as Rutgers's star player, felt especially pressed to make a good showing. He was good, but he was also black, which meant he would be in the spotlight, watched and singled out by the southern team. Shortly before the day of the game, the rumor spread that the Mountaineers would refuse to play if Robeson appeared in the lineup. Perhaps if Paul had been the inexperienced sophomore he was when the issue came up with Washington and Lee, Rutgers might have acquiesced. But with Robeson a prospective all-American and the team's most valuable player, Rutgers flatly refused and, as the team's student manager put it, "told them [the West Virginia team] to get lost."[87]

With Robeson definitely in the lineup, word spread that the Mountaineers "were out to get that nigger," and according to the film critic and documentary filmmaker Pare Lorentz, who at the time was a young West Virginia fan attending the game, play had barely begun when "a number of Mountaineer fans began hollering 'Kill that nigger! Kill that nigger!' If Paul heard it, and it was certainly loud enough to be heard, he didn't look in the direction of the jeers and didn't appear fazed by them."[88] However, before the game had ended, Robeson vented his anger on at least one of his West Virginia opponents. Years later Paul described the incident to theater critic Heywood Broun: "When we lined up for the first play, the man playing opposite me leaned forward and said, 'Don't you so much as touch me, you black dog, or I'll cut your heart out.' Can you imagine? I'm playing opposite him in a football game and he says I'm not to touch him. When the whistle blew I dove in, and he didn't see me coming. I clipped him sidewise and nearly busted him in two and as we were lying under the pile I leaned forward and whispered, 'I touched you that time. How did you like it?' "[89]

The contest ended in a 7-to-7 draw. Rutgers continued its winning spree, leveling Springfield College (61 to 0) and Philadelphia's United States Marine team (27 to 0). On November 24 at Ebbets Field in Brooklyn the Scarlet Scourge faced its stiffest challenge of the season: the all-powerful Newport, Rhode Island, Naval Reserve team. Dubbed "invincible" and star-studded with all-Americans, this team of seasoned veterans was unbeaten and unscored on, downing easily the likes of Brown, Colgate, and Dartmouth. And facing them was "little" Rutgers, its eleven men averaging just slightly over nineteen years in age and outweighed by their Reserve opposition by at least ten pounds per man. "The Naval team had eighteen all-Americans," recalled Rutgers's Thug Rendall, "and when we met in the locker room those Navy guys were riding us, calling us tiny high school boys. I got nervous and wanted Paul to stand up and shut them up with his size. But Paul shrugged his shoulders and said he hadn't heard them talking. Whatever Paul had to say, he'd say it on the field that day."[90]

Although the Naval Reserve team had the advantage, it was Rutgers's finest hour that afternoon, as before an estimated crowd of 15,000 the Scarlet Scourge trounced their opposition in a stunning 14 to 0 upset. Between the halves stunned and jubilant Rutgers students snake-danced around the gridiron, shouting school cheers and singing rousing choruses of "On the Banks of the Raritan," while deliriously happy alumni in the stands threw their hats and scarves into the air. The final victory came quickly and easily, as the Naval Reserve team had never really been in the game, managing only two first downs. Frost-bitten fans rocked the stands, cheering themselves hoarse: the Scarlet Scourge had buried the noses of Cupid Black and his other all-Americans. It was Rutgers and Robeson all the way, the *New York Times* reported: "The work of Robeson, Rollins and Whitehill on the defense was so brilliant that they broke up the Naval Reserve's plays in the making."[91]

Robeson's pivotal role in Rutgers's surprise defeat of the Naval Reserve team provided a tailor-made occasion for the larger-than-life, lavish sports reportage so popular in those days, and sportswriters made the most of it. "A tall, tapering Negro in a faded crimson sweater, moleskins and a pair of maroon socks ranged hither and yon on a wind-whipped Flatbush field yesterday afternoon," wrote an enamored Louis Lee Arms of the *Sunday Tribune*. "He rode on the wings of the frigid breezes: a grim, silent, and compelling figure. Whether it was Charlie Barrett, of old Cornell and All-American glory, or Gerrish or Gardner who tried to hurl himself through a moving gauntlet he was met and stopped by this blaze of black and red. The Negro was Paul Robeson of Rutgers College, and he is a minister's son. He is also nineteen years of age and weighs two hundred pounds. Of his football capacity you are duly referred to 'Cupid' Black of Newport and

Yale. He can tell you. It was Robeson, a veritable Othello of Battle, who led the dashing little Rutgers Eleven to a 14–0 victory over the widely heralded Newport Naval Reserves."[92]

It was a great win for Rutgers, and the team easily maintained its dominance for the remainder of the season, scoring an average of thirty points per game. Of the season's nine contests Rutgers won seven, lost one, and tied the other. Six of the team's victories were shutouts, with Rutgers totaling a whopping 295 points against their opposition's paltry 28. Walter Camp — Yale legend and the architect of the all-American football team — speculated on the possibility of a national championship match between Rutgers and the Georgia Tech Yellow Jackets, a team boasting a perfect record of nine wins and no losses, and the *New York Sun* placed seven of the Rutgers eleven on the all-East team, led by Paul Robeson. More than anything Paul would accomplish at Rutgers, this single event, the surprise drubbing of the Naval Reserve team, skyrocketed him into the national limelight, as sportswriters across the country dubbed him the best of the best. Walter Camp perhaps most succinctly summed up the acclaim when he called Robeson "the greatest defensive end ever to trod the gridiron" and officially acknowledged his outstanding performance by naming him all-American, thus selecting him to join the ranks of football's all-time greats for all-around ability and performance in football.

Like Fritz Pollard the year before, Paul had earned fame for himself and recognition for his race. The black community, justifiably proud, crowned Robeson with its own laurels. Few things did more to fire hope for the future than publicizing the accomplishments of gifted young blacks like Robeson. Black weeklies like the *New York Age,* the *Chicago Defender,* and the *Philadelphia Tribune* eagerly sought out such information as it documented, individual by individual, racial progress. "Last Fall it was Frederick Douglass Pollard of Brown who shone forth as the most brilliant of the football stars," wrote Lester Walton of the *New York Age.* "I now take pleasure in introducing to you Mr. Paul Robeson of Rutgers College, New Jersey, another gentleman of color, who has become the sensation of the present football season. For two successive years the Negro has carried off the highest honors on the gridiron, which in the vernacular of the turf, 'is going some.'"[93]

That year Paul returned "home" to the black communities of Somerville, Princeton, and New Brunswick a hero, not only for his dazzling feats on the gridiron but equally so for his less-heralded academic achievements. Robeson had made national sports headlines and been selected for membership to the Phi Beta Kappa honor society, and this while still in his junior year. "I knew of Paul many years before I met him," said one black northern New Jersey friend. "As young kids we were in grammar school and he was in college, but we all knew his activities. We all wanted to be like Paul who had proven himself both as a student and as an athlete. We thought that anybody in college was the greatest thing. We thought of him as a giant."[94]

Robeson was a giant, the fulfillment of the black community's fondest hopes. Carlton Moss, whose family had been one of those to migrate north in the 1890s explained, "I was from Essex County which includes Newark, Montclair, and the Oranges. You had after the turn of the century a small black community, some of the extremely courageous blacks who left the rural South and started branching out. My dad was one of them. He didn't want New York because it was already becoming a crowded center. So, he and other blacks like him went into these very small New Jersey communities. Scattered up the East Coast from Trenton on up all the way to Jersey City were pockets of black families, and they were all striving families. They came at a time when 95 percent of the black population lived in the South. These were pioneer people and their whole emphasis was on finding a solution to the problem of getting an education. They felt that the further north they came, the better opportunity their kids would have. You had this tremendous drive on the part of parents to work so that their kids would have an opportunity to go to high school and then to college."[95]

By the time Paul began his college education he was already well known in these northern New Jersey black communities. His high school successes marked him as one of the community's promising prospects, and, as Moss put it, "to top it all, Paul was going to a white college and a good one. There was great status attached to attending a white college. Most of us who went to college attended black schools like Morgan, Howard, and Virginia State. We always thought of going to a white school like City College. At that time, when you were growing into adulthood, you talked about those things. For some reason we all went to black schools. But Paul was out of the ordinary. He competed with whites and was head and shoulders better than them."[96]

While the press of both races heaped accolades on him, at white Rutgers Robeson maintained the unassuming manner he had always presented. His "Review of the 1917 Football Season" (*Rutgers Alumni Quarterly*) eulogized Coach Sanford and praised individually every team member, from veteran seniors and underclassmen who would lead the team the following year, to the scrubs and assistant coaches, Wittpenn and Nash. But about himself and his own accomplishments Paul wrote nothing.[97] Any acknowledgment of his own contribution, however slight, might have been interpreted as boasting and thus link him with "uppity niggers" like Jack Johnson rather than with fellow athlete Fritz Pollard, described by the white press as a "modest . . . gentleman of color [who] always shrinks from the spotlight of all athletic demonstrations."[98]

That summer, in fact, a white guest at Narragansett would chastise Robeson for what the guest viewed as just that kind of unseemly "boasting." Robeson recalled:

> I was waiting on a table in a very swank hotel. The other waiters were very proud of me. We were all Negroes. One elderly waiter, a roly-poly, good-natured fellow . . . was so proud, he'd tell everyone, "that waiter there is Paul Robeson of Rutgers, All-American end."
>
> Some guests decided that I must be an uppity kind of guy, so they proceeded to insult me at every turn. Nothing was right, and the scorn on the man's face — his insistence upon my being a "servant" not an All-American — was ugly. Finally, in order not to throw the tray in his face, I quietly left my tray on the stand, and went to the waiters' room, took off my waiter's jacket and started toward the waiters' quarters. Someone ran after me. I refused to answer. They said, "You'll lose your job." And I answered nothing.
>
> The guests stayed for days. I stayed in the quarters and played baseball. The headwaiter — I shall never forget him — came over to me that first evening. Patted me on the shoulder, and said "I understand. Take it easy until these folks leave, then come back."[99]

Robeson had learned that if one wanted to get along in the white world modesty was a required trait. Thus it should come as no surprise that Paul said nothing when he was overlooked as the logical choice for captain of the next year's team. Robeson as team captain would have presented one problem after another: a black man doing the coin toss before games, speaking at pep rallies, meeting alumni, shaking hands with opponents — all almost impossible to imagine. It would take Robeson years to get over the practice of discounting (and later embellishing) his achievements according to what made whites comfortable. It would prove a psychologically costly habit, one that interfered with his ability to assess himself and heightened his sense of inferiority in that it inextricably linked his sense of self-worth to what whites thought of him.[100]

In the spring of a year that should have been among Robeson's happiest, Paul suffered a crushing loss. During the early part of the year his father, now seventy-three years old, had begun to fail noticeably. Paul visited his father regularly — there was no one he loved and respected more — but while he was sick Paul pushed himself to the limit to keep up with his studies while traveling back and forth from Rutgers to care for William. Gerry Neale spoke with great feeling as she remembered how wrenching and difficult this period was for Paul. "He and his father were all alone. There was just the two of them — no one else. Paul went back and forth from Rutgers to Somerville nursing his father while he was going to school. By the spring Paul was really exhausted." On Friday morning, May 12,

1918, William Robeson died.[101] Again, Paul's extraordinary devotion to his father moved Gerry Neale:

> Rutgers had an oratorical contest for every class level. Paul had won in his freshman and sophomore year and had another contest coming up in the middle of May. His father, sick as he was, remembered this and had told Paul, "Whatever happens to me . . . I don't care what happens to me . . . I want you to go and give your speech and I want you to win." And really, before the contest came off his father died. Actually on the day of the contest his father was lying in state before the funeral.
>
> I went with a couple of friends to the contest. What we saw was this giant, fatigued-looking human being. The subject of his speech was the Negro and the Constitution. He won . . . but I think the remarkable thing was the high standard his father had always set for them all. Imagine winning an oratorical contest while his father was lying in state. But that was his father's philosophy for all his children: whatever you do, do it best, don't take anything that's second best.[102]

Right up until the very end, William Robeson goaded Paul to achieve, demanding in this case that his son put aside even grief, at least long enough to win first prize.[103] That the ties between this father and son were unusually strong was obvious; even casual observers noted it.[104] Paul worshiped his father and would have done anything for him. Indeed, as Robeson writes in his autobiography, the desire to please his father would persist long after William Robeson's death. As late as 1958 Robeson, reflecting on his own life, still wondered, "'What would Pop think?'. . . Often I stretch out my arms as I used to, to put it around Pop's shoulder and ask, 'How'm doin' Pop?' My Pop's influence is still present in the struggles I face today."[105]

Robeson's loyalty to his father became all the more resolute in the wake of his passing. Shortly after William Robeson's death, the Bustills decided to re-establish contact with the Robesons, specifically with Paul whose accomplishments had not escaped their notice. After years of silence, in the summer of 1918 his mother's relatives invited Paul to their famed annual family reunion held at a private picnic grounds (Maple Grove) in Philadelphia. According to one member of the Bustill clan allied by marriage but not by blood, "Paul was not at the Bustill picnics until 1918, but don't mention my name when you write that or I'll be thrown out of the family." The annual Bustill picnic drew not only nearby family but people from all over the East Coast. It was an elaborate all-day event including a huge feast, entertainment, and the traditional celebration of the Bustill family genealogy complete with a reading of the family history by Robeson's cousin, Annie Bustill Smith, and orations by various family members, including, that year, Paul.[106]

The Bustills had apparently decided to bestow on Paul the legitimacy they had denied his father. It was a victory of sorts, but coming as it did so close to his father's death it was a bittersweet triumph at best. It is unclear what motivated Paul to accept the invitation or how he felt once he was actually among his mother's relatives. Did, for example, the misspelling of his name on the program — "Roberson" instead of "Robeson" — add salt to old wounds?[107] Robeson chose as the subject of his speech "Loyalty to Convictions" because, as he later explained, "it was the text of my father's life." Whatever else he did that day, Robeson took pains to make it clear that he credited his own success *not* to his mother's elite progenitors but to the ambition and striving for excellence he had learned from his father.[108]

Forty years later, recalling that day in his autobiography, Robeson makes little attempt to hide the old anger and bitterness. He treats the occasion with calculated indifference, informing readers that he would have forgotten about the event entirely had he not come across a copy of the program in a college scrapbook. Robeson does mention the misspelling of his name, noting with amusement that the error highlighted the one aspect of William Robeson's life the Bustills would have most preferred to forget: his slave heritage. "It is likely," Robeson writes, "that 'Roberson' was [in fact] the ancestral name of the slave-holding Robesons from whom my father got his name."[109]

With his father gone, Paul felt not only loss but an anguished sense of root-lessness. His older brothers had lived away from home for years and were now fairly well settled. Not so for Paul. For so long his father had been his only anchor; without him there was no place that felt like home.

In between the time his Rutgers classes ended and his work at Narragansett began, Paul worked briefly at a shipbuilding plant in Newark, New Jersey, doing his "bit for Uncle Sam."[110] By 1918 he knew his way around Narragansett and was among old friends. "Everyone knew him, black and white," remembered Joe Nelson. "All you had to do was be around him and you could see why he was so admired. He was so big and in such good shape physically. Then, on top of it all, he was so modest, even a bit embarrassed about his own accomplishments. Everywhere he went people wanted him to sing. Even then his voice was magnificent. Any time a group got together it was almost a given that we would ask Paul to sing."[111]

On their way back to college, waiting at the train station in Providence, Paul and Joe Nelson talked about the coming year. "While we were talking we saw soldiers' coffins being sent home for burial. The soldiers who died — most of them — had not been killed in battle, but died from influenza. There was an awful influenza attack in the country then, but it seemed to kill men in the army more than anyone else. It was frightening. We both were afraid of being drafted. We were the same age and eligible, but neither of us had registered yet. So we decided the first thing both would do when we got back to college was volunteer and sign up right away for SATC [Student Army Training Corps] just to be on the safe side."[112]

Patriotic fervor ran high at Rutgers that fall, fired by President Demarest's "high noon" speech to the student body, urging a wholehearted backing of the war abroad. Occasionally, this enthusiasm assumed a sinister tone. When a naive freshman publicly denounced the sale of Liberty Bonds, for example, irate students seized him, held him for several hours in a room in Ford Hall, and then turned him over to a mob to be stripped, covered with molasses and feathers, and paraded through the town.[113] Rutgers students exhibited ardent devotion to the ideal of democracy abroad but, like the nation as a whole, showed little concern over its uneven application at home. Few whites saw the irony of American blacks volunteering to "keep the world safe for democracy" and then being confined to segregated units.

By the time classes began in the fall, the SATC had all but taken over the college, converting fraternity and other buildings into military housing facilities so that the school looked more like a military camp than an educational institution. Robeson, along with 450 Rutgers men, joined the SATC that fall and was inducted in a formal ceremony held on the campus on October 1, 1918.[114] Rutgers's new "soldiers" were paid thirty dollars a month by the government for their services and followed a rigid schedule that began with a 6:00 a.m. reveille, followed by room inspection, rifle drills, and kitchen police duty.[115] Robeson, unlike most black servicemen, underwent his SATC training alongside his white classmates. This arrangement predated President Truman's executive order integrating the armed forces by some thirty years. First appointed squad leader and later assigned the rank of corporal, Robeson became one of the few blacks not required to undergo his officer's training at a segregated center.[116]

The issue of blacks fighting in the war for "democracy" was hotly debated by black leaders of the period. Dating back to the American Revolution, blacks, segregated and the victims of gross discrimination in the military (most recently the excessively harsh treatment black soldiers received in the aftermath of the 1908 Brownsville, Texas, riot and the 1917 Houston altercation), were used as soldiers only when absolutely necessary. Nonetheless, there are many instances when they stepped forward — during the Civil War, as Buffalo soldiers in the West, in the Spanish American War, and with Theodore Roosevelt in Cuba — willing to fight in battles with the hope that whites might at last accept them as full citizens. In July 1918 W. E. B. Du Bois (according to biographer David

Levering Lewis, after soul-searching and the offer of a commission in the army's Military Intelligence) publicly announced his support of the war effort in what may have been his most famous and eloquent *Crisis* editorial, "Close Ranks." Some black leaders, including William Monroe Trotter, editor of the *Boston Guardian*, Archibald Grimke, and A. Philip Randolph, were outraged, but neither Paul nor his brother Ben, who served as a chaplain for a segregated unit, were among those objecting. Had the war continued and Robeson received his commission, he would have been placed in a segregated unit.[117]

The new SATC-enforced military schedule forced the cancellation of many of Rutgers's extracurricular activities. Football, however, was not among them.[118] Team members, taking their lead from Coach Sanford and backed by school officials and the military men on campus, went through the paces of their training with an energy quickened by patriotism. Like Walter Camp himself, Sanford believed that football developed character and experience: players would demonstrate on the battlefield the same courage they exhibited on the gridiron. "The men who had gone into the opposing football line when their signal came went 'over the top' with the same abandon," Camp wrote in 1919. "Those who had made a stand on the last five-yard line in the grim determination of the gridiron field faced the scrimmage of war with the same do-or-die fortitude."[119] As Sanford saw it, winning would be Rutgers's contribution to the war effort. And with Robeson on the team the Scarlet Scourge would be unbeatable.

Beginning the season three weeks late due to a severe influenza epidemic, Rutgers won against Pelham Bay's Naval Reserves, but by a disturbingly narrow margin of 7 to 0. Coach Sanford worked the team relentlessly for its next game, and his efforts paid off. Rutgers mauled Lehigh, 30 to 0, with Robeson leading the way. Gathering still more momentum, Rutgers crushed the Naval Transport Unit of Hoboken, 40 to 0. By midseason not one of Rutgers's opponents had yet succeeded in gaining a first down. Statistically, if all the plays scored by Rutgers's opposition had been made consecutively, the total would have amounted to a mere eighteen yards. Rutgers's defense, led by the invincible Robeson, was superb. Undefeated in its first five games, Rutgers fully expected to surpass its spectacular 1917 record.

But the Scarlet Scourge was stopped, dramatically and decisively, in the final two games of the season. Playing on Brooklyn's Ebbets Field, where only a year before they had routed the invincible Navy Reserve team, the Scarlet Scourge suffered a crushing loss, 54–14, its first in two years, at the hands of the Great Lakes Naval Station. With that, its championship climb was halted in what the *Alumni Quarterly* described as the "greatest upset of the decade."[120]

In the season's final game against Syracuse, played two weeks later, the team's superb defense once again shone as Rutgers limited Syracuse to only three first downs from scrimmage against Rutgers's own thirteen. Outplayed, Syracuse still managed to blank Rutgers, 21 to 0. The surprise collapse of the team disappointed fans and alumni. Some have conjectured, and Paul himself on occasion admitted, that at the time when both his prowess and national recognition peaked Robeson stopped enjoying the game. "When you had it hammered into you . . . that you must beat such and such a team, the emphasis was too great. Instead of playing for the love of it, you then were playing only to win," Robeson said years later. "Nothing was quite the same for Paul after his father's death," Art Van Fleet remembered. "I just don't think his heart was in football. Besides missing his father, the game had lost some of its glow. Let's face it, playing under Sandy was tough. And then, too, Sandy expected more of Paul than of the others: he was an all-American and had better play up to that standard. Opponents really wanted to get him and, big as he was, Paul got pretty beat up his senior year."[121] Robeson's performance, if not his personal best, was still outstanding, and for the second year in a row Rutgers's star player was named to Walter Camp's all-American team. In other school sports he had amassed an enviable record as well, earning an unprecedented twelve varsity letters, four in football, three in basketball, three in baseball, and two in track.

Of Paul as a track man, teammate Feitner reminisced: "Paul may not have had correct form or technique for a weight man in track but his natural athletic ability and raw strength made up for that and enabled him to achieve anyway. Paul and I both threw the javelin. Neither of us was that good, but we held our own and the team managed to go undefeated senior year and against some pretty stiff competition."[122] In his junior and senior years Robeson sandwiched track between baseball practice and games. He was the team's third top scorer for the 1919 season, with one of his most memorable feats the javelin throw in Rutgers's 1919 match with Swarthmore, when he "hurled the javelin 137 feet, 5 inches [five inches better than his nearest competitor], and this against a fairly strong wind."[123] Teammate Wittpenn remembered: "He [Robeson] just picked up the javelin, heaved it against the wind, and off it went. That was sheer strength."[124] In April of his senior year Paul traveled alone to Philadelphia to represent Rutgers in the Penn Relays and the next day to Schenectady where he played catcher for the Rutgers baseball team. In Philadelphia, facing some of the toughest track competition in the nation, Robeson finished tenth in the running broad jump (18', 5.5" against the winning 20', 3.5") and fifth in the javelin throw (127', 10" to the winning throw of 147', 05").[125]

In baseball the story was much the same. Paul played catcher's position for three years, occasionally filling in as an outfielder. "He certainly made a big target behind the plate," said teammate A. F. Eschenfelder. "The pitcher really had someone to throw to. And he talked it up behind the plate, too; that voice was that powerful even then. Paul was not the greatest hitter to come down the line, but you knew he was there when he was catching."[126]

In basketball ("Rutgers wasn't much beyond the peach basket stage in those days," said one player, "a little running, no fast breaks, two-handed sets—not much action") Robeson filled any position, as needed, and his play figured fairly consistently in Rutgers's victories.[127] "Paul was not one of the quickest men on the court, although he was fast for his size," remembered three-year basketball teammate Calvin Meury. "He was used mainly at center and forward, acting as muscleman under the boards. He stood out like a sore thumb . . . one of the few big men in the game, then. Most were five feet, ten or so."[128]

Robeson's desire to "do it all" athletically was not without its humorous moments. In May 1918, for example, he competed in a Rutgers track event against New York University while playing catcher for Rutgers's baseball team on an adjoining field. In both events Robeson performed well, placing second in the shot put and the hammer throw and holding his own on the diamond as well. Art Van Fleet said that his most vivid memories of Paul in sports were "not of Robey on the gridiron" but of having the baseball game held up while "Robey sauntered across Neilson Field over to the track meet for the javelin or hammer or shot event and then sauntered back to continue the baseball game."[129]

Much had changed since that warm September day in 1915 when Robeson, a nonentity, an ambitious black youngster from rural New Jersey, first made his way across the Rutgers campus. Four years later, "Robey of Rutgers" was the pride of both the black community and the class of 1919. The black press across the country sang his praises while, locally, the New Brunswick YMCA presented him with a purse as a gesture of the local black community's respect and admiration. Among his graduating class at Rutgers no one could compete with Robeson for all-round achievement—academic honors; athletic excellence and versatility (he earned an unprecedented twelve letters in Rutgers athletics); membership in Phi Beta Kappa; the coveted Skull and Cap award (a senior fraternity made up of the four men who best-represented the ideals and traditions of Rutgers); and oratorical prizes. A front-page eulogistic commentary in the June issue of *Targum* said it all: "May Rutgers never forget this noble son and may he always remember his Alma Mater."[130] The student yearbook likewise crowned Paul a Rutgers great:

> All hats off to "Robey"
> All honor to his name
> On the diamond, the court or football field
> He brought old Rutgers fame.

To those looking on, it appeared there was nothing that Robeson could not do. His astounding versatility helped to create the larger-than-life image many of his classmates remember: Paul Robeson was a phenomenon. Perhaps his friend Earl Schenck Miers best expressed the sentiments of the class of 1919 when he wrote many years later: "The hero of the campus was Paul Robeson . . . in my generation Rutgers men said proudly, 'I go to Paul Robeson's school.'"[131]

Classmates would remember Robey as never having earned less than an A. He was "the most brilliant student at the college," said one classmate, and another, "He led his class. None of us could hold a candle to him. He was pure black and proved beyond any doubt that a black man can have the highest intelligence."[132] But, contrary to the legend, Robeson did not earn perfect grades. He did receive both the Ann Van Nest Bussing Prize and the Monsignor O'Grady Prize for oratory and extempore speaking, but he did not win any of the academic "Special Subject" prizes and earned third rather than first or second academic honors, graduating with a solid B average.[133] Although he was one of several commencement speakers, Robeson was not among those first selected for the honor; rather, he was asked at the last minute to replace a student suddenly taken ill. And finally, his senior thesis, "The Fourteenth Amendment: The Sleeping Giant of the American Constitution," submitted on May 29, two weeks before graduation, while creditable was far from brilliant.[134] A straightforward account of the history of the Fourteenth Amendment with special stress given to Article I — how citizenship is defined, the privileges and immunities of U.S. citizens, due process of law and equal protection of the law — the essay was what one might expect from an undergraduate but not particularly profound or exceptional. That Robeson chose the Fourteenth Amendment as his subject matter (he was one of a handful of students who chose a sociopolitical subject) indicates he was thinking about his own and his people's status as citizens. But, though he might well have criticized white America for its failure to enforce the amendment, he chose instead to cite numerous legal cases that proved that properly enforced the amendment provided protection from the changing tides of state legal codes. His approach was logical, reasoned, moderate, and conciliatory. He meticulously avoided editorializing in the essay, to the extent that one must read carefully between the lines to sense the plea made on behalf of himself and his people for enforcement of the amendment.[135] In short, Robeson was not a flawless student. But his overall performance at Rutgers — in terms of both breadth and quality — was indeed remarkable, a testament not only to his many and wide-ranging talents but equally to his dogged pursuit of success.

Commencement services for the class of 1919 began on the morning of June 9 with Class Day exercises: the reading of the class poem, prophecy, and history, which saw Robeson as governor of New Jersey, dimming even "the fame of Booker T. Washington" as a "leader of the colored race in America."[136] The high point of the first day of festivities, however, took place in the afternoon, with the Rutgers–Princeton baseball match. Alumni and students — a total of over 1,000 fans — hoping yet again to rout the southern team (Rutgers had failed to beat Princeton at any major varsity sport since 1869), paraded over to Neilson Field led by Angus Fraser and his Scotch Kiltie Band. Finally Rutgers got its win, and fans and alumni went wild. On the heels of a poor season, the Rutgers team pounded out thirteen hits (one of which was a single by catcher Robeson) and downed Princeton 5 to 1. The fifty-year jinx had at last been broken, and no one was happier with the win than Paul. For the team it meant the defeat of a powerful rival; for Robeson "the defeat of a long-hated institution."[137] Robeson reaped well-deserved praise in the *Targum* for his performance, which proclaimed Rutgers's "overwhelming victory over Princeton . . . a fitting climax to [his] great career."

June 10 was a warm, sunny day. The academic procession for the 153rd Rutgers commencement formed on the Queen's Campus at 11:15 a.m. From there the sixty-nine graduating seniors proceeded to the Second Reformed Church for the 11:30 graduation exercises. Class of 1918 graduates who had missed their own commencement because they had enlisted had returned and were seated with Paul's class, eagerly awaiting formal reception of their diplomas. The mood was optimistic and upbeat: the war was over; democracy had triumphed; theirs would be a better world. Robeson, along with the two classmates also scheduled to speak, waited his turn and then walked slowly to the podium. He looked out at a sea of white faces — faculty, parents, alumni, and friends — and in that rich, sonorous voice that had won him one oratorical prize after another, began.

In his speech, "The New Idealism," Robeson outlined the process by which he and other blacks would achieve their rightful place in American society. As in his senior thesis, his approach to his topic was measured, gently admonishing but never directly criticizing the "favored race." Robeson predicted that the same spirit that had won the war would lead to a "reconstructing of American life" at home. This "new spirit" would create a sense of national unity and a renewed determination to make freedom and equality realities for all Americans, including the "less-favored race." Having proved its allegiance in the war, American blacks were now ready to take their place among other full-fledged American citizens.

"We of the less-favored race realize that our future lies chiefly in our own hands," Robeson assured his audience. "On ourselves alone will depend the preservation of our liberties and the transmission of them in their integrity to those who will come after us." Negroes, Robeson predicted, would raise themselves up by practicing those virtues most typically American: "self-reliance, self-respect, industry, perseverance, and economy." Exhorting white America to live this "new spirit," Robeson stressed the importance of practicing Christian principles and cooperation between the races. Only when "black and white shall clasp friendly hands in the consciousness of the fact that we are brethren and that God is the father of us all" would this new idealism be achieved.[138]

In his speech Robeson exhibited those qualities whites not only admired but expected from exceptional blacks: dignity, decency, and, above all, modesty. His racial philosophy, as articulated in this commencement address, had changed little since high school. Had he been less successful at Rutgers, had the racial etiquette he learned growing up not worked for him, Robeson might have been forced to move beyond the strategy of patience, self-effacement, and hard work. But the etiquette had worked and worked spectacularly for Robeson. Ironically, then, it was success that retarded (and would continue to retard) Robeson's personal and political growth and kept him bound to a racial etiquette that helped reinforce his sense of racial inferiority.

Robeson returned to his seat amid thunderous applause. According to the *Sunday Times,* "Some declared that no commencement orator in all the tradition of old Queens had ever received such applause for an oration."[139] Robeson's was a message of hope, with none of the admonishments of the first speaker, classmate John W. Armstrong, who warned radicals and others enamored with Russian socialism about presuming to criticize the American way of life. "We have no room for idle dreamers, for scheming demagogues or for rabid Bolsheviks. . . . the Trotskys and Leninists must seek a more congenial clime. Other nations may succumb to their influences, but in America they will have no effect."

Of all those gathered for the 1919 graduation ceremonies there was no one to whom this remonstration would one day more aptly apply than Paul Robeson. But on this day, the eve of the Red Summer of 1919 and the subsequent Palmer raids, Robeson was far removed from the political awareness that in later years would so alter the course of his life. Robeson in 1919 applauded, enthusiastically and loudly, along with other members of his graduating class Armstrong's patriotic sentiments.

4
Harlem

1919-1922

It was more than saying good-bye to college glory days that made the move to Harlem difficult for Robeson. By his senior year Paul had carved out a niche for himself at Rutgers: he was accepted and well liked; he knew what to do and how to behave and, in that sense, fit in. With Rutgers's close-knit, small-town atmosphere, pleasantly reminiscent of Westfield and Somerville, virtually every place he wanted to go — classes, football practice, downtown New Brunswick — was within easy walking distance, and wherever he went people stopped and spoke with him. Especially during the year following his father's death, Rutgers had been home to Robeson.

Robeson had decided to attend New York University's Law School, but for reasons that remain unclear. He did not want to become a minister; he had known that much since high school.[1] Coach Sanford and others encouraged him to pursue a career in law, and it may be that Robeson did not know what else to do. Law was a respectable profession and, in the eyes of upper-class blacks, a step up from the ministry. As to his choice of New York University, Robeson's grades may not have been good enough for a better school or he may not have made up his mind until the end of the summer and thus had no other choice.

In Harlem Paul found himself forced to exchange the fame and familiarity of Rutgers for the infinitely more prosaic challenge of trying to make ends meet. The scholarships were gone, and although he received some financial assistance, according to Rutgers classmate John Wittpenn and others, from Coach Sanford and Leonor Loree, he still had to shoulder the major portion of his tuition and living expenses himself.[2] Outside of Harlem few knew him, let alone recognized him as Rutgers's great gridiron star: Robeson was simply one of a sea of blacks seeking refuge and opportunity in the North.

Harlem was yet to reach its full promise when Paul arrived in the late summer of 1919, but the elements necessary to set into motion that intense flow of black creativity — the Harlem Renaissance — were rapidly falling into place. The same forces that drew rural southern blacks to cities like Chicago, Detroit, and Philadelphia lured them to Harlem during the war and postwar years. Between 1910 and 1920 Harlem's population increased by 66 percent (91,709 to 152,465) and from 1920 to 1930 would escalate an astounding 115 percent (152,465 to 327,706).[3] By the end of 1919, the area bordered by 130th Street on the south, 145th Street on the north, and extending west of Fifth to Eighth Avenue was almost entirely black.

Six months before Paul's arrival, on a cold February morning, more than a million well-wishers jammed the parade route from Manhattan to Harlem to welcome home the 1,300 black soldiers and eighteen white officers of New York's celebrated 369th Negro Infantry Regiment, formerly the Fifteenth National Guard. The rousing welcome was well deserved. The "Hellfighters," as the French in whose divisions they fought for almost ten months called them, had endured continuous fire longer than any other American unit in World War I (191 consecutive days in the trenches), distinguished themselves as the first American unit awarded the croix de guerre, and won from the French High Command the supreme honor of being chosen among all the Allied forces to lead the march across the Rhine. The return of the 369th Regiment was a great moment for the black community: these men were a phenomenon; their heroism legendary. Led by Lieutenant James Reese ("Big Jim") Europe's sixty-piece band, the soldiers marched in tight formation down Fifth Avenue, wave after wave of straight-backed men, legs flashing and arms swinging in perfect unison. Past the reviewing stand at Sixteenth Street they marched as New Yorkers, "mightily impressed" by their "magnificent appearance," cheered themselves hoarse, and then on to 110th Street and north up Lenox Avenue into the heart of Harlem.[4] When they reached the unofficial reviewing stand at 130th Street Colonel William Haywood ordered open formation and Europe's band broke into "Here Comes My Daddy." The crowd "went wild."[5]

Nor was New York's warm welcome an isolated occurrence. In cities throughout the country — Buffalo, Chicago, St. Louis, and others — record-breaking crowds greeted returning black soldiers. When the call had come to support the war effort, African Americans nationwide heeded the counsel of leaders like W. E. B. Du Bois ("*first* your country, *then* your rights"), who assured them that this time when the war ended patriotic blacks would reap the benefits; this time it would be different.[6] It was not. The jubilation faded quickly, and by midsummer race riots raged throughout the country. More than seventy Negroes were lynched in the twelve months after the Armistice. Ten of them were soldiers, still in uniform.[7]

Economic unrest, racial and ethnic intolerance, and a chauvinistic resolve to protect America from foreign influences were the immediate legacies of the war. Rising prices coupled with management's refusal to raise wages sent American labor on strike in epidemic numbers. "Loyal" Americans, suspecting foreign instigation, began to believe ugly rumors of a Bolshevik-planned conspiracy to overthrow the government. Attorney General A. Mitchell Palmer pointed the finger at radical aliens and devised a simple solution to America's economic woes: terrorize and deport the aliens responsible for stirring up trouble. In August 1919 Palmer created the antiradical division of the Justice Department, chose J. Edgar Hoover to head it, and began the hunt. From August until January the Department of Justice conducted surprise raids on the headquarters of radical organizations, seized membership lists and correspondence, detained suspects under astronomical bails, and refused them legal advice before cross-examination. In the final week of January federal agents arrested 3,000 alleged Communists in thirty-three cities. Many were imprisoned; 550 were later deported.

The Red Scare of 1919 meant little to Paul or, for that matter, American blacks in general, most of whom were remarkably untouched by the radical "isms" of the day. But, inevitably, the search for scapegoats, of which the Red Scare was symptomatic, widened to include them. An impotent Ku Klux Klan revived itself, promising to protect the country not only from blacks but from Asians, Catholics, Jews, Socialists, Communists, bomb-throwing anarchists, and foreigners as well. Within a year its membership skyrocketed from a meager 1,000 to a vigorous 100,000. In the South lynching and other forms of racial violence reached levels rivaling those of the 1880s.

By July when Paul delivered his now month-old Rutgers commencement address at Brooklyn's black YMCA, it was clear the temper of the nation had turned full circle. Even as he spoke, another of the summer's riots raged, this time in Longview, Texas. Later in July, an even more violent riot broke out in the nation's capital. At the end of the month, Chicago was rocked by the summer's most serious riot. It took thirteen days to restore order to the city, and the violence left 38 people dead, 537 injured, and more than 1,000 homeless. For the first time a number of black spokesmen openly advocated the use of violence for purposes of self-defense.[8]

In Harlem there was anger and bitterness but not despair. While race riots erupted in all parts of the country, Harlem remained calm — which is not to say reaction in Harlem lacked intensity. The NAACP's fight to secure passage of a federal antilynching bill, the education program launched by the Interracial Cooperation Association, Marcus Garvey's Universal Negro Improvement Association, and A. Philip Randolph and Chandler Owen's Socialist critique in the

Messenger, all reiterated the same message: blacks would no longer meekly submit to racial humiliation.

The vast majority of Harlemites, however, had no intention of taking literally Jamaican-born poet Claude McKay's passionate call to "face the murderous crowd, the cowardly pack . . . dying but fighting back."[9] Most, like Paul, were politically conservative with middle-class values and aspirations.[10] Thus the cooler heads of the NAACP and Charles S. Johnson's Urban League, both of which supported a tempered, practical approach to racial injustice, prevailed during that long, hot summer. There were problems to be sure. Unemployment was high; those employed worked at low-paying and unskilled jobs; landlords charged exorbitant rents. But these were eclipsed by the city's unquenchable optimism. In Harlem the goals of self-improvement and economic advancement appeared within reach. In Harlem, as in no other part of the country, there was hope.

Key to Harlem's future prominence was its strategic location, as Claude McKay put it, "holding the handle of Manhattan."[11] Many of New York's prominent and wealthy blacks already lived in this city nestled within the most influential and cosmopolitan city in the nation—the Reverend Dr. Adam Clayton Powell Sr., Bert Williams, James C. Thomas, Charles W. Anderson, and Mme. C. J. (Sarah) Walker. Virtually all major black institutions had moved from their downtown quarters to Harlem: fraternal orders; almost all black social service agencies, including the local offices of the NAACP and the Urban League; all the major churches; two major black magazines (*The Crisis* and the Socialist *Messenger*) and two black weeklies, the *New York Age* and the *Amsterdam News.* For many new arrivals the exhilaration they felt as they stepped into this sea of color was impossible to describe. Rudolph ("Bud") Fisher, a young Harlem author and friend of Paul's, perhaps best captured the experience in his fictional character, southern-born King Solomon Gillis, who exclaims as he exits the Lenox Avenue subway and feasts his eyes on Harlem for the first time: "Done died an' woke up in Heaven."[12]

This, however, was not Robeson's experience. The actor Clarence Muse, at the time struggling with his craft at the Lafayette Theater, shared apartment space with Paul for a short while that first year. Muse remembered Robeson as alone and unhappy, "uneasy and unsure of himself outside of Rutgers."[13] What Paul would most often recall about that first year in Harlem was how difficult it was to get along. Living in Harlem, in grand style or otherwise, was expensive: nowhere in New York were blacks charged higher rents. Robeson remembered the kindness of "the people in whose house I had a room" who fed him when he had no money for rent.[14] He also remembered being ashamed, "walking the streets to avoid the embarrassment of my condition . . . in an old army overcoat [presumably his Rutgers SATC coat], wondering if I would ever be able to clothe myself respectably."[15] He did his best, stringing together as many part-time jobs as he could handle while attending class: sorting mail nights at the post office, redcapping at Grand Central Station, singing at small recitals, acting as a sales representative for Okeh race records, helping Coach Sanford with the Rutgers freshman football team, and assisting Fritz Pollard on weekends with the varsity squad at Lincoln University. He and Bud Fisher reportedly "toured the eastern seaboard" in 1919 to earn money for college tuition. Fisher played the piano and arranged songs and Robeson sang, but they made no money. In fact, Fisher's father, the Reverend John Chauncey Fisher, had to help them out when they ran out of money and couldn't get home.[16]

To make matters worse, Paul hated New York University. It was a long trek back and forth from Harlem to NYU and the seriousness and stature Paul associated with law were nowhere to be found. "I was in the morning section composed mostly of high school students," he complained. "They were noisy and childish, so much so that Professor Aymar dismissed the class in contracts before the end of the term."[17] Frustrated and discouraged, Robeson contacted M. Harold Higgins, a former Rutgers classmate then attending Columbia Law School, and asked about the possibility of transferring there. "Paul told me that the students [at NYU] weren't very serious," Higgins said. "But I think he really wanted to get into Columbia because it was such a good school. I can't blame him for that. Columbia was just about the best law school in the country then, better I believe than even Harvard."[18] Paul persuaded Higgins to introduce him to Harlan Stone, the dean of Columbia Law School and later a Supreme Court justice. Stone met with Paul and, departing from school policy, promised to consider him for the second semester provided he kept up his grades at NYU.[19]

After all the fanfare of his last year at Rutgers the move to New York had proven a terrible letdown, and Stone's response gave Paul his first hope that his prospects might begin to improve. At the end of the year he received the news he had been waiting for; he had been accepted to Columbia Law School, and by February 1920 he was officially registered. The campus, located at 116th Street on the outskirts of Harlem atop an imposing hill overlooking Manhattan, with its austere quadrangle of red brick buildings and monumental granite and lime-stone library, exuded importance and grandeur. Attending Columbia would place Robeson in a prestigious setting and give him back that sense of be-ing someone special. It was not Rutgers; Columbia was huge and impersonal (classes were as large as 365 students), but it had the status Paul craved.[20]

His morale boosted, Robeson set to work on his studies in earnest and began participating in Harlem's athletic and social events. He refereed games for the Harlem YMCA and took part in activities sponsored by the elite St. Philip's Episcopal Church, located on 133rd Street near Seventh Avenue. St. Philip's was Harlem's wealthiest nonwhite church and the city's largest black property owner. Its largely mulatto congregation included only "the better element of colored people": its services were dignified and refined, and membership signified social recognition. Robeson joined St. Philip's choir, took part in amateur shows staged in the church basement, and played basketball for the legendary St. Philip–sponsored all-black St. Christopher's team. Robeson felt better about himself and was having fun. At one of St. Christopher's amateur vaudeville shows (the proceeds of which would help cover the cost of sending the club's track team to the Olympic Games in Antwerp) Robeson and Bud Fisher teamed up and were featured as part of the evening's entertainment. Before a full house, "both graduate collegians of national reputation . . . charmed the crowd with their songs."[21]

Friday and Saturday night basketball games followed by a social were a staple feature of social calendars in Harlem and other cities with a sizable black population, and the St. Christopher's team attracted a large and loyal following. Robeson, the "friendly giant" and a well-known name on the court, was the team's enforcer, used not as a regular starter but as a replacement when rugged play was needed. A game like that played at the Manhattan Casino at Madison Avenue and 135th Street in February 1920 against Pittsburgh's vastly superior Leondi club, a team led by the legendary player-coach Cumberland ("Cum") Posey and considered by many the best in America among black social teams, drew a packed house. The game promised not only an unusually tough contest but great entertainment as well. Market-oriented club owners like Posey made sure that fans saw aggressive, action-packed, quality basketball. In short, fans were never bored. With Leondi leading 12 to 4 at half-time, St. Christopher's tried to tire its opponents by playing them "fast." When that didn't work, the team called up Robeson, and, according to the New York Age's Ted Hooks, "then followed some of the roughest basketball ever played in the upper Harlem amusement hall. Fat Jenkins deliberately punched, tripped, and fell upon [Cum] Posey whenever the opportunity permitted, and Paul Robeson seemed to think he was back on the Rutgers' football field from the way he ploughed through his much smaller visitors."[22]

Win or lose, parties and socializing followed the game, and here, too, Paul stood out. Robeson loved to dance and he moved his huge self across the dance floor with an ease and grace that surprised many, especially those who had just witnessed his bulldozing maneuvers on the basketball court. It was at one of these Harlem gatherings, in the spring of 1920, that Paul first met the woman he would later marry, an attractive, vivacious Columbia University student named Eslanda Cardozo Goode.

Born in Washington, D.C., on December 15, 1896, Eslanda ("Essie") Goode, like Paul, had descended from illustrious forebears, one of South Carolina's most distinguished white families, the Spanish Jewish Cardozo family of Charleston. Eslanda's maternal grandfather, the urbane, splendidly groomed, and nearly white Francis Lewis Cardozo, was a freeborn mulatto, the son of Lydia Williams, a free woman of mixed ancestry, and Isaac Nunez Cardozo, a Spanish Jew and plantation owner.[23] After completing his schooling in one of Charleston's self-supporting schools for free blacks, Francis Cardozo at the age of twenty-one left Charleston to attend the University of Glasgow. Supporting himself as a part-time carpenter, Cardozo won awards in Greek and Latin, graduated with honors, and continued his education at seminaries in London and Edinburgh.[24] During the Civil War Cardozo pastored the prestigious Temple Street Congregational Church in New Haven, Connecticut, and after the war replaced his brother Thomas as superintendent of Avery Institute in Charleston. Francis Cardozo not only shaped Avery's faculty and student body but also transformed the school into an institution generally recognized as one of the strongest preparatory and teacher-training schools established by the American Missionary Association (AMA) in the South. Lauded for his tireless efforts, administrative ability, and academic excellence, Cardozo left Avery to enter politics and again proved himself remarkably adept, serving as South Carolina's secretary of state (1868–72) and its treasurer (1872–76).[25]

Francis Lewis Cardozo insisted that his children stand "ramrod straight so they could look any man in the eye" and would "not countenance any ideas of blacks' inferiority to whites."[26] Eslanda's mother, also named Eslanda, inherited her father's fair coloring, fierce intelligence, independence, and self-assurance. A stately beauty, well educated and socially prominent in Washington circles, she had her pick of suitors. Essie said that family members were not happy when her mother decided to marry John Goode, a West Indian from Chicago, because he "was a dark man, and Mama and her family are very fair. When she married a dark man, some of my relatives thought it was wrong."[27]

Essie would depict her early childhood years in segregated Washington, D.C., living in a "cold-water railroad flat" (so called because "the rooms opened into each other without a hall, like a train of cars") with her mother, father, and older brothers Frank and John, as "marvelous" and very happy.[28] Life for the Goodes, however, was far from idyllic. Her father, a lawyer and graduate of Northwestern University, soon learned that while his education distinguished him it did little to protect him from racial bigotry. Unable to find enough work to practice law,

John Goode accepted a civil service job as a postal clerk in Washington, D.C. He never advanced from that position. Disillusioned and alcoholic, he died in 1902 when Essie was six years old.

Essie's mother pulled herself together and learned beauty work, specializing in facial massage and manicures for wealthy white patrons. In 1905 she moved the family to New York where, according to Essie, she felt "she could earn a better living and educate us in non-segregated schools."[29] "Oh, she was a bold one," said Marie Seton of Mrs. Goode. "She spoke her mind and was part of the movement for women's suffrage. If she had lived during the 1960s she would have been right in the middle of the women's movement."[30] As often as Mrs. Goode's strong personality won her admiration it also irritated people. As Seton put it, "I respected her but I can't say I liked her. She was stiff-necked and could be a god-awful snob."[31]

Of the three Goode children, Essie most resembled her mother. Like Mrs. Goode, Essie was fair skinned, whereas the two boys were dark like their father. She had her mother's confidence and drive and, to some extent, her dominating, take-charge personality. Mrs. Goode took enormous pride in Essie; as one friend put it, she "worshipped her; anything she got went to Essie."[32] Essie, in turn, adopted as her own her mother's values: work hard, think for yourself, and speak your mind.[33]

And speak her mind she did, even as a young child in Washington, D.C. "One of the earliest things I remember," Essie said about her younger years, "is playing with a little boy who lived across the street from us in Washington. We lived in a mixed neighborhood then — it was about the year 1900. The boy was white but I had not yet realized that there was any color difference between us. I'm afraid I, too, was a very independent, even sassy child, and I always defended what I considered were my rights. . . . One day while we were playing I wanted my turn at something. . . . I waited for my turn but he wouldn't let me have it. I insisted and he got angry and called me a 'nigger.' I asked what that meant. He said it meant something bad — and something black. That infuriated me, for I knew I wasn't bad and I wasn't black. I pushed him and then chased him home. His mother asked me why we were fighting and I told her what he had called me and that I was going to kill him if he called me any more bad names."[34]

As a teenager in New York, Essie was equally combative. "I have always been determined never to let anyone push me around. I knew that at any moment I might have to pay for that luxury, but even if I were killed for it, I would not let anyone push me around. When I was growing up in New York City they used to refuse to serve Negroes in places like Childs', Schrafft's, and the drugstore soda fountains downtown. One day I was shopping and was tired, hot, and thirsty. There were Liggett's soda fountains everywhere. Suddenly the whole thing seemed silly to me, and I made up my mind then and there to go in and have a soda. I just walked in, sat down at the counter and in a firm voice ordered an ice-cream soda. I remember very clearly that I ordered vanilla. The counterman looked at me rather strangely, hesitantly, and I looked back at him with what must have been something like murder in my eyes. He gave me the soda, I drank it quietly, and went out feeling better."[35]

Like Paul, Essie had been raised a "striver," but an eminently practical, more overtly combative one than Paul. In high school she wanted first to be a doctor, then a scientist. Her school adviser recommended she take domestic science as her major, Essie conjectured, "because I was coloured. I thought [the adviser's suggestion] was pretty silly, because I felt I knew all about housekeeping, having kept house for our little family for several years while my mother went out to work at her facial massages."[36] Essie completed her schooling at Wadleigh High School (one of two women's classical college preparatory high schools in New York City), in three years according to her own account, and won a scholarship in a competitive examination to the University of Illinois.[37] As Essie tells the story, she was sixteen and attending a graduation party in Chicago with a boy-friend who told her about the scholarship test to take place on the following day and suggested that she also take it. "I went home and told Mama. She said quietly, 'I think you'd better study tonight and brush up for the exams.' She fixed a special dinner for me, with coffee, and stayed up with me. I took the exams the next day. I came out third on the list and won the scholarship. There were only three. The nice boy came out fourth, and missed. I felt badly about that, I remember!"[38]

Later, when Essie applied for entrance to the university, she was told she was not eligible. "The first thing that crossed my mind was that I was being refused because I was a Negro. I was determined to get in, or else tear the school down brick by brick." When she pressed officials, they told her that she had not had four years of high school and was thus ineligible. Essie felt they ought to have been impressed that she had finished high school in three rather than four years. Finally, the college accepted her, but only as a domestic science major. Essie found the course work boring and might well have quit after two years had her mother not put her foot down. The only subject she really enjoyed was chemistry, and a friendly adviser urged her on, despite the fact there were few women (to say nothing of black women) in the field. She soon transferred from Illinois to Columbia.[39]

Based on a recommendation from her Columbia professor-adviser (also a woman), Essie was offered a position as a pathologist-chemist at the New York Presbyterian Hospital while still in her senior year. Essie was intelligent, well spoken, and fair enough to pass as white: in short, unobjectionable to her white coworkers. Wartime personnel shortages also helped and allowed Essie to feel she was contributing something to the war effort. (During World War I, she had volunteered to serve with the Red Cross but had been rebuffed by a white administrator. This hurt her deeply, enough so that during World War II she hesitated before again volunteering her services.)[40] Essie was pleased and proud about her position at New York Presbyterian. "This had always been a man's job," she wrote, "and so far as I know up to that time no Negro had ever worked at Presbyterian, not even as a porter or a maid."[41] As the first black, male or female, to be professionally employed in the Columbia Medical Center, Essie's achievement was news, and the black press, especially in Harlem, made much of it.[42]

By the time she received her bachelor of science degree from Columbia University on June 2, 1920, Essie's hard work was paying off.[43] Working as a chemist and technician in the Surgical Pathology Department, making microscopic cross-sections of tissues taken from patients in the operating room, Essie performed competently and in time was generally accepted by the surgeons, nurses, and other hospital personnel with whom she had contact. Like Paul, however, she discovered that achievement inevitably meant shouldering the onerous burden of "race representative." "I knew that as the 'first' I would be considered an example of my race and sex, and that was a great responsibility. If I didn't do well at my job, it would not mean that as an individual person I was incapable, lazy, stupid, or irresponsible. All Negroes, and many women, have to fear this burden, especially those who are 'first' at anything."[44]

Paul saw in Essie qualities that made her special, a cut above other young women he had met. She lived with her friend and roommate, Minnie Sumner, in a large Italianate house on "Strivers' Row," the name given to the group of fashionable brownstones on 138th and 139th Streets designed in 1891 by the architect Stanford White. Along with "Sugar Hill" it was one of Harlem's more elegant neighborhoods, rapidly being taken over by black doctors, lawyers, and other professionals. Blacks migrating to large northern cities almost always found themselves relegated to segregated areas within the larger city, and in that sense Harlem was New York's equivalent of the nation's urban ghettos. Harlem, however, was located in uptown Manhattan, not on the periphery like most black ghettos, and its streets were not only paved but wide, clean, and tree-lined. Within its more exclusive neighborhoods Harlem tenants lived in style with the best of modern facilities — elevators, telephones, and bellboy services.[45]

"Paul lived five or six blocks further down from Essie," recalled his friend William Patterson (who was at that time dating Minnie Sumner), "and while it was a respectable living, it was not Strivers' Row. Just those few blocks made quite a difference." Patterson, who only a few years later would repudiate capitalism, join the Communist Party, and devote himself to championing civil rights and Communist causes, was during this period a striver, intent on climbing the social and economic ladder. He lived on Strivers' Row and remembered well his own education, received at the hand of his landlady, on what was expected of Strivers' Row residents. "I was a young lawyer, not making much money, trying to make ends meet with a number of other jobs. I went to work on the docks every day. Still, I was careful to arrive home properly attired with my work overalls wrapped in a bundle. My landlady said it wouldn't do. Appearance alone wasn't good enough. The doctor who owned the building wanted his tenants to do 'respectable' work."[46] Respectability was the key to life on Strivers' Row. Residents either had it or were feverishly pursuing it. Essie was no exception.

Robeson was fascinated by this pretty, energetic, and poised Columbia student. Patterson said that "in no time he was really taken, head over heels in love with her." There were other young women more beautiful: Essie was diminutive, not tall and willowy; her forehead was short, a feature she inherited from her father. But what she lacked in classic beauty she made up for in other ways. "She had something very special about her — something intangible almost," said Patterson. She excelled in school, worked a demanding job, and still found time to enjoy Harlem's parties, sing and socialize, and work as a lifeguard at the Harlem YWCA. She had tremendous energy and drive. Two years Paul's senior and city-bred, she negotiated the city with an ease that astonished Paul. Eslanda Goode was sure of herself and where she was going: she seemed capable of handling anything.[47]

Essie was similarly taken with Paul. According to one story, she first spied him, Phi Beta Kappa key prominently displayed, as she was going to De Vann's restaurant on West 136th Street, and then later met him at a Harlem party.[48] In contrast to Paul's slow, almost meditative style, Essie generally made up her mind quickly: "When she saw him she knew right away she wanted him," one friend remembered.[49] Essie herself recalled: "Everybody thought he was just one of those football players who wouldn't amount to anything. But I thought he was terrific. I said to myself, 'I'd better marry him before these other people catch on.'"[50]

Such quick decision making and focused pursuit of a goal was not Paul's usual style. Essie, however, had few inhibitions if something she cared about was at stake. Paul sensed that this woman could give him direction and the push he needed to reach his full potential. She would not settle for the mediocre, nor would she allow anything to distract her from getting what she wanted. Paul liked that about her. He needed someone with whom he could be close but also someone who would advise and guide him. In the midst of his anxiety, uncertainty, and fear that he would not be able to live up to his Rutgers fame, meeting and falling in love with Eslanda Goode turned Robeson's life around.

Over the next year Essie planned and carried out what she later frankly admitted was "a campaign to win Paul." She sensed she could not compete solely on the basis of physical attractiveness. "I wasn't pretty . . . I was short and thick, so I had to make myself—well, interesting! . . . [But] there were so many other things I could be—athletic, a good companion, gay, appreciative."[51] Essie watched other women fuss over Paul, trying to get his attention, and she decided to take a different course. "I knew that you must convince the man you want to marry that you are not especially interested in marriage. . . . I would try being casual and indifferent. It was just one of those things—it worked."[52]

While they dated, Essie thought about what she could do for this "great hulking man with little direction." She "had made up her mind she was going to make something of him."[53] She considered his athletic ability. Herself an athlete (she played basketball and taught swimming at the Harlem YWCA), Essie appreciated Paul's talent and understood his need for the acclaim playing sports offered. Still, she realized there was no real future for Paul in athletics, and Essie had her eye on the future.

According to Paul, he was half in jest, half serious when he decided in the summer of 1920 to take Essie's advice and try his hand at acting, accepting the lead in a small YWCA production of Ridgely Torrence's play *Simon the Cyrenian*. In later years Paul liked to describe himself as almost lackadaisical about his early theater experiences, and this, his first acting performance, as a happy "accident" brought about largely by Essie and the persuasive persistence of the pioneering black actress-director Dora Cole (sister of composer Bob Cole), the driving force behind the Colored Players' Guild. "How I happened to do that thing is one of those accidents that make me believe it is luck the way things come about for me," Paul explained. "I was living next door to the YWCA, so close that it was actually possible for Dora Cole to drag me in there and make me do the part. If it just hadn't happened that I was so close that I couldn't get out of it, I never would have done that thing."[54]

The opening production of *Simon the Cyrenian*, one of a trilogy of plays by Ridgely Torrence, at Madison Square Garden in April 1917, according to Harlem historian James Weldon Johnson, marked "the beginning of a new era for blacks in the theatre."[55] For the first time a white American playwright had created a role for a black man other than a stereotypical shuffling buffoon. "Simon the Tiger" was a serious, heroic figure, the native African leader of slave insurrections who helped Jesus carry his cross.

In this, as in his other early efforts, Paul learned to act by getting out on the stage and doing it and after only a few rehearsals performed the role for two nights, June 11 and 12, in the small hall with a raised platform that functioned as the Harlem YWCA's theater. A single review appeared in the black weekly, the

New York Age: the matter-of-fact comment on a promising amateur effort, noted that Robeson "interpreted his role sincerely and powerfully."[56] Despite its flaws the play gave Paul exposure, the timing of which could not have been better.[57]

Members of the Greenwich Village–based avant-garde Provincetown Theatre were in attendance for the YWCA production, among them Robert Edmond Jones and James McGowan, and possibly Eugene O'Neill. According to a widely circulated story, Robeson was approached by one of the Provincetowners concerning a role in a new O'Neill play, *The Emperor Jones.* (Accounts vary as to whether it was Jasper Deeter, who later played the cockney trader Smithers, or O'Neill himself who spoke with Paul. Though it is unlikely that O'Neill or any of the major figures within the Provincetown Theatre met with Paul, it is conceivable that one of the theater group's underlings did field the possibility.) Admittedly, Robeson had no stage experience, but this was a common problem among black actors. Though many had performed, few had ever had the opportunity to do a serious role before white audiences. Robeson had presence, a commanding voice, and, of special interest to O'Neill, who was an avid boxing fan, an impressive physique; in other words, he had real potential.[58]

Robeson turned the role down, however. According to a story Robeson repeated himself in various forms, after having a portion of the script read to him he categorically refused to have anything to do with the play. Reportedly, Robeson was appalled by the play's main character, Brutus Jones, a loose-living and superstitious escaped convict jailed for killing another black man in a razor fight during a crap game. Although it is difficult to believe that Robeson was as straitlaced and naive as he described himself, Robeson's purported response did reflect the attitude of most respectability-bound blacks of the period. The script, replete with racial epithets ("bush niggers," "trash niggers," "stinkin' nigger"), most coming from the mouth of Jones himself, lent credence to everything negative Paul had ever heard about the stage, to say nothing of white characterizations of the race. "[When] Jasper Deeter came to see me, I was studying law. I was very anxious about my life and what I would do, because I was very concerned with contributing something to my race. And of course, I was sensitive to every epithet applied to it. Added to that, I had been brought up to believe that the theatre was an evil place. And this man — Jasper I mean — came up and read me the play, *The Emperor Jones.* You can understand that my reaction was one of such anger that I couldn't breathe. The more he read me that terrible character, the angrier I got. I think I almost threw Jasper Deeter out of the house!"[59]

In the end, a twenty-year veteran of the stage, Charles Gilpin, agreed to take the part. Born in Richmond, Virginia, Gilpin had quit school at the age of twelve to do a song-and-dance act with traveling fairs. He played in minstrel shows (Perkus and Davis's Great Southern Minstrel Barnstorming Aggregation) and then toured with the Williams and Walker Company. While still a teenager he became one of the original members of the Pekin Stock Company in Chicago and worked with the Lafayette Players. There was little in theater that Gilpin didn't try at one time or another, but, aside from a single scene in John Drinkwater's *Abraham Lincoln,* a British biographical drama that opened on Broadway in 1919 (Drinkwater did not like the idea of using white actors in burnt cork), Gilpin had had virtually no opportunity to demonstrate his considerable talents in a way that would bring him public attention. He had never been able to make a living at acting and so spent much of his career doing odd jobs — portering, printing, running an elevator, barbering, and even training prize-fighters — anything to keep eating between his sporadic acting bits.[60] Then came the offer to play the lead in *The Emperor Jones,* and Gilpin scored a spectacular success. The play opened on November 1, 1920, at the Provincetowners' Playwrights Theatre and "the place rang with cheers for Gilpin," and even after the actors had taken a dozen curtain calls the audience "refused to leave." Opening night reviewers applauded the play, "the most interesting . . . yet . . . from the most promising playwright in America" according to the *Tribune*'s Heywood Broun, and called Gilpin's performance a triumph: "thrilling . . . of heroic stature" and "an extraordinarily striking and dramatic study of panic and fear." *The Emperor Jones* proved to be Eugene O'Neill's first critical success as well as the theater group's first experience of financial solvency. Word spread quickly, "and the following morning saw the first line at the box office in the theatre's history."[61] Charles Gilpin had landed a substantive role and performed it impeccably. In a single night he had achieved fame.

While Gilpin leaped from obscurity to stardom, Robeson labored halfheartedly with his law studies and part-time jobs. "Paul enjoyed the prestige that went along with being a Columbia Law School student, but he hated the day-to-day grind of courses he frankly found boring," recalled one friend.[62] Robeson helped coach Columbia's football team, and for a second year he coached at Lincoln with his friend Fritz Pollard. If nothing else, loyalty to his father and his brother Bill, both Lincoln graduates, motivated Paul to give the job his best effort, despite the school's pitifully limited financial resources. Pollard had led the team to "unprecedented success" the previous year, and Lincoln expected another good showing.[63] Paul accepted the job thinking he would be "assisting" Fritz, but Pollard already had more than he could handle playing professional ball with the Akron, Ohio, team and so seldom showed up for Lincoln's practices. On occasion, he even missed games. This left Paul by default at the helm in what turned out to be one of the most disastrous seasons in the school's history, with the worst humiliation coming at the hands of Lincoln's archrival, Howard

University, in a 42–0 debacle played before a festive Homecoming crowd in Washington.[64]

While Robeson worked fruitlessly with the Lincoln team, traveling weekends to practices and games, Pollard had earned a small fortune (Pollard claimed $1,500 per game) playing for the championship Akron team. Coaching at Lincoln "wasn't much of a job," said Pollard. "We only played a few games a season. I can't even remember how much we were paid, but whatever it was, it was peanuts. It was good to get together with Paul for a couple of days a week and help the boys. I think Paul probably did it as a relief from law school. If he was coaching at Lincoln to earn money, he was in the wrong business, that's for sure. Why, we didn't even have money for football shoes. I had to buy them myself for the team; that's how poor we were. There just wasn't money in those days for colored college football teams."[65]

Lincoln fired Pollard at the end of the season and offered his position to Robeson, but Fritz had already suggested that Paul try making some "real" money playing professionally with him.[66] Paul, wanting to keep his hand in sports and in need of money, agreed to give it a try and played briefly for Akron toward the end of the 1920 season. A few games were enough to impress the team's management. Paul was offered a permanent position for the following season, and he accepted.[67]

Meanwhile, at the Playwrights Theatre, Gilpin's performance continued to reap accolades. His success, however, did not change his color, and when news broke that the black actor was among the candidates being considered for the New York Drama League award a heated controversy ensued.[68] Those opposing Gilpin's candidacy may well have had their own reasons for wanting to prevent him from winning but would be hard-pressed to deny him the honor on the basis of merit. The real but unstated issue was that, should he win, Gilpin most certainly would expect to sit down and eat with white award recipients, and that presented a problem.

Members of the acting profession, led by Eugene O'Neill, rallied to defend Gilpin, as did others in the city. Just before the Drama League dinner, Robeson, then a second-year law student, was invited to attend Columbia's graduating class dinner at the Hotel Astor where he occupied "a seat of honor at the speakers' table." His presence at the dinner, as the white press was quick to note, "set a precedent for Columbia senior class events," and although class members denied there was any connection with the Drama League dispute, press reports intimated that university students had invited Robeson specifically to protest the Gilpin slight.[69]

Overwhelmed by protests from some of the biggest names in the theater, the Drama League eventually backed down and invited Gilpin to the dinner.[70] Gilpin expected a polite reception and intended to "stay about four minutes and then retire gracefully." When he was introduced, however, the audience surprised him, "jumped to their feet, tossed napkins in the air and cheered themselves hoarse to make the Negro feel that he was welcome at their board."[71]

Gilpin was thrilled but not naive. "I am pleased especially with the generous praise of the critics," he began. "But I don't fool myself about the stone walls that are in my way. Mr. O'Neill has made a breach in those walls by writing a play that had in it a serious role for a Negro. The Provincetown Players gave me a chance to do the part. But—what next? If I were white, a dozen opportunities would come to me as a result of a success like this. But, I'm black. It is no joke when I ask myself, 'Where do I go from here?'. . . Whatever happens, I shall have some evidence to prove that I was not a fool in thinking that a Negro can act."[72]

Gilpin's fears were well founded. Louis Wolheim, a white actor with limited stage experience, who had also won instant fame after his portrayal in a new O'Neill play (Yank in *The Hairy Ape* [1922]), went on to play the lead in *What Price Glory?*, one of the decade's finest plays, and from there to stardom in Hollywood. But Gilpin, despite his undisputed acting talent (O'Neill said that he was the only actor "who carried out every notion of a character I had in mind"), never had another leading role. By 1926 he was back to doing what he had been doing before he was selected for the role: running an elevator. In 1930, at the age of fifty-two, he died—penniless and an alcoholic—on his New Jersey farm.[73]

Gilpin's rise to fame had had a magical quality, garnering in a single stroke long-overdue recognition not only for the veteran actor but for the entire black community. Over the next two years when the play went on the road, critics continued to lavish superlatives on the actor. He was deluged with invitations, many more than he could accept, and wherever he went, he was feted. Paul witnessed the acclaim firsthand in March when he sang as part of the local talent at a reception for Gilpin held at the home of Mrs. E. P. Roberts and given by the Club Sixteen, a social group that included some of New York's and New Jersey's most prominent black women.[74] Though many blacks objected to the play's language and content, no one questioned the import of Gilpin's achievement. It was a momentous contribution to the race.

As Paul watched Gilpin from the sidelines, again and again he was reminded of the opportunity he had let pass him by. "I remember vividly picking up the paper one morning at breakfast and reading the printed eulogies," Paul later recalled. "I could not help wondering if I too should have been so acclaimed if, when my chance came, I had accepted."[75] Robeson would not repeat that mistake. He would continue with his law studies, but always with an eye open for other opportunities.

If Essie did not devise this as a strategy, she thoroughly supported it. She had made up her mind about Paul and was now completely devoted to shaping her "diamond in the rough."[76] According to Essie, she and Paul were inseparable at this point. But, as would so often be the case with this couple, in situations where Essie was sure of herself and what she wanted, Paul was ambivalent. Paul, for example, had yet to sever completely his connection with Gerry Neale, who was now a graduate student at Howard University. In fact, in August 1921 he went to visit Gerry in Freehold, New Jersey, where she was staying for the summer until classes resumed in the fall. Paul later claimed that it was he who took the initiative and broke off the relationship, explaining to Gerry that "once he met Essie he fell desperately in love and now intended to marry her."[77] Gerry, however, remembered the incident differently and claimed that Paul asked her to marry him and she refused. Either way, the matter was settled.[78]

According to Essie, she and Paul had talked about marriage and considered a formal wedding ceremony but then suddenly decided against it. In August Paul proposed to Essie and, in fact, insisted that they marry immediately. On August 17 they took the train to Greenwich, Connecticut, where they had been told they could be married quickly, but upon arrival at the license bureau they were informed they would have to wait five days before the ceremony could be performed. "Then Paul said we could be married in New York state without waiting," recalled Essie, "so we went down to Rye on an interurban streetcar and were married immediately."[79] "After we got back to the city, we stood for a few minutes on the popular corner of 135th Street and Seventh Avenue, talking," Essie remembered. "A friend of ours, a dentist whose office was on the second floor of the corner building, leaned out of his window and called down to us, 'What are you two up to?' and I remember saying to Paul, 'Wouldn't he like to know?'"[80]

What precipitated Paul's sudden proposal and the couple's hasty marriage is unclear. Although Essie wanted Paul and was not above manipulating or dissembling to land him, it is unlikely that she was pregnant, as Robeson biographer Martin Duberman has suggested, or that she tried to make Paul think she was as a way of trapping him into marriage. By many accounts, Essie was too proper, some would say "prissy," to have let Paul take her to bed before marriage.[81] It may well have been as simple as that. Essie set certain rules; Paul abided by them and finally gave in. Once he had made the decision to marry her, there was really no point in waiting.[82]

Essie and Paul kept their marriage a secret for some time, maintaining their separate living arrangements (Essie continued sharing a studio apartment on Strivers' Row with Minnie Sumner, and Paul had his flat), letting all but a few close friends think they were still only dating, possibly so as not to invite embarrassing questions. At Christmas, when they were ready to begin living together in their one-room apartment, they announced their marriage at the annual conventions of Paul's fraternity, Alpha Phi Alpha, and Essie's sorority, Delta Sigma Theta, held over the holidays in Philadelphia.[83]

In the meantime, Robeson returned to classes and his first season of professional play for the Akron Pros. Essie was working and felt she could support them both if need be on her monthly salary of $150, but (according to Essie) the idea of her supporting them both embarrassed Paul. Professional play paid well (most earned about $75 per game plus expenses, and Robeson and Pollard as all-Americans may have earned much more than that; Robert Nash, on the Akron team himself, conjectured they may have been paid "as much as $300, about the highest a player ever got paid"), but Robeson would work hard for whatever he earned.[84]

Like others in the newly formed American Professional Football Organization, the Akron team took in stride frustrations today's players would find unthinkable. Most squeezed in games on weekends after a full week of work elsewhere. Contests were hastily set up or canceled depending on anticipated gate receipts. Equipment was limited to what was absolutely essential for play. "There were no organized practices and players tried to stay in shape during the week as best they could."[85] For Paul that meant "coaching" at Columbia University. What he was really doing was practicing with the college team to keep himself in shape for the Sunday games.

If Paul was looking for the accolades and glowing press coverage of his Rutgers days, he got none of them playing for Akron. In fact, if anything, there was considerable stigma attached to playing professionally. "Professional football was just beginning," explained Bob Nash:

We didn't have much of a backing in the Eastern seaboard cities where they rooted for their Harvards, Yales, and Princetons. They thought we were some kind of outcasts giving football a bad name because we played the sport for money. But those midwestern towns, maybe a cut below Cambridge or New Haven, with their iron and coal and rubber workers, they took a liking to us. Most of those folks in Akron, Canton, or Milwaukee had never seen a college football game. Hell, they were working on Saturday. But they came out to see us on Sunday. We had our college All-Americans, but we also had a lot of local boys playing, like Tony Latone, the hero of Pottstown, Pennsylvania, and the fans came to cheer for them. Those folks worked hard and they wanted to see us play hard. No finesse, just hard-nosed, two-way football.

To show you how poor we were, . . . our uniform consisted of a jersey. Nothing else. The helmet had a leather crown — soft; it fitted snug against the skull so you would feel every crack, every hit. The shoulder pads were thin; it was as if you were wearing a sweatshirt. Even the football itself was different then, almost watermelon shaped and difficult to pass. It was unheard of that any game would require more than one football. If it went into the stands, the game was held up until the ball was recovered.[86]

Rules were even more flexible than the game schedule. "Anything short of murder went without penalty. We just lined up against each other, face to face, and it was nothing short of war," recalled Scotty Bierce, a scrappy 160-pound all-American end from Dartmouth, who played for Akron.[87] Jim Thorpe's "dirty gridiron tricks" were legendary and included such maneuvers as inserting sheet metal into his shoulder pads in order to knock his opponents senseless. Not only did the games attract a tough, roughneck crowd, decidedly a cut below collegiate fans, but the press (most notably, the *New York Times* and *Yale Daily News*), backed by football immortals like Amos Alonzo Stagg, berated players as inept has-beens and denounced professional play as nothing more than "organized brutality."[88]

As black players Robeson and Pollard had special problems.[89] "You had to put up with a lot," Pollard admitted. "In Dayton, where the team stayed overnight, we were told there were no more rooms left. Hell, I knew beforehand they wouldn't take us in, so we just went to the colored section and slept there. But the next day I deliberately took my time getting to the ball field and held up the game for over an hour. They waited for me that time."[90]

Whether they were applauded or derided at games, Robeson and Pollard would be subjected to a volley of racial epithets. Pollard, recalling the number of southerners who had settled in the area in the years following the Great War, described Akron as "just like Mississippi in those days."[91] Some hometown fans—redneck townies, a hard-working, hard-drinking crowd—cheered "the gold dust boys," while others jeered Akron's "niggers" and "coons." Akron fans found it impossible to praise "the dusky boys" without resorting to demeaning stereotypes. At home games, when Pollard, the "dusky shifter," scored, the hometown jazz band struck up its "coon" song, "The Dark Boy Blues," and after a win the *Akron Press* could be depended upon to print its "black boy" cheer:

> Signals of the Pros are there,
> But the one that gets the call,
> Is seven come eleven,
> When the black boy totes the ball.[92]

"You had to be tough as nails to play in that league," Fritz Pollard said. "And that went double if you were black because they really came after us."[93] Pollard, explosive and excitable, retaliated by taunting spectators and players alike, electrifying them with daring punt returns and sensational broken-field runs even as they shouted "Kill that nigger." "They would scream from the sidelines, 'We're going to get you on that playing field, nigger, and kill you,' and I would yell back, 'If you can catch me.'" Paul, however, refused to let his feelings show. As far as he was concerned, he never heard the jeering, never noticed his "special" treatment. Robeson did his job, but with a vengeance, letting his playing do all his talking.[94]

The Akron management began the season confidently, certain that with the addition of Robeson, "one of the biggest warriors on the professional gridiron," they would win a second championship.[95] Initially, this confidence appeared justified. The combined power of Pollard's running game and Robeson's defense shook even the most stalwart opponents, and Akron remained undefeated and unscored upon for its first seven games.[96]

By the middle of the season, however, injuries began to take their toll. Robeson, nursing torn ligaments, did not start the game against the Canton Bulldogs, but when it became clear that Akron was going to have a tough go of it, he hobbled off the bench to play. "With the ball on Akron's 15-yard line [Robeson] leaped into the air, grabbed a Canton forward pass out of the atmosphere and ran to Canton's 33-yard line before his 210 pounds were hauled to the earth." The play was a glorious one for Paul and saved Akron, as local sportswriters were quick to note, "from probable defeat," but it did little to help his leg injury.[97] Consequently, he was used sparingly in the next contest, a dazzling 19–0 victory for Akron against the Rochester Jeffersons. A brutal contest against undefeated Buffalo, played to a scoreless tie in arctic cold on a field caked with ice, proved the turning point of the Pro's season. Although Akron did not lose the contest, the team suffered key injuries that affected play for the remainder of the season.[98] In Dayton, when Akron lost its first game of the season, the Akron press singled out Robeson, injured but still playing, for its sharpest criticism, implying he had feigned injury: "If anyone sits on the bench Sunday to make room for Corcoran on the line, it will be Robeson," local commentators snapped.[99] Two successive defeats — a Thanksgiving Day pummeling (14–0) at the hands of the Canton Bulldogs and a rematch with Buffalo (14–0) — knocked the team out of contention. The final win against Chicago was meaningless, and the Akron management canceled the team's last two games and, agreeing with the press, blamed the club's downfall on "several members [of the team who] failed to keep in condition toward the lag end of the season."[100]

By the time the season ended Paul was exhausted, injured, and disillusioned. After a week of classes and studying, he would board the train at Grand Central Station usually on Friday night, travel an average of twenty-five hours to the team's destination, play a grueling game, and then arrive home battered and bruised late Sunday night or Monday morning. Monday mornings he generally went to Columbia's Furnald Hall dormitory to get notes for the classes he had missed, trudged off to the library to copy them, and then began the cycle again on Fridays.[101] He tried to use the travel time to study and catch up on missed classes but often was simply too tired. In time, his school work suffered. In the meantime, he had seen little of Essie, who was herself worn out after a full week of work and weekends spent doing housework and (because she was very particular that Paul be well groomed) washing by hand and ironing Robeson's huge shirts.[102] Most often Paul returned home bone-tired and "just collapsed in a heap," leaving Essie to pick up the pieces.[103] The team's losses had consequences beyond disappointment and athletic humiliation: specifically, the cancellation of remaining games. And so, for all of his efforts, Paul ended the season bothered by insinuations that he was among those who had "dogged it" and with less money than he had counted on earning.

While Robeson labored in class and on the football field, an all-black musical opened at New York's Sixty-third Street Theatre that fall, the product of two separate creative teams — the actors and writers Flournoy Miller and Aubrey Lyles and the songwriters Eubie Blake and Noble Sissle. Initially, it appeared that *Shuffle Along* would not make it.[104] Trial runs at the Howard Theatre in Washington, D.C., and the Dunbar in Philadelphia had left the company $18,000 in debt, forcing the cast to make its New York debut "in borrowed costumes, on a narrow stage, in a small house" located considerably uptown from Broadway audiences. But *Shuffle Along* surprised everyone. Within a few weeks of opening it skyrocketed to success, breaking all previous attendance records and making the run-down Sixty-third Street Music Hall just west of Central Park "one of the best known houses in town." *Shuffle Along* was New York's biggest hit of the season.[105]

The first postwar musical with casting, music, choreography, lyrics, and production entirely in the hands of blacks, *Shuffle Along* revolutionized the theater world's conception of black entertainment. The show was basically an expanded version of a Miller and Lyles vaudeville sketch, "The Mayor of Dixie," which recounts the story of two crooked pols vying for top office and their ultimate defeat by the honest Harry Walton. *Shuffle Along* sported a fair share of minstrel antics and stereotypical coon gags. In fact, the show's plot was little more than an excuse for black jokes, songs, dancing, and attitudes. But *Shuffle Along* also introduced something new. For the first time in American theatrical history, black performers were not limited to the comic music white audiences had come to expect, but performed serious love songs as well. The ballad sung by Sissle, "Love Will Find a Way," for example, was not a coon song but a touching and lyrical testament of love. *Shuffle Along* pushed the limits but never too hard.

Blake recalled a wonderful illustration of this measured pushing. Blake's orchestra (like that of the famous conductor James Reese Europe) played without sheet music. The reason was not — as whites liked to believe — that black musicians couldn't read music. Blake, like Reese (whose orchestra Blake said "was filled with readin' *sharks*"), had learned the importance of catering to some white expectations. (Both orchestras used sheet music but clandestinely and only during rehearsals.) As Blake explained it, "All the high-tone, big-time folks would say, 'Isn't it wonderful how these untrained primitive musicians can pick up the latest songs instantly without being able to read music?' "[106]

Shuffle Along was fresh and exciting. Brilliantly choreographed by Lawrence Dea and Charlie Davis, it introduced jazz and ragtime to Broadway. It included memorable songs like "I'm Just Wild About Harry" and "Bandanna Days" and had a cast brimming with talent: ingenue Lottie Gee; comedienne Gertrude Saunders; the phenomenal singer and dancer Florence Mills; Noble Sissle and his "take-it-from-me" style of singing; Eubie Blake on jazz and ragtime piano; the "Chocolate Dandies" chorus line; violinist Hall Johnson and oboist William Grant; and the famous *Shuffle Along* band. *Shuffle Along* did what no other black musical before it had done: it earned the wholehearted, unpatronizing approval of white theater audiences. Previous black musicals (directed and produced by whites) attracted patrons more interested in prurient thrills than in quality entertainment, but *Shuffle Along* drew sophisticated as well as vaudeville audiences. Its Wednesday midnight shows quickly became *the* place to be — "sellouts to a glamour-hungry bourgeoisie." *Shuffle Along* made that all-important breakthrough and played "white time."[107]

By the spring, when Robeson was again looking for work, an unexpected opportunity presented itself. It involved one of *Shuffle Along*'s most popular features, the Harmony Kings quartet, "a big attraction in Vaudeville bookings" and well known in the black musical world as the best of the close-harmony groups.[108] The Harmony Kings — I. Harold Browning, Exodus Drayton, Horace Berry, and W. H. Hann — had joined *Shuffle Along* in the summer of 1921. Performing selections like Bruno Huhn's arrangement of the William Ernest Henley poem "Invictus," and "Snowball," "Ain't It a Shame," and Stephen Foster's "Old Black Joe," the quartet soon became one of the show's highlights. "They were sensations," said Eubie Blake. "All college men, not only could they sing, but they were very polished and stylish. They came out on the stage dressed in gray evening clothes. The suits were cutaway, and their top hats, ties, and shoes were also matching gray. They had everything. After their performance, Flo Mills had to be behind to top them. No one else could follow — that's how great they were."[109]

When the quartet's bass singer, William Hann, had to leave the show temporarily, the group began looking for a substitute. According to I. Harold Browning, the lead singer of the Harmony Kings, Paul sought the spot. Browning recalled, "We were walking down Seventh Avenue about 11 p.m. — me, my wife, and Paul and Essie — after a show. When I mentioned to Paul that our bass singer was leaving the show for a short time and that we had to find a bass to replace him, Paul looked at me and said, 'You're looking at a bass singer!' Paul was quite emphatic about it, and when I told him to stop kidding, he said, 'I am not kidding; I am your bass.' So I told him to come to the show and see Eubie and me, and he did. After Paul sang about seven or eight bars, Eubie jumped up and exclaimed, 'That's the man!'"[110]

Eubie Blake added his own comical twist to Browning's story: "Both Browning and I agreed about Paul's voice. He was able to learn the songs and small speaking parts in a matter of hours, but moving his massive body around that stage was a challenge." Blake chuckled, "Paul stood out like a sore thumb," so much so that Sissle, watching him, shook his head in dismay and sighed, "That guy's too big!"[111]

Noble Sissle's concern proved well founded. At the theater that Monday night, Blake, in an effort to prepare Paul for performing on stage, took him to the peephole in the curtain. "We looked at the audience filling up and I pointed to the spotlight in the back of the hall. I cautioned Paul that when he came out onto the stage, above all, he was not to look at the spotlight, because it would blind him. But, sure enough, when they came out onto the stage, Paul looked straight into the spotlight and was blinded. Just what I told him not to do," laughed Blake. "He fell right into the footlights, which sloped down into the stage gutter, and pop, pop, pop went the broken lights. Down he went like a ton of bricks, but you know, it never phased him; he got right up and went into the songs. It takes guts to do what that guy did. I've known people who had been on the stage for years, and they couldn't have pulled that off."[112]

Although Paul was lumbering and ungainly on stage, his singing was smooth — just what the audience wanted. "The white audiences — these were all white audiences — liked him," Blake remembered. "Paul sang some of Hann's solos, including 'Invictus,' 'Mammy' (we sang a lot of mammy songs in those days), Will Marion Cook's classic 'Rain,' and a favorite of Paul's, 'Old Black Joe.' 'Old Black Joe' was our last number and Paul just loved it. Paul was still huge on the stage; he was so big that we had him sit down while we sat around him on stage. But you could see that Paul, awkwardness and all, was going to be a hit, even then."[113]

Robeson had performed with the Harmony Kings for only a short while when he was offered the lead role in a serious dramatic production, scheduled to open in the spring of 1922, Mary Hoyt Wiborg's *Taboo*. Although in an interview three years later Paul made light of the offer ("I was broke ... and it was far better than working in the Post Office for a month or so"), at the time he took it seriously enough that he went immediately to Browning to tell him he would have to leave *Shuffle Along*.[114] "Paul wanted to be very gracious about it all," said Browning, "and explained that he had an offer but did not want to desert the job. But by this time Hann wanted to return anyway, so it was OK for Paul to leave."[115] *Shuffle Along* was the talk of the town, but *Taboo* would offer Robeson a chance to act and occupy center stage. He would not again dismiss any acting opportunity as beneath him or take it upon himself to predict how any theater venture might fare.

5
Beginnings of a Career

1922-1924

On a stormy night in the early 1920s, four up-and-coming young black men were traveling in a taxi from Manhattan to Brooklyn. The passengers were Edwin Coates, Frank Turner, Rudolph ("Bud") Fisher, and Paul Robeson; these men would become, respectively, an educator, an educator-administrator, a physician and writer, and an actor, singer, and political activist. It was windy and raining heavily and the driver, also young and black, made several fish-tailing stops. As the cab recovered from one of these near misses, Robeson leaned forward and in a solemn and serious voice warned the driver, "Be careful. If anything happens to any of us, you will set the race back three generations," and then sat back, chuckling to himself. The driver got the message and eased up on the accelerator.[1]

As this story illustrates, there was more to Robeson than the serious, earnest, and naive personality he so often presented to the public. In settings like this, when he was with friends — other young blacks with whom he could let down his guard — we see a Robeson quite capable of laughing at himself and even at his exalted place in "the future of the race." This is not to say that Robeson did not take himself seriously. He did. But his sense of humor would prove an invaluable asset during these early years of his professional career when he would have to do and put up with so much.

If Robeson was hoping for a role to equal O'Neill's *Emperor Jones,* he did not find it in *Taboo.* Written by Mary Hoyt Wiborg, the daughter of Frank Wiborg, a wealthy Fifth Avenue financier, the play showed all the signs of an amateur effort. Set on a plantation in antebellum Louisiana, the plot revolves around a severe drought and its impending threat to crops. Superstitious plantation slaves blame the drought on a curse placed on the mute grandchild of the plantation mistress, Mrs. Gaylord (played by Margaret Wycherly), and decide the child must be sacrificed. A wandering minstrel, Jim (played by Robeson), intervenes. Through many confusing twists of plot, the setting moves to a compound on the coast of Africa many generations earlier. (In his review, Heywood Broun frankly admitted that he could not follow the story.) Here, Jim is transformed into a voodoo king, the plantation mistress into his queen, and the origin of the voodoo rite being practiced by the Louisiana slaves is explained. In the end, the child speaks, rain descends at precisely the last moment, and all ends happily.[2]

The New York production opened on Tuesday afternoon, April 4, 1922, at the Sam Harris Theater on West Forty-second Street. Margaret Wycherly was the only white woman in the cast and Robeson played the lead; other roles were filled by black actors and African students from Columbia University, gathered by the Colored Players' Guild's indefatigable Dora Cole.[3] Black ticket holders attending the performances were escorted to balcony seats while whites were seated in the orchestra section, a practice New York blacks, including the NAACP's James Weldon Johnson, still took in stride.[4]

The play did not lack for action with its voodoo chants and incantations; an African dance performed by C. Kamba Simango, a native of Mozambique who was attending Columbia; and music provided by the Clef Club Orchestra. Nonetheless, reviewers panned the production, citing as its major flaws Augustin Duncan's poor direction, Margaret Wycherly's "monstrously stagy and sepulchral" performance, a confusing plot, and a stereotypical portrayal of "the Negro . . . as a primitive animal giving expression to himself only in an orgiastic community's leapings and shriekings." (There are photos from the London production that show Robeson as a minstrel version of a plantation worker in gaudy, floor-length checked pants and as a stereotypically frenzied African chief.) *Taboo* closed after four matinee performances, but not without giving Robeson, who impressed even hostile critics, timely exposure. Burns Mantle praised his "veristic and technically artistic" characterization; the *New York Age's* Lucien White singled out his singing and acting as "distinct features of the performance"; and Charles Darnton noted "something of the Gilpin power that made *The Emperor Jones* so gripping and so pitiful." The *New York Sun's* Alexander Woollcott found himself so fascinated by Robeson that he applauded him even while bemoaning his "brutal" performance and later invited him to his apartment on West Forty-seventh Street for a personal chat.[5]

What he had seen of theater life Paul liked. Little in his experience compared with the thrill of rubbing shoulders with Eubie Blake, Noble Sissle, and Florence Mills or seeing his name mentioned in the New York theater columns, even if in a bad play. For two years now Paul had been flirting with acting and singing, giving informal recitals, often with his friends Bud Fisher or May Chinn, a pianist and music major at the Teachers' College, Columbia University, whom

Paul first met through Fisher.[6] Although Robeson may not have aggressively pursued the theater, neither did he let his legal studies interfere with opportunities to perform.

In the summer of 1920, for example, while Paul missed a final examination for one of his law courses (personal property), he found time to sing at a vaudeville show given by the St. Christopher Club as well as perform the lead in the Harlem YWCA's revival of *Simon the Cyrenian*.[7] In September he wrote to Dean Stone (on stationery from the Imperial Hotel at Narragansett Pier) requesting permission to make up the test sometime later in the fall, explaining that a "physical and mental inability to continue" had prevented him from completing the course and forced him to go to Narragansett to "recuperate."[8] Permission to postpone the test was granted, but the autumn came and went without Paul's making up the exam. The incomplete course hung over Robeson's head until March 1922 when he again appealed to Stone, this time setting the date for April, which would allow him time to attain the credits he needed to graduate with his class. Robeson included with his request a medical statement from a Dr. C. B. Powell (who, coincidentally, worked with Essie, as the stationery was headed Presbyterian Hospital, Medical Laboratory X-Ray Pathology) verifying "that Mr. Paul L. Robeson was under my care from August 2nd, 1920 to August 16, 1920 [the summer that he originally missed the exam] and not able to follow studies."[9] But in April Robeson was busy with *Taboo* rehearsals and, apparently still not prepared, again failed to take the test.

As a result, Robeson did not graduate with his class in 1922.[10] Such procrastination was not conduct his father would have condoned, nor, for that matter, would the black community in general, and Paul knew it. One night, after *Taboo* had closed, Paul returned to Columbia's Kent Library to study. On his way into the alcove he noticed the Law School dean, Harlan Stone. Portly, with a broad face and a mop of hair hanging down over his forehead, Stone had been more than patient with Paul. Robeson, certain that by this time he had exhausted even this agreeable man's forbearance with his repeated scheduling and rescheduling of that final exam, was embarrassed and tried to avoid meeting him. Stone had already spotted Paul, however, and came up to him and in a half-complimentary, half-admonishing manner said, "Congratulations. I hear you are an actor now."[11]

Robeson was not yet ready to admit his career aspirations had changed and even less that he had elected to change them. Law lacked the glitter of theater, but for a young man with idealistic goals and a sense of racial responsibility it was the logical choice.[12] That Robeson felt conflict around this issue is clear: for years, even after he was professionally respected and well established, he denied that personal ambition played any role in his choice of career. Throughout his professional career he would most often describe himself as unusually lucky and his theater opportunities as a series of happy accidents. Thus, when he recalled how he happened to get the lead role in the play *Taboo,* Paul told biographer Marie Seton: "Lo and behold, in 1922, Miss Mary Hoyt Wiborg asked me to play *Taboo,* a play about the South and Africa. Again, I knew little of what I was doing, but I was urged to go ahead and try. So I found myself in rehearsal at the Sam Harris Theater in New York, in a cast directed by Augustin Duncan, brother of Isadora Duncan, playing opposite the famous English actress Margaret Wycherly."[13]

Although *Taboo*'s poor notices disappointed Paul, when he was asked to perform the role again that summer in England he jumped at the chance. Perhaps Robeson hoped that with new direction (the British version of the play, retitled *Voodoo,* would be directed by one of London's theater greats, Mrs. Patrick Campbell) the play would earn better reviews. He had unfinished course work to make up at Columbia, but he was not about to turn down the opportunity to go to England. He would take his chances with the play, and in the meantime Law School could wait.

Paul left for London, traveling third class aboard the S.S. *Homeric* in early July, and Essie remained at home. Just before his departure, Essie had been told she needed surgery to remove adhesions from an old appendectomy. Essie did not tell Paul, however. She saw him off at the pier, wrote out some twenty letters, arranged to have friends send them off to Paul at appropriate intervals, and then checked herself into Presbyterian Hospital.[14]

Robeson, in the meantime, arrived in London and, like most visiting American blacks of the period, stopped first at 17 Regents Park, home of black American baritone John C. Payne. "See Johnny and you'll be all right," was the advice generally given to visiting American blacks. Dubbed London's "unofficial ambassador to the court of St. James," Payne had first come to London in 1919 with Will Marion Cook's Southern Syncopated Orchestra and decided to remain there permanently. In London he was befriended by Lady Mary Cook, wife of the wealthy businessman and art collector Sir Herbert Cook and a woman with a special fondness for blacks. Lady Cook subsidized Payne, provided him with a spacious home, and together with Payne gave elegant parties and entertained at a Sunday evening open house that became a virtual institution among London's black artistic community.[15]

No matter what their origin, blacks visiting London invariably met other blacks from all parts of the world and with a broad range of experiences. Britain's black population in the 1920s consisted primarily of students from the Caribbean and West Africa; West Indian and African seamen and sailors, many of whom had settled permanently in seaports like Cardiff, Liverpool, Bristol,

North and South Shields, and along Tyneside in general; and American black musicians and performers. It was a small and dispersed population and for this reason, as much as anything else, one that welcomed newcomers and visitors. The "Versatile Three" (Anthony ["Tony"] Tuck, Augusto ["Gus"] Haston, and Charles Johnson); composer and violinist Clarence Cameron White; clarinetist Sidney Bechet; composer and conductor Will Marion Cook; composer and arranger Will Vodery; musician James P. Johnson; pianist and composer Lawrence Brown; pianist and composer Eubie Blake; lyricist and actor Noble Sissle; composer and singer Shelton Brooks; and singers Alberta Hunter, Roland Hayes, Ethel Waters, Marian Anderson, Turner Layton, and Florence Mills — all spent time in London. Whether they stayed for a short time, for years, or returned for regular visits, these American black performers and musicians became part of Britain's black community.[16]

England astounded Robeson, especially the courtesy and lack of prejudice he experienced there. Talking with and observing other American blacks in London, many of whom had chosen to remain there permanently, only confirmed his initial impressions. Payne was one such expatriate and Lawrence Brown, a musician recently returned from a European tour with tenor Roland Hayes and staying at Payne's home, was another. Five years Paul's senior, quiet, reflective, and thoroughly devoted to his own work — transcriptions of formerly unrecorded spirituals — Brown was a revelation to Paul. Despite his outward timidity, on certain matters Brown would not budge. Returning to lynch-crazed America after having experienced life abroad was one such issue. As far as Brown was concerned, England was now his permanent home.[17]

Paul did little talking with Brown (although in a few short years he and Brown would begin a lifelong working relationship), as meeting the demands of his talented, eccentric director, Mrs. Patrick Campbell, took almost all his time that summer. Hers was a name that would become as synonymous with the English theater of her day as Ellen Terry's and Sarah Bernhardt's had been in the late Victorian and Edwardian eras. By 1922 "Mrs. Pat" had already earned a reputation as an innovator, a flamboyant and unpredictable actress and director, and a woman of charm, beauty, and intelligence. She had experienced breathtaking triumphs (she played both the original "Second Mrs. Tanqueray" and Eliza Doolittle) and unqualified failures, enough of them so that her contemporaries never tired of arguing over whether she was a true genius or simply a clever and occasionally lucky amateur. One of Britain's first actress-managers, she showcased such controversial talents as Ibsen, Björnson, Sudermann, and Maeterlinck. Her personal life offered ample evidence of both extravagance and disarming appeal. Authors Arthur Wing Pinero, James Barrie, and W. B. Yeats, whose talents she fostered, all wrote plays for her, and for over thirty years George

Bernard Shaw carried on in letters a tempestuous flirtation with her and, like her other famous admirers, dedicated numerous works in her honor. One never knew how projects under Mrs. Campbell's direction would fare. High-strung and unpredictable, she was inclined "to take violent dislikes to members of the cast" and make "their lives miserable with her razor-sharp wit." Much to Paul's relief, she liked him immediately.[18]

Mrs. Campbell did her best to redeem Miss Wiborg's script, principally by having Paul sing as much as possible. The idea came to her during rehearsals. One scene required Paul to fall asleep and start whistling in a dream. Because he could not whistle, Robeson improvised and began to hum. Mrs. Campbell, standing in the wings, whispered, "Sing it louder, sing it louder." So Paul fell asleep again and sang "Go Down, Moses." From that point on, whenever anything in the production went awry, she expected Paul to jump in and save the day with his singing. As Robeson himself admitted, the play quickly "turned into an unaccompanied concert—with some dramatic action." *Voodoo* played in Liverpool, Glasgow, and Edinburgh but fared no better in these locales than it had in New York. It received scant mention in British theater columns, but when it did attention generally focused not on the play but on "the wonderful singing of that fine looking Negro in the cast."[19]

In the meantime, unknown to Paul, Essie had had her surgery but suffered complications (phlebitis) that kept her hospitalized. His letters home to her were warm, at times effusive, expressions of devotion. (It would become a hallmark of their relationship that distance sparked renewed affection in Paul while prolonged proximity dampened it.) Between declarations of love and assurances he was not "slumming" (suggesting that Essie suspected his behavior once he was out of her reach), Paul begged Essie to help him think through his professional plans, particularly as prospects for a successful *Voodoo* run dimmed. "You'll know what to do—you always do." In time, Essie's prewritten letters began to make less and less sense, especially as they failed to address any of the problems Paul had posed in his own letters. By the end of August Paul knew something was wrong. "All my questions unanswered," Paul's telegram read. "Worried. Is anything wrong. Love, Paul."[20]

Only then did Essie tell him the truth. The news so shocked and upset Paul that he was ready to take the next boat back. It embarrassed him as well. All the time he had been writing Essie, on one occasion complaining bitterly about catching a cold and having to struggle through without her there to look after and "spoil him," she had been hospitalized and never said a word.[21] When Essie finally did reply, she urged him to stay, but *Voodoo*'s early closing settled the matter, and by the end of September Paul was bound for New York.

Within weeks of Paul's return York Essie was well enough to leave the hospital and begin her recuperation. In November the Harlem community gave Robeson a belated welcome home, treating him like a minor celebrity as 150 members of leading black society attended a reception in his honor at the University of Music on Michigan Avenue. It was a gala evening with entertainment provided by *Shuffle Along*'s best: Noble Sissle, I. Harold Browning, and William Hann.[22] Financial considerations, however, weighed heavily on Paul that fall, especially with Essie still unable to work. As Robeson later confided to reporters, "I had lost my enthusiasm for law school and I waited around for a chance to get into theater."[23]

Nothing materialized. While he waited, the Milwaukee Badgers, coached by Fritz Pollard and former Rutgers teammate Budge Garrett, asked Paul to play for them. Robeson was not enthusiastic. He had had his fill of professional football and had no desire to spend the winter in frigid Wisconsin. He hated the cold, and with Milwaukee a full twenty-four-hour journey by train, commuting was out of the question. But he had no other immediate prospects, and funds were scarce. In the end, the only way Robeson could complete his law course and earn any significant money was to accept the offer. This he did, attending nearby Marquette University during the week and playing professionally on weekends.

The Badgers got off to a slow start, losing 3 to 0 to the Chicago Cardinals. The following week Robeson joined the Badgers in Toledo. Milwaukee led throughout, but in the final forty seconds of the game the Toledo Maroons scored a touchdown, ending the game in a 12–12 tie. Then in Milwaukee, Robeson and Pollard starred, defeating the Racine Legion Belles 20–0.[24]

"We were practicing more regularly during the week," recalled Pollard, "not like in the earlier days. Now there was the real possibility of an organized professional football league, and those midwesterners were just the crowd to whoop it up and put it across." The Milwaukee team played "hard-nosed, two-way football" but paid dearly for it in injuries. "Hurt or not, we played that next game if we wanted to be paid," said Pollard, who himself played hurt throughout the season. By the time of the Rock Island contest, ballyhooed in the press as a duel between "two giant men of color," Paul Robeson and former Iowa University great Duke Slater, the Badgers were hobbled with injuries, and neither Pollard nor Robeson was up to snuff.[25] Paul had taken the long trip home to New York earlier in the week, having received word that Essie was sick; once reassured that she was not seriously ill, he rushed back, arriving just in time for the Sunday afternoon showdown. Fifteen thousand fans sat shivering in the stands, waiting for the game to begin, as the wind from Lake Michigan howled over an ice-caked gridiron, but the contest was called off due to the abominable freezing weather. Reaction from the die-hard Milwaukee fans was predictable: they booed and hissed players they had lionized only weeks before. The *Journal,* reflecting local sentiment, sneered, "Drag out these 'parlor babies'—where are the big-time Badgers?"[26]

Robeson, however, made his best showing of the year in the next week's contest against the Ooorang Indians of Marion, Ohio. Led by Jim Thorpe, the Ooorang band of mighty warriors—"Black Bear, Red Fang, Dead Eye, Laughing Gas, and Lone Wolf"—reportedly were on the warpath and "out to scalp" the Badgers' star black players, Robeson and Pollard. Coach Budge Garrett's strategy—Robeson passing and Pollard receiving for the one-two scoring combination—worked, and before a homecoming crowd of over 6,500, the Badgers whipped the Indians, 13–0. It was Robeson's hour to shine. "In the thick of every play, he stood out, head and shoulder over every lineman in the game," glowingly recorded the *Milwaukee Evening Sentinel.* Robeson scored both of the Badgers' touchdowns, one on an Ooorang fumble recovery in the end zone and the second a pass reception, "which the big end grabbed among a flock of Indian backs, running 20 yards to a touchdown." The victory was sweet but costly. Fritz Pollard remembered it as "the toughest, meanest game I ever played in. Budge Garrett was carried off with a broken leg, I was knocked cold, and Robeson's leg injury was worse than ever." In the games that followed the roof fell in on the Badgers as the club suffered three straight losses and a final humiliating 40–6 defeat by the Canton Bulldogs. Both Pollard and Robeson missed the final game. The *Canton Daily News* reported that Pollard had suffered several broken ribs, while Robeson "evidently got lost en route."[27]

Paul ended the season tired, injured, and disappointed with the team's final showing. Fritz had told him it would be easy money, to which Paul, who had not lost his sense of humor, replied, "That's the hardest I ever worked for easy money!" Still, Fritz talked him into stopping off in Chicago for one more contest, this one pitting the talents of all-star Negroes against a team of white players. Robert Abbott, *Chicago Defender* publisher, and cafe owner Bill Bottom conceived and sponsored the event, intended primarily to draw attention to the unheralded achievements of blacks in sports. The black team, led by local hero Fritz Pollard and appropriately dubbed "Fritz Pollard and his All-Stars," boasted a breathtaking lineup that included Ink Williams of Brown, John Shelbourne of Dartmouth, and Iowa's Duke Slater, with the remainder of the players gathered from the Lincoln Athletic Club. The *Defender* touted the December 16 game at American Giants Park as a great racial confrontation and predicted that a crowd of thousands (at two dollars a seat) would attend. In fact, the "showdown" proved a fiasco. The white team failed to attract comparable names or talent, and the game was played not at Giants Park but forty-five minutes late before a small, shivering crowd at Scherling's Park at Thirty-ninth Street and Wentworth Avenue.[28]

Paul headed home, relieved to have the season over. Once home, however, he was greeted with an avalanche of stories detailing his superhuman prowess in the gruesome Badger–Indian duel. The colorful hard-fought Badger–Indian game made a good story, especially as pregame rumors had it that the Indians were out to "kill Robeson." According to one of the most often repeated stories, one of the Ooorang players tried to stick his fingers in Paul's eyes, and Paul retaliated by knocking him unconscious. Alexander Woollcott lent the incident enough detail to build a legend:

> At that, the opposing eleven fell upon him as one Indian. Out of the corner of his eye, Paul could see his own one-hundred-percent Anglo-Saxon teammates discreetly leaving the scene. It looked as if he might have to beat up all those Indians single-handed. Before intervention became effective, he had entered upon this chore with such a genuine pleasure and such concentrated destructiveness that the story of his quality as a fighter spread over the country before nightfall. Drooping fight-promoters were galvanized into sudden action. Within a week, more than a million dollars had been confidentially pledged to back him as the prospective heavyweight champion of the world.[29]

Professional boxing was in its heyday, thanks to fight promoter Tex Rickard (who had just finished building Madison Square Garden), champion Jack Dempsey, and the million-dollar gate. Dating back to the 1880s and heavyweight champion John L. Sullivan, professional boxers had refused to cross the color line. In the past, Dempsey himself had refused such a match, but in 1920 he announced his willingness to fight a black man — Harry Wills or whoever else came his way — and in no time a rumored Robeson match became a hot sports item. (Rickard did arrange a Wills–Dempsey bout, but in the end Dempsey's manager, Jack Kearne, would not allow it. Rickard was forced to pay Wills a $50,000 forfeit.) By January the sports gossip mill revealed that "men from Chicago" had approached Robeson in the locker room following the Indian game with a Dempsey–Robeson fight proposition. A sure million-dollar draw, Robeson was promised that, "win or lose, you'll make enough so you'll never have to work again."[30] Reportedly, Robeson said he would think it over.

Sportswriters were divided about the idea. Robeson's black friends and college classmates warned him not to accept the offer. Rutgers alumni were not happy to see "Robey of Rutgers" playing professional football to begin with.[31] Did he want to become another Jack Johnson and throw away the chance to contribute something substantial to his race? The rumors and insinuations upset Paul. Even Columbia law students had heard them, and at least one class-mate assumed Robeson earned his tuition by boxing professionally.[32] Although Robeson rarely corresponded in writing, in this instance, not wanting the Jack Johnson label pinned on him, he did. In a strongly worded letter to the Rutgers Alumni Association, Robeson said that reports of a Dempsey–Robeson match (in particular, sportswriter Lawrence Perry's widely reprinted version of the story) were "absolutely untrue and unfounded." Likewise, he strenuously denied having ever seriously considered professional fighting. "I can't see any credit to Rutgers in a prize-fighting legal failure," he said. "My real ambition [is] to be a lawyer."[33]

The 1922 football season and the rumors of a professional boxing bout ended Robeson's athletic career. Paul was listed on the roster of Harlem's 1923 Commonwealth Five basketball team, but he played so seldom that one "disgruntled" fan in a letter to the sports editors of the *Amsterdam News* insisted Robeson's name be dropped from the roster and replaced by someone who at least showed up for games.[34]

Paul completed his final course in law and graduated with the class of 1923, but the prospect of looking for work in a law firm failed to arouse his enthusiasm. Instead, he contacted Augustin Duncan, director of *Taboo,* who wrote a letter of introduction to Eugene O'Neill, at the time working on another play that required a black man for the lead role. (Robeson's request for such a letter to O'Neill again suggests, contrary to the stories Robeson later told concerning his initial refusal of the Brutus Jones role, that O'Neill did not yet know Robeson.) "My dear Eugene O'Neill," began the letter dated February 23, 1923. "This will introduce you to Paul Robeson who is desirous to meet you in regard to a part in your new play." Robeson also wrote to the legendary patron of the arts (and of the Provincetown Players, in particular), the wealthy banker Otto H. Kahn. It was in his capacity as trustee of Rutgers College that Robeson made his appeal to Kahn, indicating his interest in pursuing a theatrical career and asking Kahn's assistance in the process.[35]

In the meantime, Robeson continued to perform at informal recitals, with Will Marion Cook's Clef Club Orchestra, and as part of the chorus of a new show, *Plantation Revue,* produced by Lew Leslie and starring the immensely popular Florence Mills. *Plantation Revue* began as a floor show at Sam Salvin's cabaret, the Plantation Room, and proved such a success that it soon moved to the more upscale Forty-eighth Street Theatre. There were very few theater opportunities that did not require black performers to don, at least in part, the minstrel mask. *Plantation Revue* — with a set that simulated minstrelsy's version of an actual plantation complete with log cabins, a huge half-watermelon moon that emitted beams of light at various intervals, and Aunt Jemima flipping flapjacks—was no exception. Robeson, along with the other three chorus members, wore the stereotypical minstrel garb—flashy stripped overalls, checked ascot, and a large straw hat. Still, he remembered it as a happy time and years later recalled, "humming the last strains of 'Little Gal,' that lovely song of Rosamond Johnson's set to the words of Paul Laurence Dunbar, and then rushing from the old Plantation Room into the subway train at Fiftieth Street and Broadway. There across the aisle, was dear Florence Mills, the simple nightingale-voiced star, and how proud I was when she gave me a nod and a smile of recognition." If the company of Florence Mills thrilled Paul, being billed as "the late star of *Taboo*" alongside Gilpin when he performed in May with Cook's Clef Club Orchestra at the Lafayette Theater set his hopes soaring.[36] Wherever he went, Gilpin, recently returned from a "spectacular" six-month tour of the western and southeastern United States, electrified black audiences whose pride in his achievements seemed boundless. Standing in the Gilpin aura, as Robeson did so many times during this year, reminded Paul that fame was indeed within reach.

As he weighed the theater against a staid but dependable career in law, Robeson knew what the black community expected of him. Despite the fanfare over an occasional exception like Gilpin—black weeklies happily touted such bright meteors—most blacks believed that equality would be won in the plodding struggle to make gains in respectable professions. Robeson knew what most respectable blacks thought of theater—a fast life in smoke-filled cabarets—no life for a minister's son.

On the other hand, not only Paul but Essie also (her own father's experiences a grim reminder) recognized that his prospects for real success as a lawyer were bleak. "You have to remember, there just weren't that many black lawyers in New York in those days," said Paul's friend William Patterson, at the time himself a "striver" still trying to make it as an attorney, as he recalled Robeson's disenchantment with law:

Clients were slow in coming because of the discrimination against black lawyers and within the court system. When important cases came up whites certainly would not consider a black lawyer. Even a black man in need of a lawyer, believe it or not, thought twice about hiring a fellow black. Most blacks could not afford lawyer's fees, but if they had to pay sizable sums of hard-earned money, they preferred a white attorney, who, because of the inherent advantage of color, stood a better chance of winning the case. You couldn't blame them. The NAACP didn't even use black lawyers. For important cases they chose white names like Arthur Garfield Hayes and Clarence Darrow. Black lawyers almost inevitably encountered prejudice—even in the North. So most black lawyers operated within the confines of the black community. They may have begun with high hopes and expectations, but with few exceptions most ended up handling small cases for small fees — deeds and wills, property claims — cases not likely to come before a jury or judge. So, you see, most black attorneys had to find some other means of supplementing their income. Practicing law just wouldn't do it.[37]

Paul often stopped by the office of Dyett, Hall, and Patterson at 2303 Seventh Avenue just off 135th Street to talk with Patterson. One of the few black firms in Harlem, Dyett, Hall, and Patterson was a favorite gathering spot for young black lawyers and would-be officeholders. Conversations usually centered on city politics — the means many black lawyers chose to stay afloat — and the future of the race. Robeson enjoyed the talk, but the intrigues of city government did not interest him at all. "Paul had no sense of politics whatever then," Patterson recalled. "I don't even think he voted. He was not then what he would later become. He was like so many others, a striver, just trying to get ahead."[38]

Over and above the huge roadblock of color, with his academic record at Columbia (two-thirds of his grades were C's), missed and incomplete courses, and late graduation, what chance did Robeson stand of receiving the rave recommendations he would need to get started in the field? Former classmate Steve White recalled meeting Paul in New York City weeks before Robeson's graduation. "I asked him what his plans were. Paul, almost in resigned jest, replied, 'I guess I'll be a lawyer and settle back in Harlem with some political patronage.' I could see right then his heart was not in law."[39]

Essie, recounting this period in her biography of Paul, focused on the frustration Paul experienced trying to secure work and attributes his unwillingness to pursue a career in law to the rank prejudice he initially encountered in the field. According to Essie, Paul accepted a position in a firm specializing in estates, the Stotesbury and Miner law office, offered to him by Louis William Stotesbury, a Rutgers alumnus and trustee. Essie claims that Paul worked hard, showing such interest that it was suggested he draw up a brief on a phase of the Gould case, then being handled by the firm. Although he meticulously prepared a brief good enough to be used when the case was brought to trial, clerks and other members of the firm objected to the presence of a black man in the office (Robeson was the only black employed by the firm) and eventually forced his resignation.[40]

Essie's account, intended for public consumption, reflects embellishments both she and Paul routinely indulged in during their years in England. The truth was far more prosaic. In fact, the Gould case was a well-publicized, long-drawn-out series of suits and countersuits instigated by a number of the aspiring heirs to the original Jay Gould fortune which, left in the hands of his ostentatious spendthrift grandson, George Gould, had been badly mismanaged. With

George Gould's death in 1923 the battle was on. Litigation dragged on for over seven years and involved at least ten major law firms. If indeed Robeson participated in any of the proceedings, as a black man (even the fair-skinned Robert L. Vann, an established lawyer, experienced city official, and editor of the *Pittsburgh Courier*, had a hard time getting any cases) and a recent graduate with an unimpressive record, he would not have been trusted with anything more weighty than clerking and researching. Paul himself never mentioned the case, thus leading one to question Essie's claim that he was intimately involved with some important aspect of the case.[41]

There is no doubt Paul did shop around among friends for a legal position, but he did not work hard at it. He applied for the New York Bar exam, but by March 1924 when the test was scheduled he had apparently changed his mind and never took it. Former Rutgers classmate Harold Higgins said that Robeson called on him shortly after he (Higgins) had secured a clerkship in a well-known Newark firm. "Paul asked me about taking the New Jersey Bar exam. Then I told him there was a six-month to one-year clerkship available at between thirty-five and fifty dollars a week where I was, but he was not interested. 'I can make that much one night singing,' he said, and I never heard from him again."[42]

Sculptor Antonio Salemme said that Paul talked with him on several occasions about what his pursuing a career in law would mean: constant rebuffs from whites unwilling to be represented by a black lawyer. "He said with great feeling that it was then and there he decided, 'If I'm going to face this all my life, I might as well get out.'" But Salemme, like others, privately concluded that whether or not Paul experienced prejudice he would have never been happy as a lawyer. He "was simply temperamentally unsuited to the profession. He was a true Renaissance man with far-reaching interests. Law was too cramped; it would have absolutely stifled him."[43] A look at Paul's years in Harlem supports Salemme's assessment. In fact, Robeson had been drifting away from law almost from the first day of classes in 1919, always looking for something else—professional football, a chance in the theater, singing, anything but law.

Had he not been the subject of so much adulation in college, Robeson might well have been satisfied with a respectable Harlem law career. Having tasted success, however, Paul wanted more of it. Essie shared and encouraged Paul's ambition, but his lackadaisical attitude toward getting work (in either theater or a law firm) irked her. "Uncertain as to what to do next," Paul seemed content to wait for something "to turn up," while she supported them both, she later recalled. Steady, logical, and more practical than reflective, Essie had little understanding of, let alone patience with, Paul's need for quiet and periods of seeming inactivity. Even when in retrospect she was forced to admit the "practical" benefits of waiting it out, she found it difficult to talk about what appeared to her to be complacency—or, even worse, laziness—without an edge of sarcasm. Such inaction was antithetical to Essie's makeup. Others, like Paul's brother Ben, spoke of Robeson's meditative style with more understanding, observing that Paul, who "moves by inner revelations" would wait until he felt the answer but then follow through with absolute certainty. Joe Andrews said the same: "Paul needed quiet, space—sometimes days by himself—in order to make up his mind about anything important."[44]

Paul took the time he needed that spring and involved himself in a wide range of Harlem activities, all seemingly unrelated to the problem at hand: getting a job. Many days he spent reading at the 135th Street Harlem branch of the public library along with Countee Cullen and other Harlem hopefuls. Under the guidance of an energetic and visionary librarian, Ernestine Rose, the library had become a local cultural center, housing exhibitions of African and American art and, in the evening, hosting discussions, poetry readings (by Jessie Fauset, Countee Cullen, and others), lectures on current issues (led by Columbia University's John Dewey or the brilliant and versatile Jamaican and "Dean of Harlem Orators," Hubert H. Harrison), and, occasionally, small theatrical productions.[45] Often, cultural activities included socializing or singing in the basement auditorium, which housed an old but functional piano. There Paul took advantage of the opportunity to do what he wanted to do most: perform.

"Harlem was much smaller then," recalled Mrs. E. B. Marques, a white librarian who worked with Miss Rose. "The young Negro writers had no place to go, and so Miss Rose provided a place for them. They came and read during the day. They all knew each other. At night there were speakers—Walter White spoke on lynchings in the South; Du Bois often spoke too. Paul and Essie—she was charming, well dressed, and completely devoted to 'her angel'—both came to the library, but Paul spent much more time there."[46]

One can well imagine that Paul's leisurely routine of hanging around the library and other Harlem gathering spots ("Essie tried to keep him on a rigid schedule," said Mrs. Marques) quickly became a source of annoyance to Essie, whose steady plodding at Presbyterian Hospital made it all possible.[47] Essie thought it "rather wicked laziness" to sleep past 8:00 a.m. and tried in vain to adjust Paul to her own 7:00 a.m. to 11:00 p.m. schedule. For a brief time it appeared she had succeeded, but soon she discovered that, although he would get up with her, as soon as she left he crawled right back into bed again.[48] Not only did Paul sleep late but, equally disconcerting, he thought little about staying out until 2:00 or 3:00 a.m. (his schedule) socializing and, Essie assumed, carousing.

However, if a career in the arts was what Robeson wanted, he could hardly have positioned himself better. It would be another two years before Alain

Locke, the dapper erudite Rhodes scholar and professor of philosophy at Howard University, would officially usher in the "Renaissance" with his landmark publication, *The New Negro*, but the bright burst of Harlem talent had even this early made its presence felt downtown. *Shuffle Along* marked the end of decades of blackface and slapstick buffoonery and the beginning of a wave of fresh, innovative, uninhibited black productions, each backed up by a stunning display of talent. Miller and Lyle's 1921 *Runnin' Wild* introduced the Charleston to audiences at the Colonial, while Florence Mills won theatergoers by the score at the Plantation Club.

Already, "knowledgeable" whites had discovered that some of the best of Harlem was to be seen not in theaters but in Harlem's cafes. Clubs limited to white clientele, like Connie's Inn and the Cotton Club, or the mixed establishments like Small's Paradise often put on better shows than anything offered downtown. It was not unusual at Arthur ("Happy") Rhones's plush upstairs club at 143rd Street and Lenox Avenue to see Noble Sissle acting as impromptu master of ceremonies for a first-rate floor show, with celebrities like John and Ethel Barrymore, Charlie Chaplin, W. C. Handy, and Ethel Waters sitting among the audience. And while music abounded in Harlem's clubs, dancing extravaganzas to the tune of Fletcher Henderson's polished jazz took place weekly at the aging but still majestic Rockland Palace (the old Manhattan Casino).

Poet Langston Hughes had not yet published *Weary Blues*, but Jean Toomer's *Cane* and Claude McKay's *Harlem Shadows* had gained some acclaim. Harlem intellectuals Charles Spurgeon Johnson, national director of the Urban League's research and investigation division and editor of its monthly journal, *Opportunity*, and *Crisis* editor W. E. B. Du Bois encouraged young artists, as they were convinced that the intelligent and creative elite, the race's "Talented Tenth," would play a key role in improving race relations. If the arts were the only arena for achievement not entirely ridden with proscriptions designed to keep blacks in their place, then books, poetry, drama, and music would provide the race with its most potent weapons in the battle for racial equality.

Finally, Robeson's waiting paid off, and something worthwhile did "turn up." In the summer of 1923 Eugene O'Neill offered Robeson the lead role in his new play, *All God's Chillun Got Wings*, as well as an invitation to perform in the London production of *The Emperor Jones*. Ironically, it was Gilpin's fall from grace that paved the way for Robeson's ascent. Gilpin had a difficult time handling his sudden fame. Reportedly, he had been "acting the Emperor all over Harlem." His tampering with O'Neill's script, substituting the words "Negro" and "colored man" for the original "nigger" and "black boy" infuriated O'Neill who threatened to fire and "beat the hell" out of Gilpin, all with little effect. By the summer of 1923 O'Neill had reached the end of his patience and raged in a letter to Michael Gold: "Honestly, I've stood for more from him than from all the white actors I've ever known—simply because he was colored! . . . I'm 'off' him and the result is he will get no chance to do it in London. He was drunk all of last season and, outside of the multitude of other reasons, I'd be afraid to risk him in London. So I've corralled another Negro to do it over there . . . , a young fellow with considerable experience, wonderful presence and voice, full of ambition and a damn fine man personally with real brains." With Robeson, O'Neill felt certain he could avoid a repeat of the Gilpin problems, as Paul reportedly did not drink, had expediently recovered from his earlier abhorrence of racial epithets, and showed no evidence of the "smoldering rage" characteristic of Gilpin in his later years. The young and optimistic Robeson found Gilpin's virtual throwing away of all he had earned difficult, if not impossible, to comprehend (as veteran actor Leigh Whipper put it, "Gilpin was like the cow who made a bucket of milk and then kicked it over"). Only later, as an older man himself, would Paul begin to understand the fury that consumed and ultimately destroyed Charles Gilpin.[49]

As far as theater was concerned, Robeson could not have hoped for a better opportunity. O'Neill had earned a reputation as one of America's most brilliant innovative playwrights, with eight of his works, including *The Emperor Jones,* *Anna Christie,* and *The Hairy Ape,* already produced. Perhaps more important for Paul was O'Neill's crucial role in Harlem's artistic and literary renaissance. Whatever its failings, the 1921 production of *The Emperor Jones* caught the attention of New York's white theater world and almost overnight black themes and subject matter became not only acceptable theater fare but, better yet, avant-garde.

O'Neill was one of a score of white writers and disillusioned postwar white intellectuals, distressed with the superficiality of traditional American middle-class values, who found in black themes fresh and challenging subject matter. The playwright's work was controversial, eliciting responses ranging from soaring panegyrics (Brooks Atkinson's claim that modern American drama began with O'Neill) to bitter denunciations (that O'Neill had irrevocably debased American theater, according to Columbia University president George C. D. Odell).[50] Accepting the lead in an O'Neill play promised to put Paul's name in the limelight. Notoriety was perhaps not what Robeson had in mind, but he quickly won it nonetheless, and long before he ever walked out onto the stage.

All God's Chillun began as a one-act drama written by O'Neill at the request of theater critic George Jean Nathan. Notoriously flamboyant and contemptuous of the "stupidity of Broadway," Nathan wanted a biting, polemical piece to launch the premier issue of the *American Mercury,* the journal he and H. L. Mencken had created to succeed the *Smart Set.*[51] The *American Mercury* published *All God's Chillun* long before the play ever appeared on stage and, as Nathan had hoped, debate over its controversial subject matter (interracial love) ensued almost immediately. On January 31 the *New York Herald* announced that *All God's Chillun* would be produced with a black in the lead role, rather than a white man in blackface, and with that, what had been academic wrangling escalated into a fanatic crusade to prevent the play from ever being staged.

Charges and countercharges mounted as New York City's fifteen dailies gave the issue close coverage, mercilessly picking apart the content of the play, the personal integrity of its actors, and the moral fiber of its author. The news syndicate published photographs of lily-white Mary Blair, the play's female lead, and an avalanche of protests followed. The long-standing tradition barring the casting of a black man in a major role had indeed been broken with Charles Gilpin, but in a play that made no attempt to deal with issues of love and sexuality. O'Neill's insistence on portraying interracial love was bad enough, but to those opposing the play his decision to have a real black man fill the lead was absolutely intolerable.

The controversy brought together strange bedfellows as conservative blacks, anxious that only the "proper" image of the race appear on stage, suddenly found themselves aligned with die-hard segregationists. Theater devotees and women's church groups, civic leaders and housewives, laborers and intellectuals, all jumped into the fray. The specific demands of the various factions varied, but on one point they were all agreed: immediate action must be taken to prevent the play from being staged.

Sensing a story with real news potential, New York's *Morning Telegraph*, a "sheet dedicated chiefly to the edification of horseplayers," along with the equally notorious Hearst *American,* led the way in fanning the sensationalist flames. Openly biased, they published stories crammed with innuendo and distorted facts. On March 2 the *American* disclosed that theater patron Otto Kahn, as well as theater benefactor Mrs. Willard Straight (wife of the editor of the *New Republic*), had elected to withdraw support from the Provincetown Players. (In fact, while the controversy was at its most intense, both parties increased their aid to the Greenwich Village theater group. Kahn contributed an additional $1,000, and Mrs. Straight $2,500.) Stories claimed that the hand-kissing episode would be dropped and that Mary Blair would be replaced by an octoroon. "Men in leading roles will refuse to play with Mary Blair," warned the *American,* "on the grounds that 'lips that have touched lamp black will never touch mine.'" Not to be outdone, the *Telegraph* reported unusual interest in Harlem, where large numbers of Negroes "just itching for the opportunity of witnessing a white woman kissing a black man's hand and engaging in love scenes with him" were

Maria Louisa Bustill. (Paul Robeson
Collections, Moorland-Singarn Research
Center, Howard University, Courtesy
Paul Robeson Jr. Hereafter PR Jr.)

William Drew Robeson. (PR Jr.)

Somerville elementary school, 1910. Paul is in the second row, fourth from left.
(Paul Robeson Archive, Akademie der Künste der DDR, Berlin. Hereafter PR
Archive.)

Somerville High School football team, 1913.
Paul is in the second row, fourth from left. (PR Archive.)

Somerville High School baseball team.
Paul is in the first row, second from right. (PR Jr.)

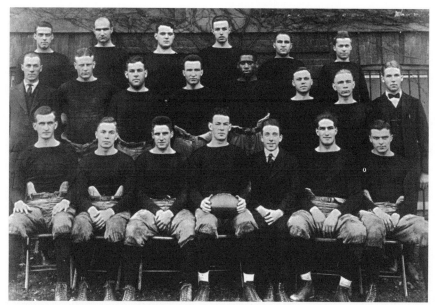

Rutgers football team, 1917. Paul is in the second row, fourth from right. (PR Jr.)

Robeson with Rutgers football team members, 1918.
Left to right: Neuschafer, Feitner, Robeson, and Breckley. (PR Jr.)

Robeson making a long run,
Rutgers vs. Naval Reserve,
Ebbets Field, 1917. (PR Jr.)

Robeson, Rutgers junior
year, 1918. (PR Jr.)

Robeson with five friends at
Narragansett, Rhode Island, 1918.
(Courtesy of Bertha Recklin.)

Robeson and two friends at
Narragansett, Rhode Island, 1918.
(Courtesy of Bertha Recklin.)

Robeson, with
Phi Beta Kappa key,
1919. (PR Jr.)

Robeson in *Plantation Revue,* 1922.
(PR Jr.)

Robeson in *Voodoo,* London,
1922. (PR Jr.)

Robeson with graduating class, Columbia Law School, 1923. (PR Jr.)

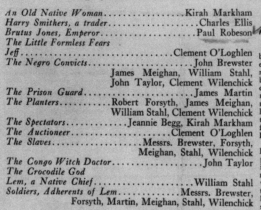

PROVINCETOWN PLAYBILL

A Leaflet Issued with Each New Production at the Provincetown Playhouse—Season 1923-24 No. 4

A Congo Mask

THE EMPEROR JONES

A Play in Eight Scenes

By Eugene O'Neill

Directed by James Light

Settings by Cleon Throckmorton

An Old Native Woman................Kirah Markham
Harry Smithers, a trader................Charles Ellis
Brutus Jones, Emperor................Paul Robeson
The Little Formless Fears
Jeff................Clement O'Loghlen
The Negro Convicts................John Brewster
    James Meighan, William Stahl,
    John Taylor, Clement Wilenchick
The Prison Guard................James Martin
The Planters................Robert Forsyth, James Meighan,
    William Stahl, Clement Wilenchick
The Spectators................Jeannie Begg, Kirah Markham
The Auctioneer................Clement O'Loghlen
The Slaves................Messrs. Brewster, Forsyth,
    Meighan, Stahl, Wilenchick
The Congo Witch Doctor................John Taylor
The Crocodile God
Lem, a Native Chief................William Stahl
Soldiers, Adherents of Lem................Messrs. Brewster,
    Forsyth, Martin, Meighan, Stahl, Wilenchick

The action of the play takes place in a West Indian Island not yet self-determined by white marines. The form of government is, for the moment, an empire.

Scene 1—Midafternoon. The Audience Chamber in the Palace of the Emperor

Scene 2—Nightfall. The end of the Plain where the Forest begins

Scene 3—Nine o'clock. In the Forest. The Moon has Risen

(Continued on page 6)

TRAGEDY

By John Masefield

TRAGEDY at its best is a vision of the heart of life. The heart of life can only be laid bare in the agony and exultation of dreadful acts. Commonplace people dislike tragedy, because they dare not suffer and cannot exult. The truth and rapture of man are holy things not lightly to be scorned. A carelessness of life and beauty marks the glutton, the idler, and the fool in their deathly path across history.

The poetic impulse of the Renaissance is now spent. The poetic drama, the fruit of that impulse, is now dead. Until a new poetic impulse gathers, playwrights trying for beauty must try to create new forms in which beauty and the high things of the soul may pass from the stage to the mind. Our playwrights have all the powers except that power of exultation which comes from a delighted brooding on excessive, terrible things.

That power is seldom granted to man; twice or thrice to a race perhaps, not oftener. But it seems to me certain that every effort, however humble, towards the achieving of that power helps the genius of a race to obtain it, though the obtaining may be fifty years after the strivers are dead.

Provincetown Playhouse Playbill, 1923–24, *The Emperor Jones*. (Courtesy of Patti Light, private collection.)

Lawrence Brown. (PR Archive.)

Robeson and Antonio Salemme in Salemme's studio, Greenwich Village, 1926.

Robeson as boxer in *Black Boy,* 1926. (PR Archive.)

Untitled nude.
Photo by Nicholas Muray.
(Courtesy of Patti Light,
private collection.)

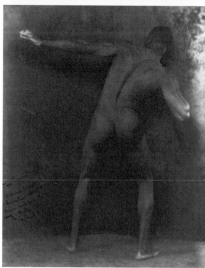

Untitled nude.
Photo by Nicholas Muray.
(Courtesy of Patti Light,
private collection.)

becoming subscribers. "It is certain that the Provincetown Theater will not be large enough to accommodate the negroes who will flock there."[52]

As the scheduled March production date grew closer, headlines predicting large-scale violence increased. "Race Strife Seen If 'All God's Chillun' Is Staged," warned the *American* on March 15. "'All God's Chillun' May Never Appear—Mixed Cast Protest and Possible Police Action a Factor," chimed in the *Herald* two days later. As if their dire auguries were not enough, both papers took pains to remind readers that this "unwholesome, revolting and disgusting" play had offended women's and church groups throughout the country and gave the protests of the Legislative League, the Century Theater Club, the Federation of Women's Clubs, and other such groups generous coverage.[53]

In March O'Neill issued a lengthy press release intended to clarify the content of the play and explain his purpose in writing it. Dismissing the critics as "sensation mongers and notoriety hounds," most of whom had "not read a line of the play," O'Neill insisted *Chillun* was not "a 'race problem' play. Its intention is confined to portraying the special lives of individual human beings. . . . To deduce any general application . . . is arbitrarily to read a meaning into the play which is not there." O'Neill defended the pairing of Robeson and Blair. "Right in this city two years ago, at a public theater, he [Robeson] played opposite a distinguished white actress, Margaret Wycherly, in a play called 'Voodoo.' In one of the scenes, he was cast as the king and she as the queen. A king and queen are, I believe, usually married. Mr. Robeson afterwards continued in the same role in England with Mrs. Patrick Campbell. There were no race riots here or there. There was no newspaper rioting either."[54]

But the controversy continued unabated with reaction extending far beyond New York City. The southern press predicted nothing less than citywide catastrophe should *All God's Chillun* be produced. The *Tampa Tribune* headlined the play as "Going Too Far," the *Greensboro Daily News* warned it was "Inviting a Lynching," and the *Birmingham Age-Herald* sputtered: "Ash Can Is the Place for O'Neill's Play."[55]

Many blacks were repulsed by the play, primarily because it fell so abysmally short of their standards, which required that only the race's best face appear on stage. The white press snatched news of black opposition as eagerly as it did black approval of the play; both made good copy. "O'Neill Disgusts New Jersey Negroes," announced the March 17 edition of the *Telegraph*. "No self-respecting Negro could have written it, and no such Negro can lend himself to stage it." According to a *New York American* story, headlined "Negro Clergy Bitter at Play," the Reverend Adam Clayton Powell, pastor of Harlem's Abyssinian Baptist Church and at that time the most influential black minister in the country, charged the play was "harmful, because it intimates that we are desirous of marrying white women." The *Telegraph* reported that Boston blacks, led by William H. Lewis, former assistant attorney general under President William Howard Taft, had mounted a campaign to ban the play in all the New England states. Like Robeson, Lewis was a lawyer and a collegiate football all-American, but unlike Robeson he had chosen to pursue a "respectable" profession, distinguishing himself as one of the nation's most outstanding black attorneys. The sentiments of Boston's blacks echoed those of conservative blacks throughout the country: selecting Lewis as their spokesman, they, by implication, rebuked Paul for his choice of theater over law.[56]

Robeson wondered at this point just what he had agreed to. Far from the acclaim accorded Gilpin, he had incurred sharp reproaches, and all this with the play yet to be staged. Although some black weeklies like the *Philadelphia Tribune* urged a more objective appraisal, even moderate black responses were far from approving.[57] On the other hand, if theater was what he really wanted, Robeson would have to accustom himself to misunderstanding from fellow blacks. "In those days," as veteran actor Leigh Whipper (who, like Robeson had a law degree and had practiced briefly before pursuing a theatrical career) matter-of-factly put it, "a good play was one that makes money. Even though we had a fine legitimate theater at the Lafayette, black theater still had the stigma of being low-brow, and maybe it was at places like the Lincoln. With occasional exceptions like *Shuffle Along,* we almost never made money. If Paul was ever to succeed, it would have to be 'in white time,' and never would he have a greater chance of doing so than he would working with Eugene O'Neill."[58]

Against the backdrop of the avalanche of criticism from black individuals and organizations, a few black leaders did champion the play. O'Neill's statement had barely made it to the press when NAACP secretary James Weldon Johnson issued an announcement defending O'Neill, the play, and Robeson's part in it; accusing certain New York newspapers and city officials of "trying to foment a race riot out of the affair"; and pointedly reminding readers that, "when colored citizens protested against the *Birth of a Nation,* these same officials stated they had no authority to interfere [and] simply arrested the colored protestants."[59] *Crisis* editor W. E. B. Du Bois likewise praised O'Neill, in particular his effort to break through the shell of "what most people think the Negro ought to be" and challenge the black community's imperative that only a "perfect and proper and beautiful and joyful" picture of the race be presented on stage.[60]

Robeson made no public response whatever. "Paul was pretty quiet initially, maybe just trying to digest what was really going on," remembered Province-town actor Walter Abel, at the time playing in *Spook Sonata.* "But even when he was talkative, he seldom said anything about racial issues. What I remember him talking about most was how frightened he was about performing. He was terrified he wouldn't be able to do it, so he just stayed out of the fray. He had all he could manage, I can assure you, just trying to learn to act."[61]

Scheduled to open as the Provincetown Players' third program in March, the long-awaited performance had to be postponed when an overwrought Mary Blair contracted pleurisy. The delay was a severe blow to the cast and all those connected with the production. The weeks of waiting had been difficult enough; a postponement of another month and a half was almost too much to bear. In the interim not only O'Neill but Robeson and Mary Blair received threatening letters. Jimmy Light, the play's director, recalled that "a great many" of these letters "were obscene or violent or both" and that he held them to prevent Mary and Paul from seeing them. "I remember one in particular to Mary—really filthy—pathological. And Gene had a letter from the KKK in Georgia, on their official stationery, signed by the Grand Kleagle, which began reasonably enough and then got increasingly worse. 'You have a son,' it said. 'If your play goes on, don't expect to see him again.' You know what tiny handwriting Gene had—well, he returned the letter after writing at the bottom in a large hand: 'Go fuck yourself!'" Another letter from the Klan in Long Island was unsigned. It said, "If you open this play, the theater will be bombed, and you will be responsible for all the people killed."[62] Threats from the Klan, which had never been more powerful, were not to be taken lightly. (Delegates at the 1924 Democratic National Convention failed to muster sufficient votes to condemn the Klan openly.) Robeson knew about these letters and even read some of them but did not appear to be bothered by them. "I don't remember Paul saying anything about the letters, even the ones from the Klan," Walter Abel said. Robeson may well have said nothing, but he never forgot this brush with Klan justice. He referred to it throughout his performing career and took pains to avoid a repeat of his experience by turning down all southern engagements.[63]

In the interim Robeson accepted the lead role in the revival of *Roseanne,* a play, like *Taboo,* written by a white woman (Nan Bagby Stephen). Originally staged in December 1923 with a white cast in burnt cork, the play failed. The Lafayette Players' revival featured an entirely black cast; Charles Gilpin initially played the lead role but was replaced by Robeson.[64]

The play promised Robeson not only relief from the interminable *Chillun* controversy but also some badly needed stage experience. A comedy-drama set in the South, *Roseanne* tells the story of a wayward preacher, Cicero Brown, played by Robeson, and of his avenging congregation, in particular the earthy and religious Roseanne, played by Rose McClendon (who would later distinguish herself but never achieve the fame she might have, had opportunities to act been more available to her).[65]

Robeson's name was to be *Roseanne's* chief drawing card, and he was given top billing in a play advertised in the black weeklies as featuring an "all-star" black cast of twenty-five. But even with a good script, fine actors, and considerable preproduction buildup, *Roseanne's* engagements at the Lafayette in April and later in May at the Dunbar Theatre in Philadelphia drew small and nearly all-black audiences. Its poor showing confirmed what actor Leigh Whipper and black theater critics Theophilus Lewis, Joel Rogers, and Lester Walton had been saying for years: whites would not attend, and blacks generally did not support the projects of black theater groups. Theater columns in the *New York Age,* the *Amsterdam News,* and the *Messenger* were replete with news of black theater groups. Whether long-standing enterprises like the Lafayette Players or more short-lived groups like the Lincoln Players, the Alhambra Players, or the National Ethiopian Art Theater, these groups labored under perennial financial distress and the frustrating and impossible dilemma of trying to cater to both white and black audiences, what James Weldon Johnson called "the double audience . . . with [the] different and often opposite points of view [of] white and black America."[66]

Charles Gilpin in a conversation with Lucien White recounted an incident that illustrates well this dilemma. Gilpin had given a special production of *The Emperor Jones* under the auspices of the Howard Players in Washington, D.C., for a black audience. Things seemingly went well (the audience's silence perhaps persuading Gilpin they were with him) until the climax of the play, "an intense moment when the poor creature's heart is wrung with fear, his body writhing in pain and his soul lost in despair." At that moment "the Washington audience laughed." Black critic Loften Mitchell tells a similar story (attributed to Langston Hughes) involving actor and baritone Jules Bledsoe playing Brutus Jones in a Harlem revival staged at the Lincoln Theater. At the play's climax the hallucinating Jones runs through the forest. Negroes from the audience shouted, "Man, you come on outa that jungle! This is Harlem!"[67] With Eugene O'Neill plays, in particular *The Emperor Jones,* the complexities of various audiences' tastes, expectations, and sensitivities came into sharp focus. Certainly *The Emperor Jones* was "art" and represented for the black actor a historic first in American theatrical history: the opportunity to play a serious dramatic lead role on the legitimate stage. At the same time, for black audiences looking to the play for some statement about the race (hard not to do, given the play's constant allusions to Africa) it must have appeared as a silly piece indeed, having very little to do with the lives of real African Americans.

While Robeson busied himself with *Roseanne,* the Provincetowners, looking for something to fill the gap left by the postponement of *All God's Chillun,* decided on an April revival of *The Emperor Jones* and asked Robeson to play the lead. From the theater group's perspective the move was a wise one, in that it shifted attention away from *Chillun* and focused instead on Robeson's acting.[68] For Paul, however, the prospect of playing Brutus Jones, with so little time to learn the part and rehearse, was terrifying. Still, he accepted the role. How could he refuse such an opportunity? Lester Walton, drama critic for the *New York Age,* recalled talking with Paul about the upcoming production. Robeson, he said, was nearly paralyzed with fear, and although Walton did his best to build his confidence, Paul remained unable to shake the feeling that he could not handle the role.[69] When one considers Robeson's limited acting experience, his panic becomes understandable. Here he was, beginning his acting career at the top, undertaking a complex and taxing role that demanded not only refined acting ability but also sufficient emotional intensity to carry an audience through a sustained hour and a half of monologue. Gilpin's performance had been almost flawless; how could Robeson, so inexperienced, hope to compete?

Fortunately, Paul was not left to flounder. James Light, the production's talented, intelligent young director, came to his rescue. To Robeson's relief, Light did not believe that blacks, as the *American Mercury*'s George Jean Nathan put it, were "born actors . . . better fitted naturally for the profession . . . than [their] white brother[s]," imbued with an almost magical ability to walk out on a stage and perform. Light took Paul's fears seriously, acknowledged his inexperience, and understood he would need careful guidance and preparation. More than any of the directors Paul would work with in his career, Light succeeded in this and later performances in eliciting from Robeson his best.[70]

Paul later recalled his initial attempts with the role as "rather hopeless." Nevertheless, under Light's "most curious and oblique" tutelage, he improved vastly. Essie, who helped Paul memorize the lines and took notes at all rehearsals, remembered: "When Paul had trouble with a speech, Jimmy would sit down on a soap-box beside him on the empty stage, and they would analyze the speech thought by thought, word by word."[71]

Whenever Paul began to stiffen up on stage, "Jimmy would call out, 'Let yourself go, Paul. Don't hold yourself in; you look as though you're afraid to move.' 'I am,' Paul would answer; 'I'm so big I feel as if I take a few steps I'll be off this tiny stage.'" Light taught Paul how to relax and control his anxiety by fixing his concentration on the emotions of the character he portrayed. "I had to give him confidence in his ability to act," Light told Marie Seton. "The problem was to build up concentration in the character and Paul's emotions so that the physical tensions built up by his fear of the stage would melt away under the emotional experience he was to evoke. No amount of pure routine could accomplish this end."[72]

On opening night at the tiny, run-down MacDougal Street theater the mood was tense and expectant. The familiar deep orange walls and indigo ceiling of the theater evoked memories of Gilpin when he first swaggered across the stage, brandishing the now legendary pearl-handled revolver. The curtain opened to a familiar scene: Charles Ellis playing Smithers, the cockney trader, the role he had made memorable when the play first opened in 1920. A huge black man dressed in the Emperor's red and blue uniform and patent leather boots, in size a striking contrast to the short and stocky Gilpin, emerged from an inner room, adjusted his gold epaulets, and slumped into his throne. "Who dare whistle in my palace? Who dare whistle dat way in my palace?" Robeson began in a booming voice. The audience sat tensely, with little show of reaction through the two opening scenes as the physically massive Robeson, the island's self-declared Emperor, swaggered, ordered Smithers to "Light me," and boasted: "Dere's little stealin' like you does, and dere's big stealin' like I does. For de little stealin' dey gits you in jail soon or late. For big stealin' dey makes you Emperor and puts you in de Hall o' Fame when you croaks." By the third scene the audience began to warm up. In the six scenes that follow, the ominous beat of the tom-tom pursues Jones / Robeson, and he loses his battle with the natives, the jungle, and himself. After entering the jungle confident that, with his escape route already mapped out, he could once again outwit the natives, the Emperor becomes increasingly more entangled and lost in the jungle of his own imaginings. Haunted by frightful images of his criminal past, he fires in panic at ghostly encounters from that past until, finally, he is reduced to the primitive state of his Congo forebears.

The audience "whistled, stamped its feet and canes, and yelled 'Bravo!' and called for Robeson, who returned to the stage in an old bathrobe, tired, bathed in sweat, but relieved and happy, for a total of four curtain calls." But despite this thunderous show of approval, Robeson stayed up all night, unable to sleep until he read the verdict in the next day's theater columns (such bouts of insomnia would plague him for much of his professional career). The critics did not disappoint him. Almost all were struck by his "dominating appearance" and "towering bulk."[73] Although many thought he lacked the "mellowness" and the "subtlety" of Gilpin, most felt his performance added a new dimension to the role, "a more primitive strength . . . a greater tumult of immemorial fears." The *New York Telegram and Evening Mail* called him "as fine an actor as there is on the American stage," and the *New York Herald Tribune*'s Frank Vreeland ventured that "physically this full-blooded Negro fitted the role better than Gilpin."[74]

The "presence" that so struck critics encompassed more than just an admirable physique. Robeson conveyed tremendous power on stage — in his physical build, the way he handled his body, his beautifully resonant voice, and his impeccable diction. Even in these, Paul's earliest theatrical roles, reviewers and audiences record experiencing this power. They also hint at an equally intense and perhaps disquieting sense of that power restrained (an experience that would continue to move Robeson audiences profoundly). For many, the theater felt too small to contain what was happening within its walls. "I can't explain or put into words the power of that huge voice in such a tiny theater." "One felt that if he turned loose his full vocal powers the walls of the tiny Provincetown would fairly bulge." "He fired his revolver at the ghosts with such tremendous conviction that he seemed likely to blow out the sides of the tiny playhouse."[75]

In spite of his own meager acting experience, the difficult role, and the history-making precedent set by Gilpin, Robeson had done it. In this one-man show he had held his audience on the edge of their seats for the entire performance. He had succeeded, and his name was in the limelight. Paul was elated, but Charles Gilpin, who had traveled from his farm in Trenton, New Jersey, to watch the opening, left the theater that night bitter and disappointed, realizing full well Robeson's achievement. Later James J. ("Slim") Martin, one of the Provincetown Players, caught up with Gilpin and, sensing his mood, invited him for a drink. "No, Slim," answered Gilpin, "I feel kind of low. I created the role of the Emperor. That role belongs to me. That Irishman, he just wrote the play." To some extent Gilpin was correct. Reviews were replete with comparisons of the two performers; it was, as the *Pittsburgh Courier* noted, "next to impossible to mention or even think about this play without speaking or thinking about Gilpin." But, although even O'Neill would later admit he thought Gilpin performed the role better than Paul, once Robeson had played the part, it was his.[76] Within a short time Gilpin's masterful rendition would be forgotten by all but serious theater historians. As he would do years later in *Othello*, Robeson so identified himself with the role, so convinced audiences he was Jones, that to this day mention of *The Emperor Jones* immediately conjures an image of Paul Robeson.

The rush and excitement of *The Emperor Jones* production left Paul little time to worry about the outcome of *Chillun*. But, as the scheduled opening date grew closer, the opposition redoubled its efforts and demanded official action, while municipal officials insisted they were powerless to act.[77] In a last-ditch effort to prevent production, the *American* editorially charged Mayor John F. Hylan with ultimate responsibility for imminent race riots. Only hours before opening night, the mayor's office uncovered a technicality it hoped would halt the production: a local ordinance that required all theaters, even unlicensed ones, to obtain permission to use child actors. The opening scene of *All God's Chillun* called for the use of several children, and two days before the play opened the Provincetowners applied for the required authorization. On the afternoon of May 15 Mayor Hylan's chief clerk denied the theater approval. No explanation was given. This unexpected development left the Provincetowners, already keyed up and nervous, temporarily stunned. In the flurry of panicked suggestions that ensued, someone suggested that midgets be used to replace the child actors.[78] Mercifully, reason prevailed, and the group decided to have Jimmy Light explain the situation to the audience and, with its permission, read the opening scene.

The presence of uniformed police conspicuously stationed outside the theater confirmed this would be far from a routine opening night. "There will be some kind of mobbing or terrors," wrote theater patron Hart Crane to friends, "and I expect to be there with my cane for cudgeling the unruly!" Critics had second thoughts about attending, and Heywood Broun in a later review admitted he carried a revolver for protection. Anticipation mixed with apprehension. Everyone — actors, audience members, and police — was tense.[79]

Rather than rely on the "impartiality" of the police, the theater group had taken its own precautions. Slim Martin, who had a small part in the play, corralled seven of his friends — huge, six-foot, unemployed steelworkers — for "police" duty, stationing them at strategic spots, one in each dressing room, two at each end of MacDougal Street, and one across the street in Sam Schwartz's place. The situation was not without humorous aspects, as Slim Martin noted, recalling one steelworker's reaction to "protecting" Robeson. Known locally for his willingness to "box anybody on earth for a twenty-five dollar purse," he looked at Paul and then turned to Martin and asked incredulously, "Is that the big ape I'm supposed to guard? Well listen, if anything starts, you and me just get out of his way and pile up the ones he knocks down."[80]

Robeson was extremely anxious as well; not about the threat of violence but at the thought that he might not be able to handle the role. "Even though he had done so well with *The Emperor Jones,* Paul was still not at all sure he would succeed in this new role," said Patti Light, wife of the director. "He was so frightened and there was nothing you could say to reassure him. Only getting through it and good reviews would do that for him."[81]

The audience — reviewers, theater subscribers, and, according to Burns Mantle, some "hand-picked and slightly colored patrons" — was seated without incident and waited nervously for the play to start. (As had been the case with *The Emperor Jones,* the audience for *All God's Chillun* was integrated, a fact worth remarking on because even *Roseanne,* with its nearly all-black cast, had segregated seating.) Finally, Jimmy Light stepped onto the stage and announced that the opening scene requiring children would not be performed. The curtain lifted with the audience left to imagine from Light's reading the interchange among innocent youngsters that sets the stage for the scenes that follow.

Robeson played Jim Harris, a weak man unable to free himself from either his own sense of inferiority or his demented wife's taunts and racial gibes, with all the pathos the role required. He grovels before Ella, begging her to marry him so that he can be her slave; he makes excuses for her childishness and blatant bigotry, and ultimately he lets her destroy him rather than admit she does not and cannot love him. The supporting black cast—Frank Wilson as Jim's friend Joe, Lillian Greene as Jim's mother, and Dora Cole as Jim's sister Hattie—gave superb performances and would earn exceptionally fine reviews. But, after months of preproduction buildup, what happened at the theater that night was the one thing that no one anticipated: the play went smoothly, without incident, from beginning to end. Far from the large-scale riots predicted in the press, *All God's Chillun*'s opening was distressingly peaceful, a letdown in fact. "Nothing at all happened, not even a senile egg," O'Neill later complained to a friend.[82]

Critics agreed the play was not O'Neill's best. Most white reviewers found it "tiresome." Heywood Broun judged it one of O'Neill's "downstrokes, . . . a strained, wanton and largely unbelievable tragedy." Burns Mantle said it was "an interesting exhibit," and Percy Hammond called it an "overdone and breath-less . . . vehement exposition of a marriage between a stupid Negro and a stupid white woman."[83]

Black critics complained that O'Neill "held back a part of Jim Harris' story, or else he did not know it at all," and that it seemed inconceivable that a man of Jim's stature and potential would throw away his life and career for an Ella Downey, a white girl "about as lost as he [O'Neill] could make her," a girl not only outside of Jim's race but "outside of his class" as well. Many resented having to watch "a big, respectable and cultured character [become] the slave of a slim, depraved and silly white woman."[84]

All God's Chillun did fail to deliver its promised lurid tale of interracial love and miscegenation. However, as veteran actor Leigh Whipper said, "It meant work, not only for Robeson but for Dora Cole, Frank Wilson, and Lillian Greene. You can't imagine how important a role like that in even a bad play was to black actors of the period."[85] In addition, the work is hardly devoid of racial content. Despite what O'Neill insisted was his intent, *All God's Chillun* is more than a psychological study of the "special lives of individual human beings" and their troubled marriage. From beginning to end the couple's mutual mental disturbance (Ella Downey's need to abuse and feel superior; Jim Harris's need to be abused and humiliated) finds in America's twisted race relations an apt vehicle through which to play out its inevitable downward spiral. As children, the blonde, fair-skinned Ella and her black friend Jim breathe air thick with the stench of racial epithets. By the age of eight, Jim daily drinks a mixture of chalk and water, hoping that in time it will turn him white. As a young adult, Ella, having long ago forgotten her childhood friendship with Jim, joins local white thugs as they taunt him for graduating from high school, "gettin' stuck up," and "trying to buy white." Jim's black friend Joe warns him to stop "denyin' you's a nigger" and forget about law school. Five years later, alone and abandoned by her white friends, Ella seeks Jim's help. Jim and Ella marry and move abroad, and Jim promises "to serve you [Ella] — to lie at your feet like a dog that loves you . . . to become your slave!"

Two years later, the couple returns home and visits Jim's mother and his strong-minded, outspoken sister Hattie. Hattie is everything that Ella is not — intelligent, educated, strong, and ambitious. By this time it is clear that Ella is not in her right mind. Hattie almost immediately realizes that the combined effect of Ella's illness and racial hatred will eventually destroy her brother, and she urges him to leave her, at least until he passes the bar exam. Later, Hattie tells Jim that Ella called her a "dirty nigger" and warns that soon she'll do the same to him. Jim refuses to believe it and frantically tries to explain himself to his sister: "I'm all she's got in the world. I've got to prove I can be all to her! I've got to prove worthy! . . . I've got to prove I'm the whitest of the white!" With this, Hattie tells Jim he is a "weak-minded fool" and "a traitor to his race" and leaves.

Six months later, Hattie's worst fears are realized. Jim is unable either to sleep or to study, as Ella walks the house day and night talking to herself, carrying knives, and threatening to kill him. In a long monologue directed at the Congo mask that lies on a stand in the room where Jim studies, Ella reveals the full depth of her racial hatred. "How dare you grin at me? I guess you forget what you are! That's always the way. Be kind to you, treat you decent, and in a second you've got a swelled head, you think you're somebody . . . why, it's got so I can't even walk down the street without seeing niggers, niggers everywhere. Hanging around, grinning, grinning — going to school — pretending they're white — taking examinations."

Jim again fails the bar exam. Though he hates himself for even having tried, his wife is relieved and happy. "Pass? Me? Jim Crow Harris? Nigger Jim Harris — become a full-fledged Member of the Bar! Why the mere notion of it is enough to kill you with laughing," Jim tells her. Dancing up and down with childish happiness, Ella exclaims, "Oh, Jim! I knew it! I knew you couldn't! Oh, I'm so glad, Jim! I'm so happy! You're still my old Jim — and I'm so glad!" Ella admits that she purposely tried to scare Jim and prevent him from sleeping or studying and even prayed that he would fail the exam. The play ends with Ella pretending they're both children again and Jim asking God to make him "worthy of the child You send me for the woman You take away."

James Weldon Johnson may have been right when he attributed the play's lack of verve to a failure of nerve on O'Neill's part: "It may be that as the play began to grow, Mr. O'Neill became afraid of it . . . side-stepped the logical question and let the heroine go crazy; thus shifting the question from that of a coloured man living with a white wife to that of a man living with a crazy woman."[86] Perhaps. But O'Neill did not sidestep or gloss over American racism — the matter-of-fact separation of the lives of blacks and whites. Racism — pernicious and accepted — blights the lives of the play's characters, both black and white. Racism was not a subject that Renaissance stars and their white friends wanted to talk about. Possibly because it was not as outrageous a theme as miscegenation or, perhaps, because it cut much closer to the bone (New York restaurants, theaters, and clubs were still, for the most part, segregated; even the "enlightened" Greenwich Village did not rent to blacks), neither white nor black critics made much of O'Neill's relentless exposition of that American institution.

One might well ask: Where was Robeson in all of this? How did he feel about playing the role of Brutus Jones or Jim Harris, a young man who, as he himself would soon do, gives up a career in law? In truth, it is difficult to find evidence of Robeson's personal thoughts and reactions about either the role or the controversy surrounding the staging of *All God's Chillun*. One has the sense that, as he did during his college years, Robeson focused completely on the task at hand, in this case succeeding in two difficult stage roles. Certainly, he had only to think of Gilpin's intense but short-lived fame to understand the precariousness of his position. He might never again have the opportunity to act in a first-rate play. Paul along with Harlem's other "New Negroes" found himself in a very different position than that of "lost generation" white writers and artists. Black artists were not "lost" but suddenly "found" and with no idea how long their good fortune would last. Always, they were skating on the edge, in danger at any moment of falling back. Thus, indulging in the blazoning of truths — even privately — was a luxury most of them felt they could not afford. Taking advantage of the vogue meant, of necessity, donning the mask. Concerning the Harlem scene, black pianist Sammy Price said, "It's too jumbled . . . and fragmented. Nobody ever told it straight — even as it was happening, we was inventing it. And don't think that was not accident neither." Langston Hughes similarly recorded the masquerading required for continued white patronage: "The Negroes said: 'We can't go downtown and sit and stare at you in your clubs. You won't even let us in your clubs.' But they didn't say it out loud — for Negroes are practically never rude to white people."[87]

All God's Chillun played in repertory with *The Emperor Jones* through the beginning of June and then for an additional month, until July 5.[88] After a brief respite, it reopened on August 18 at the Greenwich Village Theater where it played for another two months and then periodically throughout the fall of 1924. In December Robeson did a radio broadcast of a scene from the play and sang some spirituals as well.[89] Box-office sales were boosted by publicity highlighting the play's controversial history and the continuing efforts of newspapers like the *Herald* to milk whatever sensationalist appeal remained of the whole affair. It had, after all, as Provincetowner Kenneth Macgowan observed, "received more publicity before production than any play in the history of American theater, possibly the world," and the contention it provoked proved to be its chief, possibly only, drawing card.[90]

Robeson's few months with the Provincetowners changed his life. Far from the seamy stereotype of theater people he had grown up with, the group Paul had discovered consisted of serious and knowledgeable professionals, almost fanatically dedicated to their craft and their commitment to revitalize the American imagination by offering an alternative to the commercial stage manager's interpretation of public taste. In these early years the theater group did not have an easy time of it: even with the gifted and prolific Eugene O'Neill, productions were always a gamble, each punctuated by almost perpetual financial distress.[91]

Working closely with the brilliant and sensitive Jimmy Light, Paul saw first hand the group's literate and artistic underpinnings. Light and the other Provincetowners looked upon him as an equal and treated him as such. In this setting Robeson let down his guard. Never before had he been so intellectually stimulated, inspired, and emotionally involved. During rehearsal breaks the theater talk continued, often in the more relaxed atmosphere of Romany Marie's, a small restaurant/coffeehouse upstairs from the playhouse run by a cheery Russian Jew, Marie Marchand. As he listened, Paul found himself intrigued by the group and its avant-garde ideas. Essie later credited the Provincetowners as being most responsible for Paul's decision to abandon law. He quickly "fell under their spell," she wrote, "and through them has remained under the spell of theater ever since."[92] Working with the group of talented and seasoned professionals, Robeson found a setting in which his artistic temperament thrived. Law could offer nothing comparable.

Throughout the long months preceding the O'Neill productions, Robeson responded to neither white nor black criticism of the plays. In the case of *All God's Chillun* Paul followed the lead of the rest of the cast and maintained a low profile as the best defense. *The Emperor Jones* presented a different problem. Protest about this play had come almost exclusively from blacks, who were shocked by its language and puzzled as to why Robeson agreed to perform in it.

By the summer, after he had proven himself and the dust had settled, Robeson was ready to speak and began to do so in press interviews, at public events, and in writing. His response was studied, clear, and definite. To those who accused him of forsaking a respectable law career for the slick theater life, he defended O'Neill, cogently pointing out the artistic merit of his work. And to those who bemoaned his loss to the race, Paul answered that, far from abandoning racial obligations, he had chosen a more effective means to fulfill them. Theater, he argued, would afford him much more opportunity than law to make something of himself and advance the status of the race.

Most audiences listened patiently, but occasionally his remarks sparked an angry response. In June Robeson broached the topic at a reception hosted by the 135th Street branch of the New York Public Library. The event began innocuously enough as Robeson recounted a recent conversation with a former Rutgers classmate who objected to his choosing theater over law, warning him that such a choice would ruin his prospects for success at anything else. Robeson repeated for his audience the explanation he had given this college acquaintance, namely, that race loyalty moved him to choose theater over law. In the discussion that ensued, however, it became clear that Harlem's black community would accept no glib explanations from Paul. George Schuyler, the radical *Messenger*'s "black Mencken," started the ball rolling, ridiculing those who had predicted a *Chillun* catastrophe. He singled out audience member Cleveland G. Allen for his most pointed barbs. Not surprisingly, Allen took offense, reaffirmed his objections to the play, and then launched into a personal attack on Robeson. Robeson rebutted, using almost word for word O'Neill's own defense of the play when he argued that the "play was a reaction of one Negro to his environment and in no way could be construed as representing the entire race." Several members of the audience rallied to defend Paul, but the discussion ended in a shouting match, with both sides more firmly entrenched than ever in their respective positions.[93]

In a July interview Robeson again defended himself, this time for a mixed audience of black and white *New York Herald Tribune* readers. "I don't in the least minimize what I am up against as a negro. And yet, as an actor, I think I have less to buck against than as a lawyer," he told his interviewer. "I may be a bit optimistic, but I think if I'm a good enough actor . . . I can go pretty far. . . . If I do become a first-rate actor, it will do more toward giving people a slant on the so-called negro problem than any amount of propaganda and argument."[94]

Finally, in December, Robeson made one last effort, this time in a full-length article published in *Opportunity* magazine, Charles S. Johnson's Urban League showcase for Harlem's literary and artistic talent. Robeson praised O'Neill without reserve ("To have had the opportunity to appear in two of the finest plays of America's most distinguished playwright is good fortune that to me hardly seems credible") and stated unequivocally his view that *The Emperor Jones* was "one of the great plays, a true classic of drama, American or otherwise . . . a play of great strength and beautiful spirit," chronicling nothing less than "the exultant tragedy of the disintegration of the human soul." To those who resented O'Neill's failure to create a "truly heroic role, one portraying the finest type of

Negro," Paul responded, "I honestly believe that never will I portray a nobler type than Jim Harris or a more heroically tragic figure than Brutus Jones, excepting Othello."[95]

Paul's experiences with the Provincetowners had given him his first real taste of success since college, and he liked it. But it hadn't earned him much money ($1,782.15 for 1924), and when *All God's Chillun* closed at the Greenwich Village Theater in the fall Robeson's "theater career" (with the exception of a brief *Emperor Jones* revival in January) ground to a halt. Robeson wanted to act. As he said years later, "I could never be a Supreme Court judge [but] on stage there was only the sky to hold me back."[96] At the same time, he understood he could not build a career waiting for more O'Neill roles. "I realized even then," Paul said, "that the number of roles I might ever be able to act were so few, and so far between, that I might starve to death no matter what the critics said about me!"[97]

Before the year was over, however, another acting opportunity did come Robeson's way. The aggressive and energetic Oscar Micheaux, soon to become the most successful and prolific black movie producer of the period, asked Robeson to star in his new film, *Body and Soul,* offering him a salary of $100 per week for three weeks and 3 percent of the gross after the first $40,000 in receipts. Robeson accepted.[98]

Robeson's own unsteady professional and financial status was probably enough to convince him to take the part; if not, Micheaux's persuasive charm filled in the gap. Micheaux, born on a farm near Metropolis, Illinois, in 1885, the fifth child of former slaves, worked first as a Pullman porter and then as a homesteader in South Dakota before beginning his career as a novelist. Micheaux formed his own company to publish his writing and pursued an aggressive promotion campaign to sell his books, traveling to all parts of the country lecturing and promoting his work. This hefty six-footer, in later years given to wearing long Russian coats and wide-brimmed hats, applied the same chutzpah and brassy charm to the making and promotion of his films, often personally carrying the stills of a recently completed film (or what he advertised as a completed film) to managers throughout the country, especially in the black belt. He was a convincing talker, skilled entrepreneur, astute businessman, and supreme promoter with a knack of turning everything to his advantage.

Micheaux began his film career in 1918 on the heels of D. W. Griffith's fifteen-reel, three-hour polemic for white supremacy, *The Birth of a Nation* (1915). Set against this backdrop Micheaux, along with a handful of other filmmakers, answered Griffith's racial monstrosity by presenting a truthful picture of blacks. Micheaux did not fall into the trap of attempting to show only the race's best face; instead, he tried to provide for his black audiences truths about themselves on film. Although he often worked with stock Hollywood plots, substituting black stars for Hollywood's white film idols (Lorenzo Tucker as the "black Valentino," Bee Freeman as the "sepia Mae West," and Slick Chester as the "colored Cagney"), his films focused on the concerns and experiences of the black bourgeoisie and dealt with the often controversial and taboo themes he felt were of interest to this group: color caste, professionalism, passing, the tragic mulatto, self-improvement, interracial romance, and social problems among blacks.

Throughout his career, Micheaux labored under perpetual financial crises. Movies were generally completed within six weeks, with a minimum crew and a cameraman hired one day at a time. Filming on location, in actual homes or offices, was standard procedure. The result was at times brilliant, at other times amateurish. While Micheaux produced his films unhampered by the sense of whites eavesdropping (it was his aim "to view the colored heart from close up"), many of his (black) critics (whites seldom reviewed his films) never lost their sense of this omnipresent other audience. Initially, Micheaux won high praise from black critics, but in time they took him to task for depicting the seamy side of black life. Conservatives criticized him for not creating an "elevating" story of "high moral aim" (a response to Micheaux's 1920 *Brute,* which featured Sam Langford in combat against a southern lynch mob), while intellectual urban blacks frankly admitted being embarrassed by his technical ineptitude.[99] Nonetheless, while other black producers fell by the wayside, between 1918 and 1940, Oscar Micheaux produced and distributed nationally and in Europe more than thirty black-cast films.

In the silent film *Body and Soul* Robeson starred opposite Theresa Russell and played the dual role of a depraved convict posing as a preacher (Isaiah T. Jenkins) and his good, look-alike brother Sylvester.[100] *Body and Soul* offers a rare opportunity to see the twenty-six-year-old Robeson in a film portraying such a virile and blatantly sexual character. Future, white-produced films will gradually exorcise any sense of Robeson as dangerous, powerful (Brutus Jones in the end proves more a buffoon than a danger), or sensually virile. In *Body and Soul* he is all of these and more. The film likewise suggests the extent to which future film roles left huge portions of Robeson's acting potential untapped.

As Isaiah, Robeson portrays a thoroughly corrupt human being who uses the power of the pulpit and the naive trust of his congregation to get free access to liquor and, in time, to Isabelle (Theresa Russell), the daughter of Martha Jane, one of his most devout parishioners. The film is typically melodramatic in that it pits opposites — evil and good, body and soul, dreams and reality, sensuality and respectability — against each other, with "good," in the persons of Isabelle, Martha Jane, and Sylvester, triumphing in the end.

In terms of plot, Isaiah is clearly evil and not to be admired. At the same time, however, his power and sensuality are presented in a way that is at least intriguing if not attractive. The good brother, Sylvester, appears infrequently and is a less well-developed, less interesting character than the sinister Isaiah. Robeson as Isaiah "fairly oozed . . . strength and sexuality." In addition, as critic Richard Dyer notes, the film encourages viewers to feel that sex appeal.[101] In the rape scene, for example, Isaiah and Isabelle find shelter from a raging storm in an abandoned shack. Isaiah leaves the room and instructs Isabelle to take off her clothes so they can dry while she is sleeping. A series of cross-cuts shows Isabelle's bare head and shoulders and Isaiah's huge, long black shoes inching forward to the door of her room. The scene combines the eroticism of Isabelle's undressing with the tension of Isaiah's steady movement toward her. The final shot, before the camera discreetly fades, is not of a cowering Isabelle but of Isaiah — menacing, powerful, and in control — smiling at her.

Although future film critics would hail *Body and Soul* as a breakthrough in that it "wrestled with the complex nature of the black community," Robeson, like many of his contemporaries, apparently saw little artistic or intellectual merit in it. Micheaux's films never became a part of the cultural explosion of the Harlem Renaissance. As a critic from the *Amsterdam News* put it, "White theater managers in Harlem have from time to time played Oscar Micheaux pictures more from the mistaken idea of a sentiment which they feel they should exhibit in a colored community than because of the worth of the pictures. With an opportunity of viewing the best things along picture lines, it is hard to expect colored people to accept these Micheaux pictures here in Greater New York or Northern New Jersey, and they don't."[102]

Though Robeson was not above earning money by working with Micheaux, his part in the film clearly embarrassed him, and for years he kept his brief association with Micheaux a closely guarded secret.[103] Robeson might well have been able to deal with the criticism of "respectable" blacks (who objected to the film's airing of dirty laundry, i.e., portraying the stereotypical "jackleg" preacher exploiting the deep religiosity of poor blacks) had Micheaux earned the intellectual regard of a Eugene O'Neill. He had not. Worse yet, the film's distribution was limited to black theaters (*Body and Soul* opened in Harlem and made the rounds of segregated Negro theaters but was never seen by most white theatergoers), which both doomed its financial success and branded it second-rate.

6

Concert Stage

1924-1925

"My impression . . . was, what we in show business call a 'heat wave,'" said musician Eubie Blake of Harlem in the mid-twenties. "The white people were coming up to Harlem to hear this music. And . . . we would go downtown and play for millionaires." Some, like Paul's friend Bud Fisher, found the sudden onslaught unnerving. "The best of Harlem's black cabarets have changed their names and turned white," Fisher complained in 1925. He particularly lamented the loss of the Oriental, a Chinese restaurant on 136th Street (formerly Hayne's Café) where whites never came "except as guests of Negroes" and where he, Robeson, Fritz Pollard, Henry Creamer, Turner Layton, and a half dozen others regularly gathered in 1919 and 1920. At a little table just inside the door the great comedian Bert Williams ate his supper every night and sometimes joined the group singing songs and lampooning the Actors Equity Association, which years before had barred the comic genius because of his color.[1]

For black musicians, artists, and writers the "Negro vogue," as Langston Hughes called the white fascination with blacks, meant Broadway hits, publications, and skyrocketing club attendance: success on a breathtaking scale.[2] Harlem intellectuals had serious doubts about the staying power of a nascence so dependent on the whims of white audiences and financial backers. Almost all the black revues that followed *Shuffle Along*, for example, were produced by whites, shown in white-owned theaters, or financed by whites, often a combination of the three. The prolific Lew Leslie (*Plantation Revue*, 1922; *Dover to Dixie*, 1923; *Dixie to Broadway*, 1924; and *Blackbirds*, 1926), whose success rested largely on his genius for discovering (and exploiting) black talent from Florence Mills to Ethel Waters, was white, as was the producer of *Scandals* (1922) and *Runnin' Wild* (1923). The *Messenger*'s drama editor, Theophilus Lewis, in 1926 estimated that whites controlled 50 percent of Harlem's theaters and 70 percent of its patronage.[3]

Harlem's Socialist *Messenger* spelled out its concerns in its first issue of the new year, which was devoted entirely to the future of blacks in the performing arts. Theophilus Lewis, Otto Kahn, and Eugene O'Neill detailed the danger signals: the absence of black playwrights and stable Negro theater companies, the dilemma of retaining racial identity in an atmosphere dominated by white tastes and money, and the inevitable waning of the vogue. Robeson, however, consulted as an "expert" by virtue of his recent theatrical successes, expressed few of the misgivings of other contributors. Like *Shuffle Along's* sensation, actress-performer Florence Mills (interviewed by George Schuyler for the issue), Robeson exuded hope while prudently crediting his personal success to luck and the generous assistance of [white] friends. "As I have met people in various circles I find they are pulling for me. Especially my friends at the Provincetown. I honestly feel that my future depends upon myself. . . . True—plays are not easy to get, but they come from the most unexpected sources. We who start on this rather untrodden way need all the support and encouragement we can possibly get. I approach the future in a happy rather adventuresome spirit. For it is within my power to make this unknown trail a somewhat beaten path."[4]

Robeson evidenced no bitterness, none of the smoldering rage of actor Charles Gilpin who struggled in obscurity for years before attaining even a modicum of recognition. Compared with the experiences of blacks before him, theater had been extraordinarily kind to Robeson. Bert Williams had made headlines a decade earlier when he received feature billing in the Ziegfeld Follies, but he paid a high price for that success: specifically, he had to adhere to minstrel stereotypes and himself perform in blackface. Of the period's many black musical performers, only a few, like Florence Mills and Josephine Baker, achieved any lasting success. Other prodigious talents—composer, conductor, and violinist Will Marion Cook; musician and producer Ford Dabney, who toured with James Reese Europe and for twelve years led the orchestra for Florenz Ziegfeld's Midnight Frolics; composer and arranger Will Vodery, who wrote material for Bert Williams and William Walker as well as for the Ziegfeld Follies; pianist and composer Eubie Blake; and lyricist and actor Noble Sissle—had all struggled to make a living in music and never earned the recognition they deserved.[5]

Robeson, by contrast, in the earliest years of his career, had landed first-rate roles in white productions and performed to critical applause. He was "grateful," but his public posture notwithstanding, he was not naive. He understood the limitations of theater, especially for black actors. Quality roles (O'Neill's work a notable exception) were virtually nonexistent. Now that he had won a modicum of success, the problem was how to sustain it.

One black performer, tenor Roland Hayes, had already earned the renown and community respect Robeson sought for himself. Hayes's rise to fame read, as A. Philip Randolph put it, "like a romance," and his career stood as an almost flawless example of artistic excellence working in unison with racial uplift. Never had his name been associated with anything cheap or tawdry. Hayes set the pattern for other black performers, first earning recognition in Europe with plaudits in the States soon following. In 1923 the black tenor landed the ultimate British honor, a summons to perform for the king and queen of England, and, on the other side of the Atlantic, an invitation from conductor Pierre Monteux to give a solo performance with the Boston Symphony Orchestra.[6]

Hayes typified the type of artistry that James Weldon Johnson, Alain Locke, Charles S. Johnson, and other Renaissance intellectuals believed would demonstrate "the intellectual parity" of the Negro and, in so doing, win political, economic, and social equality for the race. And indeed, the young black tenor's Boston appearance and the three-month cross-country tour that followed marked a breakthrough for black American vocal artists. Hayes's mastery of German and French classical pieces along with an impeccable rendering of his own people's spirituals, proved that blacks could perform "far beyond the reaches of a Blind Tom" and shattered the stereotypical notion that because blacks sang "naturally," they lacked the ability to master classical music. "At first . . . the white people could not believe their ears," began one typical Hayes review.[7] Hayes's virtuosity had forced white critics and audiences to rethink their assumptions concerning all black vocalists: it was a momentous achievement.

Similarly, black composers of the period, trained in conservatories like Oberlin in Ohio, the New England Conservatory, and the National Conservatory in New York, challenged prevailing racial stereotypes with their mastery of European style. Some, like Harry T. Burleigh, R. Nathaniel Dett, and Clarence Cameron White, composed music for the concert stage; others, like Will Marion Cook, Robert Cole, and J. Rosamond Johnson, for shows, dance, and entertainment. Invariably they all drew on the folk music of their own people as a source of inspiration.

Although it was the Fisk Jubilee Singers, beginning with their first national tour in 1871, who first brought the spirituals to the attention of American and European audiences, it was the work of composers and arrangers like Burleigh, Dett, Hall Johnson, James Weldon Johnson, and Lawrence Brown who established the spiritual as an art form suitable for solo performance in concert halls. Burleigh's 1916 and 1917 arrangement of "Deep River" — the first known arrangement of a black spiritual for solo voice with independent piano accompaniment — began a new era, one in which a generation of black vocalists would showcase arrangements of their own native songs side by side with their mastery of European classics.

There are several conflicting versions as to how Robeson's first formal concert appearance came about. One credits the Provincetowners with taking charge and making the necessary arrangements after Essie convinced them "she had discovered the greatest voice in America." Essie claimed that she took the initiative and, with the assistance of an enamored Carl Van Vechten, got the event off the ground. Robeson's accompanist, Lawrence Brown, told still another version. Biographer Marie Seton, a close friend of Brown's, said that Brown told her that when the time came it was Robeson who made the first move.[8]

A talented musician, arranger, and accompanist to Roland Hayes, Brown first met Robeson in England in 1922 when Paul performed in *Voodoo*. It was a brief acquaintance, not to be renewed until the spring of 1925. As Brown tells the story, he had returned to America in March for his father's funeral and ran into Robeson one night at the corner of 135th Street and Seventh Avenue. After exchanging hellos, Robeson asked him to have dinner and then come with him to Greenwich Village to spend the evening with Jimmy Light. Paul mentioned how much he liked a volume of spiritual arrangements Brown had sent him and suggested that Larry play some songs while they visited Light. Later in the evening, Paul told Jimmy that he and Larry wanted to sing for him two of "the spirituals Brown had arranged, 'Swing Low Sweet Chariot' and 'Every Time I Feel the Spirit,' with Brown joining in as the second voice." Brown recalled: "It was completely spontaneous. My joining in excited Jimmy Light. He said, 'Why don't you fellows give a concert?'"[9] Within three weeks a concert program was arranged and rehearsals for an April 19 performance were in progress.

Robeson's teaming up with Lawrence Brown, ultimately the result of several chance meetings and some last-minute engineering on Robeson's part, would prove enormously important in Paul's creative and musical development. Although within a short time the quiet, diminutive Brown would be overshadowed, both personally and professionally, by the towering Robeson, in 1925 it was Robeson's coup to have persuaded Brown to perform with him. Singer, actor, and journalist I. Harold Browning, a member of the Harmony Kings with whom Robeson sang in 1921, said that in these early years, "Paul leaned on Brown for everything. He did not consider himself a great singer and felt that the 'hard work' was arranging the music, which Brown did extremely well."[10]

With Roland Hayes as his model, Robeson wanted to be more than an entertainer: he aspired to art, if not in theater, then on the concert stage. Robeson had never acquired the musical education, the classical background, and the years of study and training of a master like Hayes, but Brown could supply the intellectual and scholarly underpinnings in music Robeson lacked. Few people understood spirituals better than Brown. As Robeson put it, "Brown had mastered the secrets of negro music." As an arranger Brown had already grappled with the problem of adapting these songs intended for group singing, with chorus and verse alternating between a leader and a congregation, for a solo or duet performance. If anyone could assure the artistic success of a concert composed entirely of spirituals, it was Lawrence Brown.[11]

Born in Jacksonville, Florida, on August 29, 1893, Brown was a gentle, quiet, and reserved man who never got over the experience of southern racial violence. Larry's father, like Robeson's, had been born a slave. As a young child Brown witnessed a nearby lynching and watched the murdered body hang for hours unattended because no one dared to remove it. The experience proved traumatizing. Brown never married. He told Marie Seton that he simply did not want to bring children into "a world like this one." To others, he explained he was homosexual, although there is no reliable evidence of Brown's having had an intimate relationship with either a male or female partner. It is possible, given the traumas of his childhood, that Brown used his professed sexual orientation to protect himself from white women, more specifically from the dreaded accusation of rape. Throughout his life he harbored a deep distrust of nearly all whites. Even Carl Van Vechten, who managed to win over the tough-minded, not easily impressed Ethel Waters, never earned Brown's confidence. When questioned by Van Vechten concerning Brown's "inexplicable" dislike for him, Essie did not know what to say but felt it was not personal and so explained it as Larry's "black and white complex."[12]

As soon as he could (1914) Brown left the South and moved North, vowing never to return. He worked in Boston as an elevator operator and later won a scholarship to the New England Conservatory of Music for full-time schooling in music. He continued his studies in musical composition in England at Trinity College, where he published the first of his more than 400 arrangements of Negro folk songs, work songs, gospel pieces, and spirituals. In London he received music and voice training under Amanda Ira Aldridge, daughter of actor Ira Aldridge, the African American who won European fame as the first black to play the role of Othello. For four years Brown accompanied Roland Hayes as the legendary tenor steadily built a reputation in England and throughout the Continent. The experience broadened and matured Brown, putting him in contact with all types of audiences and with musicians from all parts of the world. Brown most likely had contact with African musicians, as he and Hayes included a Nigerian folk song performed in the original Yoruba on the program of an April 1921 concert held in Wigmore Hall. He became friends with the American-born John Payne and the British composer Roger Quilter, who introduced him not only to his own music (light and popular songs, many using as lyrics classic pieces of British literature, as in "Three Shakespeare Songs," "Love's Philosophy" by Shelley, and Tennyson's "Now Sleeps the Crimson Petal," which Robeson and Larry Brown would later perform) but to English, Scottish, Welsh, and Irish folk music as well.[13]

Larry Brown would be Paul's first music mentor, the person who revealed to Robeson the artistry inherent in the "songs" he had been singing all his life. To Robeson's raw talent and intuitive feeling Brown added breadth of knowledge, technical competence, and conceptual understanding. His arrangements were sensitive and vibrant, his accompaniment flawless, and his spirited tenor a complement to Robeson's deep organ tones. Many educated blacks of the period were defensive and even embarrassed by the spirituals (recall the refusal of students at Howard University in 1909 and again in 1919 to sing spirituals). Brown quietly and intelligently helped allay whatever mixed feelings Robeson may have had about his own native music. Brown's arrangements eliminated the spontaneous call-and-response and the intense emotionalism, shouting, groaning, and cries of ecstasy that often accompanied this music in black churches. Adapting the spirituals for the concert stage inevitably "civilized" them and transformed the music into something palatable to Euro-American tastes.

Five years Paul's senior, Brown, as a result of his own stable, retiring, and essentially cautious personality, was able to bring balance to the impulsive, gregarious, naive, and impressionable younger man. (In personal matters as well, the two men complemented each other. Concerning his personal life Brown exercised an almost obsessive discretion; Robeson, likewise, was extremely protective of his privacy. While neither understood or, perhaps, approved of the other's personal affairs, they could depend on each other not to interfere.) Paul trusted the artistic sensibilities of this refined man — a meticulous dresser, perhaps even a bit prim, with elegant dining tastes — who had not let his "education" make him ashamed of his racial heritage. For thirty-eight years Brown would painstakingly devote himself to his own craft and to perfecting their music together, complementing Robeson's often runaway enthusiasm with his own steady and methodical perseverance. He understood Robeson's limitations as well as his strengths and was always looking for new music for him. Even in later years when Robeson insisted on taking risks that unnerved Brown (performing in the South or in behalf of political causes), Larry Brown remained loyal.[14]

The idea of a concert might never have moved beyond talk had it not been for the cadre of influential promoters Robeson had gathered during his brief tenure with the Provincetown Players. Foremost among these early backers was Walter White, the sophisticated and articulate assistant to NAACP executive secretary James Weldon Johnson. Fair enough to pass easily for Caucasian, White moved with confidence in white circles and exercised enormous influence among blacks. Ambitious both for the race and in his own behalf, White had a cockiness about him that amused fellow blacks: it was only half in jest that they described him as being on a first-name basis with every well-known white in America. Witty, worldly, and eager to seize the possibilities of Harlem's nascence, White cultivated power and influence and then dispensed it to worthy causes.[15]

White spotted talent and character in Paul, joined the Robeson cause early, and remained one of Paul's most loyal and indefatigable promoters during the early years of his career. As an NAACP officer and a writer himself (his novel on southern racism, *Fire in the Flint,* was published by Knopf in 1924), White saw it as his mission to promote talented blacks. Thus White took Robeson under his wing, as he did Roland Hayes, Jules Bledsoe, Claude McKay, Countee Cullen, Langston Hughes, Hale Woodruff, and others, advising him, introducing him to the right people (Carl Van Vechten, Heywood Broun, Konrad Bercovici, Mark and Carl Van Doren, and Arthur and Joel Spingarn), and seeing to it he received prime coverage in the black weeklies. With his many contacts in the New York art and literary world, White proved a valuable ally. Not only was he invited to the best parties, but with his beautiful wife, Gladys, he entertained at elegant evenings at his charming and exclusive apartment at 409 Edgecomb, a citadel of stately apartment buildings on Sugar Hill, overlooking the Hudson and Harlem's smartest residential area. Essie, in particular, appreciated it that whenever the Whites had "guests of any interest or importance they always took care to include Paul." For new black talent, like Robeson, the nod from Walter White provided instant entrée to New York's select white and black artistic circles.[16]

Supporting gifted African Americans was the rage in 1925, and Robeson, like other blacks in his position, reaped the benefits. The motives of Harlem's "Negrotarians" (author Zora Neale Hurston's irreverent term for whites specializing in Negro uplift) varied widely, ranging from friendship, genuine humanitarianism, and fascination with Negro exotica to a desire to make money while the vogue lasted. Lost-generation artists and intellectuals, political radicals, business liberals, and WASP and Jewish philanthropists all jumped on the Negro bandwagon, each for his own reasons eager to support black talent.

Among white theater critics, Robeson had already won over two of the most influential in America: the *New York Sun's* Alexander Woollcott and the *Tribune's* Heywood Broun. Woollcott wrote a lavish, almost effusive review of Robeson's 1924 *Emperor Jones* ("the kind of evening in the theater you will remember all your life") and remained solidly in the Robeson camp from that time on. Heywood Broun also saw Robeson's *Emperor Jones* but left the theater more taken with Robeson as a person than as an actor. "Woodie was crazy about Paul," remembered Broun's secretary, Mildred Gilman. "He just loved him." Years later

Broun said he recognized immediately that Robeson was a man "touched by destiny." Both critics considered themselves friends as well as mentors to Robeson; both urged him to develop his singing voice, and both later claimed credit for Robeson's decision to sing professionally.[17]

Carl Van Vechten, the six-foot-tall, blond, and handsome former music critic for the *New York Times*, first met Robeson through Harlem's indefatigable intermediary, Walter White, and decided at once to take him on as one of his special charges. Famed as Harlem's "most enthusiastic and ubiquitous Nordic" and credited with knowing "more about Harlem than any other white man except the captain of the police station," Van Vechten served throughout the twenties as white America's tour guide through the black metropolis.[18] Van Vechten's contacts, in both publishing and theater circles, were many, and he worked assiduously to use them in Robeson's behalf.

But of all those who promoted and encouraged Robeson, none worked harder than Essie to cultivate this "diamond in the rough." There is no doubt she encouraged Paul to move away from law and into the theater. Her friend Louise Hayes recalled receiving "progress reports" from Essie detailing how "the boys" were doing during these early years. "Essie put Paul straight on his feet and made him walk. She was his backbone . . . his right arm," always planning, criticizing, offering suggestions, looking ahead, and making sure Paul met the right people and kept in contact with them. Robeson, in turn, consulted her, took her advice, and depended on her confidence when his own flagged. Robeson's friend Malcolm Pitt went as far as to say that Essie "almost determined Paul's career . . . he needed a push and she gave it to him." On this point Robeson agreed. As he said to friend and writer Glenway Wescott, "Without Essie, I'd be singing now, but on a sidewalk curb rather than a concert hall."[19]

Nearly all Robeson's early promoters believed they had been instrumental in convincing Paul to pursue a singing career. Robeson's modest demeanor led many to conclude he had little sense of his own talent and hence to the idea that without their prodding he might never have thought of singing professionally. But Robeson was neither as unambitious nor as ignorant of his ability as he appeared. He had always liked to sing. Whether in his father's church, at home with his brothers, socializing with friends, before or after games with his Rutgers football teammates, or at informal recitals accompanied by friends like Malcolm Pitt, Fritz Pollard, Bud Fisher, and May Chinn, Robeson sang whenever the opportunity presented itself. George Hayes, a black lawyer, later to become a leading civil rights advocate, and his wife, Louise, friends of Paul's since the early 1920s, recalled that Robeson along with Bud Fisher often visited them at their home in Washington, D.C. "They'd come down and stay for three or four days — go out to the country, take hay rides and sing. Whatever they did, they always ended up singing. Paul and George often had a few drinks at our bar before dinner, then wine with dinner, and then they'd start to sing. 'Water Boy' was one of our favorites. I don't know why Paul encouraged George. Really, George had such an awful voice. But Paul's voice was like something from another world — sweet — if you can talk about a man's voice being sweet."[20]

In the black community, Robeson's singing abilities had been well known for some time. When the famous and beloved orchestra leader, musician, and composer James Reese Europe died suddenly, at the height of his career, from a knife wound, twenty-one-year-old Paul Robeson was asked to sing at a memorial service held in Washington, D.C. In addition to appearances in *Shuffle Along* and at the Plantation Room and the singing he had done in five of the six plays he had appeared in, in the summer of 1924 Robeson sang at the McDowell Colony in Peterborough, New Hampshire, in November of the same year at Boston's Copley Plaza Hotel, in December at Rutgers's Ballantine Gymnasium, and on various radio broadcasts throughout 1924. Robeson did lack the self-confidence of later years and so relied on the encouragement of friends, but as to the question of who discovered Robeson, Provincetown actor Walter Abel perhaps gave the best answer: "We all promoted Paul," Abel said, "his talent was so obvious."[21]

Once a date was announced for the concert, friends rallied to Paul's assistance, each scrambling to help plan the event on a few weeks' notice. The Provincetowners financed the performance and gave Robeson and Brown use of their theater for operating costs only; Jimmy Light and Gig McGhee volunteered their services for lighting; and the theater group's Stella Hanau and Katherine Gay made arrangements for advertising, circulars, mailing lists, and posters. Carl Van Vechten wrote personal letters to influential friends, urging them to attend. Walter White made the rounds of his contacts and used his access to the black weeklies through NAACP press releases to advertise the event nationwide. Finally, on the morning of the concert, Heywood Broun, in his *New York World* column "It Seems to Me," sang Robeson's and Brown's praises, promising concertgoers an evening of rare entertainment: "I have heard Paul Robeson sing many times, and I want to recommend this concert to all those who like to hear spirituals. . . . Into the voice of Robeson there comes every atom of the passionate feeling which inspired the unknown composers of these melodies. If Lawrence Brown's arrangement of 'Joshua Fit de Battle ob Jericho' does not turn out to be one of the most exciting experiences of your life, write and tell me about it."[22]

As an artist, Robeson would be most remembered for his breathtaking performances of black spirituals and work songs, adapted for the concert stage by some of America's best trained black musicians. But singing this music would thrust Robeson into the maelstrom of America's twisted race relations. It would take him years to find his way through the maze of black and white discourses on the subject and to come to his own understanding of himself as a performer of the ancient music of his race.

At the heart and soul of the spirituals is the trauma of black slavery—an experience white America did not want to confront and most blacks of the period preferred be put in the past. Among a people denied the freedom to speak explicitly their thoughts and feelings, the spirituals were, as W. E. B. Du Bois put it, the slave's "articulate message to the world." Whether pure folk or arranged adaptations, they tell the story "of an unhappy people, of the children of disappointment; they tell of death and suffering and unvoiced longing toward a truer world."[23]

James Weldon Johnson refers to the spirituals as a "miracle," created by slaves and through which slaves found a way to sustain their spiritual selves, a miracle that emerged from the forced encounter of three worlds: traditional African life, evangelical Protestantism, and the white American South. Music and dance were vital dimensions of the world from which black slaves were torn. They could not bring physical cultural artifacts with them, but they could, and did, bring their extensive and complex expressive cultures. African expressive modes such as call-and-response, textual improvisation, pentatonic and modally ambiguous melodies, and African-derived rhythmic conventions would feature prominently in the new art form created by slaves.[24]

At the same time, the spirituals reflect and derive from enslaved Africans' experiences in their new environment. Slaves were taught Christianity primarily because it was thought religion would offer slave owners an additional means of control. Enslaved Africans, however, were never passive recipients of Christianity and rejected the attempt to reduce Christianity to an ethic of pure submission.[25] Instead, they carefully chose and took as their own those biblical texts that related directly to their experiences. Slaves recognized striking parallels between their situation and that of Old Testament Jews. The story of Jewish enslavement and freedom provided a rich array of characters, settings, and experiences—symbolic language that the slaves would use to articulate the realities of their own lives. It is impossible to grasp the essence of the spirituals without understanding this Old Testament bias. Old Testament figures—Daniel, David, Joshua, Jonah, Moses, and Noah—predominate.[26] Again and again the Old Testament stories recounted in the spirituals show the deliverance of the oppressed, the victory of the downtrodden and weak, the defeat of the powerful and proud. God parts the Red Sea to allow the Hebrew slaves to pass through and then abruptly closes it, drowning the mighty armies of the pharaoh; tiny

David humbles the giant Goliath with a stone; blind Samson brings down the mansions of his conquerors; Jonah is rescued from his confinement in the belly of the whale through faith.

The God that the slaves sang of in their spirituals was, by and large, the God of the Hebrews — immediate, intimate, just, and active in the lives of his people. There was no doubt in slaves' minds that, like the Jews, they were God's chosen people. The vast majority of spirituals identify their singers as "de people dat is born of God." Not only did slaves believe they were the chosen, but there is also evidence that many of them believed their owners would be denied salvation: a basic idea running through the spirituals is that slavery is a denial of God's will.[27] The escape-to-freedom motif is omnipresent: slaves are always sailing, walking, riding, rowing, climbing, crossing rivers and mountains on their way to heaven, Canaan, the Promised Land — freedom. If "my Lord delivered Daniel," the slaves reasoned logically, then "why not every man?" Their God, like the God of Moses, would take them out of Egypt and to the Promised Land.

> He delivered Daniel from de Lion's den,
> Jonah from de belly ob de whale,
> And de Hebrew children from de fiery furnace,
> And why not every man?

For all the sadness, loss, and suffering recorded in these songs, they are characterized much more by a feeling of confidence and hope than of despair, a belief that contemporary power relationships would not last forever. These songs helped slaves preserve their sense of autonomy and worth, affirm the reality of their suffering, transcend the degradation of present lives, maintain communal connections, and hope for a better future. There is implicit protest in them all. Their hope is not a denial of history but rather a belief that history is in motion always moving toward divine fulfillment.[28]

On the evening of the concert Robeson and Brown arrived to find the lobby and sidewalk in front of the theater already filled with black-tied, evening-gowned, and bejeweled concert goers waiting to take their seats. (New York's white avant-garde had acquired a taste for black expression and what was understood to be genuine black folk music was in demand: in 1925 and 1926 eleven books were published on black spirituals, folk songs, and oratory.) The performance was sold out; latecomers would have to stand in the wings to hear the program. Larry Brown remembered that he and Paul were "both scared to death." A formal concert composed exclusively of black folk songs and spirituals had never been tried before, and no one could predict how an American audience, even in New York, would react. Furthermore, despite the widely held notion that blacks sang spirituals "naturally," more than one black soloist had floundered trying to render these seemingly simple pieces. They were not, as James Weldon Johnson wrote, "concert material for the mediocre."[29]

"I never saw Paul so nervous," said Walter Abel. "He was terrified, so much so he allowed no one, not even Essie, near him in the dressing room." Robeson and Brown had planned a short program divided into four sections of four songs each: spirituals, folk and dialect songs, and two more groups of spirituals (all of these arranged by Brown). It was a carefully planned but brief program—at best, between thirty-eight and forty-eight minutes of actual singing. Possibly it was all that Robeson and Brown could prepare on such short notice; more likely it was an accommodation to Robeson's singing voice, which was not strong (a fact that would have surprised many given his massive frame) and possibly might not last longer than forty-five minutes.[30]

A roar of anticipatory applause greeted them as Robeson and Brown stepped up to the stage, impeccably but simply dressed in tuxedos (Paul's was the tuxedo he had purchased as an undergraduate at Rutgers). They assumed their positions, with Paul standing to the side of the piano, resting one hand on it. Their entrance, classic in its simplicity, immediately hushed the audience. Visually the two men complemented each other—Brown slight and sprightly, Robeson gigantic and powerful. When Paul was ready to begin, he simply nodded to Brown. "I have never seen a more civilized, a more finished artistic gesture than his nod to his accompanist, the signal to begin his song," one observer commented. In his "luscious, mellow, bass-baritone" Robeson began.[31]

The program opened with the stirring "Go Down Moses," a spiritual so direct in its call for freedom that the singing of it had been forbidden on many plantations. It is God, interceding on behalf of his people, who commands Moses to "Go down . . . way down in Egypt Land" and "Tell ole Pharaoh, Let my people go." Robeson began the song gently, but with each succeeding verse intensified the power and emotion of the command "Go down, Moses, way down in Egypt land," enough so that by the final verse Robeson's deep bass indeed sounded like the voice of God demanding long-overdue justice.[32]

It would have been nearly impossible to listen to Robeson sing and continue to think of the spirituals as quaint or little songs. Whether an understated lament like "By an' By," a richly poetical portrait of God's liberation like "Swing Lo, Sweet Chariot," an anguished cry of despair like "Nobody Knows the Trouble I've Seen," or a joyous statement of faith like "Every Time I Feel the Spirit," there was nothing small about these songs. They were passionate acts of will on the part of a people determined to rise above their bondage; they were acts of "soul-making" from an anonymous and invisible population obsessed with freedom;

they were courageous explorations of the dark side of the human condition, of the meaning of suffering, of the necessity of resisting.[33]

The emotion these songs summoned from Robeson was obvious from the minute he began to sing. They evoked memories of family, friends, his father and his father's church, and the black communities of his youth. (In his 1958 auto-biography, *Here I Stand*, Robeson would use the words "A Home in That Rock," taken from one of the spirituals he sang at this concert, to title the chapter describing his boyhood years and his deep affection for his father.) The spiri-tuals articulated in rich imagery the essentials not only of Robeson's racial past but of his own experiences as well. Themes that appear again and again in the spirituals — the yearning for home, loneliness, separation from family, the tra-vails of the motherless child, and the longing for freedom — were themes that also dominated Robeson's own life. The spirituals were, as one critic put it, "part of Robeson's being," and he sang them on this night, as he would in the years to come, with great sincerity and feeling, handling each word of each song with exquisite care.[34]

In addition to the spirituals, the program also included Harry T. Burleigh's humorous "Scandalize My Name," two love songs, "Li'l Gal" and "Down de Lovah's Lane," and Avery Robinson's arrangement of "Water Boy." The work song, "Water Boy," is built around the cry for water of a gang of condemned and laboring men. Robeson sang the refrain (the water cry itself, "Water boy, where are you hidin'?") a cappella and very softly, and the verses themselves with the tempo picked up and Brown accompanying. The result is a haunting and plain-tive evocation of men condemned to a life of hard labor, but men, nonetheless, still capable of bitter humor and moments of braggadocio. Both love songs — "Li'l Gal" (arranged by James Weldon Johnson) and "Down de Lovah's Lane" (arranged by Will Marion Cook) — were written by blacks about blacks and both use as lyrics the poetry of Paul Laurence Dunbar. Here again, Robeson and Brown departed from the norm as they sang simply and without the slightest hint of ridicule two delightful songs about young black lovers.

By the time Robeson and Brown began the spirituals that made up the last half of the concert, Robeson had established with his audience the unique bond and emotional connection for which he would be remembered throughout his career. Robeson and Brown began their third set of songs with the beautiful "Steal Away," one of the many signal songs for runaway slaves, which Robeson sang like a guarded secret in almost a whisper. This they followed with the lively "I Know de Lord's Laid His Hands on Me." About their next song, "Sometimes I Feel Like a Motherless Child," Mrs. Walter Abel, who attended the concert, had vivid recollections. "The tears were running down Paul's face by the time he finished. And I was crying too, and so was half the audience. Paul *was* a mother-less child. Listening to him sing, for the first time in my life, I understood something about the pain of being a child without a mother and I couldn't stop crying. It was a very powerful experience."[35]

The concert ended with the rousing "Joshua Fit the Battle of Jericho" and its powerful image of the righteous shout of God's people bringing down the walls of the city. As Robeson and Brown took their bows, the audience applauded without restraint, shouting "Bravo! Bravo!" and pleading for encores. As they had planned, they complied, repeating five pieces, adding three more, and "taking so many bows that reviewers lost count of them." Still, the audience was reluctant to leave and did so only after the house lights were turned up.[36]

Reviews, without exception, were enthusiastic. "It is his intense earnestness which grips his hearers," said one, and another, struck by Robeson's "fine stage presence," paid Paul the supreme compliment of likening him to the Russian dramatic and singing genius, Feodor Ivanovich Chaliapin, widely regarded as the finest operatic bass and actor of his time.[37]

Comments on Brown's performance were equally laudatory, most concurring that he "played the accompaniment perfectly" and well deserved "parallel billing with Mr. Robeson . . . not only for pianism but for his vocal assistance."[38] Word spread, and the two succeeding Robeson–Brown concerts (on May 3 and May 17, also at the Provincetown Playhouse on MacDougal Street) again drew packed audiences of urbane New Yorkers, as actor Walter Abel put it, "the sophisticated carriage trade — all very elegant and chic."[39]

Although only a few Harlem blacks made the trek downtown to MacDougal Street, black weeklies gave the Robeson–Brown concerts glowing and detailed coverage. The *New York Age*'s Lucien White faltered only in his search for superlatives. Mark Whitman of the *Amsterdam News* was similarly moved: "They [Robeson and Brown] raised these songs, which many of us but a few years ago did not care to hear, to a higher degree of artistry than they have ever enjoyed before." With their success came requests to perform for private engagements as well as a spate of articles in the black press lionizing Robeson and Brown for their contribution to improved race relations. Typical was the reaction of the *Amsterdam News* to a special Robeson–Brown performance on May 13 for 3,000 students at the Bushwick High School in New York. After singing, Robeson spoke with the youngsters (something Paul enjoyed and would continue to do throughout his career) and held his audience spellbound as he recounted his experiences acting in *The Emperor Jones* and his athletic career at Rutgers. And the *Amsterdam News* wrote proudly: "Again let it be said that Robeson and Brown are 'tumbling down' the walls of misunderstanding between us and other groups by sheer personality and their wonderful art."[40]

Robeson and Brown were both delighted. Paul, in particular, "was surprised and happy that people liked his singing and were taking him seriously. 'Now, I'll be able to buy two overcoats!' he said, only half in jest." In the meantime, front-line backers like Walter White and Carl Van Vechten continued to sing their praises. Van Vechten started pushing Robeson's records nationwide and in an article published in *Vanity Fair* in February 1926 promised that "To hear him [Robeson] sing Negro music [would be] an experience allied to hearing Chaliapin sing Russian folk songs."[41]

Robeson and Brown enjoyed other coups that spring. They secured the services of a white agent, James P. Pond, which, according to veteran black actor Leigh Whipper, was a huge achievement in itself. "Most of us got work through TOBA [Theatrical Owners and Bookers Association, an organization that booked black acts on a regular basis in some eighty blacks theaters across the country] — we called it 'Tough on Black Ass,' and, believe me, it was tough — working for less than nothing, sometimes not even getting paid, being stranded in cities when a show folded. It was hard enough to get work, let alone an agent willing to risk handling a black performer." And in May Robeson received a contract offer (arranged with the assistance of Walter White) from the Victor Talking Machine Company of Camden, New Jersey. Victor was a prestigious recording label, and among black performers of the period, most of whom — if they recorded at all — recorded for black audiences on "race" labels like Okeh and Black Swan, such an offer was virtually unheard of. The yearlong contract required Robeson to perform a minimum of six selections of solos and duets and offered an advance of $100 per record against a royalty of one cent for each face, with Robeson supplying accompanist Lawrence Brown at his own expense (by the end of the year they had grossed $1,125.12 in royalties and advances from the discs).[42]

One of the contradictions of Harlem's renaissance — and there were many — was the belief that Harlem's artistic nascence marked the beginning of a new period of improved race relations, though the day-to-day racial experience of blacks showed little, if any, evidence of such change. Ordinary Harlemites, most of whom worked hard, struggling on low wages to make ends meet, had few illusions about relations between the races. As Langston Hughes put it, most "hadn't heard of the Negro Renaissance. And if they had, it hadn't raised their wages any."[43] Even in Harlem, expensive nightclubs like the Cotton Club and Connie's Inn, both of which drew a large white clientele, frowned on the patronage of blacks, unless of course they were celebrities. Similarly, the "vogue" had done little to alter the pattern of racial segregation downtown. Blacks were still relegated to balcony theater seats ("progressive" houses like the Provincetown Playhouse excepted), barred from restaurants, refused rooms in the city's hotels, and (a particularly annoying point for Essie) prohibited from renting even in the Village.

Harlem's artistic elite sensed the wide gap between whites' image and Harlem as it really was. (As one young black writer recalled, "So thousands of whites came to Harlem night after night thinking Negroes loved to have them there, and firmly believing that all Harlemites left their homes at sundown to sing and dance in the cabarets.")[44] At the same time, Harlem's young artists found it difficult to resist indulging in the belief that things were improving racially. Few of the vogue's beneficiaries were willing to admit that only the specifics of the stereotype had changed — from lazy, shuffling Negro to exotic, sensuous African — while the proclivity to judge on the basis of race remained intact.

Harlem's stars "at least for the moment were above the color line," that is, until they were faced once again with the inevitable racial slight.[45] For them, instances of blatant prejudice often occurred side by side with their precedent-breaking successes. Financially encouraged and supported by whites for their Negro-ness, they were just as often treated with contempt because of their color. Despite the rhetoric of racial pride, however, Harlem artists and intellectuals as a group were not racially militant. On the contrary, they shared with their "less-enlightened" counterparts a distaste for confrontation as a way of dealing with race problems. The situation created a dilemma for Harlem's stars, and most resolved it by behaving as if the millennium had already come, dismissing racial incidents as temporary aberrations and avoiding any undue emphasis on or discussion of the race problem.

In Robeson and Brown's case, a glaring example of the inevitable slight occurred in May, almost coincidental with the signing of the Victor record contract. It involved the Dutch Treat Club, an exclusive gathering of writers, columnists, playwrights, actors, and singers who met for lunch every Tuesday at noon at the Hotel Martinique to listen to speakers or be entertained. At the end of April Robeson and Brown were asked to perform for them. Such an invitation signified selection by the group for honorary membership, which would be formalized with the awarding of a plaster of paris medal hung on a red ribbon. After waiting outside in the hallway until the meal was finished (a slight in and of itself), Robeson and Brown sang for the 130 club members and all appeared to go smoothly. But when they had finished their performance, the club's president, George Mallon, made no mention of any honorary membership, even though three medals were displayed conspicuously at Mallon's table setting. British explorer Major K. Forbes, the other invited guest, spoke briefly and was awarded his medal, which he promptly put around his neck, but the other two medals remained undisturbed, and with that the day's events ended.[46]

Initially, the news was slow in reaching the public, rating only a small notice in the *New York Times,* which matter-of-factly reported that "negroes Paul Robeson and Lawrence Brown had been denied honorary membership in the Dutch Treat Club." When the black press picked up the story, however, "a wave of indignation," according to James Weldon Johnson, "swept the city." The *New York Age,* in particular, gave the incident meticulous coverage, calling George Mallon "a spineless creature . . . lacking moral courage" for permitting "Paul Robeson and Lawrence Brown to be made the subjects of an insulting slight." When challenged, Mallon explained that to avoid controversy he had acquiesced to the wishes of a southern-born club member by omitting the awards for Robeson and Brown. The southerner in question, however, writer Irvin Cobb from Paducah, Kentucky, emphatically denied having voiced any objection: "I accepted them as artists regardless of color. I should have had no objection to sitting with them. I would have applauded their being given honorary membership in the club. The only reason I did not sit at the speakers' table was because I had made previous arrangements to sit elsewhere with two other friends."[47]

While the black press rallied to Robeson's defense, Paul minimized the event, claiming he had been unaware club members had slighted him. "He said that he had no knowledge of the Dutch Treat Club's customs, and that he accepted the invitation . . . thinking only that he was going to sing some of his songs to a group of newspaper men," reported the *New York Age.* Later, in the wake of ensuing protests, Robeson could claim no such ignorance. Still, he said little about the incident and made it clear he did not want to make an issue of the affair.[48]

Like most American blacks of the period, Robeson kept his reaction to racial slights in check, especially in the presence of whites. Brown, although he had performed with Roland Hayes before royalty and in all the major European capitals, also said nothing publicly about the incident. It was a strategy that Harlem Renaissance thought, with its emphasis on achievement, supported and one that enabled Robeson, like most of his contemporaries, to maintain the racial etiquette of the grateful and personally unambitious "striver." As Robeson explained, "From an early age I had come to accept and follow a certain protective tactic of Negro life in America, and I did not fully break with the pattern until many years later. Even while demonstrating that he is really an equal (and, strangely, the proof must be *superior* performance!) the Negro must never appear to be challenging white superiority. Climb up if you can — but don't act 'uppity.' Always show that you are grateful. . . . Above all, *do nothing to give them cause to fear you.*"[49]

Since his days at Somerville High, Robeson had won friends with his easy, affable manner in situations where his success might well have made him enemies. No one liked or wanted to work with an "uppity nigger," however talented. For both personal and professional reasons, Robeson did not want to appear critical, overly ambitious, or unappreciative of the many opportunities that had come his way. Although he willingly lent his talents to political and charitable causes (in May 1927 he helped raise money for industrial workers in Sierra Leone, West Africa, and in July of the same year he performed in behalf of a home for Negro actors; he added his name to the Citizens Committee of One Hundred, formed to support the Brotherhood of Sleeping Car Porters, and also to a letter of appeal to Massachusetts governor Alvan T. Fuller protesting the execution of Sacco and Vanzetti), Robeson was not politically oriented or active at this time. His friend Malcolm Pitt said that he doubted Robeson even voted during these years. When he extended himself, he did so primarily because it was a decent thing to do. What most absorbed Robeson at this point was developing himself as an artist. When interviewer Mildred Lovell asked him in 1927 if he thought he could accomplish more for his people as a lawyer or politician, Robeson's reply was substantially the same as it had been in 1924: "No. I studied law only because I felt the practical need of a profession. And as to political influence, an individual cannot be instrumental in eliminating inherent race prejudice. A man like Roland Hayes, for example, is doing more to uplift the Negro race through his artistic contribution than any reputed Negro lawyer or politician."[50]

Thus Robeson took the convenient and practical position that his art was more powerful than bigotry and even the cowardly acquiescence of a handful of "liberal" whites. Robeson was not visibly upset that white friends like Woollcott and Broun, both of whom knew well several Dutch Treat Club members (Robert Benchley, Ring Lardner, Robert Sherwood, Marc Connelly, Rube Goldberg, and George S. Kaufman, who were all also part of the Algonquin inner circle), said nothing about the incident. When he was interviewed, Marc Connelly had no memory of such an incident: "It could have happened, but if it did there was not furor over it." Lowell Thomas, at the time on the board of the Dutch Treat Club, said that as he remembered it, no one received honorary memberships. "Those who performed were given a special medallion, and I'm sure Paul Robeson received one." One would have thought that Broun, in particular, with his impressive list of liberal credentials (in 1927 Broun crusaded for Sacco and Vanzetti, for example), would have rushed to Paul's defense, but he did not.[51] Paul did not want to draw attention to the matter. Perhaps experience had taught him the wisdom of such an approach; it certainly had taught him (his first lesson coming at the hands of Rutgers's Coach Sanford) to expect only limited support from whites eager to foster his talents.

Examples abound of well-known blacks similarly going out of their way to avert or downplay racial incidents. When Roland Hayes was selected to receive the NAACP's coveted Spingarn Medal in 1924, he initially refused the honor. Walter White informed James Weldon Johnson of Hayes's decision as diplomatically as possible: "Roland wants no personal honor; applause and an audience are enough for him." Only after White managed to convince Hayes that the award would draw attention not to his color but to his talent and achievements did he agree to accept the medal.[52]

In 1924 Walter White was himself prepared to sue New York's Cafe Lafayette after he and Hayes were refused service there, but he was persuaded by his friend and NAACP official Joel Spingarn to drop the matter. (Spingarn agreed White had a solid case but warned him that to make it a cause célèbre "would do a great deal of harm to Roland.") John Wolforth (the husband of Mildred Gilman, Heywood Broun's secretary and Paul's friend) recalled that James Weldon Johnson took comparable pains to sidestep racial confrontation. Wolforth and Johnson planned to have lunch together at the Algonquin Hotel. Johnson arrived impeccably dressed in a Panama suit but nervous that he would be questioned about his color (the NAACP secretary was fair, although not light enough to pass) and not allowed entry. Wanting to avoid a scene, Johnson devised a plan. As they walked by the maître d', he began conversing with Wolforth in French. The ploy worked. The maître d', assuming Johnson was French rather than an American black, decided against questioning him and let him in.[53]

Invariably, success combined with the "proper attitude" provided Harlem hopefuls entrée to exclusive white and black social circles, and Robeson's case was no exception. "It was a period when almost any Harlem Negro of any social importance at all would be likely to say casually: 'As I was remarking the other day to Heywood —,' meaning Heywood Broun. Or, 'As I said to George —,' referring to George Gershwin," contemporary Langston Hughes remembered. By 1925 the Robesons were high on the guest lists of both uptown and downtown gatherings of the new artistic elite. There were Harlem parties — some, like L'Lelia Walker's, outrageously elegant; others, like author Jessie Fauset's Seventh Avenue gatherings, serious literary soirées. Downtown, Arthur and Mrs. Spingarn, Eddie Wasserman, Muriel Draper, and Rita Romilly held gatherings where one met as many blacks as at a Harlem party. Heywood Broun entertained at many spirited get-togethers on the disheveled first floor of his home on Eighty-fifth Street, with most of his guests the writers and "wits" of New York: Woollcott, Benchley, Margaret Leech, Gilbert Gabriel, Dorothy Parker, Mabel Norman, Russel Crouse, Harold Ross, George Jean Nathan, George S. Kaufman, Marc Connelly, and, occasionally, Langston Hughes and James Weldon Johnson. Robeson, according to Broun's secretary Mildred Gilman, "was a clear favorite."[54]

When he wasn't reveling downtown, Carl Van Vechten and his wife, Fania

Marinoff, invited Harlem to the West Side for one of those lavish "integrated" parties of Renaissance lore. Celebrities — Tallulah Bankhead, Theodore Dreiser, Adele Astaire, Eugene O'Neill, Dorothy Thompson, George Jean Nathan, Cole Porter, Noel Coward, Alfred and Blanche Knopf, F. Scott Fitzgerald, Elinor Wylie, Rudolph Valentino, and Bessie Smith — were legion at these affairs, as well as so many black guests that Van Vechten parties were reported "as a matter of course in the colored society columns, just as though they occurred in Harlem instead of West 55th Street." Here also the Robesons were frequent guests, with Paul as much in demand for his singing as George Gershwin, another regular, was for his magic at the keyboard.[55]

Paul and Essie enjoyed the socializing as a venue for work and as an event in and of itself. In July they played host themselves, taking Eugene O'Neill (itself a coup as O'Neill generally preferred hell holes in the Tenderloin district) along with Provincetowner Harold ("Gig") McGhee and his wife, Bert, for a gala evening uptown. Beginning with cocktails at the Robesons' apartment on 127th Street, the group proceeded to Craig's for dinner, to the Lincoln Theater to see Johnny Nit dance, back to the Robesons' for more cocktails, out again for the midnight show at the Lafayette, from there to Small's cabaret, at 5:30 a.m. to the Vaudeville Comedy Club, and then finally back to the Robesons' where after breakfast the party broke up at 9:00 a.m.[56]

No one was more pleased with their new social prominence than Essie, who meticulously recorded in her diary their growing list of celebrity acquaintances.[57] But she was also worried that somehow Paul was moving beyond her. Though in many respects she and Paul had been ideally suited to each other when they married in 1921, as early as 1924 their marriage began to show signs of strain. Ironically, it was Paul's stage success, so encouraged by Essie, that increasingly put distance between the couple. It was more than having less time to spend with each other. Paul entered a new world when he began performing, one that departed radically in values and perspective from the one he had grown up in and had, for a time, shared with Essie.

Essie would have said some of their trouble began in 1924 when Paul started posing for sculptor Antonio Salemme at his studio overlooking Washington Square in Greenwich Village. Perhaps. But others close to Paul believed that the onslaught of adulation and attention that followed his concert and theater successes simply "overwhelmed him." In many senses, Robeson did it backward: he married first and then began to find himself emotionally and sexually.[58]

Salemme, at the time a fairly well-established artist, was told by friends about this "magnificent man" performing in *The Emperor Jones* and so he went to the play the next day to see for himself. What the artist saw was not an actor but a breathtaking body, "beautifully formed and glistening with sweat. I knew immediately I had to sculpt him. When I asked him about it — I wanted to do a life-size, seven-foot nude statue of him — he just grinned, looking at me as if we were both school boys. 'It's hard work,' I told him, 'you have to pose.' 'OK,' he said, and came back to the apartment with me where we had tea with my first wife, Betty [Hardy]. He settled into the couch, was right at home, and to us it felt as if he had been coming by like this to visit all our lives."[59]

Salemme was one of those at the center of life in Greenwich Village, an artists' haven, famed for its defiance of convention and off-beat lifestyle, that began at approximately West Fourteenth Street and Fifth Avenue and extended south in a maze of curving streets and alleyways, a jumble of apartment buildings, small shops, decorated and repainted store fronts, eating places, churches, and night clubs. Beginning in the early 1900s artists, writers, clerks, and teachers flocked to the area, drawn primarily by its low rents (in 1910 a partially furnished room cost between two and three dollars a week and the spacious top floor of an apartment building as little as thirty dollars a month) as well as its seclusion from the rest of the city and its Old World charm (the Village was one of the few sections of Manhattan untouched by the building spree of the late 1890s). While their conservative Irish and Italian neighbors looked on in horror, these new-comers transformed the area into a bohemia, teeming with renegade artists, radical writers, anarchists, and libertarians.

In the years before the war, the Village was aflame with radical ideas and almost frenetic creativity. Artists gave themselves to love and work with equal passion and abandon. Emancipated women, living alone or in freewheeling alliances, smoked and drank in public. Mabel Dodge, recently separated from her husband, set up her salon with the help of friends (Carl Van Vechten, Hutchins Hapgood, and Lincoln Steffens) on the second floor of General Daniel Sickel's house at 23 Fifth Street.[60] Radical small-press publications (*The Masses, The Little Review, The Seven Arts, The Bohemian, The Pagan,* and *The Quill*) as well as avant-garde theater groups (the Washington Square Players and the Province-town Players) likewise found in the Village the congenial climate they sought. Although by the twenties Greenwich Village had tamed down considerably, it still served as an oasis for creative talent. As a Midwest transplant, a fictional character in an Edmund Wilson short story ("The Road to Greenwich Village"), put it, "Another thing is that nobody cares what you do down here — nobody expects you to cook or go to church. . . . I tell you, the West is all right, but it's a great relief to get some place where you can feel a bit free."[61]

Robeson had already been superficially introduced to the Village ethos through his association with the Provincetowners, happily discovering that with these people there was no "racial etiquette" to maintain; it was sufficient simply to be himself. Singer Ethel Waters (who would meet Robeson for the first time in Salemme's studio a few years later) recalled feeling a similar sense of ease in the Village. "These bohemians were like my own people, and I liked them. Your color and your bank account made no difference to them. They like you for yourself." Characteristically, in the beginning Paul said little but observed and listened carefully. In time, however, he began to relax and talk about himself — something he had never before done among whites.[62]

Robeson began posing for Salemme while performing in *The Emperor Jones*, taking the short walk from the MacDougal Street theater to the studio where he would stay for two to three hours at a time. Salemme, a wiry 150-pound man, in his youth a neighborhood tough, took to Robeson immediately. The two talked at length as Salemme moved slowly and painstakingly through a series of preliminary sketches and then on to the French clay with which he would shape this gigantic statue, the two men becoming in time, as Salemme put it, "intimate friends." Salemme cooked for Robeson and educated him on art, often relaxing by taking him to the Metropolitan Museum to look at the works of Cézanne and Picasso. On occasion Robeson reciprocated, and the two went to a baseball game, this time with Paul explaining to Salemme the basics of the sport.[63]

Robeson discussed his work with Salemme: how much he wanted to act and whether he should make the move toward singing. Paul felt uneasy about his theater prospects but was even more apprehensive about singing. "One day during a posing session he began practicing 'Deep River,' with his arms outstretched, gesturing the song's deep emotions," Salemme said. "It was wonderful; his singing left me almost speechless. He had this magnificent voice but just the same didn't believe in himself. The thought of performing publicly really frightened him. He always appeared so relaxed that people thought his acting and singing was innate, that it came with no effort at all. What they didn't realize was how hard he worked and how terrified he actually was of appearing on stage."[64]

When word spread that Robeson was posing nude for Salemme, people began flocking to the studio to watch. "They would ring the bell, come up three floors, and ask if they could stay. I would have preferred we work alone, but Paul never refused anyone. He loved the stimulation — both intellectual and social. He would sit there in his bathrobe, stretched out on the couch like a king, then take off his robe, pose for about two to three minutes (he didn't work very hard), and then back to the couch again. Women were just crazy about him; they fell all over him. He could have his pick, really. That's the kind of effect he had on them."[65]

The more Paul saw and experienced of Village life, the more he wanted to be a part of it, and the Villagers were eager to let him in. His obvious talent and breathtaking physique fascinated Village whites; his shyness and modesty, his emphasis on luck in recounting his own rise to fame, and his largesse concerning racial insults put them at ease. "Paul had such magnetism," Salemme remembered, "and wherever he went he belonged. When he was in a room, everyone knew it. He had that kind of presence. He never raised his voice, in fact, he was soft-spoken, but no one ever had to lean forward to hear him. He was charming, almost boyish, and loved to tease people, but he was no common person. Everybody wanted to be around him."[66]

While Paul learned the freedom of the artist's life, Essie worked from nine to five in the basement of Columbia's Presbyterian Hospital more than 100 blocks uptown, pursuing those middle-class values for which the Villagers had such disdain. Even had their schedules allowed her to share more of Paul's life, it is unlikely Essie would have enjoyed the company of Paul's new friends. At heart Essie was a pragmatist; loose-flowing lifestyles, erratic work patterns, and stereotypically "artistic" temperaments did not put her at ease.

At first Essie went with Paul to Village parties as well as to midtown parties at Van Vechten's or Heywood Broun's, but she did not mix as easily as Paul, especially in the Village (certainly few were interested in her work as a pathologist), and, unlike her husband, made little effort to spare whites' feelings concerning racial issues. The "enlightened" stance was to avoid such discussion and behave as if there were no race problem. "We just didn't talk about race," one regular said.[67] But Essie never forgot a racial slight and spoke openly with whites about her anger over such incidents. It made everyone uncomfortable.

Robeson, however, almost completely refrained from any mention of race. Salemme recalled Paul conversing amicably with conservative and obviously bigoted southerners who had come to visit the studio, and this without the slightest hint of discomfort. Paul relished the intellectual stimulation and emotional excitement and saw little point in bringing up a topic that made everyone ill at ease.[68] But Essie never let him, or anyone else for that matter, forget that the "liberal, open-minded" Village still would not rent to blacks. Nor did she hesitate to express her resentment when she sensed whites intruding in black affairs. What one might, in retrospect, admire in Essie as spirit and pride, whites of the period most often interpreted as bitterness. Walter Abel expressed the feeling of many of Paul's white friends when he observed, "Paul was happy, proud of the purity of his blood, but Essie always had a chip on her shoulder."[69]

What made it doubly difficult for Essie was that the liberated women attending these parties, unimpressed with and certainly not deterred by her status as "wife," blatantly flirted with Paul. Women found him astonishingly attractive. His boyish gentleness and manly reserve could disarm even the most sophisticated female. And Paul genuinely enjoyed women's company. He took his time, listened, and treated them as intellectual equals. "When he talked with you it was as though there was no one else in the room," remembered Jimmy Light's wife, Patti. "He had a wonderful sense of humor, never deriding. Sometimes he reminded you of a mischievous young boy; he had that look in his eyes when he was about to tease. He could be very funny and had a wonderful smile, and such a hearty laugh. You were the center of his attention and he made you feel very special." "When Paul entered a room everyone noticed," said Mildred Gilman. "He had such an infectious smile and no enemies whatsoever then. Paul was invariably asked to sing, which he always did. He never refused. Everyone adored him. He had such a magnificent voice. It just poured out of him. He was always the center of attention. I don't think Essie really liked the parties. She was lively and bright, but so straitlaced. She could hardly stand it — sharing him — as she was forced to do at these parties. She was just too prim, too do-goodish, too earnest to fit in."[70]

At first the Villagers' liberal sexual attitudes shocked Robeson ("Everyone dated and slept with everyone else, or at least talked that way. Certainly no one would give it a second thought if Paul — black and married as he was — did the same"). He found it difficult to grasp the idea that it might be acceptable for him to socialize with white women. It was only five years earlier that, despite his superb singing voice, he was excluded from the Rutgers Glee Club because of the socializing that followed performances. At the same time, Paul found the attention from white women flattering and the thought of crossing that forbidden boundary exciting. Walking hand in hand down Broadway with the petite Patti Light, Paul often joked about the malicious stares they elicited from passing whites. "'You'd better hold my hand, Patti, so no one will hit me,' Paul teased. You could almost feel the hate in the stares of whites affronted that I was walking alongside such a conspicuous black man," she recalled. "Paul would just laugh, unbutton his overcoat and say, 'Patti, hide in my overcoat, and people won't know you're with me.'"[71]

One can well imagine Essie, so sure of herself, so certain about the "correct" way to do things, suddenly thrust into this bohemian milieu. It was not her nature to suspend judgment: she did not approve of the excesses glibly accepted and encouraged in the Village and other artistic circles. As she sensed Paul slipping away from her, she tightened her grip. In public settings she fawned over her "darling," complaining that her "sweet boy" stayed out too late and needed to be taken care of. Her motherly behavior embarrassed Paul. In a story recounted by several of Paul's friends, Paul asked her for money for cab fare (Essie handled their money) and she gave him a dollar. Annoyed at the paltry sum, Paul snapped back, "Oh for once be a Nigger and not a Jew and give me five!"[72] (While some found such stories amusing, the joke was at Essie's expense and insulted not only her but her Jewish heritage as well.) Langston Hughes told another story (an anecdote he claimed was lore among Harlem wits) recounting how Essie "at a great public ball [in Harlem] after one of Paul's concerts . . . went around . . . closing all the windows so 'her baby' wouldn't catch cold. Then she took him home—on time!" Glenway Wescott concluded simply: "She was so ambitious for him and all that with so little understanding of his art. Most of the Villagers found it all a bit crass."[73]

Essie pushed, planned, and hustled, but she just was not part of New York's artistic genius, nor was she particularly interested in that genius. Wescott said, "Paul once told me, 'The trouble with Essie is that she never had an education.' When I looked at him puzzled, reminding him of her degrees in science, he said flatly, 'But science doesn't count in the type of education I mean.'"[74]

In time Essie attended fewer and fewer parties, although she maintained close contact with the Whites and Van Vechtens and would continue to do so for years to come. With his wife conspicuously absent, it did not take Paul long to develop a reputation as a lady's man. Some of the gossip was true; how much is hard to say. But, real or imagined, the reputation had begun in earnest.

Salemme had parties at his apartment: dinner and a shared barrel of wine. "People would arrive at 6:00 p.m. and leave in the morning," Salemme remembered. "We'd talk and sometimes listen to a recording of Bessie Smith. Paul was almost always there and sometimes stayed the night. He'd tell Essie he was posing. The trouble was everybody I knew, male or female, liked Paul. Paul slept around, but so did we all. It was difficult for Essie. I'm sure she suffered, and that probably added to her aloofness. She was always faithful and stood by him no matter what. Matriarchal. Looked after his every need. I never warmed up to her. She just couldn't meet people halfway. She didn't have the ability. You never wanted to put your arms around Essie. Paul, meanwhile, was lionized. It always seemed as if she had a chip on her shoulders, while he had made his peace with whites."[75]

"Essie just had no idea of what she had in Paul," Mildred Gilman concluded. "We [Robeson and Gilman] were very close. Paul told me how unhappy he was, and from time to time intimated he was considering divorce. He was so physical and sexually alive. Essie had no appreciation for that side of him. She didn't even realize the physical beauty of the man." In time Robeson was more open about his liaisons with white women. Gilman said that he even went as far as to take her dancing at Harlem's Savoy Ballroom. "Paul and I both liked to dance, but Paul's black friends, especially, did not appreciate his bringing me—a white woman—to the Savoy and asked him not to do it again," remembered Gilman.[76] Although whites frequented the Savoy, Harlemites did not appreciate having their dirty laundry aired in full view of "slummers." It was one thing for Paul to have his private affairs but quite another for him to ignore established etiquette and flaunt them publicly. The Village's cavalier disdain of convention did not sit well with Harlem blacks, most of whom were struggling to achieve the lifestyle Village intellectuals disdained. In short, the revolt against middle-class values was a luxury only whites, who had choices in the matter, could afford.

Essie had heard rumors that Paul was seeing other women, and as she saw less and less of him her anxiety mounted. Isolated, if for no other reason than the geographical distance between Strivers' Row and Greenwich Village, she had few people she could turn to for help. Once she paid Salemme a visit, ostensibly to ask him about his coffee (which Paul loved). "She said Paul raved about my coffee, and always complained about hers. I felt sorry for her; there was much more to it than the coffee. She wanted so badly to please him. She would have done, I think, anything I suggested, so long as I said Paul would like it."[77]

Essie had always been protective of Paul—"more a mother to him than a wife"—but as rumors of his philandering spread she became even more so.[78] Mildred Gilman complained that "she tried to build a wall around Paul and 'protect' him from everyone. As a result the marriage was on and off." Most of Paul's friends (men in particular) disliked Essie and agreed with Rutgers classmate John Wittpenn that she was "bad medicine for Paul." They all had their stories. Wittpenn recalled an incident told to him by Eleanor Garrett, the wife of Budge Garrett, who had played football with Paul at Rutgers and professionally. "'Essie,' Eleanor said, 'was so uptight about her status that she would be affronted if I (a white woman) got into the car before her.'" Wescott agreed. "Essie pushed Paul, but . . . she went too far."[79]

In the summer of 1925 Essie quit her job at Presbyterian Hospital in order to devote herself full-time to managing Paul's career. Certainly there were sufficient practical considerations to warrant her decision, but one cannot help conjecturing that emotional factors (as Essie saw it, fighting for her marriage) proved at least equally compelling. An agreement, signed on July 31, 1925, spelled out Paul's, Larry's, and Essie's respective responsibilities and financial shares for this first concert tour: Robeson and Brown would each receive 45 percent of the income, and Mrs. Robeson 10 percent.[80] In retrospect one wonders if Essie could have done anything that would have made a difference. Her close monitoring of Paul did not help their marriage; it probably introduced more tension. For the next eight years she would fight to hold Paul, and Paul, chafing, let her do the planning and organizing while he looked elsewhere for the emotional compatibility and excitement he found lacking in his marriage.

Essie's first priority was to get financial matters under control. Being in the limelight had not made them much money, and there were bills to be paid. Paul had earned some performing at private functions and, later in the summer, at a scattering of concerts (Peterborough, New Hampshire, and Provincetown on Cape Cod) arranged by Pond, but it was not enough. Without Essie's income it would have been impossible to make ends meet. Enlisting the aid of Carl Van Vechten, in June Essie secured a loan of $5,000 from the wealthy Otto Kahn, to be repaid at the end of two years.[81]

With money matters at least temporarily settled, in September the Robesons left New York bound for London and a British run of *The Emperor Jones*. Essie was thrilled. Professionally, the trip promised yet another feather in Paul's cap, and personally, for Essie, a chance to keep a close eye on Paul, enjoy with him the social life that went with his performing, and perhaps get their marriage back on its feet. On the eve of their departure, Essie told reporters from the *Amsterdam News* that she and Paul planned to use the time abroad for a long overdue "second honeymoon."[82]

Robeson was unknown in England, but Eugene O'Neill was not. Anyone who followed London's theater columns had heard of this American playwright and his penchant for doing the unthinkable on stage. Reaction to O'Neill ran the gamut from disgust to genuine interest. Backers worried but believed this play would at least fare better than an earlier London staging of *Anna Christie*. Scheduled for a three-month run under the direction of Sir Alfred Butt, *The Emperor Jones* opened in London at the Ambassador Theatre on September 10.

Initially, the play did well, with the second night's takings just three pounds short of the Ambassador's record, but the production failed to sustain its momentum and closed after less than a month on October 17, 1925. Most British reviewers panned the play. *Gentlewoman* dismissed it as evidence of America's puerile fascination with and fear of Negroes and complained that "Negro plays do not evoke the same emotions in London that they are understood to in, say, Kentucky, and the sight of a half-naked wretch gradually becoming more demented leaves an English audience cold." "Good ideas spoilt by wrong treatment," was the verdict of the *New Statesman*. "Too long and drawn out . . . a series of delirious soliloquies," said the reviewer for the *Daily Sketch*. Many mentioned an overdone and ineffective use of tom-toms, with *Time and Tide's* Cicely Hamilton suggesting the device had been introduced because Robeson's "producer, apparently, could not trust him to carry his audience from scene to scene."[83]

But even those most adamant in their objections to O'Neill praised Robeson, and despite its disappointingly short run *Emperor Jones* proved a personal triumph for Paul. The *New Statesman* judged the play worth seeing "mainly . . . because of Mr. Paul Robeson. . . . Where the author was good, he was magnificent." Reviewers for the *Daily Sketch* and the *Star* agreed: "the applause last night, which was considerable, was all for the actor."[84] Described as "a magnificent figure of a man," with "a wonderful voice," Robeson was credited with "astonishing emotional powers," "extraordinary capability," and a "masterly," "almost overpowering," performance that held "the audience in an absolute grip of fascinated interest."[85]

This exposure, albeit in a failed play, earned Robeson considerable attention and, at the end of October, an invitation from the new British Broadcasting Corporation to sing on nationwide radio, thus beginning a long relationship between Robeson and the British people, most of whom would never see him but would be won nonetheless by the magnificent voice they heard on radio and phonograph records. Interviewed before the broadcast, Robeson could hardly contain his excitement: "And I hope you will believe me when I say that I am thrilled at the prospect of talking and singing to — how many is it? — ten million British listeners. . . . The delight of it almost scares me." The *Star* praised Robeson's singing voice, calling him "the Chaliapin of the coloured race," and Paul responded by unveiling his plan to pursue a concert career, explaining that "you can easily exhaust the dramatic roles that a negro can choose from" but "there is no end to the songs one can sing if one has the voice."[86]

A rash of press interviews followed. Initially, Robeson was puzzled by the openness and interest he sensed among the British press. Like so many black performers before him, he did not find in England the attitudes he had come to expect from whites. On the one hand, London reviewers thought little of using the word "nigger" in reference to Brutus Jones but, on the other hand, they consistently referred to Paul as "Mr. Robeson," a courtesy seldom extended to him in the States.[87] Interviewers sought his opinion on important matters and expressed what appeared to be an unpatronizing interest in his career plans.

It was thrilling for Paul to have an audience willing to take seriously a black man's account of himself and life in the United States, and he took pains both to present himself favorably and to clarify British misconceptions. In an interview with the *Star,* Robeson exposed the Jack Johnson image as a stereotype: "People are apt to think that all men who are big and strong are fit to fight, especially if they are coloured. We are not all Jack Johnsons, no sir." Similarly, he explained the unique problems black performers faced in the United States. "You see, it is difficult for a coloured actor to make a name on the stage. Folks won't believe he can act and prefer to see Al Jolson or Frank Tinney blacken his face and imitate us." While projecting the modest demeanor required of American blacks, Robeson let slip sufficient information for reporters to conclude they were in the presence of an intelligent and athletically and musically gifted black man. He described himself as "a great reader," especially of "the modern writers. . . . Sometimes people express surprise that a negro should be an intellectual. The negro as artist surprises them even more. This is because there still remains so much of the old false ideas of the negro's limitations." He recounted his problems as a black law graduate trying to practice his profession. "I have studied law, but law in New York is not as dignified a profession as it is in London: it is too mixed up with politics and if I could not get a leading part such as I have created in two or three O'Neill plays I should probably drift into vaudeville or cheap stock companies and nobody would ever hear of me."[88]

"Paul was a different person in London," remembered Walter Abel, who was in London at the time. "He was exuberant and willing to talk about his past — his father, his experiences growing up, his lack of opportunity as a barrister." Robeson recalled his own meager beginnings and the lessons that his father, "one of the old liberated slaves . . . passed on to my young receptive mind." When asked by interviewer Reginald Pound if the slavery stories told to him by his father had left him with bitter feelings, Robeson replied, "Why no! Those stories my old dad used to tell me are vivid in my memory; but — well, those bad times are over. What we have got to do is to go forward. There is still too much wild talk about the colour question; some of it wounds me deeply, but I don't let myself get morbid about it. I conserve my energies for my work as an actor. I realize that art can bridge the gulf between the white and black races, though they cannot mix either their blood or their ideals."[89]

The deference Robeson received from members of the British press he also found in his living and working environs. The Robesons rented a flat in Chelsea (12 Glebe Place, the two upper floors of a three-story house, complete with maid service), one of the city's favorite retreats for artists. "There were few inconveniences for him [Paul]," Essie later recalled. "He did not have to live in a segregated district; . . . he dined at the Ivy, a delightful restaurant with marvelous food, directly across from the theatre where he was playing; he ate at many other restaurants in town with his white or coloured friends without fear of the discrimination which all Negroes encounter in America. . . . So here in England, where everyone was kind and cordial and reasonable, Paul was happy." The simple courtesies the British extended as a matter of course meant a great deal to Robeson. Essie remembered how much Paul enjoyed the more "leisurely and deliberate pace of life . . . the whole-hearted friendliness and unreserved appreciation of audiences and of the public at large. . . . He became an enthusiast about cricket and many warm sunny days found him sitting lazily in the stands at Lord's or at the Oval watching and enjoying the test matches." "You could see it in his demeanor; he was almost transformed," Patti Light, herself in London at the time, recalled. "In England he could let down his guard. He was still ill-at-ease with the role of Brutus Jones, but Jimmy [Light] was there, to direct and reassure him. I never saw him more relaxed or confident. Paul was not as overpowered by the glitter and the glamour of it all as Essie. For Paul it was simply a great relief to be himself and feel so accepted."[90]

Essie herself admitted that she and Paul "reacted very differently to London, although [we] both loved it." She was most taken with their new lifestyle, and in letters home to friends she cataloged an impressive list of new acquaintances. On opening night *The Emperor Jones* celebrations included a number of high-spirited fetes, followed by a more leisurely round of friendly meals and gatherings. Throughout it all, the talk was stimulating, the company impressive. Mr. Harwood, producer of the play, gave a party at his "charming flat" in Adelphi Terrace, and Paul, Jimmy Light, Harold McGhee, and M. Eleanor ("Fitzy") Fitzgerald all attended. There the Robesons met Harwood's friends and discussed German theater with Fitzy, who had just returned from a tour of the Continent. Emma Goldman, also in London, invited the Robesons to dinner — roast goose — and talked about "her disheartening experiences in Russia." The Robesons, in turn, tried to cheer this "big hearted, motherly woman, isolated in London" with casual conversation and "all the home news." Assisted by a letter of introduction from Carl Van Vechten, Paul met and dined with British celebrities like novelist Hugh Walpole. The Robesons socialized with black friends in London as well: John Payne and the Turner Laytons. J. Turner Layton and his musical partner Clarence "Tandy" Johnstone, an orthopedic surgeon who pursued a musical career as a drummer and singer, had been in England since 1924. They performed (Layton played the piano and Johnstone sang) in evening dress, and their refined technique met with instant success. On several occasions the pair entertained the Prince of Wales at St. James Palace. In addition to the good company and welcome respite from English food (Payne treated Paul to dinners of southern fried chicken; the Laytons served him "marvelous Boston baked beans as a special favor"), black friends confirmed the Robesons' own favorable impression of London: it was a good place for black performers.[91]

In November after *The Emperor Jones*'s early closing, Paul and Essie left England for vacation and travel in Paris and on the Riviera, a welcomed change for Paul from England's rain and cold. They were armed with letters of introduction from both Walter White and Carl Van Vechten, and their itinerary was predictable, the required fare for any aspiring creative talent: pilgrimages to the Left Bank and 27 rue de Fleuris (Gertrude Stein), James Joyce's apartment, and Sylvia Beach's shop at 12 rue de l'Odeon. Robeson "charmed a small group of Quarternites at one of Sylvia Beach's and Adrienne Monnier's Sunday afternoon salons, singing spirituals and negro workmen's songs," and Van Vechten's letter gained him access to Paris's high priestess of art and culture, Gertrude Stein. Stein trusted Van Vechten's judgment, describing as "delightful" his habit of "giving letters of introduction to people he thought would amuse" her. Robeson "interested Gertrude Stein," who observed that he "knew American values and American life as only one in it but not of it could know them." In her typically cryptic and authoritative manner, Stein instructed Robeson on singing the spirituals: "They do not belong to you any more than anything else, so why claim them?" she asked.[92]

Robeson was not particularly impressed by this mountainous, mannish woman, despite her reputation in international artistic circles. Later, talking with friend and writer Claude McKay about the visit, Paul said simply that Stein "was all right." Still, Robeson encouraged McKay, who had not yet met Stein, to do so, explaining that he "shouldn't neglect such an opportunity, as she knew all the literary people who counted." McKay, however, declined, as he told Paul, because of his "aversion to cults and disciples. I like meeting people as persons, not as divinities in temples."[93]

From Paris, Paul and Essie moved on to Villefranche on the Riviera. With its single movie house operating only once a week and telephone service that shut down temporarily at noon and completely after seven at night, Villefranche had a primitive charm that appealed to artists and writers (among them Max and Eliena Eastman, an unknown and broke Ernest Hemingway, John Dos Passos, Archibald MacLeish, Robert Benchley, and Scott and Zelda Fitzgerald) who flocked to the area from 1925 through 1929 before it was "discovered."[94]

During their ten-day stay the Robesons were guests of writer Glenway Wescott whom Paul had met in 1924 at the time of his debut in *The Emperor Jones*. It was a wonderful time for Essie, who thoroughly enjoyed the socializing and having Paul, at last, to herself. Paul met writer Frank Harris, dined with movie director Rex Ingram, stumbled upon poet Claude McKay while strolling along the Promenade at Nice, and then lunched with him at a cafe where McKay introduced Paul to Max Eastman. Through Wescott the Robesons were introduced to actress Mary Garden at her villa in Beaulieu where they had tea in the garden and discussed the curative powers of the sun. This was a particular thrill for Paul who in his Rutgers college days had listed Mary Garden as his favorite actress. Rebecca West recalled one particularly enjoyable evening when Wescott's talented protégé, Frank Norris, invited the Robesons to dinner, after which Paul sang in the dining room, all in all, according to West, "a marvelous time."[95]

Rebecca West and G. B. Stern, both staying at the same hotel as the Robesons (the Welcome Hotel), stopped to visit, but Paul had gone off by himself to see friends farther up the coast. West had already met Paul briefly, sometime between 1920 and 1922 when he was on the bill with Florence Mills in *Plantation Revue*. Nonetheless, Essie urged the two women to stay for dinner because, as she put it, waiting to speak with her husband ("the grandest man in the world

[with] the most remarkable gifts . . . so intelligent and with it all so modest") was "worth it." West remembered Essie as "so in love with Paul, so proud of him, and so happy to be with him. No one could possibly be as perfect as her Paul."[96] Essie's enthusiasm was apparently contagious. West and Stern waited for Paul to return.

Essie would remember their stay at Villefranche as a wonderful romantic interlude.[97] In fact, it would be one of the last times she could even manage the pretense of "having" Paul. The tension between them, by this time part of the fabric of their marriage, was never far from the surface and even in Villefranche on more than one occasion erupted openly and publicly.

Claude McKay, who saw quite a bit of Robeson in Villefranche, particularly disliked Essie. McKay, a dark-skinned Jamaican who neither liked nor trusted light-skinned mulattoes, could barely tolerate being around her. He saw Essie as a stereotypically narrow-minded striver, bourgeois and pretentious, critical of whites but desperately seeking their approval. He found her cloying solicitude for Paul particularly irritating. The distaste ran in both directions; Essie saw almost nothing to commend in McKay. Loud, earthy, and occasionally boorish, McKay not only drank heavily but frankly admitted his homosexuality and talked openly about his 1923 bout with syphilis. A bellicose political radical and expatriate, always trying to write but in the meantime living off benefactors and the kindness of friends, McKay represented almost everything Essie detested.[98]

Midway through the Robesons' stay, McKay dropped Paul a note, inviting him to dinner along with the Eastmans. Max Eastman, an old friend who had edited *The Masses* with McKay, had been responsible for persuading McKay to go to Nice and finish his work, and McKay was anxious to have Max and Paul meet. When the invitation arrived, Essie opened it and responded, as Paul ignored mail and never or almost never wrote to anyone. She informed McKay they would both be there for dinner (even though McKay had clearly asked only Paul) "because they [she and Paul] just couldn't breathe without each other."[99]

Frank Harris, who had visited the Robesons that afternoon, took himself along to McKay's, also without being invited. McKay had not talked with Harris for years and particularly did not want to see him that night, as Eastman and Harris detested each other. As McKay relates it, the evening was a complete disaster. Harris, in long discourses based on his own firsthand observations of Russian life, demeaned Eastman's latest book, *Since Lenin Died,* and Eastman was unable to reply because Harris never stopped talking. Harris, liberally lubricated with a case of French wine McKay had hauled out from under his bed, was overbearing, loud, and aggressive. When the evening finally ended, all, with the exception of Harris, were glad and relieved to leave.[100]

Glenway Wescott, also at the dinner, remembered the evening differently and insisted that McKay's behavior ruined the evening:

His manners were abominable; he was loud, raucous, and drank quite a bit; Essie was appalled by it all. A few days later McKay called on Paul, having arranged beforehand to meet him. When he arrived, Essie, politely but coldly, informed him that Paul had gone to Paris, when in fact Paul had only stepped out for a walk. McKay thought this odd as Paul had told him he would be there in the afternoon, but at Essie's insistence finally left. When Paul returned from his walk and McKay failed to arrive, he asked Essie about it. Essie told him what she had done. McKay was a rowdy, cheap and loud, and not the kind of person he ought to be associating with, Essie informed Paul. Enraged, Paul set out immediately for Nice to find Claude and went with him from one bar to another until three a.m. when he finally returned home. Paul was furious and embarrassed that Essie would try to control who he chose as friends.[101]

A short time later the Robesons invited the Eastmans, McKay, and Wescott to dinner. Perhaps the best that could be said for the evening was that Harris was not there. By this time McKay's distaste for Essie was rock-solid, matched only by her thorough abhorrence of him. In later accounts of the evening McKay made no effort to hide his contempt for what he saw as pretentiousness on Essie's part. "Now that Frank Harris wasn't there," McKay wrote, "the women had their chance to luxuriate in talking. It was the first time Mrs. Eastman had heard the American negro voice. She whispered to me that she was fascinated and, like a happy eager child, she engaged Mrs. Robeson in conversation. Presently Mrs. Robeson exclaimed mockingly to Mrs. Eastman, 'But Darling, where did you get that accent? I do adore your way of using our English language. It's just lovely!'"[102]

Max Eastman also disliked Essie. Robeson's "strong minded wife," as he later described her, has "all the faults without the virtues of a revolutionary engineer." Eastman even went as far as to blame Essie for Robeson's later rigid pro-Communist politics. "At least I've always thought she was at the wheel when Paul, a man with a gentle heart and magnanimous understanding of America's slow progress toward race equality, veered from his path, and became a blustering yet manipulated advocate of totalitarian tyranny over all the races."[103]

Wescott perhaps best summarized Paul's dilemma with Essie. "Paul wanted Essie around," he said, "but not too close." Although Essie's handling of his personal affairs in the case of McKay infuriated Robeson, in other instances he depended on Essie to plan and arrange his schedule. No one understood better than Paul how much Essie had done for him. "I never had the heart to say no to anyone, but I needed time to myself," Robeson years later admitted to concert manager Fred Schang. "Essie could do it; she sent people away and made sure that I got paid when I sang."[104]

So Robeson put up with Essie's management of both his personal and his professional life. He found it difficult to put his foot down and say no, but more than that, he wanted it both ways: he wanted his personal freedom with Essie taking care of the details of his professional life. It was Essie, after all, who had already paved the way for his return to America by sending on to Walter White news of Paul's London successes, which White promptly condensed and sent through the NAACP offices to black weeklies throughout the country.[105]

7

Touring America

1926-1927

The Robesons returned home in December 1925, and by January James Pond had booked eight concerts, the beginning of Paul and Larry's first "nationwide" tour. Whether or not Paul felt ready, he was about to test himself as a singer.

Robeson would end the tour in March, exhausted, sick, frustrated, less sure of himself, and uncertain as to what, if anything, he had accomplished. From the start, it was a difficult task he, Larry, and Essie set for themselves, more difficult than any of them had imagined. In New York City where the vogue continued unabated, Robeson and Brown easily enthralled white audiences. But, outside of New York City, what most whites knew about black music was confined to minstrel caricatures. First performed for white audiences by white actors in blackface who claimed to have learned their art by observing southern blacks, minstrel show performers took the trauma of slavery and plantation life and transformed it into a comic subject. The staples of the minstrel show — shuffling, irresponsible, wide-grinning, loud-laughing blacks speaking nonsense in heavy dialect and performing musical renditions of "darky life on the Old Planta-tion" — ridiculed African Americans: their culture, their religion, and their experience. With this as their frame of reference, most whites, even those kindly disposed toward blacks, looked upon the spirituals as an interesting, perhaps amusing, artifact of a backward race. The attitude of many educated blacks was often not much better. For some, the spirituals were an uncomfortable reminder of a past they wanted to forget. Others, determined to debunk once and for all the "stage Negro," abandoned spirituals and anything else that suggested or appeared to confirm the minstrel stereotype.[1]

But Robeson's presentation — classic in its simplicity, self-possessed, and emotionally riveting — would move white audiences to look beyond the stereo-types and appreciate these songs as art. By winning the respect and approval of white audiences Robeson and Brown would, in turn, make it possible for blacks to reclaim their music and listen to it without shame or apology. More than any singer of his time, Robeson dethroned the caricature, moving black spirituals and work and folk songs out of cheap, second-rate minstrel shows and into the concert halls. In short, his performances forced a serious appraisal of the artistic value of this long-demeaned music.

The tour opened at New York's Town Hall on January 5, 1926, before "a capacity house as enthusiastic as it was large."[2] Robeson and Brown's almost completely white audiences were eager to hear that "racial quality [and] lusciousness rarely found outside the throats of colored men and women," that "deep feeling," "unembarrassed forthright frankness," "spontaneity," and "almost complete avoidance of artistic sophistication."[3] They were not disappointed: audiences laughed, cried, and called for encore after encore, with the favorite "Water Boy" repeatedly requested. In response to the overflow crowd, Robeson and Brown gave a second concert at the Selwyn Theater, again to a predominantly white audience. Critics commended their performance, noting it effected so "perfect" a "comprehension" between the two races that audience members could "feel the solution to the 'negro problem' in a way they could never reach it through their intellects."[4]

The spirited send-off was heartening as Robeson and Brown prepared for a winter of traveling that included concerts in the Northeast and throughout the Midwest (but no southern bookings). Robeson worried about his voice and if it would withstand the winter weather. To prevent strain he and Larry again planned a program less than an hour in length and divided into four sections of four songs each.[5] If the concert went well and Paul's voice held out, they could then "generously" give numerous encores. It would prove good psychology, as it spared Robeson's voice while making audiences feel they had been treated lavishly.

Robeson and Brown understood that in America's heartland, in cities like Detroit, Indianapolis, and Pittsburgh, there was no "Negro vogue." In fact, the Ku Klux Klan commanded a considerable following in many parts of the Midwest. With no classical pieces to soften the racial content of the program, the pair anticipated difficulties not only from whites but also from "a certain mistaken element among . . . 'the Negro intelligentsia' [that] narrow-mindedly imagines that an educated Negro singing our distinctive songs, sacred or secular, is somehow holding the race up to ridicule by making capital out of distinctively racial music."[6]

The Robesons and Brown left New York determined to reshape old racist stereotypes and in Detroit Robeson spoke with great feeling about his desire to implant in audiences across the country "a new and better concept of the quality of our people's songs." Critical comment following the January 28 concert in

Detroit's Orchestra Music Hall was reassuring in this respect. Cyril Player of the *Detroit News* congratulated Robeson and Brown for their work as "missionaries" spreading word of this rich art form throughout America. Critics frequently included explanatory material on the history or performance of spirituals in their reviews. "To listen to Negro spirituals is to realize what folk music is and to understand that it requires no artificial fostering. . . . Such music must be born of deep racial feelings, usually of suffering," Clifford Epstein of the *Detroit News* concluded. Only a Negro could convey adequately its "latent humor, sorrow, religiousness and credulity."[7] Although praise from white critics was more often than not laced with racial stereotypes, judging from his comments to the press, Robeson was more encouraged by reviewers' goodwill than annoyed by their ignorance. Indeed, in retrospect it is difficult to appreciate the radical change any serious, let alone positive, commentary represented.

Part of Robeson's success was his "massively rich" bass voice; part his impeccable diction and flawless phrasing; part his presence, an arresting combination of size, strength, reserve, and intellectual and emotional intensity. Set next to the diminutive Brown, Robeson awed audiences. "Bedrock; fundamental; primitive," said Harvey Gaul of the *Pittsburgh Post*, and the *Pittsburgh Press*: "A huge man physically, Robeson's voice is as great . . . and . . . when he chose to release it to its full power, he fairly shook the hall with its volume." That same voice also had a "haunting beauty," capable of eliciting from audiences the tenderest emotions. Reviewers spoke of an "inescapable . . . spell," "an ingenuous charm," "a penetrating pathos," "a wistful longing," "an indescribable seeking for something . . . beyond the intellectual . . . that sets the heart strings vibrating." Some attributed this evocative power to Robeson's race; others noted a religious quality to his singing, "as sincere and beautiful as the most elaborate church music of the white race."[8]

Despite the accolades, touring proved exhausting and frustrating. The strain of performing coupled with traveling long distances in the dead of winter on drafty trains bound for some of the nation's coldest states—Iowa, Michigan, Illinois, and Wisconsin—left Robeson physically worn and more susceptible than ever to colds and laryngitis. Equally tiresome was the battle to secure accommodations, which in each city began anew. Essie generally made all the arrangements. As manager it was her "job," and, if necessary, she could at least pass as white. While Essie never deliberately hid that she was black (she wore her hair straight up on one side and down on the other, showing the kink on her temple, thus making it clear she was not trying to pass), she did use her fair skin to its best advantage. On trains Essie most often managed to "get berths right in the center of the car, whereas Robeson, without her, would have likely been seated over the wheel."[9]

On more than one occasion concerts were so poorly advertised that Robeson and Brown found themselves singing to a handful of people. In Burlington, Iowa, not only was the audience minuscule, but the Methodist church hall was cold and drafty. In Chicago also, only a small group of people, most of whom were personal friends, even knew Robeson was performing, and bitter cold and heavy snow on the night of the performance further diminished attendance. "We have had such a bad time this trip," Essie confided to Carl ["Carlo"] Van Vechten and his wife, Fania. Friends had come, but "of course [they] were lost in the hall." Nonetheless, Paul "made up his mind to give these few people as fine a recital as he could" and, according to Essie, "sang better than he ever sang in his life—just got mad and opened his lungs and sang!" Reviews in the white dailies confirmed Essie's observation, with Glenn Dillard Gunn's exuberant comment in the *Chicago Herald Examiner* typical: "I have just heard the finest of all Negro voices and one of the most beautiful in the world. . . . In the soft mellow resonance, in sympathetic appeal, in its organ-like ease and power, it is distinguished among the great voices of the present. By quality alone it exercises a spell that is inescapable." Essie, delighted, immediately relayed the good tidings to Walter White who, as usual, issued press releases ("Paul Robeson . . . Has Triumph in Chicago") through the NAACP news office to the black weeklies.[10]

Two days later in Milwaukee's bitter February cold the trio faced more frustration. Upon their arrival at the Northland Hotel, the manager (only when he saw them did he realize they were black patrons) informed the Robesons and Brown their reservations would not be honored. An argument ensued and Essie, incensed, contacted Pond and demanded that he plead their case. Grudgingly, the hotel proprietor backed down and gave the Robesons and Brown their rooms, provided they agreed to stay on the first floor and use the side stairs rather than the main elevator. "The boys," Essie said, "were furious." To make matters worse, a short while later they discovered that the organization that had booked the concert, the Booker T. Washington Social and Community Center, was in fact "a little colored lodging house for the blind, with about twenty inmates," and that to accommodate this meager population Pond had leased the Milwaukee Auditorium, "a huge arena for the horse and auto shows and athletic games [that] holds 10,000 people. Those poor ignorant people," Essie said with ill-disguised disdain, "hadn't advertised and only our friends (most white) made up the audience." Again Robeson rose to the occasion and "sang very beautifully."[11] But by mid-February even the indefatigable Essie was discouraged and in letters to friends ("It's a hell of a life") made little attempt to conceal her feelings.[12]

After a hiatus of nearly two months with no engagements, the trio arrived at Boston's Back Bay Station early on a cold, sleety March morning for a concert at

Symphony Hall. Robeson was sick with a heavy cold, and the three disembarked from the frigid train "worried, weary, and depressed." They had breakfast at the station and then began the search, by cab, for lodging but were refused in hotel after hotel. "This had a most depressing effect on them [Paul and Larry], and as [we] drove about . . . Paul's cold grew worse." Essie decided to "take a chance" and asked the taxi driver to take them "to the finest hotel in town, the Copley Plaza." There, finally, they were "received and with every courtesy."[13]

By the time of the concert Robeson's throat was so sore and raw that he had decided to cancel the performance. Larry Brown, who thought of Boston as his hometown, pleaded with Robeson to try at least a song or two before calling the concert off. Robeson agreed but, as Essie recalled, was "so frightened that he walked on the stage in a trance." Paul's first instincts had been correct. "He never sang so badly in his life," Essie wrote sadly. "His rich, lovely voice was tight and hard and unrecognizable." Disheartened and embarrassed, Robeson left the stage vowing he would never sing in concert again. Boston reviewers proved more tolerant of a performance obviously hampered by a sore throat than Robeson. The *Transcript* noted "imperfections": a "baritone of a not large range," with "none of that magic or silver of Hayes' voice," by contrast "almost harsh at its lower edges," but considered this of "minor consequence" in comparison with Robeson's exquisite renditions of "Steal Away" and "Water Boy" and the "intuitive and finished accompaniment of Lawrence Brown." Nonetheless, Robeson remained adamant and canceled his two remaining New York concerts.[14]

When the "tour" (in fact, a sporadic series of concerts) ended in the spring, Paul, Larry, and Essie breathed a collective sigh of relief. With Pond taking a 45 percent commission and the rest divided equally among the three, they made little money. The ordeal left them all unsettled and worried, especially Robeson, who was more aware than ever of the fragility of his voice. Stories abound of Essie protectively "bundling the boys up" and fretting over drafts and open windows while Robeson looked on, seemingly unconcerned with such details. But sculptor Antonio Salemme, who spent a good deal of time with Paul, said that when Essie was not there to take care of things, Robeson worried as much as, if not more than, she about the dreaded cold. "The incongruity of a man of Paul's size being frightened of drafts amused me," Salemme said. "There he was, this giant, standing nude with his arms lifted and stretched out in front of him, glancing around nervously at an open window, complaining that the studio was drafty."[15]

But Robeson knew he could not risk harming his voice. His first phonograph recordings, four double-sided records released simultaneously late in 1925 in the United States and England, had sold 50,000 copies within four months and earned Robeson more than $1,100. The tour had convinced him that he must protect his voice and that this involved more than avoiding drafts. He needed voice training — someone to teach him how to take care of and strengthen his voice, do warm-up exercises, and use his diaphragm properly. He wanted someone who would not "touch his voice as such" but would "just show me how to use my voice without ruining it." With limited financial resources and time (Robeson was scheduled to begin rehearsals for a play in the fall), Essie sought the assistance of someone she knew personally, Teresa Armitage, an accomplished voice specialist and singing teacher Essie had met while in high school.[16]

What good, if any, this limited coaching did is debatable. Reginald Boardman, Roland Hayes's accompanist after 1938, heard Robeson at his 1926 Boston concert and later observed that as far as voice training was concerned there was not much Robeson could learn in two months. "His teacher might have been able to teach him how not to strain his voice while retaining his own style, but that kind of training takes time," Boardman said emphatically. "He may have been overenthusiastic both with his program and encores and thus pushed himself and strained his voice, and a good teacher could have helped him learn to pace himself, but never in such a short period of time. It takes years to learn that kind of pace. Years, not months."[17]

Essie, in the meantime, had additional concerns. Assuming responsibility for keeping "the boys'" spirits up and taking care of all the "dirty work" — scheduling, buying train tickets, arranging accommodations, collecting fees — had taken its toll. "When Paul first finished his tour, I was simply dead beat," Essie confided to Carlo and Fania in July. "Both of you know how I try to make the boys comfortable, look after everything; literally singing with them (silently) in the concerts. So I was tired."[18]

Once home, Essie looked at herself and decided change was in order. "As soon as I got my breath I turned Paul out into the green pastures of Harlem and the Village to romp and relax. He's doing it and it's doing him untold good. He's lost all his tension and is just the merry graduate sweet Baby he used to be. I sat down and took stock of myself. I found my color was bad, too fat, sluggish and generally uninteresting. So Paul being disposed of, I decided to spend the summer on myself. First I went on a strict diet and spent the time sewing. Lost a lot of weight. Joined dancing classes. By September, when Baby is a star, I shall be a star's wife. . . . I haven't had time to pay attention to myself for four years and I find I need it badly."[19]

Whether she let Paul loose or Paul simply went without her permission is a matter of conjecture. Dropping the weight and making herself over failed to allay Essie's insecurities. She was thirty years old, aging faster than Paul, and again frightened that he was moving away from her. For two weeks in May, on the heels of a visit from Paul's brother Ben, she and Paul argued steadily, ostensibly about money (specifically, seventy-five dollars Robeson had lent to a friend without Essie's permission). The disagreement was heated (friends confirm that Paul and Essie both had hot tempers and quick tongues), protracted, and serious. Essie ordered twin beds, and Paul stayed out nights drinking and partying. Finally, in the summer, they reconciled, at which time, according to Essie, she brought up the subject of having a baby. Robeson's reaction, reportedly, was a firm no. "You know you're not strong enough. I'll never forgive you if you ruin what is left of your health for a baby . . . you're more than enough. I'm perfectly satisfied. I say, NO."[20]

Robeson may well have, as Essie claims, couched his refusal in "I'm doing this for your own good" protestations. In any event, neither broached the real issue of a marriage in trouble, as apparent to Essie as it was to Paul's friends in the Village. It was common knowledge that Robeson was seeing other women. He talked with friends about his unhappiness and frustration, occasionally even intimating he was considering divorce. Whether or not the talk was serious, Robeson was restless and had no intention of tightening the marital knot with a baby. Securing the marital truss, however, was precisely what Essie had in mind ("I'll take a chance . . . and I may end up with two Pauls"), and in time, owing no doubt to their mutual reluctance to talk honestly, she wore Paul down and became pregnant with or without his consent.[21]

Robeson badly needed a professional victory and hoped to get his footing back with a new theatrical production, *Black Boy,* due to open in the fall. One wonders if he read the script carefully, or at all, before accepting the role. Hopelessly melodramatic and hackneyed, *Black Boy* recounts a humble black man's dream of winning the world heavyweight championship and with it wealth, power, and, the final plum, the love of a white woman. The protagonist, a black vagrant goaded into challenging the prizefighting favorite, succeeds and within two years wins the title. The similarities to the life of Jack Johnson are unmistakable but, unlike Johnson, Black Boy (the character is never given a real name) succumbs easily and quickly to his "rightful" fate. The black boxer follows the stereotypical path; booze and the high life undo him and a double-crossing manager hastens the fall. He loses the big fight because he is drunk and retreats into utter despair when he discovers that his "little white missy" (Irene) is not white but a "nigger" like him. The play closes with the champion reduced to his former state, a vagrant with his harmonica, facing grubstakes and the open road.

The script forced Robeson to swallow a host of indignities. It called for him to sing a spiritual while shining the shoes of his manager's mistress, Irene; to say lines like "no good nevah comes ov niggahs fightin' white men"; and to follow such stage directions as "your eyes dance, you begin to strut and feel your muscles — an animal-like grin comes over your face." Could it have cost Robeson less emotionally to play this role than it did to appear in his high school minstrel show? Was *Black Boy* any less of a caricature?

Perhaps Robeson had relied on the authors' (rather questionable) credentials: Jim Tully, despite his unorthodox background, had already written one play (*Outsider Looking In*), and Frank Dazey, a Harvard graduate and motion picture writer, were coauthors of the play *Peter Weston*. Or he may have pragmatically accepted that white audiences could be counted on to patronize yet another version of the tragic downfall of a big black prizefighter. In either case, Robeson felt he had little choice; he had no other offers and as he told reporter Percy Stone, "he could not live without working." He had tried other avenues. At the urging of Walter White, he applied early in 1927 to the Juilliard Foundation for a grant to study and interpret Negro spirituals but, despite White's rave recommendation, did not get the fellowship.[22]

In an effort to prevent snags or, worse yet, a replay of the *All God's Chillun* controversy, producers Horace Liveright and Donald Friede elected to cast a light-colored black actress opposite Robeson in the role of Irene, rather than the white woman called for in the script. The search for an experienced actress of the proper shade proved almost impossible, as black actresses typically confronted the same difficulties getting experience on the legitimate stage as their male counterparts. Even Carl Van Vechten, one of Liveright's many talent scouts, met with little success. In the end, Friede and Liveright settled for a high-yellow ingenue, a dancer with virtually no stage experience, twenty-two-year-old Fredi Washington.[23] Thus, in their cautious tiptoeing around white sensibilities, Friede and Liveright had placed on Robeson primary responsibility for carrying the show. Indeed, Liveright and Friede saw Robeson as their ace in the hole, and almost immediately after they announced that Robeson would play the lead, interest in the play picked up. "It was obvious that this huge athlete's body would strip well on the stage," said Friede, "and his resonant and beautiful voice could not help but add meaning to his lines."[24]

Despite their business savvy, Liveright and Friede had little experience working with black actors and were caught off guard when within days the inevitable "incident" occurred. To celebrate the contract arrangements they invited the Robesons to lunch. Liveright gave little thought to where they would dine and, when warned by Friede that they might run into a problem, brushed aside his concerns. Friede, however, insisted that they call ahead. "And I was glad I had; not only did that speakeasy inform us that they would be unable to serve us if we came with the Robesons, but we got the same answer from every restaurant and speakeasy we called. Even the Algonquin asked if we would mind eating in a private dining room they would be happy to put at our disposal." Liveright was furious, but the lunch problem still had not been solved, and the Robesons were due to arrive momentarily. Finally, Friede called home and arranged to have lunch there, but not without first double-checking. "What if our colored cook should object to serving the Robesons? That would be the final calamity. I called her and put the question to her point blank. She laughed aloud at my doubts and assured me that nothing would make her feel prouder. And she magically turned out a magnificent lunch on less than an hour's notice."[25]

The two producers ran into similar problems scheduling the play's trial runs. Robeson needed lodging and, as Liveright and Friede discovered, virtually every decision had to take race into consideration. In the end, *Black Boy* opened in Mamaroneck, New York, primarily because Friede had a large summer home nearby where Robeson could stay. "Even then," Friede remembered, "I had to shut my eyes to what our ultra-conservative neighbors would think about our house guests."[26]

After testing its wings in mid-September, first in Mamaroneck and then in Stamford and Hartford, Connecticut, *Black Boy* opened on October 6 at New York's Comedy Theater. Robeson devotees Carl Van Vechten and Fania Marinoff, Mary Blair, and Jimmy Light were on hand as well as other celebrities including Dorothy Peterson, Judith Anderson, Lee Schubert, David Wallace, Fannie Hurst, Cyril Hume, and Winthrop Chandler. Despite the opening-night fanfare, however, the play's reception was lackluster. Tully, described by the *Morning Telegraph*'s Burton Davis as the new "Jack London . . . spokesman for the hobo," had relied on coarse language to add realism to his portrayal of the prizefighting world, but, in the end, what the script showed most vividly was its authors' ineptness with dramatic form. Critics complained about the blatant attempt to milk white fascination with the seamy side of black life and the authors' failure to penetrate beneath a showy, melodramatic surface. The *Brooklyn Daily Eagle*'s Arthur Pollock charged it had "plot a plenty, but . . . so badly pieced together . . . as to leave many small but essential truths untold," and *New York Evening World*'s E. W. Osborn dismissed it as "tawdry." Burns Mantle predicted it would attract two audiences, "One . . . interested in drama slumming. One . . . interested in Paul Robeson, with neither . . . entirely pleased." Some blamed the play's failure on Fredi Washington's "mechanical" acting.[27] Others, like the *Mercury*'s George Jean Nathan, pointed the finger at the producers for catering to a white "audience [that] would resent the spectacle of a big Negro . . . indulging in amorous contacts with a white woman." Thus, said Nathan, "the script was duly altered [and] the whole point of the play was thus got rid of at one swoop."[28]

Most reviewers enjoyed the "radio scene," which featured Major J. Andrew White, an expert in the still novel field of broadcasting (who had himself announced the recent real-life Dempsey-Tunney fight in Philadelphia), reporting the play's fight as Black Boy's girlfriend heard it over her own radio. Casting White, with his easily recognizable voice, proved quite effective as he succeeded in holding theater audiences, as he had in the past held radio listeners, "on the edges of their seats." But it was Robeson whose presence saved the production from total disaster. The script called for him to sing several songs, and most reviewers agreed with Alexander Woollcott that "when Robeson sings . . . the play is just pushed to one side." "No play which has Paul Robeson can be unexciting," said *Life*'s Robert Benchley. "His rich and becoming personality swings you along whether you meant to be swung or not."[29]

Black Boy's audiences were almost totally white, but the play sparked debate among blacks nonetheless. The *Messenger*'s Theophilus Lewis and George Schuyler berated its demeaning portrait of the black man as a "lovely ignorant perverse child surrounded and victimized by scheming whites of little morals or character." Virtually all critics objected to the play's language, but the repeated use of the word "nigger" in particular "nauseated" black reviewers.[30]

With the furor over Carl Van Vechten's recently published *Nigger Heaven* still fresh (even the "artistically enlightened" Du Bois, Walter White, and Alain Locke found Van Vechten's use of the word "nigger" offensive), black reaction to the use of the detested word in yet another widely publicized work is not surprising. Robeson's contemporary, Langston Hughes, summed up the feeling of many when he said that for blacks of high and low station alike the word "nigger," "like a red flag to a bull," evoked "all the bitter years of insult and struggle in America."[31]

Robeson, however, evidenced little concern over *Black Boy*'s language. Nor had he been among Van Vechten's many detractors. In fact, he sent Van Vechten a telegram in July congratulating him on the publication of *Nigger Heaven* ("Amazing in its absolute understanding and deep sympathy") and publicly reiterated these sentiments in an October 1926 press interview. Neither was Robeson particularly shocked, as were so many others, by the controversial black journal *Fire!* published in late 1926. Its creators, Harlem's radical literati — Langston Hughes, Zora Neale Hurston, Wallace Thurman, John P. Davis, and Bruce Nugent — all came under attack from the black literary establishment. Their intention had been to "burn up a lot of old, dead conventional Negro–white ideas of the past," but most blacks found pieces like Wallace Thurman's story of a sixteen-year-old prostitute and Bruce Nugent's impressionistic rendering of androgyny, drugs, and creative decadence ("Smoke, Lilies, and Jade") disgusting.[32] Nugent said that once *Fire!* was published, a segment of Harlem's middle-class social set deliberately snubbed the journal's contributors. "Thurman and I were in Craig's one night when some of this set walked in and past us with their noses high in the air. Robeson was with them, at the rear of the party, and as they filed past he looked at us, grinned, and winked, almost as if to say, 'Aren't my friends silly?'"[33] Just the same, whatever he thought privately, Robeson played it safe and kept his opinions to himself. He was not about to court disapproval by brashly identifying himself with any radical (conservative or liberal) group.

Regardless of where one stood on the language debate, the fact was that *Black Boy* bored whites and infuriated blacks. Incredibly, starring in it did little to damage Robeson's reputation. White critics praised him and black reviewers, caught in the dilemma of wanting to support on principle any black actor in a lead role on the legitimate stage, did the same. Thus Theophilus Lewis, George Schuyler, Joel Rogers, Floyd Calvin, and Romeo Dougherty wrung their hands in dismay over the dearth of quality plays and the absence of viable black theater but, as far as Robeson was concerned, agreed that "If it weren't for Paul, there wouldn't be any show."[34]

When *Black Boy* closed after only three weeks, Robeson announced to the press that he was through with theater. He claimed that it was not the play's early closing that bothered him. "I have just gotten to where I can command a real salary," he said with no small show of bravado, and "I can make good with my singing." In truth, *Black Boy*'s aborted run left Robeson unexpectedly out of work with no way to make up for the money he had counted on earning. Both Salemme and Patti Light remembered how disappointed Robeson was when the play closed. Paul was experiencing what the "old-timers" knew only too well: there were very few roles out there even for the most talented blacks.[35]

Essie, typically quick to respond in a crisis, hurriedly put together a twelve-page, single-spaced brochure, crammed with photos and rave press reviews (over fifty) of Robeson and Brown's 1924–26 concerts and sent the leaflet to music halls, theaters, colleges, black churches and organizations from New York to Kansas. (The Robesons apparently had a falling out with Pond over *Black Boy,* perhaps concluding, as did most blacks under white management, that despite the exorbitant rates he charged, Pond failed to address the special problems of a black performer.) Essie's brochure billed Robeson and Brown equally, stressed their "IMMEDIATE" availability, and included instructions to contact "Manager Eslanda Goode" for further information.[36]

Robeson's comeback concert took place on November 25 at New York City's Comedy Theater. Robeson needed to put the *Black Boy* failure behind him and connect himself with a success as quickly as possible, and he hoped that a solid New York performance would set the tone for a better year in 1927. Complimentary tickets were sent to those drama critics who a month before had panned *Black Boy* but written favorably of Robeson's singing.[37]

Robeson and Brown easily won over their audience "of hypercritical whites" on the lower floor (blacks were confined to the balcony), "a good many figures well known in the arts . . . many of them hearing the songs for the first time." The *Morning Telegraph*'s Burton Davis commented in detail on each of the four groups of songs. He applauded the humor in the first group, which included Brown's arrangement of "Ezekiel Saw de Wheel," noting that "Robeson was often interrupted by irrepressible gusts of laughter particularly during the gyration of the big wheel that runs by faith while 'the little wheel runs by the grace of God.'" Of the second group consisting of Negro folk songs, Davis commended the "haunting melody and the bitter humor and braggadocio of 'Water Boy,' [which] brought the concert to a halt, until Robeson promised to sing it again later [and] 'Scandalize My Name' [which] sent the Yankees into gales of laughter and the Southerners among us into reminiscent chuckles." In the third section Robeson and Brown returned to spirituals, and the concert closed with four of Brown's arrangements, including "Joshua Fit de Battle ob Jericho," which Davis described as "the majestic, exulting, comic tour de force." The opening New York performance was, as Robeson had hoped, a smashing success. He and Brown left their audience clamoring for more, in fact, steadfastly refusing to budge until they had been treated to two additional songs.[38]

From New York the trio traveled to Worcester, Massachusetts, an industrial city made up of Yankees, Irish, and newly arrived East European immigrants, but very few blacks. Initially the concert looked promising; like their New York debut it had been sold out. But, as the *Worcester Telegram*'s "favorable" review illustrated, outside New York, in mainstream America, even laudatory reviews were replete with racist stereotypes. "Two colored singers descended on Worcester yesterday, as typical of two distinct types of their race today as if they had been picked out of the pages of *Uncle Tom's Cabin,*" the Worcester review began. Touching briefly on the performance ("poignantly beautiful and richly musical"), the reviewer quickly returned to his opening theme. "Robeson, the taller and stockier of the two, looks the personification of sadness. He does not quite understand, but yet acknowledges with a splendid and aloof dignity. He has poise, reserve, and restraint. His shorter accompanist has the regular expressive face of the pickaninny of the movies who senses something wrong with his lot, especially when he steals a watermelon, and is caught, but forgets it immediately as soon as the pain of punishment is over."[39] Publicly Robeson said nothing about such reviews (How could he? They applauded his singing, and certainly he was "grateful" for that), but one can well imagine his confusion, frustration, shame, and anger at finding himself forced to "accept" such demeaning commentary in exchange for praise.

Although Essie had done her best on short notice, her mailings had elicited meager responses, with the majority of bookings limited to black churches and organizations and small local groups. The January–April portion of the tour, in particular, included many out-of-the-way and geographically disparate engagements. In large cities Robeson could rely on receiving his $1,000 guaranteed payment, but in the smaller towns and particularly at concerts sponsored by local black organizations he had no such assurance. This meant that someone (in most cases Essie) had to haggle with sponsors to keep Robeson and Brown's fee as high as possible and then make sure the money was collected. (In later, more prosperous years when Robeson was managed by Robert Rockmore and booked by Fred Schang, Rockmore would insist Schang not accept bookings with black civic organizations, fraternities, and churches, as some could not honor their financial commitments and those that did often persuaded Robeson to make a "donation" and give most of the money back. Rockmore made Schang promise that he would never reveal this to Robeson as he would most likely object to the idea.)[40]

As Paul, Essie, and Larry made their way from Worcester across the country to Wichita, Kansas, and Kansas City, Missouri, their troubles only got worse. Robeson's refusal of southern bookings, initiated specifically to sidestep the possibility of real trouble from the Klan stemming from his 1924 appearance in *All God's Chillun* (also because Larry Brown absolutely refused to go "back to that hell-hole"), did not spare him the humiliation of having to appear before segregated audiences. In racially segregated midwestern cities with large black populations the problem was particularly distressing. In Wichita, Robeson's upcoming concert (held at the local high school, sponsored by the Committee on Interracial Goodwill, Wichita Council of Churches) was announced in the white press with the reassuring note that "sections of the auditorium will be reserved for colored people. . . . The white and colored people will not be seated together."[41] Robeson, as Roland Hayes had before him, swallowed the insult and performed. (As for accommodations, they never even tried to secure hotel room in Wichita, but stayed instead at the home of Dr. and Mrs. F. O. Miller on 1025 North Avenue.)[42]

In Kansas City they faced a different problem. Roy Wilkins, at that time editor of the black weekly, the *Kansas City Call,* and a member of a committee formed specifically to bring Negro artists to the area, booked the concert and was thrilled that Robeson had "agreed to come to us for $750," as the group reportedly had few financial resources and would have to depend on ticket sales to pay the fee. The white newspaper, the *Kansas City Star,* carried notices of the concert (to be held at Grand Avenue Temple, a white church that hosted many of the city's cultural affairs) but refused to include Robeson's photograph either in the news item or in the advertisement.[43] Nonetheless, the seating for the Kansas City concert was integrated. Wilkins remembered local whites causing "quite a hullabaloo about the seating arrangements, [but] being a Negro committee promoting a Negro artist and appealing primarily to the Negro community for support, we could not (just from a business standpoint, aside from all the moral values involved) — we could not agree to any segregation." As a result ticket sales lagged as a fair number of white persons stayed home because the open seating arrangements might force them to sit beside a black person. The committee did make Robeson's fee (Wilkins recalled "anxiously . . . count[ing] the box office cash, [trying] to meet his stipulation that he . . . be paid his full guarantee before he went out on the stage"), but just barely. Reviews in both the *Kansas City Times* and the *Kansas City Journal* abounded with accolades, but the praise was undermined considerably by the omnipresent lower-cased "negro" set beside the conspicuously capitalized "Caucasian" and by a steady stream of comments implying that Robeson, like all blacks, sang "naturally." "His songs and his singing are unencumbered by any 'arty' filigree. . . . He simply sings, as one singing teacher says, 'As God intended him to.'"[44]

The most distressing problem Robeson faced in Kansas City, however, came not from whites but from blacks who were offended and humiliated by his exclusive use of black music. Among those voicing the most articulate protest was one Mrs. L. J. Bacote, a local music teacher who had studied at both the New England and the Kansas City conservatories of music. The *Call* featured her lengthy critique in a front-page article headlined "Paul Robeson Not an Artist, and Recital of Negro Songs Here Was 'Humiliating' Says Mrs. Bacote." "Since he [Robeson] was advertised as a high salaried artist," Bacote said, "I expected to hear some classics. A varied vocal program should include the 18th century bel canto, or grand opera — arias from oratorios — a chance for linguistic demonstration whether in Italian, German, Spanish, French, or Russian — something other than the native tongue. . . . There should be representative concert numbers involving all kinds of dazzling technique, high class ballads and spirituals." Robeson's "apparent stage timidity," his obvious lack of "musical education" and contact with "teachers in voice culture," the words of some of the songs, and Lawrence Brown's "style of performance at the keyboard" all were cause for profound embarrassment for Bacote, especially as "those of the Caucasian race were there [at the concert] in large numbers." By way of example, she cited a selection "containing words 'about the shooting of dice'" and Brown's "stage antics" (his worst, keeping "time with the pedal"), which elicited "grins of sarcasm" from whites in the audience. "We [Negroes] do not wish to be confused as clowns for the other race."[45]

However narrow-minded Bacote's objections to the Robeson–Brown performance might appear in retrospect, her thinking reflected the views of a substantial number of educated blacks who were convinced that uplift depended on the race proving itself intellectually and aesthetically the equal of whites. Like the vast majority of whites, Bacote believed that, having been denied access to learning and art, her race had no culture of its own and would improve its status only after educating itself and acquiring (white) culture. Small wonder Robeson's concert enraged her. Despite their formal attire, Robeson and Larry Brown had demonstrated ignorance of the worst kind in posing as real musicians when, in fact, all they knew how to do was to sing songs composed by "ignorant" blacks. As Bacote saw it, Roland Hayes's performances were significant; Robeson's were an embarrassment.

The Kansas City music teacher's attack did not go unchallenged. The following week the *Call* printed a number of responses, all lauding Robeson. "Let me say here if an 'extensive musical training' is going to make the Negro ashamed of the songs of their fathers; songs whose soothing melodies buoyed up the sinking souls of the oppressed; songs that placed in their hearts the hope of a better day and lifted from their shoulders the drudgery of slavery; songs upon which our race had been built — if such must be the result — God grant that the Negro may be denied the privilege of an 'extensive musical training,' and just sing for me the soul-inspiring Negro spirituals as they were sung by our fathers — and by Paul Robeson." Another reader observed that even "if Mrs. Bacote was humiliated," no one else seemed to be; in fact, "everyone . . . went away pleased and could have heard more music if he [Robeson] had given it."[46]

After the Kansas City concert Robeson and Brown had two months with no engagements before they resumed touring. Unfortunately, the second half of the year looked no more promising than the first, with bookings again unevenly spaced and sponsored largely by small local groups (for example, the Rochester, New York, Women's City Club) and organizations with which Paul had special ties (the Middlesex County YMCA, New Brunswick) or conducted as benefits for small black churches (St. James African Methodist Episcopal Zion Church, Ithaca, New York; Paul's father's church, Witherspoon Street Presbyterian in Princeton; and the Flemington [New Jersey] Baptist Church). In short, they would perhaps tide Robeson and Brown over, but they were hardly breaking new ground. A March 12 concert in Columbus, Ohio, for example, sponsored by the Charles Block American Legion Post (colored), drew a disappointingly small audience of 400 with "only a sparse gathering of white people." To make matters worse, the Robeson–Brown recital had been planned as an opener to the evening's main event: the post's formal presentation of a silver cup to a local AMEZ pastor who had won a Legion-run church attendance contest. Still, as the *Columbus Citizen* was quick to note the following day, Robeson and Brown gave an impressive performance and the audience, small as it was, roared its approval, demanding no less than six encores.[47]

In May the tour finally and mercifully ended, with Robeson, Essie, and Larry, despite their public optimism, privately profoundly discouraged. Continually bucking the onslaught of white stereotypes proved wearing, and again they had little money to show for their efforts. (The press, however, painted a different picture. In February 1927 *Variety* listed Robeson as one of twenty-one top-paid U.S. performing artists, and a September 1927 article in the *New York Herald Tribune* reported that Robeson along with several other black performing artists planned to purchase land in Bar Harbor, Maine, and set up a Negro colony there. The second story had no basis in reality. Blacks named as prospective buyers denied having ever heard of the proposition or having ever taken it seriously, and Robeson quickly disassociated himself from the rumored project.)[48]

Throughout the tour whenever he spoke with reporters Robeson had refuted the one-dimensional view of spirituals as sad, gloomy songs, pointing out that many of them are "so bright a vein that they could be syncopated" and that "Negro music is . . . full of hope, faith, courage, and exultation."[49] But neither Robeson's performing nor his explanations appeared to have altered mainstream American stereotypes. As late as October reviewers noted "the strain of almost blind hopelessness" present in these "delicate and pathetic melodies."[50] If Paul was laying the groundwork for some future new appreciation of black arts and culture, he had little evidence of it on this tour.

To confuse matters further, in the spring Essie told Paul news that threw his domestic life into chaos: she was pregnant. Paul had not changed his mind about not wanting to become a father. According to Essie, he said little when she told him the news. One can only guess at his feelings. At best the year had taught Robeson painful lessons regarding the precariousness of touring; at worst it had led him to doubt himself and his art. Shaky in the marriage to begin with and unsure of himself professionally, Robeson now found himself shackled with additional responsibilities: a pregnant wife and soon a small child entrusted to his care.

Robeson responded by focusing his energy on the more solvable problem: earning money and developing himself as an artist. He agreed to appear in an American black revue, to be produced by Caroline Dudley Reagan, a rich white socialite originally from Chicago, the following year and received an immediate $500 advance, enough to pay for his own and Larry Brown's passage to Paris where they would begin a European concert tour managed by the white impresario Walter K. Varney. By the time the tour began Essie was almost eight months pregnant, but Paul sailed for Europe nonetheless, leaving his wife in the care of her mother in New York. Typically, once he got away from Essie, Paul recovered warm feelings for her. Aboard the S.S. *Majestic* Paul wrote to her, effusively pledging his love: "So hard for me to leave you sweet. Seems as tho you are me. . . . Of course I love you more than I love my very self."[51]

The scene of the earlier triumphs of Roland Hayes and host to the sensational Josephine Baker, Paris was hardly unacquainted with *le musique nègre,* but even this seasoned audience viewed a concert made up entirely of black spirituals as, at best, a novelty. Still, at their opening concert at Paris's Salle Gaveau, Robeson and Brown got the recognition they had hoped for in America. Robeson, plagued with a cold and bedridden for four days before the concert, recovered on time and performed well. Their first song, "Wade in de Water," "drew . . . a hearty round of applause"; by the time Robeson and Brown sang "Go Down, Moses" the "applause was deafening"; and "Joshua Fit de Battle ob Jericho," the last number on the program, "brought down the house."[52]

The *New York Sun*'s Thurston McCauley was especially struck by the improvement in Robeson's voice: "His range has increased amazingly . . . his concert engagements have added greatly to his poise and ease in obtaining the desired effect without loss of dramatic feeling and expression. . . . [He] is the present reigning favorite of the Parisian amusement world." And judging from the array of European and American celebrities who crowded the lobby before the concert — James Joyce, Michael Strange, Ludwig Lewisohn, Sylvia Beach, Howard Sturgis, Blair Fairchilds, Mrs. Cole Porter, Roland Hayes, Howard Jordan, and Alberta Hunter — McCauley had not exaggerated. The concert drew a crowd of 1,700, with standing room filled and 500 people turned away at the doors. Immediate plans were made for a second concert to accommodate those unable to get into the first. Noted black historian, observer of the arts, and critic-at-large Joel A. Rogers, also in attendance, sent news of Robeson's Paris success back home to the black weeklies, making particular note of the many celebrities in attendance.[53]

While Robeson enjoyed the Parisian accolades, back home in New York City, unceremoniously and almost unnoticed, on November 2 Essie gave birth to their son, Paul Jr., at Long Island College Hospital in Brooklyn. Paul, in the meantime, wrote to Essie, assuming because he had not heard differently that all had gone well (in fact, she had a difficult time and secondary complications), said little about the baby, but was lavishly affectionate to her. "Nothing matters but you . . . and I'm so anxious to show you a new love — just like the old one but so much sweeter — kinder — more love — more considerate."[54] He picked her brain as to what course he should pursue professionally and complained that Europe, for all its acclaim and prestige, did not pay the bills. "They come and rave over our program . . . and they feel well — if he can sing so grandly (like Chaliapin) I should do the things he does — Boris Godunov etc. They say I'm almost wasted upon simple music—no matter how much they enjoy it. So I can't make money doing what I am—I'm sure. . . . But we must have money." Possibly work in Europe should be confined to only a few months per year with the rest of the time spent in America, Paul suggested, promising Essie that from now on he would "turn things over" to her and "trust in you and your judgment wholly."[55]

But while Paul mused by letter with Essie about his professional prospects, her physical condition deteriorated. Six weeks after giving birth she developed a breast abscess and a severe case of phlebitis. Finally, an exasperated Mrs. Goode took matters into her own hands and informed Paul of Essie's condition. Robeson booked passage immediately and was in New York by the day after Christmas. Essie recovered slowly and was not even allowed out of bed until the end of January. But she had what she wanted: a baby, her second Paul.[56]

Since the early twenties Paul had enjoyed the spotlight, while Essie, in the background, worked an uninspiring job and took care of the mundane practical tasks that made it possible for him to perform. For Robeson it had been important that he not appear too ambitious, too hungry for success. Essie was a different matter. She arranged, argued, haggled, looked for and capitalized on opportunities, all in Paul's behalf. But in this instance Essie wanted something for herself and was determined to have it with or without Paul's consent. Whether Robeson was angry with Essie or just unable to face his new responsibilities, he chose not to make the birth of his first child a priority in his life. Essie had her baby, but for Paul family considerations, for some time to come, would play second to career commitments.

8

Show Boat

1928-1929

Robeson returned to America, worried. Paris had received him warmly, but once home he faced a host of new troubles: a new baby, a sick wife, and few professional prospects. He had agreed to perform the lead role in a black revue but now was having second thoughts about it. He and Essie had seen Caroline Dudley Reagan's *La Revue Nègre,* in Paris in 1925 and were not impressed. Essie found it offensive. "We saw the revue twice — rotten — that is between us," she wrote to Carl Van Vechten. "I hate to run down our own stuff, but the only good thing is Larry [Louis] Douglas. . . . The American scene is splendid and all fine until Josephine [Baker, who created a sensation in Paris in the role] does this ridiculous, vulgar, and totally uncalled for wiggling. . . . They [Parisians] are crazy about it. . . . They seem to adore the music and the color and the crudity of it all."[1] The earthiness and unapologetic sensuality of Josephine Baker — bare-breasted with a satin bikini covered by pink feathers, her hips, stomach, and rump gyrating so violently that even Parisians were shocked — embarrassed Essie, as it did many other "respectable" blacks, among them the "dean of black musicians," violinist, composer, and conductor Will Marion Cook, who despised the production, calling it and other black revues betrayals of black culture, "all rank and weak imitations of sordid unfunny white plays." Cook blamed the American socialite producer, Caroline Dudley Reagan, for "this Paris abortion." As he saw it, she simply knew nothing about genuine black culture.[2]

Robeson, while not personally offended, had reservations: he wanted to be known as an artist, *not* a dance hall entertainer, and he worried about his reputation should he involve himself in a similar revue. But with Essie still recuperating from the birth of Paul Jr. and an American concert tour out of the question as Larry Brown was still in England, financial considerations loomed large. Reagan, anxious to reassure Robeson, had promised an "intimate revue," one that reflected black values rather than prurient white interests. In the end, Reagan and her lucrative salary offer ($500 a week once the show began, and 5 percent of the gross from $10,000 to $20,000, and 10 percent over that) proved impossible to resist.[3]

In January 1928 Robeson concluded final contract arrangements for the Reagan revue. Still, he had a six-month interim with no work. In March he was contacted about replacing Jack Carter in the part of Crown in DuBose and Dorothy Heyward's hit musical, *Porgy,* at a salary of $500 a week. Robeson accepted the offer immediately, despite the beating the black press had given the production. An episodic musical set in Cat Fish Row, Charleston, South Carolina's black fishing tenement, *Porgy* presented a vivid but stereotypical portrait of the area's multifarious poor black residents, according to the *New York Times,* "an ebony carnival of crap-shooting, murders, blaring picnics, comedy bits, passionate spirituals, a hurricane." The musical's plot centers on Porgy (Frank Wilson), a crippled beggar who gets around in a tiny goat cart, and his romance with the drug-addicted Bess (Evelyn Ellis). Crown, the role Robeson would fill, is a murderer and Porgy's cruel nemesis. Physically Robeson fit the part (a man "dat Gawd start to make into a bull den change He min") perfectly and so impressed producers with his singing that they hurriedly reinstated several of the musical numbers omitted when Carter played the role.[4] Working with a talented cast, Robeson was once again in the limelight, and after playing the role only a short while he was offered another part, the role of Joe in the London production of the Jerome Kern–Oscar Hammerstein classic, *Show Boat.*

Paul was thrilled, accepted immediately, and rushed home to tell Essie. Although *Show Boat* had scored a surprise hit in an otherwise lackluster season in New York the previous year, grossing $50,000 a week in an impressive run of 572 performances, neither Paul nor Essie expected a similar reception in England. As they had learned in 1925 with the London production of *The Emperor Jones,* shows that did well in America often fared poorly in England. Still, they felt confident *Show Boat* would at least tide them over until the Reagan revue in the fall.

Robeson left for London at the beginning of April. Essie, whose health had improved considerably, planned to leave Paul Jr. in the care of Grandmother Goode and join Paul in May. Concerned that he had neglected Larry Brown who had remained in London, Paul wrote to him from the ship to apologize for not having contacted him sooner (although Essie had) and to reassure him that *Show Boat* would eventually generate work for both of them. In the meantime, he promised to pay Brown out of his own salary, "which is only fair. . . . My musical career with you is by all odds paramount. . . . I took this job only because it brought me back to my concerts with you. . . . I'm here to take up my work and keep it up no matter what happens."[5]

Rehearsals began in April, with a cast that included the well-established star of light stage productions, Edith Day, as Magnolia, Cedric Hardwicke as Captain Andy, Marie Burke as Julie, Howett Worster as Ravenal, Colin Clive as Steve, Alberta Hunter as Queenie, Paul Robeson as Joe, and an American dance troupe of twelve "high-yellow" blacks. *Show Boat*'s story, based on Edna Ferber's novel, spans a period of forty years and revolves around the lives of the players and workers aboard the *Cotton Blossom,* in particular the romance between Captain Andy's daughter Magnolia and the handsome gambler Gaylord Ravenal. The show boat's leading lady, Julie (a mulatto who has passed for white), leaves suddenly after being accused of having Negro blood and takes along with her the show's leading man (Steve). Life on the *Cotton Blossom* continues as Magnolia and Gaylord assume Julie's and Steve's places in the show. Soon the two fall deeply in love and elope to Chicago. In time Gaylord's gambling sours the marriage, and he deserts Magnolia, leaving her to raise their daughter, Kim, alone. Years later Magnolia applies for a job at a cabaret where Julie, now a drunkard, sings. Julie recognizes her old friend and sacrifices what is left of her own career to help Magnolia start hers. Eventually Captain Andy finds his daughter and persuades her to return with him to the *Cotton Blossom.* And, finally, an aging Gaylord Ravenal also returns to the show boat, where, to his surprise, he is welcomed back by Magnolia.

Although *Show Boat*'s London producers worried how British audiences would respond to the musical's plot, in particular its use of the tragic-mulatto theme, they were determined to retain the show's authentic American flavor. Blues singer and performer Alberta Hunter said that she won the role of Queenie over a "big, fat, white Englishwoman" because Hammerstein "wanted the real thing . . . *Show Boat* didn't want that English jive. *Show Boat* wanted America." Advertisements promoted the musical as "ultra American entertainment," a theatrical extravaganza, bearing the Ziegfeld stamp of speed, opulence, and dazzle, and preproduction publicity promised the largest, most elaborate show ever launched at the Drury Lane Theatre, with a cast of over 160, a full eighteen different scenes, more than 1,000 costumes, and a host of memorable musical numbers.[6] The promotion strategy worked, and patrons began queuing up in front of the box office a full twenty-four hours in advance for the 200 half-crown, two-shilling, unreserved opening night seats.

The Drury Lane Theatre with its huge, graceful porticos was ideally suited for an elaborately staged romantic musical, and the curtain opened to reveal a steamboat inching its way along the Mississippi. Soon the scene shifts to the wharf where Joe, carrying a sack of flour, appears for the first time. Magnolia, suddenly realizing that she has fallen in love with Ravenal, talks with Joe, who suggests that she "ask ol' man river what he thinks." Magnolia exits and Robeson, sitting beside the sack of flour and whittling, sings what will become the most memorable feature of *Show Boat*'s London engagement, "Ol' Man River." In the next scene Queenie, Joe's wife and the show boat's cook, sings "Can't Help Lovin' Dat Man" to Joe while Joe stands with his arm affectionately on her shoulder. Joe does not reappear until the end of the play when, as an old man, he sings "Ol' Man River" once again and then in the finale when he leads the chorus in a reprise of the song.

Described by Queenie as a typically "lazy nigger," Joe does little to advance the plot, but instead functions like a Greek chorus, silently observing and occasionally commenting on the actions of the major characters. Despite the brief amount of time Robeson actually spent on stage, reviewers almost unanimously concurred that he stole the show, and this in a musical whose plot focuses almost entirely on the fate of the separated white lovers. London reviewers, who nearly all panned the production as "dull" and "too long," agreed that Robeson "dominated the show" and his singing aroused "the only enthusiasm . . . of the evening." Edith Day, Cedric Hardwicke, and Marie Burke received applause for their performances, but the plaudits given to Robeson eclipsed them all. "The thing that will be remembered first and last — the thing that held it all together and will be on everybody's lips before many days are over is the song 'Ol' Man River'!" Even the *Times*'s revered James Agate, who judged the play "a piece of story-telling . . . as inept as anything I have ever seen on any stage," praised Robeson and suggested that "half an hour . . . be cut out of the show and filled in by Mr. Robeson with his 'Steal Away,' 'Water Boy,' and other Negro spirituals."[7]

"Ol' Man River" was not a song that Robeson found easy to perform even though, as several sources claim, Jerome Kern wrote it with him in mind. Initially Paul was not even sure he liked it and, as Essie confided to Carl Van Vechten, he "worried about the monotony of it. . . . But he practiced on me for a few days and we worked out a nice variety. The first verse and refrain, full voiced and strong, the second verse and chorus in his nice medium voice. Then later, as the old man, he does it with that lovely soft voice of his that he uses for 'Weepin' Mary' and similar songs."[8]

In fact, Essie vastly understates what Robeson's interpretation added to the song. "Ol' Man River" did represent a departure in its sympathetic portrayal of black workers struggling to survive in a racist and segregated South. But, unlike a true spiritual, the song expressed the emotional tone and reality *whites* most often heard in spirituals — sorrow and a melancholy resignation to suffering. The lyrics do include references to suffering and oppression but these are ripped from their historical context (institutionalized slavery) and further blunted by the repeated suggestion that some unnamed fate is responsible. The implication is that it is the destiny of the black man to suffer.[9]

The jazz critic Nat Hentoff said of Billy Holiday that "to instrumentalists, playing with Lady Day was like jamming after hours among themselves. She moved inside a song the way they did." The biographer Pete Hamill described Frank Sinatra as inhabiting "a song the way a great actor inhabits a role, often bringing his own life into the music." And Robeson himself, giving advice to aspiring singers, cautioned them to "sing songs which you completely understand and in which you completely believe." Before Robeson could sing this song he had to find a way inside it; he had to massage and reshape it so that it stirred something deep inside him and spoke the truth about his experience.[10]

Just before sailing for England, Robeson recorded "Ol' Man River" backed up by Paul Whiteman's orchestra and chorus. In the Whiteman recording Robeson sings "Ol' Man River" without coloring or interpretation. The result is jauntily paced (Jules Bledsoe in the 1927 New York production also sang the song quickly) and light hearted, with the plucking of banjoes figuring large in the background. The differences between the Whiteman recording and those of the London production only a few months later are startling and a dramatic illustration of Robeson's interpretative genius. They are in fact recordings of two totally different songs.

For the London production Robeson slowed the pace and performed the song in an almost ambling manner, his body gestures mirroring his vocal interpretation and giving the effect of the slow but constant flowing of the river about which he sang. To add depth and take advantage of his rich bass, he sang it in E-flat, which meant reaching a bottom low of F rather than the G of Jules Bledsoe. And, finally, he gave special attention to the lyrics. Kern had consciously imitated black folk music, and from the start Robeson treated the song as a folk product, altering its words and emphasis as his view of himself and the world changed. For the 1928 London production the only words he changed were the demeaning "*Niggers* all work on the Mississippi" to "*Darkies* all work on the Mississippi." (In later years Robeson would make more substantive changes to the text until he had totally expunged from it all of its benign resignation and transformed it into a militant statement to fight for full freedom.)[11] But he completely altered the emphasis and direction of the song with his interpretation. What Robeson knew both emotionally and intellectually was that Joe's sufferings were a product of the historical reality of slavery. Sculptor Antonio Salemme once said that Robeson "seethed when he thought of what his father had had to put up with [as a slave]." Robeson reconnected the song with its historical context by lingering over the lines dealing with oppression ("Body all *achin'* an' *racked* wid pain" and "*Bend* your knees / An' *bow* your head, / An' *pull* dat rope / Until you' *dead*") and giving the verbs special emphasis (an emphasis even more apparent in recordings of the song in which Robeson is not accompanied by a chorus). He sang slowly, reverently, and with great feeling the lines about the river Jordan, the only lines in the song suggesting Joe's longing for freedom:

> Let me go 'way from the Mississippi,
> Let me go 'way from de white man boss,
> Show me dat stream called de river Jordan,
> Dat's de ol' stream dat I long to cross.[12]

For those who were willing to hear, Robeson revealed the person beneath Joe's mask, a person who knew where he came from and who longed for freedom. The effect on his almost totally white British audiences was overpowering, as one reviewer put it, "tears spring unbidden." Robeson's interpretation of the song changed the face of the entire musical, transforming it from a *white* production replete with racist stereotypes and built around the overdone theme of the tragic mulatto to a show in which Robeson in the minor part of Joe was the main attraction. He brought such power and dignity to this song that no one who heard him ever forgot the experience. Once he had performed it, "Ol' Man River" would be forever linked with Robeson's name.[13]

"He tied that show up in a knot," Alberta Hunter remembered. "There was something about his voice that was almost alarming." "People went out of their minds about him," said the actor Bernard Sarron (later Unity Theatre stage manager). The song proved so popular that producers had the words written on a cloth curtain that was lowered between scenes, so that audiences could see as well as hear them. Time and again the musical was stopped by demands for yet another chorus from Robeson. "Nothing like this had ever happened in London before," said Sarron. "People came a half dozen times just to hear Robeson," said another observer. "I remember meeting a woman outside of the theater having a cigarette between acts who told me that this was her fourth time seeing the show. She came only to see Paul and went outside and smoked through the rest of the show and then went back to the theater when it was time for Paul to sing again."[14]

Show Boat, the biggest moneymaker to date in the history of the Drury Lane Theatre (the show ran for 350 performances and earned close to $32,000 a week), drew Britain's most prestigious theatergoers, including, in June, the king and queen of England. Alberta Hunter spoke of playing before royalty as a "thrill" that she and the production's twelve chorus girls "would long remember." Not so for Robeson. Like most performers, he had off days, and for that particular performance "Paul got off pitch and never got himself back on," Hunter sadly remembered. "Afterward he cried like a child."[15]

Despite an occasional bad night, however, Robeson triumphed in *Show Boat*, and his popularity among Londoners — the smart Mayfair set, elderly patrons of the theater, the "intelligentsia" of Bloomsbury and Chelsea, and young people from Clapham and Tooting — soared, so much so that theater manager Sir Alfred Butt decided to make arrangements for Paul, accompanied by Brown, to give two special matinee concert performances of some twenty Negro spirituals and folk songs at the theater in July. "Paul and Larry will do their usual four groups with the Drury Lane Orchestra doing a twenty minute interval of really fine music between the first and last two groups," Essie, who had joined Paul, wrote home. "That will stretch the program to its proper length, without overworking the boys. We expect to make some real money on that. Sir Alfred seems terribly keen on Paul and says the show largely depends on him. Everyone seems to like Paul, as usual."[16]

The Drury Lane Theatre was packed to overflowing for the first concert on July 3. The curtain opened to an entirely bare stage except for Larry Brown seated at the grand piano. While the audience waited, Robeson, no longer clad in the stevedore Joe's work clothes but formally dressed in a dark suit, walked with his "curious rolling gait" onto the stage. Leaning back against the piano, Robeson looked at Brown, nodded his head, and began to sing.[17]

With his first song Robeson "took the audience and put it in his pocket . . . and kept it there," Essie recalled. "They stomped, cheered, and applauded all through the program and demanded him to repeat songs and give many encores. It was really thrilling." Concert favorites included Harry T. Burleigh's arrangement of "Deep River," and "Water Boy," "Lil David," "By and By" and "Steal Away." Audiences loved the humor in pieces like "Scandalize My Name," and "Ezekiel Saw de Wheel," for which Brown joined in the singing. Poignant selections so moved listeners that many wept openly, and Robeson overcome by emotion himself, wiped tears from his eyes. The audience begged for "Ol' Man River," the obvious encore, and initially Paul refused, explaining that he was not allowed to sing it because it was part of the show, but finally he gave in. It brought the house down.[18]

Critics had a difficult time accounting for the powerful emotions stirred by this "shy looking giant in a black suit." "It was queer," wrote the reviewer for the *Daily Sketch,* "to see that 'brilliant' audience moved to tears by his singing of 'Water Boy' and 'Deep River.'" Several paid Robeson the supreme compliment of likening his "simplicity and restraint as well as tempestuousness" and the "indescribable richness of [his] bass tone" to the world-renowned concert and operatic genius Feodor Chaliapin, who, several days before, had performed *Boris Godunov* in London.[19] It was not a comment to be taken lightly (and, indeed, Essie would later use it to full advantage): Robeson, with almost no formal training and at the beginning of his career, was once again being compared to a man many saw as the greatest bass of the century, a highly trained singer of tremendous range, as at home with the challenging *Boris Godunov* as with Schubert's lieder.

James Douglas of the *Daily Express* lavished praise on Robeson in a review so laudatory it was subsequently printed in full on the programs for the second Drury Lane concert and Robeson's later English concert tour, as well as in the American black weekly, the *Amsterdam News*. In his long, lyric account, Douglas likened Robeson's singing to a religious experience, a "spiritual spell," "mystical," "divine witchery," the "seventh heaven of faith." Robeson's performance was a "revelation," intense enough to "melt the worldling's heart and renew the worldling's withered mind. . . . We laughed and wept. He broke our hearts with beauty. As he wiped the tears from his eyes we wiped the tears from ours. He shook some of us into sobs. . . . there were seconds when his face was alight and aflame with seership. We saw the rapt mysticism gathering in intensity until it reached the height of the mood . . . dominated, . . . captivated, . . . transfigured, . . . swept along the path of prophecy. [We became] like little children [as we] surrendered to his magical genius." Douglas was struck by the ease with which Robeson, standing "in a plain tweed suit, holding a piece of paper in two immobile hands," enraptured audiences. "He is a giant, an athlete, a rugby player, and a man of culture," Douglas concluded, "more than a great actor and a great singer . . . a great man."[20]

Robeson took London by storm and at a time when negative feeling about the presence of black American entertainers had grown quite pronounced. Before the mid-1920s, British exposure to blacks had been limited to West Indian and African students and black laborers like those working in the Cardiff dockyards.[21] Most English people, on the basis of this scant experience, assumed that all blacks with the exception of occasional students and professionals were uneducated and culturally inferior. Drifting, unemployed black dockworkers (especially in Wales) were a case in point: most British viewed them, as well as the white women they married, as lower-class and trashy. In 1919 race riots broke out in Liverpool, Cardiff, Manchester, Barry, Newton, and Hull, all seaports or industrial cities with a sizable population of West Indian and West African blacks. Ostensibly the issue was job rivalry, but sexual jealousy over blacks marrying white women was in fact an equally intense source of animosity.[22] (These sentiments persisted well into the twenties. Jimmy Light recalled a remark to this effect made to him concerning Robeson during rehearsals for the London run of *The Emperor Jones* in 1925. "You must have a hard time teaching Robeson all his speeches," the stage manager of the Ambassador Theatre said sympathetically to Light. "Well, isn't he illiterate?" Light told the theater manager, "Robeson is a barrister, and Phi Beta Kappa man — that is the highest

American academic honor." Puzzled, the stage manager asked, "Well, if that's the case, what is all this race business you have in America?") [23]

By the mid-1920s the same Negro vogue that swept New York had also left its mark on London as black American entertainers became not only acceptable but fashionable. (Edwina and Louis "Dickie" Mountbatten, married in 1922, honeymooned in America, and returned to England with "a stack of sheet music for the Charleston and Black Bottom," and the Prince of Wales reportedly saw Florence Mills perform thirteen times when she was in London.) As white Londoners' interest rose, so did the number of black American performers eager to make their way in England. "London is full of Race artists at the moment," wrote Ivan H. Browning in the *Chicago Defender* in 1928, "and to see them strolling through Leicester Square, Piccadilly and other streets reminds one of 7th Avenue in New York." With unemployment among British musicians and performers at an all-time high, issues of job rivalry as well as propriety (the British never took to Josephine Baker the way the French did) and racial and class distinctions all played a part in the growing resentment among some British of this latest American import. [24]

Groups like *Shuffle Along*'s star quartette, the Harmony Kings, seldom encountered criticism ("these gentlemen are college men," reported the *Kent and Sussex Courier* in 1929), but the gaudiness and sensuality of revues — even the well-received *Dover to Dixie* (1923) and *Blackbirds* (1927) — consistently elicited disapproval. Persuaded by the vitriolic pen of the *Daily Express*'s eccentric, sensationalist, and outspoken Hannen Swaffer, England's "cultured" theatergoing public dismissed black revues as coarse, crude, and, in some cases, clearly offensive. Some, like Albert Voyce, chairman of the Musicians' Federation, defended those few "respectable and decent" Negro performers "who behave themselves and keep their place," but, for the most part, all black performers suffered from revue artists' generally unsavory reputation. To make matters worse, white American visitors and tourists encouraged this type of overgeneralization, urging their British friends to stay away from these and other black ne'er-do-wells. By 1923 the issue had become so heated that when the question of licensing an all-black cabaret at the Empire Theatre was brought before the London County Council, permission was granted only when the proprietor, Sir Alfred Butt (the same Butt who now arranged for Robeson's Drury Lane concerts), promised "that a rail would be put around the portion of the room in which the show was staged," thus making it physically impossible "for the black artists to mix with the audience." [25]

Against this backdrop, Paul Robeson was a revelation. A college graduate, a Phi Beta Kappa scholar, an athlete, a barrister, and an actor who performed not only legitimate theater but the avant-garde works of Eugene O'Neill as well,

Robeson could hardly be categorized as either uneducated or culturally bereft. He understood full well how much his intelligence and education had helped him to win British approval. "When I first arrived in London [1925] I was greeted first as a barrister and not as an actor, and all my work was judged by intelligent people with my scholastic training in mind," Robeson told the *Pittsburgh Courier*'s Floyd Calvin in 1927. Robeson concluded that his education was "the primary reason for my achieving a fair degree of success in such a comparatively short time. . . . In nearly every case where I go out to sing for the richest and most highly cultured white people, after my program I am invariably invited to meet the guests socially. This is because they know I am a university man, and they know I have background."[26] Robeson's Drury Lane concert performances, both restrained and powerful, exuded a similar air of refinement. His impeccable diction, his sonorous speaking voice, his regal and dignified presentation—austerely bare stage, simple black evening dress, a single nod breaking the stillness as he gestured to Larry Brown to begin—proved a stark contrast to the abandon and excess many Londoners associated with black performers. Again and again, British papers reminded readers that Robeson was an "exceptional" black man, a point that even the most proper of critics—the *Times*'s James Agate, Sydney Carrol of the *Daily Telegraph,* and the *Daily Sketch*'s John Blount—were forced to concede.

In some British circles it was considered chic to cultivate the friendship of an exotic Indian rajah or a gifted black (as many British had a low opinion of colonials, it made a difference that Robeson was an American black, rather than an African or a West Indian), and among such people Robeson was looked on as a fascinating addition to an evening's guest list. Thus Robeson, as one observer put it, "was feted by the Trite Young Things and implored to go to every cocktail party north of the New Cut."[27] In June Paul sang at one of Lady Ravonsdale's elegant dinner parties in Westminster, touted as "among the best private entertainments in London," and, later, at a series of receptions given by the powerful, conservative owner of three London newspapers, Lord Beaverbrook. By July, writing home to Van Vechten, Essie could happily list "tea with Lady Colfax" and a "command to sing before the Prince of Wales" as among the Robesons' most recent social coups. "Everyone wanted to know Paul and to be seen with him, especially some of our so-called society ladies, 'gawd elp us,'" remembered *Show Boat*'s Marie Burke. "During the run of *Show Boat* I didn't see much of Paul socially; he was just too busy recording, meeting people, and being lionized."[28]

By midsummer the number of fans eagerly waiting outside Robeson's dressing room before and after performances for a glimpse of the star, an autograph, or a word with him had become a problem. The attention was flattering, but

Paul was generally extremely nervous before performances and needed at least a full half-hour alone to collect himself. Theater manager Sir Alfred Butt, aware that Robeson had a difficult time turning people away, decided that he needed assistance—a dresser to look after his personal needs and monitor the flow of fans and autograph seekers, especially before performances. Thus began an association and friendship that would continue for over three decades between Robeson and his dresser, Joseph ("Joe" or "Andy") Andrews.[29]

Andrews was thirty years old, a slim, almost gangly, five-foot, eleven-inch, jack-of-all-trades with dark eyes and thick black hair, when he and Paul first met in 1928. Born in Grenada on March 8, 1898, the same year as Paul, and proud of his West Indian heritage, Andrews had had a varied, if somewhat unstable, work history. He had moved to New York City as soon as he finished high school in the West Indies and there learned American racial mores the hard way as he fought his way from one menial job to another, contending with not only bigoted whites but often hostile American blacks as well. Andrews left New York abruptly in 1920 on the heels of a racial incident with an American black but found the situation in Chicago no better. Frustrated with boarding at the YMCA and barely making ends meet, he took a job as waiter on a Lake Michigan boat. In 1922 his brother, Gordon Andrews, who had set up an import-export business in London, sent for him, offering him employment in his new company. Andrews accepted the offer, but once again things ended badly. By 1925 the company was bankrupt, and Joe was out of work. For the next two years, from 1925 to 1927, he worked in France, drifting again. "There was nothing to do about it," the even-tempered, philosophical Andrews later reflected. "So I just folded my arms and waited for what might happen next."[30]

When a friend suggested Andrews audition for the chorus of the *Show Boat* production, Andrews was ready to give it a try. "Work was work. I was lucky not to be chosen," Andrews recalled in his clipped English accent, "for later I was selected to look after Paul. I was introduced to him during rehearsal and after a brief chat we took to each other instantly." Soft-spoken and initially reserved, Andrews would for some twenty years function as Robeson's man Friday, his scheduler, his secretary, the one who let people in and out. In contrast to Essie, who was so often abrupt, Andrews, distinguished-looking in his dark blue suit, treated the people he turned away with such respect and courtesy they seldom felt slighted. Everyone, it seemed, with the notable exception of Essie, liked Andy. (Later, when Paul and Essie's marital difficulties resurfaced, Essie accused Andrews of helping to arrange and cover for many of Paul's clandestine meetings with other women.)[31] Throughout his long association with Robeson, Andrews's loyalty remained unqualified. He seldom questioned or criticized anything Paul did, and in time, he won Paul's confidence. Over the years, on those occasions when Robeson felt overwhelmed and at a loss to express his feelings it was Joe Andrews to whom he talked.[32]

With his *Show Boat* and Drury Lane concert successes Robeson had won acceptance and a life hardly imagined by blacks in America. No one was more surprised and pleased by this turn of events than Robeson. Patrons came specifically to hear him, and reviewers consistently gave him top billing. Essie wrote to Carl Van Vechten in July that they both were feeling "as though at last we are at the end of a long journey. Paul is so happy he grins and jigs . . . is tickled to death and greatly relieved." For the first time he and Essie enjoyed mobility—the freedom to live, entertain, walk, or dine wherever they chose, and this they did with great relish. In September they moved to a fully furnished apartment on 76 Carlton Hill in one of London's loveliest areas directly facing Regent's Park in the St. John's Wood section, and throughout the summer Paul found himself "piloted to the best tables in cafes, invited to select Mayfair drawing rooms," and made "the guest of honor in the night clubs."[33]

Most American blacks who spent time in England felt a striking and unfamiliar sense of racial ease. But what Essie and Paul experienced went far beyond racial freedom. Britain's upper class fell in love with Paul that summer and, once hooked, courted him unabashedly. Joe Andrews remembered how quickly London society took to Paul. "He was shy but had earned great honors in academics and in sports, and at six feet, two inches, was considered an exceptionally fine specimen of a man. In short, he brought to England qualities most admired by the British: education, intelligence, athletic ability, and modesty."[34]

It was thrilling to be courted by a social group so select it snubbed many white Americans, but amid the excitement the Robesons lived with the fear of suddenly losing the favor they had so unexpectedly won. Thus, in press interviews, Robeson filtered and occasionally altered details of his life, stressing his mother's genealogical heritage (he now began referring to himself as Paul *Bustill* Robeson), his father's repute as a minister, and his own academic and athletic achievements, love of scholarship, and deep racial pride. Absent was any mention of his childhood poverty (Paul told the press he had been given everything he needed as a child and "was never kept short"), his father's humiliating dismissal, the movie *Body and Soul,* Paul's late graduation from Columbia, or anything that might possibly detract from his image.[35]

In particular, Robeson was careful to make no mention of his contract with Caroline Dudley Reagan. Flattered by the respect accorded him by Britain's elite, Robeson at the same time was haunted by their disdain for black revue entertainers. Had he, like Roland Hayes, confined himself from the start to "high" art, the issue might not have been so pressing. But, in fact, Robeson owed much of his recent success to the kind of entertainment that evoked such scorn among his present admirers. Revues like *Shuffle Along* and Lew Leslie and Will Vodery's *Plantation Revue* had given Robeson experience, exposure, and money at a time when he needed all three. Even when white Rutgers classmates complained about his "singing and acting funny" and asked Paul directly how, with all his promise, he "could apparently sink so low," Robeson stuck it out.[36] And now, even as he nodded in agreement with his British friends that such revues were crude and vulgar, he himself was slated to perform in one in the fall.

In July Robeson received a curt telegram from Reagan reminding him of his coming obligations. The timing could not have been worse. Only weeks before the Robesons had been dealt a grim reminder of racial realities awaiting them back home. Every prominent white American in England had been invited to the American embassy's annual Fourth of July celebration; the Robesons, however, received no invitation. It is inconceivable that Robeson's presence in London could have been inadvertently overlooked; among the British there was no American more talked about that summer. Thus Paul and Essie interpreted the omission as deliberate, in all likelihood instigated by white Americans who would have been offended had the couple been invited. "Paul was not surprised at this obvious snub from white America," Joe Andrews recalled, "but he worried that it might affect his reputation in Britain. But you know Paul, he never spoke of such things publicly. He always tried to be bigger than them [racist whites] and kept his worries to himself."[37]

Within a short time Reagan's worst fears were confirmed when she heard that Robeson had agreed to appear in a fall run of *Show Boat* in England. Furious, she wired Robeson immediately, demanding to know the exact date on which he planned to begin rehearsals for *her* revue. Paul replied by cable: "All plans indefinitely postponed. Sending Essie soon to discuss arrangements." Reagan contacted Frank Gillmore, the executive secretary of Actors' Equity, who joined her in cabling Robeson, again inquiring as to his intentions regarding the revue. Paul replied tersely that he was "under no contract obligations until September 1st. Wrote Dudley today, stating firmly my position."[38]

In late August Essie returned to the United States to shoulder the unpleasant task of explaining her husband's position to an angry Reagan and her crew of Equity supporters. Essie offered several explanations for Paul's change of heart. He "did not consider himself an actor anyway, but a singer [and] does not like the idea of having to sing blues in a revue. He does not think that sort of singing would be good for his voice or his reputation." Robeson, according to Essie, also objected to spirituals in a revue. "My husband feels they would be out of place, that he would not have the proper atmosphere for the singing."[39]

In an effort to garner support from the black community Essie agreed to an exclusive interview with the *Amsterdam News* and again tried to justify Paul's position. He had signed a contract, Essie admitted, but since then concern over straining his voice combined with his reluctance to sing spirituals in a revue had forced him to rethink these arrangements. When Larry Brown (who saw his own career in jeopardy) said that he also thought Robeson should cancel the revue, the matter was settled. Paul then sent a cable to Reagan stating his intentions, returned his $500 advance salary, and even offered to "buy the contract [and] pay the cost of the damages to Mrs. Reagan."[40]

Safely ensconced in England, Robeson spent much of the fall outlining his position to his newest and most unlikely supporter, the drama critic for the Beaverbrook presses (the *Daily Express, Sunday Express,* and *Evening Standard*), Hannen Swaffer. Eccentric—he dressed in late-1890s Edwardian attire with his long gray hair draped over his stiff collar, chain smoked, and regularly attended seances—Swaffer was best known for his brilliance as a newsgatherer and his intimate form of gossip writing (he always told "the inside story"). He rejected the solemn and ponderous stance of most drama critics, electing instead to write from the viewpoint of an ordinary audience members. The public, in turn, trusted Swaffer and believed that "nothing could stop him from telling the truth as he saw it." A favorable notice from him would seal a play's success and set it on a run of at least several months, and a negative notice spelled disaster: at the height of his fame Swaffer was barred from twelve London theaters, so wary were owners of his negative judgments.[41]

Justifiably disliked and distrusted by American blacks in England for his years of heavy-handed attacks on American "nigger shows," Swaffer, once won over by the educated and cultured Robeson, championed his cause with the same energy and passion he had in the past so effectively used to berate black revue performers. He sympathetically enlarged on Robeson's thoughts in lengthy articles published in one of the most widely read papers in England, the *Sunday Express,* and reprinted in *Variety,* while vigorously asserting his own opinion that, whatever the cost, Robeson's talents ought not "to be wasted on some cheap-jack show."[42]

Robeson squirmed, weaseled, and rationalized in arguments delivered by Swaffer and tailored for British consumption, using as his major defense Swaffer's own objections to black revues. Robeson told Swaffer that in his initial talks with Reagan she had emphasized the high-class nature of the revue: he was to do a dramatic sketch, sing some blues, and appear in a skit written around some Negro spirituals. At that stage, they had even talked about enlisting the services of Jerome Kern and perhaps Irving Berlin. But, in time, plans changed, and it became clear to Paul that the Reagan revue would be no different from all the rest. "I began to realize that I could not sing vulgar blues depending on risqué catch lines to get them over, that I would be no good in a revue." Furthermore, he added, "My religious spirituals would have been insulted in a jazz show."[43] The offer to do the revue had come at a time when he was under pressure, Robeson told Swaffer. "My wife was ill then, and I was worried, and I signed a contract which frankly I do not feel capable of doing." As Robeson saw it, Equity should handle the matter entirely. He would accept their verdict, whatever it was, and pay whatever money he owed. As far as the money was concerned, Paul said, "Money does not interest me. I am turning down valuable contracts all the time." (Essie offered a perhaps more honest explanation in a letter to the Van Vechtens when she said simply that they would pay what they had to pay in order "to avoid a suit in England because of Paul's 'noble' reputation.")[44]

Equity, however, saw Robeson's explanations, dutifully communicated by his wife and manager, as thinly veiled excuses for release from contract obligations he no longer wanted to keep and treated them as such. Equity representatives met with Essie and demanded that she cable Paul, which she reluctantly agreed to do, adding that she could give Reagan no assurances that this would have any effect. The Equity council requested a reply from Robeson within two days, but the deadline came and passed with no response.

On September 6 Equity's executive secretary cabled Robeson at the Drury Lane Theatre and informed him that he had been placed under temporary suspension and had until October to defend himself. "If by that time," the cable concluded, "no satisfactory reply has been received . . . the temporary suspension will be changed to one for an indefinite term." Concerning Paul's sudden aversion to singing blues and spirituals in a revue, the association reminded him that he had yet to find out "just what Miss Dudley [Reagan] is planning for him."[45]

Langston Hughes *did* know something about the revue, and his account contradicts Robeson's claim that it was hastily put together and second-rate. Hughes, by this time established as a writer, earned his living during the summer of 1926 composing lyrics and sketches for the revue along with Paul's friend and Harlem novelist Rudolph Fisher. The revue was truly "Negro," presenting "many of the then unexploited Negro folk-songs with all the materials music and sketches [done] by Negro writers," Hughes said. Armed with the performing talents of Paul Robeson and music critic and singer Nora Holt and backed up by first-rate writing, the production promised to be something new, artistic, and totally respectable. As Hughes observed, it was not the quality of the revue but Robeson's mind-boggling success in London that had finally persuaded him to rescind his contract obligations. That this was the case was fairly obvious to everyone involved. Essie's efforts to defend Paul, forcing her, as Hughes humorously recalled, "to flee over the Harlem rooftops with baby Paul in her arms, like

Eliza in *Uncle Tom's Cabin* in order to escape the clutches of Mrs. Reagan's process servers," failed to persuade anyone differently.[46]

Equity representatives tried repeatedly to impress on Robeson the seriousness of his impending suspension. Finally, the association played its trump card when it suggested larger racial ramifications should Robeson refuse to return. "The Association believes," an Equity editorial warned, "that it would be a very great pity if this outstanding member of his race should take such a narrow view of the obligations he incurred when he signed the contract."[47] At this point, official overseer, information disperser, function arranger, mentor, and confidant for blacks in America, Walter White, stepped into the picture, entreating Paul for the sake of the race to fulfill his contract obligations. White, who had so often in the past fought for Robeson, personally advancing Paul's career through his position in the NAACP, now pleaded with him by letter not to let the race down.

> Dear Paul:
>
> This is going to be one of the most difficult letters I have ever had to write. On September 6 I sent you the following cablegram:
> AS FRIEND LET ME ADVISE MOST CAREFUL CONSIDERATION CONTRACT MATTER. REACTION ALREADY VERY BAD. FEEL WILL HURT YOU AND ALL US.
>
> I enclose a clipping from "Equity" which is self-explanatory. Our mutual friend, Arthur Spingarn, sent this to me and he feels very strongly as I do — that whatever the immediate financial or other sacrifices which may be involved that to do other than to live up to your contract would be a very great mistake.
>
> I realize that in writing you I am doing a most risky thing in interfering in a matter which is personal. On the other hand, I feel that I should be derelict in my duty to you as a friend if I did not let you know what the sentiment here is. Gladys and I attempted to convey to Essie when she came to see us our feelings when first we heard of the difficulty and that feeling has been greatly intensified by the additional facts which we have learned. Some of the very best friends that you have feel that to do otherwise than the right thing would irremediably injure you and would react upon all of us.
>
> May I give you one illustration of this. I was asked to do a certain thing by a prominent white person. I agreed to do it. Two or three times the question was asked, "Now can I really depend upon you?" Becoming irritated I said quite sharply that I had given my word and that was enough. The reply was, "Your people are not strong on keeping their promises are they? — Look at what your friend Paul Robeson is doing." . . .
>
> Finally, let me urge that whatever you do, answer Equity's cables.[48]

If Walter White could not persuade Robeson to change his mind, no one could. And, indeed, White's pleas proved fruitless, and Robeson bowed out of the contract. Despite the solemnity with which Equity pronounced his suspension, the association's ruling — adverse publicity notwithstanding — would have little effect on his activities in England, and Robeson knew it. Though he regretted disappointing Walter White, he would not allow White or Equity to force him to leave England.

When the matter was finally settled, Essie sent for Pauli and her mother while Paul wrote to White in an attempt to smooth things over. Cordial but restrained, White replied: "You are right in saying that we can disagree and yet remain the same friends. We [Gladys and Walter White] do both sincerely hope that the matter is going to work out all right for both the present and the future."[49] In fact, Walter White understood Robeson's position far better than he was able to let on and thus continued, their disagreement notwithstanding, to tout Robeson's British stage and concert achievements through NAACP news releases sent regularly to the black weeklies.[50]

Reagan, meanwhile, infuriated that Robeson had "gotten away" with breaking his contract, attempted to issue an injunction preventing Paul's continued appearance in *Show Boat,* arguing that because he had broken his contract with her he ought not to be allowed to perform anywhere. Sir Alfred Butt fought back, insisting that "if Mr. Robeson is forced to leave the cast of *Show Boat,* there is a possibility the rest of the production may come to an end."[51] Florenz Ziegfeld briefly got into the fray, siding with Robeson and Butt.[52] The issue was eventually brought to court and on October 3, 1928, was finally settled in Robeson's favor. Said the judge: "The only effect of the injunction in such a case would not be to benefit the plaintiff, but to drive the defendant out of employment."[53]

Since the early 1920s Robeson had given eloquent lip service to the ideal of artistic achievement as a means for improving race relations. And until 1928 Robeson's personal ambitions had been in perfect accord with the larger, nobler endeavor of race advancement. But the Reagan contract issue had forced him to choose between personal goals and what, at least in the minds of many vocal race leaders, was of benefit to the race. Had *Show Boat* folded quickly, as expected, Robeson would have returned to America to do the revue, happy to have work. But, in fact, *Show Boat* and the Drury Lane concerts gave Robeson recognition unlike anything he had dreamed possible. With the production reopening in the fall, a 1929 Celebrity Concert Series tour of Britain already contracted with Lionel Powell (manager of Paderewski, McCormack, Chaliapin, and Kreisler), talk of his starring in a British film, and a projected tour of the Continent in the planning stages, Robeson would have little to worry about professionally.[54] In short, Robeson had found what he longed for, respectability and the opportunity to work and enlarge himself as an artist, and he had no intention of giving up any of this new life.

Robeson's breaking of the Reagan contract and subsequent decision to remain in England posed dilemmas for blacks in America. A few, like the Harmony Kings' Ivan H. Browning, who had himself experienced life in England, defended Robeson. Browning and his group were playing in London during the *Show Boat* run, and in his spare time Browning acted as a correspondent for the *Amsterdam News,* sending home news concerning black American performers in London for his column "Entertainers in Europe." Writing to Romeo L. Dougherty, drama editor of the *Amsterdam News,* Browning argued that the real villain was not Robeson but white America and its treatment of black performing artists.

> When you think of the opportunity they give to Negro artists in Europe as compared to the way they treat such a wonderful artist as Bledsoe [in the United States], it is really disgusting, and I wish all of our real class artists in America were over this way, where they could go just as high and far as their ability would let them. They've idolized Scott and Whaley for years in England, the Versatile 3, Layton and Johnstone, Florence Mills, Josephine Baker, and now it's Robeson. . . . America will never give our artists the chance they deserve. . . . I think the Negro press should get right behind Equity and let them know that, after all, it isn't that they are really a protection to the Negro but "Robeson" happens to be doing a bit "too well" for the American Ofay. . . . Imagine an American newspaper carrying photos of a Negro in the manner they are doing Robeson and they did Miss Mills in the same way, also Miss Baker. O, well, the Negroes must keep digging, sad when they can't have success in America, Europe is certainly the place to have it on an unusually large scale.[55]

Leigh Whipper, a veteran black actor who had been at the craft since 1899, agreed. "Acting was no easy job, I can assure you," said Whipper, reminiscing about his own early theater days.

> My first break in legitimate theater came with *Those Who Walk in Darkness,* and through that play I eventually became the first black member of Actor's Equity. I had sent in my application [to Equity] by mail under my own name, Leigh Whipper, and when I went by the office to pick up my card, the secretary was somewhat alarmed by who, or what, she saw. She looked up the records and found a membership for a "Miss Whipper," but nothing for me, a Negro male. I assured her that I was the one and only Leigh Whipper, and, dumbfounded, she gave me the card. I suspect that if they had known be-

forehand I was Negro, they would have refused me. But now, I was at least in the door. When the disturbance with Robeson came along, there were still very few colored people in Equity. Even though there was a brief rush in the 1920s, it was still tough for black actors. Paul's decision may have temporarily hurt him, but it would have been foolish for him (or me for that matter) to have turned down the British contract, especially given the way white theater has treated us in the past.[56]

Most blacks, however, were caught between dismay over the racial repercussions of Robeson's decision and pride in his success. Some railed against Robeson for having agreed to perform in *Show Boat* at all, with its demeaning stereotypes and flagrant use of the word "nigger."[57] But the same black weeklies that editorially censured Robeson for taking part in the musical documented in lavish detail in their society pages Robeson's wooing and winning of London's upper classes. The European careers of Noble Sissle, Layton and Johnson, Leslie Hutchinson, the Four Harmony Kings, and John Payne had long been a popular feature of black weeklies, but the Robesons' life in England, as recorded by itinerant reporter Ivan H. Browning and others, read like a fairy tale to blacks in America.

Where else but in England would it have been possible for the Robesons to give a racially mixed party and have it described in London's (white) society pages side by side with other high-society fetes? In America the white press remained "strangely silent"[58] about the Robesons' social life, but black weeklies like the *Amsterdam News* jumped on the story of this "delightful party" given in honor of Mr. and Mrs. Carl Van Vechten. Readers were walked through the Robesons' London home, beautifully decorated with masses of lilies and carnations, and given sufficient detail to experience vicariously the entire elegant evening. "Guests arrived shortly after 11:00 p.m., many having just left the theater," and Essie, "dressed in a beautiful banana-meat transparent velvet evening dress," received them in the foyer. From there a "trim [white] maid took the guests to an upper floor, where the men left their wraps in Mr. Robeson's spacious bedroom, and the ladies in Mrs. Robeson's equally spacious bedroom." The gathering, "one of the most distinguished and unique in London . . . numbered among its guests the elite of London's art and social worlds," including "one of the most influential men, politically, in England today," *London Express* and *Evening Standard* owner Lord Beaverbrook, "patron of the arts and one of the wealthiest men in the world." The guest list went on: the Harmony Kings, Ivan H. Browning and his wife, publisher Alfred Knopf, Chicago tenor George Garner and his wife, Turner Layton, Edith Day, Fred and Adele Astaire, Mrs. Patrick Campbell, Leslie Hutchinson, Alberta Hunter, John Payne, and

Lady Ravonsdale, daughter of the late Lord Curzon and "one of the most beautiful, distinguished and popular peeresses in England. . . . After the guests had been served every sort of delicacy in the dining room," they found their way to the library "where champagne, cocktails, wines, whiskey and soda were served, and then returned to the drawing room. Robeson spoke to them for a few minutes of his great friendship for Van Vechten and then sang about an hour." Guests did not leave until 4:00 a.m., and the Robesons "surprised them all by informing them that this was their first party. . . . And to be sure it was a most beautiful affair and one that will be remembered by everyone who attended."[59]

It was difficult to argue with the Robesons' success. Essie, in particular, was thrilled. So often suspicious of whites and intent on earning the approval of black society, Essie saw the party as proof that they had, in fact, "made it." Walter White wrote immediately to extend his congratulations, not only for Paul's professional achievements but also for the couple's equally important social prominence.[60] By the end of the year there was little doubt in either Paul's or Essie's mind that they had made the right decision. Breaking the Reagan contract had opened a whole new world of possibilities. Life was better than either of them ever dreamed it could be, and the struggle required to survive in America seemed far away indeed. If, for the present, American blacks mistook Robeson's motivation, they would later realize he had made the best decision for himself and for the race, or so Paul and Essie hoped.

9

The Toast of England

1929-1930

Walter Abel, who with his wife visited the Robesons near the end of the *Show Boat* run, was stunned by Paul's popularity in England. "He was so incredibly admired. Women, especially, were crazy about him." To reinforce his point, Abel recounted Robeson's arrival at a party given by Mae Knuckle, a London cellist. "When Paul came in the whole atmosphere changed. Everyone's attention was fixed on him. His presence was electrifying. He said 'Hello,' sat on the floor in a corner with his knees crossed, and we just waited for him to sing. He did, of course. It was positively amazing. And great fun."[1]

Having publicly announced in January their plans to remain in London, in March the Robesons moved from St. John's Wood to a newly purchased house located in the fashionable London suburb of Hampstead Heath. Enclosed by ancient chestnut and oak trees, set off from the road and facing the heath, it was elegant, tasteful, and spacious. Essie completely refurbished the largest room in the house as a nursery for Pauli. At the top of the long winding staircase, Paul had a large room that adjoined his own bedroom converted to a library-sitting room, complete with a massive collection of books, solid masculine chairs, expensive rugs, and dominating it all, sculptor Salemme's famed bronze bust. "We had known Paul in his impoverished days with the Provincetowners," said Abel, "and now here he was at Hampstead Heath having splits of champagne. Paul was God Almighty and admired by everyone. It was all the best for Paul, then."[2]

The vivacious twenty-two-year-old Dorothy West, one of an inner circle of young black Harlem writers that included Langston Hughes, Claude McKay, Zora Neale Hurston, Countee Cullen, and Wallace Thurman, had vivid memories of the Robesons' style of life. West recalled a dinner party at the their new home in 1929.

They had five white servants. I wasn't there long before I got the distinct impression (although nothing specific was said to indicate this) that the servants looked down on me and some of the other young black guests. I guess we did not belong, or at least didn't seem to belong, to the "titled group." It was almost a class thing. The servants were not necessarily against us for being black, but they made it perfectly clear it was the Robesons they were working for. The Robesons were "gentility" as much as the whites these servants had worked for in the past, and we were not. It was almost funny. We were all on our best behavior in front of the servants. In the dining room itself, when the servants were present, we [the guests] and the Robesons talked in low voices, a very measured conversation. One of them served tea. You know, I did not take milk in my tea, but I took it then so as not to offend the servants. But when the servants went back into the kitchen, leaving us to ourselves, we felt free to talk in a louder, more normal tone of voice, laughing and joking with each other. Then, when the servants returned, we quieted down again. It was almost as if we had to prove to the British servant class that we were worthy of being served by them.[3]

Abel had mixed feelings about the changes he observed. "Essie was so proud of that house and their tasteful furnishings, and, almost embarrassingly, she pointed out the white servants waiting on *them*. She was like a schoolgirl, just thrilled with things she never had before. As soon as we got there she ushered my wife upstairs to show off her new dresses, all the latest fashion. And yet, it struck me all poignantly as not ostentatious but an overstriving for something they had longed for in America but had been unable to achieve." Abel felt that Paul on the surface adjusted more gracefully, although in his own way, "Paul was as awed with it all as Essie."[4] Robeson more often than not treated their new status lightly and with humor. When, for example, Jimmy Light came to dinner one night at Hampstead Heath, Paul nudged his old friend and with a feigned seriousness said, "I hope you're not offended by the *white* servants."[5] But Robeson was not joking in 1929 when he began referring to himself as Paul Bustill Robeson rather than Paul Leroy Robeson: it was a move deliberately designed to bring attention to his own elite — Bustill — heritage.

Show Boat closed in March 1929, and on April 6 Paul, Essie, and Larry Brown left for Vienna and their first continental tour. As usual, Larry Brown arrived at the train station well ahead of time while the Robesons were late. "The Robesons," as Essie put it, almost always "just made trains by fractions of a minute" and on this occasion they missed their train — not because they were late, but because of a mistake on Essie's schedule. Essie was enraged — she would have to get new tickets and send wires ahead to Brussels—and roundly "scolded" the officials at the train station she held responsible for the mix-up. Larry and Paul laughed the incident off and could easily afford to do so, knowing full well that with Essie in charge they did not have to worry about such details.[6]

Robeson and Brown's first stop was Vienna, a cultural mecca, home to some of the world's greatest classical musicians—Mozart, Hayden, Beethoven, Schubert, Mahler, and Strauss—and, in 1929, a city plagued by postwar poverty and economic crisis. When Paris's sensational discovery, the alluring and provocative star of *La Revue Nègre*, Josephine Baker, performed there the previous year, her presence had "aroused an anti-negro feeling that Vienna never knew existed." A right-wing student group that earlier had attacked socialists and Jews staged anti-Baker demonstrations and vowed to prevent "colored artists from performing in Vienna." The Catholic Church agreed that Baker was a moral threat and supported efforts to keep her off the Vienna stage. Hitler would not assume power until 1933, but his racist manifesto, *Mein Kampf* (1925), was selling briskly. The fact that "decadent" jazz musicians (jazz being the very opposite of Wagner, military sacrifice, ecstatic death, and Aryan domination, and the collaborative effort of two despised groups—blacks and Jews) could make good livings in Austrian and German cities rife with poverty and unemployment particularly galled conservatives who viewed jazz as a pernicious influence on German values. The result was that Baker was banned from the Ronacher Theater where she had been originally booked and was forced to perform in another smaller theater, the Johann Strauss.[7]

Certainly Robeson and Brown hoped their classic presentation would prevent any repeat of the Baker disturbance. Nonetheless, they had no idea how a program of black spirituals and folk songs, however elegantly presented, would be accepted in this city so steeped in classical music. But whatever "cheap sensation" and jazz influences skeptical audiences at the Mittlerer Konzerhaus-Saal might have anticipated, they found instead "Africans dressed in European evening clothes, and with a phenomenal voice" and were delighted. Robeson and Brown drew a packed house, and they were, as Essie put it, "a sensation" with "Weeping Mary," "By and By," "Water Boy," "Deep River," and "Witness" drawing passionate pleas for encores. At the end of the concert, audience members "crowded up to the stage . . . and shouted and stomped for just one more. Even after lights out people remained applauding furiously."[8] In Budapest Robeson and Brown again filled concert halls and left audiences begging for encores and autographs. Budapest reporters, applauding Robeson's "refined and perfect legato" and "genuinely virile voice," were particularly taken with his "fantastic religiousness . . . [and] mystical manifestation of the soul of a race." Two final performances in Vienna and Prague (April 16 and 19) definitively answered any lingering questions Robeson and Brown may have had about their ability to hold European audiences.[9]

Despite the rave reviews, the tour was hardly worth the effort from a financial point of view. While the great Chaliapin commanded the handsome fee of $3,000 for a single concert in Prague, Robeson and Brown received a mere sixty-dollar guarantee and 50 percent of the net in the same city. Such was the case in other European cities as well. Budapest hailed Robeson "a Negro Helge Lindberg" (a Finnish baritone, known throughout the Continent for his interpretations of Bach and Handel), but paid him poorly: only 50 percent of the net and with no guaranteed fee whatsoever. Still, the Robesons and Brown were not overly dismayed. Essie, who had made all the arrangements with European managers and agents, knew well in advance they would not make money. The purpose of the tour had been to establish Robeson and Brown on the Continent. And, as Essie's handwritten log, in which she meticulously recorded expenses, weather conditions, hotel accommodations, concert hall facilities, audience composition and reaction, and numbers encored, confirms, they intended to return. The money would come later.[10]

At the end of April, Robeson and Brown were scheduled to give their first performance in London's most prestigious concert auditorium, the Royal Albert Hall. "Paul worried about that performance for weeks," Joe Andrews recalled. "A solo performance there was an awful ordeal and few singers attempted it." A massive, oval-shaped, glass-domed amphitheater with a seating capacity of 10,000, the Royal Albert Hall was originally conceived in 1853 by Albert, husband of Queen Victoria, to be the cultural center of the Kensington Gore Estate. With the green of Kensington Gardens to the north, the gardens of the Royal Horticultural Society to the south, and the Kensington Arcades on the east and west, it was an imposing structure that lacked any semblance of intimacy. To put a proper perspective on its gargantuan dimensions, consider that during the 1920s and 1930s the Royal Albert Hall housed boxing matches, suffragette meetings, the Ford Motor Show, and marathon runs. As one longtime patron mused, "What Victorian megalomania imagined that a *concert* hall should provide seating for over 10,000?"[11]

The prospect of filling a hall that size troubled Robeson. Would they draw a respectable showing? And if they did, would their audience be content with an entire concert of spirituals? Just a few years earlier a group singing spirituals had reduced Albert Hall patrons to gales of laughter. There was also a problem with the hall itself: its "infamous echo" (which was not remedied until 1969) handicapped even seasoned performers because they heard everything they sang twice, the last words of each sentence reverberating well into the next sentence.[12]

Robeson and Brown came close to filling the cavernous auditorium — an achievement — and attracted a high caliber of patrons as well, "comparing favorably with those [of] Kreisler and John McCormack." Many were people who made a habit of going to the Albert Hall on Sundays; others, like Marie Seton, went because they had seen Robeson in *Showboat*. Seton recalled being startled by the contrast between Robeson as he appeared in *Showboat* — dressed in a shirt with rolled-up sleeves and patched and torn work pants — and his presentation on the stage of the Royal Albert Hall — regal and imposing in tails, a stiff white shirt, and a white tie. "His presence filled the hall, yet he stood reverently, as if dedicated to the thing he was about to do." With a nod from Robeson to Larry Brown, the concert began.[13]

The concert drew a spirited ovation, lasting over twenty minutes. This did not stop Paul from loosing a night's sleep waiting up for the verdict of the press. The morning papers brought good news: reviews oozed superlatives.[14] But a scattering of unflattering comments among the generally laudatory reviews, the first of what would become repeated complaints concerning his limited repertoire, marred the event's success for Robeson. The *Daily Express* put it subtly when it suggested it was Robeson's personality rather than his music that drew thousands to Albert Hall. The *Daily Telegraph* was more direct and commended Robeson for having "kept the programme of Negro spirituals . . . within reasonable bounds." And the *Daily Mail* was blunt: "After ten minutes . . . one wished that Mr. Robeson had some more intellectual sort of music on which to exercise his noble and hauntingly beautiful voice."[15]

Anticipating that his repertoire would soon become an issue, Robeson had begun studying French and German language and classical music at the beginning of the year. Other black concert performers — Roland Hayes, Marian Anderson, and Jules Bledsoe (who had recently added *Aida* and "El Toreador" from *Carmen* to his repertoire) — all performed classical music and Robeson himself was convinced that his continued professional status depended on whether he could make similar additions to his repertoire.[16]

Many people underestimated just how important the professional and personal status he had earned in England was to Robeson. The adulation fed more than a performer's need for audience applause. To the extent that approval from the elite of the white English-speaking world quieted a gnawing sense of racial inferiority, Robeson had to have it and would do what was necessary to protect and preserve it. The prodigiously talented musician, singer, and composer Noble Sissle — who, with Eubie Blake, was responsible for the landmark musical *Shuffle Along* (1921), which included Sissle's famous "I'm Just Wild About Harry" — had, like others, assumed that Robeson was only responding to outside influences when he began learning classical music. As a friend, Sissle empathized with Robeson and objected to those who insisted that he change his concert program. In an effort to help, Sissle presented Paul with lyrics (his own) for a song he was sure would be a hit. But Sissle's offer offended rather than flattered Robeson and he indignantly turned the song down. Sissle was first surprised and then annoyed. As one observer recalled, "He did not appreciate what he saw as Paul's new affectations, apologetic attitude and high-brow taste, and let him know as much."[17]

In the meantime, a spring and summer tour of British seaside towns directed by Lionel Powell drew less critical audiences, made money, and generally lifted Robeson's spirits. (Under Powell, who managed Robeson's British concerts from 1929 until his death in 1930 when Harold Holt took over, Robeson did well, earning 70 percent of the box office gross, with 10 percent going to Powell.)[18] Most people in these seaside towns had never seen Robeson but had some knowledge of him from hearing him on the wireless and phonograph records. He won them over, effortlessly it seemed. In concert, the contrast between his huge and magnificent voice and his simple, understated style thrilled audiences. He walked onto the stage with smooth long strides, stood with his feet apart, leaning his weight on his right foot. Tipping his head as though in thought and glancing at a folded slip of paper, he nodded to Lawrence Brown, threw his head back and began to sing.[19]

Throughout the summer, audiences in these seaside towns accorded Robeson the respect of a foreign dignitary, with town hall receptions, presentation of the city keys and welcoming ceremonies hosted by the mayor and other city officials standard fare. People turned out in large numbers to welcome him at train stations, and cabbies routinely refused payment. "Seldom has a Tunbridge Wells audience been so wild with enthusiasm," wrote one reviewer, "and even after Mr. Robeson had added an encore . . . the house refused to leave its seats." "The giant negro, undergraduate, footballer, lawyer, actor and singer stands in a class alone by reason of his beautiful voice," said another of Robeson's June 19 concert at Southsea. "Last night he packed the South Parade Pier to the doors, the audience standing three and four deep round the promenade [and] held them spellbound." Pejorative comment on his limited program appeared sporadically ("No singer can make a reputation . . . on this very restricted and cheap form of vocal composition"; "Personally I am unable to judge Mr. Robeson's abilities as a singer, as I have not yet heard him sing anything that requires singing"), but in general Robeson was personally idolized and professionally lauded.[20]

It was wonderful to be appreciated for and judged by the quality of his art rather than the color of his skin, and although he often spoke about the deplorable bigotry of the United States, Robeson expressed only admiration for British race relations. By any standard American black performers fared better in England than in the United States; still, England was hardly free of racial bigotry. For the vast majority of England's black population, most unemployed sailors and dockworkers living in working-class areas in London, Liverpool, Swansea, Manchester, and Cardiff, racial bigotry and chronic unemployment were facts of life.[21] The saying, common among Britain's black working class, was that "in the States the Negro is the last to be hired and the first to be fired; in Britain he isn't even hired." One could not move in British upper-class circles without being exposed to patronizing attitudes concerning colonials. And even if Paul had wanted to remain ignorant, Essie, so outspoken on racial issues, would have made it impossible for him to do so. Still, Robeson never publicly criticized British racial mores. Personally he had not experienced prejudice and in press interviews said as much.[22]

But an incident occurred in the summer of 1929 while Robeson was on tour that called into question his heartening accounts of British racial tolerance. It involved another American black, as successful in his own field as Robeson was in his: Robert Abbott, the wealthy owner of one of the largest and most influential of the black American weeklies, the *Chicago Defender.* Abbott visited England with his wife in the summer of 1929 as part of a five-month business-vacation tour of Europe. The experience proved a racial nightmare. The difference in the couple's color—Abbott was very dark and his wife, Helen, fair enough to pass as white—caused problems from the start. According to Abbott's biographer, people "gaped" and "treated [them] as freaks." And that was just the beginning. The Abbotts arrived, reservations in hand, at the West End's prestigious Savoy only to be told the hotel did not cater to Negroes. Abbott tried to get into several other hotels by sending his fair-skinned wife in ahead of him to make arrangements while he waited in the car. But in each instance, when Abbott tried to enter he was halted at the desk and informed he would have to leave. Hotel after hotel (a total of thirty) refused the Abbotts admittance. Finally, the couple gave up and in desperation accepted the hospitality of Jamaican-born Louis Drysdale, a black singer and voice coach living in London.[23]

The *Daily Express* gave the story front-page coverage and a three-deck headline: "London Hotels Colour Bar / Ordeal of Negro Millionaire / 30 Refusals" and explained that "Mr. Robert Abbott, a wealthy American Negro reported to be a dollar millionaire, has been refused admission at so many London hotels that he has given up trying to find hotel accommodations in London." Abbott was flooded with personal calls and letters protesting his treatment, some from as far away as remote sections of Africa. Parliament member James Marley spoke personally with the Abbotts about the incident, a group in Scotland invited Abbott and his wife to stay with them, and the Society of Friends in London organized a series of meetings to deal with the race issue in England.[24]

Robeson knew about the Abbott case; it received such wide publicity it would have been impossible for him to miss it. Nor was Abbott's treatment an isolated incident; other accomplished blacks had been similarly mistreated.[25] Still, Robeson said nothing, even when a short time later when he allegedly experienced a similar slight at London's swank Savoy Hotel.

There are several versions of what happened to Robeson at the Savoy. According to the most widely told account, shortly after the Abbott rebuff, Robeson was invited to the Savoy as the guest of Lady Colefax, a British socialite and one of London's most successful hostesses who often gave parties for musicians and actors either in her home or at the restaurant. Paul had dined at the hotel many times and on several occasions taken guests there, without ever encountering a problem. On this occasion, however, he was informed by the manager that the Savoy no longer served Negroes and he was not allowed in.[26]

Within a short time James Marley, M.P., received a letter that recounted in detail Robeson's experience at the Savoy. Although the letter was signed by Robeson, it is unlikely that Paul wrote it because he seldom read his own mail, let alone engaged in lengthy correspondence, and he and Essie had sailed for New York a few days after the incident was reported to have occurred. The letter writer in the Robeson family was Essie, and she, much more than Paul, was prone to speak her mind on racial issues. Furthermore, the letter specifically states that Essie was with Paul when the incident occurred, a detail that at least one source contradicts. (Director Andre Van Gyseghem said that Robeson arrived not with Essie but with a white friend, Jean Forbes Roberts, who later married Van Gyseghem.) "You can imagine how embarrassed we both were," the letter read. "We have never gone to any place like the Savoy except at the very urgent invitation of white English gentlemen. We prefer much quieter places. On this occasion the manager had to send into the grill room for the friend who was awaiting us, and he and his party of six people had to get up and come out with their drinks to find out what was the trouble. They were all indignant and went to several managers, etc., but it seemed there was no doubt about the ruling against Negroes, and we all had to leave. The rest of the party was all white."[27]

Marley read the protest missive at a gathering at the Friends' Meeting House on Eustace Road (a meeting that Essie's mother and Sir George Henschel, one of Robeson's voice trainers, both attended) and used it to hammer home the point that racial discrimination in England was growing. He cited a report from William F. Nicholson, secretary of the Society of Friends, documenting some twenty hotels in the Bloomsbury section that regularly excluded people of color.

Paul and Essie with Charles Johnson (an African studies tutor) on the set of *King Solomon's Mines*, 1936. (PR Archive.)

World premier of *The Song of Freedom*, 1936. (PR Jr.)

Eslanda and Paul Robeson Jr. in Buganda with Mulamuzi and the son of Kabaka, king of Buganda (from *African Journey*), 1936. (PR Archive.)

Paul Robeson Jr. with Pygmy elder statesman, Congo, 1936. (PR Jr.)

Eslanda Robeson
in Uganda, 1936.
(PR Jr.)

Robeson with
Princess Kouka in
Jericho, Egypt, 1937.
(PR Jr.)

Robeson in *Jericho,* 1937. (PR Jr.)

Robeson with Henry Wilcoxon and Wallace Ford at the pyramids near Cairo, during the filming of *Jericho,* 1937. (PR Jr.)

Robeson as Umbopa in *King Solomon's Mines,* 1937. (PR Jr.)

Robeson singing for troops of the International Brigade, Madrid, 1938. (PR Jr.)

Robeson with soldiers in
Spain, 1938. (PR Archive.)

Robeson with Loyalist troops, Spain, 1938. (PR Archive.)

Robeson with
black members of the
International Brigade,
1938. (PR Archive.)

Paul Robeson Jr. showing salute of
Spanish Loyalists, 1939. (PR Jr.)

Robeson in Spain with
Communist leader Dolores Ibarruri
(La Pasionaria), 1939. (PR Archive.)

Herbert Marshall, Fredda Brilliant, and Paul Robeson, late 1930s
(Marshall Collection.)

Plant in the Sun program cover. Photo by John Vickers, London.
(Marshall Collection.)

Robeson (*center*) with Herbert Marshall and *Plant in the Sun* actors, 1939.
© Dudley B. Gordon, Brixton. (Marshall Collection.)

Plant in the Sun rehearsal: Robeson (*right*), Herbert Marshall (*center*). Photo by John Vickers, London. (Marshall Collection.)

(*opposite*) Robeson as David Goliath in *The Proud Valley*, 1939. (PR Jr.)

Robeson in the mines in *The Proud Valley*, 1939. (PR Jr.)

In two of the cases cited, hotel managers indicated they might have reconsidered if the applicants had been Indian instead of Negro and if, once admitted, they would have agreed to separate themselves from the rest of the guests. Marley noted also that well-known entertainers like the Harmony Kings were admitted to first-class hotels but only "as members of the staff who assisted at entertainments and not as guests." Marley even went so far as to bring the matter of racial discrimination before Parliament for discussion and wrote to Prime Minister Ramsay MacDonald for support on the issue.[28]

The press, invited to attend the Friends' meeting, subsequently printed the Robeson letter in October under the title "The Colour Bar in England." When the news of the Robeson rebuff broke, London was outraged. "That Paul Robeson, that cultivated, sensitive spirit whose wonderful voice has sung itself into the minds and hearts of Great Britain, should be so insulted ought to bring matters to a head," raged the October 25 edition of the *New Leader.* "When one remembers the white trash which is habitually given the freedom of West-end grill rooms and lounges, this latest insult to a distinguished gentleman of colour is all the more outrageous." (The Robeson incident, however, did little to change racial attitudes in London. Four years later, Duke Ellington and his orchestra arrived at London's Waterloo Station and were greeted by thirty-seven photographers. But when the fanfare died down and the group looked for a place to stay for the night, they discovered that no decent London hotel would rent to them because of their race.)[29]

Robeson made no public comment about either the Abbott incident or his own racial slight and was out of reach, with Essie aboard the Cunard liner *Tuscania* on his way to the United States for a six-week concert tour when the story broke in England. Between the time of his departure and arrival in the United States the news had reached the American press, and judging from his reaction Robeson may well have not known the letter had been published until he stepped off the boat and was besieged by questions from reporters about it. According to Joe Andrews, "No one was more surprised than he was to see the letter published in the American press." Robeson told reporters that he had wanted to let the incident die quietly but that an Englishwoman and friend of his to whom he had recounted the story took it to the British press. The black press, especially, hounded Robeson to explain how such an incident could have occurred in England. Finally, realizing he could not avoid the question indefinitely, Robeson agreed to speak with reporter L. Baynard Whitney of the *New York Contender* about the matter. Robeson's "explanation" was predictable: the incident may have taken place in England, but the fault lay with American racial attitudes. "To my mind there is only one answer. Whatever influence has been brought to bear could not have been English, for I had not only been served at better and finer places everywhere in London, but many of them considered it an honor to have me present. The influence of American race prejudice was responsible for the affront. My English friends had repeatedly told me that England would never stoop to such an act."[30]

Black American journalists did not chastise Robeson directly for his refusal to acknowledge the experience of "ordinary" blacks abroad, although, had he spoken up, the issue may well have been aired in the white press as well. Nonetheless, they made it clear they did not share his view of England as a racial paradise and urged their readers to exercise caution: "Negro travelers and sojourners in Europe are apt to be carried away by the ordinary courtesy which every hospitable people extend to strangers," said the *Amsterdam News*'s Kelly Miller. "Because France or Italy treats a Negro tourist without harshness does not imply that they want him as their neighbor, companion or fellow countryman. Tolerance for the exceptional man does not mean acceptance of the multitude." Robert Abbott, meanwhile, still seething, published in his own widely read *Chicago Defender* a series of twelve articles entitled "My Trip Abroad" in which he angrily concluded: "The average Englishman feels that England is a white man's land and that a black man has no business there, except as an occasional tourist. . . . Nearly every Negro I talked with was bitter against England and said that he much preferred the American white man who at least was not a hypocrite."[31]

Robeson refused to be goaded into making an issue of the Savoy incident, particularly in America where, for him, the oppressiveness of racial intolerance weighed so much more heavily than in England. It had been two years since his last visit, and from the moment he set foot on American soil he was apprehensive. In a diary he kept for several days during his first New York engagements (one of the very few times he so recorded personal reactions), Robeson noted the "strange feeling" he had sitting at the theater one night. "I was almost afraid to purchase orchestra seats for fear of insult — when in England my being in the theater is almost an event. . . . I do hate it all so at times . . . I feel so oppressed and weighted down."[32]

His concert tour, managed by the impresario F. C. Coppicus (who had handled the American tours of Caruso, Chaliapin, and Rosa Ponselle), had been well publicized and news of Robeson's British and Continental successes amply documented in the black weeklies. The opening November 5 concert at Carnegie Hall drew a full house and an enthusiastic response. The *Daily Eagle* praised the "ease, simplicity and . . . restraint of his voice"; the *Evening Sun* Robeson's ability to create "moods of sentiment, passion and suffering" that "thrilled his listeners"; and the *Herald Tribune* his "strong voice . . . gestureless manner and . . . avoidance of extravagance." Although the word "monotony" was used by more than one critic, and others lamented a "loss of power and bloom" and an "excessive reserve," Robeson's second Carnegie Hall concert several days later was also sold out and a thousand people turned away at the door. Throughout the country the story was much the same: almost all superlative reviews. In Toronto and Chicago the Chaliapin comparison reappeared. His flawless diction ("so clean cut that scarcely a syllable escaped one's hearing"), his perfectly timed hushes and hesitancies, and his ability to move from the painful poignancy of "Sometimes I Feel Like a Motherless Child" to the humor of "Scandalize My Name" particularly impressed critics. "Even his mere speech is rhythmic. It is a joy to hear him announce his encore number or tell the story of a song," said one reviewer. And another: "You don't know whether you are impressed most with his voice, his bearing, his personality, his repose, his engaging air, or what. He thrills you, that's certain."[33]

No amount of audience applause, however, could quiet the unease Robeson felt being back in America. Because life in England had allowed him to relax his racial guard, Robeson found himself vulnerable to insults he had at one time been able to take in stride. He understood well in advance that touring would mean battling to secure hotel accommodations, but in contrast to earlier American concert tours, in 1929 he was refused accommodations in cities whose population came out in record numbers to hear him sing. In Madison, Wisconsin, Robeson and Brown entertained 3,000 concertgoers at the city's Universal Stock Pavilion — only Fritz Kreisler and Sergei Rachmaninoff had attracted audiences this large — but they still could not get lodging in any of the city's hotels. "Last Tuesday, the city of Madison . . . entertained two distinguished guests," wrote an out-of-town reporter. "One was Paul Robeson. . . . The other Bull Montana, whose main claims to public fame are an ugly physiognomy and gorilla physique. Robeson was in Madison to give a concert, Montana to engage in a wrestling bout. All Madison hotels were closed to Robeson . . . Montana, on the other hand, swaggered into the best hotel in the city, received immediate homage and attention, and was assigned one of the best rooms in the hotel." In England Robeson entertained and dined with Lord Beaverbrook; in the United States he had to go to friends or to the colored section of town to find a place to stay. In time he would learn to adjust even to this schizophrenic set of realities, but in 1929 he still entertained the hope that success in America, might, as it had in Britain, ameliorate racial restrictions. It did not.[34]

Two years later Robeson told the *Kansas City Call's* Roy Wilkins that the entire 1929 tour had been a "very unhappy" experience for him. Even in New York he had felt the need for "[white] friends with whom to go around, who would act as bumpers, so to speak, between the prejudice and their colored friends." Robeson said much the same after his hugely successful November 18 concert at Rutgers College — an event that reportedly roused "interest and enthusiasm unprecedented in musical affairs" and filled Ballantine Gymnasium, with 5,000 patrons turned away. After performing, Robeson met with old college friends—Mal Pitt, John Wittpenn, and Steve White. White remembered it as "a wonderful evening. We were all so pleased for Paul. We had a grand time, talking, telling stories, and singing the old Rutgers songs." Later, Robeson spoke candidly with his old classmates about what it felt like to be back in America, apparently assuming they would understand. They did not. "He was angry about the way he was treated in America," Steve White recalled. "'I'm staying in England,' he said. 'I'm sick and tired of being pushed around.'" Paul's attitude disturbed White, who found his frustration and apparent lack of gratitude puzzling. Robeson had achieved so much. What did he have to be angry about? "I was surprised," White said, "because nothing really had changed racially in America. What had changed was Paul. He had been away from it all. He was just not the same old Robey anymore."[35]

Not only did he not get "pushed around" in England, but in England Robeson had professional opportunities unthinkable for a black man in America. In 1930 the opportunity was the role of Othello for which Robeson had signed a contract with London theater magnate Maurice Browne just before sailing for America.

London's theaters were in a serious slump, but while other British theater managers went under, Maurice Browne had been able not only to keep his head above water but to establish himself as a producer of international repute as well. After years of financial floundering with small theater groups, in particular Chicago's Little Theatre (founded by Browne and his wife Ellen Van Volkenburg and one of the first experimental theater groups in America), Browne earned fame and financial success with his 1929 Savoy production of R. C. Sherriff's *Journey's End,* a riveting dramatization of British soldiers in the trenches during World War I. This sudden turn of fortune stunned even Browne, who wrote incredulously in his autobiography, "For a moment I had become—God forgive me—the most powerful theatre magnate in the English speaking world."[36] The money Browne earned—£80,000 from *Journey's End*—he used to fund new theater ventures, staff expensive offices, and purchase the Globe and Queens' Theatres. By 1930 his reputation was such that any play he masterminded, often simultaneously in his two theaters, was "news."

Like many others who saw Robeson in *Show Boat,* Browne almost immediately pictured him in the role of Shakespeare's Moor, and early in 1929 wrote to Robeson suggesting "that we talk over plans once more—*The Emperor Jones, All God's Chillun* . . . and my beloved *Othello.*"[37] Initially, Robeson was flattered but refused, explaining that he was not yet ready for such an undertaking. Like any aspiring actor, Paul dreamed of doing Shakespeare, but only after he had gained sufficient experience. He was familiar with the play, but no more than any educated person would be: he had read it, performed parts of it in high school, and seen it on stage. Browne, however, found it difficult to imagine a Robeson failure and so pressed on, dismissing Paul's misgivings as evidence of that modesty that so charmed London. As Browne saw it, Robeson needed someone who would push him beyond his insecurities. And that Browne did relentlessly.

Browne proved difficult to resist. Six months later he was still pressing Robeson, and in that interim Robeson had become less sure about his own prospects, in particular the direction he should take in his concert work. Mastering lieder was proving far more difficult than Robeson had anticipated, and quality theater roles were scarce. Perhaps agreeing to do *Othello* was no more risky than playing in O'Neill's *Emperor Jones* had been in 1924. Browne promised Robeson competent direction, an excellent supporting cast, and an astounding $15,000 a week. In time the offer, particularly the salary, became increasingly enticing. Joe Andrews said flatly, "It was a question of contracts, and that meant something in terms of maintaining the standard of life on which Paul had already embarked."[38] And so Paul acquiesced and, just before leaving for America in the fall of 1929, agreed to play the role.

The Robesons' "standard of life" included a personal valet (Joe Andrews) for Paul, a live-in Scottish nanny for Pauli, and their new home purchased in 1929. Perhaps the Robesons were living beyond their means. For the past year an old benefactor, the imperious Otto Kahn, had been pursuing them with increasingly unfriendly reminders concerning a 1925 loan of $5,000 that still remained unpaid. In December 1928, on the heels of Robeson's widely publicized *Show Boat* success, Kahn in a registered letter demanded an explanation, since the Robesons had assured him the loan would be paid at the end of two years and had worked out a series of periodic installments to that effect. Essie replied, took full blame (Paul is "very angry with me because he thought I had written ages ago"), itemized exactly how their money, in particular Paul's $600-a-week *Show Boat* salary, was being spent, and promised to attend to the loan immediately. Kahn was temporarily mollified, until January when, for the second time, he was forced to cover the premium on Paul's $5,000 life insurance policy, which the Robesons in their original agreement had used as collateral for the loan. In October 1929, Essie wrote to Kahn again (nothing as yet had been remitted on the loan), explaining that their Equity settlement with Caroline Reagan had caused yet another delay in repayment.[39]

By the time Paul returned to England, Browne was ready to launch an extensive promotion campaign designed to keep the play and Robeson's name prominently in the public eye. Browne's casting of a black man in the role of Othello, the first time a black man had played the part since Ira Aldridge almost a century before, elicited considerable attention in the press and resurrected a long-dormant controversy regarding the playwright's intention regarding the race of the Moor. Soon everyone, it seemed, from university professors to housewives, was writing letters on the topic to the London dailies. The debate, vociferous and energetic, continued until it became tiresome and finally died quietly without ever being resolved.[40] All in all, it was good publicity, giving Robeson a ready-made opportunity to demonstrate his intellectual virtuosity and giving the public another reason for coming to see him in the role.

Included as part of the publicity was a series of press interviews (crammed in between Robeson's concert engagements), carefully planned to show Robeson as a cultured, erudite family man. Held at Robeson's new home at Hampstead Heath, these interviews took place at regular intervals throughout the first half of 1930. Their format varied little. Reporters were introduced to Essie, who with a new mother's pride showed off their young son (her "little white angel," as Essie liked to call Pauli) and began a tour of the house, which invariably included a perusal of Robeson's well-stocked library. Reporters were predictably impressed and in the write-ups that followed approvingly commented on Robeson's "library . . . stacked to the ceiling with books on a thousand subjects."[41]

With the press Robeson struck a confident pose, conspicuously fingering the Phi Beta Kappa key on his watch chain as he spoke about his efforts to refine even further his understanding of the great English dramatist, the complexities of Shakespeare's text, and the finer points of interpretation. Privately, however, Robeson was uneasy. In truth he was far from a Shakespeare scholar and, to make matters worse, had little time for any serious textual study. Robeson understood the role emotionally and interpreted it largely in a racial context. Othello's all-consuming jealousy becomes plausible, he reasoned, only if Othello is of a different race and therefore "feels himself quite apart from the Venetian." This difference makes it "easier for Iago to get the seeds of suspicion sown. . . . It is because he is an alien among the white people that his mind works so quickly for he feels the dishonor more deeply. His colour heightens the tragedy."[42]

On occasion, Robeson's textual analyses proved somewhat facile, as when he tried to draw an analogy between Othello's dilemma and that facing blacks in America: "He [Othello] was a general, and while he could be valuable as a fighter he was venerated, just as a Negro who could save New York from disaster would become a great man overnight. . . . So soon, however, as Othello wanted a white woman, Desdemona, everything was changed, just as New York would be indignant if their coloured man ever married a white woman." But, on the whole, Robeson impressed reporters as he argued that his race made him more rather than less suitable for the part (an "English [white] actor would have to spend at least three-fourths of his time convincing the audience that he is really black") and would prove an asset even in the mastery of Shakespearean English: "The rhythm of Shakespeare has come easily to me, for it is pure music. Some of the words have been easier for me to learn to pronounce than they would have been for many Americans, for there is a similarity between English words as they are spoken by the English and by the American Negro." He preferred studying from his Furness Variorum *Othello* rather than the modern version, Robeson told reporters, because it helped him to get "the full value of the words and the true pronunciation . . . seeing in print such words as *chaunce* and *demaunde* pulls me up and makes me say them the English way."[43]

Thus Robeson succeeded in creating exactly the impression Browne thought necessary to assure *Othello*'s box office success. He presented himself as scholarly, serious, and intellectual—as one interviewer put it, "one of the most cultured men I know." But, although Paul had persuaded the public, he had not convinced himself, and privately he remained acutely apprehensive. The entire prospect terrified him: he was not even sure that he could master Shakespearean English without a slip, let alone perform the role artistically. Already there was talk of producing the play in the United States following the London run. The American producer Jed Harris heard about the production and rushed off to London to discuss with Robeson the prospect of doing the play in America, suggesting Lillian Gish (the female lead in D. W. Griffith's archetypal defense of white supremacy, *Birth of a Nation*) for the role of Desdemona. Essie wrote delightedly to White: "Imagine the interest Lillian Gish would arouse, and wouldn't she make a marvelous Desdemona."[44]

Robeson maintained a heavy concert schedule, studying the play as he traveled by train for a tour of the provinces that included stops in Bristol, Glasgow, Edinburgh, Sheffield, Manchester, and Cardiff. Throughout the tour, Paul was feted not only for his radio appearances and gramophone recordings but also as *Show Boat*'s star and as a performer of international renown as well. Stepping off the train, impeccably dressed in a huge black overcoat and hat, Robeson cut an imposing figure as he greeted well-wishers gathered to welcome him. Invariably he gave a first-rate interview at the station, easily charming locals with a word or two about *their* people or town (in Dundee, for example, their lovely "rolling hills"). A Bristol reviewer described it as a "typical Robeson gesture" when Paul interrupted his performance, turned around, and gave "the front row of girls sitting on the organ pipes [who for most of the concert saw only Paul's huge shoulders] a song all to themselves."[45]

With the tour concluded and opening night for *Othello* only a short time away, Robeson announced that he would miss several weeks of rehearsals because he had agreed to go to Switzerland to star with Essie in *Borderline*, a low-budget, silent, experimental film, and from there to Germany to play in *The Emperor Jones,* and finally to Dublin and Belfast for several more concert engagements. Was Robeson so intimidated by the role that he wanted to put off beginning rehearsals as long as possible? Perhaps. Or anticipating the worst, he may have counted on the concerts and a successful art film to save him. Or he may have wanted to use lack of rehearsal time as a way of excusing a bad performance. In any event, he would not return to London to begin work on *Othello* until April 10, only six weeks before opening night.

When *Borderline's* producer, experimental film director Kenneth Macpherson, first approached Robeson about the project, Robeson hesitated. "Nothing in the nature of cotton-picking!" Robeson reportedly told Macpherson. Macpherson assured Robeson that *Borderline* would be art, "treat the Negro as a sensitive and intelligent being," and, unlike Robeson's earlier and well-hidden *Body and Soul,* show in white as well as black theaters. Macpherson's promise to avoid stereotypes combined with the novelty and artistic possibilities of being part of an experimental film appealed to Robeson, and he agreed to take the part.[46]

Macpherson was at the center of Pool Productions, the avant-garde group that wrote and published the film journal *Close-Up.* The group's intent was to cut through the commercialism of conventional film, encourage and support experimental filmmakers, and use the medium of film to make rich symbolic statements about life and social problems. A forty-page essay released by Pool Productions explained the group's intentions with respect to *Borderline* and commented extensively on the unconventional camera work intended to underscore the film's symbolic imagery. White characters in the film represented "sordid exploitation and unbridled jealousy," while black characters stood for all that was pure and natural. *Borderline's* plot revolved around the parallel lives of two couples, one black and the other white. Astrid (credits list Helga Doorn, in fact, the poet Hilda Doolittle) is a neurotic white woman and her husband, Thorne (Arthur Gavin), an alcoholic. It was Macpherson's plan to demonstrate that, while the black couple, Peter (Paul Robeson) and Adah (Essie Robeson), are racially confined to a borderline existence, Astrid and Thorne also find themselves on society's edge because of their personal problems. The result was intended to be a visual poem showing life "on the cosmic racial borderline" with Robeson the icon of blackness.[47]

The Robesons arrived in Territet on March 20, completed the filming, did some sightseeing, and were off to Berlin by March 30. Privately shown, what little notice the film attracted when it was released in October 1930 focused on Macpherson's ambitious use of innovative and poetic cinematic techniques. Of the few who reviewed the film, most panned it, dismayed that an idea so "full of promise" should produce such "absurd" and "disappointing" results. The *Evening Standard*'s Clive MacManus advised Macpherson "to spend a year in a commercial studio" before attempting something as difficult again.[48]

In early April Robeson performed *The Emperor Jones* in Berlin at the Kuenstler Deutsches Theater in an otherwise all-white production directed by Jimmy Light. Berlin between the wars was really two cities. One was still reeling from postwar poverty and years of staggering inflation, strikes, riots, and unemployment. The other was a cultural phenomenon that drew artists from all parts of Europe. Even more exciting and permissive than Paris, the city boasted superb orchestras, 120 newspapers, theater (over thirty-two legitimate houses) unrivaled anywhere in the world, and avant-garde directors like Leopold Jessner, Erwin Piscator, and the Deutsches Theater's own master impresario, Max Reinhardt. Berlin hosted lavish musicals including the black show, *Chocolate Kiddies* backed up by a jazz band led by Sam Gooding. The nightclubs of Berlin — the Blue Angel, the White Mouse, the Cabaret of the Comedians, Smoke and Sound, Kata Kombe, Megalomania — offered revues with naked women, men dressed as women dancing together, and an abundance of prostitutes. Essie reported that both she and Paul were "crazy" about Berlin, and indeed Berlin's artistic life was breathtaking, as impresario Sol Hurok put it, "the greatest renaissance in this century." But Patti Light remembered Paul's reaction to Berlin differently. "Yes, Berlin was alive artistically, but its decadence really bothered him," she recalled. "Prostitutes in their high boots, charging more money if they took their boots off, and male prostitutes and homosexuals everywhere. It all unnerved him."[49]

Robeson, however, did enjoy working with Jimmy Light, who not only directed but played the part of Smithers in this unique production in which only Light and Robeson spoke English. If agreeing to take the role had been in part a delaying tactic, it at least raised Robeson's confidence, perhaps warming him up for the task that lay ahead. He received fine reviews, with critics hailing him as "the first great American actor in Germany." Eugene O'Neill wrote to Essie expressing his congratulations: "Jimmy [Light] told me Paul knocked them dead! I knew darn well he would. . . . All the wishes there are to Paul and you and the heir [Pauli] always."[50]

But Robeson could put off beginning *Othello* only so long, and after concerts in Dublin and Belfast he returned to London to begin work on the play. "Right from the beginning Paul felt he could not do the role," Joe Andrews said. Performing Shakespeare in London was a far different matter than singing "Ol' Man River" and Robeson knew it. This was England's greatest playwright. Robeson had done what he could to prepare for the role, including uncharacteristically learning his lines more than seven months before rehearsals began and seeking out Shakespearean actor Frank Benson to help him with his voice, manner of speaking, and proper intonation.[51]

Rehearsals, however, only confirmed his worst fears. Browne had promised Paul an expert Iago and intense and competent direction.[52] Robeson got neither. Instead, Browne cast himself in the role of Iago and chose his former wife, Ellen Van Volkenburg, to direct the production. Browne did assemble a competent and talented supporting cast, however. Twenty-two-year-old Peggy Ashcroft, an athletic Danish-German-Jewish beauty, was chosen to play Desdemona. Although she had been acting professionally for less than three years, she had recently scored a huge success as Naomi in Ashley Duke's adaptation of Lion Feuchwanger's melodrama, *Jew Suss* (1929). Robeson and Essie had seen her in the role and both agreed she would be wonderful as Desdemona. Ashcroft auditioned and, despite the fact that she could not sing (as Desdemona she would have to sing the Willow Song), got the part.[53] Dame Sybil Thorndike, an actress of remarkable talent and versatility and one of the most skilled tragic actresses of her day (she had been performing in Shakespearean productions, as well as in other classical and modern plays, for well over thirteen years) was selected to play Emelia; a young Ralph Richardson played Roderigo; and Max Montesole took the part of Cassio.[54]

Maurice Browne remembered the Dartington rehearsals idyllically, with Robeson at the day's end singing spirituals "unaccompanied, by the light of a great log-fire in the music room," but Robeson and Peggy Ashcroft had no such warm recollections. "Rehearsals were a fairly horrific experience," said Ashcroft with feeling.[55] Admittedly, Ellen Van Volkenburg did have years of theater experience, but most of it was in modern experimental theater. In fact, Van Volkenburg boasted that hers would be a "fresh" *Othello* as she had never even read the play before consenting to direct it. Browne had complete confidence in her and gave her carte blanche both financially and artistically, an unfortunate move since almost all her major decisions proved disastrous. "Paul was treated abominably," said Ashcroft. While Paul had wanted individual attention from someone with the patience, experience, and temperament of Jimmy Light, Van Volkenburg's "method" was "to sit actors down and lecture them like a school-mistress." Sybil Thorndike found Van Volkenburg's direction adequate, but Thorndike with her years of Shakespearean experience hardly needed direction. "It was evident after a few rehearsals," Ashcroft said, "that we were going to get no help from the director. As inexperienced as I was, I could see she knew very little Shakespeare."[56]

From the start Robeson had problems with the scenes involving Desdemona. Both Robeson and Ashcroft had received letters objecting to a black man kissing a white woman, and although Ashcroft made it clear in press interviews that she, like most Londoners, found the issue a bit foolish ("I consider it a great honor to be acting with Mr. Paul Robeson . . . and any discussion about my kissing and being kissed by him seems merely silly to me"), the mail so upset Paul that he found it difficult to let Ashcroft near him and instead kept backing away. "I was a little disturbed," Robeson later admitted to reporters. "In my heart I [had] felt that in London trouble could not possibly arise on racial grounds." As it turned out, there were no serious problem in London, but even a few dissenting voices were enough to make Paul extremely self-conscious, as he later put it, like a "plantation hand in the parlor — that clumsy."[57]

Robeson faced an undertaking that, as he said himself, "I did not then consider . . . I was capable of" with virtually none of the assistance he had been promised. Joe Andrews recalled vividly Paul's absolute terror over the entire affair. Othello, "the noble Moor," a man "all-in-all sufficient," greatly feared by all who had traffic in the Mediterranean, was a professional soldier who knew nothing of doubt and uncertainty because both are foreign to the soldierly mind. It was a life and character almost completely alien to Paul's personal experience. "He explained to me how difficult, almost impossible, it was for a Negro coming out of America, where he was expected to be deferential and humble, suddenly to walk on stage and effect the assertiveness and confidence of a general. I have never seen Paul as frightened about anything as he was of that role."[58]

Robeson complained but Browne did little but blithely insist Paul's "natural" ability would carry him through. Robeson later reflected that in this, as in other productions, "directors assumed that I knew what I was doing, when the fact was that I had no technique at all. They no more questioned my 'technique' than they would that of a Hindu dancer." In the end, it was Essie who got Paul the help he needed when she persuaded Max Montesole (the veteran Shakespearean actor who was playing Cassio in the production) to work with him outside of rehearsals. Jimmy Light was also summoned to the cause, but in the day-to-day task of learning individual lines it was Montesole who saved the day. "Each evening Max worked with us," said Ashcroft, "sometimes at my little flat in Piccadilly, other times at the Chestnuts in Hampstead. We were not popular, as you can imagine, with Browne or the director, but we did have Sybil [Thorndike] as an ally. There were a lot of hard feelings between Paul and the Browne–Van Volkenburg team."[59]

Even with the support of Montesole and Light, Robeson could not shake his extreme apprehension. Repeatedly he tried to get out of the part — once, only two weeks before opening night — and repeatedly Browne convinced him to continue with the production. "You do not know how worried I was," he later confided to Hannen Swaffer. "I expected in my first Shakespearean part to have real guidance. . . . I was so worried I nearly gave up the idea." Robeson later said, "I could not feel it, . . . and I have to feel a part to play it."[60]

On opening night, in the foyer of the Savoy Theatre, dashingly dressed celebrities and British notables rubbed elbows with the sizable number of colored patrons in attendance. It was a sight seldom seen in any London theater. Jacob Epstein's rugged, textured, thirteen-inch, slightly larger-than-life sculpted head of Robeson greeted arriving patrons, and prominently displayed playbills for the great coal-black African Rossius's 1833 portrayal of *Othello* reminded them that this performance would make theater history. Well-known theater and literary personalities — Anna May Wong, Hugh Walpole, Mrs. Ronald Balfour, Lady Diana Cooper, Lady Ravonsdale, and Lord and Lady Plunkett — turned out in force as well as "plainly dressed women in horn-rimmed spectacles" and "exotic creatures wearing weird ornaments and decoration." Critics in large numbers also attended and their reviews devoted as much attention to the "spectacle" of playgoers (including Essie, "a striking looking woman" in "a white satin evening dress") as to the performance on stage. To assure the production would be greeted with rousing applause, Browne had stacked the audience with unemployed actors, most seated in the stalls.[61]

London loved Robeson, and this opening night audience in particular wanted very much for him to succeed. The play, however, got off to a shaky start as the curtain opened to almost total darkness and Iago's bitter outburst to Roderigo set far back on an inner stage behind the Savoy's proscenium arch. Whereas the practice with Shakespeare is generally to bring the action as far forward as possible, for this production *all* the play, with the exception of Desdemona's death scene, took place on this distant inner stage. Throughout the lighting remained dim, so much so that Richardson carried a torch in his sleeve to illuminate his own face as well as to find his "way through the stygian darkness of the set." "Unconscionable noise" made in shifting scenery (the "willow scene was played to a veritable bombardment behind the back cloth") further distracted audiences. The overall effect was to make the action remote and frigid and the audience "detached spectators, rather than impassioned participants."[62]

Robeson first appeared in the second scene, mustached and bearded (a concession to those who argued Othello was not black but Arab) and dressed in dark, heavy, fur-trimmed robes. Ashcroft felt that Paul had been "betrayed by the clothes designer" as the dark robes he wore through most of the play overaccentuated his long arms. Robeson was obviously nervous. One reviewer noticed his fingers twitching, another that he appeared to be holding "himself greatly in check, and was at a loss as to what to do with his arms, which hung listlessly by his side." Although he spoke the famous Senate speech with a "quiet authority," there was also a certain "monotony" and "wooden attitude" in his delivery. To make matters worse, Van Volkenburg had liberally altered the text, cutting the play from five to four acts, the result being most evident in the badly slashed and disjointed first two acts.[63]

In the second half of the play, beginning with the heart-rending cry "Confess — handkerchief. O devil," Robeson came alive. Dressed in snow-white robes, he physically dominated the stage. When the lines required passion, he was terrifying: "The blow on Desdemona's face cut the house like a whip." When he raged his whole body shook and swayed, speaking "all the horror of an obsessed mind." In Desdemona's death scene, despite the clumsy staging ("Othello find[s] himself marooned in a distant corner [and] has to push a candle off stage and fetch his dagger from the wings — all awkward business"), Robeson acted with both dignity and pathos, like a "priest about to perform a holy rite."[64]

When the final curtain fell, "cries for Robeson came from all parts of the house," and thunderous cheering rocked the theater. The curtain was raised again and lowered "a full twenty times before the frenzy subsided." Robeson came on stage and faltered for words. "I am very happy," he said between "staccato sobs of joy." Still, the audience had not had enough. Their spirited appeals finally brought forward Peggy Ashcroft, Sybil Thorndike, and the director, Ellen Van Volkenburg. Again, the applause was deafening.[65]

Opening night reviewers showered Robeson with accolades, describing his portrayal as "richly poetical . . . one of the great moments in the history of Shakespearean drama," "acting genius," "Herculean in . . . dignity of strength," "magnificent," "great," "remarkable," "without question . . . the most impressive *Othello* this generation has known." Peggy Ashcroft, likewise, received nearly unanimous plaudits for her "beautifully simple and sincere" Desdemona. "For once we have a Desdemona worthy of the great Othello," said the *Evening News*. Others agreed: "the perfect Desdemona," "beautiful beyond qualification," "the Desdemona of one's visions." And Sybil Thorndike's Emelia was hailed as "the second triumph of the evening," her performance in some instances even competing with Robeson. "Her outburst in the death scene [was] one of the finest pieces of realism in the whole production," said one reviewer; and another, "Of all the performances at the Savoy, Sybil Thorndike's Emelia is the best."[66]

But as the glow of opening night wore off, reviews took on a more judicious tone. The "much-feared" James Agate, whose years of intelligent and incisive commentary had earned him the respect of London's theatrical community and the role of London's chief arbiter of taste, was the first reviewer to accord Robeson serious and unbiased scrutiny. Although Agate has been accused by some of racist attitudes (for example, his remark that "there is no more reason to choose a Negro to play Othello than to requisition a fat man for Falstaff"), Agate did not assume that Robeson or any other actor for that matter achieved the craft "naturally" and accorded Robeson the professional respect of a lengthy, detailed, and honest review. Agate judged Robeson's performance as he would that of a seasoned actor. The result was a scathing assessment, which appeared in the *Sunday Times* nearly a week after opening night and set the tone for almost all subsequent commentaries. In comparison with other Othello's, Agate found Robeson's sorely lacking. In particular, Robeson failed to effect the bearing of a great general (precisely what Paul himself feared he would not be able to do). "Though in the mere matter of inches he [Robeson] towered above everyone else, it was a tower which cringed. He walked with a stoop, his body sagged, his hands appeared to hang below his knees, and his whole bearing, gait, and diction were full of humility and apology, the inferiority-complex in a word. . . . The first thing Othello must possess is majesty, a majesty compounded of pride of race . . . sovereign assurance . . . and self command . . . the actor who does not convey the higher elements of spiritual beauty in the character does not convey Shakespeare's Othello. . . . Mr. Robeson, alas, failed not only to show mastery of the grand style, but also to indicate any idea of its existence."[67]

Although Agate conceded that "in hot display of purely animal frenzy, Mr. Robeson was exceedingly fine," his final judgment was that he "failed to be Othello" and displayed none of the "highly civilized quality" needed for the fifth act in which "Othello's passion rises to the heights of philosophic conception, and Othello's pain gives place to the moral affrightment that such things can be." In short, Robeson's Othello lacked the manner of a man "familiar with the heavens. Throughout the play this Othello had his forehead bent not only figuratively but literally to earth."[68]

Agate complained that Browne had "shockingly manhandled [the text] to the ruination of the verse and often of the meaning." And while he praised Sybil Thorndike and Peggy Ashcroft's "exquisite" Desdemona, added that apart from their performances "the acting was . . . on a dismal level." Browne's Iago, "like Jack Point in a temper, some schoolboy whipping a top, some incommensurate gnat," in particular, irked him.[69]

Subsequent reviewers now did an about-face and concurred that Robeson lacked "the bearing of a general and administrator [and] at the end of the first act . . . slunk off the stage between his soldiers with the air of a pickpocket who is being run into Vine Street between plainclothes detectives"; he "seems de-pressed from the moment he enters the stage"; he was "the underdog from the start"; he performs "with the cares of 'Ol' Man River' . . . still upon him." Critics so ridiculed Iago ("just about as devilish as a chartered accountant," "a cipher, insignificant and meaningless") that Browne gave up the role three weeks into production, conceding that his portrayal was abominable.[70]

Ellen Van Volkenburg's direction was singled out repeatedly for criticism, with many blaming her ineptitude for flaws in Robeson's performance. "Many beautiful lines were quite unnecessarily cut out," complained one reviewer, and her inclusion of "a most annoying 'artistic Chelsea' dance . . . was quite out of place."[71] In the last scene, according to critic William Disher, "the verse sweeps the actor along . . . Robeson . . . awakened us to the accustomed thrill of 'It is the cause, it is the cause my soul . . .' and then by a stroke of crass stupidity for which Ellen Van Volkenburg as producer must take the blame, he stopped, walked slowly right across the stage, and lost all the impetus of this profoundly moving soliloquy."[72]

Robeson had not succeeded in effecting an intellectual, subtle, or confident Othello, but, as even Agate admitted, he did portray an emotionally vibrant one. Several reviewers, like *Weekend Review*'s Ivor Browne, felt this was reason enough to see the production. "You will see an Othello as may never be found again, an Othello whose passion rises and falls with the ease of a wave, whose voice is rich music allied to language." John Dover Wilson, Shakespearean scholar and professor emeritus of English literature at the University of Edinburgh, agreed: "Paul Robeson's performance as Othello was a revelation to me and I think its absolutely right. The critics complained that he didn't know how to stand on the stage, but that didn't matter; the voice, the dignity, the greatness of the man, that's what we wanted, that's what I felt."[73]

Sybil Thorndike felt that inexperience, more than anything else, limited Robeson. "Blacks had so few opportunities to perform serious stage roles, and for that reason Robeson had no choice but to sing and perform any roles that came his way. The movie roles he later accepted did him no good and were a terrible waste of his talent. He was potentially a first-class actor, but he did things emotionally rather than with artistic technique. With more steady and quality theater work and competent direction Robeson could have become a great actor. In 1930 he did not have pace or technical skills, and as a result he quickly exhausted himself — the pools of sweat on the floor during the *Othello* production were clear examples of this. If only he had had the opportunity to learn and refine his technique — because he had all else: the physical presence, voice, appearance, emotion, and imagination."[74]

For the first two weeks of its run *Othello* grossed $20,000 a week, but negative reviews eventually took their toll as audience attendance sagged steadily and receipts fell dramatically. In June Browne admitted to reporters that *Othello* had indeed "been a costly production" and one that had begun to "lose money."[75] By the time *Othello* closed Jed Harris had abandoned plans to have Robeson play the role in America. Privately Robeson was relieved; publicly he explained that racial considerations forced the project to be shelved. Robeson was not ready to do *Othello* in America. Nor was America ready to accept a black Othello.

IO

Uncouplings

1930-1931

As if the later, less flattering reviews of *Othello* were not enough, Robeson had another distressing problem to contend with: Essie had written a biography of him, which was released (in an "ingenuously arranged" promotion effort) the day before his *Othello* opening. Robeson was furious. Essie had managed to upstage him in an account that depicted him as lazy and childlike and herself as wearing the pants in the Robeson household. And with this preceding him, Robeson was to go on stage and play the noble and thoroughly manly Othello. Rebecca West remembered Paul storming out of the house and threatening to cut off Essie's allowance. Joe Andrews confirmed Robeson's anger. "But, he didn't say much," said Andrews. "What could he do? It was already out."[1]

It was her intent, Essie had told mentor Carl Van Vechten in June 1929, to "work out exactly the picture of Paul I want people to have."[2] And from beginning to end, it is Essie's portrait not only of Paul but of herself and their life together this biography details. If anything characterizes the work it is its steady assault of motherly rebukes and petty carping, all couched in a saccharine overlay of fawning praise. The result belied Robeson's larger-than-life public image, depicting him as helpless and completely dependent on his wife.

The biography begins benignly enough, chronicling Robeson's rise to fame from the parsonage in Princeton. Essie takes pains to explain the importance of Paul's black heritage (beginning with the title, *Paul Robeson, Negro*) and outlines in detail the social, religious, and cultural significance of the black church. She traces William Robeson's humble beginnings and later prominence, writes at length about Maria Louisa Bustill's impressive family history, idyllically describes Paul's relationship with his father as well as his ties with Princeton's black community, and records with pride Paul's athletic and intellectual achievements at Rutgers. She devotes an entire chapter to Harlem, a chapter, one suspects, intended in part as a cautionary note to white women infatuated with her husband. ("It's one thing for him to be running around with his own kind," she told Glenway Wescott, "but his cavorting with white women means that black women are inferior, not good enough, just more 'nigger trash.'") The chapter traces Harlem's historical development, explains its attraction to whites and, most important, its inner life accessible only to blacks. "One knows without being told that the white person occasionally seen in the streets of Harlem does not really belong there. . . . Only Negroes belong in Harlem, and they actively resent . . . white tourists."[3]

The tone of the biography changes with chapter 5, which covers Robeson's early theater and concert career as well as his courtship of Essie. Throughout the biography Essie refers to herself in the third person, but despite this annoying pretense of objectivity her presence, at once doting, parental, and judgmental, is painfully obvious and especially so beginning with chapter 5. It is here that Essie first describes Paul as "extremely lazy," a point she belabors whether referring to his work habits or his decision-making processes, using the adjective eleven separate times in reference to him. She devotes three pages at the end of the book to detailing examples of Robeson's "Laziness with a capital L": He is "too lazy to send . . . a card or write . . . a letter" to friends; waits "until the last moment" to learn the lines of new plays; "won't learn a new song until [he] can't sing the same old programme any longer"; is "too lazy to dig in and work, and so . . . say[s] 'I'm a special interpreter of the music of my people' because no work is required" for him to sing these songs "really well"; and is so "everlastingly lazy" he won't even consider playing Othello because it would mean taking the time to "learn the role, learn how to walk in strange clothes, learn how to talk in a strange idiom, . . . and read . . . about Shakespeare."[4]

Essie credits Paul's first successes to "his usual good luck" and "his precious instinct," which seem "at first glance to be almost pathological laziness [but] successfully [steer] him past nearly all the wrong turnings straight on to his goal." While acknowledging the Provincetowners' talent, she speaks with ill-concealed disdain of their work habits, values, and influence on Paul. "Their complete lack of any routine appealed to him deeply. Their leisurely, lazy life suited his own temperament perfectly."[5]

Given her own background—a strong-willed mother, an alcoholic father, and two less than successful brothers—it was perhaps inevitable that as an adult Essie would continue to perceive men as helpless and in need of the steady hand of a decisive woman. She certainly saw herself as filling that role in Paul's life and, one senses, resented not being given credit for pushing Paul to overcome his "characteristic laziness" and achieve success. Whether acting as manager, nurse, confidante, or secretary it is Essie, according to this work, who takes care of the day-to-day needs of this "small boy," this "blessed, confounded, adorable nuisance," whom she will "treat as a man" as soon as he grows up. Robeson behaves "passively," is unable "to think out what he would do or wanted to do," and has "no trace of aggressiveness in his make up," whereas she, as one reviewer put it, is "the power which plans and arranges the lives of both Big and Little Paul."[6] Essie handles the money, pays the bills, and makes travel arrangements, usually securing "three of the best seats in the [Pullman] car" and hotel rooms where Robeson and Brown might otherwise have been refused. When *The Emperor Jones* closed unexpectedly in London in 1925, it was Essie who answered Paul's "What will we do now?" She encourages him after bad performances, arranges for him to have voice lessons in the mid-twenties, and later pushes him to study German lieder and undertake Maurice Browne's *Othello.*[7]

Among the most disquieting portions of the book, and those that most embarrassed Paul, who so jealously guarded his privacy, were the sections dealing with the Robesons' intimate life together. Had Essie been a better writer, she might have handled the subject more deftly. Instead, what these passages reveal most poignantly is Essie's need to be seen as sexual, uninhibited, and passionate: a wife as well as a helpmate. When she talks about their monthlong stay at Villefranche, she mentions nothing about their explosive arguments but instead portrays the vacation as a long and wonderful romantic interlude. She describes herself as having "disturbed the quiet of Villefranche by washing her hair and sitting on the balcony to dry it in the sun" and how the sight of her usually carefully coifed hair, "standing in an enormous semi-circle straight out from her head and face, like a huge black wool-silk halo" caught the attention of many an amazed passerby, including Glenway Wescott. It was Essie as the outside world seldom saw her, or so she would like her readers to believe. Wescott, seeing her, remarked, "Makes me think of the jungle," to which Essie replied, "You forget that way back somewhere I am the jungle."[8]

One senses her casting about for examples sufficient to prove her point, as when she describes herself and Paul getting out of their beds (apparently they slept in separate beds) "to sit just within their balcony window, nude, for their daily sunbath." Set down in Essie's matter-of-fact, reportorial style, even suggestive details fall flat; worse yet, they call into question the very assertions concerning her sexuality and her relationship with Paul that they were intended to support.[9]

Similarly, she chooses not to sidestep the issue of Paul's extramarital affairs, painting herself as the worldly-wise wife, so sure of her husband's ultimate commitment that she can and does allow him the freedom to stray occasionally. In a re-created discussion that included her, Paul, and a mutual friend (Marion Griffith), she has Paul, presumably for Marion's benefit, list what he considers to be his major faults: cowardice, dishonesty, and perhaps marital infidelity.

Essie, true to the persona she has maintained throughout the book, defends her husband. Her rationale, presented, one suspects, once again for the benefit of the other women in Paul's life, is that even if Paul had "consummated" a passing "interest" or "fascination" with another woman, he nonetheless remained faithful to her "in the all important spirit of things." The "conversation" continues, and Essie turns to Paul and reminds him: "I am the one woman in your life, in your thoughts, in your love. No matter what other women may have been to you, and you to them, they have in no way walked in my garden. We have kept that sacred to us. I'm not a fool. I love you so much, and understand you so well, and have been so close to you all these years, that I should have known, I should have felt, if you were in any way slipping from me. If there have been others, they have, strangely enough, brought us closer together."[10]

Many British readers found Essie's "startling frankness" unnerving. The biography reeks of repressed anger given vent in revelations, as one commentator put it, "if . . . discussed in other Hampstead houses [are] certainly not set down for publication." Most London reviewers chose the safe route of commenting only on the valuable insights the work offered regarding the "difficulties that Mr. Robeson, a highly educated man, had to fight on account of his colour." And a few drew unflattering conclusions about the race as a whole and apparently felt justified as they merely echoed the views of Mrs. Robeson herself: "Robeson has the quality of laziness like most men of huge physiques and negroes whether they have physiques or not"; and "His wife has written a book . . . delightfully true to her race in its naiveté of enthusiasm."[11]

In most cases white reviewers in the United States also handled the work gingerly, while blacks, especially those like Walter White with personal as well as professional ties to Robeson, refused to make any comment whatsoever. The few who paid Essie the courtesy of genuine critical scrutiny, like Langston Hughes, panned the work: "A chatty, informing and naively intimate book" that reveals as "much about Mrs. Robeson as . . . about Paul — and a good deal about them together." Hughes commended Essie for her opening chapter on the Negro church, "some sound and sensible pages on Harlem and the Negro problem," as well as on "Paul's life in two worlds . . . uptown and down, black and white," but took her to task for her endless name-dropping ("The book is dotted with Glenways and Genes and Hughes and folks like that") and her characterization of Robeson as "tumbling from one success to another, working hard when he is interested, and being lazy in between time, enjoying life in the careless Negro fashion."[12]

Hughes was critical but not cruel, but Stark Young, the white Texan whose review appeared in the *New Republic*, ridiculed not only the work but Eslanda Robeson as well. "Its mediocrity spoils the fine material it attempts; its trite and somewhat specious plausibility invites a certain approval that is only another kind of condescension," Young wrote. "There is not in the whole book a word or a phrase or a reaction that betokens the depths, common sense, simplicity of nature and artistic sense that he [Robeson] undoubtedly possesses. Not even the Negro dialect . . . is good. . . . The whole tone is dead, implausible and learned from the worst type of pious biographical rubbish."[13]

Inept and painfully desperate as it may have been, the biography represents Essie's attempt to fight for her marriage and, to the extent to which her own identity was defined by that bond, her life. Although most intelligent readers would easily recognize the degree to which hurt and anger over a failed marriage drove Essie's portrayals of both herself and Paul, there is no evidence that Paul ever expressed any understanding or empathy for his wife's position. "More than anything the book embarrassed Paul," Joe Andrews said frankly. "Criticism of any kind upset him deeply, and he worried that because of the book people would think less of him. He had always been so careful in England about how he behaved and what he said and didn't say. It troubled him that people might be offended or shocked by Essie's revelations or her blunt discussion of their personal life." The biography did suggest an unflattering underside to Robeson's seamless public persona, one that contradicted press portrayals of a picture-perfect Robeson family life. For all but the most naive the book amounted to a public admission that all was not well in the Robeson household.[14]

That British white women found Robeson immensely attractive and he, for his part, returned the compliment was well known in Britain, with accounts like that recorded in the 1929 diaries of British diplomat and writer Sir Robert Bruce Lockhart of Robeson dancing "with all the white women" at a Beaverbrook party commonplace. Ethel Mannin in a 1930 biographical sketch of Robeson talked about his magnetism: "When he comes into a room something happens . . . irresistibly people look at him; he radiates the intense vivid life in himself." His voice, whether singing or speaking, was an integral part of the magic: "The best description [of his voice] I ever heard . . . is unprintable, since sexual imagery in this country is verboten." Dorothy West, with no prodding, talked about "the other woman Paul was in love with" at the time. She remembered the Robesons renting a flat (before he and Essie moved to Hampstead) from a titled family in London and conjectured that a woman Paul was in love with owned the house. Glenway Wescott said the same, and Essie herself discussed the matter of Paul's love affairs with the Van Vechtens at the time of the Robesons' party in 1929.[15]

If Pauli had been intended, in part, to save a faltering marriage, Robeson made certain the ploy did not work. Paul often told friends that "the boy," as he almost always called Paul Jr., was "Essie's child. . . . She had him against my wishes," and that being the case "she should do with him as she wished." Robeson lavished attention on other people's children (frequently at Heywood Broun's parties Paul sang Broun's son "Woodie" to sleep) that he often denied his own son. Only later, when Paul Jr. was an adult (and no longer the sole remaining marital link), would his father show him real attention.[16]

Glenway Wescott, Dorothy West, Antonio Salemme, and Malcolm Pitt each remarked on what appeared to be an astounding indifference on Paul's part to his son. "Paul resented the way Essie and her mother doted on him [Pauli], maybe because his own childhood had been so hard, just scraping by," said Pitt. In the middle of the *Othello* run, two-year-old Pauli became seriously ill with tonsillitis, a bowel fissure, and stomach cramping and eventually had to be hospitalized. Pitt, who was visiting at the time, recalled vividly Essie's distress. "Paul was busy and she was beside herself, so I sort of took Essie over, trying to distract her and cheer her up by taking her out and to the theater. She really had to do it all — both the mothering and the fathering of that child."[17] As Robeson's life in London became increasingly hectic and he saw less and less of Pauli, the issue became a source of tension and, in many respects, a metaphor for Robeson's lack of commitment to the marriage. In 1930 when the *Daily Herald*'s W. R. Titterton asked Robeson what he would do if his vocation as an artist were to come into conflict with his family obligations, Paul responded thoughtfully but firmly, "Then my family must suffer."[18]

Not surprisingly, the issue of Paul's relationship with his son also showed up in the book. Unwillingly to admit her own deep disappointment with Paul, Essie makes her point by depicting her mother as harboring the secret thought that "Paul saw far too little of his baby, and . . . was strangely lacking interest in the child," and Paul himself admitting he has "no fatherly instinct about him [Pauli] at all." At one point in the book Essie has Paul put the question to her bluntly and ask why, when he's so busy, he should be forced "to take up a lot of time with him."[19] Whatever Essie's intent, the book only widened the marital breach, entrenching the couple all the more firmly in their respective positions: Essie would continue to alternate between prying and blithe ignorance and Paul to use silence and secrecy as a way of safeguarding his freedom.

Robeson's reputation, meanwhile, appeared to have weathered both *Othello*'s early closing and the book, and at the end of the year he was selected for inclusion in the 1931 British *Who's Who*. Publicly Robeson continued the confident posturing that had characterized the pre-*Othello* publicity campaign. "*Othello* has taken away from me all kinds of fears," Robeson said in June 1930, "all sense of limitations, and all racial prejudice. *Othello* has opened to me new

and wider fields; in a word *Othello* has made me free." Robeson talked gran-
diosely and often unrealistically of future plans and projects. According to the
Paris Tribune, he intended to found a theater of his own in London where he
could give recitals of Negro spirituals, act in all kinds of roles ("If I can play
Othello then I can play other Shakespearean parts. . . . If I can play Shakespeare
then I can play Ibsen, Strindberg, Tolstoy, Gorki"), and widen audience access
by providing "a good number of cheaply-priced seats."[20]

In other instances Robeson told the press he was studying Russian, working
out a number of Shakespearean songs with his "friend" Sir Roger Quilter,
whom he had met through Larry Brown, progressing with his study of German
lieder, and making plans to live in Germany in order to perfect the language and
study acting and the music of Schumann, Beethoven, and Schubert. As early as
February 1930 Robeson reported that he had already learned "many classics . . .
Schumann, Schubert, and other masters and very lovely I find them."[21]

The truth, however, was different. Initially Robeson tackled German lieder
enthusiastically, purchasing a metronome to use while listening to gramophone
recordings, assuming, as he told Essie, that the easy rhythm of Negro music had
made him "careless of the value of notes."[22] Throughout his life, Robeson was
able to combine his raw talent with a rudimentary amount of training to carry
him through even the most challenging projects, and so he assumed that with
some time and effort he would also easily learn lieder. He soon discovered
otherwise.

"I never heard the music of Mozart, Schubert, and Brahms as a child — and
now it is this great cliff that I cannot climb," Robeson told Rebecca West.
Reginald Boardman, a voice teacher of Roland Hayes's, said bluntly that Robeson's efforts were doomed from the start, primarily because he was unwilling to
give the project sufficient time and concentration:

> Studying such music is a very taxing thing, and Robeson was not intellec-
> tually oriented toward great classical music. . . . Hayes worked at it for
> years, at Fisher, then in Boston and Vienna with the Brahms expert George
> Henschel, and even he only knew *some* lieder — he was certainly not what I
> would call a student of lieder, like Lotte Lehmann or Fischer-Dieskau, both of
> whom had hundreds of pieces at their disposal. But for Robeson, well, with-
> out about ten years of real study it would have been impossible for him to
> sing lieder. And opera? That would have also taken a tremendous amount of
> time and study, especially an opera like *Boris Godunov.* Robeson had Chal-
> iapin's great physical presence, but his voice was untrained. There is quite a
> difference between making an impressive sound singing "Water Boy" or "Go

Down Moses" and doing the same in a difficult opera where you have to know the language, the music, and the acting part.[23]

Paul's friend Glenway Wescott remembered Robeson's early efforts with lieder as almost pitiful:

He began studying in Paris and tried to sing Schubert's lieder, but he never enjoyed it. "I don't feel comfortable with the language," he kept saying to me. "It just doesn't feel natural. The words, the rhythms don't feel natural." I played the piano for him and was just amazed. His rhythm was off, his voice strained and tight. It was really awful. I knew then that Paul would have to study long and hard if he were to sing classical music really well. Once he found out how hard lieder was, he lost his enthusiasm. He was far from itching to work on it and, in fact, put it off as long as possible. In the meantime, if some other acceptable medium came along — theater, films, whatever — so much the better.[24]

Caught up in the pressure he felt from critics, audiences, and even his own concert manager, Harold Holt, to broaden his program and his growing realization that he might never master the classics, in 1930 Robeson began publicly and aggressively to promote the artistic and cultural value of the music he already sang. He told interviewers of his scholarly interest in "the origin of Negro melodies" and of his discovery of 150 spirituals "hitherto unknown to him."[25] At the same time, he went to great lengths to distance *his* music from its crude and vulgar American variant, jazz ("Jazz to my mind has no spiritual significance . . . it will [not] have any serious effect on real music"), and made clear his resolve to move far beyond "Ol' Man River," assuring reporters he did not even like the song and would never have consented to perform it had he known it would stereotype him and the production would drag on for so long. "London, half full of gold, would not tempt me to take part in another musical show."[26]

Repeatedly, Robeson pointed out the cultural significance of the spirituals. "I was quite amazed," Robeson told reporters after a concert in Paris, "to find how such simple music appealed to the sophisticated French public. . . . Ravel and several other French composers have based some of their music on African melodies and rhythms." He found "enormous interest in negro songs" while on his Continental tour and "made some fascinating discoveries" as well. "A well-known Polish musician proved to me that the melodies of Central Africa have influenced European music. . . . In Paris a Prince of Dahomey . . . told me that in his country there are whole families who devote their lives entirely to song. We are on the eve of great discoveries with regard to Negro culture."[27]

Despite his confident demeanor, however, Robeson was discouraged and at a loss as to what to do next. By the summer public affectations yielded to private realities, and, opting for the familiar over branching out, Robeson summoned Larry Brown from America (where he was collecting new music) for a summer–fall tour to open at the Savoy Theatre and include stops in industrial centers like Birmingham, Sheffield, and Manchester. The program they pulled together ("Robeson's 'New Experiment'") was a good reflection of Robeson's professional ambivalence. Their weeklong August engagement at the Savoy, for example, included an abridged version of *The Emperor Jones* (with Max Montesole playing the "foul-mouthed little cockney wastrel," Smithers) sandwiched between a hodge-podge of opening and closing musical numbers (spirituals, Stephen Foster selections, "Ol' Man River," and some German lieder).[28] The classical music Robeson sang included Beethoven's "Die Ehre Gottes aus der Natur"; Schumann's "Die Beiden Grenadiere" and "Wenn ich in deine Augen seh"; and Mozart's "O Isis and Osiris." Savoy audiences tolerated Robeson's lieder and critics noted it, but without enthusiasm ("[There was] some lieder, which Mr. Robeson does not sing very well").[29] What earned Paul applause were old triumphs: *The Emperor Jones* selections and, as always, the spirituals and work songs.

After the Savoy concerts Robeson eliminated lieder from the tour. His program for the rest of the summer was often interrupted by "acts" from other performers: in Manchester a one-act play (Stanley Houghton's *Fancy Free*); in Sheffield a ventriloquist, "feats of strength by the Three Caesars," an impressionist, and dance routines; and in Bradford magicians and comedians.[30] The tour won Robeson the rave reviews and applause he craved, testifying at best to his many talents, at worst to his lack of confidence and fear of failure. "Paul was making lots of money (and needing it), singing 'Mighty Lak' a Rose,' as he put it, 'Anything to make a buck,'" Glenway Wescott recalled. "But it was more than that. He tried lieder off and on for a while, but it just never worked for him. Eventually he just gave it up and began studying Russian instead."[31]

Not only was Robeson locked in a virtual stalemate professionally, but personally he felt almost equally trapped as smoldering tensions between him and Essie erupted again in the fall after Essie discovered and read a love letter to Paul from Peggy Ashcroft. As had been the case earlier in the mid-1920s, when Robeson roomed with Gig McGhee in the Village (ostensibly because McGhee's apartment was close to the Provincetown Theater on MacDougal Street), in England, likewise, Paul felt the need for separate living quarters and so earlier in the year had rented a flat in London. Apparently, Paul and Essie had discussed the possibility of living in the flat together, and while Paul toured the provinces (Pauli and Essie's mother were in Territet, Switzerland, where *Borderline* had been filmed and where Essie planned to buy property) Essie stayed in the apartment and while there intercepted the Ashcroft note. Essie had not suspected the young and newly wed Ashcroft of having any romantic interest in her husband and on discovering otherwise was enraged. She left immediately for Territet and once there wrote to Paul. Her letter has not survived, but Robeson's response to her, one of the few lengthy letters he ever wrote, has.

I am very sorry, of course, you read that letter. You will do those things. You evidently don't believe your own creed — that what you don't know doesn't hurt you. It makes things rather hopeless. It must be quite evident that I'm likely to go on thusly for a long while here and there — perhaps not. I'm certain I don't know, but the past augurs the future.

I've tried to explain to you that no mail addressed to me — telegraphed, cabled or otherwise — is so important that it must be opened. You knew I was coming in Sunday, and you could have held it until then. . . . Its my fault for having mail reach me there, but you were not living there as yet, and I felt for the time being it was my apt. It makes matters rather difficult, as I must have a certain amount of privacy in my life — and my mail must be inviolate. . . . So, I see nothing but to leave you the apartment and go to an hotel. I'll keep my front room and come in to see you. I most probably will be at the Adelphi — and you can have the girl live at the house; either that, or we can rent it out and you remain in Switzerland. I could come over for a couple of weeks before going to America.

In our present condition it appears it would be better also for you to remain in England or Switzerland then (When I go to America). We'll need every penny, and I'll be so busy with my work, I'll not be able to see much of you — you might feel happier there with the boy.

The work on this music must be done, and I can see my way clear if I can concentrate.

As for that letter — I'm sure you haven't destroyed it, and I must not only request but demand you send it to me. Please send it all, as I shall have it verified. Just how it helps you to do these things, Essie, my dear, I do not know. But I must have the letter. What I feel about this and that I'm sure I don't know. I am in a period of transition — where I shall finally finish is of little consequence to me. I would like to get on with my work. To do that I think I need to be alone and to be as far as possible absolutely free. I thought in spite of past misunderstandings it might be possible tho we happened to be in the same apt. But if these things can continually happen, its quite impossible and will only be bad for you and me. I'd suggest you remain with the mountains and lakes, and I'll come there when I can feel so disposed.

There's no need of beginning something (the apt. scheme) we know will not work out as we wished.

I'm sure that deep down I love you very much in the way that we could love each other. It could not be wholly complete because we are too different in temperament.

But however as it is, we haven't helped each other very much. I feel spiritually starved. You became almost a physical wreck. Something's wrong — maybe my fault, maybe yours — most likely both our faults. There's no need rushing ahead, repeating the same mistakes. . . .

I'd love to come to Switzerland for a short while when I'm thru and see you and Mother before going away. We'd be more likely to understand each other better there. If you must come to see about the flat and business, all right. If you feel you want the flat — all right. You determine that. But the financial strain must be considered. Love to the boy. Do tell me about him and how he's going along. Of course I'm interested. Write me always as you feel. I often feel extremely close to you and want to see you and talk to you and perhaps weep on your bosom. Let's hope all will come out right. Love, Paul.[32]

Paul's letter only rekindled Essie's rage, especially because she was convinced he only wanted her to stay in Switzerland "so he can carry on with Peggy."[33] She was correct in assuming Paul's primary motivation was not financial but incorrect in guessing it was Ashcroft with whom he wanted to spend time. In fact, the Ashcroft affair was brief, with Paul and Peggy parting amicably.[34] But, for almost two years by then, Paul had been romantically involved with an English white woman, whose identity he had kept a secret, and that relationship, in contrast to his other flirtations, showed every sign of being serious.

Essie stayed in the London flat while Paul finished his tour of the Provinces and visited her on weekends. For the first time they talked seriously of divorce, and initially Essie was inclined to agree it would be best. At the end of December 1930 Robeson sailed for America (without Essie) for a coast-to-coast tour. Reports of his British and European successes — *Show Boat, Othello,* the Albert Hall concerts, Continental tours, and the addition of German lieder and English folk music to his repertoire — preceded him, thanks largely to Walter White. Still, Robeson was apprehensive. A sold-out opening concert at New York's Carnegie Hall laid many of his fears to rest, as he held "the audience spellbound" and earned superlative reviews for the "sincerity," "manly fervor," and "natural resonance" of his voice; his "admirable" and "ever clear and smooth" diction and enunciation; his "superb" stage presence; and the "gusto, exaltation and fervid simplicity" of his renderings of spirituals.[35] When after four encores the audience still showed no inclination to leave, Robeson added two extra vocal groups and closed with the show-stopping "Ol' Man River." So intense was the crush to talk with him after the concert that it took until well after midnight to clear the hall.

The black press (in particular the *New York Age*) applauded Robeson for at last including lieder. "For the first time upon the concert stage Mr. Robeson . . . presented a program which included a group of classics, including a Beethoven composition, 'Die Ehre Gottes aus der Natur'; the air 'O Isis and Osiris' from Mozart's 'Die Zauberfloete' (both in German); an English song by Purcell, 'Passing By,' and the old favorite, 'The Two Grenadiers,' by Schumann, also in English." Clearly, Robeson's time in England, "with its atmosphere of culture, seems to have brought . . . a smoother polish, a more sophisticated interpretation." But Robeson's predominantly white audiences asked for no encores of his classical music, and critical comment in the white press on these pieces was at best reserved. Noting that Robeson had expanded his repertoire to include "singing in other languages than English and in other dialects than that of the Negro," the reviewer for the *New York Times* commented unenthusiastically that Robeson "did full justice to his text as well as the music."[36] What moved audiences and earned rave reviews were the spirituals, a point not lost on Robeson; for his remaining American concerts he eliminated German lieder and by the end of the tour had dropped all classical pieces from his repertoire.

From Carnegie Hall Robeson and Brown went on to the Midwest (St. Louis, Kansas City, Chicago, Minneapolis), to the West Coast (Portland, Seattle, Los Angeles, San Francisco, and Oakland, with a special engagement at Stanford University), to Denver and Toronto, and finally back to New York City. Overflow audiences greeted them throughout, frequently applauding the pair into "double and triple encores." At San Francisco's Philharmonic Auditorium over a hundred chairs were placed on stage to accommodate the overflow; audience attendance at San Francisco's Dreamland Auditorium set a new record; and in Denver "even the extra chairs placed in the orchestra pit could not accommodate all who wished to hear the singer, and scores stood while many were turned away."[37]

Still, criticism of his repertoire plagued Robeson. He was sensitive about the issue and when questioned often responded defensively, especially if the criticism came from the black press from whom he apparently expected more understanding. According to Nannie H. Burroughs (writing for the Associated Negro Press), blacks who supported Roland Hayes often refused to do the same for Robeson because they objected to his reliance on spirituals.[38] In New York the previous year fewer than 300 blacks had attended Robeson's homecoming concert at Carnegie Hall, and in 1927, in Kansas City, Robeson and Brown had received a pummeling at the hands of the city's black elite, many of whom complained bitterly about the "embarrassing program" consisting only of spirituals. Throughout Robeson's 1929 tour—in New York, Detroit, Pittsburgh, and Chicago—there were fewer blacks at his concerts than at Hayes's performances.

Robeson said little at the time, but he did not forget such slights. In a 1932 interview he would angrily refer to those well-placed Philadelphia blacks who "won't come to hear me sing because I limit my program to Negro folk songs," and on this, his return trip to Kansas City, he kept an audience of 500 waiting for over an hour because local promoters were $700 shy of his agreed-upon fee of $2,000. J. Francis Smith, traveling manager for New York's Metropolitan Music Bureau, insisted that Robeson not begin the concert until he had been paid his full fee. But at 9:15, with the issue still unresolved, Robeson decided to sing rather than disappoint those who had come to hear him, and "looking moody and morose" he finally appeared on stage.[39]

Although virtually all black intellectuals of the period affirmed the importance of artistic achievement as a way of improving race relations, they were often at odds as to what form this achievement should take. Black audiences, likewise, were not of one mind on the issue. *Messenger*'s theater critic Theophilus Lewis on more than one occasion expressed his mistrust of the aesthetic sensibilities of upper-class black audiences and his belief that Victorian censorship ought not to be confused with discriminating taste. To further complicate matters, almost all black performers had to deal with the perennial problem of a double audience of blacks, on whom they relied for emotional support, and whites, who in most cases supplied the financial backing. White nostalgia for the "primitive" and the desire among many middle-class blacks to affect white "culture" further clouded the issue. Like virtually all his contemporaries, Robeson would be forced in the course of his own professional development to take a position and define artistic achievement for himself. In Robeson's case, initially that stand would be determined not as much by conviction as by the simple acknowledgment of his own limits and preferences.

As the tour continued, Robeson grew increasingly impatient with the criticism and more than once lashed out at members of his own race.[40] On the eve of his return to England, in a press interview in White Plains, New York, where he had performed with the 700-member Westchester Negro Choral Union, Robeson made his strongest statement on the subject to date:

> It is refreshing to come back to New York to discover that here, within an hour of the metropolis, is a band of 700 singers, rehearsing and training under capable leadership, devoting their time to the singing of the spirituals. Throughout the country, with few exceptions, I found a contrary condition

to be true. I found a special eagerness among the younger and, I am sorry to say, the more intelligent Negroes, to dismiss the spiritual as something below their new pride in their race. It is as if they wanted to put it behind them as something to be ashamed of—something that tied them to a past in which their forefathers were slaves.

Robeson explained that whenever he performed for large black audiences they invariably demanded he include German, French, and Continental classics.

It always makes me unhappy to do this. I prefer a program entirely made up of spirituals, because I know therein lies our sound and enduring contribution. I know that in the concession to the music of other peoples in our Negro programs, magnificent and masterly though they may be, lies the eventual obliteration of our own folk music, the musical idioms of our race. By accepting the white man's music we are passing out of the scene as creators and interpreters of the finest expression and loftiest that we have to offer. Either we must encourage more groups like that in Westchester to preserve our folk-music, or we must leave this country, those of us who want to see our music preserved, and go to Africa, where we can develop independently and bring forth a new music based on old roots.[41]

It was a difficult period for Robeson, as he floundered in his search for a personal and professional life that would fit his new status while allowing him to grow and find himself artistically. Robeson complained that the press frequently misquoted him, but in fact his views and plans fluctuated from month to month, so much so that often by the time his quoted statements found their way into print he had changed his mind yet again. To make matters worse, he almost always tailored his comments to his audience, thus creating discrepancies between remarks made to white and black or American and British audiences. Taken as a whole, his press statements reveal little more than his own deep ambivalence. Robeson loved England, for example, but there were aspects of life in America he missed. Thus, in a January *New York Herald* interview with Richard Reagan, he complained about the pressure he felt in England to be "strictly an intellectual," abandon the spirituals, learn German lieder, and even quit concert work altogether and return to the practice of law. With Reagan, Robeson insisted his roots were in America and that another two years in Europe would leave him "dead artistically." But, once he had returned to England, Robeson told the British press he could never live in America as it meant facing the day-to-day humiliation of racism; London, he said, was his home because "in London every man is a potential friend and people are unprejudiced and fair."[42]

Robeson was genuinely glad to be "home" in England, however. Whatever pressure he might feel to conform was more than compensated for by the phenomenal adulation he received in return. The arrival of the black American baritone and actor Jules Bledsoe, for example (who was also aboard the *White Star* liner with Robeson and was scheduled to appear at the Palladium), went virtually unnoticed whereas Robeson's return was announced in all London's major papers. Although in many respects the careers of Robeson and Bledsoe had followed parallel lines — both were preachers' sons, both made their concert debuts in 1924, both won acclaim in the role of Joe in *Show Boat*, both struggled with the repertoire issue, and both conducted European tours in an effort to position themselves as continental stars — in England there was only one Paul Robeson. The great impresario Sol Hurok had managed Bledsoe's career, and Bledsoe, in contrast to Robeson, had already added opera to his repertoire, but in London Robeson stole all the headlines. Once Robeson had established himself in England it was next to impossible for another black to upstage him. Bledsoe had never really won British audiences; his "Ol' Man River," such a hit in the States, hardly made an impression in England. As a matter of fact, not a single British critic compared Bledsoe's rendering of the song to Robeson's.[43]

Once home, Robeson began work on a London production of Eugene O'Neill's *Hairy Ape*, made famous in America with Louis Wolheim in the lead role. On paper, prospects looked promising. Robert Rockmore (soon to be Robeson's business manager), a New York attorney and a friend of Eugene O'Neill's and Jimmy Light's and reputed to have made a hobby of producing plays (including Hall Johnson's *Run Little Chillun!* in 1933, which enjoyed a profitable 126-performance run at the height of the Depression), agreed to finance the project, but only on the condition that Robeson be cast in the lead. With veteran Jimmy Light directing, Robeson in the role of Yank would be flanked by a talented English cast: Norah Balfour as Mildred; Lawrence Hanrey as Long, the cockney stoker; and Sidney Morgan as Paddy.[44]

From almost the first rehearsal the production encountered difficulties from the lord chancellor and censor, Lord Cromer. The censor's "sensitivities" reflected a long-standing discomfort among British audiences with O'Neill and in this case resulted in the deletion of some thirteen expletives from the text. Like the role of Brutus Jones, the part of Yank required Robeson to act the primitive, in this case baring his teeth with uncontrolled animal energy. Precisely because the role was such a departure from the Robeson the British knew, the production attracted attention. Newsmen invited to watch rehearsals reported that Robeson's "hungry snarl, sneering challenge and scornful shout of cheated defiance . . . roused emotions that startled and thrilled."[45]

The action of the play focuses on the gargantuan Yank Smith, stoker aboard a transatlantic liner. Physically powerful, brutal, and earthy, Yank takes great pride in his work: he is a crucial part of the machinery that keeps this huge vessel moving at twenty-five knots. All that changes after a chance encounter with one of the first-class passengers, Mildred Douglas, an idle young white woman with a halfhearted taste for social service, who upon seeing Yank at home in his searing inferno, stripped to the waist, bathed in sweat, and swearing and grunting like an uncaged animal, gapes, recoils in disgust, and faints. Her look of horror does not escape Yank, who is suddenly covered by an unfamiliar feeling of shame. The "Hairy Ape," as his friend Paddy calls him, becomes sullen and morose and abandons his position in the stokehold, determined to get even with that woman and the moneyed class she represents, all to no avail. The wealthy aristocratic strollers on Fifth Avenue whom he insults ignore him. When Yank finally does attract attention, he is arrested. He tries to join the IWW (Industrial Workers of the World), but even the labor organization rejects him. At the zoo standing before a gigantic caged gorilla, Yank finds briefly the sense of belonging he longs for. In a self-deprecating tone, Yank points out all that he and the gorilla have in common, jimmies open the cage, offers the animal a "Pardon from de governor," and extends his hand for "de secret grip of our order." But something angers the gorilla, and he grabs Yank, crushes his ribs in a violent hug, drops him to the floor of the cage, shuts the door, and walks away. "Even him didn't think I belonged," moaned the dying stoker. "Christ, where do I get off at? Where do I fit in?"

It is interesting that Robeson's comments to the press indicate that he almost completely missed the political and social implications of the play. The hero, Yank, is a worker, isolated, and ultimately destroyed by warped social values and modern technology. Robeson mouthed conventional interpretations of the play ("capitalism is his [Yank's] only enemy") but showed little understanding of the special resonance this play would have had in industrial areas of Britain, hard hit by unemployment and virtually ignored by the government.[46]

With his British contacts limited largely to the upper classes, Robeson moved in a rarefied atmosphere, a world completely removed from the devastating labor crisis plaguing England's "distressed areas." Personally, Robeson was so self-absorbed, so concerned with finding his own niche, and literally hustling to keep up with living expenses that he had little room for anything else. Thus, from the outset Paul appeared primarily focused not on the content but on defending his suitability, as a black man, for the role. In a January interview with Richard Reagan, Robeson said that O'Neill was rewriting portions of the play specifically to accommodate him (as a black man) in the role; later, after no such revisions were made, Robeson stressed the universality of this "strong and forceful . . . fighter, a king among his own kind." When a reporter from the

Manchester Evening Chronicle asked him if *The Hairy Ape* would play in the industrial provinces and "distressed areas" of England, Robeson addressed the question solely in terms of the play's likely financial prospects in those places. He responded that he would like to take the production to Liverpool, Manchester, Cardiff, and Glasgow, and then asked ingenuously, "Do you think the venture would be successful?"[47]

The Hairy Ape opened Monday, May 11, at the Ambassador Theatre to an audience that had willingly paid twenty-four shillings, double the usual price.[48] The curtain parted, showing the cramped forecastle of a transatlantic liner sailing from New York, crowded with men dressed in dungarees and heavy shoes, shirtless, cursing and singing—and almost all drunk. Robeson, seated in the foreground, dominated the scene, swaggering and grunting in a voice loud enough to be heard above the din of grinding machinery.

Robeson was at his best in the first half of the play where, stripped to the waist and drenched in sweat, he showed his magnificent form to full advantage. Physically, he fit the part of this fierce, truculent powerhouse who made "the old tub run" perfectly. The third scene, which follows Yank's fateful encounter with the elegant and easily distressed Mildred, brought the loudest applause of the evening as Robeson, "huge shoulders glistening in the red light of the furnaces . . . made a fine Rembrandtesque picture." But for the second half of the play the fully dressed Robeson was less impressive, enough so that the final scene where the giant gorilla crushes Yank was almost anticlimactic.[49]

Despite their avowed "disgust" with the play, London audiences found the spectacle of Robeson acting the primitive engaging, and when the final curtain fell the house rocked with the "utmost enthusiasm." The next day's reviews rehearsed a familiar Robeson story: faulty production rescued by a stellar Robeson effort. Although a few critics admitted interest in O'Neill's techniques, the vast majority ridiculed the playwright's use of symbolism, obscenities, oblique psychological references, and expressionistic-impressionistic style (using masks to portray society as uniformed marionettes and bathing the audience in red light during the scene set in the stokehold). Several suggested the subject, inappropriate for London, was the play's major flaw ("In any of the industrial centres of the North" it would have found "more appreciative audiences than the Mayfair audience who politely received it last night"). In the end, consensus judged the play so poorly constructed that even Robeson "could not entirely disguise [its] weakness."[50]

Still, reviewers gave Robeson "an ungrudging tribute of admiring applause" for his "powerfully impressive . . . splendidly vital" performance, "so real that he makes the play . . . anemic," "a one man show," "the dominating voice in the profane chorus of stokers." Several admiringly commented on his physique. Said

Frazier's: "That Mr. Robeson should be stripped to the waist is my first demand of any play in which he appears."[51]

There were some inevitable observations about Robeson's suitability, as a black man, for the role. Several suggested that his portrayal transformed the character from O'Neill's "Hairy Ape" to a "Bronze Ajax" showing little of the "thick-witted, dangerous and ugly" attributes of the original character. Others contended that Robeson's color altered the direction of the play, making it "difficult to think of [it] other than a piece of racial revolt."[52]

The play had been running for only five days when Robeson suddenly took ill with a cold and laryngitis and withdrew, forcing the production to close and purchased tickets to be refunded. To the press Robeson explained he had looked forward to a long run, regretted the way things turned out, and was particularly upset about having thrown a number of English artists out of work. Some found it difficult to believe that this magnificently endowed man could be laid low by something as trivial as a cold, and soon the rumor circulated that Robeson was trying to "malinger his way out of difficulty" (a doomed production). Most, however, thought otherwise and explained Robeson's "sudden indisposition" matter-of-factly with no unflattering insinuations, reporting that after consultation with doctors it was decided that further performances would be "madness as far as Robeson is concerned" and might permanently injure his singing voice. Several recounted speaking to Robeson in a hospital bed and noted he had been unable to manage more than a whisper. "My voice is coming back slowly, and I am feeling better, though still weak and tired," Robeson said. "The rehearsals nearly killed me, I am supposed to be a strong man. Yet I couldn't stand up to the strain on my physical strength. When I came to the first night I had no physical reserve left. My voice went."[53]

For the first time in ten years Robeson was functioning apart from Essie, who had always been there to monitor his activities so that he did not tire himself and, when he fell ill, nurse him back to health. But since their separation Essie could do little but stand back and watch as Paul overextended himself and suffered the inevitable repercussions. "He [Paul] stepped on the ship in New York immediately following the hardest concert tour he has ever done," Essie, still defending Paul, wrote to the Van Vechtens in May, and "stepped off the boat on this end and jumped right into rehearsals. He worked like mad and opened [*Hairy Ape*] after two weeks of rehearsing. The consequence was he was tired out, began yelling, and after opening Monday night, had to be put to bed in a nursing home the following Friday suffering from strain, nerves, laryngitis and no voice at all. In bed a week, treated with inhalators and ordered complete rest by the doctors. Looks thin and tired but with his voice intact. They closed the play and will not reopen it fearing Paul will ruin his voice."[54]

As much as Essie had threatened Paul's privacy, her presence in his life had also protected it. She had freed him by attending to professional and personal details, and their marriage sanctioned activities of his that might otherwise have been judged questionable. But by 1931 all that had ended, and despite considerable support from the British press, rumors concerning the "real reasons" for Robeson's sudden withdrawal from *The Hairy Ape* continued.

Reports of white English women infatuated with Paul were not new, but following the Robesons' separation, stories of this type increased and acquired a decidedly less deferential, more titillating tone. During Robeson's American tour, for example, the *New York News and Harlem Home Journal* published a front-page article headlining the couple's separation, spiced with the additional news that "a beautiful English woman enamored of Robeson, [an] untitled, middle-class woman . . . said to be living hard by Robeson," had followed him to New York City, and "the battle is now raging . . . between the two women [Essie and the English woman] for Robeson's affections." In London the *Daily Mirror*'s account of the fans lining the corridor outside Robeson's dressing room after one performance of *The Hairy Ape* was similarly enticing: "Then in the ensuing rush," the *Daily Mirror* reported, "four beautifully dressed English and American women got first into the little room and warmly kissed—and were kissed by—the giant Robeson."[55]

Such innuendoes, scattered as they were, did not bode well for Paul. Robeson's experience had mistakenly persuaded him that in twentieth-century England racism did not exist. But it was precisely because he did not fit the stereotype (and not because the British were above stereotyping on the basis of race) that Robeson had been treated so well. Between the English settlement of the New World and its fumbling attempts to reconstruct colonial governments out of former slave societies, Englishmen had to conjure up a variety of rationalizations (primarily various defects characteristic of the colored races) in order to justify black importation, enslavement, and eventual emancipation. Among these rationalizations was the idea that the darker races were promiscuous and strongly sexed, indolent, unintelligent, unmanageable, untrustworthy, and inclined to be musical. (Stories that fed the stereotype of the African's superhuman prowess were legion. Black troops had not been allowed to take part in the coronation of George V because reportedly English women had lavished so much attention on black soldiers at the time of the coronation of his father, Edward the VII. Similarly, in 1925 at the Wembley exhibition, several young and muscular African men on "display" as part of an exhibit of an African village, daily drew crowds of admiring white women. As a result the Africans were barred from touring London with the rest of the exhibit for fear the British white women would "capture" them.)[56]

Old myths die hard, and in those areas of England with heavy black populations such racist assumptions were often held to be fact and, among those British with little first-hand contact with blacks, American movies filled in the gap and perpetuated the stereotype. Thus the English were not surprised that Robeson could sing but amazed that he had a law degree. When he first came to London in 1925 to do *The Emperor Jones,* local theater workers had assumed he was, "like all blacks," illiterate.[57] Robeson's capacity for deep emotion was also presumed a racial characteristic, but the restraint, poise, and reserve with which he expressed that emotion was not. Physically and sexually Robeson had the appeal the British associated with the African, but with Robeson it was controlled and proper.

Robeson sensed enough danger to be worried, but in fact he had little idea how damaging suggestions of sexual impropriety could be to his reputation. Thus far, he had been the perfect exception: sexual but not promiscuous, not overly ambitious but far from indolent, emotional but restrained, simple but intelligent and well educated. But, should he slip, particularly in the area of sexual conduct, Robeson ran the risk of becoming "one of them" and thus of finding himself excluded from the inner circles of Britain's upper class.[58]

The public, with some exceptions, took in stride Robeson's sudden departure from *The Hairy Ape.* Paul meanwhile moved into bachelor quarters in London (Essie remained at the flat on Buckingham Street), and then he disappeared. Such disappearances were not out of character for him, but in this case his timing was poor. For a solid month there was virtually no mention of his activities in the British press, and for the remainder of the summer he surfaced only occasionally to do a concert in one of the small towns on the seaside of southwest England where he was resting and spending time with the woman he loved.[59]

Essie, meanwhile, struggled to maintain composure while bearing the brunt of unkind gossip. At times she tried to be patient, hoping that if she behaved as Paul wished and kept out of his way things would work out. She made excuses for his moodiness ("Big Paul is not very well and not very happy. . . . I think he has growing pains") and for the little time he spent with his son. Essie visited Pauli often in Kitzbühel, Austria, where he was living with her mother or had the pair stay with her in London, but Paul seldom saw his son during this time. When Essie heard about photographs Van Vechten had taken of Paul, she hurriedly wrote him in July: "Please, please may I have the pictures. . . . I'd simply love to see them and Pauli will probably try to eat them up." In December Paul backed out of his plans for a long overdue visit with his son. "He is way behind with his Victor recording contracts," Essie explained to the Van Vechtens, "so he asked Mama if she would bring him [Pauli] over [to London]. . . . Pauli hasn't seen him since last Christmas. He will get the surprise of his life."[60]

On other occasions Essie tried to make Paul jealous, once by sending for an old friend, the handsome, elegant West Indian Harold Jackman. One of Harlem's most eligible bachelors but widely rumored to have his eyes fixed on the young poet Countee Cullen, Jackman nonetheless cut a striking figure and made an enviable escort. Jackman complied, sailed from New York to London, and stayed for about two weeks, all to no avail. If Paul noticed or was bothered by his presence, he never let on.[61]

When all else failed Essie brazenly fought for what she felt was rightfully hers. Glenway Wescott remembered an incident that occurred in 1931.

> Paul asked me what I thought about him getting a divorce. I said it would be difficult but someone had to do it. "Yes, it would be hard," Paul said. "But I'm not sure. I don't want to be a martyr. I want to sing all over the world and I'm having fun here." Then he asked me if I would do him a favor. "Call on Essie and give her a chance to tell her side." I said "No" but later gave in. Pauli was there — very polite and shy. It took Essie awhile, but once she got started she just poured out her anger, assuming, I guess, I would admire her for her possessiveness. She blamed the other woman completely and told me that she intended to cause a scandal and put that white woman in her place. She felt completely justified in doing everything she could to humiliate her. Whatever it cost, Essie was determined not to give Paul up — especially to a white woman — without a fight.[62]

In November Robeson did the unthinkable and canceled a scheduled performance at the Royal Albert Hall. Headlined by the *Daily Express* as "Incredible News," Robeson's cancellation left 6,000 stunned and disappointed ticket holders who refused to go home quietly and "demanded to be admitted to hear all about it." In short, the audience found the news incomprehensible: "Round the pavement circling the building men and women were running, shouting out the news to each other. They did not seem to believe that there was no entertainment for them."[63]

The reason given was again a cold that this time had developed into influenza. But such a cancellation was unheard of at Albert Hall, a course of action other professionals almost never considered. "Very bad cold, perhaps mild attack of influenza," Essie reported to the Van Vechtens, "such as he often has when he is careless and doesn't take care of himself. . . . It does seem too bad he won't be reasonable. But I am not allowed to tell him not to go to parties just before a big concert as I used to, so he just goes and does these things and gets into trouble. Don't worry, nothing wrong with his voice. It seems to improve with age and naughtiness."[64]

Joe Andrews said that the Albert Hall incident occurred at a time "when all things in Paul's mind were accumulating." He and Essie had finally agreed in October to divorce, which left Paul free to marry if he wished. "Paul did have laryngitis, but he never liked performing in Albert Hall either," said Andrews. "It was too big and the acoustics inadequate. He had his usual worries about his voice and whether it would carry, and with everything else it was all too much for him, and so he backed out." When pressed on the issue, however, even Andrews admitted that Robeson "was probably not too sick to appear on stage."[65]

Londoners, who had treated Robeson as a professional, expected him to act as one. (Sybil Thorndike, herself a consummate professional, on the subject of backing out of a performance said, "If I had been shot through the brain, I would have done the show first and then died shortly thereafter.") Even Larry Brown was embarrassed by and annoyed with Robeson's behavior. The furor over Robeson's last-minute cancellation intensified when the news spread that on the night before the concert he had apparently felt well enough to attended a "smart set" (Evelyn Waugh, the Plunkett-Greens, and Noel Coward) party. Robeson's performance at the Palladium on November 23, less than two weeks after the Albert Hall cancellation, did little to ease the hard feeling among Paul's London following, but it did reassure Paul. Though he may temporarily have lost his status as the darling of the Albert Hall crowd, he was still adored by other segments of British society. The reviewer for the *Daily Sketch* noted that "hundreds of women admirers besieged the stage door of the Palladium and mobbed Paul Robeson after his recital. . . . They clutched him by the arm, thrust autograph books into his hand with cries of 'You wonderful man,' and clambered onto the footboard of his car until the police cleared a passage for him and his accompanist, Lawrence Brown."[66]

Five weeks later, in December, Robeson did sing at Albert Hall. As if to reprimand him, many who ordinarily might have attended refrained from doing so, leaving Robeson singing to a "half-empty" hall. Paul recognized the admonition and "despite the warmth of his reception," according to one reviewer, "sounded embarrassed for the first two songs." He did his best to please those who had come, however, with a program composed primarily "of those unsophisticated songs in which he excels, those Spirituals of his race, which in recent years have had such a vogue all over the English-speaking world." The audience responded especially well to "Water Boy," "I Want to Be Ready," "Were You There When They Crucified My Lord," and "Ol' Man River." Robeson included only two Russian songs: Alexander Gambs's "My Prayer" and Gretchaninov's "The Captive." To further placate patrons Robeson acceded to a whopping ten encores; even as the audience began slowly streaming out, he was cajoled into a final rendition of "My Old Kentucky Home."[67]

II

Coming of Age

1932

In January 1932 Robeson arrived in America for a three-month concert tour. From New York City's Town Hall, where the tour opened on January 18, throughout the Northeast, Midwest, and Canada Robeson performed for full houses, this despite the countries' economic woes, and earned superlative reviews. His program varied little from his British repertoire and included the usual fare of spirituals and folk songs as well as two Russian songs (Gambs's "My Prayer" and Grechaninoff's "The Captive") and two European pieces (John Ireland's "Sea Fever" and Christian Sinding's "Light"). Life in England had left its mark: Robeson returned to America confident, polished, and at ease with the adulation. In Des Moines, an audience member during intermission asked if Robeson would sing "St. Louis Blues." The response from his travel manager was crisp and a bit put out: "Mr. Robeson never sings blues!"[1]

Meanwhile, on the other side of the Atlantic, unsavory rumors concerning Robeson's personal life had begun to mar Robeson's cultivated image of artist and scholar: of late Paul Robeson figured as prominently in British gossip columns as he did in the society and theater pages. The gossip subsided while Robeson was on tour in the United States, but once he returned to the Continent in March, his whereabouts for the next two months unknown, the rumor mill picked up pace again. The most anyone knew was that Paul had spent some time in Paris, presumably in connection with work but in fact in a rendezvous with the unnamed woman with whom he was in love. The press still expected Essie to know Paul's whereabouts even though the couple no longer lived together, but in this case she was as much in the dark as everyone else. When asked on April 11 about reports that Paul had signed a contract to star on the Paris stage during the winter of 1933 and that he planned to collaborate in the writing of the play for that production, Essie had little to say: "I have not heard anything about my husband's collaborating with Sacha Guitry and Yvonne Printemps.

He was, however, in Paris a week or so ago before he sailed for New York." Robeson was scheduled to return in the spring to New York for a Broadway revival of *Show Boat;* that much was known. But Robeson's personal plans, of much more interest to the British public, remained a mystery.[2]

In New York the talk was all of Ziegfeld and his decision to take a pre-Depression hit out of mothballs and present it on a New York stage already hard hit by economic decline. Edna Ferber, author of the novel on which the play was based, lambasted Ziegfeld's plan, calling it "as bad an example of showmanship as I have ever known," and predicted that "no one would come to see it [the revival]." Ziegfeld, despite his bravado, had his own concerns. Robeson was to be the drawing card (handsomely salaried at $1,500 a week, almost $1,000 more than Jules Bledsoe had received in the original 1927 production), flanked by almost all the original hit's cast. Still, both Ziegfeld and director Jerome Kern wondered if Robeson's delivery was perhaps too sophisticated, too slow, and "fetching a gallon of pathos" for American audiences.[3]

Edna Ferber was so convinced the production would fail that she summarily announced she would not attend the May 19 opening at the Casino Theater, but at the last minute she changed her mind. "There was what appeared to be a mild riot going on outside the theatre and I immediately decided that infuriated ticket purchasers were already demanding their money back. Sure enough, as I fought my way inside there was a line in front of the box office, though the play had begun. They were milling around and thrusting their hands forward toward the man in the box office. He was saying over and over, in a firm voice, 'NOMORESEATSNOMORESEATSNOMORESEATSNOMORESEATS.' . . . I went in, leaned against the door and looked at the audience and stage at the very moment when Paul Robeson came on to sing 'Ol' Man River.' . . . In all my years of going to the theatre . . . I have never seen an ovation like that given any figure of the stage, the concert hall, or the opera."[4]

Reviews of Robeson's performance far outdistanced those earned by Jules Bledsoe in the 1927 American production. Robeson "never seemed more appealing" and "stopped the show with his magnificent rendition of Old Man River," wrote Maurice Dancer in the *Pittsburgh Courier.* "Having revived *Show Boat* at the Casino, Mr. Ziegfeld should make up his mind to keep on reviving it from now until Doomsday," suggested the *New York Times's* Brooks Atkinson. "After four and one half years, it still seems like a thoroughbred. . . . Mr. Robeson has a touch of genius. It's not merely his voice. . . . It is his understanding that gives 'Old River' an epic lift." "Mr. Robeson's celestial voice could almost not be heard above the din of applause last evening as he began the notes of 'Ol' Man River,'" wrote Percy Hammond of the *New York Herald Tribune,* and the *New York World Telegram's* Robert Garland concurred: "Knowing nothing about voices, but knowing what I admire, I admire the voice of Paul Robeson more than any other voice I can think of. It is a voice in which are beauty and strength and the quality not even a musical critic can put a finger on."[5]

The big story, however, was not Robeson's latest professional coup but new and substantive rumors, this time in the United States, about the women in his life. Nancy Cunard, the slender (almost to the point of emaciation), rash, only child of an American society hostess and an English baronet and heiress to the vast wealth of the Cunard Line, arrived in New York just before *Show Boat* opened to gather material for her now famous collection, *Negro: An Anthology.* Notoriously unconventional, Cunard courted publicity, particularly the type that would embarrass her American-born mother, Lady Cunard (formerly Maud Burke of San Francisco). Lady Cunard had earned a name as one of London's most brilliant hostesses, but the repeated unseemly escapades of her intransigent daughter threatened to topple her from her hard-earned position. Nancy, disdainful of her mother's social pretensions, flaunted her own eccentricities — outlandish dress, a bohemian and promiscuous lifestyle, radical and brash political views, and an extreme fascination with the Negro race. The conflict between Cunard and her mother became front-page news with the 1931 publication of Nancy's controversial essay, "Black Man and White Ladyship: An Anniversary," which both chronicled her two-year relationship with an unnamed black man and spelled out her bitter appraisal of her mother as a narrow, snobbish woman consumed by class and racial prejudices.

Several days after Cunard arrived in New York the Hearst *Daily Mirror* announced that Paul Robeson was the unnamed Negro in "Black Man and White Ladyship" and the reason for Cunard's visit to New York. As the *Daily Mirror*'s reporter James Whittaker saw it, Cunard's taking up residence in Harlem's Grampion Hotel (the same hotel where Robeson was staying) was more than coincidence. Cunard, Whittaker concluded, "has elected to throw her special lot in with the Harlemites, who have welcomed her as a friend of their leader, Paul Robeson."[6]

The press jumped on the Hearst story, and within hours reporters crowded outside the hotel ready to record every Cunard–Robeson move. Robeson denied the story immediately and threatened to sue the tabloid, charging the *Mirror* had deliberately substituted his name for that of the black man in question, musician Henry Crowder, because the Robeson name made "better copy." "It was the rottenest and most disgraceful piece of journalism I have ever encountered," Robeson told reporters.[7]

Cunard was out of town when the story broke, but when she returned, the fiery young heiress responded quickly in an angry telegram to the *Mirror*: "Racket my dear sir, pure racket, heiress and Robeson stuff. . . . Call Monday one o'clock give you true statement." At a press conference the following day, Cunard handed out a typed statement refuting the rumored liaison: "I am astounded at your story of myself and Paul Robeson. You must correct this immediately. I met him once, in Paris, in 1926 at the Boef sur le Toit cabaret, and have never seen him since." (Antonio Salemme, however, claimed that Paul had had an affair with Cunard and that on one occasion he had taken her to Salemme's studio. Joe Andrews admitted that Cunard had met with Robeson more than once but insisted that if there was anything between them, "it was not serious. She was too aggressive and boastful for Paul.")[8]

Scandal did not frighten Cunard; most often she welcomed it, and in this case managed to turn even this situation to her best advantage, using the unexpected publicity to headline her support for the Scottsboro boys and her own forthcoming book. While denying the rumored affair with Robeson, Cunard baited reporters with the identity of the "Negro friend" in question but then refused to reveal his name. "The more mystery there is, the better I like it," Cunard frankly admitted. "I'm getting out a book. . . . and this is what you Americans call ripping ballyhoo for the volume."[9]

The Cunard incident, however, paled in comparison with another scandal brewing simultaneously in England. What had started as unflattering innuendo, fed by Robeson's mysterious disappearance after his return to the Continent in the spring, mushroomed into a widely publicized rumor that Robeson was romantically involved with Lady Edwina Mountbatten. News of the alleged relationship first broke into print in England on May 29 (only a few weeks after the *Daily Mirror*'s disclosure) in *The People,* a sordid rag specializing in lurid gossip, murder stories, and exposés. Although the article mentioned no names specifically, few of the paper's readers (it claimed a circulation of three million) would fail to guess the unnamed participants. The scandal "which has shaken Society to its very depths" concerns "one of the leading hostesses of the country, a woman highly connected and immensely rich," the article revealed. "Her associations with a coloured man became so marked that they were the talk of the West End. One day the couple were caught in compromising circumstances." Suggesting 1930 or 1931 as the period during which the alleged affair took place, the author offered the now-exposed liaison as an explanation for Queen Mary's 1931 decision to send Edwina away for a two-year "rest" on the island of Malta where her husband, naval officer Lord Mountbatten, was stationed. "The Society woman has been given the hint to clear out of England for a couple of years to let the affair blow over; and the hint came from a quarter which cannot be ignored."[10]

Beautiful, unconventional, adventurous, and strong-willed, Edwina Mountbatten had never found the role assigned to her — supporting her husband in his career—satisfying. Travel to such places as Syria, Iraq, Transjordania, and Persia provided some outlet for her restless spirit, but not enough. Her thirst for the exotic soon brought her well beyond unusual touring itineraries and made her fodder for London's gossip columnists. The rumor was widely bandied about that she adored men of color, and, indeed, her activities in Harlem, which she visited as recently as 1930 with her cousin Majorie Jenkins, appeared to bear this out. Although Harlem "slumming" was tolerated and considered a fashionable pleasure among European high society, Edwina indulged with far less caution than her similarly stationed contemporaries. She "regarded 'proceeding with care' as only half living," but her quest for adventure proved a costly pastime as the press took it as their duty to scrutinize her activities. Thus Edwina Mountbatten acquired for herself a reputation, and for her husband the lamentable role of keeper of a wayward wife.[11]

The response to the scandal, presumably initiating from the crown, was swift and decisive. Lady Mountbatten sued Oldhams Press and *The People* editor Harry Ainsworth for libel. She and her husband returned to London from Malta and prosecuted the action before the High Court of Justice. Edwina Mountbatten denied any untoward relations between her and the black man, unnamed in court but assumed to be Robeson, insisting, "I have never in the whole course of my life met the man referred to." The case was decided in Lady Mountbatten's favor, and upon receiving a full apology from the publisher, she did not press further for financial damages. As a public gesture of support and goodwill, the king and queen received Edwina and her husband for a visit and luncheon. Despite a surface cordiality, however, the incident had caused considerable animosity and "a noticeable cooling of relations for some time after the case, which Edwina strongly resented."[12]

The Cunard incident annoyed Robeson, but the Mountbatten scandal deeply disturbed him. Whether he could succeed in squelching the rumors was not the point. There was no doubt he had of late relaxed his initial strained propriety in British social settings. In fact, one could say that as his confidence grew Paul had become lax in this regard, so much so that his reputation as a lady's man was all but carved in stone. In either case—the Cunard or the Mountbatten affair—he fit the part. Robeson wanted no more advice like that given to him by the singer and Parisian nightclub hostess Bricktop (Ada Smith), who traveled to London specifically to warn him that an interracial marriage would ruin his career. Similarly, Robeson had no intention of being lectured to in the United States and, for the time being, saw no other recourse but to keep busy professionally, avoid talking about the subject, and hope that the whole nasty business would die out of its own accord.[13]

While Paul all but hid in America, Essie fought her own battles in London.

On June 25, in the thick of the Cunard and Mountbatten scandals, she announced she was suing Paul for divorce. For almost eight years now Essie had struggled to hold the marriage together, hoping until the very end that Paul would decide to remain, if not faithful, at least married to her. At his insistence, she had rid herself, as she told the Van Vechtens, "of a lot of silly young ideas I used to be boarded up with" and tried to understand the notion of "artists being free."[14] She kept herself busy, working on a novel and a play and socializing as much as possible. It had not been easy. Essie, for so long the planner and decision maker, by 1930 did things as Paul wanted them done. Paul would see whom he wanted to see, go where he wanted to go, and Essie was not to meddle.

By the summer of 1932 Essie had resigned herself; things were just not going to work out. Paul Jr. said that "from my mother's point of view it was just one affair too many." "It seems impossible to please him," Essie wrote sadly to Carl Van Vechten. "I hemmed and hawed and put off the evil day [the divorce] as long as I could hoping something would happen, but he insisted that he MUST have his freedom, and that I just HAD to give it to him, so I felt I must. I had a long talk with Fania [then in London visiting Essie] about the divorce and she agreed that I had to get it since he insists."[15]

"It is all perfectly friendly," Essie informed reporters after announcing the news, "and we will keep on being friends, but we've seen so much of each other and both are just a bit tired and want our freedom. . . . I am not giving the name of the co-respondent because I don't know and I don't care who she is. . . . It is most incredible, though, that people should be linking Paul's name with that of a famous titled Englishwoman [presumably Edwina Mountbatten], since she is just about the one person in England we don't know. I even had a friend come to me in Paris and say that if the Queen wanted me to drop this thing to do it. It is just too amazing and all very ridiculous."[16] Essie tried to maintain her poise and self-assurance in the face of an almost constant barrage of press inquiries, but Paul's activities often made this difficult. Only a few weeks after announcing the divorce, Essie learned that Paul had registered himself and "Mrs. Paul Robeson" at a hotel in New York. The woman in question could have been either white or black as the real Mrs. Robeson could easily pass. When questioned about this by the press, Essie could do little more than state the obvious. "All I know," she said, "is that there have been a Mr. and Mrs. Paul Robeson staying around New York hotels."[17]

A few days after Essie's announcement, Robeson held a press interview following a Saturday *Show Boat* matinee. Although it had been at his urging that Essie initiated divorce proceedings, Robeson gave the impression that it was Essie rather than he who wanted to end the marriage. "I have been expecting this," Paul told reporters. "I am sorry, but I guess it had to be. . . . I have made my plans well in advance." Robeson went on with considerable self-assurance to reveal what gossip columnists had suspected all along: he was in love with another woman. "It has not been much of a secret abroad," Robeson said smilingly, adding, "When I was in London last we were seen together much of the time and made no bones about our attachment." Insisting that the woman was neither Nancy Cunard nor Peggy Ashcroft, Robeson said only that she was white, British, and of high society. "I can't mention the name now," he said, "as I don't know if she still wants me." Paul assured the press he had decided to marry a white aristocratic English woman only after careful thought and was "prepared to leave this country [the United States] forever" if such an interracial marriage required it. Whatever the reaction in America, Robeson felt confident the marriage would be accepted in England.[18] His bombshell dropped, Robeson returned to *Show Boat,* apparently intending to say no more about the matter until he had finalized plans with the woman in question.

Robeson kept himself busy that summer with a crowded public and professional schedule that included engagements ranging from an appearance as guest artist on NBC radio's "G.E. Circle" program and a midnight benefit performance for the Harlem Children's Aid Society at the Lafayette Theater, to a concert before an audience of 9,000 (the largest of the season) at Lewisohn Stadium. The deluge of rumors had done little to damage his popularity in America, and awards, honors, and invitations greeted him wherever he went. By far the most gratifying of these was Rutgers's decision to award Paul an honorary masters of arts degree, making Robeson the first person in the arts, black or white, and the youngest ever to be chosen for such an honor. "What was even more pleasing to me," Paul said in a later London interview, "was the knowledge that it would do the Negro race an immense amount of good all over America, giving them just that confidence and self-respect they need so badly."[19]

In years to come it would give Paul great satisfaction to recall that among the others receiving honorary degrees from Rutgers that afternoon was the president of Princeton University. The irony of his being feted alongside this prestigious representative of the university did not escape Robeson. It represented, as Hannen Swaffer later described it, "the triumph of the son of a slave" over the sons of southern aristocracy, who by and large composed the student population of the university. "One of my older brothers thought of trying to get into Princeton," Robeson recalled in a press interview. "He was told that if he got in there he would be extremely lucky to get out alive." Neither Paul nor his brothers, nor any black for that matter, had been able to attend Princeton. Robeson could hardly have hoped for a sweeter vindication. "Nothing," Paul said in 1933, "can ever take away from me the glorious satisfaction of that hour. I am continually looking back on it with exquisite pleasure; it gives me poise and confidence in my own future and in that of my people."[20]

In the meantime Paul studiously avoided people and situations that might require him to talk about his personal plans. For old friends as well as professional colleagues this meant that although Robeson was in the public limelight he was virtually impossible to contact privately. The Van Vechtens wrote to Essie complaining that they could not reach Paul. "I'm sorry that you haven't seen much of him," Essie responded from London in June. "I hear on all sides that he is very depressed and I'm sure the reason he hasn't seen you is because he's so unsettled mentally, and is afraid to talk to anyone he really cares about, because he doesn't know his own mind. When he gets his divorce he may get himself together. I hope he does, poor lamb. I hate the idea of him being unhappy and disorganized." Initially, old friends were not surprised when efforts to reach Paul failed. Robeson was notorious for missing appointments and almost hopeless at attending to mail. He would pick it up, put it on the table or desk, vow to read it, move it aside, and then finally give up on it. Anyone who knew him understood that without Essie or someone to take care of these matters, the phone would ring off the hook and the mail remain untouched, piling up at Harold McGhee's apartment downtown at 25 Van Dam Street, Paul's address for the summer.[21] The truly persistent eventually contacted Walter White, certain that as a long-time friend White could reach Robeson.

Lawrence Studios wanted Robeson for an operatic version of *Tom-Tom* and telegrammed White in April: "We must have Robeson. Will you help convince Robeson of the importance of accepting the role. They have already approached his manager." Musician Werner Josten and playwright Donald Haywood, each with projects of his own, also tried going through White. Josten had composed a pantomime opera, *Batouala,* which White later confided to friends would have been perfect for Paul. Alexander Woollcott had spent the summer gathering material for a biographical piece on Robeson for *Cosmopolitan* (later published in *While Rome Burns,* a book recounting the accomplishments of twelve living Americans) and needed additional background information only Robeson could supply. "I wish we could get together sometime next week," Woollcott wrote to Robeson in June. "Lunch, tea or supper would be alright with me. . . . What do you say. . . . I wish you would call me sometime tomorrow and let me know."[22] In all likelihood, Paul never even saw the letter. In any event, he never responded, thus forcing even Woollcott, such an indefatigable supporter in the early years of Robeson's career, to solicit Walter White's assistance.

White, who wanted to talk with Paul about playing the lead in a dramatization of his novel, *Fire in the Flint,* was having his own troubles. "I have tried to reach you several times by telephone, but without success," White wrote to Paul in March. And again, in August: "I have tried to reach you by telephone today, but they told me you were out of the city until tonight. Telephone me Tuesday morning, won't you, when you get up."[23] Letters, phone calls, and telegrams to Paul—even from Walter White—all produced the same results that summer: no reply, no answer.

At the end of the summer White finally managed to arrange a short meeting with Robeson but found him so concerned about personal matters he was impossible to talk with or pin down about anything. In August White wrote apologetically to Woollcott: "I know you think me the world's worst promiser. After I promised you to see Paul I tried for some time to see him, but was never able to catch him in. I then went away for a short rest as I was pretty near the popping point. On my return I went to the theater one afternoon to see Paul and we made a date to talk a bit later. I kept the date and tried my hardest to bring the conversation around to a discussion of his early days but Paul was so filled up with the present contretemps [sic] with Essie! There she is entering our lives again. . . . Thus I wasn't able to get anything which I thought would help you."[24]

The news that Robeson would leave *Show Boat* in September (as stipulated in the original contract) elicited a fresh flurry of speculation. Pressed by reporters for information, Paul gave vague, often contradictory accounts of his plans. While the *Pittsburgh Courier* reported Robeson had returned to France in search of material for a new show slated for New York's winter season, the *New York World Telegram* stated he had slipped out of the *Show Boat* production to appear in a new musical in London written especially for him.[25]

In fact, Robeson was indefinite because he did not want to reveal his plans. He left New York in September, as the *Courier* had reported, headed for France, but not to gather material for a new show. Having announced publicly his affection for the unnamed English society woman, he could endure the waiting no longer. The time had come for her to make her decision and for the two of them to finalize their plans. Marie Seton, Miki Fisher, and Joe Andrews confirm that this was Paul's purpose in going to Paris. Meeting in London was out of the question because Robeson's alleged affair with Edwina Mountbatten still "was the talk of London society," and his far from inconspicuous physique made privacy impossible.[26] And, while Paul was willing to declare his feelings publicly, his unnamed intended had given every indication she was not. Thus the two planned to meet in secret.

Robeson was prepared for intolerance and bigotry in America, but until recently he had felt he would always be "assured of a following in England." The Mountbatten incident had shaken that confidence, however. Generally, Paul managed to maintain poise under stress, but this situation had completely unnerved him. The journalist, critic, and Caribbean theorist C. L. R. James, a friend of Robeson's at the time, recalled running into Paul as he walked to the British Museum:

> I saw Paul's magnificent figure coming down the street and, as usual, I stopped to talk to him: it was always a pleasure to be in his company. He was a man not only of great gentleness but of great command: he was never upset about anything. But this day Paul was bothered. "James," he said, "do you hear what all the people are saying about a colored singer and a member of the British Royal family? It's not me, James," he said passionately. "It's not me." I started to laugh. Paul looked at me somewhat surprised and he said: "What is there to laugh at? I don't see anything to laugh at." I told him "Paul, you are a Negro from the United States; you are living in England and you say that people are linking your name to a member of the British Royal Family. That, my dear Paul, for you is not a scandal, it is not a disgrace. I laugh because you seem so upset about it. That is very funny." . . . Paul was so passionate in his denial and so disturbed by the accusations. Most men whom I know, nearly all, might have denied it but in all probability would have given the impression that they were not displeased, certainly not bothered one way or another. But not Paul. He was absolutely unyielding on the subject. "They got the wrong Nigger in the woodpile, this time James. It's not me — Hutch maybe — but not me!"[27]

"Hutch" was Leslie Hutchinson, a tall, handsome Grenada-born singer and cabaret star who mixed effortlessly in fashionable society and boasted ladyloves drawn almost exclusively from *Debrett's Peerage*. Even as an older man he had a perennial youthfulness that allured the daughters and even the granddaughters of women he had dated years earlier. According to C. L. R. James, part of Hutch's charm was a haughtiness, an indifference to the elite audiences he entertained, who found his particular kind of snobbishness interesting and attractive. Edwina Mountbatten had given Hutch a cigarette case with her name engraved on it, and most people with any inside information assumed it was Hutchinson and not Robeson with whom Edwina had been romantically involved.[28]

A scandal involving Lady Mountbatten was about as close to the crown as one could get. If the king and queen were unhappy with Edwina, what effect would this have on Paul, his reputation, and his marriage plans? Robeson had worked hard to earn British approval and now, as he was on the verge of marrying into white British society, he needed that affirmation more than ever. Robeson knew only too well from his father's experience in Princeton the destructive potential of rumor and innuendo. In the end, it made little difference whether the gossip was true: it could still permanently discredit him and bring to naught all he had worked so hard to achieve. Illicit affairs would perhaps be tolerated in a lower-type cabaret entertainer but not in Paul Robeson, artist, scholar, athlete, and gentleman.

One of the few people who knew the identity of Paul's intended was Joe Andrews, Robeson's dresser. Andrews had worked for Paul since 1928 and had become one of his close confidants; on many occasions, by Andrews's own admission, he covered and made excuses for Paul. When interviewed about the woman Paul was in love with, Andrews without hesitation revealed her name. "It was rumored that it was Lady Mountbatten or Peggy Ashcroft, but they were both married. It was none of the women Paul was rumored to be seeing. The woman he was in love with was Olivia Jackson [actually, Yolande Olive Jackson; Andrews, however, knew her only as Olivia, the name Robeson presumably called her], the daughter of William ["Tiger"] Jackson, a high court judge in India, whom Paul had first met through John Payne, a friend of Larry Brown's. The family was very well placed; Olivia's brother Richard, also a barrister, later became head of Scotland Yard."[29]

Besides being a great beauty Olivia was, according to her niece Virginia Lloyd, spirited and passionate—as Lloyd put it, "wild when she was young." She had previously been engaged to a Frenchman whose hobby was jazz music. The Frenchman formed a small jazz group with a number of Americans, and Olivia ran away with one of the Americans. That marriage lasted only three weeks and shortly after it ended she first met Robeson.[30]

"They were very much in love with each other," Andrews said. "Paul had been invited many times to Worthing to visit her at her family's home. The Jacksons were very well to do; they had at least twenty Indian servants at Worthing, two a penny. But as it became apparent that Olivia was serious about Paul, pressure from her family and friends mounted. Her parents objected strongly to her marrying Paul. You understand how it is. It is all right, even a bit of a coup, to have an affair with a famous black man, but in her social circle marriage to a black man was simply out of the question. Paul was a little naive about all this and right up to the end believed their love would win over her parents' objections."[31]

But such was not to be the case. The couple met in Paris in September, and there Olivia Jackson refused Paul, explaining that she was going to marry someone else. According to Joe Andrews, "Sir Victor Sassoon, of the Sassoon brothers, who himself wanted to marry Olivia, warned her that marriage to a black man would never work. In the beginning she fought, defending Paul to her parents and calling Sassoon a 'carpetbagger.' But in the end, they won out and Paul lost. When it came right down to the hard reality of actually going through with the marriage and living with the consequences of that decision, she just couldn't do it."[32]

Olivia Jackson's refusal devastated Paul. He had anticipated difficulties, but not from her; he never seriously thought she would turn him down. And there was not only the deep personal loss to deal with but the exposure as well. Paul had been so sure of her he had done everything but announce her name publicly. One can only guess at the embarrassment and humiliation he felt. One wonders whether Robeson had read Evelyn Waugh's belittling and sarcastic portrayal in *Decline and Fall* (1928), if not of him, of a remarkably similar ambitious young black man in England, fictionalized as Sebastein ("Chokey") Cholmonley. A scathing caricature of blacks, in particular ambitious American blacks like Robeson, Chokey lacks even the most rudimentary level of sophistication. He naively confuses social banter with genuine interest and does not have the common sense to recognize when he is being humored and patronized. At a formal luncheon Chokey tells his British acquaintances about himself and why he likes England:

> When I saw the cathedrals my heart just rose up and sang within me. I sure am crazy about culture. You folk think because we're coloured we don't care about nothing except jazz. Why I'd give up all the jazz in the world for just one little stone from one of your cathedrals. . . . I've seen Oxford and Cambridge and Eton and Harrow. That's me all over. That's what I like, see? I appreciate art. There's plenty coloured people come over here and don't see nothing but a few nightclubs. I read Shakespeare. . . . *Hamlet, Macbeth, King Lear.* Ever read them? . . . My race . . . is essentially an artistic race. We have the child's love of song and colour and the child's natural good taste. All you white folks despise the poor coloured man.[33]

Did Paul now take a second look at his "friends," in particular this group of intellectuals who made a game of collecting colored artists and other exotica? Had they all along viewed him only as a curiosity, a novel party addition they could later imitate and make sport of?

"Paul went into a very deep depression," Joe Andrews sadly recalled. "It was terrible. For the first six weeks he refused to see anyone. He stayed alone in his room with the curtains drawn. He would not talk, go out, or do anything. I had never seen him so upset, and there was nothing anyone could do for him."[34] Olivia Jackson's rejection resurrected feelings of shame and inferiority that Robeson's success had led him to believe were long gone. He had always feared being typed as a physically arresting but brainless and unsophisticated black man. Hence the great effort, sometimes painfully obvious, to portray himself as intellectual and urbane: an artist, not merely an entertainer. There was the personal heartbreak to contend with, but beyond that the sense of having walked into his own worst nightmare: being publicly exposed as just another naive and sexually attractive black man.

Essie was one of the few people Paul agreed to see during the fall of 1932. Whether she came to Paris of her own accord or because Paul had sent for her, she was there, ready to pick up the pieces. It was a difficult time because Paul oscillated between a profound melancholia and furious bouts of anger with himself for being black and with Olivia for refusing him because he was black. Essie had always had strong feelings about black men dating and marrying white women and said as much in her 1930 biography of Paul. When Joel Rogers of the *Pittsburgh Courier* asked her in an interview in October 1932 how she felt about Paul's proposed marriage to a white woman, Essie responded with an emphatic declaration of personal racial pride: "I am always a Negro, and my family traditions go back as one. A public school at Washington D.C. was named in honor of my grandfather, Francis L. Cardozo, who was educated in Edinburgh and Oxford, and won prizes for Latin and Greek which I am saving for my boy, Paul."[35] The implication was clear: as Essie saw it, Paul's feelings about himself as a black man and his decision to marry a white woman were so intertwined as to be inseparable.

Robeson had played the game according to the rules established by whites and it had worked for him. He had behaved with perfect decorum — in speaking said all the "correct things," denounced low-brow jazz, and performed only "cultured" artistic music. In all things he had tried to conform to the idealized image the British had created for him. He was as they saw him: a physical Adonis with a captivating presence and charm; an erudite scholar; an awe-inspiring artist, yet almost boyish in his modesty; a talented athlete; and a cultured and poised gentleman. He had not stepped out of line to advocate radical causes, joined hunger-strikers' marches, or confronted the upper classes with the harsher realities of life. He had not denounced British racism even though he was well aware that other blacks did not fare as well as he. He was exceptional and, in turn, was treated exceptionally. In England Robeson experienced the ease of living in an environment where he was respected and accepted, an experience afforded few blacks of his time. Why should he have not assumed that this acceptance would also follow when he asked for the hand of a white British woman in marriage? But when it came to the final test Paul discovered that he was still a "nigger" in the eyes of those whites he had tried hardest to please. As musician and black critic Rudolph Dunbar later reflected, "Paul had almost, but not quite, accomplished the impossible. He had transcended class in

England—so very important a consideration to the British at that time. And he almost transcended race. But race was something even Paul Robeson could not transcend."[36]

By the time Robeson emerged from his self-imposed isolation, he had begun to reconcile himself to the loss of Olivia Jackson. But as he came to grips with the meaning of her rejection, his feelings about England changed; the old enchantment was gone. As far as the general public was concerned, Robeson had all but fallen off the face of the earth. The few activities he did undertake that fall were carefully chosen and, in retrospect, reflective of a new attitude. In October, interviewed by a friendly Hannen Swaffer, Robeson discussed his professional plans and his decision to remain in England. Later in the month Paul gave his first public performances since returning from the U.S. production of *Show Boat,* not at Albert Hall or some equally prestigious locale, but in a setting in which he could count on being accepted enthusiastically and without question—at a variety theater, the London Palladium, in a weeklong engagement at the top of the variety bill, and at Manchester's Hippodrome the following week. His program included singing six pieces, sure crowd winners: "I've Got a Robe," "Lindy Lou," "Water Boy," "Scandalize My Name," and the finale, "Ol' Man River." He earned rave reviews for both engagements. The *Daily Sketch,* the *Daily Mail,* and the *Evening Standard* all agreed: the huge audiences loved Robeson. Robeson later admitted the concerts had been an ordeal (undoubtedly, by this time he badly needed the money), but he added that the audience response had made it worthwhile. "Dignity is not out of place in the halls," wrote Wilson M. Disher of the *Sunday Referee.* "That is proved, if it needed any proving, by Paul Robeson's appearance at the Palladium."[37]

With the press Robeson refused to dole out the optimistic and gracious "line" reporters had been primed to expect. Interviewers saw another side of Robeson, a sadness and melancholia he made little effort to disguise. "Now and then his face and eyes fall into a brooding contemplation," observed a reporter from the *Manchester Guardian* in November. "I am a very melancholy person by nature," Paul confided, adding with an uncharacteristic candor that "he hated concert work . . . though he was glad to find he was not the failure he feared he would be in variety . . . he did not feel he wanted to stay there for good either. . . . 'The idea of going round and round the concert halls for the next twenty years appalls me,'" he said.[38]

In short, Robeson had stopped trying to become what the British wanted or expected him to be. He had gone further than any black man before him but had learned the bitter lesson that even in England he was a black man. There would be no more passionate courting of upper-class approval, no more trying to fit his personal history and professional ambitions into a mold prescribed by white British aristocracy. Following the breakup with Olivia Jackson, the education of Paul Robeson began in earnest.

Later, recounting the breakup to friends, Robeson would claim that it was he who recognized in Olivia a racially superior attitude and called an end to the relationship. According to one of these stories, Paul's moment of awakening occurred while he and Olivia were being chauffeured about by one of her employees. "As they talked, Olivia made disparaging remarks about lower-class people — the Irish, Welsh, one of those groups. Paul turned to her and asked her please not to talk that way, especially in front of the chauffeur as these kinds of comments were really an insult to him. Olivia laughed at Paul and explained, 'Oh, its really quite all right, Paul, he's only one of the servants.'"[39] Revels Cayton heard essentially the same story from Paul, but remembered the interchange having taken place in a more intimate setting. "Olivia and Paul were engaged in a passionate embrace," Cayton said, "when one of the servants walked in. Startled and embarrassed, Paul, almost on reflex, jerked away from Olivia. Surprised and a bit amused by it all, she told him not to be alarmed; it was quite all right as the intruder was only a colored servant."[40]

Robeson's retrospective accounts of the breakup represent more than just an effort to save face; they reflect a new political awareness. Robeson told friends that repeated incidents like this made him realize he could not marry Olivia Jackson. Her attitude toward servants — as if their presence had no significance at all — bothered him. It bespoke a habit of mind disturbingly similar to that of southern whites who had from time immemorial treated their black slaves and later their manumitted servants in the same manner. Had not his father also been a bondservant? Was he not himself descended from the working class? Were not English servants and the working classes of England suffering privations similar to those of his fellow blacks in America? To have married Olivia Jackson would have been to deny his own kinship with these people. It would have amounted to renouncing his own identity.

But despite what Robeson told friends, these were insights Paul gained only in retrospect and after he had fully assimilated the meaning of Olivia Jackson's rejection. Joe Andrews said that when things were going well between them Paul's attitude had been quite different. "There were many Indian servants at Worthing, and Paul was in complete wonderment at it all. He found it strange and sometimes awkward to be in a situation in which he, as a black man, was lionized in a household filled with servants bowing and scraping to him, but he was not at all angry about it all. It just amazed him."[41]

Robeson's thinking concerning his professional goals underwent an equally dramatic transformation. For the first time Paul began talking about what he wanted to do, rather than what British society thought he ought to do. It is hard to say whether it was Robeson who first turned his back on the British upper classes or they who first snubbed him. The Albert Hall cancellation spelled the beginning of the end of a five-year romance. Perhaps, as with Olivia Jackson, Robeson began to understand how tenuous his acceptance in such elite circles had always been. Joe Andrews remembered Paul's later reflections on the party he attended the night before the canceled Albert Hall performance: "I think initially he went to cushion the fear of the next night's concert. He was unsure of himself socially and trying to decide which direction that part of his life would take. It took him time, but he was in the process of forming some opinions. This particular party stuck out in his mind because afterwards he connected it with the Albert Hall cancellation. In time he got to the point where he felt that such gatherings, where black and other artists were shown off like rare jewels, were frivolous. But that was later."[42]

Robeson now addressed the question of his professional and personal future with a new intensity and honesty. No amount of "correct" behavior would win for him the acceptance he had so fervently sought, and he knew it. He was who he was. In many senses, Paul had come full circle. When he asked himself what it was he wanted to do on the stage, what it was that made him happy, it was the memory of his early days with the Provincetowners and their inspired dedication to fine art that most moved him. Robeson told one interviewer that he intended "to take a West End theatre, surround myself with a really first-class company, and put on plays in which I have always been interested." It was his hope to act in parts "that are not Negro parts," and he said that he was "enormously interested in Russian drama." A small repertory theater would offer him the opportunity to perform before smaller, more intimate groups, something he had always preferred to performing before large audiences.[43]

As early as November 12, 1932, authentic sources, according to the *New York Age,* had revealed that Paul and Essie Robeson were on the verge of reconciliation. They had a child and, according to Revels Cayton, primarily for that reason agreed to remain married. "Essie convinced Paul that he would never safely cross the color-line and so, in many respects, staying married was a face-saving arrangement for both of them."[44] To judge from what Robeson did and said at the time, he emerged from his depression personally beaten down and convinced that the one thing that was important to him and over which he did have some control was his career. Never again would he be hurt as he had been by Olivia Jackson.

Both Essie and Paul had changed during the last several years. There was no going back, and they both realized that. Reconciliation, humiliating as it was for Paul, meant at the least an end to public scrutiny of his personal affairs. Essie, likewise, did not have everything she wanted, but she did have a friendship with Paul and the Robeson name. It was enough. As Cayton observed, "She was ambitious and whatever she might achieve on her own, she could never reach Paul's pinnacle of fame, and she wanted that fame."[45] Essie would no longer attempt to control all facets of Paul's life; in this respect she understood he had clearly grown beyond her. The Robeson marriage had lost its romantic spark, and reconciliation would be, as Dianne Loesser put it, "amicable but not passionate."[46] It represented a compromise, but one that both Paul and Essie could accept. Paul had his career and Essie a life independent of his, and on that basis they would remain married.

12

The Emperor & Screen Images

1933-1934

It would take Robeson time to lay the matter with Olivia Jackson to rest and put the trauma of 1932 behind him. Her rebuff devastated him and this overwhelming personal defeat forced him to rethink entirely the direction of his life. The sudden cessation of what had been almost ten years of extramarital liaisons — from casual affairs to intense romantic involvement — liberated Robeson, and for the time being he had little interest in new romantic pursuits. In many senses it was a relief. Freedom from worrying about clandestine meetings, unsavory gossip, damage to his reputation, and bitter quarrels with Essie created the psychological space he needed to reflect on himself and his life. For the next several years he did just that, developing himself personally and professionally and, in the process, discovering the roots of his identity. During this time Robeson would undertake an array of new projects — repertory theater, movie making, and language study. He would make his first trip to the Soviet Union, embrace his African heritage, alternately adopt and abandon England as his true "home," turn his back on critical admonitions by announcing folk songs as the mainstay of his concert repertoire, and reach out to larger, less elite audiences as his perception of himself changed from concert performer to "people's artist." Although he would remain conspicuously removed from politics for the next few years, this period of self-scrutiny set the stage for Robeson's later passionate and irrevocable political commitments.

The new year brought two unexpected professional opportunities. One, a film version of *The Emperor Jones,* offered a lucrative salary, widespread exposure, and Robeson's first serious opportunity in the medium. The other, a repertory run of *All God's Chillun Got Wings,* paid next to nothing but would prove deeply satisfying and Robeson's best acting performance to date.

John Krimsky, a young, ambitious, and relatively inexperienced film producer, traveled to London early in 1933 to meet with Robeson and try to persuade him to star in an American film version of O'Neill's *Emperor Jones*. Krimsky went directly to the Dorchester House in Mayfair where Robeson was staying and upon arrival was asked to wait in the study as Robeson was entertaining guests in the drawing room. Robeson introduced Krimsky to his guests, apologized to him for the delay, and promised to begin their discussion momentarily. Although he had been warned it would be difficult to convince Robeson to come to the United States, even if for only a short time, Krimsky was hopeful. Eugene O'Neill's literary agent Richard Madden had assured Krimsky that O'Neill would sell him the film rights provided he cast Robeson in the lead (producer Samuel Goldwyn had earlier offered O'Neill a large sum for the film rights, but O'Neill refused when he found out that Goldwyn planned to cast the white opera singer Lawrence Tibbett, who had recently sung the operatic version of *The Emperor Jones* in blackface at the Metropolitan Opera), and O'Neill himself had already written to Robeson urging him to take the part.[1]

After the guests left, Robeson opened a bottle of champagne — he loved Krug champagne — and the two men talked. Krimsky made up his mind about Robeson within minutes after meeting him. "My first impression . . . was overpowering — he *was* the Emperor Jones — regal, charming and authoritative . . . the only person to play Jones"; beside him "all other performers paled into insignificance." Robeson was less eager. He "was terse and to the point," Krimsky remembered. "He explained" — perhaps belaboring the many difficulties involved to enhance his bargaining position and assure he would be treated well in the United States — "that he would have to give up many concert engagements to undertake the filming, but his great enthusiasm for the part and Gene O'Neill's strong recommendation had made up his mind to accept — but on one condition, that under no circumstances would he be required to enter the southern part of the United States. This stipulation was to be expressed in legal terms as 'south of the Mason and Dixon line.' All other details such as compensation were to be left to his attorney in New York. I immediately agreed . . . and we shook hands."[2]

Krimsky was elated, so much so that two days later he sailed on the return crossing of the *Aquitania* for New York, eager to begin contract arrangements with Robeson's attorney and business manager, Robert Rockmore. His enthusiasm faded somewhat after talking with Rockmore, who "drove a very hard, in fact, a bit harsh, bargain." Throughout his career Robeson had studiously avoided dealing with financial matters himself, first letting Essie and now Rockmore, do the "dirty work" of salary negotiations. Many people assumed Robeson did not care about money and, left to his own devices, would have worked gratis. Such was not the case. If anything, the fact that it *did* matter embarrassed

Robeson and made it difficult for him to fight on his own behalf. In addition, in the United States especially, the assumption was that if you were a black man, you were lucky to have work. Period. It was not only unseemly, but worse yet "ungrateful" for a black man or woman to negotiate the issue of salary. Able, hard-nosed, and scrupulously honest, Rockmore, the son of Russian Jewish immigrants and a World War I veteran, proved an invaluable ally to Robeson in this respect. With Rockmore acting as "hatchet man," Robeson could convey indifference *and* be paid well. When the legendary jazz musician Louis Armstrong in 1922 was getting ready to leave New Orleans to go north to play in King Oliver's band, a man described by Armstrong "as the toughest Negro down there" gave him this advice. "When you go up North, Dipper, be sure to get yourself a white man that will put his hand on your shoulder and say, 'This is my nigger.'" The man's advice (which Armstrong took) was not a judgment of Armstrong's business ability but rather an acknowledgment of and strategy for dealing with the practical realities of American racial mores. Rockmore was Robeson's "white man."[3]

The contract, signed in February 1933, stipulated that Robeson would receive $15,000 for six weeks of work and, in the event that the filming extended beyond that time, an additional $2,000 per week. Over and above this, Rockmore demanded $1,000 for travel expenses as well as all lodging expenses (which were to be first class) for the Robesons and Joe Andrews. Robeson was to have complete and sole rights to reject songs assigned to him, be present at all showings or "rushes," and be listed as the "star" of the film. Finally, the contract spelled out in very specific terms Robeson's stipulation that none of the filming require him to go to the southern part of the United States.[4]

Coincidental with the Krimsky meeting, the manager of London's Embassy Theatre, Roland Adam, approached Robeson about a repertory production of *All God's Chillun Got Wings*. Adam had already secured the services of the talented young leftist avant-garde director Andre Van Gyseghem, who at the time was studying experimental proletarian theater techniques in Moscow. Intrigued with the social and political implications of O'Neill's work, Van Gyseghem had agreed to return from Moscow to direct the production, again on the condition that Robeson play the lead role. Adam, however, was nervous about approaching Robeson. Like most experimental theaters, the Embassy "was being run on a shoestring" and could afford to pay Robeson only a meager ten pounds a week. But, while compensation issues had loomed large in the *Emperor Jones* negotiations, Robeson brushed aside the matter of money with Adam. Robeson had always enjoyed performing in small, intimate settings and relished the intellectual stimulation of working with people whose primary consideration was not money but art. After months of talking about starting his own repertory theater, *All God's Chillun* appeared to be just the opportunity he had been waiting for, and Robeson agreed on the spot to take the part.[5]

When Robeson first played the role nearly ten years earlier he himself had had little experience of the personal defeat that ultimately destroys the character Jim Harris. He was twenty-six years old — a nationally known athlete, an award-winning scholar, a hugely popular figure in Harlem, and a law school graduate just beginning a career on stage. For the 1924 production two large problems overshadowed everything else for Robeson: proving himself as an actor and withstanding the intense controversy the play had provoked. But in 1933 Robeson brought to the role not only more stage experience but considerably more life experiences as well: Jim Harris's despair over lost love and his failure to transcend race was something with which Robeson could all too readily identify.

As Robeson worked on the play, so the play worked on Robeson. What must it have been like for him after Jackson's rejection to play the part of a man who would nearly sell his soul to win the love of a white woman? A man who denied, overlooked, and made excuses for this woman's blatant racism simply because he loved her and wanted to be with her? A man whose identity and heritage — symbolized by the African mask given to him by his sister as a wedding present — evoked in this white woman he loved only scorn, derision, and terror?

With the Old Vic's talented and newly risen star Flora Robson cast in the part of Ella, rehearsals for the March opening began. "Nearly all of us who work in theatre have one unforgettable experience," Robeson later told biographer Marie Seton, "something which at the time makes so profound an impression upon us as to exert a permanent influence. Such an experience was mine during the production of *All God's Chillun.*"[6]

Almost everyone involved with the production had similar recollections. "Robeson was Jim," said director Van Gyseghem,

and the result was terrifying in its intensity. Time and time again directing Flora and Paul I had the feeling of being on the edge of a violent explosion. I had touched it off, but the resulting conflagration was breathtaking. They literally shot sparks off each other. Seldom have I seen two performers fuse so perfectly. It was so intimate and intense that I felt, at times, I should apologize for being there. Watching it was sometimes more than one could bear at such close range.

Robeson's technique was not Flora's. She was an expert actress with tremendous emotional power. She absolutely hushed audiences as she stripped the meager soul of Ella. But her technically superb performance found a perfect foil in Robeson's utter sincerity. Within this gigantic body that he didn't quite know how to handle was a tremendous humanity, a spiritual side; that was what came through. He had the facility for making imagination visible; his magnificent voice seemed to vibrate with truth and take control of his body until one was blinded by naked suffering made solid and tangible. His awkward and ungainly movement seemed to make his tenderness and humility more moving and truthful. He was, instinctively, a great artist.[7]

In addition, Robeson was by all accounts a pleasure to work with, according to Van Gyseghem, "never obstructive in any way. He was our ticket, our drawing card, and he knew it, but you wouldn't have known it watching him at rehearsals: he was no prima donna. He listened carefully and took direction very well." When a last-minute financial crisis threatened to cancel the production, it was Robeson who stepped in and saved the day. Roland Adam had assumed O'Neill would ask the standard 5 percent, but when Jimmy Light arrived to settle the matter he informed Adam that O'Neill wanted 10 percent and an additional $1,000 as well. Adam had no way of getting the money together in time for opening night. Finally, at the end of one of the last rehearsals Adam's assistant, Eric Somers (Adam was out of town for a few days), informed Van Gyseghem the play could not open because they did not have the money to pay O'Neill. Robeson overheard the conversation and followed Somers back to his office. "Will this be any help?" Paul asked as he handed Somers a check for £100. The play opened as scheduled, and on opening night Adam handed Jimmy Light, along with a program, a check for the remainder of what the theater owed O'Neill.[8]

From the time the curtain opened, Paul and Flora Robson held their audience spellbound. Robeson was especially moving in the church scene in which Jim leads his cringing wife past lines of staring white and black faces and helps her to hold herself together with a sermon of his own, so painfully removed from reality that he is near hysteria by the time he finishes it. Flora Robson handled with excruciating skill Ella's inexorable descent into madness, especially her savage colloquy with the African mask, in which she is tossed back and forth between love and manic hatred for her "dirty nigger." The final scenes, where Ella spits out her venom at a broken, ever-patient, and groveling Jim, were so moving that the audience "had positively to pull itself together before it could offer its tribute of stormy applause."[9]

As a rule, British audiences found O'Neill's work offensive and his plots difficult to understand. This play was no exception. Reviewers almost all panned *Chillun,* and even those favorably disposed toward America's "chartered libertine among dramatists" were confused over exactly what effect O'Neill had hoped to create. *Punch* judged the play "unnecessarily untidy . . . wavering awkwardly between symbolism and the starkest realism." "Horribly good," said the reviewer for the *Morning Post*. "A great deal of feeling and very little craftsmanship," said the reviewer for *Weekend Review*, and another, "too . . . devoted to the creation of atmosphere." But the performances of Paul Robeson and Flora Robson won unreserved accolades. As one critic put it, "acting of this caliber overleaps the limitations of the play." "Two perfect players," said another. "No acting equivalent . . . has been seen for a long time in London."[10]

"I couldn't have believed Paul could rise to such heights of poetry," Rebecca West wrote to Alexander Woollcott. "He seems to be just beginning. . . . it was as if his imagination and his body did not know what fatigue was." Reviewers concurred it was perhaps the best performance of Robeson's career, "infinitely finer" than his 1930 *Othello*. "Intensely moving . . . flawless," said the *Times*. "Jim Harris must suffer and, when Mr. Robeson suffers it is as if the entire nation were groaning in eternal and infinite duress," wrote the *Weekend Review*'s Ivor Browne. "Virtuoso acting," concluded the *Star*'s A. E. Wilson. Robeson "unfolds the part of Jim . . . with infinite pathos." Reviewers were equally struck by Flora Robson's "terrific power" and "indescribably intense and poignant" performance. "To make us feel the torments and at the same time to explain what lies behind them is a task of utmost delicacy. Miss Robson achieves it with a triumph."[11]

Even the grand actress of the English stage herself, Dame Sybil Thorndike, judged Paul's and Flora's performances nearly flawless: "When I saw Flora, I thought to myself, here we have the making of one of England's greatest tragic actresses. Flora was not beautiful in the conventional sense; in fact, she was rather plain. But she took the role of Ella beyond racial themes and portrayed the devastating love/hate relationship between the couple to the point that it was almost too painful to watch. And Paul was brilliant as Jim. His performance was a smashing example of just how much talent he really had. He was focused and concentrated his full attention on the role. In a way, it made me realize what a shame it was that his full talent was so rarely used. He could have been one of the world's great actors if he had only given his craft more attention and time and there had been more roles for him and other Negroes in those days."[12]

All God's Chillun played for three weeks at the Embassy and in June moved to the larger, West End Piccadilly where it ran for another three weeks at reduced ticket prices. Artistically, the production was a success; financially, it cleared expenses with a profit of ten pounds, two, and sixpence — one of the few "profits" Adam earned in those days.[13] For Robeson it was a pivotal experience, both personally and professionally.

On paper *The Emperor Jones* project looked equally promising; the credentials of the leading players outstanding. The film's producers, two young upstarts, John Krimsky and Gifford Cochran, a mild mannered, independently wealthy Yale graduate, began the venture confidently, buoyed by the coup of winning the film rights over the legendary Samuel Goldwyn. Neither Krimsky nor Cochran lacked self-assurance. Their first film, a remake of Leontine Sagan's controversial *Maedchen in Uniform* (an experimental art film portraying discipline and lesbian relationships in a Prussian boarding school for girls), had proven a dazzling financial and artistic success, despite considerable censorship in the United States, and now these "two cocky twenty-four-year olds" anticipated an even greater victory with *The Emperor Jones*. DuBose Heyward of *Porgy* fame had written the film's prologue, and the equally talented J. Rosamond Johnson composed the score, an intertwining of African, Gullah, Harlem jazz, and voodoo motifs. The white Dudley Murphy, who had experimental film projects and several black films to his credit (among these RKO's 1930 *St. Louis Blues,* which, according to Thomas Cripps, the author of the definitive study of African American film, *Slow Fade to Black,* was the "finest film on Negro life up to that time"), would direct the film. The cast was superb, with Dudley Digges as Smithers and Jimmy Mordecai, Frank Wilson, Fredi Washington, and Ruby Elzy in supporting roles. With a quarter of a million dollars backing (an almost unheard of sum for an independent film), the project was off to an auspicious start.[14]

But Robeson was not looking forward either to returning to America or to beginning work on the film. Long before he ever got near the set, Paul was annoyed as he anticipated the inevitable volley of racial indignities. His misgivings were not ill founded: the Robesons had no sooner stepped off the celebrity-filled *Olympic* and onto American soil when the racial slights began. Krimsky and Cochran met Paul and Essie at the pier. "We planned," Krimsky recalled, "to eat at one o'clock at an expensive, socially prominent restaurant but we were delayed at docking and customs. I phoned and changed the reservations to two o'clock and mentioned to the owner that we were bringing as our guest Paul Robeson. I never dreamt there would be a problem; we ate there every day ourselves. But the owner informed me he would have to cancel my reservation. 'If I allowed a Negro to have lunch here I would lose my entire southern clientele,' he said. So Gifford [Cochran] hurriedly called his butler at Beekman Place and Fifty-first and had him set up lunch there. Robeson didn't know about any of this. If he had, I'm sure he would have turned around and taken the first boat back to England."[15]

Paul might indeed have taken the first boat back, but not because the incident surprised him. Such exclusion was a fact of life for American blacks. Robeson simply had no intention of exposing himself to such humiliation. His contract spelled out that determination in legal terms, and his attitude, first with Krimsky and Cochran and later with others, made it clear that should he be slighted there would be trouble. Robeson's irritation showed in his moodiness during film takes, his aloofness with the cast, and his readiness to take offense. Although Krimsky later described the set as a happy one, others complained, especially about Robeson's temperamental behavior. Indeed, an outside observer would have had a difficult time recognizing Robeson as the actor Van Gyseghem described only months earlier as such a joy to work with.

Shortly after rehearsals began, Krimsky asked Robeson if he would consider allowing some of the scenes to be shot in Charleston, South Carolina, on a piece of property owned by Cochran's cousin called Magnolia Gardens — according to Krimsky, a perfect location for the jungle scenes. When Robeson jokingly told Krimsky he would, provided Krimsky could get him into the best hotel in Charleston, Krimsky naively went ahead and made inquiries at Charleston's Fort Sumter Hotel. "If I allow a Negro in this hotel, I might as well burn it down," an exasperated manager told him. DuBose Heyward, himself from Charleston, offered to let Robeson take over his house, but Robeson refused. "I wouldn't want to embarrass you," Robeson reportedly told Heyward to which Heyward, drawing himself up his full 5 feet 3 inches said coldly, "Nobody in Charleston could possibly embarrass a DuBose or a Heyward and certainly you couldn't."[16]

One senses in this tense exchange both Robeson's railing against the status quo (Why was it acceptable that Charleston's best hotel refuse him lodging?) and the southern-born Heyward's chagrin with the suggestion that any black man could ever succeed in embarrassing him. The United States was not England. If Robeson, as much an international celebrity as he was, were refused service in a New York restaurant no public outcry would ensue as it had in England at the time of the Savoy incident. Most of those involved with *The Emperor Jones* film found Robeson's rage, his refusal to accept America's racial etiquette, difficult to fathom. From Robeson's perspective, however, the issue was clear: if he was not treated as a man in the United States, he would see to it he was treated as a *star.*

In the end, the "dismal swamp" — in fact, the entire film with the exception of two scenes — was shot in New York's old Paramount Studio in Astoria, less than an hour from Harlem and one of the few studios still remaining on the East Coast. Scores of technicians were recruited to compensate for the facility's unsophisticated equipment. Plants and trees, hanging moss and swamp vegetation were shipped in from the Everglades and other parts of Florida. Pigs, chickens, geese, goats, and donkeys roamed the set for use in other scenes. On more than one occasion devotion to verisimilitude reached ridiculous proportions. To make the jungle look steamy, technicians shot digestive oil into the air with an insect sprayer. For one of the cabaret scenes 250 etherized flies were used to add an authentic tropical touch. During shooting of the saloon scene Dudley Murphy served the actors (one of whom was the young songstress Billie Holiday) real liquor instead of the customary tea in a highball or cocktail glass, the result being a cast so unmanageable that not one of the scenes was ever printed. In the end, despite all efforts, the scenery, in particular the jungle set, looked fake. As Krimsky later quipped, "When critics commented on the phony crocodile, they were right. That's what it was—a phony crocodile. Today movie authorities revel in the surrealism of it all. Believe me, we were not trying to be surrealistic, but were just doing the best with what we had."[17]

Krimsky insisted that every effort be made to accommodate Robeson on the set, including heating the water used for the jungle swamp scenes so that Paul would not catch cold. At Robeson's request Krimsky hired former all-American Frederick ("Fritz") Pollard, at the time operating a booking agency for local black talent (Sun Tan Studios), as a casting assistant and to play a bit part, but primarily to function as Robeson's dresser on the set. Pollard worked to help get Robeson into shape (Robeson was "a little flabby," said Krimsky) and saw to it that someone brought lunch daily, including a bottle of fine champagne, to Robeson's dressing room, where Paul ate alone, with Essie, or occasionally with someone else he might choose to invite.[18]

After about the fourth or fifth day of shooting Robeson let Krimsky know he was not happy with Dudley Murphy's direction. Recalled Krimsky:

Fritz came to me, complaining on Paul's behalf about Dudley. Fritz said that Paul thought Dudley was too preoccupied with camera work, especially in the jungle scenes, which they redid again and again, and not enough with acting. "Dudley thinks that everyone with black skin is a born actor," Paul complained. He wanted direction and wasn't getting it. "I'm not an actor," he insisted, "I'm a singer and I need direction." Paul just got more frustrated by the day and near the end of the second week of a five-week timetable things went from bad to worse. So we hired William De Mille, Cecil B. De Mille's brother, and had him work with Paul on his lines and movement on the set. De Mille, an actor and playwright himself, was good. He was a big help, especially with the jungle monologue, which had given Paul so much trouble earlier. The most important thing, though, was that Paul was pleased with the arrangement. That made things easier for everyone.[19]

Krimsky defended Robeson. "Really, things went as smoothly as they could considering everyone knew Robeson couldn't go outside the shooting location and get served in a decent restaurant or night club." True, he kept to himself, never sat at the round table with the production's key personnel, or had lunch with the rest of the cast, but "he arrived on the set promptly every day and worked hard. He wanted the hour and a half off to relax, not because he was affected or temperamental. Let's face it, he was a star."[20]

Others saw it differently. "An unadulterated son of a bitch," is what Gifford Cochran's wife said of Robeson on the set. "He really fouled up everything. We were offered Magnolia Gardens for the jungle scenes, but he wouldn't go below the Mason-Dixon line. He flatly refused to set foot in the 'swamp' unless it was exactly the right temperature. This fellow from Brown [Fritz Pollard] did everything but lie down and sleep for Robeson. He was demanding, extremely difficult to work with, and continually complained. And, his wife, Essie, if anything was worse than he was."[21]

"This was not the Paul I had known in college or in pro-ball. England changed him," said Fritz Pollard. "He was angry — really in a terrible mood — and part of my job was to try and keep him under control. I was glad for the work, it was the Depression and all, and times were tough. But Paul was almost impossible to work with. I tried to get him to exercise. Just moving around the set winded him — too much of the good life in England. He wouldn't do it — exercise. He was in a horrible mood. Blacks in Harlem were annoyed with him and thought he was putting on airs. I don't think it was that at all. He was just not going to let people treat him like a second-class citizen. He wasn't going back to that again."[22]

By late summer Robeson was finding it difficult simply to keep himself under control. When problems arose he had little resilience. Questioned by an interviewer in August as to his mood on the set, Robeson snapped: "Temperament? Yes, the film studios are full of temperament, and I know why. It is the long waits. I could have been temperamental . . . but I controlled myself. . . . When I was kept waiting an hour or more for lights and cameras, I was so tired that I went to my room and rested. Making the film taught me a lot about myself — revealing many little faults. My wife did the rest, and her advice has been invaluable."[23]

It was 1924 when Robeson first took the heat for challenging white America's racial-sexual sensitivities in *All God's Chillun,* and now, nearly a decade later, little had changed. The Will Hays office, at the time the industry's censoring agency, after viewing amorous scenes between Robeson and the fair-skinned Fredi Washington, told Krimsky he would have to reshoot a scene that showed a black man in close proximity to what appeared to be a white girl. "They warned us," said Krimsky, "that the sequences would eventually be cut out if we didn't make the corrections. So, we had to daily perform the ludicrous task of applying dark makeup to the beauteous [but light-complexioned] Miss Washington." Similarly, Manoedi Maskote, a genuine African chieftain and one of the players employed for the jungle voodoo sequences, was informed that he was too light-skinned. Maskote protested that Africans came in many shades of black, but to no avail. He was told he would have to be blackened up in order to give moviegoers the distinct "safe" differentiation of color.[24]

Film critic Richard Dyer points out other alterations in the script for the film version that suggest similar adjustments made to suit white sensibilities. If one of the possible meanings of atavism is return to the primordial jungle, another is return to a violent racial memory — in the case of Brutus Jones, the historical experience of slavery. The stage version suggests as one interpretation of Jones's breakdown, his terror when faced with the racial memory of slavery, whereas the film allows for no such reading of Jones's experience. Similarly, the chain-gang scene as presented in the play shows the cruelty and sadism of the white guard who Jones later kills, whereas the film does not.[25]

America's casual acceptance of institutionalized racism, its fetish with color, and its horror at even the slightest hint of sexual contact between the races infuriated Robeson, as did the producers' insistence that the film cater to white sensibilities. By the end of his stay he had reached his limit, and on at least one occasion he came close to retaliating physically. The Robesons had been invited to a black-tie dinner party given by Pauline Munn. When they arrived at the Park Avenue address, the doorman refused to let them ride the elevator and directed them to use the servants' entrance instead. In former days Robeson would have brushed the affront aside, but not that summer. Upstairs, someone informed Krimsky of a commotion and he rushed to the scene where he found Robeson in his tuxedo and inches away from "punching out the doorman." Krimsky told the doorman off and then personally escorted the Robesons to the elevator and upstairs. There was no mistaking Robeson's mood.[26]

Despite these and other difficulties, the finished film proved a turning point in black film portraiture. For the first time in American cinematic history a black actor played the lead role in a full-length class-A film. Admittedly, Brutus Jones was far from the "hero" the black community wanted, but he was light years removed from the usual shuffling stereotypes and Stepin Fetchit buffoons. Brutus Jones lied, murdered, gambled, swore, and took advantage of the naiveté of fellow blacks. But he also blackmailed his white employer on a private Pullman car, forced the white cockney trader Smithers to "talk polite" to him and light his cigarette (the famous, "Smithers, a cigarette"), brazenly took control of the island, and assumed the role of Emperor with both style and daring.[27] As Krimsky later put it, "In the pre-*Shaft* days, a film didn't show black men asking for anything except would Mr. Sir like a shoe shine. When Jones had the white man light his cigarette the audience recoiled."[28] Nothing like this had ever been shown on the American screen.

Throughout the film Robeson strode like a colossus — whether singing spirituals in a Georgia church, shooting craps in Harlem, presiding over his island kingdom, or forcing Smithers to grovel in his presence. In Robeson's hands Brutus Jones transcends the stereotype of the crap-shooting, loose-living, violent, and irresponsible black as well as that of the primitive foolishly trying to affect civilized behavior. Robeson depicts the naive and ambitious Brutus Jones showing off his shiny-buttoned porter's uniform to relatives and friends with both humor and understanding. He unveils Jones's ultimately tragic combination of foolhardiness, extravagance, and ambition (Jones listens with rapt attention as Jeff teaches him "high finance," i.e., the shoe shiner's art of increasing tips by studying white passengers' shoes) without ever losing sight of his essential dignity. Jones makes mistakes, but he is not a fool. Even when the script appeared designed to make Jones look ridiculous (as when Jones, working on a prison chain gang, bursts into strains of "Water Boy," backed up by Hall Johnson's full black choir), Robeson maintains his character's stature.

In the last half of the film, Robeson is brilliant. As Emperor he swaggers, struts, and exploits his "bush nigger" subjects as if he had been king all his life. His portrayal of Jones's final flight in the jungle is both powerful and agonizing. In frenzied gestures Jones rips off the trappings of civilization, beginning with his embroidered coat down to his magnificent black patent-leather boots, and flings them into the forest. Stripped to the waist, his strident diction flags, then deteriorates to a pitiful whine. The former Emperor sweats and stumbles, incoherent and humbled by his own terror. Apparitions of his past life pursue him, and he begins to shoot at his fears. Hallucinating a service at his old Baptist church, Brutus sings the poignant "Daniel in the Lion's Den" and prays for forgiveness. He wastes his final bullet on a crocodile and staggers out of the forest, the relentless voodoo beat following him, to meet his fate. The cynical Smithers discovers the Emperor collapsed over a voodoo drum and sneers, "Well they did for yer right enough, Jonesey, me lad! Dead as a 'erring." But even Smithers finds it hard to maintain his mocking tone. Win or loose, Jones was the Emperor and died like one, as Smithers put it, "in the 'eighth o' style."

When it came time to show this groundbreaking film in the United States, it was "business as usual," racially speaking. *The Emperor Jones* opened on September 19, 1933, but in two New York theaters simultaneously—one catering to whites and the other to blacks—the Rivoli on Broadway and the Roosevelt in Harlem. The Roosevelt's owner Frank Schiffman slashed theater prices from the usual forty to twenty-five cents for matinees and thirty-five cents for evening performances, a gesture patently designed to keep black patrons away from the white Rivoli.[29]

The opening at the Roosevelt drew such a crowd that an additional showing was offered to handle the overflow. Interest continued to exceed expectations, enough so that the management held the film over a full week to accommodate the demand. When Jones finally closed at the Roosevelt, blacks went downtown to the Rivoli to see it, which, according to the *Pittsburgh Courier,* finally convinced the Rivoli's management to close the show.[30] Similar scenarios were repeated in other cities with sizable black populations. One patron, a sociologist at Howard University, said that in Washington, D.C., "blacks attempting to see the film in white theatres were stopped at the door by black bouncers hired specifically to keep Negroes out. I was so angry about it all that I just made up my mind: they were not going to keep me out of their white theatres for this film. I did get in, too. I lost myself in the crowd and managed to get by the bouncers. But the whole situation was awful—especially that we subjected ourselves to such degradation."[31]

Robeson attended neither opening, having made certain he was bound for England as soon as the film was complete and long before its September 19 opening. Given his frame of mind it was a wise decision. Three years before, Richard Harrison, "De Lawd" in the black musical *Green Pastures,* had faced a similar dilemma when that play opened to a segregated white audience in Washington, D.C. Blacks were enraged and pressured Harrison to refuse to perform. Harrison's compromise—he performed at the segregated Washington opening but added a special benefit showing for black audiences—failed to satisfy his critics.[32] In short, it was a no-win situation, and Robeson had no intention of involving himself in a similar fray.

Critical evaluation of the film was mixed. In general, white critics heaped accolades on Robeson and applauded the performances of Dudley Digges, Fredi Washington, and Frank Wilson as well. "Another victory . . . he [Robeson] dominates the picture," said the *New York Daily News.* "Compelling," and "magnificent," said others. "The finest acting ever seen on stage or screen" said an effusive Regina Crewe of the *New York American.* Others noted flaws. "Robeson is too civilized to catch the brutish qualities in this character," said the *New York Evening Post*'s Thornton Delaney. "Less effective in the role than the late Charles Gilpin" judged the *New York Herald Tribune.*[33] Critics were divided in their assessment of Heyward's half-hour prologue, although most agreed it did not work well with the rest of the script, which had been taken almost word for word from O'Neill's stage version. Others complained that the juxtaposition of Heyward's Hollywood rendering of the Georgia church, Harlem cabaret, and chain-gang scenes with the stark jungle scenes created a jarring, unsatisfying effect. Similarly, reviewers noted technical flaws: an ineffective use of double exposure as a method of portraying Jones's hallucinations, a "phony"-looking jungle, unbelievable spirits, and singers appearing in shadow boxes. But, on the whole, white reaction to the film was favorable.[34]

The real "story" in terms of reaction to the film occurred within the black community, as an initially favorable response quickly gave way to heated debate. Director Dudley Murphy had pleaded with NAACP secretary Walter White to screen the film, hoping that the nod from White would ward off just such negative reaction. In the past the NAACP willingly acted as judge and arbiter for plays and movies; NAACP files are replete with correspondence on various film controversies. Less than a year earlier White had vigorously protested the Metropolitan Opera's decision to cast Lawrence Tibbett in burnt-cork makeup (rather than Robeson or Jules Bledsoe) as the lead in the operatic version of *The Emperor Jones*.[35] But on the issue of *The Emperor Jones* film, White, perhaps feeling slighted by Robeson, perhaps too mired in the Scottsboro case to take on anything controversial, maintained an uncharacteristic silence. Initially, he claimed he was too busy to view it. In the end, he never did publicly take a stand on the issue.[36]

Krimsky would later blame *Pittsburgh Courier* reviewers for leading the attack against the film, but in fact the person around whom the eye of the storm centered was Joel A. Rogers of the *Amsterdam News*. The *Courier* did criticize the film, but it was the assault from the generally measured and thoughtful Rogers that ignited the black community. In an emotional review, Rogers dismissed the movie and condemned Robeson for agreeing to perform in it. "O'Neill . . . does not know Negroes," Rogers stated flatly. "*The Emperor Jones* struck me . . . as being written for morons . . . the monotonous beating of the tom-toms in the theatre gave me a headache. . . . Imagine hunting down a fugitive with a drum, thus letting him know always where you are. [*The Emperor Jones*] is commercialism of the worst sort. . . . its crap shooting, lewd women, gin-guzzling and the like [makes] one feel like making a dive for the garbage can after seeing it."[37]

Rogers's critique triggered a barrage of replies in black weeklies, and the battle over the merits of the movie raged for months. Black scholars attacked Rogers for his lack of "cultural acumen." "All that he [Rogers] can see . . . is the word 'nigger' . . . and the portrayal of Jones as a crapshooter, pullman porter, convict and finally as a superstitious darky." Theophilus Lewis, one of the few black critics to maintain equilibrium on the issue, set the tone for a more balanced assessment as he humorously, tongue-in-cheek, chastised Rogers and others for their overly emotional response. As he had done almost ten years earlier when the play first opened, Lewis commended O'Neill's work, adding that the movie version was even more effective. Likewise, the *Amsterdam News*'s Romeo Dougherty (one of the few to defend Robeson during the 1928 Reagan contract dispute) took issue with the Rogers attack and pointed to the unwillingness of blacks to support black talent as the real issue. "There are even Negroes foolish enough to believe that the white man is going to invest his money to propagandize the greatness of Negroes. Those [blacks] who look at life through sane eyes and with appreciation for the truth . . . realize that we have got to create and support our own artists if we want to see . . . things in the theatre which will satisfy us."[38]

The response of black audiences evidenced equally ambivalent sentiments. Most took pride in Robeson's achievement. At the same time, parts of the film offended and embarrassed them. Not since Carl Van Vechten's *Nigger Heaven* had the issue of black portraiture elicited such furor. Nonetheless, in Harlem *The Emperor Jones* played to standing-room-only audiences and the Roosevelt grossed over $10,000 on the film in a single week. As the *Amsterdam News*'s Ted Poston observed, black reaction was more complex than it appeared. "Despite the fact that Brutus Jones was a killer, despite the fact that he exploited his Negro subjects far more ruthlessly that the white man who preceded him, the [black] audience — or the major part of it — fairly worshipped him. Worshipped him with continuous applause even after he had done the unforgivable thing — said to a white man 'We niggers understand each other.' Every utterance of the banned epithet brought a chorus of 'tch-tch-tch-tches' of course, but this didn't dampen the fans' ardor for the next step upward of the Emperor Jones." But, as Poston noted, by the time the same audiences exited the theater their reaction had come full circle. "One thought apparently remained in the minds of those who had momentarily ridden to a vicarious triumph with the Emperor Jones. . . . This thought was expressed by the argument of a little man who was escorting a tall woman from the theatre. He said, 'I got my opinion of a nigger who would stoop that low and use that word on the screen for those white folks.'"[39]

That word was "nigger," and Brutus Jones used it a full fourteen times. Its use shamed and enraged black audiences, many of whom assumed that Robeson agreed to play the role simply because he lacked the moral fortitude to refuse it. A letter to the editor of the *Amsterdam News* expressed well this sense of betrayal. The author, Bill Coleman, recounted how proud he had been of Robeson and his achievements. He had heard much about the film and looked forward to seeing it until he had the following conversation with a white Jewish friend. "Bill, your stage idol is a great singer," his friend told him. "He is also a great actor. Surely this idol of yours is not hungry. If he were I might find an excuse for him. Can you tell me why throughout this picture he called himself 'nigger'? I'm a Jew, Bill, and if a cheap producer sought to low-rate me and my people, even if I was starving I would have spit in his face and walked out." Coleman concluded his letter with the poignant comment: "So you can see why I was mortified, why my face was red, even though it is of black hue. I will never praise another colored person to white people again until after they [*sic*] are dead. I know then they can't move me to tears."[40]

Responding to the criticism, the Roosevelt showed for a limited engagement, beginning on November 20, a modified version with the word "nigger" deleted. William Nunn Jr., a columnist for the nation's leading black weekly, the *Pittsburgh Courier,* acknowledged that *Jones* was a film "every man, woman and child of the Negro race should see," but urged fellow blacks to view the altered version "where you can maintain your race-pride and self-respect without having to be insulted or offended."[41] When the dust cleared the controversy remained as unresolved in 1933 as it had been when the play first opened in 1924. If anything, it was even more difficult in 1933 for black performers to secure work than it had been in the twenties. The dilemma for black actors had not changed: they were damned if they accepted certain roles and unable to work if they did not.

For all the contention it provoked, financially *The Emperor Jones* did not do as well as hoped, perhaps confirming, as DuBose Heyward's biographer Frank Durham put it, "the old truism that all-Negro pictures die quietly." Production costs, according to Krimsky, had exceeded the half-million dollars projected (newly introduced sound added complicated problems and unforeseen financial burdens), forcing Krimsky to invest $100,000 "above the line" to defray the additional expenses. According to Krimsky, United Artists' distribution of the film was inept and the fear among white theater owners that showing the film would attract black patrons hurt as well.[42]

While still in America Robeson said little about either himself or the film. Once safely back in England, however, he almost immediately began to vent the anger he had such a hard time controlling during filming. In a provocatively headlined article, "Paul Robeson's Amazing Attack on Americans," published in August in London's *Daily Express,* Robeson excoriated white America, calling it the "lowest form of civilization in the world." This, however, was only a preface to Robeson's major attack, which he aimed unsparingly at fellow American blacks. "The news that a negro in Haiti had succeeded in turning himself white excited the American negroes more than anything I can remember," Robeson informed the British press. "If they knew his secret I am convinced they would all turn white too. . . . All American negroes want to be exactly like whites." It was not his task, Robeson said flatly, to try to "counteract . . . prejudice against the Negro." Rather, it was to "educate . . . the negro to believe in himself. . . . I am going to produce plays, make films, sing chants and prayers, all with one view in mind — to show my poor people that their culture traces back directly to the great civilizations of Persia, China and the Jews."[43]

Later the same month, Robeson again raised the issue of "the inferiority complex of American Negroes," this time in reference to standards for measuring artistic achievement. In one dramatic gesture Robeson summarily dismissed black critics who over the years labeled him an artist of limited talent for his failure to add German lieder and opera to his repertoire, citing this as yet one more example of blacks' servile adherence to white standards. "It is part of the inferiority complex of the American Negro . . . to consider . . . it . . . an achievement for a Negro singer to sing in a white man's opera house. . . . But what does that prove? I fail to see how a Negro can really feel the sentiments of an Italian or a German, or a Frenchman, for instance. So I really can't see where the achievement is in singing in an opera in any of these languages. . . . I will not do anything I do not understand. I do not understand the psychology or philosophy of the Frenchman, German or Italian. Their history has nothing in common with the history of my slave ancestors. So I will not sing their music."[44]

H. De La Tour in his column, "Our Performers Abroad" in the *Amsterdam News,* predicted that Robeson's "purported interview" in the *Daily Express* would "bring the colored columnists and others to the front with a roar," and it did.[45] American blacks did not take kindly to Robeson's patronizing attitude or to his lecturing them from the other side of the Atlantic Ocean, and by September the *Amsterdam News* had struck back in kind:

> We believe that Paul Robeson is a distinguished actor [and] a fine singer, and as long as he sticks to singing and acting, Paul is a pleasant fellow. But, unfortunately he is not content to be a distinguished actor and fine singer. Mr. Robeson, if one is to believe his statements in recent interviews with several white periodicals, has became a Race Leader, A Chinese Philosopher and an Opera Critic.
>
> The singer qualified for the first position by announcing his ambitious program to overcome the inferiority complex of the whole Negro race and to save it from its insane desire to become white. He assumed his second position by proclaiming his inherent understanding of Chinese, Hebrew, and Russian philosophies and by stating that he must find a great work in one of these languages as he will never again sing in French, German or Italian. He draped himself with the third mantle by attacking the desires of Negroes to "sing in a white man's opera house. . . ."
>
> We still believe that Mr. Robeson is a distinguished actor. We are convinced that he is a fine singer. But when he turns leader, philosopher and critic, we cannot continue to regard him as a pleasant fellow.
>
> If Mr. Robeson would accept advice from a Negro-owned periodical (which is probably suffering from an inferiority complex), we would say, "Stick to your singing, Paul, for when one strays too far from his given field, one is likely, if you will pardon our English, to jolly well make an ass of one's self."[46]

For blacks the "dismal decade," as Walter White called the thirties, was marked not only by hardship and poverty but also by increased racial tensions, a wave of lynchings (twenty-four in 1934), and the infamous Scottsboro case. The winter of 1932–33 had been the worst in U.S. economic history; unemployment continued to skyrocket, and Roosevelt's New Deal was just beginning to demonstrate tangible results. Few groups were harder hit than "first-fired, last-hired" American blacks, who not only bore the brunt of unemployment but also served as easy targets for white frustration and despair.[47]

There had been a noticeable cooling of feeling for Robeson among some of his black American following in the years after his decision to remain in England. Some felt that he put on airs; others, that he shirked his responsibility to the race. (In a *Pittsburgh Courier* poll tallying the most popular male performers of 1932 the Mills Brothers ranked first [880 votes], followed by Richard Harrison [760], Bill Robinson [610], Chilton and Thomas [600], Stepin Fetchit [520], Paul Robeson [370], and four others, including Clarence Muse [220].) When Robeson returned to do *The Emperor Jones* Harlem held no gala affairs in his honor. Robeson, likewise, no longer felt as much at home in Harlem as he had in previous years, and he did little to make himself available to old friends or to show much sensitivity to the problems of a Depression-ravaged population of American blacks.[48]

Outside the entrance to Harlem's Lafayette Theater stood the Tree of Hope, an elm tree whose roots were buried under the cement of Seventh Avenue and 132nd Street. The word was that rubbing the tree would bring good luck — a job or a gig. "Rub the buds off," newcomers were told. "Tree won't give you any luck unless you rub it bare." During the Depression when work for blacks — any kind of work — was practically nonexistent, the tree became a gathering spot. At any moment a saloon keeper or a booker for the Lafayette Theater might come by looking for a last-minute replacement. Most nights no one came by, but that didn't stop a crowd from gathering and rubbing the tree for luck. Harlem blacks in all occupations struggled to eke out a living, while Robeson, by contrast, not only had work with superb pay but a role in a class-A film, an unheard of achievement for a black man. But instead of being grateful for his good fortune, Robeson behaved as if he were doing people a favor and, to many it seemed, was impossible to please.[49]

Remarks ascribed to Essie in an interview with Ted Poston of the *Amsterdam News* (an interview devoted largely to promoting *her* new novel and play) only confirmed the impression that the Robesons were far removed from the problems of ordinary American blacks. Comparing the Depression in England and the United States, Essie expressed sincere empathy for the plight of England's displaced elite but almost none for the far more desperate situation of America's hungry and unemployed. "Here [the United States], everyone talks about the depression. We, who are only a generation removed from washtubs — and who can go back to tubs if need be — are loudest in our lamentations. Over there [England] the situation is very much worse. Lady So-and-So cannot very well apply for a job as someone's maid. Her presence would be embarrassing — even if someone would employ her." Such seeming indifference combined with Robeson's proclivity to air the black community's dirty laundry from a safe distance and in the white press infuriated many blacks.[50]

American blacks provided a safe target for Robeson on which to vent his rage over racial realities. And, although he spoke from the depths of his own experience when he chided them for emulating white tastes and values, he did so as one who had already passed through the fire and for whom the struggle with inferiority was long a thing of the past. In truth, it was not. As the writer James Baldwin would do years later in Paris, Robeson had found in England a haven from the social forces in America that threatened to destroy him. But, like Baldwin, he would discover that the forces he tried to flee "became interior" — that he had dragged them across the ocean with him. In time Robeson would discover that the answer to who he was would be found only within himself.[51] But he was not there yet and, to the extent that Robeson himself still wrestled with a sense of inferiority, it enraged him to see it mirrored in the behavior of American blacks.

But in England Robeson's popularity was at its apex, and a public uproar ensued when the BBC sliced time from Robeson's New Year's Eve radio program to accommodate the Bach Cantata Club Choir's "Christmas Oratorio," which was running about fifteen minutes late. In the days that followed, irate listeners flooded the BBC with complaints concerning its "just stupid" "blunder." "The BBC saw the Old Year out with a terrible 'bloomer,'" wrote one irritated patron, and another wrote: "I could have flayed the executive alive . . . when the recital of Paul Robeson was delayed by ten minutes by the never-ending choral siege of Bach."[52]

Secure, at least for the present, of his following in England, Robeson was determined to find a niche that fit his own professional and personal needs, even if that meant floundering for a period of time. At times the result bordered on chaotic as Paul branched out in multiple directions simultaneously, studying and searching for something he would know only when he found it. He was passionately interested in (and would remain so throughout his life) discovering links between seemingly diverse cultures and told reporters he believed "the best means of discovering [these] relationship[s] . . . is through the sounds of their languages, their songs and their music." To this end Robeson feverishly pursued his study of languages — Russian, Hebrew, Gaelic, Chinese — stealing time while traveling (aboard ship on his way home to England after filming *The Emperor Jones*, for example), at rehearsals breaks, even during intermission at the theater to study.[53]

Early in the year Robeson told interviewers he had undertaken a study of ethnology and that he intended to write a book that would "prove scientifically . . . that the Negro heritage is as glorious as that of other peoples." He was learning new folk songs — Scottish, Welsh, and Somerset traditional airs — and, at the end of 1933 he began studying (in his own words, "quite haphazardly") East Coast African languages (Swahili and the Bantu group) at the London School of Oriental Languages, keeping copious, often disorganized notes, written in shorthand and on small scraps of paper, covering technical and philological problems (the positioning of the tongue for making particular sounds, the use of phonemes, various language groupings) as well as broader ideas elicited by his language studies.[54]

In January 1934 Robeson began a long concert tour of the British Isles (January–May, July, and August), part of the Harold Holt Celebrity Series. Although he ranked equally with other Celebrity Series concert performers for the season (Yehudi Menuhin, Paderewski, and Vladimir Horowitz) and was billed as "The World's Greatest Negro Actor Vocalist," Robeson stepped outside the customary itinerary for artists of his stature by including engagements in industrial centers such as Newport, Manchester, Sheffield, Liverpool, and Yorkshire. He made significant changes in his repertoire as well, eliminating classical pieces and concentrating on folk songs — those of his own people, most selected and arranged by Larry Brown ("Water Boy," "Go Down, Moses," and often as an encore "Deep River"), and Russian ("Oh, Ivan"), Hebrew ("Shor Somrin"), English ("Oh No John!"), Scottish ("Loch Lomond"), and Finnish ("The Wanderer") songs as well. "This is a permanent departure," Robeson said in one of the many interviews he gave on tour. "Negro songs, Russian, Hebrew and Slavic folk songs, all have a deep lying affinity . . . folk songs are the music of basic realities, the spontaneous expression by the people for the people of elemental emotions. . . . I am appealing not to the highbrow and not to the lowbrow, but I am singing for . . . common humanity."[55]

He also began including in his concert repertoire a number of popular tunes — Stephen Foster's "Poor Old Joe" and "Old Folks at Home," Hoagy Carmichael's "Lazy Bones" and "Snowball," Wood and Wolfe's "Shortnin' Bread," and White and Trinkaus's "Mammy's Kinky Headed Little Boy" — some minstrel tunes, others tin-pan alley songs, still others an amalgamation of the two with stereotypes of the "stage Negro" sprinkled liberally throughout. Listening to Robeson sing these pieces is startling — it is difficult to imagine the fiery Robeson of later years performing "Poor Old Joe," for example. Why did he sing them? Robeson was still looking for ways to enlarge his repertoire, and these were all popular songs his audiences wanted to hear. "Dad was torn between the purity of his art and reaching a mass audience," Paul Robeson Jr. said. "Mother argued that you've got to do some of the garbage — if you want to call it that — if you want to reach a large audience. You do that with radio, you do that with vaudeville, you do that with musicals."[56]

Joe Andrews once said of Robeson that everything he did "had class and dignity. There was nothing cheap or tawdry about him. In his hands even the simplest song or play became something noble, something more than it had been." And in this respect, listening to Robeson sing even "plantation" pieces is a revelation. There is humor in his renderings, but never ridicule. It may have been his classic manner, his flawless diction, or his rich bass that added depth to songs generally given a much shallower treatment. Because he sang with such sincerity and unashamed sentiment, audiences were not so much laughing at the song's characters as with them. He managed this even with a song like "Lazy Bones," a light-hearted tune about the stereotypically lazy southern black. The song is laced with stereotypes ("as long as there's watermelon in the vine, everything is fine"), but listening to it you identify with the singer of the song, the "lazy" son's frustrated father. Robeson lent to these pieces a quiet strength, an understanding touch, and an infectious conviction that transformed them into "something more." "He recorded all kinds of popular songs," Paul Robeson Jr. said, "plantation songs, yet . . . I have to confess that as a little kid my favorite song was not 'Deep River' or anything like that. It was 'Mammy's Little Baby Loves Shortnin' Bread.'"[57]

Robeson drew overflow audiences and, especially in the provinces, received a regal reception. Although some audiences — those in Sheffield and Yorkshire, for example — were initially cautious, Robeson quickly won them over. He touched his listeners personally, and they responded in kind. Throughout the tour, Robeson made it a point to talk with and learn as much as he could from the people for whom he sang, particularly in the industrial areas. Each new connection he made whetted his appetite to learn more. In the textile center of Manchester, hard hit by the Depression, he spoke with a worker whose father and grandfather wove cotton that had been picked by slave workers in America. "The workers of Manchester had supported the side of the Abolition in the Civil War," Robeson later reflected, "though the Union blockade of the South cut off the supply of cotton and resulted in greater hardship for them, while at the same time the millowners and their government had supported the side of Slavery." Jan Carew, a student in London at the time, remembered Robeson actively seeking out African students to talk with after concerts and also recalled that Robeson's concert agent would generally have someone assigned to follow him around. Without this precaution "Robeson would get in with some group of students and . . . spend days with them, forgetting all about his concert[s]."[58]

Larry Brown remembered that in Dublin during their 1934 tour, "something happened which made me see Paul in a new light and realise that he had a power beyond that of an ordinary singer. After our concert several young Negro medical students — I think five of them — who were studying in Dublin, came to see Paul. . . . I've never forgotten the expression on the faces of these young Negroes as they looked at Paul. How shall I describe it? They seemed to worship him. Although they came from so many different places they all looked at him as if he were a man they could trust and who, in a sense, they regarded as Moses."[59]

In Sheffield a man asked Robeson as a special favor to recite William Blake's poem, "The Little Black Boy." Robeson had read the poem as part of his BBC New Year's Eve program and, as the man explained, that poem was the last thing his young brother heard before he died. Robeson willingly complied, explaining later that Blake, an outspoken abolitionist, particularly appealed to him and that he felt the poet "must have understood the mind of the Negro to an amazing extent." "The Little Black Boy," one of Blake's *Songs of Innocence,* is narrated by a black child, an innocent who accepts the world as he finds it. But the author of the poem and, presumably, his listeners are not. Thus, the poem, and especially its last stanza, which might easily be read as being about the all-too-familiar and patronizing "black skin but white soul" longing for white acceptance, becomes a poignant and ironic statement, pitting the innocence of a black child against the cruelties of the world. It was a message Robeson both understood and appreciated.[60]

Audiences were enthralled with his reading of the poem, his "direct delivery," his "feeling for the beauty of the English tongue," and his diction so perfect as to put "many English elocutioners to shame," and Robeson recited it frequently for the remainder of the tour. As he did with many of his songs, Robeson introduced the poem with some brief explanatory remarks: "Regarding the second line of the poem, I am sure if Blake were alive today, he would gladly admit that souls have no color, neither white not black."

> My mother bore me in the southern wild,
> And I am black, but O! My soul is white;
> White as an angel is the English child,
> But I am black, as if bereav'd of light.
>
> My mother taught me underneath a tree,
> And, sitting down before the heat of day,
> She took me on her lap and kissed me,
> And, pointing to the east, began to say:

"Look on the rising sun: there God does live,
And gives His light, and gives his heat away;
And flowers and trees and beasts and men receive
Comfort in morning, joy in the noonday.

"And we are put on earth a little space,
That we may learn to bear the beams of love;
And these black bodies and this sunburnt face
Is but a cloud, and like a shady grove.

"For when our souls have learned the heat to bear,
The cloud will vanish; we shall hear his voice,
Saying: 'Come out from the grove, my love & care,
And round my golden tent like lambs rejoice.'"

Thus did my mother say, and kissed me;
And thus I say to little English boy.
When I from black and he from white cloud free,
And round the tent of God like lambs we joy,

I'll shade him from the heat till he can bear
To lean in joy upon our father's knee;
And then I'll stand and stroke his silver hair,
And be like him, and then will he love me.[61]

While he was reciting Blake; talking with British, Welsh, Scottish, and African workers; studying at least four languages simultaneously; and adding new popular and folk songs to his repertoire, Robeson was also learning everything he could about Africa. Throughout the year he talked and wrote about Africa and African culture, ostensibly to educate others but in the process exploring, clarifying, and refining his own thought. Intuitively he had come to understand that his own identity was linked to his understanding of Africa, that as an American black he had absorbed without even realizing it racist stereotypes of the "Dark Continent," and that what he actually knew about Africa was painfully limited. Again, it was as much as anything the recognition of his own lack of knowledge that prompted Robeson to lecture American blacks for their "regrettable and abysmal ignorance" concerning their ancestral home: "I have met Negroes in the United States who believed that the African Negro communicated his thoughts solely by means of gestures," Robeson wrote in 1934, "that, in fact, he was practically incapable of speech and merely used sign language! It is my first concern to dispel this ignorance."[62]

Robeson was so focused and absorbed with what he was learning that everything else took second place. In January, on his way to a studio recording appointment, he stopped to consult a book at the British Museum. He had left with time to spare to make his appointment, but once he had the book in front of him, he became completely engrossed. Meanwhile a large orchestra waited in the studio, mechanics double-checked their equipment, the director watched the clock, and Robeson never showed. Robeson arrived home late that night still deep in thought and utterly unaware that he had kept the studio staff and orchestra waiting for hours.[63]

At the same time, Essie enrolled at the London School of Economics (LSE) where she began studying anthropology under the distinguished professors Bronislaw Malinowski and Raymond Firth. In this relatively new science Malinowski was the most sought-out anthropologist in Europe and a leader in the movement to make fieldwork among native peoples and understanding natives' conceptual processes essential components of anthropological research. LSE was widely regarded as *the* place to study anthropology. With its superb faculty and innovative courses covering topics such as the principles of social structure, kinship, religion and ritual, and political organization, it attracted students from all over the world, many of whom went on to become well-known anthropologists in their own right.[64] Although Essie audited courses rather than enrolling in a degree program, she quickly made her presence felt (years later Raymond Firth still had vivid recollections of her in class) and saw to it that Paul met scholars in the fields of interest to him. "I don't recall her even reading a paper, a seminar requirement," said Prince Peter of Greece, himself a student at the school. "But she had a considerable amount to say outside of class. I saw her mainly with her husband at Professor Malinowski's home. She and Paul also often had dinner at my house. She was lively and very racially minded, in a continuous state of revolt against white supremacy."[65]

In the first half of 1934 an event occurred that would give Robeson's effort to synthesize his developing racial and professional identity the direction and focus it needed. Hungarian film producer Alexander Korda, who had single-handedly put the British film industry on the map with his phenomenally successful *The Private Life of Henry VIII* (1933), and his brother Zoltan Korda showed Robeson portions of some 60,000 feet of film Zoltan had taken during six months in the Congo, Uganda, and Sudan in the hope that they could persuade Robeson to star in a film set in Africa and based on an adventure story by the prolific and popular Edgar Wallace.[66] Robeson watched the footage — which showed African native life, scenery and animals, and battles, dances, and rituals never before seen by Westerners, including a remarkable scene involving thirty war canoes, each manned with a crew of eighty warriors in full war paint, shooting the rapids at Stanleyville — and was stunned. It was spectacular, but more than that it documented a vision of Africa that cut to shreds the Western stereotypes he had been taught to accept as fact. Robeson was so impressed that he agreed immediately to take the part.[67]

Work on the film, *Sanders of the River*, began in the early summer at Shepperton Studios on the Thames River just outside London. The well-known and versatile English actor Leslie Banks was cast in the role of Sanders and the twenty-year-old American beauty, Nina Mae McKinney, best known for her hugely successful portrayal of the seductive temptress Chick, in King Vidor's film *Hallelujah!* (1929), was chosen to play the role of Lilongo, Robeson's wife in the film.[68] Nearly 250 blacks — native African laborers, unemployed drifters and dockers gathered from the ports of Bristol, Liverpool, and Cardiff, and a scattering of students and professional and out-of-work actors — were hired to play the African extras. Extras were paid as much as a guinea a day, a handsome sum for working-class blacks struggling to make ends meet.[69]

From the first rehearsal Robeson was relaxed, enthusiastic, and eager to work, certain that the film would offer blacks, in particular American blacks, a picture of the "Dark Continent" in which they could take pride. He got along famously with everyone and actually enjoyed the waiting periods between filming because they allowed him time to mingle with other members of the cast extras — black Cardiff dockers from Tiger Bay and Africans representing the Acholi, Sesi, Tefik, Jeruba, Mendi, and Kroo tribes. (Among cast extras, more than twenty different African languages were spoken.) For Robeson, it would be an exhilarating experience, as much a personal and intellectual odyssey as a professional challenge. The synergistic effect of his daily contact with Africans on the set, his own study and research, Essie's academic work, and the academic contacts he made through her would provide one of the most intellectually and emotionally stimulating experiences of his life.[70]

Often, during filming breaks Robeson persuaded African extras to sing for him while he jotted down notes on scraps of paper. Other times he had natives teach him Yoruba and Twi. The connection Robeson felt with these Africans was an experience so startling and intense that he would talk about it for years to come. "I was astonished listening to them [the African extras], at the closeness of our own racial derivation. One day on the set I overheard one of them speaking his native dialect. To my amazement I was able to understand much of what he said. I spoke to him at once, and do you know he was from the Elbo tribe in Nigeria — the very tribe and country from which my father's own family came. Surely, I must have heard a word or two of that language, that crept into my father's speech and that he himself had inherited." Robeson compared the experience to a homecoming. "I felt that I had penetrated to the core of African culture when I began to study the legendary traditions and folklore of the West African Negro."[71]

After they had exhausted the ranks of African laborers, casting recruiters for the film, desperate to fill the African parts, combed London for African students, aspiring intellectuals, and musicians and artists in need of some extra money. Among these recruits was the tall, powerfully built West African Orlando Martins, a beginning actor-singer and African nationalist. Born in Lagos, West Africa, in 1900, Martins first came to England to join the British navy and fight for the crown in World War I, but when he was turned down because of his youth he joined the merchant marine instead. After the war, Martins remained in England, making his living as a wrestler, a "super" in the ballet, a snake charmer, and an extra in silent and talking films. (Later Martins would earn fame as a radio-stage celebrity in Nigeria, singing many songs Robeson made famous, copying Robeson's style quite precisely.) Martins was not a trained intellectual, but he had a fine mind and was one of "a handful of Africans who really 'knew' English ways." Friendly and hospitable, Martins gladly assisted Paul's "research," lending him books and entertaining him for hours with African folk tales.[72]

Much has been made of Robeson's association with the young Johnstone (later Jomo) Kenyatta, the legendary hero of Kenya's independence movement, who was also hired as an extra on the *Sanders* set. Stories vary as to how the two men first met: Joe Andrews remembered their being introduced through Essie (both Essie and Kenyatta were attending Malinowski's seminar at the London School of Economics); others, among them Kenyatta's biographer, Jeremy Murray-Brown, claim the two first met on the *Sanders* set. Kenyatta had a long road to travel before achieving his later fame, and in 1934 he was one of many African students living hand-to-mouth, struggling to make ends meet. What singled him out in these early years was not his nationalistic fervor but his controversial defense of the much maligned East African Kikuya tribal ritual of clitorectomy, or female circumcision, which he published first in a 1934 article and then in 1935 in greater detail in his proud account of Kenyan life, *Facing Mount Kenya*. Although the book was a financial failure, it gave Kenyatta exposure, especially the chapter explaining clitorectomy, which shocked and horrified many British. Kenyatta made the most of the notoriety, changing his name from Johnstone to the tribal Jomo Kenyatta and adopting the image of a Kenyan warrior, bedecked in animal skin and brandishing a spear borrowed for the book jacket photograph from a fellow Kikuyu, Prince Peter Mbiyu Koinange, son of the senior chief of Koinange.[73]

Kenyatta, with his flair for the theatrical (he once arrived at a formal LSE summer school gathering dressed in tribal dress long before such clothing was familiar wear for African nationals), fascinated Robeson, but in truth the friendship between the two men was a casual and temporary one based largely on Kenyatta's financial needs, Robeson's burgeoning interest in Africa, and their mutual fascination with the potential of the new film medium. Murray-Brown describes Kenyatta as "very poor in those days and certainly not above trying to get to know Robeson simply because Paul was such an important person with so many influential contacts" and conjectures that Kenyatta may well have viewed friendship with Robeson as a way of getting started in a film career. Robeson gave Kenyatta some of his records and a gramophone, and Kenyatta talked with Robeson about Russia and colonial Africa. They visited each others' flats, Robeson's "bookish" and "unpretentious" set of rooms on the Strand and Kenyatta's modest bed-sitting room near Victoria Station. Lord Fenner Brockway, a friend of Kenyatta's and a leader of the British Independent Party, remembered Kenyatta and Robeson meeting for tea at the Strand. When they got up to leave, they clasped and heartily embraced each other much to the surprise of British onlookers. Most observers agreed they enjoyed each others' company but were "not close" (almost all of Robeson's African friends were West rather than East African), although there was "much accord" between them. As for the rumor that the two were roommates for a time, Joe Andrews said emphatically that he doubted such an arrangement ever took place. "Paul liked his privacy. It is not likely that he would have let anyone share his flat on the Strand." By the late 1930s contact between Robeson and Kenyatta had ceased; if there had been a falling-out it may have been over their differences with respect to the Soviet Union.[74]

By far Robeson's most important "discovery" that summer was confirmation that Africa did have a culture, a culture that African Americans had inherited but that was lost to them because they were for all practical purposes unaware of its existence. "Africa is a Dark Continent not merely because its people are dark-skinned or by reason of its extreme impenetrability, but because its history is lost," Robeson wrote in 1934. "In the country of his adoption . . . he [the American Negro] is an alien . . . he believes himself to have broken away from his true origins; he has, he argues, nothing whatever in common with the inhabitant of Africa today — and that is where I believe he is wrong."[75]

Simply talking about African culture was a radical move for the times. And Robeson not only affirmed the existence of African culture but outlined ways in which it was superior to Western culture. He spoke with great admiration of the "flexibility and subtlety of a language like Swahili, sufficient to convey the teachings of Confucius," and announced his intention to "make these qualities and attainments of Negro languages known in the Western world." Western culture, like all cultures, Robeson observed, has its limitations. "The white man has made a fetish of intellect and worships the God of thought; the negro feels rather than thinks, experiences emotions directly rather than interprets them by roundabout and devious abstractions, and apprehends the outside world by means of an intuitive perception instead of through a carefully built up system of logical analysis." Above all, Western culture lacked the spiritual dimension of Eastern thought. "Somewhere, sometime — perhaps at the Renaissance . . . a great part of religion went astray. A blind groping after Rationality resulted in an incalculable loss of pure Spirituality. Mankind replaced dependence on that part of his mind that was brain, intellect and intuition . . . we grasped at the shadow and lost the substance. . . . Now the pendulum is swinging back. . . . Mankind is gradually feeling its way back to a more fundamental, more primitive, perhaps truer religion. . . . This religion, this basic culture, has its roots in the Far East, and in Africa."[76]

Robeson was no anthropologist, and had his writing been taken seriously by the anthropological community it most certainly would have been challenged, as it so directly contradicted prevailing academic thought, especially on the subject of African Americans. With few exceptions anthropologists from Franz Boas at the turn of the century to Ruth Benedict and Ashley Montague in the thirties and forties, as well as sociologists like Robert E. Park and E. Franklin Frazier, held that African Americans shared the same culture as white Americans. Seeming cultural differences between the two groups were explained as the result of environmental deprivation and cultural "stripping." The assumption was that American blacks were cultureless, with the exception of what they had managed to assimilate from the white mainstream. Thus Gunnar Myrdal was merely reiterating long-held assumptions when he observed in his 1944 *An American Dilemma* that the American black is "not proud of those things in which he differs from the white American" and cited as examples of the "distorted development, or pathological condition" of black life such things as the "emotionalism" of their churches, the "unwholesomeness" of their recreational activities, "the plethora of Negro sociable organizations," and "the cultivation of the arts to the neglect of other fields." In Robeson's mind there was no question that African Americans had a culture and that this culture was essentially African in origin. The question was whether they would be able to embrace that culture and use it as a source of power and identity.[77]

Working on *Sanders* had been a tremendous learning experience for Robeson, and when he considered the opportunity the film presented for communicating his new understanding of Africa on a large scale, he found it almost impossible to conceal his excitement. In contrast to Hollywood's superficial and self-serving depiction of African "savages," the Kordas appeared seriously committed to truth and accuracy. In the construction of the set, described by the *London Illustrated News* as "one of the most remarkable . . . ever put up for the cinema," no effort was spared. Alexander Korda had over fifty reed-thatched huts to house the village's 200 natives built from scratch, so determined was he to capture the authentic detail of African life. He imported shields, calabashes, and spears from Africa and had everything else in the village hand-crafted, including conical huts, kraals, and canoes. Robeson's songs ("The Canoe Song," "The Killing Song," and "Love Song") as well as the "Congo Lullaby," sung by Nina Mae McKinney, were based on recordings of authentic African chants gathered by Zoltan Korda. The Kordas even went as far as to construct a full-scale replica of the stern wheeler, *Zaire*, familiar to Edgar Wallace readers as the stern-wheel paddle steamer in which Sanders with the assistance of native Haussas could rapidly reach and restore order among rebellious natives.[78]

It may well have been this focus and enthusiasm — reporters looking for Robeson during the filming of *Sanders* most often found him at the end of the day in his London flat, beating out the rhythms and cadences as he listened again and again to recordings of African speech and music — in part at least, that prevented Robeson from seeing warning signs that the film might not turn out to be all that he hoped. The first and most glaring of these was the script itself. Producer Alexander Korda had from the beginning envisioned a film pro-Empire in emphasis. Hungarian by nationality, Korda was an ardent Anglophile nonetheless, "as staunch a champion of the British Empire and the White Man's Burden as if he had been brought up on Kipling instead of the Hungarian classics," who saw *Pax Britannia* as the world's "greatest bulwark" against the rising tide of fascism. On more than one occasion, Alexander Korda's devotion to British imperialism caused contention with his more liberal brother Zoltan, who felt their films should explore native experience objectively and stay out of politics. One of their arguments revolved around whether a white man would thank a native by shaking his hand. Alexander Korda thought not; Zoltan insisted the contrary and in this instance won his point, although most often it was Alexander's point of view that dominated their films. *Sanders,* like Alexander Korda's subsequent films — *Four Feathers, Fire over England,* and *The Drum* — not only justified British imperialism but sanctified it, portraying the Empire builders as the embodiment "of the most noble traits in the English character and spirit."[79]

Edgar Wallace, on whose *Congo Raid* the script was based, by far the best-known and most widely read fiction writer of the period, had written a series of stories about the film's protagonist, Sanders, the British commissioner who controlled a quarter of a million warring cannibal Africans living on the fringes of Togo country in West Africa by flogging miscreants, sending them down the river in irons, or hanging them from convenient trees. Korda altered Wallace's Sanders to make him more benevolent — a character more in keeping with the glorified view of colonialism Korda wanted to portray.

The film is built around the imperialistic theme of conflict between reasonable and kindly British colonial officers ("the Keepers of the King's peace") and warring and barbaric Africans. When the commissioner first meets Bosambo (Robeson), he recognizes a potentially valuable ally and cultivates his friendship. Bosambo works hard to demonstrate his loyalty; he embraces Sanders's Christian religion ("I am a Christian for Lord Sandi") and promises to send his own son to England to learn Western ways. When Bosambo saves the commissioner's life, he is promoted to the position of Sanders's "man," a job requiring him, assisted by his own warriors, to help Sanders in all aspects of his administration. Bosambo (did Robeson miss entirely the "Sambo" in Bosambo?) has no authority except that given to him by Sanders. Bosambo elicits admiration chiefly because he is cooperative and well behaved. His "kingship" is a sham.[80]

Before Sanders returns to England to be married, he gathers the tribal kings before him, who bow, scrape, and listen intently to his instructions (Kenyatta played one of these kings).[81] "Obey Lord Ferguson [his replacement] as if you were his own children. . . . You will be loved by Lord Ferguson just as you were loved by me." In Sanders's absence two rascally English traders inflame the African natives with gin and firearms and spread the rumor that the mighty Sanders is dead. A rebellious king murders the new administrator and captures Bosambo, who throughout has maintained his British loyalties. The film climaxes when Sanders, returning with his new bride in tow, rescues Bosambo from the clutches of a treacherous old king. The message is clear: order will prevail only under the white authority of Lord Sandi, "hater of lies" and "righter of wrongs."

Despite their enthusiasm, Paul and Essie were neophytes, just beginning to learn about Africa. Joe Andrews remembered an incident that clearly demonstrated this point. Most mornings Essie drove Paul to the *Sanders* set for rehearsals. Often, she stopped to pick up Africans along the way. "It never occurred to her to consider whether they were East or West Africans before she let them in the car, which shows really how little she understood them and their prejudices," Andrews said. In fact, rivalries among West and East Africans, West Indians, black students, and black laborers were commonplace, and much of the contention related to the extent to which the various groups had adopted British attitudes and prejudices. West Africans, for example, typically looked down on East Africans as inferior and backward (barbarian, actually, as East Africans practiced such atrocities as female castration) and wanted nothing to do with them. "More than once she had the East African Kenyatta and the West African Orlando Martins jammed with others into the car. Neither Kenyatta nor Martins was happy about the situation. When Paul realized there was a problem, he asked Essie simply not to pick up anyone. It was just easier that way."[82]

Flora Robson, who had starred with Robeson in *All God's Chillun* the previous year, recalled a similar blunder on Robeson's part. A prince of Ashanti, at the time attending Oxford, was annoyed with Paul for appearing in *Sanders* nearly naked except for a leopard skin. He asked Paul, "'What do you wear a leopard skin for?' So Paul said 'Well, what do *you* wear in Africa? Tweeds?' And the Prince said, 'Yes, we do.'"[83]

In addition, Robeson had for years failed to appreciate the discrimination colonials routinely experienced in England, which, as the West Indian Hugh Scotland, who attended law classes in London in the early thirties, put it, "in practical terms meant that if you went to a restaurant as a coloured colonial you expected to have to wait a long time; the same thing for a haircut. Robeson was treated like a king, and we were still trying to get a haircut."[84] As late as the spring of 1933 Robeson described the "colour bar on this side of the Atlantic" as "a very mild affair. Almost everywhere, the Negro, or any man of colour, can move amongst his fellows on terms of almost complete equality. Such restrictions as exist are too petty to annoy a man with any philosophical outlook on life."[85]

Over and above the issue of discrimination, Robeson did not understand — because as an American black it was not his experience — what it meant to be born a colonial. Twenty years later writer James Baldwin was still struggling to fathom what he described as the "gulf which yawns between the American Negro and all other men of color." Baldwin suggested as an explanation an immense difference, the product of experience, in the psychology of the American blacks. "We had been born in a society, which . . . was open, and, in a sense which has nothing to do with justice or injustice, free. It was a society . . . in which nothing was fixed and we had therefore been born to a greater number of possibilities, wretched as those possibilities seemed at the instant of our birth," Baldwin wrote. "This results in a psychology very different . . . from the psychology which is produced by a sense of having been invaded and overrun, the sense of having no recourse against oppression other than overthrowing the machinery of the oppressor. We had been dealing with, had been made and mangled by, another machinery altogether. It had never been in our interest to overthrow it. It had been necessary to make the machinery work for our benefit and the possibility of its doing so had been, so to speak, built in."[86]

In this situation, as in so many others he faced in life, Robeson had no role models to follow and he discovered this "gulf" the hard way. It was an important piece of knowledge to be missing and perhaps more than anything else accounts for his failure to see the film for what it was. Friends noticed this gap in Robeson's understanding and were initially surprised. "Occasionally Robeson spoke before the West African student Union and the India League as well," said the West Indian C. L. R. James. "But through it all, I think he never really understood Britain's imperialism. He just didn't get it." Fenner Brockway agreed.

"Paul was an American and he *had* a country. He had participated in its 'events' —football, college, life in Harlem. He may not have liked his country very much, but he *was* a citizen. West Indians, Africans, and Indians didn't have a country. This was something that Paul had never experienced."[87]

Even after the film was completed Robeson remained confident about it. He had not expected an overnight miracle, just a fair shot, and felt that *Sanders* would succeed in both attracting a mass audience and positively portraying Africa "in a really magnificent way. I have seen all the African and Balinese films that have been made, and I've not come across anything like it. We know something about the rhythm of Negro music, but these records of Korda's have much more melody than I've ever heard come out of Africa. And I think the Americans will be amazed to find how many of their modern dance steps are relics of an African heritage—a pure Charleston, for instance, danced in the heart of the Congo. It's a great opportunity for me to break new ground in my singing."[88]

For the remainder of the year Robeson continued studying and performed a small number of concerts. By the end of 1934, however, it became clear that something in his thinking had decidedly shifted. In December 1934, he spoke before the student-aid and political organization, the League of Coloured Peoples (LCP), at Memorial Hall on Farringdon Street. Founded by the Jamaican-born Dr. Harold Moody in 1931 to provide practical aid for West Indian and African students and their families in England, the LCP had by 1933 expanded its activities to the political realm by backing the Scottsboro campaign, formally protesting the American lynching of blacks, and supporting self-government for the West Indies.[89] In his speech that evening, entitled "The Negro in the Modern World," Robeson rehearsed themes he had been talking about throughout 1934: the richness of African culture, the importance of owning one's racial and cultural heritage, the cultural alignment of blacks with Eastern cultures, and Robeson's sense of himself as African.

He urged his audience and all people of African descent to be proud of being called "African" or "Negro" and reminded them that whatever institution or system they developed must have the stamp of Africa on it. He told them that they could not be de-Africanized by exposure to other cultures because they *were* African and advised them to take what was best from other cultures and mold it to their own needs. And finally he both urged and cautioned them not to limit themselves to the study of European culture but to examine the cultures of the East as well—in particular the cultures of China and Russia. Discussing his own success, Robeson admitted frankly that in the early days of his career his color had been an asset: to the extent that whites underrated the race as a whole, his achievements had seemed all the more impressive to them.[90]

Then, before this unsuspecting audience, Robeson let fall a bombshell and announced that he was "unquestionably leaving" England, explaining that in spite of his position in the performing world, he had grown tired of Western values. "I refuse to live under the sword of Damocles all my life," Robeson said. "I want to be where I can be African and not have to be Mr. Paul Robeson every hour of the day." While acknowledging that *he* had "found perfect freedom and peace" in England, he added, "it has not been so with my friends — companions of my own race. Where I am welcome they are not. . . . I am tired of the burden of my race, which will be with me so long as I remain here. I must cast it from me and go to live where I belong."[91]

Describing himself as "a Negro wandering through the world," Robeson was vague about where he was going but quite clear that he intended to leave. His announcement left his audience stunned. One can only conjecture as to what motivated him. If it was a reaction he wanted, he got it. The British press jumped on the story and gave it widespread coverage. In fact, nothing Robeson had said during the past two years concerning Africa and Western culture had elicited a comparable response. When a reporter from the *Star* accused Robeson of running away from the race problem in England, an Indian student quickly came to Robeson's defense. "I do not see any 'running away' in Mr. Robeson's statement. He is tired of your 'white civilization.' . . . As an Indian, I feel the same very much myself . . . the problem of the colour bar is nothing short of living hell in this country. Suppose our young men go back to India with bitter memories and resolve to work and find ways to redress the grievance and not to pocket the insults. Will that be running away? Surely not!"[92]

One has the sense that throughout 1933 and 1934 the British public listened politely as Robeson spoke and wrote about Africa, but actually paid little attention to what he said. One of several articles he wrote on the subject, "Paul Robeson on My Dark Race," appeared in *Forum* in March 1934 and included a photo caption characterizing Robeson in the same stereotypical manner he had always been characterized. "He leaves a trail of friendliness wherever he goes, this Paul Robeson, Negro, who with his typical Negro qualities — his appearances, his voice, his genial smile, his laziness, his childlike simplicity — is carving his place as a citizen of the world, a place which would most certainly have made his slave-father proud."[93]

Robeson had complete freedom to speak as he wished in England. But as an "exceptional" black, he constituted no danger. Talk as he might, Robeson neither threatened nor changed British ideas and values.

13

The Search for Home

1934-1935

Robeson's December announcement may have shocked the British public, but leaving England, or, perhaps more accurately acknowledging publicly that he "would not live out [his] life as an adopted Englishman," was something that Robeson had been thinking about for some time. For ten years the British public had treated him regally, following his personal and professional life with a parent's interest and lack of objectivity. But, increasingly, Robeson felt dissatisfied with his life in England. To friends he complained that he was "tired of the shallow life," of his horizons limited to a relentless cycle of touring, filmmaking, and theater work. Intellectually, he felt frustrated. In the past, when he spoke about race relations in England he had felt that his views were taken seriously. Now, as he came close to questioning the Empire, the public's response was often condescending and patronizing.[1]

Robeson wanted time to read and reflect. He longed to learn languages, not just as a tool for enlarging his repertoire but thoroughly, with true fluency the goal. He wanted to retire, study, and perhaps write a book.[2] His vast collection of phonograph records and textbooks as well as attendance at various language schools had only whetted his appetite. "He always seemed most content when he was alone, studying, jotting down similar words in other languages," said Joe Andrews. "Often his pockets were filled with notes written on scraps of paper. On tour he always took along a briefcase, full of books and more notes."[3]

Africa was not, however, as many surmised, Robeson's destination. In November 1934, friend, screen critic, and journalist Marie Seton, recently returned from Moscow, joined the Robesons for dinner. Seton first met Robeson in 1930 after a matinee performance of *Othello,* and she would remain friends with him and Essie throughout their lives. Between 1932 and 1934 she spent considerable time in Russia, working as the Moscow correspondent for the journal *Film Art* and interviewing the Russian film director Sergei Eisenstein, in preparation for a biography she was writing of him.[4]

Seton brought with her to that November dinner a letter for Paul from Eisenstein. Eisenstein wanted to make a film with Robeson about Toussaint L'Ouverture and in the note invited Robeson to visit him in the Soviet Union to discuss the possibility.[5] Robeson had long been interested in the Russian language and culture and had intended to visit the Soviet Union, but he had never had a definite reason for going. Eisenstein's invitation was just the impetus he needed, and he accepted.[6]

Robeson began studying the Russian language in the early 1930s, initially as part of an overall effort to expand his repertoire. He studied on his own and also with the Russian composer Alexandre Gambs, and in 1932 and 1933 with the black musician G. Ruthland Clapham of the Southern Syncopated Orchestra. Clapham accompanied Paul for a short time in 1933 when Robeson and Brown had a brief falling out, but he didn't keep the job for long because he had a habit of overdrinking, which on at least one occasion embarrassed Robeson. Clapham was, however, a skilled musician who knew the Russian language and Russian music well, and Robeson rehearsed regularly with him for several years. He later told Andrews that he "got more from 10 minutes with Clapham than he would from years of study with some of the great teachers of voice."[7]

In contrast to German, Russian was an easy language for Robeson to learn, and in fact he rather speciously claimed he learned the language in six months. He gave the matter of his uneven success with language studies a good deal of thought and concluded it was a matter of affinity, of likeness of experiences expressed over time in language, that accounted for his facility with Russian. Robeson had noted years before an affinity between the music and historical experiences of American blacks and Jews, and in the early 1930s he began talking about a special kinship between Russians and American blacks and adding Russian pieces — many sung in Russian — to his concert program. Robeson explained this special kinship to Roy Wilkins in 1931: "The Russians have experienced many of the same things the American Negroes have experienced. They were both serfs and in the music there is the same note of melancholy, touched with mysticism. I have heard most of the great Russian singers on the gramophone [Joe Andrews said Robeson owned many Chaliapin recordings and listened to them often and avidly] and have occasionally found whole phrases that could be matched in Negro melodies. . . . I found at once that the language and the music seemed to suit my voice and I think there is a psychological explanation. . . . I know that I am going to be able to sing the music of Moussorgsky as if I had been born in Russia."[8]

Robeson had heard personal accounts of Russia's vibrant artistic life and its remarkable racial liberality from friends and theater associates. Andre Van Gyseghem (with whom Paul had just recently worked in *All God's Chillun*), talked at length with Paul about Soviet arts. At the time one of the few English-speaking authorities on Soviet theater (he made five trips to the Soviet Union between 1933 and 1935, one of which included a year's work at Moscow's Realistic Theatre), Van Gyseghem wrote numerous articles on Russian theater for the *Moscow Daily News* and credited much of his own professional expertise to the education he received in the Soviet Union.[9]

If others like Marie Seton had not already done so, Van Gyseghem introduced Paul to the Soviet-published *Moscow Daily News*. Against a backdrop of consistently denigrating reportage in the British mainstream press, this publication offered an equally biased but laudatory portrait of life in the new Russia. Tailored specifically for Western readers, the *Moscow Daily News* detailed Soviet advances in science, agriculture, education, athletics, and industry and developments in the arts as well as the rise of Russia's minorities from a virtual feudal existence to civilized modern life. Readers of the newspaper saw a Russia in which minorities — Chinese, Manchurians, Uzbeks, Kazakhs, Jews, Mongolians, and Georgians — most of whom were located hundreds and thousands of miles from Moscow, were treated as equals and encouraged to participate in all aspects of Russian life.[10] "Son of Slave Tells of Kazakhstan, Old and New" ran the headline of one typical account, in which forty-year-old Tusuy Kuzembayev explained how the new Soviet regime saved him from a life of misery and servitude.[11] Not only minorities but Russian women as well experienced new freedom and opportunity, working side by side with men in the factories.[12]

Robeson had heard similar stories from an East African — in all probability Kenyatta — who had visited the Soviet Union, traveled east, and "seen the Yakuts, a people . . . classed as a 'backward race' by the Czars [and] been struck by the resemblance of the tribal life of the Yakuts and his own people of East Africa." The East African's account fascinated Robeson. "Well, I went to see for myself . . . in 1934 how a people like the Yakuts would fare freed from colonial oppression and part of a socialist society," Robeson wrote in his autobiography. "I saw how the Yakuts and the Uzbeks and all the other formerly oppressed nations were leaping ahead from tribalism to modern industrial economy, from illiteracy to the heights of knowledge."[13]

American blacks who visited or lived in Russia during the late twenties and early thirties were uniformly awestruck by the treatment they received. Two friends of Paul's, Claude McKay and William Patterson, had already visited Russia: McKay in 1922 and Patterson in 1927. Both were impressed with the freedom from prejudice they experienced there. "Never in my life did I feel prouder of being an African, a black," said McKay, and Patterson agreed: "It is as if one had suffered with a painful affliction for many years and had suddenly awakened to discover that the pain was gone." Henry Lee Moon, at the time a young journalist (later he wrote for the NAACP), lavished praise on the Soviet Union in June 1934 in an article published in the *Nation.* "I have never felt more at home among a people than among the Russians, and I think this is a common experience of Negroes who have visited the Soviet Union." Langston Hughes, one of a group of twenty-two blacks invited to the Soviet Union in the spring of 1932 to make a Soviet-financed movie on American race relations (the film was never completed; despite their good intentions the Soviets understood almost nothing about American race relations), wrote with great affection of Soviet warmth and hospitality. White tourists generally bemoaned the abominable living conditions and short supply of even basic necessities, but as a black man Hughes felt only the exhilaration of being freed of the burden of race, a joy that more than compensated for material shortages. "There *was* no toilet paper," Hughes admitted. "*And* no Jim Crow."[14] Two members of the Hughes group, actor Wayland Rudd and Homer Smith, an aspiring black journalist whose degree from the University of Minnesota got him no further in the United States than a desk job in the post office, elected to stay in Russia.[15] Others, like writer and educator Louise (Patterson) Thompson ("[we are living] like royalty. . . . Everywhere we go we are treated as honored guests . . . and offered the best") and Matt Crawford, returned home but never forgot the experience. "I realize how much being in Russia has affected me," Crawford wrote to his wife. "Unconsciously I have lost that depressing subconsciousness of being a Negro. The ever-present thought that my dark skin must circumscribe my activities at all times."[16] By 1934 American black weeklies like the *Afro-American,* the *Chicago Defender,* and the NAACP's *Crisis* regularly featured reports on the Soviet Union's exemplary treatment of its minorities, most written by Homer Smith under the name of Chatwood Hall for the Associated Negro Press in Moscow.

The experiences of American blacks living in the Soviet Union hit close to home for the Robesons as Essie's two brothers, John and Frank Goode, were among those who fled America in search of work in Russia. John, who had lived in Russia for some time, worked as a bus driver at the Foreign Workers' Club, while the towering and powerfully built Frank, more recently arrived, planned to tour with circuses and carnivals as part of a wrestling troupe, which billed him as "Black Samson."[17] Essie remained in close contact with her brothers (Frank Goode named his daughter after her), corresponding regularly with them. Their letters home to her and Mrs. Goode included not only long lists of items impossible or difficult to procure in the Soviet Union (underwear, typing paper, a scrubbing brush, Thermos bottles, brooms, mops, carbon paper) but also detailed accounts of how good life was for blacks there. "You will be coming to a country that is absolutely devoid of racial prejudice," John Goode would write to his mother in the summer of 1935. "In fact, they lean the other way and favor the races who have been oppressed. . . . It is a country where there is no unemployment. And the lot of the Worker is getting better every year. . . . It is true that in living conditions they still have some distance to go before they catch up with America, [but] when you take into consideration the millions out of work there, the Worker here is far better off. . . . For Paul, the fact that he will be able to play anything he wants, sing anything he wants, do anything he wants, something which he has been denied all his life, should count for something."[18]

Although Robeson expected to like Russia long before he actually went there (in a 1933 interview with William Lundell, Robeson said he anticipated finding "absolutely no color prejudice" there), none of what he had heard adequately prepared him for *his* experience of the Soviet Union. The journey that would permanently alter the course of his life began on December 20 when Paul and Essie, accompanied by Marie Seton, left London bound for Moscow, with a day's layover in Berlin.[19]

Paul had not been in Germany since 1930 and on his return in 1934 he found in Berlin a city he barely recognized. The blatant homosexuality and prostitution that so repulsed him in 1930 were gone but so also was the vibrant theater life that had drawn gifted and ambitious artists from all over Europe. In its place was militarism and an atmosphere of profound distrust that Robeson sensed almost as soon as he stepped off the train. Adolf Hitler, who in 1930 had been an inconsequential dissident fanatic, had been in power now since March 1933. Storm troopers were everywhere, swarming through the Friedrichstrasse Station and striding confidently down the streets. Robeson was certainly aware that the producer Max Reinhardt, whom Robeson knew from the 1930 production of the *Emperor Jones* at Reinhardt's Deutsches Theatre in Berlin, had been forced into exile when Hitler assumed power, his theaters confiscated by the Nazis. In fact, many of the leaders of Germany's avant-garde theater world were Jewish (Leopold Jessner, the Rotter brothers, Fritz Kortner, Elizabeth Bergner) and among the first forced to depart Hitler's Germany.

Experiencing firsthand the effects of Hitler's rule deeply disturbed Robeson. According to Marie Seton, Essie sensed Paul's anxiety and on their arrival looked up a Jewish man Paul knew and asked him to come to the hotel to visit. Although he was happy to see Paul, their visitor was noticeably nervous and finally asked that they talk outside, walking in the streets. Essie and Marie went with him, but Paul stayed at the hotel, convinced it was no longer safe for a conspicuously black man to walk the streets of Berlin.

The next morning the Robesons and Seton arrived at the train station an hour early. Essie went to collect the luggage while Paul and Marie located the train. An older white woman glared at Robeson and then spoke to the uniformed men standing on the platform. The men turned and looked at Paul, who read "hatred in their eyes" and thought immediately of a lynch mob. Robeson stepped toward them, and inexplicably they backed away. Marie Seton, in her biography of Robeson, makes much of their layover in Germany and its traumatic effects on Paul. Whether or not Seton exaggerated, Robeson's first exposure to Russia's racial liberality would impress him all the more, coming as it did on the heels of what he himself later described as a "day of horror" in Berlin.[20]

"Old Man Winter was running amok and sweeping the town with his most stinging blasts," wrote Chatwood Hall of the day Robeson arrived at Moscow's White Russia Station. Robeson stepped off the train, a virtual unknown in the Soviet Union. But even with temperatures plunging well below thirty-three degrees below zero, a sizable group had gathered to greet the Robeson party, among them Sergei Eisenstein and his Scandinavian cameraman Edward Tisse, British actor and director Herbert Marshall (at the time studying with Eisenstein), actor Wayland Rudd, John and Frank Goode, Celestine Cole and Coralie Arletitz, Soviet playwright Alexander Afinogenov and his mulatto wife, Genia, and officials of Intourist and VOKS (Society for Cultural Relations with Foreign Countries).[21]

Foreign visitors of note were routinely greeted by representatives of various Soviet organizations on their arrival in Moscow. By the mid-1930s the Soviet Union had developed a vast network of organizations and agencies specifically charged with assuring that foreign visitors left with a good impression. The Communist Party served as the hub for these organizations, some of which were organs of the Soviet government, while others were under the direct supervision of the Comintern. VOKS serviced foreign intellectuals and artists; state organizations like Intourist catered to ordinary tourists and minor intellectuals; and the Bureau of Revolutionary Literature dealt with foreign writers already identified as possessing revolutionary sympathies. VOKS had diverse goals and activities, but its major aims were to popularize Soviet culture abroad and mobilize foreign intellectuals in the event of a military attack on the Soviet Union. VOKS saw to it that foreign dignitaries were greeted at the train station (for example, in 1931 George Bernard Shaw had been welcomed by a huge crowd and a brass band), supplied with interpreters, feted with sumptuous banquets and receptions, and given wide coverage in Russian newspapers. If an important foreign visitor needed an audience for any reason, VOKS provided it.[22]

Robeson had no record releases in the Soviet Union (among the items Frank Goode repeatedly requested from Essie and her mother were records) and, in fact, had brought along several recordings as a way of introducing himself. Despite its recent modernization, Russia still experienced chronic shortages of certain foods and most consumer goods, in particular those produced outside of the country. Foreign books and phonograph records were simply unaffordable or unavailable. John Hammond, at the time just beginning what would be a brilliant executive career in music, visited Russia in 1935 representing the American Record Company and was amazed at how technically and musically bereft the Soviets were. "They had no money to pay for American recordings and their own recording equipment was 'rudimentary.'. . . They were just experimenting with electrical recording, a ten-year-old art in the rest of the world." Hammond characterized the heads of the Soviet Gramophone Trust with whom he spoke as musically uninformed, people who "disapproved completely of contemporary Soviet music . . . [and] had no interest in American popular music. I'll bet they had not even heard of Paul Robeson in 1934. That's how backward they were."[23]

If Robeson arrived an unknown he would not remain one for long. In press interviews he turned on the charm, speaking (through an interpreter) of his love for the Soviet Union, in particular its language and art. He explained the special affinity he felt for the Russian language, talked enthusiastically about Soviet theater, expressed his desire some day to play the title role in the great *Boris Godunov,* and said that he looked forward to observing, even on this short visit, the "national minority policy of the Soviet Government in action . . . in Moscow." Finally, Robeson added, although he intended this visit primarily as a holiday, he might be persuaded to sing on Soviet radio. (The single controversy connected with this Russian trip involved Russian radio and occurred before Robeson ever arrived in the Soviet Union. Apparently, the All Soviet Broadcasting Committee had played one of Robeson's spirituals but then quickly apologized publicly for having subjected listeners to the religious "Steal Away." The *London Times* reported that Soviet authorities had assumed the inclusion of this particular piece was part of a plot intended to spread anti-Soviet propaganda. The Soviet press, however, clarified Robeson's intent, explaining that, although the piece was semireligious, it should be interpreted as a protest against the treatment of the black man in America under the capitalist regime.)[24]

The Soviets responded to Robeson kindly and from the moment he stepped off the train treated him regally, but although he appeared confident and at ease, Paul was neither. He was no stranger to affectionate greetings. For years his warmth and charisma had made him welcome in places where days before he had been a stranger. And, while he was intrigued by what appeared to be an almost complete lack of racial consciousness among the Soviets, Robeson's initial response was a cautious skepticism of "the genuineness of the Soviet welcome." As he later told *Daily Worker* interviewer Vern Smith, "even in the capitalist world some of the bitterest aspects of Jim Crowism . . . [were] not applied to him," but most often this was because in his case "a condescending exception had been made." Robeson was not about to be fooled into assuming that the friendliness and goodwill he experienced in Russia necessarily meant anything significant in terms of general racial attitudes.[25]

The Robesons stayed at the historic National Hotel in a suite occupied the year before by William C. Bullitt, the first American ambassador to the USSR, and began what would be a busy and exciting three weeks of sight-seeing, shopping for books and clothing (Paul brought home a sable coat), attending Russian theater, talking with Russian artists and workers, and visiting hospitals, factories, and nurseries. This included, of course, the inevitable round of receptions and introductions to dignitaries and artists: Si-lan Chen Leyda (the daughter of Eugene Chen, the first foreign minister of the Chinese Republic under Sun Yat-sen, and the wife of Eisenstein's American student, Jay Leyda); an Indian student, D. G. Tendulkar (who later completed a monumental biography of Mahatma Gandhi); the Soviet minister of foreign affairs, Maxim Litvinov, and his British wife, Ivy, with whom the Robesons spent Christmas Eve; dramatist Alexander Afinogenov (who had been part of the welcoming committee); writer Muriel Draper; and Soviet representatives of the Commissariat of Public Education.[26] Robeson had not as yet mastered Russian: he could speak adequate textbook, "Pushkin" Russian, but still needed an interpreter to converse. Essie's brother John, at the time living in Moscow, was helpful in this respect, as were others, like Herbert Marshall, Eisenstein, and Marie Seton. But Robeson's lack of confidence showed. Si-lan Chen Leyda on first meeting Robeson found him distant, in conversation given to rambling "off on an endless comparison of Chinese and African sculpture," and concluded he felt "unsure of the unfamiliar surroundings." Later, when Paul felt more relaxed, the intellectual posturing abated and the talk became more genuine.[27]

Similarly, Robeson was guarded as he toured the city, anxious to find out for himself what the Soviet Union was all about. The Soviet people did stare at Robeson—he was so huge and so black—but with a wonderment untarnished by condescension. One day as Paul walked through Pushkin Square with Essie and Marie Seton on his way to the Kamerny Theatre, a little girl playing in the snow with some other children suddenly spotted him—a black giant in his furlined coat and fur hat—and with a scream of delight ran to him, flinging her arms around his knees. The other children followed, and within moments a mountain of squealing bodies had descended on him, tugging at his coat, grabbing his hands, and trying to climb up on him. They had never seen such a big man, so dark against the white snow. Paul greeted them in Russian and they begged him to stay and play with them. But finally, to the children's dismay, their mothers returned and rescued Robeson. The incident made a deep impression on Paul, who said simply but incredulously to Marie Seton, "They have never been told to fear black men."[28]

Observing life in Moscow, Robeson quickly caught the city's upbeat spirit, what one *Moscow Daily News* reporter described as "the feeling that the people . . . are facing the morrow with [a] courage and happiness . . . difficult to find in other countries today."[29] In comparison with 1933, when the Soviet Union experienced devastating losses, 1935 would be a good year for the economy of the country. Stalin regularly awarded medals to workers for setting new production records and after a good crop in 1934 people in Moscow were no longer starving. A traveler returning to the Russian capital after a ten-year absence would hardly have recognized it, so dramatically had it changed. In the twenties, Moscow was in shambles, its dilapidated buildings a mute testament to the ravages of revolution, civil war, and, finally, the chaotic efforts of Stalin to consolidate power and effect his first Five-Year Plan. By 1934 one saw little evidence of the previous decade's bitter struggles. Modern buildings, a new metro system joining the Sakolniki suburban area northeast of Moscow with the Krimskaya Ploshohad near the Park of Culture and Rest in the southwest (completed in record time and with equipment built in Moscow factories), construction of the Moscow–Volga Canal, and varied and lively cultural life confirmed that Moscow was a city on the move. There were hardships, but observers like Robeson who toured only Russia's major cities invariably sensed a determination to grow that was in stark contrast to the economic paralysis gripping Europe and America.[30]

The Robesons arrived at the height of Moscow's theater season and during preparations for an international celebration of the fifteenth anniversary of Soviet cinema, which was to culminate with a weeklong International Film Festival in Moscow at the end of February.[31] To Robeson, the abundance and variety of available drama—special theater for children, collective farmers, Jewish and other minority groups—made British and American dramatic offerings seem anemic by comparison. Moscow's Kamerny Theatre had already produced O'Neill's *Hairy Ape, Desire under the Elms,* and *All God's Chillun;* John Dos Passos's *Fortune Heights;* and Sophie Treadwell's *Machinal;* upcoming productions would feature Elizabethan plays (including two of Shakespeare's), an adaptation of Dickens, and several modern American plays.[32]

Robeson particularly enjoyed (he later described it as "one of his happiest impressions") the Moscow Children's Theatre production of *The Negro Boy and the Monkey,* a popular story about a little African boy who comes to Russia in search of his lost monkey, as it demonstrated Soviet interest not only in blacks like Toussaint L'Ouverture, Ira Aldridge, and their own Alexander Pushkin but in

Africa and African life as well. At the theater children had their own foyer in which to play games and hold festivities, and a team of actors and actresses devoted themselves exclusively to performing children's plays. Fifteen hundred children had gathered for the Sunday afternoon performance that Paul and Essie attended. During intermission Robeson got up to walk around and was quickly surrounded by children who saw the likeness between him and the play's African character, Kojo. A small boy of eight rushed up, hugged Paul's knees, and said with great excitement, "I'm so glad you've come. You will be happy here with us. Don't go." Robeson was so moved by the experience, both the play itself and the young Russian audience, that he was in tears by the final act.[33]

What Robeson saw of the Soviet National Minority Theatre likewise touched him deeply as it evidenced a radically different attitude toward minorities than anything he had previously experienced, even in England. The task of representing the USSR's more than 150 nationalities on stage was itself a monumental undertaking. Nonetheless, by the mid-thirties more than forty languages could be heard on various Soviet stages, and in Moscow, with its permanent National Minority Theatre, performances were given in Tartar, Jewish, Lettish, and gypsy languages.

The existence of a state Jewish Theatre had a special meaning for Robeson who had always felt an almost "mystical" connection with Jews and, according to Herbert Marshall, "was sometimes more Jewish than a Jew. He wore a yarmulke when he studied and asked me to teach him the Kaddish — in fact, he chanted Yiddish rather well."[34] Given Russia's long history of anti-Semitism it was remarkable. The *Moscow Daily News* frequently reminded readers how much life had changed for Russian Jews, who under the czars could not even own land without first serving twenty-five years in the army to earn the privilege. Historically barred from living in large industrialized cities or in villages in central Russia and from studying in centers of higher learning, the vast majority of Russian Jews had settled in small towns, the *mestechka,* where they eked out a living as tradesmen. Set against this backdrop, a state-sponsored Jewish Theatre was indeed, as one writer for the *Moscow Daily News* put it, something "the greatest dreamer . . . could hardly dream."[35]

At the time of Robeson's visit, the Jewish Theatre was deep into preparations for what would be a landmark production of *King Lear,* in Yiddish, with Solomon Mikhoels in the lead, all part of the gigantic fifteenth-anniversary celebration. For Robeson, this unusual production demonstrated a flexibility and broad-mindedness muted in England and totally absent in "democratic" America, which still continued to refuse a black Othello, to say nothing of a black man playing a Shakespearean or other role presumably intended for a white actor. But here, in Russia, what Robeson had only imagined as possible was actually happening. If a short Jewish man like Mikhoels, with "the face of a gnome, . . . slanting eyes, a dome-like forehead, and lips that have a curious sculptural sensuality," could play the great King Lear, and in Yiddish, why not a black man in the role of Hamlet?[36] "The *Lear* production really excited Paul," Herbert Marshall recalled. "In a way it opened up a whole new world of creative possibilities for him. It just amazed him; he had never seen anything like it." Small wonder, then, that by the end of his visit Robeson was talking about returning to Russia to play Othello or perform *Stevedore* with Uzbek and other Central Asian artists playing the parts of Negroes. This brief introduction to Russian arts had set Robeson's imagination soaring. In the Soviet Union, with racial and class distinctions seemingly obliterated, all things were possible.[37]

Speaking with American and British artists living in Russia only confirmed Robeson's impressions. Herbert Marshall, the cockney son of a bricklayer from London's East End, a cheery ginger-haired giant of a man who was almost as tall as Robeson, met Robeson during this visit, Paul's first trip to Russia. The two quickly became friends. Marshall was thoroughly taken with the Soviet Union, not only because it afforded him the opportunity to study with filmmaking giants like Eisenstein, Pudovkin, Dovzhenko, and Vertov, but also because of the artistic freedom and opportunity he experienced there. In England, the minute he opened his mouth his cockney accent branded him lower class, but in Russia the accent betrayed nothing and even if it had, the Soviet Union was free of Britain's stultifying class distinctions.[38] The young Londoner's ambition, daring, and dedication (he had worked his way to Russia and taught himself the language in order to gain admission to the Academy of Cinema and study with Eisenstein) impressed Robeson, and his knowledge of Russian arts and language made him an ideal guide and translator. Robeson, then, saw much of Moscow through the eyes of this wide-eyed artist, a young man who, by his own admission, was "dogmatic, even fanatic" in his loyalty to the Soviet Union.[39]

Marshall, however, did not sugarcoat his account of the hardships under which Russian filmmakers labored: "We had very little film; even professional filmmakers, Pudovkin and others, were all very hard up. . . . We were short of apparatus. Quite often in those early years we never got a piece of film. . . . I remember working . . . on a two shift system . . . working at night in the Moscow film studios [with] the heating . . . off . . . for economy. The actresses . . . were wearing summer dresses, but they kept their Russian fur coats on until the last moment. . . . Then they threw off their furs and had to play in this fantastically cold studio."[40] Even when Marshall was a sixty-year-old man who had long since "given up, abjured, recanted, defected and even cursed to eternity" his youthful devotion to Russia (he had been a member of the Communist Party), remembering that period left him "continuously shocked . . . by my naivete and . . .

enthusiasm." But, he added emphatically, "Those were our youthful idealistic days. We wanted to be there. We felt that a movement that could produce such clearly outstanding works of art must be a movement of worth."[41]

While Marshall educated Robeson on the Russian arts, Paul's old friend William Patterson, who had come to Russia to recover from tuberculosis, introduced him to Soviet politics. Although ill (Essie thought he was "near death's door"), Patterson was animated on the topic of U.S. race relations and life in the Soviet Union. Much had changed for both men since they had parted ways after Paul's law school days in Harlem. California-born and educated, Patterson initially appeared destined for a comfortable life among Harlem's professional class. But he soon wearied of the limited and tedious work available to black lawyers. Listening to radicals like black Communist Party member Richard Moore, who occasionally attended "bull sessions" at the law firm, left Patterson feeling even more restless. In time, he began meeting regularly with Harlem Communists. While Robeson made a name for himself professionally in the arts, Patterson spent three years in the Soviet Union, returned to the United States a champion of the Soviet way of life, and joined the Communist Party (CPUSA). As International Defense League secretary he played a major role in the CPUSA's championing of the Scottsboro boys, and in 1932 ran as the Communist candidate for mayor of New York City.[42] Patterson had a politician's understanding of black organizations and willingly worked through them to advance Party objectives; in short, he never let his political loyalties marginalize him. In the Scottsboro case, Patterson skillfully used the issue to build up Party credibility in Harlem.

"It was wonderful to talk with him [Robeson] again and to contrast our impressions of democracy under socialism and the democracy we had both experienced in the United States," said Patterson. "We discussed Scottsboro a great deal. Paul had followed the case, but not closely, and as we talked he began gradually to understand the enormous differences racially between the U.S. and the Soviet Union." Patterson explained to Paul why he had rejected what he viewed as the NAACP's bourgeois, middle-class mishandling of the case. "Let's face it," he said bluntly, "the CPUSA was the only major organization willing to fight seriously for civil rights."[43] And, in fact, no major party in either Britain or the United States had ever accorded racial matters top priority, while the Communist Party time and again proved itself willing to give the principle of equality more than lip service, to the point where, on more than one occasion, it expelled members found guilty of racial bigotry.[44]

Patterson's observations verified what Robeson had himself surmised. He had heard stories like that recounted by Jamaican-born Robert Robinson contrasting the treatment he received in a Ford automobile plant in America with his experience doing similar work in the Soviet Union. In both countries Robinson's color made him an oddity. In the United States, the only black toolmaker among 699 whites, Robinson found himself ostracized and "surrounded by complete silence," but in the Soviet Union workers welcomed him warmly. "This whole new attitude became especially apparent to me when on the Volga boat going to Stalingrad a peasant Russian girl invited me to dance. This simple act . . . made a deep impression on me. . . . A strange land, this, I thought. A white girl invites a Negro to dance in the presence of other white people and no one is surprised."[45]

Exchanging views with people like Marshall and Patterson was stimulating and intriguing, but by far the high point of Robeson's visit was meeting the brilliant cinematographer Sergei Eisenstein. Physically the two men stood in sharp contrast to each other: Robeson gigantic, dark, and towering; Eisenstein short and stocky, with a great leonine head, a shock of unkempt curly hair, and deep-set, intense eyes. Emotionally and intellectually, however, they had much in common. Born in 1898, the same year as Robeson, Eisenstein was an intellectual, fluent in several languages, a filmmaking genius but with eclectic interests ranging from esoteric language studies to Agatha Christie murder mysteries. Like Robeson, Eisenstein was of a "minority" race (his father, Mikhail, was a Jew), and like his black guest, he had achieved international acclaim at a young age for his work: *Gas Masks* (1924), *Strike* (1924), *Potemkin* (1926), *October*, or *Ten Days that Shook the World* (1927), and *Old and New*, or *General Line* (1929).[46]

Robeson and Eisenstein saw each other almost every day, and on more than one occasion talked far into the night, unimpeded by an interpreter as Eisenstein spoke fluent English. Eisenstein lunched with the Robesons the day of their arrival and, later, went to great lengths "to make his room homey" on the evening Paul and Essie came to supper, "lighting it with candles in antique candle holders and borrowing comfortable chairs and a white linen tablecloth. . . . He, too, was transformed. He wore a plain, dark suit which he had just bought." In their talks the two men covered a wide array of topics: the evolution of languages, preliterate expression, and music as an indicator of comparative cultural development, as well as Eisenstein's proposed film. Eisenstein introduced Paul to the work of philologist and archaeologist Nicholas Y. Marr, in particular his research on the formation and evolution of language and cognitive development, and Robeson, in turn (undoubtedly advised by Marie Seton who knew Eisenstein's reading tastes), recommended to his host Marcel Granet's *Le Pensée chinoise.* One evening, Paul played the African and Siamese records (impossible to get in Russia) he had brought Eisenstein as a gift.[47]

Sometimes their conversations were intense, covering complicated language issues or the difficulties of artistic commitment, other times playful and light-hearted. As to whether the Robeson–Eisenstein conversations were pedantic or an exercise in academic name dropping, Herbert Marshall said emphatically, "Certainly not, particularly on Eisenstein's part. He was a voracious reader, a real scholar. And Paul was a willing learner, curious, always looking for new reading on the nature and background of language." One evening they discussed the aboriginal tongues of Australia and the dialects of Africa and China, competing with each other as they acted out in the small space between the bed and the window of Eisenstein's cramped room what they guessed were the expressive words devised by early man to convey physical movement. On several occasions Eisenstein accompanied Paul to the theater and during the day took time to show him some of his own films and those of other Russian film directors. Concerning his new film project, *Black Majesty*, a portrayal of the life of Toussaint L'Ouverture, Eisenstein said he intended to depict this dramatic figure as a man whose actions reflected a particular stage of cultural revolution, specifically "the developing genius of the Negro people," and had sought out Paul because he felt "Robeson was an artist whose qualities would respond to his own creative methods."[48]

Eisenstein, however, mentioned nothing to Robeson about political considerations that made completing the film and securing Robeson for the lead role particularly pressing. Of late the director had fallen out of favor with Stalin, ostensibly because he overstayed a 1931 trip to Mexico while working on *Qué Viva México,* causing an enraged Stalin to telegraph film backer Upton Sinclair and order the "deserter" Eisenstein to return immediately. After a long delay, Eisenstein went back to Russia in the spring of 1932, but once home he found his artistic freedom dramatically curtailed. He was allowed to teach but nothing more. By the time he and Robeson met in 1934, Eisenstein had gone four years without completing a film. He needed and wanted to work but in order to do so had first to win back Stalin's favor and he hoped that this new project with Robeson would accomplish both ends.[49]

Robeson, unaware of these pressures, observed Eisenstein, his routine of rigorous study, and the intellectual energy he brought to his work. The experience inspired Paul, who had for so long felt trapped by his schedule and frustrated by his inability to pursue in any depth his own academic interests. Robeson discussed his theories on Eastern cultures with the Russian film director who, much to Robeson's delight, appeared to take him seriously. This alone boosted his confidence tremendously. Robeson saw evidence of Eisenstein's dedication and willingness to make due with meager resources in other Russian filmmakers as well. Their spirit appealed to his idealism. Not since his earliest theater days had Robeson been exposed to such intense artistic energy. He was anxious to work with Eisenstein and left Moscow with the understanding that as soon as they had settled on a date they would begin filming *Black Majesty* and possibly a Russian version of the American play *Stevedore*.[50]

But such was not to be the case. Eisenstein never did do a film with Robeson, according to Herbert Marshall because "they wouldn't let him." In fact, from 1929 until 1937, when *Alexander Nevsky* was completed, Eisenstein's films were not even shown in the Soviet Union. So complete was Eisenstein's fall from grace that he later even denounced himself. Aside from teaching, Eisenstein remained without a position.[51]

In the meantime, Paul and Essie, in a festive mood, ushered in the New Year with an exhausting round of parties. (Indicative perhaps of Robeson's buoyed spirits, the same Robeson who in England complained constantly about the damp and raw weather, worrying he would catch cold and damage his voice, never once objected to the Soviet Union's bitter, thirty-degrees-below-zero cold.) The evening began with a private showing of Pudovkin's *End of St. Petersburg* and *Storm over Asia,* followed by a midnight celebration with Eisenstein at Dom Kino (GIK), the House of Cinema Workers, and topped off by a surprise visit in the earliest hours of the New Year to the Moscow Foreign Workers' Club, where Essie's brother John worked.[52] The Robesons' entrance brought the jazz band and dancing to a sudden halt, as throngs of young Americans surrounded them. Paul promised a later, more lengthy visit and as proof signed up to play catcher for the club's baseball team on his return. It was a warm and raucous celebration during which the Robesons joined in many a toast to "the New Year, the third of our Second Five-Year Plan," and Paul was inducted as the Foreign Workers' Club first new member for 1935.[53]

If Robeson needed further confirmation of the Soviet Union's success in creating a new and equal society he got it in Leningrad, the Robesons' final stop before leaving Russia. Paul saw no theater in Leningrad but instead toured the Koganovitch ball-bearing plant where he witnessed not only Americans working alongside Russians but blacks and whites and women and men working together as well. Again, Robeson was moved and sang to the thundering applause of the plant's Russian and foreign workers.[54]

Russia proved the perfect tonic for Robeson's sagging spirits, and after a hurried tour of the Scandinavian countries he returned to England in mid-January, revived and ready to begin his seventeen-city February–April tour of the British provinces. There had been little fanfare in the Soviet Union over Robeson, the performer, as he gave no public concerts (although he did sing privately before small groups), and few Soviets had heard his recordings. Thus Robeson felt accepted in Russia for who he was and nothing more. It was an exhilarating experience. "I was not prepared for the endless friendliness, which surrounded me from the moment I crossed the border," Robeson said. "I was rested and buoyed up by the lovely, honest, wondering looks which did not see a 'negro.' When these people looked at me, they were just happy and interested. There were no 'double looks,' no venom, no superiority. . . . this joy and happiness, this utter absence of embarrassment over a 'race question' is all the more keenly felt by me because of the day I spent in Berlin on the way over here. . . . In Soviet Russia, I breathe fully for the first time in my life."[55]

Once home Paul dove into his work, performing and singing at a breakneck pace. As Joe Andrews and others confirmed, "He was like a new man, at his best, optimistic, full of ideas and energy." Russia had changed him, enlarging his vision of the world and what was possible for him as a creative artist.

14

Film & Its Limits

1935-1936

Once Robeson returned home, the wave of rumors that began with his December announcement picked up pace again. Both the British and South African press, egged on largely by a story circulated by W. G. Ballinger, a British trade union activist in South Africa, reported that Robeson had decided to move to Africa, "share the life of the natives," and work for the rights of "his people" there. Ballinger, who originally came to South Africa in 1928 to advise Clements Kadalie, the charismatic leader of the International and Commercial Workers' Union (ICU), stayed following the union's disintegration to practice his own brand of advocacy journalism. In Robeson's case, Ballinger fed the gossip mill by inferring political meanings in any mention Paul made of Africa. "He [Robeson] has become much more politically minded lately," wrote Ballinger in the South African *Argus,* and "is coming to South Africa, not only to study its music, but to see the conditions of the black man and whether he can do anything to help them [*sic*]."[1]

Robeson's concert agent, Harold Holt, was not pleased with this kind of publicity, and in January both he and Paul vigorously denied that Robeson had any political interest in either South Africa or, for that matter, Russia. It was not unusual for Paul in his enthusiasm with a new discovery or insight to speak before he had really thought things out. In this instance, Holt covered for him, and Robeson claimed he had been misquoted, explaining that when he did visit Africa his sole purpose would be "to find some pure African music and songs. . . . It is not true that I am going to bury myself in Africa and cut myself off. What good would that do to the negro?" Robeson also denied having ever referred to Russia as his "spiritual home" or that he had he any intention of resettling there. Once the rumors were laid to rest, Robeson refused to engage in further discussion of his personal plans, mentioning Africa and Russia only in the context of his professional work and his desire "to discover some common element in folk music which extends all the way from the Hebrides to the Congo."[2]

Although Robeson was not yet willing to jeopardize himself professionally by publicly giving an all-or-nothing embrace to either Africa or the Soviet Union, his interest in the Soviet Union was definitely growing. His brief visit there had afforded him a glimpse of what his personal and professional life might be like with the burden of race eliminated — to Robeson it was a vision well worth pursuing. Ironically, it was just as Robeson's interest in the Soviet Union was beginning to blossom that disillusioned anti-imperialists one by one permanently parted ways with Moscow. The experience of George Padmore is illustrative in this respect. Padmore (Malcolm Ivan Meredith Nurse), born in Arouca, Trinidad, was boyhood friends with C. L. R. James. He studied sociology and political science in the United States, joined the Communist Party in 1927, and in 1928 began to write for the *Daily Worker* in New York. Padmore's interest in the Party stemmed largely from its liberal racial attitudes and, beginning in 1927, its rigorous defense of the anti-imperialist cause. In 1929 Padmore was invited to Moscow where he was treated as a minor dignitary, made a member of the local soviet, appointed head of the Negro Bureau of the Red International of Labour Unions (Profintern), and asked to help organize the first International Conference of Negro Workers, held in 1930. The Party's support of the colonials' cause, initially undertaken as part of an overall effort to garner allies against the established order was short lived and ended in 1934 when Stalin instituted the policy of collective security against fascism. It was a shift in direction that required close collaboration between the Soviet Union and Western powers and, as a result, the Soviet Union discreetly dropped its support of revolutionary nationalists in Africa and Asia. Padmore and other Marxist anti-imperialists were enraged. "He arrived at my flat early one morning, completely discouraged," C. L. R. James said, recalling Padmore's reaction to these events. "Germany and Japan have no colonies in Africa," Padmore said sadly. "How can I attack them? Britain and France are the ones with colonies in Africa." The Soviet Union's tacit alliance with the West ended Padmore's Party involvement.[3]

Other anti-imperialists soon followed suit, especially in the aftermath of Mussolini's invasion of Ethiopia. Initially, the Soviet Union came off well, publicly supporting the Ethiopian cause as part of its overall antifascist effort. But in April 1935 Maxim Litvinov, the Soviet delegate to the League of Nations, refused to condemn Mussolini's aggression, and in the fall of the same year the news leaked that the Soviets had been selling coal, tar, wheat, and oil to Italy at below market prices. Among colonials, Russia's position as archdefender of

freedom fell precipitously. On both sides of the Atlantic anti-imperialists condemned Russia's shameless opportunism, and many, unable to explain why
Russia had "sold Ethiopia out," abandoned their Party allegiance altogether.

Robeson was preparing for his visit to the Soviet Union when Mussolini,
using as a pretext a border incident between Ethiopia and Italian Somaliland,
began his campaign to turn Ethiopia into an Italian colony. This wanton annexa-
tion of the symbol of Africa's past greatness and one of the few independent
states remaining in a European-dominated Africa shocked and galvanized racially conscious blacks around the world.[4] At the time London was home to a
formidable anticolonial lobby; besides Padmore and James, some of the other
most important black anti-imperialist activists of the twentieth century used
London as their base — among them future president of Kenya, Jomo Kenyatta,
and the West African trade union organizer I. T. A. Wallace-Johnson. Within this
population, reaction to the invasion was swift and unambiguous. Organizations
like Harold Moody's League for Coloured Peoples (LCP), founded in 1931,
and the West African Students' Union (WASU), begun in 1925 by Lapido
Solanke, a Yoruba law student outraged with the degrading presentation of
Africans at the 1924 British Empire Exhibitions staged at Wembley, had long
provided venues for both students and the long-oppressed population of black
seamen and dockworkers in the Cardiff area to meet and talk. Ethiopia rapidly
politicized both groups, driving the traditionally conservative LCP to fight on
behalf of Cardiff's black seamen and provide in its journal, *The Keys,* a forum for
radicals like C. L. R. James. WASU, which published its own journal (*Journal of
the West African Students' Union in Britain*) from 1929 to 1935, opened a hostel
at 63 Camden Road in the borough of St. Pancras, London, in 1933. It quickly
became a popular meeting place for anticolonial activists.[5]

Robeson had contact with the LCP (*Keys* published news of Robeson's activities and on several occasions Robeson spoke before the organization) and
with WASU to which he offered financial support in 1935 by enrolling as an
organization sponsor. He knew Kenyatta and was friends with C. L. R. James as
well. Despite these ties, however, he did not become deeply involved in the
anticolonial movement in Britain, even at the time of the Ethiopian crisis. In
fact, it was not until his association with Max Yergan, the quixotic former
YMCA official and founder in 1937 of the Council on African Affairs, that
Robeson truly became engaged in African politics. In 1935 Robeson's relationship with people active in the movement centered primarily around his own
interest in African cultures and languages — and not on African political issues.[6]

Early in 1935 Robeson began his two-month Celebrity Series tour of the
British provinces, Ireland, Scotland, and Wales. Essie accompanied Paul for part

of the tour, primarily because she had research to do in Manchester and in Ireland and Scotland.[7] In interviews with the press, Robeson quickly laid to rest any latent rumors concerning his future plans. His repertoire, which included longtime audience favorites like "Go Down, Moses," "Deep River," "Water Boy," "Witness," "Steal Away," and "Ol' Man River," as well as plantation songs like "Shortnin' Bread," "Poor Old Joe," "My Old Kentucky Home"; Russian pieces like "Labourer's Plaint" (sung in Russian) and "Ivan O Ivan"; the Finnish "The Wanderer"; the English ballad "Oh No, John"; and recitals of Blake's "The Little Black Boy" further reassured audiences that nothing had changed. Record-breaking crowds welcomed him throughout the tour. In Leicester he drew the "largest audience of the season," and in Neath a crowd, "almost frightening in its size," greeted him at the train station. Headlines for the Belfast concert read "All Records Gone . . . Ulster Hall Booked Out . . . Thousands Disappointed," and one prominent citizen remarked that "in all his thirty years experience he had never remembered such pressing demand for seats at any celebrity or other concert." Reviewers echoed local ebullience, heaping praise on this "modest celebrity," this "famous . . . singer of the people's music . . . recognized as a first-rate scholar," a man of "intense culture" who with his "thousands of gram-ophone records" "revels in languages" and (as Robeson frequently told inter-viewers) "has studied almost every European language."[8]

Paul felt at home with his audiences, and in Ireland and Wales, especially, he met people who knew hardship and with whom he felt a special tie. Wherever he went, Robeson worked his audiences with the finesse of a seasoned politician. "Never in my life have I been so moved by a reception," Robeson said in Neath. And in Belfast: "I appreciate that Irish audiences have a certain warmth . . . and quite naturally I have always been attracted to such audiences." At the same time he was utterly sincere when he told local concertgoers: "I have been made to feel that your people understand me, and the warmth of the welcome has gone to my heart." With reporters Robeson reiterated his interest in Scottish, Welsh, and Irish folk music and his continuing language studies — Russian, Siberian, Chi-nese, and African dialects. His audiences, it seemed, could not get enough of him, no matter what he sang.[9]

Robeson's first British film, *Sanders of the River,* was scheduled to open on March 29, and for weeks preceding that date publicity notices touted the film's exoticism and adventure, rare footage of African tribal dances and rituals, and recordings of native music never before heard in the West — "The Mad Charge of War Canoes . . . The Capture of Beautiful Slave Girls! . . . The Congo Death Dance! . . . The Black Magic of Witch Doctors!" Despite the lurid promotion effort, the film's opening drew a far from common crowd, "the better sort" of

London picturegoers.[10] Record sums were spent in advance ticket sales, the proceeds of which were to be donated to the Newspaper Aid Fund, a cause for which the recently deceased Edgar Wallace had had great sympathy. *Harper's Bazaar* announced that "all the world is going" to the *Sanders* opening, and, indeed, police had difficulty containing the huge crowd gathered outside the Leicester Square Theatre to watch the spectacle of arriving stars.[11] Under the glare of purple and green searchlights shining from across the street and into the theater's foyer, the awaited procession of motorcars began, pausing just long enough to deposit their bejeweled and lavishly gowned occupants at the theater door. Standing with arms linked to prevent the crowd from mobbing the arriving notables, policemen were unable to withstand the surge that attended the arrival of the Robesons. Fans broke through the cordon shouting "Good old Paul" and within seconds had surrounded the Robeson car. The police regrouped, regained control of the crowd, and Essie and Paul hurriedly edged their way into the theater.[12]

The Robesons sat in the front row and watched the film, "apparently quite content" with what they saw.[13] Deafening applause shook the theater at the film's conclusion. Leslie Banks (who played the British commissioner, Sanders) took the stage briefly, and then a piano was hastily pushed onto the stage as the audience, by this time clamoring for Robeson, shouted "Song! Song!" Robeson declined, explaining he was too nervous to sing, but the pleas continued for "Ol' Man River" and the new film's "Canoe Song." Finally, Paul came on the stage, according to the *Daily Mirror* "trembling . . . literally shaking with . . . fright." Recovering his poise, Robeson acknowledged writer Edgar Wallace's kindness toward him and returned to his seat. For one of the few times in his career Robeson refused to sing.[14]

Visually *Sanders* was breathtaking, filled with "attractive panoramas of herds of game galloping over the grass-lands," and virtually all British reviewers hailed it a "great cinema spectacle." With so little known in the Western world about the "Dark Continent," the African footage alone made this film worth seeing. "What we see is much more impressive than what we hear," wrote the reviewer for *Reynold's Newspaper.* "But for the strains of Paul Robeson's rich bass the film would have been almost as good in silent form."[15] *Sanders* represented a departure, "a dramatic film with a 'documentary' authority — an illuminating study of a primitive civilization with full-blooded adventure to provide the maximum emotional thrill." "Intensely spectacular," said the *Irish Independent* in a glowing review; "a film of exceptional interest . . . [with] novelty and nobility of theme," said *Film Weekly.* "Sanders and his story are occasionally in danger of being ousted by something closely akin to a travelogue," but it is "a grand travelogue . . . full of movement and primitive passion." Even James Agate, whose acid commentary ranked the film second-rate, acknowledged "the breathless interest it aroused" in a house "packed from floor to ceiling by an audience of every height of brow."[16]

If the film was a spectacle, Robeson was one of its major tableaux. Leslie Banks's rave notices almost all commented on Robeson's "outstanding," "authoritative," "impressive" acting performance; his "magnificent physique and terrific voice," his Adonis-like presence, his "splendour of stature and bearing which transforms the spirit of the jungle into majesty."[17] Some reviewers complained about lags in the action; others faulted the film for departing from the original Wallace story, creating instead "a sort of western plot, complete with last-minute rescue and other well-known cow-boy effects." Nina Mae McKinney's portrayal of Bosambo's wife, Lilongo ("one feels that she probably must have driven straight to Nigeria from Fifth Avenue"), likewise drew criticism. She brought the "appearance and atmosphere of Harlem cabaret into genuine African surroundings," so that "at any minute one expected her to break into some sophisticated dance band number." And, more than one critic poked fun at Paul's songs, "a weird blend of adapted Congo melodies with English lyrics."[18]

Exactly when Robeson realized *Sanders* had failed to present the picture of Africa he had envisioned is debatable. Biographer Marie Seton, elaborating on a story published in the *Daily Mirror,* claimed it was at the film's premiere. (The *Mirror* reported that while the film was running "Mrs. Robeson noticed [Paul] slip out, and . . . went to look for him, only to find that he had left the theatre. She got into a cab and found him at home very perturbed at the prospect of his personal appearance at the conclusion of the film. . . . Eventually Mrs. Robeson got him back to the theatre.") According to Seton's account, accepted as gospel thereafter, Robeson left the theater consumed with anger because he had been tricked; last minute changes and edits had ruined *Sanders.* "Robeson stared at the spectacle on the screen" and to his horror found "it was entirely different from what he had hoped." At the end, when he was asked to come to the stage and make a speech, "He rose—a tower of ice-bound fury—and walked out of the theatre in protest."[19]

But recollections of others do not bear out this story. Among the press, only the *Daily Mirror* mentioned Robeson's disappearance, and no newspapers, including the *Daily Mirror,* reported any noticeable displeasure on Robeson's part. Several commented on his uncharacteristic refusal to sing, but if Robeson was angry no one in attendance noted it. Robeson told the *Daily Express* that he had excused himself, explaining that after seeing and hearing him "as a lion on the screen" it would hardly be fair to fans "to hear him as a mouse down there on stage."[20] Had Robeson truly been "a tower of ice-bound fury," as Seton claims, others, especially newspaper reporters present in large numbers for the premiere, would have commented on it.

Friends of Robeson's all remembered his extreme apprehension before a performance of any kind, but particularly at movie openings, where the best he could do was to sit helplessly, hope that things went well, and then stay up all night waiting for the critics' verdicts in the morning papers. Furthermore, Joe Andrews, when asked about Robeson's storming out of the *Sanders* premiere, was taken aback and genuinely puzzled by the question, having never seen or heard reference to the Seton account. "That does not sound like Paul," Andrews replied thoughtfully. "He was too much of a gentleman to have done such a thing. And, surely, I would have known about such a big thing as his storming out of the theater. The subject was never raised, and Paul at the time did not seem to me to be unhappy about the film."[21]

By virtually all accounts (excepting Seton's) Robeson expressed no dissatisfaction with the film until faced with a storm of protest from a small but vocal group of West Indians, Africans, native members of the India League, and white anti-imperialists who condemned the film for its pro-Empire bias and Robeson for agreeing to appear in it. Embarrassed at having his own political naïveté so publicly exposed, and by a group of people whose opinion he valued, Robeson defended himself as best he could, insisting that objectionable material had been added to the movie without his knowledge or permission. Although Robeson's explanation did not ring true, no one was more convinced than Paul himself that he had been tricked. Something had gone wrong, and he could find no other way to account for what had happened. Whether Robeson had begun to sense the extent to which he had internalized white Western culture and values is unclear. The experience definitely unsettled him and, for the time being, he rationalized his part in it.[22]

The film, according to Trotskyist writer and historian C. L. R. James "caused one hell of a row" among politically active West Indians and Africans. Yusuf Dadoo, an Indian anti-imperialist then studying medicine at the University of Edinburgh (later he worked as an anticolonialist in South Africa), recalled how profoundly disappointed he and African students were with the film and with Robeson. Set against the backdrop of Europe's passivity in the face of Mussolini's invasion of Ethiopia, the intensity of their reaction is not surprising. "We had so admired him. After the film opened I went with some of my friends from South and East Africa and the West Indies to a Robeson concert in Edinburgh. When the performance was over we met him at the stage door and told him how we felt. Robeson was friendly, listened to what we had to say and even agreed with us. He, too, had been disappointed with the film; it had turned out differently from what he had expected and he said he was ashamed of his part in it." The controversy did not die out quickly. More than a year and a half later, Marcus Garvey's publication, *The Black Man,* published a scathing indictment of Robeson and charged that the only Africans who supported him in this matter "were young men who have not yet started to think in the highest sense of racial integrity and pride. . . . Paul Robeson ought to realise that the growing prejudice against Negroes in England, or Great Britain for that matter, is due largely to the peculiar impression moving picture fans obtain from seeing such pictures."[23]

Although portions of the film undoubtedly were cut during the final edits, even a cursory viewing of *Sanders of the River* reveals that no additions or last-minute changes could account for the film's imperialistic bias: it is blatant and pervasive. "When Paul said he did not know that scenes had been added to the movie, initially the West Indians and Africans did not believe him," James remembered. "They asked, 'How could Robeson be the star of the movie and not know what was in it?' But even those most opposed to the film did not come down too hard on Paul because he had done so much that was positive before *Sanders.* I myself think the explanation was more simple. As an American black, Paul did not understand the colonial situation. Even though it had similarities with his own experiences in America, he just didn't get it."[24]

Robeson was not the only one with a blind spot in this area. One could hardly have expected Essie to have publicly criticized Paul for performing in the film, and when questioned about it she either praised it and London Film Productions as "the greatest of its kind in the world" or reiterated Paul's contention that editorial changes had ruined an otherwise good film. The black American press, whether owing to insensitivity, ignorance, or simple relief at seeing a black other than Stepin Fetchit in a leading role, initially ignored the film's imperialistic bias. When the movie first opened in August at Loew's Victorian and the 116th Street Theaters, the *Amsterdam News* described it as a "great drama," a "brilliant story, . . . full of action, suspense and tremendous scenes." Some white reviewers, like the *New York Herald Tribune*'s Howard Barnes noted an "ungainly synthesis of melodrama, operetta, travelogue and straight propaganda" and took issue with the blatantly patriotic message and the assumption "that the white man's rule makes a virtual paradise of the African hinterland." In America, censure of the film was by and large limited to the Communist *New Masses,* which noted that even in England the best Robeson could do was to play a "stoolpigeon to Sandy, a black man who betrays his own people to the English."[25]

In fact, the imperialist bias of the film is set quite explicitly in its prologue: "Sailors, soldiers, and merchant adventurers were the pioneers who laid the foundations for the British Empire. Today their work is carried on by civil servants — the Keepers of the King's peace." In short, civilization in the person of the quiet, pipe-smoking, good-humored, and authoritative Sanders will over-come savagery—the continent itself and its unruly natives, in particular the war-bent African chieftain Mofolaba.

Ironically, for all Robeson's talk about giving a true picture of Africa, the character he portrays is more British than he is African. Bosambo is the "good African," identified not with Africa, which is presented in the film as the primitive and violent "other," but with Western "civility" and peace. The inside of Bosambo's tent evokes the domestic arrangements of the British middle class; his wife, Lolingo, is never shown bare-breasted as are native African women in the film; and his rousing songs sound more like British and American marching songs than African chants. Bosambo is the exception—docile and childlike, trained by whites, loyal to whites, and essential to the colonial enterprise.

In fairness to Robeson, the magnificent footage and the Korda brothers' insistence on authenticity in the form of genuine artifacts (conical huts, kraals, calabashes, shields) and actual recordings and footage of real African dances and rituals may well have convinced him that the film would present a similarly authentic portrait of Africa. "Authenticity" was one of the film's major selling points, but these artifacts communicate little real information about Africa, sandwiched as they are between a paradigm that is Western in outlook and sympathy. The African dances and rituals, for example, have complex meanings, but in the film they are neither explained nor examined. Thus they remain remote, mysterious, exotic, and primitive in the unflattering sense and serve primarily to support the film's selectively constructed and positive view of British colonial administration.

That the film was produced in England, where Robeson had always felt relatively safe, had further reassured him. Historically British filmmakers had shown themselves capable of moving beyond Hollywood's glib stereotypes and, on occasion, of even making fun of their own cherished British ideals (for example, the 1938 Marcel Varnel–directed *Old Bones of the River,* a comedy and, as the title suggests, an obvious satire of *Sanders of the River* starring Will Hay and Graham Moffat, with Robert Adams looking remarkably like Robeson in the role of Bosambo).

And despite its many failings, *Sanders* did mark a milestone in black portraiture on film. It featured a black man—not a comic Charles Laughton in black face as originally planned—in the role of Bosambo. As late as World War II whites in blackface still played the roles of African blacks with real blacks used primarily as "scenery props." Ustane in the 1925 thriller *She* was played by the white Mary Odette; the pygmies in the 1932 *Tarzan the Ape Man* were all played by whites in blackface; and Tondelayo in *White Cargo* (1942) was played by the white Hedy Lamar. The wonderful scene in *Sanders* when Nina Mae McKinney sings the lullaby "Little Black Dove" to her child was another first. Showing a black mother's feelings of love and tenderness for her child and suggesting by extension an emotional life for her husband as well was an image hitherto denied blacks on the screen. Finally, Bosambo, by virtue largely of Robeson's own persona, has moments—moments that James Baldwin describes as "created, miraculously, beyond the confines of the script: hints of reality, smuggled like contraband into a maudlin tale, and with enough force, if unleashed, to shatter the tale to fragments"—that show strength, sophistication, and intelligence. Bosambo clowns, but he is not a fool. He understands British colonialism, but rather than fight it he chooses to adapt himself to it, manipulate it, and make it work to his advantage.[26]

Criticism of the film from Africans and West Indians bothered Robeson, especially with the white press giving his portrayal of "Bosambo's dog-like devotion to Sanders and trust in the magic of the King's law" glowing reviews. For the rest of his life Robeson would regret having played the role. Interviewed by Rick Roberts of the *Pittsburgh Courier* years later, Robeson claimed he had given every dollar he earned from the film to charity. "I hate the picture. I have tried to buy it but because it is a tremendous money-maker, have not been able to do so. . . . I committed a faux pas which, when viewed in retrospect, convinced me I had failed to weigh the problems of 150,000,000 native Africans."[27]

But Robeson had little patience when the negative comment came from black Americans. "An actor cannot eat his ideals," he said in October 1935. Questioned on the film by a reporter from the *Amsterdam News,* Robeson had a similar response: "To expect the Negro artist to reject every role with which he is not in ideological agreement is to expect the Negro artist under our present scheme of things to give up his work entirely—unless, of course, he is to confine himself solely to the Left theater. Under such an arrangement, I might as well give up my singing, my concert work, everything." In addition, Robeson reminded the black press that *Sanders* would give him and other black actors future opportunities that might not have been possible had he refused to do the film. He was not just speculating. About *Sanders,* one reporter wrote, "The picture was such a great success financially that Korda has decided to film the life of King Christophe with Mr. Robeson in the title role. After this picture is completed, he [Robeson] said, he feels sure he can persuade Korda to present the life of Manelik II on the screen."[28]

Regardless of what the critics said, the public—the movie-going public, youngsters, adventure lovers, and Robeson fans—loved the film and Robeson's role in it.[29] *Sanders of the River* made Robeson a film star, his name given top billing on theater marquees throughout the country, a contender in what by the mid-1930s was indisputably the most popular form of entertainment in Britain. Although not as successful as "Ol' Man River," Robeson's "Canoe Song" proved extremely popular, and at concerts and smaller gatherings he was almost always asked to sing it. (Forty years later Joe Andrews still found it difficult to contain his enthusiasm about the song. During the interview for this book, introductions were barely complete when Andrews insisted on playing an old 78 recording of the song on Paul's own gramophone, which Andrews still had.)[30]

Outside England and throughout the Empire the film was also popular. Nigerians set up a monument for Sanders (in real life Sir Robert L. Bowen, the first British resident of Nigeria) and erected it on the highest hill in that section of Africa. Twenty-two years later, *Sanders* was still being shown in Nigeria. In Lagos it played at three "cinemas in a single week and audiences, who never tired of Paul Robeson's voice, more often than not overlooked any 'offensive' parts in the interests of entertainment." When the film was shown at Darwin, North Australia, and Bosambo chanted his war song, "the aborigines in the audience joined in, stamping their feet and clapping their hands until they turned shy at the laughter of the white members of the audience."[31]

In less than a year *Sanders* had returned £180,000 for the £100,000 put out in production costs. The film won London's Institute of Amateur Cinematographers' annual gold medal as well an award for music at the Vienna Film Exhibition and became the first of what the historian Jeffrey Richards called the Empire film genre: "great, action-packed adventure yarns, infinitely cinematic and especially suited — thanks to their reliance on stock characters and stock situations — to international distribution."[32] Empire films were the British version of the American western and the Japanese samurai films — celebrations of patriotism and myths of national identity that took the historical realities of British expansionism, colonization, and commerce and transformed them into the drama of high-minded heroes acting in the name of royal prerogatives to defend culture against anarchy: in short, the white man's burden.[33]

With his tour concluded, Robeson began work on two plays, both small theater productions. *Basalik,* a play written for Robeson by a woman using the pen name of Peter Garland, tells the story of an African chief trying to save his people from the corrupting influence of the West. Sponsored by the Theatre Arts Club, a private theater club of about 3,000 members, the play appeared promising, offering not only a heroic role for Robeson but a cast that required a dozen "real Africans" performing native dances. Basalik (Robeson) suspects the inept and alcoholic British governor of corrupt dealings with Hiram Parkes (Wyndham Goldie), an unprincipled American gold prospector. Posing as a servant in the governor's mansion, Basalik succeeds in confirming his suspicions. To prevent the governor from cheating the natives, Basalik abducts the governor's wife

(Coral Brown) and holds her hostage. The wife, meanwhile, falls madly in love with Basalik who, despite her advances, succeeds in retaining his (and her) honor, returning her to her husband as soon as the governor formally agrees not to cheat the natives of their land. Everyone is better for the experience; in short, the ending is happy and innocent. Robeson's performance won plaudits, but reviewers pummeled the play as "amateurish," "dull," and "singularly naive."[34] Margaret Webster in the role of the "dithering, gossipy wife" of a soldier at Government House (Webster later directed Robeson in the American production of *Othello*) by most accounts ran away with the play. Audiences and critics alike were disappointed with Robeson's meager role, which called for little dialogue ("monosyllables . . . in the first two acts and only a few commonplace declarations in the third") and no singing.[35]

At least with *Stevedore,* scheduled to open in May at the Embassy Theatre, Robeson would work with a first-rate script, one that had scored a spectacular hit in New York the year before with a black cast that included Rex Ingram, Canada Lee, and Leigh Whipper. American labor unrest was at its height in 1934, and U.S. audiences devoured the proletarian Union Theater's vivid dramatization of the battle of black dockworkers in New Orleans to unionize and fight racial oppression. The play so moved American theatergoers that on more than one occasion individual patrons, for the moment forgetting they were watching a play, leaped from their seats ready to defend the embattled Negroes. At one performance Bill ("Bojangles") Robinson was among those who rushed onto the stage to join in the melee.[36]

Agit-prop theater flourished in Depression-ravaged America, reaching its apex in 1935 with the Group Theatre's monumental production of Clifford Odets's *Waiting for Lefty,* and was beginning to make similar inroads in England because of the efforts of politically minded professionals like Van Gyseghem to acclimate British audiences to it. Van Gyseghem and Embassy Theatre's manager Roland Adam, the business side of the Adam–Van Gyseghem team, hoped that with Robeson in the lead they might attract new audiences, willing for Robeson's sake to give *Stevedore* a fair hearing.[37]

Robeson was enthusiastic about *Stevedore,* but for reasons that had little to do with politics. The play offered him a wonderful role — an intelligent, courageous black man who unites with whites and other blacks to battle a common enemy. Additionally, it would provide jobs for African and West Indian extras as well as for friends like John Payne, whose choir was hired for the production. "Paul was hardly a political radical then," Van Gyseghem said with an amused smile. "Oh yes, he wanted badly to work with Eisenstein and was very interested in the Soviet Union, but his focus was still almost exclusively on his art and improving himself professionally. As for seeing a connection between art and politics, well, that would come later. He liked talking about politics, but he really did not see any link between what he did — his life — and politics."[38]

Because black actors who could speak English well enough to take direction and be understood on stage were so scarce, American blacks, Africans, and West Indians with almost no stage experience (Larry Brown among them) were used to fill most minor roles. Orlando Martins, recruited for the production, turned out to be a "fair actor," but Brown, almost universally acknowledged as "a really sweet man," proved only "so-so." Adam recalled: "I had thought, quite naively, that they [the Africans] would be troublesome and quarrelsome, so in an attempt to curb any violence which might occur I hired Wilfred Adams, an African law student, a big tough man who earned money on the side by wrestling. I thought he would keep order. But there was no trouble — quite the opposite — all went, as far as order was concerned, very well."[39]

Stevedore opened on May 6, 1935, at the Embassy Theatre to a crowded house.[40] Robeson played Lonnie Thompson, the play's hero and "bad Nigger" who tries to unionize his fellow black stevedores. Thompson's organizing efforts elicit hostility not only from the white bosses but equally so from suspicious and frightened black workers. Angry whites have Thompson arrested on a phony charge of raping a white woman. He escapes the lynch mob, hiding for a day in the mud under the docks where he is finally found by friends, among them, the white union organizer. When mobs of white toughs gather to "mop up all dem wharf niggers," the frightened Negroes are tempted to flee.[41]

Physically Robeson dominated the play, towering "like the noblest tree of ebony" and making his white opposition seem "puny" by comparison. When he spoke, his resonant bass enveloped the theater. Who would not be moved by that voice urging you to stay and fight? "You got black skin. You can't run away from dat . . . you can't run away from yo'self, black man. . . . Every time de white boss crack de whip you turn and run. . . . When you gwine say: 'you can't do dat. I'm a man. I got de rights of a man. I'm gwine fight like a man.'"[42] The blacks erect a barricade and arm themselves with rusty rabbit guns, bricks, lumps of coal, and baseball bats. When the mob attacks, Lonnie is killed, but his death only strengthens the resolve of the remaining black stevedores. Morris, the white union boss, returns backed up by a group of white union members and, finally, the mob retreats.

Although the Tory press attributed a "Sinister Significance" to the date on which the play opened — May 6, the day of the Silver Jubilee celebrating the twenty-fifth anniversary of George V's ascension to the throne — and charged that the production, financed by "Moscow gold," was "obviously . . . a signal for a wicked Socialist and trade unionist revolution," conservatives had little to worry about as London audiences were hardly moved, let alone outraged, by the play's alleged political intent.[43] While New York producers had wisely compensated for the delays caused by repeated set changes by constructing two revolving stages that kept the action going at all times, Van Gyseghem and Adam took no such precautions. As a result, the action lagged, interruptions were many and long, and if patrons had trouble staying in their seats it was from boredom rather than any empathic outpouring.

Robeson's performance was hailed as "magnificent," but critics almost universally panned the play.[44] James Agate's somewhat racist remarks are a good reflection of upper-class London's ho-hum attitude concerning the peculiarly American issues raised in the play. "Let me say at once that I have never been further south than the taffrail of a liner lying off Tangier. . . . Nor at home am I privileged to know any negroes. . . . What, however, worries me is why the sentimental English should be so insistent about claiming the Negro as a brother. We do not go about asserting this particular relationship with Arabs, Aztecs, Red Indians, Maoris, Lascars, Goanese, Cochin, Chinese." Almost all reviewers disliked the play's heavy-handed propaganda; several took issue with its racial and labor bias; and even reviewers sympathetic to the politics found this production remote. Applause for the message of the play appeared in publications like the *Left Review,* the *London Daily Mirror,* and the *Jewish Chronicle,* but such reviews were exceptions rather than the rule.[45]

Perhaps a play with themes so tied to American concerns was doomed to fail in England. If not, Van Gyseghem and Adam's alterations in the script (undertaken, one assumes, to prevent such a failure) sealed its fate. What had been a militant and rousing production in America became in London what one critic called "Uncle Paul's Cabin"—a lethargic, loosely constructed piece of race propaganda, redeemed by Robeson's singing and John Payne's choir. The addition of music to the play shifted attention to Robeson but in so doing irreparably blunted its message and this, combined with the limitations of an inexperienced black cast, destroyed the essence of the original production. The London version was, as the play's author George Sklar observed, "built around him [Robeson], . . . not the 'most felicitous' way to present it." "In New York . . . real pace was established; also a real sense of heat and squalor," wrote a reviewer who saw both productions. "The production at the Embassy was too much interrupted, and I got [the] impression of semi-tropical climate where the sweat of brow and of terror are accompanied by the sweat of merely sitting still."[46]

Reviewers of the British production seldom noted the theme of oppression (the *Daily Express's* Hannen Swaffer, a man regarded by many as racially insensitive, reported being "horrified" by the racial oppression depicted in the New York production). Instead, they remarked on the "delightful atmosphere of brimming good spirits" among Lonnie Thompson's fellow black workers, the "amiable, eager animation of negro scenes," and "the extraordinary pleasant quality of their voices." Similarly, British reviewers hailed the music, from both Robeson and John Payne's choir, as the production's strongest point. "As usual," wrote one, "it is sheer delight to hear his [Robeson's] speaking or singing voice and his presence is magnetic," and another, "Although Mr. Robeson carries the show on his shoulders, Mr. John Payne's choir, both as actors and singers, provide a striking background."[47]

During the summer while Robeson and Brown conducted a leisurely tour of the coast of England, Essie received word from Universal Pictures offering Paul the role of Joe in a remake of the 1929 *Show Boat* movie.[48] Robeson, still smarting from the negative reaction to *Sanders,* had little interest in having anything to do with Hollywood, and so Essie wrote back to Universal, reportedly quoting an outrageously high salary figure, high enough, she thought, "to prohibit them engaging Paul." But, as Essie put it, Universal "fooled us and gave us the money, so we went."[49]

Robeson's decision to accept the role may have been as simple as that: Universal offered a salary he could not refuse. As Essie said in a letter to her mother in September, "We won't come to America at all unless the money is guaranteed. . . . The only thing we'll be coming for is the money." If, as Robeson said in several interviews, it was his hope to "be independent of the box office" within a few years, *Show Boat*'s large salary (Paul Robeson Jr. described the $40,000 his father received for six to seven weeks of work as "one of the biggest single pay days he ever got") was its biggest plus. Other factors may also have influenced Robeson. Whatever his personal feelings about Hollywood, one could hardly argue with its success: Hollywood offered a breadth of exposure impossible with British films. In addition, with *Show Boat* there would be few surprises. It had been tried and tested, and although blacks were not enamored with it, it would not incite the controversy of an *Emperor Jones.* Finally, should the film fail, Robeson, playing only a minor role, would not have to bear responsibility. In short, he had little to lose and much to gain.[50]

Robeson's lucrative contract arrangements underlined his "star status" and left few loopholes for last-minute changes. Although Universal refused his request for approval rights of the final version of the film (producer Carl Laemmle Jr., in a cable to Universal Pictures responded, "Impossible . . . Garbo doesn't have this privilege nor anyone else"), the studio did give him everything else he asked for: in addition to his salary, not less than fourth place in the billing, the right to refuse filming locations outside of California, transportation costs for both himself and Essie, and the right to make recordings, radio broadcasts, and concert performances in his spare time.[51]

It had been two years since Robeson last visited the United States, and so for this trip he planned to tour as he made his way from New York to Hollywood. In the late summer Robert Rockmore wrote to Walter White on Robeson's behalf, requesting that the NAACP sponsor Robeson in an October concert in New York City. White responded quickly, and in a curt letter marked "personal" and addressed to Robeson he informed Paul that the racial and economic situation in America made his request impossible. Such a concert, White said, "would not be a success. The list of people who are still solvent enough to buy tickets and who are interested in the Association is so limited that we question whether or not we could dispose of any tickets."[52]

By 1935 much more than geography separated these two men who in former years had appeared to be such firm friends and loyal allies. In this instance White saw Robeson as either ignorant of or indifferent to the economic hardships of American blacks and equally oblivious to special problems plaguing the NAACP as it battled to regain public confidence after the crushing psychological defeat of the Scottsboro case and to keep itself financially sound enough to continue the legal fight for a federal antilynching bill. The truth was that neither White nor Robeson could count on the other for support in a crisis. When debate erupted in the black community in 1934 over Robeson's part in the film version of *The Emperor Jones,* Walter White kept himself and the NAACP out of the fray, begging off with the excuse that he did not have time to see the film. Similarly, when confidence in the NAACP was perhaps at its lowest ebb, Robeson, in an interview with Julia Dorn in Moscow, denounced the organization's handling of the Scottsboro case and even went as far as to question the premise of interracial cooperation upon which the organization was founded: "I believe there is no such thing in England and America as inter-racial cooperation from the NAACP point of view," Robeson said. "Before the Negro is free, there will be many Scottsboros. The Communist emphasis in that case is right."[53] White would have been hard-pressed not to take Robeson's comments personally. The CPUSA had publicly humiliated him, and Robeson had taken his stand firmly with the Communist Party.

With the *Show Boat* filming scheduled to begin on November 18, the Robesons arrived in New York at the end of September, ready to begin their concert tour without White's assistance. In the meantime, White made several unsuccessful efforts to contact Robeson with a counterproposal, a benefit concert in Atlanta. By the beginning of November, when White still had not heard from Robeson, he began to get annoyed, complaining to Eugene Martin, his brother-in-law and head of Atlanta's NAACP, that Robeson once again had failed to leave a forwarding address when he left New York, "and a great deal of mail has piled up for him there."[54]

White wrote Robeson several more personal letters, explaining that he was "punch-drunk" trying to keep up with recent court cases and frustrated that Paul was so "elusive." Finally, on November 15 in an air-mail special delivery letter, White made a final impassioned plea: "I have a double reason for hoping you will be able to accept the engagement to sing at Atlanta on December 7th in that the benefit may be jointly for the Atlanta University Alumni Association, of which Jim Johnson and I are members, but also for the NAACP. We need it very much because we have such a terrific number of cases and because from sixty-five to seventy-five percent of our money is contributed by colored people who have been so hard hit by unemployment that they are unable to support the work of the organization as formerly. We are more hard pressed than usual."[55]

Essie responded for Paul. Her reply, or, more accurately, her retort, matched well the sharp, perfunctory tone of White's September response to Rockmore's letter about an NAACP-sponsored concert in New York. Essie viewed the Atlanta concert as an afterthought and an offer that White, above all, should have known Paul would not accept, as it was in the South. Concerning White's intimation that she and Paul had been deliberately "elusive," she snapped, "Elusive, hell. We're hard-working people, you mean." She had indeed tried to contact White, by calling both his office and Gladys (his wife), but without success. "But the next time, I'll leave my name, so I'll have an alibi," she said sarcastically. Regarding the Atlanta concert, Essie made their position quite clear: White had had his opportunity; now they were booked. "There's not a chance of our working in a concert now . . . we are hard at work on the film *Show Boat* and will barely finish in time to get our ship back to England for our concert tour there . . . [no] time to give a concert on the way out, either, because we had a full list already."[56]

The tour opened in Montreal on October 13, with cross-country stops from New York City to Portland, Oregon. Robeson and Brown's program—spirituals, popular folk songs, and an occasional Russian or English folk song—earned them favorable reviews. White's prediction, however, proved correct: they drew packed houses, but their audiences were almost overwhelmingly white.[57]

Universal, meanwhile, spared no effort in either production or expenses for *Show Boat*. From the start it was slated as a money film—a visual extravaganza and top-of-the-line entertainment, costing an estimated two million dollars and requiring more than 3,000 actors, musicians, singers, dancers, and extras. Jerome Kern and Oscar Hammerstein II, who had succeeded so brilliantly with the Broadway production, were engaged to create the screenplay and musical score. Seasoned performers—Irene Dunne (Magnolia), Charles Winninger (Captain Andy), Helen Morgan (Julie), Donald Cook (Steve), and Alan Jones

(Gaylord Ravenal) — played the lead roles. Some 500 technicians transformed the five acres of California studio into an 1885 southern town, complete with town hall, bandstand, and park. After two months of sleuthing along the shores of the Mississippi, prop scouts found an 1885 vintage showboat and steam packet of the same period, which they promptly dismantled and freighted to Hollywood to be reassembled, while technicians brought the "Father of Waters" to California by widening the channel of the Los Angeles River, which ran through the back lot of Universal City, and constructing a levee alongside it.[58]

Robeson began filming on November 18. The part of Joe was a small one, and American versions of the musical historically focused on the production's white love story. The Kern and Hammerstein alterations in script and score further diminished Robeson's role. With the ending transformed to a "happy" one in which Magnolia, her daughter, and Ravenal are reunited, the final rendering of "Ol' Man River" was eliminated altogether. Thus, Robeson would sing "Ol' Man River" only once at the beginning of the film. Although Kern and Hammerstein did add several new songs, one of them, "Ah Suits Me," sung by Robeson, the American movie was a white musical from beginning to end. The black characters Joe and Queenie (played by Hattie McDaniel, soon to achieve Academy Award fame in *Gone with the Wind*) played no significant role in forwarding the plot. Joe, for example, spends most of his time shelling peas and spilling them while Queenie, complaining that Joe "don' do nothin'," puts them back in the bowl.[59]

Still, Robeson appeared in good spirits, certainly better than his mood two years earlier with *The Emperor Jones*.[60] Only once, when he insisted on employing a recording technique he had used successfully in *Sanders*, did Robeson press a point against the advice of producers. The method required that Robeson hold the microphone close to his lips and "croon" into it rather than standing the usual ten feet back, singing at concert volume, and relying on the sound mixer to take care of volumes registering on the light valve. Robeson argued that his technique enabled him to control his own volume perfectly, so that it would never reach the blasting point. Studio technicians balked, but in the end Robeson won out and proved his point. After twenty-five recordings, engineers discovered that he sang exactly the same way each time, with perfect volume control.[61]

By the time *Show Boat* premiered at New York City's Radio City Music Hall on January 19, 1936, Robeson was back in England. A month after the American premiere, he attended the gala British opening along with Irene Dunne and director James Whale at the Leicester Square Theatre. Several of the 1928 Drury Lane *Show Boat* cast — Sir Cedric Hardwicke, Edith Day, and Marie Burke — were on hand for the event, specifically to wish London's "own Paul" well and to give the film a major send-off. It was the reception Paul wanted and one he would never have received in the United States.

American and British reviews of *Show Boat* differed substantively. In the United States the film was called an "opulent spectacular," "magnificent in scope" with an "enormously effective" score and "rich humor and pathos."[62] Acting plaudits were equally distributed among cast members; mention of Robeson was sparse and in keeping with the small amount of time he actually appeared on the screen.[63] Opening at Harlem's Roosevelt and Loew's Victoria Theaters in the summer, *Show Boat* earned favorable reviews in the black weeklies as well. By contrast, British reviewers gave the film fair to poor ratings but crowned "their Paul" its uncontested star. The *Sunday Pictorial* headlined its review, "*Show Boat* Returns, Paul Robeson Steals the Show with Ol' Man River" and the *Manchester Guardian* called it "Paul Robeson's Film from Beginning to End."[64] London's *Saturday Review* lampooned the film's "disastrous" happy ending and complained that, "instead of Paul Robeson's voice, the audience is treated to a piece of banality difficult to match."[65] James Agate predictably dismissed the film as "a silly thing . . . a mass of snippets. . . . a commonplace piece of money-making" with "only fair acting" and photography (aside from "Russian-looking" shots of porters carrying bales of cotton) "on the same artistic level as the oleographs on a cottage wall." Robeson, said Agate in a backhanded compliment, was noticed more for his absence than anything else: "And somewhere miles away Mr. Robeson, whom we have quite forgotten, and who has nothing whatsoever to do with the story, also sings."[66]

In the United States *Show Boat* fulfilled its promise as a moneymaker, grossing $93,500 in its first week at Radio City Music Hall and $73,000 in the week that followed. At the Stanley Theater in Philadelphia it earned rave notices, grossed $22,500 in its opening week, and was held over for an additional week. Boston's Keith Memorial reported "a very good $17,000" with a holdover of "at least two weeks." In Los Angeles *Show Boat* set a new season record with a gross of $10,500, almost three times the Pantages' normal take. An intense heat wave notwithstanding, the film proved Detroit's "top coin in town — $27,000." From Baltimore: "Initial week will snatch a hearty $9,500, with film likely to hold over for a month." The Fox Theater in St. Louis: "Picture got away to a terrific start, the doors opening an hour earlier than usual. House walking away from the field with $20,000 for one week."[67]

Robeson had long passed the point where all that mattered was the opportunity to play a *starring* role. "I came to understand," he later wrote in his autobiography, "that the Negro artist could not view the matter simply in terms of his individual interests, and that he had a responsibility to his people who rightfully resented the traditional stereotype of Negroes in stage and screen."[68]

At the same time, he needed to make a living. *Show Boat* may not have been professionally satisfying, but it did give Robeson the financial security he needed to pursue roles he wanted without having to worry about what they paid. Robeson wanted very much to act, to be taken seriously in the profession, and to play the same kind of challenging and substantive roles that might be offered to a similarly gifted white actor. The roles were out there, but not for a black man, and for the time being Robeson had concluded that if wanted to widen the stage opportunities available to blacks he would do so only in small, noncommercial ventures that were willing to branch out in this new uncharted territory.

15

African Journeys

1936

When Robeson returned to England after his first visit to the Soviet Union in January 1935 he was eager to begin work on Eisenstein's portrayal of the Haitian revolutionary Toussaint L'Ouverture. What Robeson did not know was that Eisenstein had barely finished his farewells to him and Essie when he was called to account for himself at the All-Union Creative Conference of Cinemato-graphic Workers, held in Moscow from January 8 to 13, 1935. After spending two years (1930–32) abroad in Hollywood, Mexico, and Europe, Eisenstein had apparently overstayed his time away and as a result he was accused of plotting to defect — in other words, he had lost favor with Stalin, a situation that spelled the end of a career for an artist. To make matters worse, he returned with the film he was working on, *Qué Viva México,* unfinished and the work-in-progress in the hands of the American writer Upton Sinclair, who had financed the project.[1]

The atmosphere in Moscow for artists and intellectuals had changed dramat-ically during Eisenstein's two years abroad. All the nation's resources both hu-man and material had been conscripted into the service of one overriding objec-tive: fulfilling Stalin's Five-Year Plan. By the end of 1932 the slogan "Social Realism," a phrase attributed to Stalin himself, ruled the arts. Writers and artists must show life as it was becoming rather than as it was (an empty ditch was a canal in the making, vacant lots were future parks, and so on). In addition, Soviet creative works must be accessible, easily understood by the masses, and, at the same time, worthy of their classic Russian and world art ancestry. (Shostakovich, for example, was asked to compose melodies that the toiling masses — building the future — could whistle on their way to work.) In short, art was now to be the clarion and apologist for the bureaucracy.[2]

In this setting not only were Eisenstein's earlier works — *Potemkin* (1926) and *October* (1927) — suspect but equally damning was his recent lack of productivity. The All-Union Soviet Film Trust, which since 1930 had controlled all branches of the movie industry, established as its primary objective production quotas (in 1932, 500 full-length films), and Eisenstein had not completed a film since 1929 (*The General Line*). The pressure of the bureaucracy on every revolutionary, intellectual, and artist was tremendous. Eisenstein's inactivity became a central theme at this conference, a gathering calculated to demonstrate the regime's control of intellectuals and to prod directors into stepping up production. Major Soviet filmmakers indulged in several days of flattery, abasement, affirmations of socialist realism, and attacks on the most famous figures in their midst. For Eisenstein, the offensive came from old friends and filmmakers whom Eisenstein had generously helped in their early careers. Only one filmmaker, the pioneering director Lev Kuleshov, came to his defense. Eisenstein was pilloried and as a result he did not secure permission to make *Black Majesty*.[3]

In the meantime, Robeson entertained several other proposed portrayals of the Haitian revolt. In 1935 he read a dramatization of the life of Toussaint L'Ouverture written by C. L. R. (Cyril Lionel Robert) James, the politically astute young West Indian journalist whom Robeson had known since 1932. James had given the script to Robeson's friend, Marie Seton, who urged him to get the play produced and offered to talk with the Incorporated Stage Society (according to James "a very exclusive society which had given first performances of . . . Shaw and many other playwrights who have become world famous") on his behalf.[4] The Stage Society agreed to do the play, provided Robeson was cast as Toussaint. Representatives from the Stage Society, including Executive Committee member Flora Robson, who had played opposite Robeson in the 1933 London *All God's Chillun*, tried to contact Robeson but failed. Finally, James, acting on a tip from Marie Seton, found Paul at a party and showed him the script. Robeson agreed on the spot to perform the role. "Paul read it and with great simplicity and directness said, yes, he would be ready to play the role," James remembered. "There were not too many parts in those days which gave a black actor, however distinguished, a role that lifted him above the servants' quarters. It was definitely a role Paul wanted to play."[5]

From a practical point of view, agreeing to perform in a play scheduled for only a two-night run did not make much sense. Robeson already had plans for a rigorous two-month tour of the British Isles (the Harold Holt Celebrity Series) from mid-January through the beginning of March. But the Toussaint production was precisely the kind of theater Robeson said he wanted most to do: a noncommercial venture recounting the story of a great black hero, the script conceived and written by a black man and requiring an almost exclusively black cast.

Robeson and the slight but equally towering (six feet, three inches) dark-skinned, and noticeably good-looking James, first met shortly after James moved from Trinidad to London. In addition to their mutual interest in theater, the two men had much else in common. James, an amiable, soft-spoken intellectual, as much at home with Shakespeare as with the Marxist classics, often found himself along with Robeson among the guests at gatherings in English homes. "We joked with each other about being London's 'better sort of blacks,'" James remembered. "There were so few of us at the time in London who were 'in' as blacks."[6] Like Robeson's, James's parents were both well educated. In Tunapuna, the small village where James grew up, his father, a schoolmaster steeped in the manners and values of inherited British culture, held a position rivaled only by the priest or minister. His mother was, as James would later describe her, "a reader, one of the most tireless I have ever met." By the age of six James was reading Shakespeare; at the age of ten he won a scholarship to Queen's Royal College, a school modeled after English public schools and the island's premiere educational establishment.[7]

Educated in the British system, a de facto part of Trinidad's plantation past, James, as Robeson had at Rutgers, learned the rules. Both men excelled in sports; both played on otherwise all-white teams (James played on the Tunapuna Cricket Club team); and both learned in the process some bitter racial lessons. Of all James's early experiences, none would teach him as much about colonialism and the pernicious quality of systematized racism as playing, observing, and writing about cricket.

> We talked quite a bit about our problems with whites athletically. Paul had gained fame as a footballer, but at a price: he was accepted on the football field but in all other aspects subjected to prejudice. For me, both in Trinidad and in England, it was much the same. As a student at Queen's Royal College, oh, how I loved cricket, much to the detriment of my studies. For the British cricket is more than a sport; it is a way of life. On the field one adopted an absolute morality of fair play and unquestionable obedience to the umpire's decision. It was a matter of honor. As a person of color, if you were adept enough at the sport, white teams would allow you to participate. They let me play as they had let Paul in America, but, for both of us there was no racial mixing after the match. That was a line that no one crossed. I knew this, and certainly Paul had learned it as well during his football days in college.[8]

Since his arrival in England, James had been working on a book about the San Domingo revolution and the slave insurrection led by Toussaint L'Ouverture. His research dovetailed with his deepening devotion to Marxism and his championing of full independence for colonials.[9] Certainly, the debates surrounding Mussolini's invasion of Ethiopia influenced James's decision to present a dramatization of a virtually forgotten example of slaves successfully rising against their masters. The story of the San Domingo revolution and of its leader, Toussaint L'Ouverture, demonstrated that colonial populations did not need to depend on leadership from Europe in their struggle for freedom. It was a timely message.

Perhaps during rehearsals Robeson and James talked about the situation in Ethiopia. It would have been difficult to avoid the topic. Mussolini's aggression had outraged anti-imperialists and nationalists around the world. The *Pittsburgh Courier* in the United States closely followed the crisis and sent historian and newsman Joel A. Rogers to Ethiopia to cover the story, and Harlem held numerous fund-raisers and rallies in support of Haile Sellasie.[10] In London, James collaborated with Amy Ashwood Garvey (a native of Jamaica who at that time had been married to Marcus Garvey for three years and was a founding member of the Universal Negro Improvement Association and an active Pan-Africanist throughout her life), Jomo Kenyatta, George Padmore, and others to form the International African Friends of Abyssinia (IAFA, later the International African Service Bureau, IASB), an organization created to rally British support around the Ethiopian cause. But whether James and Robeson talked or not, and Robeson's impassioned rhetoric on the topic of Africa notwithstanding, Robeson remained solidly in the pro-Soviet camp, which for the time being meant putting the issue of Ethiopia on the back burner.[11]

James thoroughly enjoyed working with Robeson and never let their political differences interfere with their friendship. "We worked morning and afternoon for about three hours daily during the short time we had to rehearse," James recalled. "You get to know a man pretty well in that amount of time. Robeson was here, as elsewhere, always the center of attention: not an easy role to fill. Besides playing the lead, he was his own extraordinary self, and not only players but all who were connected with the stage where we rehearsed had their eyes fastened on him and were all ears when he spoke. . . . To have spent half an hour in his company or to have ten minutes alone with him, was something you remembered for days."[12]

Robeson showed none of the temperament he often evidenced in larger, more elaborate, well-financed productions. James described him as attentive and obliging, "far more so than one or two others in the cast." (James had less kind words for Essie: "A nuisance," he said bluntly. "She watched rehearsals and was constantly offering advice as to what should be changed and rearranged.") According to James, only once did Robeson do anything other than exactly what he or director Peter Godfrey suggested. While reading a very long speech, taken directly from the material James had collected, Paul stopped halfway through, turned to James, and said, "James, I don't want to go any further. I think it should stop here." Godfrey and James agreed and cut the speech at the point

Paul had suggested. As James put it, "When so quiet a man made a definite decision, you automatically agree."[13]

As had been the case with *Basalik,* filling *Toussaint L'Ouverture*'s bit parts proved difficult. Africans like Kenyatta, who had played in *Sanders,* could not be used because, as James put it, "the moment he [Kenyatta] opened his mouth, you could tell he was an African," and so black actors like the Nigerian Orlando Martins, the American Robert Adams, and others, nonprofessionals like Larry Brown, were recruited. "Sometimes you ran into unpredictable trouble with the smaller roles," James recalled. "One poor soul who was in a very minor role and just couldn't act at all, at the very last minute simply had to be replaced. He was very upset and bitterly disappointed and begged me personally to be kept on, but I just couldn't."[14]

Toussaint L'Ouverture opened in March at the Westminster Theatre and met with mixed reviews. Critics concurred that James, a fine historian, lacked equal dramatic talent. Most found the work, which covers a twenty-year period from Toussaint's political beginnings in 1791 to his betrayal, captivity, and death in 1802, "sincere and unpretentious" but complained that it "suffers from repetition, that the dialogue is informative rather than suggestive" and that like "so many other chronicle plays . . . all the action happens 'off.'" In short, James wrote like a historian.[15]

At the same time, critics were genuinely taken with the story and with Robeson's dominating performance. Most knew little about Toussaint L'Ouverture's life, and reviewers devoted considerable space to educating readers on the topic. "Sometimes the narrative needs trimming" said the *Observer,* "but the play . . . manages to be continuously interesting because Toussaint himself is interesting."[16] The *Times* agreed: "The dramatist, having an interesting subject sticks to it, the play, in spite of its woodenness now and then, holds the stage at the Westminster Theatre."[17]

Robeson received excellent reviews. "The action is genuinely vitalized by Mr. Robeson alone," said the *Times.* Through his "vital and tremendously sincere acting, the leading character came to life," agreed G.W.B. in the *Sunday Times.*[18] "Physically he was hardly suited to the role of this forty-seven year-old ex-coachman, worn out with years of slavery, and, it is said, a man of small stature, but he played the part with quiet dignity, and in one or two scenes, with a passion and intensity that gave his words a power they lacked in themselves."[19] Robeson was pleased. Whatever its limitations, *Toussaint* did expose audiences to a great black hero, a character, as one reviewer put it, who "emerges as a man of greater capacity and a higher honour than the white men who contrived his downfall."[20]

Robeson in *Show Boat,*
London, 1928. Alberta
Hunter is fourth from left,
next to Robeson; Marie
Burke is fourth from right.
(PR Jr.)

Robeson, London, 1928.
(PR Jr.)

Joseph Andrews,
Robeson's dresser.
(PR Jr.)

Paul Robeson Jr. and Mrs. Goode,
Christmas, 1928. (Courtesy of Patti Light,
private collection.)

Eslanda Robeson and Paul Robeson Jr,
Christmas, 1928. (Courtesy of Patti
Light, private collection.)

Robeson with Peggy Ashcroft as Desdemona, *Othello,* 1930, London. (PR Jr.)

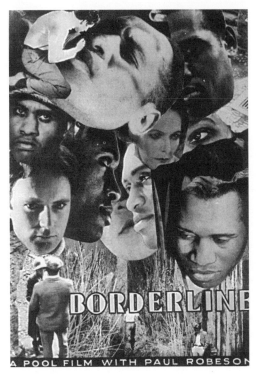

Borderline, advertising poster. (PR Archive.)

Paul Robeson Jr., 1930.
(Courtesy of Patti Light, private collection.)

Essie Robeson, 1930.
(Courtesy of Patti Light, private collection.)

(*opposite*) Robeson, London, 1930. (Courtesy of Patti Light, private collection.)

Robeson as Jim Harris with Flora Robson in *All God's Chillun*, 1933. (PR Archive.)

Robeson in *The Emperor Jones*, 1933. (PR Jr.)

Robeson with Dudley Digges in *The Emperor Jones*, 1933. (PR Jr.)

Robeson as Bosambo in *Sanders of the River*, 1934. (PR Jr.)

Robeson with Nina Mae McKinney in *Sanders of the River,* 1934. (PR Jr.)

(*opposite*) Robeson as Bosambo in *Sanders of the River,* 1934. (PR Jr.)

Robeson with Herbert Marshall and
Sergei Eisenstein, Moscow, 1934.
(Herbert Marshall Collection, University
of Notre Dame, Indiana. Hereafter
Marshall Collection.)

Robert Rockmore, Robeson's lawyer
and business manager. (Courtesy of
Robert Sherman.)

Robeson in *Show Boat* (the film), 1935. (PR Jr.)

Robeson hoped that his next film, *Song of Freedom,* would both widen acting opportunities for him and other black actors and answer the charge of his having sponsored British imperialism in *Sanders*. In *Song of Freedom* Robeson would play the part of the hero, not his underling. There would be no white overlord, no Bosambo kowtowing to every wish of his master. Furthermore, Robeson demanded and received veto rights over the final version of the film.

"'Song of Freedom' is a kind of test piece," Robeson said in a 1936 interview:

> It gives me a *real* part for the first time. I have always been up against two difficulties on the screen. The first, and less important, is that my reputation as a singer has misled producers into refusing to try me out as an actor. The second is the difficulty which confronts all coloured artists. Film producers take an attitude that a Negro must be a romaticised puppet (usually comic) or else of no interest to filmgoers at all. You saw the result in "Show Boat." I was given a sentimental "bit" which did little more than feature me in a couple of songs. I feel that I can do much more on the screen than that. . . . In this film I play the part of a coloured stevedore who wins operatic fame and then returns to his own people in Africa. The story presents me as a real man — no more romaticised than a white man would be in a similar role. It is the first step in my effort to break down the prejudice that Negroes must always be "different" on the screen.[21]

Produced by Hammer in conjunction with British Lion, *Song of Freedom* was advertised as "a dramatization of Robeson" and his West African forebears in Sierra Leone, "the actual territory in which he can trace back his ancestors for generations." Elisabeth Welch, an American-born singer and actress who began her career in New York in shows like *Liza* (1922), *Runnin' Wild* (1923), *Chocolate Dandies* (1928), and *Blackbirds* (1928) and settled in England permanently in 1930 after discovering there a more appreciative audience for her magnificent voice, would star opposite Paul, playing the role of his wife, Ruth.[22] The film opens with a flashback to the eighteenth century and the African island of Casanga where one group of Africans are battling to enslave another. One of the natives and his wife escape death by fleeing. The scene then leaps to present-day London, where John Zinga (Robeson), the descendant of the native pictured in the original scene, labors on the docks. Zinga is happily married and he and his wife, a fair-skinned black with straight hair, live in easy middle-class harmony, the only blacks in a white working-class neighborhood. (Elisabeth Welch's role was a radical departure from the stereotypical depiction of black women in films at that time.) Zinga is obsessed with a longing to visit the land of his origin. "Africa, it's always Africa, isn't it John," his wife says to him. "That's my home,"

Zinga answers. "It's where we come from. But—our people—I have a feeling they're grand people too—the people we belong to."[23]

Singing while he works ("Lonely Road"), Zinga is discovered by an opera impresario (Esme Percy) who urges him to take lessons and perform. Hopeful that a stage career might earn him enough money to make the trip to Africa, Zinga agrees and rapidly rises to fame. As he travels the world, he is heard one night by an anthropologist who recognizes in one of his songs ("Song of Freedom") something that he himself had heard along the coast of Africa. From the song and the huge medallion that Zinga wears around his neck (a medallion belonging to one of his African ancestors, the king of Casanga), the anthropologist is able to locate the tribe from which Zinga's forebears originated. Armed with this information, Zinga and his wife leave for Africa in search of his people. Zinga is disappointed to discover that what the anthropologist told him about the island and its people ("backward, uncivilized, impoverished") is true. "It's all so primitive!" he moans and then says, "It's got to be changed!" His efforts to make changes inevitably bring him into conflict with the evil witch doctor who has the natives totally under his control. At the climax of the film, Zinga and his wife are about to be put to death when the king recognizes in one of Zinga's songs something that originated in his own tribe. His life spared, Zinga gives up his career in England and resolves to live in Africa and work for the good of his people.[24]

While Robeson labored at Beaconsfield, hoping to convey the true story of Africa on film, Essie was actually in Africa, concluding a tour of the continent that had for so long fascinated them both. Like Paul, she had returned from the Soviet Union reinvigorated, and while Paul dove into his work and language studies, she pursued even more energetically her studies at the London School of Economics. By 1936 she had made up her mind: for personal as well as academic reasons, she would see Africa for herself and would take eight-year-old Pauli along for the journey.

Essie chronicled the trip in her 1945 *African Journey,* and although the book reflects her later, more mature political viewpoints it also provides an account of what drove her to make the trip, her impressions of the continent, and a striking photographic documentary. It was a remarkable undertaking, especially for a woman whose only traveling companion was a eight-year-old boy—a three-month-long journey that would take the pair from England to Cape Town (seventeen days by boat) and two days later, Port Elizabeth, then to Johannesburg and on to Mozambique, up the east coast of Africa to Mombasa, by train to Uganda, and finally to Entebbe and then home (because planes did not fly at night in 1936, this final leg of the journey would take nine days). They would endure merciless heat, dust storms, a strange diet, and illness (both Essie and Pauli became ill). The trip and the book that followed mark a unique achievement, one of the first portraits of Africa done by an African American who spent time in Africa, a portrait that combined a critique of European colonialism with a human portrait of Africans and a deep appreciation for their cultural achievements.[25]

"I wanted to go to Africa," Essie writes in the introduction to *African Journey.* "It began when I was quite small. . . . I remember wanting very much to see my 'old country' and wondering what it would be like." A more recent impetus occurred while she was studying anthropology at the London School of Economics. Essie believed the African was as capable as the European of subtle reasoning but discovered that the absence of her own firsthand experience made it impossible for her to support her point of view. "I'd just have to go out to Africa and see and meet and study and talk with my people on their home ground," she decided. "Then I would be able to say truly: I have been there too, and I *know.*"

Paul decided not to go with her, Essie explained, because "he had contracts ahead for two years and couldn't risk not being able to fulfill them." Although Robeson repeatedly told reporters it was his "burning ambition to visit Africa," he put off visiting the continent and filmed *Song of Freedom*'s African-set scenes at a tiny hamlet called "Egypt," near British Lion Studios at Beaconsfield. In fact, with the exception of less than a week he would spend in Egypt in 1938 filming *Jericho,* Robeson never visited Africa. "Paul doesn't stand the heat well," Essie explained in his defense, "changes of climate are hard on him, changes of diet and water put him off." (Friends of Robeson's all agreed: he was not the outdoors-adventure type. He liked his creature comforts and would have had little interest in "roughing it" anywhere for three months.) So together they decided it was best for Essie to go to Africa first, with Paul perhaps coming along for a second trip.[26]

In part, what convinced his parents that Paul Jr. needed to see Africa was remembering how "astonished and delighted" he was when he saw all the Africans on the set of *Sanders.* "Why, there are lots of brown people," he had remarked, and "lots of black people too; we're not the only ones." Pauli's chance comment left both Paul and Essie "profoundly disturbed by the realization that he had been living in an entirely white world since we had brought him and my mother to live with us in England. The only Negroes he had seen besides ourselves and Larry [Brown] were the occasional ones who visited at our home. His young mind had thought we were the only brown people in a totally white world." For the past several years Pauli had been living in America with his grandmother and attending various schools. Although Essie and Paul had hoped the experience would broaden his racial exposure, in many respects the change proved only "bewildering and painful." "He was slighted because of his colour," Robeson later told the British press. "Children wouldn't play with him, and he wouldn't swim in the pool. He would mope and be very sorry for himself."[27]

As reports from Mrs. Goode about racial incidents increased, Essie's anxiety mounted and even Paul briefly and uncharacteristically got into the fray, instructing Mrs. Goode from across the ocean on how matters should be handled. Sadly, the explaining, consoling, and instructing that black American parents routinely do to prepare their children for the emotionally devastating experience of racism Paul and Essie had to do in letters to Paul Jr. rather than in person. Essie reminded Pauli that both she and his father had been the only blacks at the schools they attended. "But we were both proud of being coloured. We didn't feel sad about it at all. . . . We are very proud of having a coloured son, a Negro boy of whom we can be very proud. . . . We, too, were called 'nigger' when we were young. But we didn't mind very much. We used to call names back. . . . I honestly think that white people call us niggers because they are jealous of us. They only call us nigger, when we do something better than they do, or when they are angry. . . . But you must not be unhappy, Darling. You have a great deal to be proud of and be happy about. There is love all around you."[28]

At one point, the plan was that Mrs. Goode would take Pauli to Africa in the hope that the experience would do for Pauli what living among blacks in America had failed to do. Later, perhaps due to Mrs. Goode's ill health and to Essie's awareness that if Pauli's life had been racially sheltered, in recent years her own had been too, Essie decided to go herself.[29] They had an ambitious itinerary, one that assured that she and Paul Jr. would see all kinds and varieties of black people.

Along with the preparatory inoculations, shopping, and travel reservations, there was the task of obtaining visas, which went smoothly in all cases with the exception of South Africa. After a frustrating run-around and endless admonitions that "these things take time," Essie decided to take her chances and leave without the South African visas. "Pauli and I will just get on that ship, with or without our [South African] visas," Essie told Paul. "When we get there, all they can do is refuse to let us land. If they do that, I'll set up a howl there, and you can set up a real howl here, and then maybe they'll do something."[30]

After saying good-bye to Mrs. Goode at the London flat, Paul took Essie and Pauli to Waterloo Station and settled them in the train they would take to Southampton to board the steamship *Winchester Castle*. Larry Brown also came to see them off, and Paul promised to stay close to the phone in case they ran into any problems. On May 29 Essie and Pauli set sail, arriving in Cape Town on June 15. In the interim, Paul had secured their South African visas so they had no trouble landing. Dr. Schapera, head of anthropology at Cape Town University, whom Essie had met previously in London through Bronislaw Malinowski, greeted them at the dock. After a brief round of press interviews and welcomes from various delegations, Essie and Pauli were off on a tour of Cape Town.

Throughout this three-month trip, Essie made it a point to talk with everyone — from dignitaries, scholars, and university officials to African chieftains, black African miners, peasants, and herdsmen, and even unsympathetic white colonial officials. She took particular care to study women's roles and gender relations in the various cultures she observed and throughout the trip took numerous photographs. (Paul bought her "a gem of a camera, a Rolleiflex" and wisely advised, "You can't take too many pictures.")[31]

On June 19 Essie and Pauli arrived in Port Elizabeth, where they were met by Max Yergan, an American black who had been in South Africa for the past seventeen years, working under the auspices of the International Committee of the YMCA. Yergan, a graduate of Shaw University, a Baptist college in North Carolina, was intelligent, enigmatic, and ambitious. Over the next several years he would become a conspicuous and extremely influential member of Robeson's inner circle of friends and political allies. At this point, however, Paul had met Yergan but did not know him well, and Essie had never met him at all.[32]

Yergan and his wife, Susie, first settled in Johannesburg and then later moved to Alice, just outside Port Elizabeth and close to the Fort Hare campus. Initially, he was under constant surveillance by South African police, with informers transcribing verbatim his public statements and forwarding them to headquarters for closer scrutiny. In time the surveillance abated and Yergan forged friendships with staff colleagues, support personnel, and the students with whom he worked. By the late 1920s he had concluded that the dire conditions endured by the prevailing majority in South Africa could only be improved by a total social and economic upheaval. While continuing to keep a low profile in his public activities, he privately began to encourage the construction of a new social order that would destroy capitalist relations and replace them with a more equitable distribution of material wealth. It was a perspective he maintained and clandestinely supported throughout his years in South Africa.

Yergan's political commitments, however, seldom impinged on his personal life style, and although he was acutely aware of contradictions of South African life and the suffering surrounding him, he lived very well: he and his wife had comfortable accommodations, traveled widely, dined lavishly, drove a Ford, wore expensive clothing, and sent their children to schools overseas. During their stay with the Yergans Essie and Paul Jr. lacked few amenities.

Essie "liked Dr. Yergan on sight." And with his years of experience in South Africa, he proved an invaluable tour guide. He took Essie and Pauli to the

Second Annual All-African Convention held at Bloemfontein on July 1 and showed them Basutoland, both the black and white sections. Essie saw and recorded with characteristic meticulousness and candor the ravages of colonialism in South Africa. "All through this spacious country there are European farms: neat, well-built white farmhouses," she wrote. "Definitely and considerably removed from the group of buildings are the dirty, ramshackle huts which house the farmer's Native labor. Always the cattle, chicken, and dogs are far better housed than the African worker." In the best of the segregated reserves, living conditions were barely tolerable; the worst, as she saw later in Nancefield just outside Johannesburg, were "like a village of dog kennels." Even Paul Jr. was stunned by what they saw. When they reached the Orange Free State, Pauli, obviously confused by the contradiction between the name of the place and what he was observing, asked with a child's candor, "What's so free about it?"[33]

Essie was impressed with the intellectual acumen of the Africans she met, "far more politically aware than my fellow Negroes in America. They understand their situation . . . and are firmly resolved to find a way to improve their lot." She asked an African chief what he thought of visiting (white) anthropologists and was told with a smile that he was amused but could not understand "how any reasonable person could hope to study the intimate details of a life and people . . . [knowing] nothing whatever of the language. . . . knowing the language of a people is a gesture of respect, and a proof of real interest."

Marie Seton remembered that the trip meant a great deal to Paul Jr. He relished taking care of his mother and having her all to himself for such an extended period of time. The sights and animals in the game reserves left him "spellbound" and "enthralled," and he enjoyed meeting people — dignitaries as well as African children — almost as much as his mother did. He had his father's gift for languages and "so picked up easily phrases in the various national languages and even mastered some of the difficult clicks." In Kampala he was provided with a king's son as a playmate, and "the boys hit it off together at once, and seemed to enjoy each other's strangeness. In between play and games, which after a few words of explanation on either side they understood immediately, they plied each other with questions."[34]

By the time they reached Uganda in mid-July, after a twelve-day journey by ship, train, and automobile from South Africa, the strain of traveling began to show on Essie. Pauli was also sick, but only briefly in Kabarole where he had eaten against orders an indigestible variety of banana followed by raw milk. Both were quite upset by the other's illness. Pauli had apparently never seen his mother ill before, knew her only "as the 'doctor' or 'nurse' telling everyone else what to do," and was frightened. Essie worried terribly about Pauli, wondering "what I would tell Big Paul and Mother if anything happened to him." For almost all the last month of their trip Essie fought fevers and a steady stream of digestive ailments. Still, their schedule remained unaltered: studying, touring, and even a three-day safari in the Belgian Congo. They both made it through, with eight-year-old Pauli quite proud of himself for having returned his mother home in one piece.

At home, at work in British Lion–Hammer and Gaumont's film studios, Robeson examined *Song of Freedom*'s final edits.[35] He was determined that he not again appear as a mouthpiece for British imperialism, that the film's other black characters have substance beyond the usual ridiculous stereotypes, and that Elisabeth Welch's performance not repeat Nina Mae McKinney's Western sophisticate transported to Africa.[36] Robeson carefully reviewed the first half of *Song of Freedom* but for some reason did not even look at the second half, or so he later told reporters.[37] Possibly he chose not to preview it so as to have less responsibility for its final outcome (he did tell reporters he was "afraid to see the second half"), or he may have seen it but, wishing to avoid embarrassment, publicly said otherwise.[38]

Although *Song of Freedom* was not technically an "Empire film," it employed many of the stock features of the genre and thus attracted, if not apologists for Pax Britannia, at least the fans of Edgar Wallace and Rider Haggard and other armchair adventurers seeking excitement in an exotic setting. Publicity releases, predictably, detailed the hazards of filming in an area of darkest Africa known as "White Man's Grave" and boasted footage showing the famed devil dance, an initiation rite for young natives entering manhood which was seldom seen by white men and never by white women (according to promotional releases, in Africa the penalty for a white woman's watching was death).

Song of Freedom's hero, John Zinga, represents a decided step away from the bowing obsequiousness of *Sanders*'s Bosambo. Black stevedore, concert-singer, and African king, Zinga conquers European concert halls and evil African witch doctors with equal ease. The film's story, however, was hopelessly weighed down by implausibilities and unlikely coincidences: Zinga's discovery by an Italian maestro, the timely appearance of an anthropologist to interpret the meaning of his chant, the uncovering of his regal lineage, and Zinga's rescue of his tribe from the clutches of an evil witch doctor. Robeson's hovering over the final edits could do little to remedy these defects, and thus the film that Paul promised would "give a true picture of many aspects of the life of a colored man in the West" and show "him as a real man" did considerably less than that.[39] The film's sentimental story diminished the potential strength of its hero, many times reducing him to a caricature, consistently victorious but fantastic.

Reviews of the film, which opened on August 17, 1936, at the Piccadilly Theatre's new trade show, rehearsed what was fast becoming the tired theme of

Robeson's British film career: good entertainment but poor art.[40] Critics agreed that "any film built around Paul Robeson's voice starts with a clear advantage" and liberally applauded his singing, especially his plaintive rendering of Eric Ansell's "Lonely Roads."[41] Elisabeth Welch, likewise, fared well with the press. But most complained the film lacked substance, and almost all panned the second half: "Drum thumping . . . posturing"; "In his native Africa, the . . . realism of the film dies an unnatural death"; "Pure claptrap uttered in a loud and solid voice." Several lamented the squandering of Robeson's talents. One reviewer reported being "acutely embarrassed by the sight of . . . probably the world's most cultivated and erudite singer, performing the songs of native Africa with lyric and orchestra."[42] "Pathetic," said *Bystander*'s George Campbell, not only of Robeson's latest effort but of his film career in general. Admitting the constraints of prevailing racial attitudes in both Britain ("We are too confoundedly patronizing for words") and the United States ("the negro is just a clown . . . no more entitled to serious consideration as an artist than, say, Shirley Temple") as well as the psychological cost of trying to work with and through those stereotypes ("Mr. Robeson, a charming and cultured man, feels all this acutely"), Campbell nonetheless took Robeson to task for going "to the other extreme . . . in his desire to escape from the abysmal . . . nigger roles thrust on him by Hollywood" by playing in "stories about demigods — chiefs of superhuman valour and cunning, like Bosambo — and now the hero of *Song of Freedom.*" Campbell urged Robeson to "just forget he is a negro . . . [and] simply play normal human beings." As if it were that easy.[43]

In the United States, however, the black press hailed *Song of Freedom* "the finest story of colored folks yet brought to the screen" and "everything the Negro has longed to see about himself," precisely because it countered traditional negative stereotypes with a dazzling, larger-than-life substitute, however improbable.[44] Robeson, for his part, understood all too well the fatuousness of pretending that race did not matter; what he wanted was a realistic and substantive role that would not necessarily glorify the race but simply do it justice. It would take time and four more films in quick succession for Robeson finally to give up the idea that he could significantly alter racial stereotypes through film.

While *Song of Freedom* was still in the cutting room, Robeson turned his attention to another film on Africa, Joseph Best's *My Song Goes Forth* (originally titled *Africa Looks Up*), a documentary tracing the development of the Johannesburg gold and Kimberley diamond mines, the growth of Durban, and the response of South Africans to white initiatives in education, medicine, and housing. Robeson's part in the film was small—he stands by the piano, sings, and then reads a prologue. There is no doubt that Robeson's desire to give the moviegoing public a true idea of today's Africa was sincere; he invested £250 in this production and labored over his own revisions to Best's prologue.[45] Perhaps he hoped the documentary mode would ensure the film's authenticity. But, although *My Song Goes Forth* departs from the norm in its dispassionate and nonstereotypical treatment of the African native, it does so almost entirely within a white Western framework. With its purpose, as stated in the prologue, to show "what the white man has achieved . . . [and] done for the native" in South Africa it could hardly do otherwise. Viewed now, after apartheid, it is difficult to watch.[46]

Robeson's introduction, for example, portrays the African in all respects the equal of his fairer-skinned brother, but both the prologue and the film's footage — a patchwork of documentary clips with a white voice-over noting conditions and advances — demonstrate African intelligence by documenting the natives' rapid acquisition of Western values. Proof of the "longing of . . . poor uncultured Negro[s] for the light . . . of knowledge, education and the higher things of life and civilization" is demonstrated in the film by their movement from primitive dwellings to modern (Western) living quarters and from elementary labor to skilled trades and professional occupations.[47] Similarly, the film shows wealthy white mine owners alongside Africans whose wages fall considerably below the white standard but, aside from a reference in Robeson's prologue to the parceling out of Africa "among the white races . . . for the benefit of [the white man] to obtain the wealth it contained," makes no attempt either to highlight or to comment on these economic inequalities.[48] The film's political shortcomings had little effect on its public reception, but comparisons to Paul's other films did. *My Song Goes Forth* never came close to competing with Robeson's African-set potboilers and even after several revisions received limited showings and barely managed to break even financially.[49]

In August Robeson took a brief trip to the Soviet Union, primarily to finalize contract arrangements for an upcoming December–January concert tour, arriving back in London just in time to meet Essie and Pauli as they returned from their tour of Africa.[50] Once home, Robeson dove into work on another African-set film, *King Solomon's Mines*. Again he would be the star, again playing the great African hero, again hopeful the film would combine financial success with his message about Africa. Gaumont British Film Studios anticipated a hit. In an industry dominated by Hollywood, Britain's Empire films had proven surprisingly competitive moneymakers, and this heavily budgeted version of the Rider Haggard classic more than met the genre's stock requirements with its narrow escapes, treasure hunts, perfectly timed eclipses of the sun, treacherous desert treks, tribal wars, and panoramic shots of Africa. These, combined with the

Robeson physique draped in all manner of exotic garb and the Robeson voice echoing across the mountains, all but assured producer and financial backer Michael Balcon a box-office success.[51]

Publicity releases followed the Empire-film format, promising genuine African footage shot in the hazardous "Valley of a Thousand Hills" in Natal, South Africa, by "one of the finest teams of artists and technicians that the British film industry can muster."[52] Costuming was touted as another of the film's chief drawing cards: "Four thousand natives are being employed and for their clothes, bead ornaments by the thousand have been bought and warriors' bonnets are dressed with ostrich, eagle and cock feathers."[53] Costume mistress Yvonne Alexander, after scouring London in search of native garb, secured an enormous pouch made of tortoise shells and hung with bits of hair. Sharks' teeth, tigers' claws, monkeys' paws, Zulu headdresses made of ostrich feathers, exotic necklaces and ornaments filled the studio wardrobe, as well as 12,000 "flashes" (arm and leg bracelets) made on location out of cow tails and a magnificent *caroos* (huge cape) made for Robeson out of emu feathers. The leopard skin that Robeson wore had its markings carefully set so as to decrease his size because he was, as one observer put it, in danger of looking like Gulliver among the Lilliputians.[54]

Robeson was relaxed during filming and enjoyed working with the cast and crew, enough so that he labored over what to give "the boys" (the crew) as a parting gift, finally deciding to sing and treat them to cigarettes and "a glass of excisable liquor" at the studio restaurant.[55] Robeson paid little attention to the film's plot and characterization, concentrating instead on his language studies (under the direction of the Nigerian E. I. Kpenyon) with the same single-mindedness he had shown on the *Sanders* set, where he had listened to Korda's recordings of native chants and dances. Perhaps Paul felt that the producers' attentiveness to detail, from costuming and footage to their insistence that he learn a Nigerian language, would assure the film's credibility. More likely, he welcomed the distraction studying offered as well as the reassurance that despite the film's content he was still an artist and a scholar. "I have found a curious thing," an enthusiastic Robeson told reporters on the set. "As in other primitive languages this tongue [Efik] depends largely on accentuations and inflections of the same basic word to convey entirely different meanings. The curious thing is this: the tonal 'notes' in Efik are almost exactly like those of the Chinese."[56] Onlookers were reportedly amazed by Robeson's "deep knowledge of language and ethnology," and one surprised reporter commented, "Other players find it difficult to read light novels on the set, but Robeson can study."[57]

As for its message about Africa, *King Solomon's Mines* was blighted by the same difficulties that had plagued *Sanders* and *Song of Freedom*. The Rider Haggard novel on which the film was based was a classic of the Empire genre, so imaginatively rich that it affected virtually all subsequent stock characters, with the exception of Tarzan, that would emerge out of this fiction and film genre. Haggard, who had served as a British colonial officer in South Africa in the 1870s, knew the continent well and based his fiction on personal observation filtered through the lens of his own active imagination. The result was a combination of realism and racial and exotic wish-fulfillment. For millions of readers and filmgoers before Tarzan, Africa was *King Solomon's Mines*.[58]

The setting is the as-yet-unconquered territory to the north of Transvaal. The tale, built around speculation linking the abandoned stone city of Zimbabwe and the biblical mines of King Solomon, focuses on the adventures of the great white hunter and fortune seeker Allan Quatermain (Sir Cedric Hardwicke), his companions, and Umbopa (Robeson), servant to the party and a dispossessed African king. Added to the original Haggard story is a woman, Kathy O'Brien (Anna Lee), who engages Quatermain and his companions to help her find her father who has gone off in search of gold and the legendary King Solomon's mines. Guided by a yellowing Portuguese map, the group battles the elements of desert and mountain, an evil king and usurper of Umbopa's throne (Robert Adams), a hag witch doctor, tribal warfare, and a volcanic eruption. O'Brien is found safe, and Umbopa rescues the group from the clutches of the witch doctor, returns victorious to the tribe, and sings his white friends a fond farewell. Robeson plays a heroic character, but one too naively conceived to be taken seriously. Only within the context of a romantic adventure story can one accept Umbopa's penchant for unexpectedly bursting into song (melodious Europeanized cadences), to say nothing of a harrowing encounter with death in the desert where he is not only miraculously revived but also answers in full basso the echo of the distant mountain as he leads his lagging entourage up its inaccessible peaks.[59]

Reviews lauded the film's handling of technical problems (a desert sandstorm and volcanic eruption) but took issue with its adolescent story, "guaranteed to delight youngsters" but hardly satisfying to an adult.[60] "A thundering good version of that grand epic of one's boyhood days," said the *Sunday Chronicle,* to which the *Daily Herald* added, "Unless you are something of a boy at heart, the full flavor of the film will be missed."[61] Publicity releases claimed Robeson's songs were first recorded in Africa and then brought back to the studio where composer Spoliansky "modernized the age-old tunes, and elaborated them, gradually shaping them into . . . beautifully orchestrated melodies."[62] Something evidently was lost in the translation, as critics praised Robeson's singing but poked fun at the songs ("the silliest lyrics ever escaped from the limbo of post-war song scenes") and the incongruous manner in which they were sandwiched into this adolescent yarn: Robeson "addresses the distant mountains and listens to his own echo, suddenly accompanied by a symphony orchestra of some dozen pieces popping out rather remarkably on the edge of the world."[63]

Clearly, Robeson still had not grasped some basic tenets of the genre. One was that, although Empire films stressed authenticity, they did so for the sake of entertainment and high drama, their major selling points. It was the exotic, strange, and terrifying qualities of Africa that *King Solomon's Mines* sought to replicate. Even films like *Song of Freedom* (which Robeson personally always liked), which managed to avoid a blatantly proimperialistic thrust, were riddled with a British, Western bias in that their plots invariably focused on white characters or on Africans like John Zinga, British in outlook and orientation.[64] Unfortunately, unlike Essie who personally observed the devastating effects of British colonialism, Robeson, in his self-imposed role as arbiter for the African point of view, was hampered by his lack of firsthand knowledge of the life and culture of the people he sought to portray. By October 1936 even the friendly British had begun to weary of Robeson's proselytizing in behalf of a continent he could never find time to visit. When the news broke that Paul would begin work on yet another African-set film (*Jericho*, 1938), *Picturegoer* commented: "This will be the fourth British film featuring Paul Robeson in an African setting in which he has avoided the irksome necessity of entering the Dark Continent and has had Africa brought to the studio for his convenience."[65]

Like others who visited South Africa (including the black actor Robert Adams, who was compelled to undergo six weeks of demeaning investigation by government officials before being allowed into the country to film a portion of *King Solomon's Mines*), Essie's experiences quickly disabused her of any romantic ideas she might have had of the "dark Continent." Whether describing the "dreaded pick-up vans . . . a cross between a dog-catcher's wagon and a police patrol wagon" that seized "natives" without a pass or permit, South Africa's rigid segregation of the races, the "reserves" to which "natives" were confined, or the South African mining industry, there was little sentimentality in her observations. "We saw a mine train, this time coming up from Johannesburg with its tragic burden of Africans who have served their time in the mines. Some broken in health, some with the beginnings of the dreaded phthisis. . . . Many hanging out of the train windows drinking in the sun and air. All with the pathetic little cash which will be eaten up by taxes and fees."[66] If Robeson chose to involve himself time and again in melodramatic and unrealistic films, projects that paid well but failed in the one area he repeatedly said most mattered to him—to "show the greatness of the African native in his natural home"— perhaps it was because they reflected his own romantic and somewhat naive attachment to Africa.[67]

As much as anything, the pace of Robeson's work prohibited the kind of reflection needed for any reasoned evaluation of proposed film projects. Once *King Solomon's Mines* was completed, for example, he began work almost immediately on yet another film. The most, perhaps, that can be said for *Big Fella,* as one critic later put it, was that Paul was "not playing a half-naked African chief."[68] As with *Song of Freedom,* James Elder Wills directed, Eric Ansell composed the music, and Elisabeth Welch costarred.[69] Essie played a small role (a hotel proprietress), as did Larry Brown (the script called for many black extras), which may have in part accounted for Robeson's decision to do the film.[70]

Based on a novel by Claude McKay, Fenn Sherie and Ingram d'Abbes's script was another contrived and sentimental story. Robeson plays the hero, Banjo, a happy-go-lucky dockside worker who is asked by police to help search for the only child of wealthy parents, who is believed to be lost or kidnapped in Marseilles. Banjo agrees after learning there is a sizable reward for the boy's return and finds the child, neither lost nor kidnapped but run away in search of adventure. Through many twists and turns of plot and the conniving of the white "tough," Dengal, Banjo befriends the young boy, sees to it he is returned home safely, and finally collects his rightful reward. Robeson did insist that the dialogue make it clear that Banjo worked for a living, and script writers, perhaps taking their cue from Robeson, changed the title of the film from the original *Banjo* to *Big Fella,* as the former "might lead audiences to expect a sort of 'Uncle Sambo' of the cotton plantations."[71] The film earned middling reviews (even Robeson's singing was not enough to carry it), and it faded into oblivion shortly after its opening at the British Lion Trade Show in June 1937.[72]

16

Russian Romance

1936-1937

"Some day soon I shall write at length, in the context of my life story, about the meaningful experiences I have had with the Jewish people," Robeson wrote in 1954. Although Robeson never did this, the need he felt in middle age to gather and explain in writing these experiences attests to their importance in his life. Robeson told one friend that he "had always felt an almost mystical connection" to Jewish people. The roots of this connection go back to his childhood—to memories of Sam Woldin, a Russian Jew, who extended kindness and friendship to his father; of his father and his brother Ben reading Hebrew together; and of the spirituals themselves, songs as much a part of Paul's childhood as the air he breathed, songs that directly identified the suffering of blacks with that endured by Hebrew slaves.[1]

Subsequent events in Robeson's life would only solidify this bond. In 1915, the year Robeson entered Rutgers, Leo Frank, a Jewish businessman convicted of raping a white factory worker, was lynched by angry white Southerners. Robeson witnessed the anti-Semitism of Rutgers students, and at Rutgers was allowed to room with Herbert Miskend, presumably because Miskend's Jewishness made him less than white. At Narragansett Robeson met young Jewish women who were not ashamed to socialize with blacks, and in Harlem he fell in love with and married Eslanda Cardozo Goode, who was Spanish, Jewish, and black. Throughout his artistic career he witnessed and benefited from the generosity of Jewish philanthropists like Joel and Amy Spingarn, Julius Rosenwald, and Otto Kahn, and he often acknowledged to friends in interviews how much Jews had helped him in his early days. The Jewish press, both Yiddish and English-language publications, followed Robeson's early career and lavished praise on him for his musical genius and devotion to the race. That same press, evidencing its deep interest in race and racism, regularly published news of race riots, lynchings, and legal decisions related to race.[2]

As early as 1927 in an interview with the *Jewish Tribune*'s Sulamith Ish-Kishor, Robeson spoke about the cultural kinship between blacks and Jews (a theme he would refer to throughout his career) and sang the spiritual "Go Down, Moses" to illustrate his point. By the 1930s Robeson had begun to add Yiddish songs like "Schlof Mein Kind" ("Sleep My Child") and the Hebrew "Hasidic Chant" to his repertoire. Finally, his business manager, lawyer, and trusted friend, Robert Rockmore, was also Jewish.[3]

Hitler's campaign to exterminate Jews would deeply affect Robeson. After assuming power in 1933 Hitler immediately took steps to restrict the rights of Germany's Jews by enacting the first government-sanctioned act of persecution—the boycott of Jewish businesses. In 1935 the Nuremberg Laws stripped German Jews of all political and civil rights, and by the year's end 75,000 Jews had fled Germany. After November 9, 1938—Kristallnacht, the "Night of Broken Glass"—any Jew who didn't leave Germany would eventually be confined to concentration camps.

Initially Robeson was ignorant of the plight of the German Jews, but as early as 1933 Marie Seton forced the issue on him when she introduced him to Frederick Kuh, an American news correspondent who had recently fled Germany fearing reprisals for a story he had done on the notorious Reichstag fire. Kuh's immediate problem was that he needed work and he hoped to land an interview with Robeson through Marie Seton's intervention. When they met, Kuh told Robeson about what had been going on in Germany and the subject of the conversation shifted from Robeson to those events. It was Robeson who plied Kuh with questions. In the months that followed, the several thousand German Jewish refugees who arrived in London confirmed Kuh's narrative. Seton, a member of a committee headed by H. G. Wells that had been formed in 1933 to assist the refugees, asked Andre Van Gyseghem and Roland Adam if they would give a benefit matinee performance of *All God's Chillun,* at the time playing at the Piccadilly, to help raise money for the refugees. Both willingly agreed. But when Seton approached Paul about the benefit, he surprised her by hesitating. "I'm an artist. I don't understand politics," he told her. Seton pressed on. Focusing on the issue of race, she asked Paul directly: "Do you think people will let you forget you are a Negro as long as there is racial prejudice?" According to Seton, only then did Paul agree to do the benefit.[4]

By 1936, however, Robeson was less circumspect, and when Hans Ernst Meier, a German Jewish musician, refugee, and chairman of a group of Jewish expatriates committed to exposing the truth about Nazism, asked him for assistance Robeson "was immediately favorable to the idea," Meier recalled, "and agreed to give us a £30 donation, at the time a colossal sum to us. 'I as a Negro and all my fellow blacks are oppressed,' he told me. 'What Hitler is doing in Germany is the same thing—perpetuating racial hatred. We Negroes must join those who oppose racialist, warlike, and oppressive Nazism. You can always count on my help and solidarity.' His donation proved decisive. The journal [*Germany Today: Inside Germany*] made its debut and was surprisingly successful."[5]

Interviewed by Nathan Krems of the *Jewish Transcript* just after passage of the Nuremberg Laws in 1935, Robeson said that one reason he felt so close to Jews was because "the Negro and the Jew have the same problem," the same enemy: fascism. Few events illustrated this common bond more dramatically than two great athletic contests that occurred in 1936: the June heavyweight boxing bout at Yankee Stadium between Joe Louis (the Brown Bomber) and the German Max Schmeling, and the Summer Olympics held in Berlin six weeks later. When Schmeling beat Louis in twelve rounds the Nazis crowed that no "Schwärz" could ever defeat a fine Aryan, and Minister of Propaganda Joseph Goebbels proclaimed Schmeling's victory a triumph for Hitlerism and proof of Aryan superiority.[6] Six weeks later the Olympics were held in Berlin. Liberals in Great Britain, France, and the United States urged athletes representing the Western democracies to boycott the event, and some, like the Jewish sprinter Herman Neugass and the predominantly Jewish Long Island University basketball team, did. Athletes who did choose to compete reasoned that the games would not only provide an opportunity to display their prowess but would strike a blow at German arrogance as well.[7]

Hitler intended to use the Olympics to showcase Nazi achievement, and in this context the outcome of the games was politically significant. Although German athletes would win the most gold (33) as well as silver and bronze medals and surpass the second-place Americans by a full 57 points, in track-and-field events black American athletes, ten of whom won medals, beat back the German challenge. Led by the phenomenal Jesse Owens, who himself earned four gold medals and shattered two world records in the process, these black athletes amassed another three gold medals and a total of six silver and bronze medals. Although anti-Semitic signs had been temporarily removed for the games and token Jews (the fencer Helene Mayer and the hockey star Rudi Ball) allowed to represent the Reich, Hitler's hatred of the Jews was well known. Also understood was that he viewed blacks with equal animosity and disdain. Thus the victories of black American athletes were more than athletic achievements; they decisively countered Hitler's notions of racial superiority.

Joe Andrews remembered that Robeson followed the 1936 Olympics closely: "Not only was he interested in seeing Hitler humiliated, but Paul's friend, Fritz Pollard's son, Fritz Pollard Jr., was among the eighteen black athletes competing. He was delighted to see how well the black American athletes performed and especially pleased that Pollard's son did well." (Pollard won a bronze medal in the 110-meter high hurdles).[8]

The Berlin Games made Jesse Owens a household name throughout the world and America's newest idol, but even an achievement of this magnitude did not change American racial realities. Robeson understood this better than most, and Owen's experience returning home to the United States reinforced the point that although fascism was the enemy, the Western democracies continued to be guilty also of their own long history of racist behaviors. Jesse Owens's family — his parents, brother, and wife — traveled from Cleveland to New York to welcome Owens, but they were then denied accommodations in hotel after hotel. They were able to secure a room only after Cleveland city councilman Herman Finckle, in New York himself to greet Owens, heard about the Owenses' difficulties and intervened on their behalf. Finckle vacated his own room at the Hotel New Yorker and transferred to the Hotel Pennsylvania on the condition that the Pennsylvania also admit the Owenses.[9]

As the international situation worsened Robeson's interest in the Soviet Union intensified. He had been reading Sidney and Beatrice Webb's glowing account of Soviet life, *Soviet Communism: A New Civilization?* enthusiastically, making copious notes in the margins; on a short trip to the Soviet Union in the summer of 1936 he spent an "idyllic few days" with friends who were filming on location on a collective farm some distance from Moscow.[10] Once again he was struck by Russia's treatment of its minorities and its complete absence of racial prejudice.

If initially it was the idea of freedom — freedom for himself and others to pursue their talents unencumbered by race — that endeared the Soviet Union to Robeson, it was now the realization that the Soviet Union most exemplified the shape a world without fascism and racial oppression might take. Russia, alone among the Western democracies, made bigotry of any kind a punishable crime. And looking at Russia, as Langston Hughes put it, "through Negro eyes," Robeson carefully observed how Russia treated its Jewish and non-European populations. "How can the Siberian Yakut have universities, take an important part in the great industrial and social development of the Union, while his distant cousin, the American Indian, is so unadaptable that he must languish on reservations until he dies out. . . . The answer obviously lies in the tremendous differences in the very foundations of the contrasted societies."[11]

For some time Robeson had been considering sending Pauli to the Soviet Union to be educated and by 1936 he began actively pursuing the possibility. Robeson felt that the combined effects of racial slights, Pauli's atypical foreign schooling with private tutors hand picked by his parents, and the burden of having a famous father had made his son an outsider, "shy and sensitive" with few friends. Feeling by contrast and in retrospect the racism he had been subjected to all his life and wanting something better for his son, Robeson saw Russia as a racially safe, nurturing environment — one in which his son would find an understanding of his position as "a member of one of the most oppressed of human groups" and the only one that he would fully trust with the education of his son.[12]

Juggling the demands of their own careers and what they thought was best — socially, emotionally, and intellectually — for their son had always been a problem for the Robesons. For the past two years Pauli had been living with his grandmother, attending various schools in New York. Paul had wanted his son "to go to America at regular intervals, so he will know his own people" and Essie agreed but with the caveat that his manners remain "perfect, and charming." The plan had been to get him settled in a school in the United States and have him spend summers with his parents. It was a difficult arrangement. Essie kept in close contact with her mother by letter, fretting over Pauli and overseeing the smallest details of his day-to-day life. "We seriously are worried about his wet bathing suits, his wet bedroom slippers, his unbrushed hair," she wrote her mother in 1935. "I am wild about his going swimming with only older pupils. . . . I don't care what anyone else thinks about it; I never want Pauli to go swimming, so long as I can control him, unless there is a good life guard . . . on duty. . . . We don't like the incident of the glasses of milk at 6 p.m. That means irregular meals. . . . We all know that if he puts on a damp bathrobe, wears wet leather shoes about, and has irregular meals, that very soon he will slip right back into semi health."[13]

Robeson was far less concerned with Pauli's health than he was with his exposure to or experience of racial slights, and for this reason was unhappy with having Pauli continue his education in the United States or even in Britain for that matter. There had been incidents in the United States but it was something that happened in England during the filming of *Sanders* that permanently shook Robeson's confidence in Western democracies and their ability to provide the racial environment he wanted for his son. Essie and Pauli were staying near the filming location in Beaconsfield, and Pauli spent much of his time playing with nearby white children. After a couple of days the white children were told by their nurse (who did not know that Pauli was Robeson's son) not to play with Paul Jr. Thus suddenly and for no apparent reason Paul Jr. found himself excluded. "The children's parents," Paul explained, "came from India and that's why they were so color conscious. An incident like that happening to your child must wound you very deeply," Robeson continued, "and the worst thing would be the inability to do anything about it." How Pauli reacted is unclear, but for

Robeson the incident was deeply upsetting, reviving old feelings of helplessness and hurt, and he told the story repeatedly in press interviews and at some time to almost all his close friends.[14]

The Robesons talked the matter over at length together and with friends, and they sought out the advice of people like Peggy and Eugene Dennis, American Communists who had themselves left their young son, Tim, in Russia while they traveled, performing their Communist duties. Peggy Dennis recalled that Essie "had some doubts" about the idea. In the case of political or military turmoil would they have any difficulty getting Pauli out? Although Gene Dennis, who did most of the talking that night, would not say directly that they had anything to worry about, he did urge Essie that, should they decide in the affirmative, "to make it publicly well-known and be sure the practical arrangements are such that you can take him home whenever you wish."[15]

Paul and Essie decided to take Pauli and Mrs. Goode along with them for Paul's Russian concert tour as a way of testing the waters and ascertaining if arrangements to send Pauli to school in the Soviet Union could be worked out. Paul, Essie, Larry Brown, Pauli, and "Ma" Goode arrived in Moscow at the end of December and at the height of the New Year festivities. In Moscow the mood was optimistic. The Soviet government had taken pains to publicize the host of new projects completed in 1936: the straightening and widening of the city's narrow winding streets to a luxurious 100 feet, radically improved public transportation systems, and the construction of more than 150 new schools. Work on the enormous Moscow–Volga canal progressed rapidly, and new projects—an airport for the district of Khimk (about ten miles outside of Moscow), general housing and large apartment buildings, and construction of the Palace of the Soviets, the House of the Commissariat of Heavy Industry, the Academy of Sciences, and the All-Union Institute of Experimental Medicine—were ready to begin.[16] For the second year in a row, giant fir trees aglow with Soviet stars and miniature electric light bulbs lined the streets. According to the *Moscow Daily News,* merrymaking took place throughout Russia, but Moscow with its banquets, ice carnivals, bright paper lanterns, colored lights and rows of decorated booths, outdoor athletic events, balls and masquerades, and abundant food boasted the most elaborate festivities.[17]

On the surface all appeared well. The worst effects of forced collectivization—famine and chronic food shortages, livestock depletion, mounting police severity, the deportation of whole kulak farm communities, the constant uprooting of families—had abated. There was food, and materially life had picked up. From all appearances Stalin's Russia was indeed on the move: after a rocky start, the first gigantic experiment in planned economy seemed to be working as the USSR achieved economic growth at a pace unheard of in the West. The underside of this rapid industrialization, seldom seen or noted by Western observers, was its enormous cost in human life and suffering and, of course, Stalin's purges, which by 1938 would effectively eliminate any potential opposition by wiping out two-thirds of the Communist elite of the Lenin and post-Lenin periods.

Leaving Pauli with his grandmother in Moscow where he would attend a Soviet model school on a trial basis (placing Pauli again in a privileged, protected setting, with Stalin's daughter and Molotov's son as classmates), Robeson, Brown, and Essie embarked on their first concert tour of Russia.[18] Chatwood Hall, reporting for the American Negro Press, wrote ecstatically of the tour, following Robeson in Leningrad and Moscow, through distant Kiev, and on to Odessa on the Black Sea. Robeson and Brown thrilled audiences by performing several selections in Russian, among them Moussorgsky's "Within Four Walls" from his cycle *Without Sun*. The major portion of the program, however, was performed in English. With no translation and thus no idea of what the words meant, audiences responded nonetheless: as one critic put it in his review, they felt the music and "took in the meaning of living feeling."[19] In Odessa, one audience member jumped on stage and fastened a pin bearing a picture of Lenin to Robeson's lapel. In the cultural center of Kiev another enthusiastic worker audience gave Robeson such a thunderous reception that he had to plead to be relieved from further encores.[20]

For Robeson, the tour was the thrill of a lifetime. He loved the "responsiveness and give-and-take attitude" of the Russians, who made their counterparts in the bourgeois world seem stiff and bland by comparison. "It seemed to me that I had close contact with a people who are themselves still close to their own folk traditions," Robeson said of the Soviets. "Coming here is like coming to another world; leaving it is like leaving a special, new and fresh air, the like of which nowhere else in the world exists. . . . In America I always feel that I am giving something and receiving nothing in return."[21]

One of the things Robeson received "in return" was an appraisal of his spirituals unlike anything he had ever encountered in the West. Soviet reviews acclaimed Robeson a "'mass singer'—simple, natural and human," noting approvingly that he did "not limit his repertoire to the dull framework of 'chamber music concerts'" and included selections from Lawrence Gellert and Eric Siegmeister's recently published *Songs of Negro Protest*. "By listening to Robeson one learns to regard the Negro and his art not from the exotic but from the purely human point of view," wrote the *Moscow Daily News*'s A. Constant Smith. "These compositions, reflecting the oppression of the Negroes, are impressive as social documents as well as for their intrinsic musical qualities."[22] William Patterson, in his review, stressed the theme of protest expressed through religious imagery in the spirituals and more directly in Negro work songs. "Bourgeois historians have shelved" the facts concerning the American Negro's history and "circulated a bunch of lies and slanders about the cowardice of Negroes and their worthlessness as slaves" (a situation Patterson attempted to redress by including in his already lengthy review a history of American blacks dating from 1776). "The concerts of Paul Robeson and Lawrence Brown in the Soviet Union are testimony to the close relationship between American Negroes and the Soviet public. [They] permit knowledge of the protest songs of the Negro . . . his rich treasure of revolutionary traditions . . . and especially the material conditions which provide the form and content" for these songs.[23]

But by far the most gratifying and enlightening appraisal came from Eisenstein. His review of Robeson's Moscow concert, intended primarily to teach Russian audiences about this unfamiliar American folk music (and, one might conjecture, to demonstrate Eisenstein's Party loyalties), exemplifies well the change in perspective, the "new and fresh air," Robeson experienced in the Soviet Union. Missing were the patronizing tone, the endless harangues over the artistic merit of these "simple and ignorant songs," and the praise riddled with racial stereotypes that generally characterized Western reviews. In Eisenstein's hands the spirituals emerged as much more than the pathetic chronicle of suffering. They were songs of protest, created by a people determined to fight for their freedom with whatever means were available. Eisenstein dignified the spirituals not only by demonstrating their artistic merit but also by laying bare the unassailable spirit of the slaves who created them. American blacks were not so naive as to believe that religion would somehow miraculously rescue them, Eisenstein informed his Russian readers. Admittedly the spirituals made use of biblical names and places, but they did so only as "coverings . . . [as the] outward form under which are hidden very different feelings." These are "songs which convey the desperate sorrow of overworked toilers and their hateful fury against their exploiters," Eisenstein explained. It was a condition with which most Russians could readily identify. "Hence the loud applause," even with his music untranslated, "when this black giant . . . greeted his listeners in clear Russian, saying 'Hello and thank-you.'"[24]

Eisenstein's review, indeed, the reception of Paul's spirituals in general, proved a turning point for Robeson. Looking at his own people's music through the eyes of outsiders he saw it, perhaps for the first time, without shame or apology. In the past Robeson had paid lip service to such an attitude and intellectually believed it, but emotionally he bore the scars, primarily the shame, of having internalized white American prejudices. Ironically, Robeson had to go halfway around the world and perform before an audience that couldn't even understand the words he sang to receive the affirmation he needed.

The tour proved an exhilarating experience, one that taught Robeson as well as his Russian audiences a good deal about the protest tradition of the music he had been singing all his life. There was no extenuation in Russian appraisals, only admiration for the valor and tenacity of the race. Again, Robeson felt welcomed, not because he constituted an exception to the stereotype or because he embodied Western notions of the exotic primitive but rather because he represented so well the collective experience of American blacks. Although his discovery of Africa had given Robeson a running start on the road toward racial self-acceptance, it was only that, the beginning of a longer journey. Africa as an integrating symbol did not work in the long run for Robeson. While Robeson's ancestral roots were African, his life experiences were not, as friends like C. L. R. James were quick to point out. In Russia Robeson felt embraced for what he was—an American black—without reservation and by a people he respected. Small wonder he felt he had at last come home.

Returning to Moscow, Robeson discovered a noticeable change in Pauli after just two weeks: "no longer shy, sensitive and moody, unconsciously defending himself against rebuff, being an 'outsider.' He was one of the children, he was a member of the group, and he reveled in this great experience. He held his head high; his shoulders back; the children, the school have taken him in; he 'belonged.'"[25] That Pauli's brief time in a Soviet school effected the radical transformation described by his father is unlikely. (One could conjecture, for example, that Paul Jr., who received so little focused attention from his father, would have "felt" anything in order to please him and that Pauli's new sense of "belonging" was much more related to his father than to his Russian classmates.) Without doubt at least some of the feelings Robeson attributed to his son were what he himself experienced in Russia. Almost everywhere he looked, Robeson found confirmation for his sense of Russia as home. A month before the Robesons' arrival, the Eighth Congress of Soviets had overwhelmingly approved the celebrated 1936 Constitution, declared by Stalin "the only thoroughly democratic Constitution in the world."[26] And on paper, perhaps it was. Sidney Webb, pointing out by contrast the limitations of the American Declaration of Independence, the French Rights of Man, and Bentham's "Principles of a Civil Code," rhapsodized that the Soviet document "insures to every citizen, not only protection against aggression, but also the right to remunerative work . . . to specified hours of rest and paid weeks of holiday; the right to unlimited and gratuitous education of every kind and grade; and . . . the right to full economic provision . . . in all the vicissitudes of life." Robeson was similarly impressed: "Mankind has never witnessed the equal of the Constitution of the USSR. . . . Everywhere else outside of this Soviet world black men are an oppressed and inhumanely exploited people. Here they come within the provisions of Article 123 of Chapter X of the Constitution, which reads 'The equality of the right of citizens of the USSR, irrespective of their nationality or race, in all fields of economic, state, cultural, social and political life is an irrevocable law.' "[27]

Robeson saw the Soviet Union practicing its democratic rhetoric not only at home, in relation to its own minorities, but internationally as well. Faced with the mounting threat of Fascist aggression, in 1935 at the Seventh Congress of the Communist International, the Soviet Union reversed its formerly hostile attitude toward moderate Socialists (Stalin had taken heed of the situation in Germany where antagonism between Communists and Socialists had prevented effective resistance to Hitler), adopted instead a popular-front strategy, and instructed foreign Communist parties to merge their efforts with those of more moderate groups committed to fighting fascism. In the fall of 1936 the Soviet Union began sending military equipment and personnel to aid the Republican government in Spain. Admittedly, there was little altruism in the shift in policy as it was aimed primarily at protecting Russia and keeping Hitler at bay. But from the perspective of Western liberals and anti-Fascists it meant that the USSR alone among the world's powerful governments took action to halt the spread of fascism. The unwillingness of England and France to intervene on behalf of the Spanish Republicans confirmed a moral laxity that most leftists, including Robeson, found inexcusable.

As an American black, Robeson identified with the historical enslavement of the Russian serf, the plight of the Spanish working class, and the oppression of Jews much more readily than with the colonial experience of African blacks. "Paul saw only the Soviet Union's tolerance of race and color," said George Padmore. "For him that was it. It was Russia's racial tolerance, more than anything, that won Robeson. Whatever else you might say, Soviet leaders dealt with any manifestation of racial chauvinism with great severity. Paul had never seen anything like it, and it impressed him."[28] Fenner Brockway, head of the Independent Labour Party, bluntly said much the same: "Robeson never was an African and for that reason never fully understood our position. So naturally he went along with the popular front."[29]

C. L. R. James remembered his disappointment over losing Robeson as a supporter of the anti-imperialist cause:

Paul showed such intense interest in Africa during the early 1930s, I was sure he would eventually join us in the fight against British colonialism. He was such a giant, and we expected and hoped for so much from him. But, in truth, he was not a colonial and never really understood British imperialism. In fact, it took him a long time to grasp the damage done by a movie like *Sanders of the River*. Russia really changed Robeson, and that meant the end for us. Of course, everything we were saying would become clear by the time of the neutrality pact, but before that, anyone who dared oppose the united front was condemned as a Trotskyist, myself included! Paul was an American and a Westerner, not an African. As an American I don't think he understood what the British had done in the colonies and how wrong it all was, even though it was so like his own situation in America.[30]

Thus, in a January broadcast over Moscow radio, quoting an editorial that appeared in the November issue of *Crisis,* Robeson pointed out direct parallels between the plight of the Spanish people and that of the poor, landless, and disenfranchised around the world. "Their country is being ravished, fathers, sons, defenseless civilians murdered by the invading hordes of the intervention cynically condoned by some democratic European states which scarcely lift a finger to prevent the commission of this crime against humanity. . . . I regard it as of the greatest importance that the Negro peoples of the world should fully appreciate the many times repeated statement that 'the Spanish people are defending the whole of society against the ravages of the fascist hordes.'" For the first time, Robeson spoke of the need for personal involvement in political affairs. "We, as a people, can no longer be indifferent to international events. It is to our vital interests that we should range ourselves on the side of the democratic forces of the world today, particularly those forces which are leading the struggle for peace against war, for collective security against the wars of aggression, for freedom and against the new slavery."[31]

Ironically, events that so impressed Robeson—the ratification of the landmark 1936 Constitution and Russia's intervention in Spain—occurred almost coincidentally with one of the most famous of Moscow's purge trials, that of the old Bolsheviks Zinoviev, Kamenev, and other "Zinovievites" accused of indirectly instigating the assassination of the Communist leader and Politburo member Sergei Kirov in December 1934. Although not one piece of material evidence was produced at the trial, all but one of the prisoners publicly confessed their guilt in court, and all were shot.

Robeson, like most Western observers, knew of the trials. The names of the accused were well publicized and the trials carefully covered in the Soviet press. Foreign journalists and diplomats were invited to attend and many published reports, a surprising number concluding that on the whole the trials were conducted fairly.[32] From his film experiences, Robeson knew better than most how easily words, images, and even truthful facts could be manipulated to create what amounted to lies. Although Robeson would not have, at this point, used the word "exploitation" to describe his film experiences, he had learned how his image could be manipulated to serve very different purposes from what he might have intended.

In fact, this and the other "show" trials were staged for public consumption and carefully crafted to prove the existence of an anti-Stalin conspiracy and thus set the stage for the Great Purges of 1937–38. The trials were held in the October Hall of the Trade Union House, a small hall chosen in preference to the much larger Hall of Columns, the setting for the earlier 1928 Shakhty trial. The hall had room for no more than 150 Soviet citizens (Soviet spectators — all selected by the NKVD, the People's Commissariat for Internal Affairs, i.e., the secret police — were mainly NKVD clerks and officials) and some thirty foreign journalists and diplomats. Many officials of the Central Committee were unable to attend as were the relatives of the accused.[33]

The presence of foreign journalists and correspondents was essential to the success of the trials. Stalin had himself considered the possible repercussions of world opinion when he ordered the Zinoviev trial and concluded that all that was necessary was that foreigners witness the trials. "He [Stalin] is not impressed by the argument that public opinion in Western Europe must be taken into consideration. To all such arguments he replies contemptuously: 'Never mind, they'll swallow it.'"[34]

And many did. The British Labour Party's eminent pro-Communist lawyer D. N. Pritt, who attended the Zinoviev trial, and the American ambassador to Russia, Joseph E. Davis, were both persuaded that the Soviet government's case was genuine. Davis, after witnessing the 1937 proceedings against Karl Radek, dismissed as preposterous suggestions that the trials were staged: "To have assumed that this . . . was invented and staged . . . would be to presuppose the creative genius of Shakespeare." Pritt, in his autobiography, published in 1966, long after the Khrushchev revelations, wrote that he *still* had "a Socialist belief that a Socialist state would not try people unless there was a strong case against them." Walter Duranty of the *New York Times* spoke Russian, had been in Russia for years, and knew some of the accused. Still, he concluded that "the future historian will probably accept the Marxist version."[35]

Soviet sympathizers, like Paul, saw the revolutionary Communist state as alone in ideological conflict with most of the Western world and he explained the unsavory rumors as fabrications of Russia's Western enemies or excesses of Stalin's underlings. Interviewed by Ben Davis Jr. in 1936 for the *Sunday Worker*, Robeson called the rumored "starvation of millions" in the Soviet Union "bunk," and added, "What else would you expect Hearst to say?" His views on the show trials that followed the 1934 assassination of Kirov were equally partisan. "They ought to destroy anybody who seeks harm to that great country."[36]

"You have to remember the times," said Robeson's close friend Revels Cayton when asked about Robeson's view of the purges. "Not many people liked the Russians and *they* were out to get us. We couldn't believe what we read in the

Times; they printed lies about Russia. Many of us believed the West wanted to see the Soviet experiment fail. Hadn't the Allies after World War I sent expeditionary forces to defeat Russia? There were so many examples. The U.S. conducted a red scare in the aftermath of World War I, and Hitler from the day he became chancellor outlawed the Communist Party in Germany. With everybody in the West against Russia the argument that those purged were fascist spies attempting to overthrow the state did have some credibility."[37] Within the Soviet Union one heard only praise for Stalin. Pro-Stalinist propaganda was so widespread — Stalin was the hero, the beloved leader, the supporter of the arts, the savior of the Soviet people — and so rigorously and ruthlessly enforced that even Stalin's victims participated in the cult worship. To those inside the Soviet Union survival often depended on such fawning adoration, but to the outsider the glorification of Stalin appeared genuine.[38]

The racial experience of American blacks often led them to avoid passing judgment on Stalin's excesses, so amazed were they with the government's protection of minorities and its fostering of a raceless society. Langston Hughes in an article published in *New Masses* in 1935 compared the opportunities accorded to minorities in Soviet Asia with the treatment of blacks in Alabama. The United States did not come off well. In Alabama a talented young black school teacher dies because the local white hospital refuses to admit her. In Kazakstan and Turkestan, both former colonies of czarist Russia, complete illiteracy and a total absence of education of any kind had been reversed and this within the space of ten years. "As to the purge trials," said Hughes, "the liquidations, the arrests and censorship, deplorable as these things were, I felt about them in relation to their continual denunciation in the European and American press, much as Frederick Douglass felt before the Civil War when he read in the slave-holding papers that the abolitionists were anarchists, villains, devils and atheists. Douglass said that he had the impression that 'Abolition — whatever it might be — was not unfriendly to the slave.' . . . After all, I suppose, how we see anything depends on whose eyes look at it."[39] Robeson's assessment was similar but went further. Not only was the Soviet Union "not unfriendly to the Negro," but it actually was willing to fight to establish and then protect the rights of its minorities. The Soviet Union's stand on the issue of race elicited from Robeson a loyalty equal only in intensity to the loyalty he felt to his father as a child.

For every Western detractor of Russia there was an enthusiastic adherent defending the Soviet Union as the last hope for democracy and many of these were personal friends of Paul's (Herbert Marshall, Marie Seton, Andre Van Gyseghem, and William Patterson) or people he knew through the theater. In one sense, for Robeson, then, it became a matter of whose propaganda one chose to believe, and with racial issues already tipping the scales heavily in the

Soviet Union's favor, Paul chose his side. Robeson's American concert booking agent, Fred Schang, recalled struggling to understand Paul.

> The politics threatened his business, and believe me, the money was nothing to be sneezed at. We argued about it quite a bit, and I never really did get it. In the end, Paul would always say that he was pro-Soviet because without equality liberty made no sense and because Russia was providing equality for all its citizens regardless of race or nationality. "What good is it that I have freedom just because I am famous and an exception?" Paul asked me many times. "What good is that? The vast numbers of poor people do not have equality, work, or food. People must have that first. They need to live. Gaining equality for the masses may require some temporary oppression and suppression of freedom. If this is what it takes to gain equality for the masses, then freedom must wait. Liberty without equality," he said, "was meaningless."[40]

Within days of their arrival back in London, Paul and Essie were off to Cairo. Perhaps Paul had been stung by newspaper quips concerning his past failure to visit Africa; in any event, for the first time he agreed to work on location for his next film, *Jericho*. As if to stave off further criticism, Robeson assured the press that he "should very much have liked to have gone much further south — into Africa proper . . . but unfortunately . . . didn't have the time."[41] Robeson worked hard, on more than one occasion battling sandstorms in the desert near the three great pyramids where much of the filming was done, but without his usual ebullience. He would be well paid for his time, $5,000 a week, and there the matter rested. From all appearances he wanted to get it over with as quickly as possible.[42] Absent were Robeson's sense of mission about Africa and his characteristically optimistic pronouncements.

If he was once again participating in a caricature of Africans, Robeson was at least less naive about it and more resigned. He looked at *Jericho* as another adventure story, a "boys' film," compared it to a Tarzan story, and confided that as his own son "was mad about Tarzan books," he was sure he'd enjoy the film. (Edgar Rice Burrough's Tarzan, the orphaned son of Lord Greystoke, a British colonial official, is raised by a tribe of monkeys and soon establishes dominance — not because he is human but because he is descended from English aristocratic blood. As one critic put it, Tarzan embodies the white settler myth, "a white-power fantasy of the type 'Rambo in Africa.'") Clearly, Robeson had given up the idea of effecting change through the medium of film: *Jericho* would be an adventure film and nothing more.[43]

Jericho (titled *Dark Sands* in America) recounts the story of Jericho Jackson (Robeson), a former medical student, now a Negro corporal, in the World War I American Expeditionary Forces. A ship transporting American blacks to Europe is torpedoed and begins to sink, trapping a number of men below the deck. In order to save the men, Jackson is forced to shoot a panicked sergeant. Later, his heroism overlooked, Jackson is court-martialed and sentenced to death. Jackson escapes, and his commanding officer, Captain Mack (Henry Wilcoxon), is held responsible for the escape and is dishonorably dismissed and imprisoned as punishment. Jackson's flight leads him and another fugitive, Mike Clancy (Wallace Ford), to Africa where he is befriended by the chief of the Tourag tribe, marries the chief's daughter, Princess Gara (played by a real princess, Princess Kouka), and eventually becomes chief himself. In the meantime, Captain Mack, who is finally released from Leavenworth, sees footage of the new Tourag chief, Jericho Jackson, leading his tribe on its annual trek across the desert for salt. Mack decides to capture Jackson and clear his own name, but once he locates him he abandons his plans for revenge, leaves Jackson to his tribe, and returns home.

Press releases touted the credentials of the renowned African explorer, T. A. Glover, who would head the danger-fraught expedition to obtain the mandatory footage through 2,500 miles of desert, on a route that had claimed the lives of eleven motorists the previous year.[44] A new twist was added with the casting of a "genuine" African princess opposite Robeson. The princess made news on both sides of the Atlantic, and promotional notices played up the innocence of this unspoiled beauty ("as vivid as the relentless sunshine of the Soudan") who had never been away from home and had come to Paris to complete the filming against the wishes of her African chieftain father.[45] Although her first glimpse of Western civilization reportedly "horrified" her (the princess thought European clothes "ridiculous" and "too scanty" and walked out in disgust after being taken to a cabaret), she nonetheless learned Western mores quickly enough and appeared in the film perfectly coiffed, eyebrows plucked, and makeup expertly applied.[46] Her presence added the unique "line" the film needed: a sensual, innocent, alluring, and unquestionably feminine version of the primitive.

If Paul lacked ardor for *Jericho* (according to Joe Andrews, "Parts of the film he even laughed at himself and when the reviews came out he wasn't even interested in them"), he was quite animated on the subject of Egypt, particularly as it related to his anthropological and philological studies. The Egyptian press gave extensive coverage to the Robesons' arrival, and Robeson, in turn, eagerly shared his observations concerning the Egyptian people and their kinship with Negroes.[47] In a lengthy two-part interview with R. W. Merguson, a black American newspaperman hired by the *Pittsburgh Courier* to report on the aftermath of the war in Ethiopia, Robeson said nothing about the film (or, for that matter, about the 1936 treaty of alliance between Britain and Egypt, which ensured a British military presence along the Suez Canal and in several other respects also compromised Egyptian sovereignty). Instead, he talked at length about the historical and linguistic relationship between black Africans and present-day Egyptians. As always, Robeson quickly won over the "natives" on hand to work as extras, who were both charmed and well aware that because of Robeson they had work. Fay Jackson, reporting for the ANP, recorded the reaction of one old man, hired as an extra. "Meestair Robeson he is the vair best man in the world! Not for heem I would not have eat many, many times. He got me much work in dese pictures. Vair best man in the world. We love heem . . . ahhh!"[48]

A high point of the Robesons' time in Cairo occurred when costar Henry Wilcoxon asked Robeson to come with him and visit the Great Pyramid of Gizeh. Their guide took them to the Pharaoh's Chamber located at the geometrical center of the pyramid. There, they noticed an unusual echo, and Wilcoxon suggested that Paul sing a chord. Paul did and a sound like that of a huge organ filled the chamber. When the reverberations finally died out, Robeson stepped to the center of the chamber and sang the stirring "O' Isis and Osiris" from Mozart's *The Magic Flute,* according to Paul Robeson Jr., one of his father's favorite songs. The result was breathtaking. The entire chamber vibrated with an unforgettable sound of unbearable beauty. Paul Robeson Jr.'s comment on the event is apt: "An African American singer had made a connection with African antiquity via the music of the greatest European composer."[49]

Reviews of the film, released in August 1938, gave *Jericho* grudging approval. The *London Times* in a scathing commentary lamented that Robeson had agreed to "assume one of the most ridiculous masquerades and indulge in . . . the most ludicrous dramatics to be seen this side of 'The Sheik.'" Among the many "bewildering things" Robeson was called on to do, the *Times* cited a scene where, "swathed in several yards of Turkish toweling and holding his demi-Bedouin baby, [Robeson] throws back his ebony head and solemnly sings, 'Mammy's Little Baby Loves Shortenin' Bread.'"[50] The black American press was less critical, most likely relieved to see Robeson playing a Jericho Jackson rather than a Brutus Jones. Ralph Matthews, writing for the *Baltimore Afro-American,* looked for a positive racial image and, finding it (Robeson as a "natural born leader of men"), forgave the film its weaknesses.[51]

Jericho completed, Paul and Essie left in the early summer for Moscow with plans to spend the next four months visiting Pauli and Mrs. Goode and vacationing, first at the famous Soviet health resort of Kislovodsk, from there to the foothills of the Caucasus Mountains and the Soviet Riviera on the Black Sea, and then back to Moscow where Robeson hoped to soak up as much as he could of Soviet culture, extend his Russian language studies, and explore the possibility of a Russian *Othello* or version of *Stevedore.*[52] For Paul it would be his first real holiday in years, certainly one of the few that allowed him any extended time with his son.

At school in Moscow, Pauli was doing well, but his life was still far from normal. The publicity he received in the Communist and Socialist press made him once again both a celebrity and an oddity. Robeson himself used his son's progress as an example of the superiority of the Soviet way of life, and columnists like Chatwood Hall could not resist playing up Pauli's accomplishments, even though such emphasis on individual accomplishment was forbidden in the new Russia. The *Daily Worker* and the black American press featured "international letters" from Paul Robeson Jr. to his friends in the West, while the Soviet press and *Daily Worker* regularly published stories and photos of this young "pioneer" student.[53] Pauli's "international letters," indistinguishable in tone from the *Moscow Daily News* and *Daily Worker* "news reports," confirmed that Pauli was a happy, enthusiastic, and racially well-adjusted child. "There is no race prejudice here"; "I can go to any school whose entrance exams I can pass"; "I like it that everyone is so kind and friendly and busy, too, because everyone has work." On more than one occasion Pauli articulated the Soviet point of view on a controversial issue, such as the civil war in Spain: "Gee, I hope the Republicans throw Franco into the sea!"[54] If Paul (or Essie for that matter) objected to the publicity or exploitation of his son, he said nothing about the matter publicly. Robeson did say how proud he was of Pauli, who graduated with honors to the fourth grade during the Robesons' stay. Watching the ceremonies, Paul was moved to tears when his son's classmates cheered him "thunderously."[55]

While the Robesons spent time as a family in Russia, the Republican forces in Spain continued to beat back the advance of the Franco Nationalists. More than any event in modern history the Spanish Civil War captured the imagination of Western liberals, Socialists, and Communists alike and united under a single banner the great issues of the day: defense of a freely elected government against overthrow by an armed reactionary clique, civil liberty and human rights, the universal cause of the poor against their rich oppressors, and, with Germany and Italy backing Franco, fascism versus freedom. Robeson's personal enchantment with the Soviet Union coincided with a period of marked prosperity for the Communist Party in Britain (CPGB) and throughout Europe, brought about largely by the Soviet Union's solitary defense of the beleaguered Spanish Republicans.[56]

In England, before the outbreak of hostilities in Spain, only the extreme left approved of Russia, while most moderates viewed Soviet enthusiasts as starry-eyed and naive. With the outbreak of civil war in Spain, the Soviet Union began actively to cultivate its image as the lone defender of democratic values there, and attitudes gradually changed. Historically minuscule, the CPGB saw its membership grow from 5,800 in 1934 to 15,570 by 1938, a development that had much less to do with the crude propaganda of longtime members than with international events and the apparent logic with which they pointed toward communism as *the* answer.

Much has been written about the leftist politics of students and intellectuals of the period. The rise of fascism on the Continent, the apparent collapse of capitalism, and in Great Britain the profound distress of several million unemployed workers led many to look to Marxist political philosophy for the meaning they found missing in their lives. The arrival of Hunger Marchers at Oxford and Cambridge in the late twenties and early thirties proved to be a moment of epiphany for the undergraduates of that generation and forced many of them to an understanding — however superficial — of what unemployment really meant. In contrast to student involvement in the General Strike of 1929, which many participants remembered as an "exciting" "occasion for a spree," students' face-to-face encounter with Britain's desperate unemployed was profoundly moving. For many, it was their first significant contact with workers and it left them overwhelmed by a sense of personal and social guilt. By the mid-thirties students were not only welcoming marchers but themselves marching with them.[57]

According to Paul Robeson Jr., his father had a similar experience in London in the late twenties during his phenomenally successful *Show Boat* run. Robeson was coming out of a matinee performance of *Show Boat* when he happened upon a group of Welsh miners singing in the street. The miners had walked from Wales to London, having been shut out of the mines by mine owners. Robeson listened to them "and, on impulse, fell in with them." Martha Edwards, a friend of Robeson's from South Wales, described them as men who had nothing left to loose. Their families were on the verge of starvation, and so they thought, let's go all the way to London. "They've got plenty; we've got nothing. We're like a forgotten race." Robeson listened to their story and took the group of men to their first meal in days. Later he helped raise the money needed to send a freight car loaded with food and clothing up to the mining valleys. It was Robeson's first encounter with Welsh miners (before this he "barely even knew there was a place called Wales" quipped Edwards), and it changed him.[58]

During the 1930s some of Britain's most gifted writers and poets, among them Christopher Isherwood, Stephen Spender, W. H. Auden, and Cecil Day Lewis, embraced the intellectual and political path charted in the Soviet Union. The most talented contributors to the 1934-launched *Left Review,* a literary magazine functioning under the auspices of the British section of the Writers' International, a Communist-controlled organization headquartered in Moscow, were young, new to political interests, and emotionally committed to exploring a Marxist approach to the West's economic and social problems. (Robeson wrote an article for the *Left Review* in November 1937, as did Nancy Cunard, Jack Chen, Herbert Marshall, and Andre Van Gyseghem that same year.)[59]

Not only literary intellectuals but scientists and philosophers as well, disheartened by the chaos of capitalism during the Depression, followed the lead of intellectuals like Sidney and Beatrice Webb and George Bernard Shaw and put their faith in Moscow's apparent ability to harness and organize the natural resources and manpower of a huge nation. British Jews in large numbers joined the Party during these years as well (yet another draw as far as Robeson was concerned). Before 1933 Jews supported the Party largely because it stood in opposition to the pathologically anti-Semitic czarist regimes; after 1933 Jews were drawn by the Soviet Union's unwavering rejection of Nazi Germany and its establishment in the 1930s of a Jewish national region in Birobidzhan in the Soviet Far East. The 1934 rise of Sir Oswald Mosley's British Union of Fascists made the threat of fascism distressingly immediate. The Party's reaction to and defense of Jews at the time of Mosley's giant 1934 demonstration in London and to the anti-Semitic incidents that followed, particularly in London's East End, convinced many Jews that their only real future lay with the Party.[60]

Not only did Party membership rise during this time, the caliber of recruits also improved. Many were well educated and financially well off and thus able to contribute substantial time and monetary backing to Party projects. These new recruits generally showed little interest in the endless harangues about issues and policy that in former years had so divided the Party. Most saw themselves as part of an international army engaged in a battle that would determine the future of the Western world: thus they were willing to accept Party discipline, more or less, without question.

By late 1937 the Soviets were in effect running the Loyalist effort in Spain, in particular military and internal security affairs. Russian officers and advisers controlled the armed forces, and Soviet tanks and aircraft provided the little muscle the Republican resistance could muster. In Britain, meanwhile, public opinion on the issue of Spain was divided. Some, albeit a small but powerful and influential minority, from the outset supported Franco as a patriot saving his country from anarchy and communism; the majority, however, backed the Republicans. Initially, many British supported the government policy of nonintervention, but by 1937, after such wanton atrocities as the German bombing of Guernica, public opinion changed. Passionate advocates of the Republican cause accused Labourites of deliberately dragging their feet. Still, the British government refused to budge. In May 1937 the Russian Jewish commissar of foreign affairs, Maxim Litvinov, pleaded before the League of Nations for aid in countering the aggression of Hitler and Mussolini in Spain, but to no avail. The Labour Party fell under bitter criticism — and not only from the extreme left —

for supporting nonintervention. In this setting Britain's Communist Party gained credibility. Even Labourites, with their long history of antipathy toward the Party (Communists were barred from membership in the Labour Party), now began tentatively to reassess their position. By late 1937 the "cause" had widened its circle to embrace not only British Communists and far-leftists but professionals and intellectuals, the organized working class, and the liberal-minded middle class as well.

The size and breadth of support for Spanish relief activities testifies to the passions the crisis aroused.[61] At the national level there was the National Committee for Spanish Relief (chaired by a conservative MP, the duchess of Atholl), which coordinated the activities of other organizations like the Society of Friends, the Save the Children Fund, the Salvation Army, and various trade union organizations. In individual localities the Aid Spain Committee formed the backbone of the movement, and almost every town had its own committee that collected milk, soap, and funds for medical aid and organized meetings to explain the cause of Republican Spain. The composition of individual committees varied, although most, if not Communist Party–dominated, had some Party representation. Many centered around church organizations, and in working-class districts drew representatives from local trade unions and co-op guilds. In other areas, less formal groups gathered to support a common cause. Among the professional class, subscribers to publisher Victor Gollancz's Left Book Club often formed the nucleus of the group.[62]

Robeson was invited to attend more of these benefits than he could fit into his schedule. As a fund raiser he could not be matched, but more than that, he had made no effort to hide his Soviet sympathies: in other words, Robeson was clearly in the Communist camp. "Paul was being invited to popular front functions by the Party," said Herbert Marshall, who had himself recently returned from Russia and was at the time writing and directing for Unity Theatre. "Sometimes invitations came from members locally, from the working-class people of Wales or Scotland, or from high-ranking members like Harry Pollitt. But Paul was not being used by the Party. He was with the Party because he and the Party were genuinely dedicated to the same cause. And for the Party members, it was most definitely a feather in their cap to have Paul Robeson on their side. The probing that people started doing around that time as to whether or not Paul was a Party member strikes me as irrelevant. He espoused their cause wholeheartedly, so what did it matter whether he was a card carrier or not? We were all on the same side, and within the Party we thought of him as one of us, member or not."[63]

In the late spring, while Robeson was still vacationing in the Soviet Union, he was asked to sing and broadcast a message to a mammoth international meeting, by far the largest fund-raiser to date, to be held in June at the Royal Albert Hall and organized by the National Joint Committee for Spanish Refugee Children. The event promised to dwarf all previous demonstrations and boasted the support of a wide political spectrum: Communists, Socialists, Labourites, and conservatives, as well as an impressive list of celebrities including W. H. Auden, Sean O'Casey, Jacob Epstein, Julian Huxley, Cecil Day Lewis, Stephen Spender, Dame Sybil Thorndike, H. G. Wells, Rebecca West, and Virginia Woolf. Although Robeson would be unable to attend the benefit in person, he agreed to broadcast a message from Moscow, as would Pablo Casals from Bucharest.[64]

As the date for the grand international meeting drew closer, rumors circulated that Robeson's broadcast would be banned. When the news reached Robeson that the politically conservative council of the Royal Albert Hall had canceled both his and Casals's broadcasts, Robeson made it clear that he had no intention of letting anyone, in particular the Albert Hall hierarchy, dictate how and under what circumstances he could speak.[65] Robeson shot back that he would postpone "taking his son to the Caucasus for a holiday" and return to London immediately to attend the rally in person "because he felt it an obligation . . . remembering the sufferings of his own race, to contribute his talent on behalf of Spanish democracy."[66]

To accommodate the millions of European and American listeners who had been promised a radio broadcast, Robeson recorded a message in Moscow that would be broadcast as originally planned.[67] (Making the recording was not easy. Because he had no accompanist, Robeson had to keep running from the microphone to the piano to strike a note for himself and back to the microphone again.) In the meantime, on the day before the event, apparently unaware of Robeson's change in plans, the council, in an effort to save face and placate the opposition, agreed to lift the ban on the Robeson broadcast (the ban on Casals and speakers in Madrid, however, would remain in effect) on condition that only Robeson speak and that his message be apolitical. They were too late; Robeson had already recorded his message and left Moscow.[68] By the time he reached London, a new rumor was afoot: the Germans intended to jam the relays. Again, there was no mistaking Robeson's mood: "This record will be broadcast from Moscow," he announced with feeling, "and if there is any jamming from the outside I shall continue in person from Albert Hall with the broadcast." He said later, "Nothing was going to stop me from sending or giving my message to the British public on the subject of Spain," and, indeed, nothing did.[69]

The benefit, attended by representatives of more than twenty-one countries, featured noted artists, intellectuals, and political figures as well as a moving performance by fifty Basque refugee children. But among all the celebrities and political notables in attendance, Robeson stood out. Few could compare with his ability to inspire a crowd, and for this event Robeson was at his best. As the reporter for the London *Daily Worker* later commented, his "appearance on that platform . . . was in a way the most significant of all. He was the only man not to seem dwarfed by his surroundings. Entirely at his ease, and natural, he both sang and, brushing aside the Albert Hall Council directive, spoke with a simplicity and power that carried immediately everyone away."[70] The audience, moved by Robeson's hurried trip back to London, his stirring expression of personal commitment, and his passionate twenty-minute appeal for the Spanish cause shook the rafters with cheers and opened their pocketbooks as well. It was Robeson's strongest political statement to date and his first public declaration of his own involvement and commitment.

> The artist must take sides. He must elect to fight for freedom or for slavery. I have made my choice. I have no alternative. The history of the capitalist era is characterized by the degradation of my people: despoiled of their lands, their women ravished, their culture destroyed—they are in every country save one denied equal protection of the law and deprived of their rightful place in the respect of their fellows.
>
> Not through blind faith or coercion, but conscious of my course, I take my place with you. I stand with you in unalterable support of the Government of Spain, duly and regularly chosen by its lawful sons and daughters. . . . For the liberation of Spain from the oppression of Fascist reactionaries is not a private matter of the Spaniards, but the common cause of all advanced and progressive humanity.[71]

The event proved a huge rallying point and an overwhelming fund-raising success. "Handfuls of pound notes, dollars, francs, belgas, Austrian schillings, kroner, lire, roubles — an international torrent of money — poured onto the platform table at the Albert Hall last night," reported the next day's *News Chronicle*. The enthusiasm was contagious, and at one point more than £1,500 had been laid on the table in silver, notes, checks, and promissory notes scribbled on the backs of programs.

An intensely emotional experience, the Albert Hall rally irrevocably sealed Robeson's commitment to Spain and to the cause in general. In contrast to previous performances at Albert Hall, Robeson was, according to Joe Andrews, "actually comfortable, with none of the paralyzing fear he usually felt." He had found a consuming passion: a personal, artistic, and political way of being that would replace the years of self-doubt and floundering with a clear-cut moral and ethical direction, a passion that satisfied his need for a higher calling, a passion that added a new and compelling spiritual dimension to his life.[72] Events preceding the rally, in particular efforts to block his Moscow radio broadcast, succeeded only in making the threat of fascism chillingly personal for Robeson, linking his personal freedom of speech and the larger cause of democracy in Spain. Finally, had Robeson entertained doubts concerning his own influence and charismatic appeal, the response of his rally audience dispelled them. As one of Britain's most loved and respected performers, Robeson could play a decisive role in shaping public opinion, and he was determined to do just that.

17

The World Scene: Politics

1937-1939

Robeson's professional schedule said "business as usual," with his Celebrity Series tour slated to begin in the fall of 1937. On the surface it appeared Robeson was still Britain's "good old Paul." On tour, he went through the paces, his repertoire of spirituals, work songs, popular folk music, and standards like "Poor Old Joe," and "Shortnin' Bread" virtually unchanged from previous years. Audiences appreciated the familiarity of pieces they first heard long ago, in less troubled, less volatile times. As the reviewer for Robeson's concert at Liverpool's Paramount Theatre put it, "Here is an unusual case of an artist who would be criticised [by the public] if he did resort to more originality in the song he presents."[1]

But, in fact, Robeson's focus had shifted radically. The "cause" now overshadowed all other considerations and once committed, Robeson crusaded at a frantic pace. He had discovered more than the purpose and the spiritual dimension he complained had been missing from his life. After struggling for over twenty years to earn legitimacy and respect, he had found it, unexpectedly, in the political arena. Battling on behalf of the cause, Robeson shared the stage with intellectuals and members of Parliament and was embraced by Socialists and Labourites despite his Communist Party leanings. Whether he spoke, sang, or simply lent his gigantic presence, Robeson felt accepted and his ideas taken seriously. It was a powerful experience, one that he had been waiting for all his life.

On December 19 Robeson took part in another gigantic Albert Hall rally, which occurred on the eve of one of the few Republican victories of the war, the capture of Teruel, a provincial capital in Aragón situated some 200 miles east of Madrid. The three-hour gathering, sponsored by the Labour Party, drew a record crowd of 12,000, too large for even the cavernous Albert Hall to accommodate, thus necessitating an overflow meeting at Hammersmith Town Hall.

"It was just like the old days in the Albert Hall last night, the days when there was a conscience in the land and vast crowds . . . assembled to show Britain stood on the side of democracy and freedom," reported Hannen Swaffer.[2]

Although Britain's policy of strict neutrality made political participation in Spanish affairs by British citizens illegal, a growing number of Britons had elected to ignore official policy and do whatever they could to support the Republican cause. Among these were the leaders of this rally—Labourite MPs Clement Attlee (after whom a battalion in the International Brigade had been named), the diminutive, fiery redhead Ellen Wilkinson, and Philip Noel-Baker, all recently returned from the Spanish front. Labour Party leadership was adamant in its opposition to joining forces with Communists, bitterly recalling the Party's attempts to destroy Labour in the late 1920s and early 1930s and convinced that Party members would again oppose Labour when it best served their purposes. Nonetheless a minority of Labour leaders—Labour members from North Lambeth, Stafford Cripps, Aneurin Bevan, and George Strauss, as well as Atlee, Wilkinson, and Noel-Baker—repeatedly risked expulsion by publicly supporting the popular front.[3]

One of the period's most significant illegal and "unconstitutional" acts was the formation of the British battalion of the International Brigade. Its functioning depended on a well-organized operation, carried out in England by members of the British Communist Party, who accompanied volunteers on a weekend trip to Paris (which required no passport). In Paris, the French Communists lead recruits on foot over the Pyrenees and into Spain. About half the British battalion's 2,000 volunteers were Communist Party members; the rest were Labourites, members of the Independent Labour Party, or allied to no political party. Writers, scientists, and intellectuals volunteered, as did many Jews who saw fighting for Republican Spain as their chance to take a stand against the forces of anti-Semitism. The vast majority of British volunteers, however, came from the poorer working class. From all over the British Isles they came: miners, engineers, construction workers, and even the unemployed.[4]

Labour leader Clement Atlee spoke for a large segment of the British population when he told the rally audience: "I have been criticized for going to Spain, but I care nothing for the criticism of the other side. No one need be ashamed of standing for those ideals of freedom, democracy and social justice for which our forefathers fought. . . . Our Government . . . [has] betrayed the cause of democracy." Atlee's speech drew spirited applause, but Ellen Wilkinson's "I bring you greetings from a victorious army" brought the audience to its feet and started the contributions flowing.[5]

The story had been widely circulated that Robeson had given up another engagement to attend this rally, and his appearance on stage, huge and striking, electrified the crowd. "Strike the Cold Shackles from My Leg" and other slave songs drew thunderous applause. The high point of the rally, however, came when Robeson performed "Ol' Man River." For years the song had been his calling card in England, the music the British most associated with him. But this audience heard an entirely new rendering that altered the words and, in so doing, transformed the song from a "white-person's spiritual"—a poignant lament of unchangeable fate—to a strident, unapologetic protest. The finale of the day, it brought the house down.[6]

ORIGINAL VERSION	ROBESON'S VERSION
Dere's an ol' man called de Mississippi	There's an old man called the Mississippi
Dat's de ol' man dat I'd like to be	That's the old man I don't like to be
What does he care if de world's got troubles?	What does he care if the world's got troubles?
What does he care if de land ain't free?	What does he care if the land ain't free?
You an' me we sweat an' strain	You and me we sweat and strain
Body all achin' an' racked wid pain	Body all aching and racked with pain
"Tote dat barge!", "Lift dat bale!"	"Tote that barge!"; "Lift that bale!"
Git a little drunk an' you'll land in jail	You show a little grit and you land in jail
Ah gets weary an' sick of tryin'	But I keep laughin' instead of cryin'
Ah'm tired of livin' an' scared of dyin'	I must keep fightin' until I'm dyin'
But ol' man river	And old man river
He just keeps rollin' alon'.	He'll just keep rollin' along.

By the end of the year, Essie and Paul had decided to go to Spain themselves as a further show of commitment and to offer support to the soldiers fighting there. Initially, Essie had opposed the idea. "Paul is doing some very good work for Spain, here in England . . . singing at important meetings . . . speaking and writing quite frankly. . . . Why need he go into the war area, into danger, perhaps risk his life, his voice?" But Paul had made up his mind, and Essie eventually gave in.[7] Preparations for their January trip were hurried, and Paul worked through the afternoon of their departure on January 21, recording two songs from *Porgy* at Abbey Road. He spent the few hours that remained with Pauli and Mrs. Goode before catching the 10:00 p.m. train for Paris.[8] As American citizens Paul and Essie obtained their visas fairly easily after an initial rebuff (unknown to either, however, the American State Department began keeping a file on Robeson, recording his remarks and speeches dealing with the subject of Spain).[9] Others, not American citizens, who had planned to make the trip with the

Robesons, including Jacob Epstein, Rose Macauley, Henry Moore, and Stephen Spender, were not as fortunate. After signing an affidavit indicating they would engage in no political activity, the group finally obtained permission to study the cultural life of the Republican territories. In the end, however, their visas were denied by the Foreign Office on the grounds that the object of their visit did not fall within approved categories.[10]

The Robesons arrived in Spain on January 23 on the heels of what was to be the only significant Republican victory of the war, the capture of Teruel. Republican troops had easily breached the poorly held Nationalist lines and by the first week in January had captured the town. It was an optimistic time, one of the few times when a Republican victory seemed within reach. Charlotte Haldane, author, newspaper correspondent, and Jewish American wife of scientist John B. S. Haldane, met the Robesons at the train station. A Communist Party member, working clandestinely as one of the Party's agents in Paris helping British volunteers and visitors across the border and into Spain, Mrs. Haldane acted as a guide and interpreter for the Robesons during their visit. It was her job to give the Robesons the Party's view on matters and see to it that they were introduced to all the "right" people, among them American Communist Party leaders, the sturdy muscular Texan, Robert Minor; the Kansas-born son of a Welsh homesteader, Earl Browder; and the editor of the *Daily Worker* in Britain, William Rust.[11]

With Robeson being seen regularly in the company of well-known Communists, the question once again circulated as to whether Paul was secretly a Party member. His close ties to the Soviet cause, his presence at Communist-sponsored functions, his friendship with Party members, and the attention given to him in Spain by Party higher-ups fueled the speculation. If Robeson had openly proclaimed himself a member of the CPGB it may well have soured Labour's view of him: the Labour Party worked with the Communists during these years, but members certainly did not trust the CPGB. "Party membership would have endangered his position and lessened his influence," said Herbert Marshall, who concluded that Robeson was not officially a Party member. Revels Cayton agreed: "Robeson was not a joiner and had no time for meetings and studying Marxist texts. The Party had him anyway. Why should they force him to join?" Doxey Wilkerson, himself a Party member who would later serve with Robeson on the Council of African Affairs, said much the same: Robeson was a free spirit and would not have functioned well within the Party. "It was better to take Robeson on his own terms. It didn't really matter if he was or wasn't a member. What mattered was that he was on their side." Finally, Joe Andrews, whose ties with Robeson were personal rather than political, agreed that "Paul was not a joiner" and added, "Paul was more intuitive in his decisions. It took him a long time to come to a decision but once he felt it was right he clung to it. That's what happened with Russia. Paul saw how Russia behaved in racial matters and as a result was for Russia. Does that make him a Communist?"[12]

The Robesons' ten-day itinerary included stops in Barcelona, Tortosa, Benicasim, Valencia, and Albacete, traveling inland to Madrid, back to Valencia and Barcelona, and then home through France. Driving down the Spanish coast, Essie, who kept a detailed record of their travels, noted only the striking beauty and apparent calm of the countryside ("no sign of war anywhere").[13] In Barcelona the Robesons were met by "an enormous Buick, with a smart uniformed chauffeur and a spruce young officer as aide-de-camp," sent by an appreciative Spanish government for their use. They made their first stop at the seaside village of Benicasim, formerly a resort area for rich Spaniards, recently transformed to a hospital where Paul would sing for wounded Loyalists.[14]

One soldier at Benicasim, an American black from Harlem, wounded after eleven months of fighting, "saw Paul and stopped dead and stared. When he got out of the car, he gazed, astonished, and Paul went up and spoke to him. He said he recognized Paul at once but simply could not believe his eyes."[15] The young man lost no time spreading word of Robeson's arrival (the Spaniards called him "Pablo" and, despite his enormous size, "Pablito") and within minutes Paul was besieged by American, English, Welsh, Scottish, and Canadian soldiers. Robeson sang for them as well as for the wounded in the wards. At the hospital soldiers propped themselves up in bed to listen. Those who could squatted in a tight circle around him. No entertainer of such stature had visited Spain and soldiers "went wild with joy" on seeing him. Brows furrowed, hand cupped behind his ear, he sang "John Brown's Body," "Water Boy," "Lonesome Road," the "Internationale" and the new "Ol' Man River."[16]

It was not until they reached "bombed and starving Madrid" that the Robesons began fully to understand the enormous human suffering already exacted by the war.[17] "Bomb craters in the road. . . . No women or children allowed to enter. . . . All being evacuated. . . . No alarms because they take the bombing for granted and even bet on which windows the raid will break," wrote Essie.[18] And Charlotte Haldane: "Here for the first time we saw the devastation . . . the Germans had used the war in Spain as a training ground for the Luftwaffe and for experiment with aerial weapons."[19]

By this time Spaniards in Madrid were accustomed to hardship and deprivation. Still, they gave the best of what little they had to the Robesons, taking great pains to see to it the couple was comfortable and graciously accommodated. The Robesons stayed at the Palace Hotel — its windows were barricaded to prevent shattering from bombs and its first two floors were given over to taking blood donations — and they were given a "luxurious" room equipped with "even hot water." In the evening the mayor and military commanders of the capital gave a party for the Robesons in the Town Hall where some fifteen Spanish flamenco players and singers performed for them.[20]

Such generosity on the part of people who had so little — whether Spaniards, Welsh miners, or his own people in Princeton, Westfield, and Somerville — touched Paul deeply, as did the welcome from Republican soldiers he met along the way. At the headquarters and training camp of the International Brigade at Tarragona, Robeson passed out cigarettes, candy, and letters from home and then performed at a local church that was being used as a meeting place and club for the British and American battalions and a brigade of Spanish soldiers. More than 2,000 men packed the hall. Robeson sang and then asked the men what they would like to hear. An ambitious young pianist volunteered to accompany Paul as he sang "The Song of the Volga Boat Men." It soon became obvious to Paul that it was he who was accompanying the spirited but inexperienced pianist rather than the other way around. Paul burst into chuckles and soon the whole hall joined him — his laughter was that infectious.[21]

Like Langston Hughes, who had covered wartime Spain for the *Afro-American* from July to December 1937, Robeson was struck by the sizable number of American blacks among the volunteers. As early as 1937 the Party had adopted the slogan "Ethiopia's fate is at stake in the battlefields of Spain" and asked that material aid collected for Ethiopia be passed on to Spain after the Ethiopian government could no longer receive shipments of supplies. Black newspapers — the *Pittsburgh Courier, Baltimore Afro-American, Atlanta Daily World,* and *Chicago Defender* — supported the cause of the Spanish Republic; Harlem churches and professional organizations sponsored rallies; and some of Harlem's greatest musicians — Cab Calloway, Fats Waller, Count Basie, W. C. Handy, Jimmy Lunceford, Noble Sissle, and Eubie Blake — gave benefit concerts for the Harlem Musicians' Committee for Spanish Democracy and the Spanish Children's Milk Fund.[22] When Langston Hughes asked black soldiers why they had traveled halfway around the world to fight for a country the great democracies chose to ignore, some said they fought Franco as a way of thwarting the Fascist Mussolini and others that they recognized that Spanish Fascists were the same as those who oppressed American blacks in the South.[23]

These young black soldiers joined an International Brigade integrated as a matter of course (the Abraham Lincoln Battalion, with approximately ninety African American volunteers, was the first fully integrated military unit in U.S. history. American armed forces would not be integrated for another decade). More remarkable still, the International Brigade would tolerate no prejudice within its ranks, a point of propaganda that Russian army officials made certain was well publicized; thus capable blacks served as officers with whites under their command. A white southern captain who refused to fraternize with a black officer was punished by being demoted to the rank of private. Only after long hours of punitive labor and a public apology was he reinstated to his former rank. Lincoln veteran Crawford Morgan, a native of North Carolina, found the experience exhilarating. "I felt like a human being, like a man. People didn't look at me with hatred in their eyes because I was black, and I wasn't refused this or refused that, because I was black."[24]

The Robesons' official escort and chauffeur in Barcelona, Lieutenant Konrad Kaye, told them about the legendary Oliver Law, perhaps the most widely known black hero in the brigade. Law, a black building-trades worker active in black rights struggles on Chicago's South Side, served as an officer in Spain and was killed at the age of thirty-four at the Battle of Brunete. Lieutenant Kaye spoke of Law with great affection, recalling that "many officers and men here . . . considered him the best battalion commander in Spain. The men all liked, trusted him, respected him."[25] Robeson heard similar accounts from black soldiers he met with in Albacete, Valencia, Mardis, and Benicasim, and soon after his return from Spain he announced he would produce a film based on the life of Law, with all receipts donated to the cause. Never again would he appear in a film "where the Negro race was not given equal treatment and human respect."[26]

When Robeson sang to the troops on the battlefield at Teruel he used a loudspeaker system that forced rebels to listen to him as well. Similarly, the loudspeaker used for his Madrid broadcast (which also would reach listeners in England and America) functioned both as a morale booster for the Republican troops and as a strike at the Franco forces.[27] (Langston Hughes said that one of Franco's tactics for "getting back at . . . Madrid for holding out so tenaciously was to broadcast daily, from his powerful radio towers at Brogos or Seville, the luncheon or dinner menus of the big hotels there, the fine food the Falangists were eating, the excellent wines they drank. . . . One could almost hear rebel diners smacking their lips on the radio.")[28] In the spirit of the popular front, Robeson linked the cause of Spain with that of oppressed people everywhere. "My songs," he said, "come from the lips of the people of other continents who suffer and struggle to make equality a reality. To me Spain is another homeland, because the people of this country are opposed to racial and class distinctions."[29]

Robeson returned from Spain at the beginning of February, inspired "by the doggedly optimistic spirit of the Spaniards themselves," more convinced than ever that the Soviet Union was the champion of the underdog and ready to begin what would be a year of nonstop crusading. "No one in Madrid thinks of defeat. None dreams of complaining," said an inspired Robeson to the press.[30] "I never saw him so completely wrapped up in anything," remembered Joe Andrews. "He was like a Joan of Arc, totally engaged. Nothing else mattered. For the first time since his breakup with Olivia Jackson, Paul was consumed, taken up in something beyond himself."[31] His campaign started on his return, as soon as he crossed the Spanish border into France, with speeches and a radio interview in Paris. Robeson refused to talk about theater or cinema. Spain was what was on his mind. "Je ne suis pas alle en Espagne par curiosité," said Robeson to French journalists, "mais pour apporter aux combatants républicains le témoignage de mon amitié."[32] Back in England his pace never slackened.

Reports from the front, however, became bleaker by the day. "I cannot understand why there are not demonstrations in the streets of London and Paris," Robeson said in early February 1938, speaking on the rebels' heavy bombing of densely residential areas of Barcelona and Valencia.[33] By the end of February, the Fascists had beaten back what remained of the Republican forces in Teruel and were driving them to the east and north, crushing Republican opposition in town after town. By the early months of 1938 the sheer urgency of the situation attracted new support, catalyzed longtime backers, and moved anti-Fascists in general to unite to fight the real enemy. Robeson, like others committed to the popular front, unwilling to be fettered by ideological differences among Labour, Liberal, and Communist Party members, would appear at any gathering as long as it was anti-Fascist — before a sell-out crowd at the Granada Theatre at a rally presided over by the Amalgamated Engineers' Union; at the Empress Stadium Hall for a June evening rally conducted as part of the Emergency Youth Peace Campaign and organized by the League of Nations Youth Groups; in September at a concert in Bristol (where Robeson insisted that seats be priced down so that anyone could attend); and in December at a Christmas party held by the Workers' Travel Association at Charing Cross Hotel where he sang for typists, maids, and factory workers.[34]

Local Aid Spain Committees worked assiduously throughout the year, typically conducting two-week door-to-door collection campaigns followed by rallies held at local meeting halls. Robeson frequently appeared at larger rallies of this kind; his name all but assured a large turnout and generous contributions. At the December 1 rally at the Arts Theatre, for example, sponsored by the Spanish Relief Committee of the Cambridge University Peace Council, Robeson was the star attraction and seats were completely sold out. He sang a piece in Spanish, "Els Segadors" ("The Reapers"), according to Robeson the equivalent of the Catalan national anthem, and another song of the Republican forces and recited two Langston Hughes poems. The rally proved a huge financial success, in no small measure due to Robeson, who, as one writer put it, was "the man who did most to draw the crowd and make a substantial collection possible."[35]

As the situation in Spain deteriorated and pleas for aid became more desperate, Robeson redoubled his efforts, extending himself to the limit, often appearing at two benefits in a single day or following a performance of one of his Celebrity Series concerts with an appearance at a nearby rally for Spain. Although Larry Brown was apolitical himself, he was loyal to Paul and despite his own misgivings was there to perform with Paul as needed. "I often think Paul never had a personal life except when he went to sleep," Brown said, remembering this period. "Paul couldn't say no to anyone who asked his help." Everywhere he went—whether to a benefit, a concert, or a rally—people swarmed around him. His concert tour of the provinces proved a spectacular success, "the most successful tour we ever had," said Brown.[36]

But not all of Britain was happy with the crusading Robeson. The same upper-class audiences that Robeson had so charmed with his magnificent voice and boyish modesty now read, and correctly so, an implicit criticism of them in his choice of performing venues and his support of anticolonial and anti-Fascist causes. The status and adulation these audiences had bestowed on Robeson, he now scorned. Although often indirectly stated, his message was nonetheless clear. "It costs nothing, or next to nothing now, to hear Mr. Robeson sing or to see him act," wrote one disgruntled reporter following Robeson's appearance at the program welcoming the India League's Jawaharlal Nehru back from Spain (admission to the concert was threepence and up): "His [Robeson's] platform is now definitely political, not concert." The conservative *Daily Express* lamented the change: Robeson is "a bit scornful of the coloured actors, singers, and writers called the 'talented tenth.' Anyway, he says, they probably form one-hundred-thousandth of the Negro population of the world."[37]

Robeson performed for upper-class audiences, but grudgingly and for the purse. As always, whether approving or disapproving, the British press gave Robeson ample space in which to explain himself, but in contrast to former years when he carefully avoided offending anyone, in 1938 Robeson spoke his mind in interviews and for the first time publicly stressed his own affinity with the working poor and dispossessed. "I am definitely on the side of the labouring people, because I come from labouring people. I was a labourer myself and ninety-five percent of my people are." Abandoning the emphasis of former years on his achievements as a scholar, footballer, barrister, and performer, Robeson now repeatedly reminded audiences and readers of his own slave heritage. "I have known hell," Robeson told reporters, "because my own father was a slave. He escaped and became a serf-laborer. . . . My first memory is of when I was about five years old and my home on the edge of a New Jersey slum, with a great mountain of ashes outside the window. My father, grown too old to preach, had to cart ashes for a living." In June 1938 he directly attacked the British government's role in labor violence in Kingston, Jamaica, where police broke up hostile crowds of striking laborers, trash and street cleaners and restored order only after 8 were killed, 171 wounded, and 700 arrested.[38]

Robeson received a lukewarm reception and admonishing reviews when he performed on April 3 at the Royal Albert Hall. Critics chided him for a repertoire that lacked the "fine drawn variety of effect that other forms of art bring to the Albert Hall" and said bluntly it was perhaps "exaggerated" to treat "him as a celebrity of the first mark."[39] The sense of not-being-good-enough that for years had haunted Robeson now found expression in his increasing criticism of the apathy of Britain's upper classes and of their unwillingness to get involved. In Robeson's mind they, the privileged, the "Clivedon set," had become emblematic of the problem, conspirators either directly or indirectly with the enemy. The more he identified himself with the working class, the more Robeson understood how little his personal achievement had done to improve the overall status of his race. "I used to think that if I could make a success of my own life it would help my tortured people. I subscribed to the idea of the 'talented tenth.' People said, show the world that you've got something, you negroes, and then they'll respect you."[40] Robeson's experience had taught him differently. While fame and success offered him a certain amount of racial freedom — "I can go into hotels and restaurants where other Negroes would not be admitted" — it had not done the same for other blacks.[41] "If I were the greatest singer and actor that ever lived, it wouldn't emancipate Negroes," Robeson said in 1938. "Einstein is the greatest mathematician that ever lived, but it didn't save the Jews from Hitler."[42]

Finally, Robeson made it clear he would no longer pander to audiences by attempting to sing music for which he had no feeling, by limiting himself to sentimental pieces like "Poor Ol' Joe" and "Mighty Lak' a Rose" (although he did continue to sing these songs on tour), or by playing the African lackey in imperialistic films. Instead, he would add to his repertoire black protest songs like "Strike the Cold Shackles from My Feet" as well as those of other oppressed peoples, and he would flatly refuse theater or film roles that failed to portray "realistically the plight of blacks and other oppressed groups."[43] "I loved singing before the elegant and well-dressed people in the Queen's Hall and the Albert Hall [but] I have the feeling I don't belong there," Robeson said at the end of 1938. He now believed he must make his art accessible to those "who . . . were waiting outside" of his expensive concerts because "they could not afford to go in."[44]

Performing at vaudeville and variety houses as he did throughout the year — the Tracadero Music Hall, the Elephant and Castle, and the Hammersmith —

Robeson could not have been more pleased. It was hard work (three performances daily) for little pay (at an admission of sixpence Robeson had to do eighteen performances before he could equal the salary he would have received for one performance at the Queen's Hall), but Paul was happier than he had been in years. "I am far more interested in appealing to the people by singing folk songs — even sentimental songs — which they like, than in showing off with the so-called classics," he explained in one press interview. "I would rather sing fifty concerts with the right audience than one with a tough audience who want me to give them Brahms. . . . I feel I belong more to the Elephant and Castle. than to the Queen's Hall."[45]

In the spring of 1938 Robeson's crusading for Spain took on a new contour as he began rehearsing for his first workers' theater venture, Unity Theatre's production of Ben Bengal's *Plant in the Sun*. Historically, Communist-inspired workers' theater groups consisted of nonprofessionals who, without funds or theater, performed anywhere they could find an audience — in cellars, on the backs of lorries, on street corners. Enthusiastic but disorganized, these traveling troupes viewed acting primarily as a vehicle for communicating political ideas and relied exclusively on the use of propaganda-laden agit-prop pieces to do this. Scripts followed a predictable format, using cartoonlike caricatures (the capitalist, the poor little working girl, the common laborer, the young spirited Communist) rather than complex characters. Actors spoke directly to the audience, often shouting their message through megaphones, and audiences were encouraged to participate.[46]

Unity Theatre grew out of just such a theater group, the Rebel Players, under the leadership of the Soviet-inspired producer, actor, and director Andre Van Gyseghem. A special visitor to the 1933 International Olympiad of workers' theater groups in Moscow and a Communist all his adult life, Van Gyseghem transformed the Rebel Players and saved it from the swift demise of similar groups, primarily by encouraging the group to extend its repertoire beyond agit-prop scripts.[47] In February 1936, with its 60 active and 300 associate members, the group reorganized, renamed itself Unity Theatre, and rented permanent theater space in a small chapel, St. Jude's Hall, near King's Cross on Britannia Street. In keeping with the Soviet spirit, Unity's new guidelines stipulated that all productions be a collective effort and the names of cast and crew remain anonymous. Like all workers' theater groups, Unity's aims were revolutionary: it would produce plays for and about the working class aimed at making working people conscious of their power and the need for unified action, both of which would ultimately contribute to the struggle for world peace and a better social and economic order.[48]

The core of Unity consisted of Jewish people, most the sons and daughters of families who had fled persecution in czarist Russia, Poland, or elsewhere and settled in London's East End (where they had to fight anew to stave off the anti-Semitic attacks of Sir Oswald Mosely and his British Union of Fascists). The overwhelming threat for Jews was fascism and Unity's aims were clearly anti-Fascist.[49]

Most of Unity's members were Communists, if only because outside of the Party there was nowhere else to turn. Still, as Party member and Unity player Bram Bootman recalled, "While Communists were in the forefront of Unity activities, there was no direct involvement from Moscow. The Communist Party simply took culture seriously, and perhaps never more so than during the popular front years. And we, in turn, took our new politics seriously. Unity was earnest and absolutely dedicated. There was, for example, no drinking allowed, not even from patrons during intermissions."[50] Unity Theatre, despite a strong Communist Party presence, reflected the tolerant inclusive attitude of popular-front politics and committed itself equally to attracting the middle class and intellectuals and promoting workers' culture.

Set against the backdrop of a London stage "strewn with trivial comedies about trivial people," Unity Theatre offered a "sincerity and vitality . . . refreshing after the slick posings . . . of West End Theatres": substantial drama that spoke to contemporary political concerns. Its 1936 season included several strike plays (Albert Maltz's *Private Hicks* and Clifford Odets's *Waiting for Lefty*), a satire on capitalist Britain written by a London cab driver (Herbert Hodges's *Where's the Bomb?*), and a dramatization of the fight against fascism in Spain (Ramon Sender's *The Secret*).[51] Unity's April 1937 production of *Waiting for Lefty* proved a spectacular success, in part because of the timeliness of its opening, which coincided with a massive transport strike that paralyzed London (and won sympathy from some who otherwise might not have understood what was at stake for labor), and in part because of Herbert Marshall's masterful direction. Arriving theater patrons had to push through (staged) picketing taxi drivers and, as if they were being screened by union officials at a union meeting, show identification (in this case, their Unity Theatre membership card) before being allowed into the theater. Inside, posters listing cab drivers' grievances covered the walls, and ushers dressed in working clothes led patrons to their seats. Except for a table and a few folding chairs, the stage was bare, patrolled by company toughs daring audience members to make a false move. By this time some patrons began to wonder whether they were at Unity or a real union meeting. The theater was packed with people standing on chairs and seated in the aisles. When the audience was finally settled an unannounced blackout occurred, the cast members took their places, and the play began. By the end of the play when the rehearsed claque yelled "Strike! Strike!" the entire audience joined in the shouting, even H. G. Wells with "his small piping voice."[52]

Robeson saw the *Lefty* production and was so impressed with the play and the theater group's spirit that he began talking about performing with the group himself. "When Unity's director, Bert Marshall, heard through the grapevine about Paul's interest, he almost fell over," recalled actor Peter Noble. "Paul Robeson. It was just too good to be true. Marshall knew Robeson, but certainly not well enough to approach him himself. Once he heard Robeson might be interested, Marshall contacted him and explained that Unity had no money; the group could not pay him the salary he commanded. But Paul said that was okay. He said he made his money from concerts, records, and movies and that he wanted to play with Unity for the joy of it and for the chance to do something to support the cause."[53]

"Films eventually brought the whole thing to a head," Robeson had said in one of a spate of interviews at the end of 1937 in which he explained his decision to forsake both British films and West End theaters in favor of lending his talents for no fee to theaters like Unity.[54] As Robeson saw it, the British film industry had proven unwilling to let him "portray the life . . . hopes and aspirations of the struggling people from whom I came."[55] "I thought I could do something for my race on the films, show the truth about them," Robeson said in another interview. "I used to do my part and go away feeling satisfied. Thought everything was OK. Well, it wasn't."[56]

Paul had no kinder words for the West End's "trivialities meant for a well-fed public." "I have no room for the Uncle Tom's Cabin type of Negro play. It must be a play of struggle," he said in one interview, "a role with some depth and meaning."[57] In another: "I'm through doing things I've done before over and over again in the theatre. I could get a very high salary in London. . . . But the West End is decadent because it does not reflect the life and struggles of the people."[58] Working with Unity Theatre, by contrast, said Robeson, "means identifying myself with the working class. And it gives me a chance to say something I want to say."[59]

Robeson's frustration with the British film industry had indeed reached a breaking point, but one wonders whether without Spain Robeson would have been able to free himself so decisively from the professional and personal maze of his film ventures. More than any event of the period, Spain cut through the contradictions, defining unambiguously the nature of the struggle. "It was such a crusading time," said Peter Noble, "a time when you wanted to save humanity before it came down over your ears. If you weren't progressive, liberal, or left during those times, there was something wrong with you."[60] But of all the causes it espoused, it was Unity's crusade for Spain that most endeared it to the public.

"Spain was it," said Bram Bootman. "That's how we got the middle class to come to Unity. People in Labour — Harold Laski, Ellen Wilkinson and even the aristocratic Lord Farrington — all were drawn to us first and foremost by Spain."[61]

Unity Theatre's popularity thus grew apace with Britain's mounting political tension. Within a year it had transformed itself from a floundering organization with no assets (the group could not even afford a typewriter) to a full-fledged theater company with a membership of 1,500. The following year saw more expansion as Unity began its own summer school to train actors (founded in conjunction with the Left Book Club) and the Left Book Club Theatre Guild made plans for building a new and larger theater and launched the monthly journal New Theatre. Robeson, along with Unity stalwarts, conductor and composer Alan Bush, Herbert Marshall, and Andre Van Gyseghem, attended the summer school in Leiston, Suffolk. It was a setting in which like-minded leftists could talk, socialize, and work for the cause. The atmosphere was intellectually stimulating and socially relaxed. "We went swimming one afternoon," Van Gyseghem recalled. "I swam out to the raft and there found Paul and Professor Haldane sitting soaking wet on the raft conversing quite earnestly in Russian, a language native to neither of them. I got a hearty laugh out of that."[62]

The November 1937 opening of Unity's new theater on Goldington Street in the working-class St. Pancras district marked Robeson's first formal appearance with the group. The mood inside the theater was both fervent and celebratory as well-wishers ranging from the volunteers whose muscle and skill had made the new theater a reality to celebrities like Robeson, Dame Sybil Thorndike, and H. G. Wells congratulated one another.[63] The not-quite-finished foyer wall sported numerous newspaper and other congratulatory messages including a long note from writer Sean O'Casey.[64] The evening's program featured the London Choral Union (conducted by composer Alan Bush) and the Workers Propaganda Dance Group, as well as a production of what had by this time become Unity's calling card, Waiting for Lefty. Dame Sybil Thorndike, who actively involved herself in many socialist causes, was among those scheduled to speak, with Robeson slated to end the evening with a song. Robeson's appearance on stage was greeted by an ovation that shook the former Methodist church for a full five minutes. His presence was a boost to hard-working activists, a validation of all the causes for which the group struggled, and a financial boon as well — when Robeson performed the group made money. Finally, the cheering waned, and Robeson greeted the crowd. "Thanks. I'm sure glad to be here, and from now on you'll be seeing a lot more of me." With that brief introduction he sang "Ol' Man River" (the new version) and brought the house down. Together with the group's landmark Lefty production, the presence and support of Paul Robeson would become symbolic of the best of Unity's achievements.

Plant in the Sun was a prolabor, pro-union propaganda play, but one with solid characterization and a realistic and suspenseful plot that saved it from the tediousness of so much proletarian drama.[65] Robeson played the role of Pee Wee, a candy factory laborer who tries to organize his fellow workers in the shipping department. When he is fired his coworkers rally to his defense and stage a sit-down strike. The company succeeds in breaking the strike, and in the ensuing battle many strikers are hurt. The violence, however, only serves to mobilize the entire factory, which strikes in support of the injured men. The play ends with the workers victorious, united in spite of the stool pigeons, police, and thugs. "Union talk," concludes Pee Wee, "grows like a plant in the sun."

The volatile "ex-bricklayer and carpenter" Herbert Marshall's direction followed the Russian model and used the Stanislavsky Method, which required that actors familiarize themselves with the lives of the people they would portray before dealing with the script.[66] "The actors do not just learn their lines and cues. To begin with, we have a discussion of the play, its social and artistic significance, an analysis of each character. Then there is a reading, followed by a lecture on spontaneous struggles and their expression in strikes. We viewed documentary films of 'stay-in strikes' in France. We visited two British sweet factories, one very modern, the other more old-fashioned. We studied American magazines with illustrations of sit-down strikes. We made a special study of the dialect of the East Side of New York—and then modified it somewhat for English audiences, but preserving its essential richness."[67]

Rehearsals, which took place at night or on weekends because most of the cast worked during the day, were high-pitched, exciting, sometimes close to riotous, often punctuated with liberal yelling and swearing. The theater group's devotion to realism on more than one occasion left an actor hurt or at least bruised a bit. The script for *Plant in the Sun* called for Robeson to push and shove the considerably smaller Bram Bootman, who played the play's villain. Paul regularly apologized to Bootman for handling him roughly, but in the end realism had to come first.[68]

Rehearsals were further enlivened by the group spirit of cast and crew, without equal in professional theater. Basic to the theater group's artistic and political philosophy was the conviction that cooperative work takes precedence over individual accomplishment. There were no "stars" in Unity. Thus scene changes were made by the actors themselves, who practiced until they could do it quickly and with perfect precision, even with the lights completely doused. Members abhorred elitism, the "star system" associated with capitalist theater, and to that end all actors assisted with the "dirty work" and all were to remain anonymous.

Robeson threw himself into the production and the Unity spirit wholeheartedly, his enthusiasm and eagerness to "pitch in" an inspiration to the rest of the cast and crew. "During the run of *Plant* a roster was printed naming the different blokes who were to sweep up the dressing room after each performance," remembered actor Mike O'Connell. "Paul's name was . . . omitted but when he saw me cleaning up two nights running he said it must be his turn. I said, 'That's alright I'm used to this kind of work.' He said, 'This is a team effort. We act as a team on the stage and that goes for the whole organization. I'm one of that team, so give me that broom, Man.' He was much bigger than me, so I gave him the broom."[69] Peter Noble remembered Paul as a "jovial, hard worker" who "loved what he did at Unity. He swept floors, collected tickets. He played it for fun and was willing to do whatever he could to help out."[70] Norman Bedow said much the same: "Marshall used to write directions on the script. Paul followed them to the letter, and when others would not follow the directions written in their scripts, Bert would scream out 'Paul does it, so should you!'"[71]

Robeson took time to talk with local children who waited for him every night at the theater gates and on more than one occasion visited Unity members in their homes. "Many times after the show Paul would sing. If there was no piano accompaniment, he would tap his foot until he got the beat and then sing. A constant favorite was 'Water Boy' and 'Ol' Man River.' People queued up and we played to crowds and autograph seekers outside the theater after the show; we got good publicity then. Paul wanted no part of being billed, wanted no recognition, but how could you not recognize Paul?"[72] (It proved impossible for Unity to maintain its policy of actor anonymity with Robeson. From a practical point of view, Robeson's unconcealed presence only enhanced Unity's stature, enabling it to draw an even wider, more middle-class audience. In the end, then, despite Robeson's objections, advertising flyers for *Plant in the Sun* specifically mentioned Paul Robeson by name.)[73]

Plant in the Sun opened on June 14, 1938, at the new Unity Theatre on Goldington Street. Critical reaction was uniformly positive, even among those opposed to the group's ultraleft politics. "The curtain had not been up for five minutes . . . before I realized something new had happened," wrote the *New Statesman and Nation*'s reviewer. "One is so accustomed to going to a 'Left' play with a certain apprehension. . . . But you need have no such apprehensions about *Plant in the Sun*. In the first place it is a rattling good play, continuously witty as well as [an] unsentimental and unexaggerated picture of realities in the struggle of American labor."[74] The *Times* applauded the play's "humor," and J. K. Prothero of the *Weekly Review* its "sudden breathless moments of suspense."[75] As one "prosperous-looking, grey-haired Robeson fan" put it, "not only was it better than any amateur show I have seen, it was better than ninety per cent of the professional shows running in the West End now. When I first came, I thought a 'political' play would make me feel uncomfortable, but the whole atmosphere was so friendly that I felt quite at home. It has made me think quite a bit."[76] In addition, while Robeson attracted his own entourage of fans, more than one reviewer noted that he never upstaged *Plant*'s other actors. "Unnamed amateurs who make up the rest of the cast need not fear comparison with his [Robeson's] professionalism. They are all good; it is a tribute to Robeson's genius that, great actor though he is, he never lets Pee Wee get out of hand. His comrades were able to act on a level with him in inspiring unity."[77]

Robeson's physical presence on stage was, as always, breathtaking. "Picture it," said Van Gyseghem. "Paul — huge and towering — the only black actor on the stage. He had that audience believing he was a candy factory worker on strike. Paul gave that role an authority and majesty that he just couldn't manage with the 1930 Othello. And when he spoke — what command. The audience was just spellbound."[78]

In July workers' theater advocates were invited by MPs Ellen Wilkinson, A. P. Herbert, and Lord Farrington to the House of Commons to meet with members of Parliament. Paul Robeson represented Unity Theatre at the meeting.[79] He explained how his personal disillusionment with British stage and cinema had led him to Unity and invited those in attendance to the special Cambridge performance of *Plant* on July 23.[80] The idea of Robeson, a black man, being similarly invited to speak before the U.S. Congress was almost inconceivable. But in England, and speaking on behalf of Spain, when Robeson spoke, people listened.[81]

Paul, it seemed, had time for everyone and everything except Essie and his son. Finally, Essie stepped in and explained to Marshall in June that Paul would have to leave the show because he had other pressing commitments.[82] Money *was* a consideration as Robeson was supporting two living quarters in England, Essie's brothers in the Soviet Union, and Pauli and Grandmother Goode in the United States. He could not afford to perform gratis indefinitely, and if he would not admit as much, Essie would. Whether or not Robeson's early departure from the play was Essie's doing alone or a mutual decision, he left. Perhaps he felt he had done what he had intended to do; perhaps he felt the need to return to the concert stage where he alone was the focus, the magnet, the source of electricity and energy.

Amazingly, Robeson kept up with an overcrowded concert and theater schedule as well as a wide variety of benefit and charity performances, most, but not all, to aid the cause of Spain. By the end of September 1938, only two years since the outbreak of hostilities in Spain, world events had borne out every dire prophecy concerning Hitler's and Mussolini's appetite for conquest. Austria was lost in March to the Anschluss, and in the same month Chamberlain's "appeasement" government was charged with handing Czechoslovakia over to the Nazis.

In Spain, the International Brigade held its farewell party in October in Barcelona and volunteers disbanded. The last valiant effort, the Ebro offensive, ended in mid-November with the Loyalist retreat. Barcelona fell in January and Madrid in March 1938.

Robeson continued crusading for Spain, but with each passing month it became more difficult. Of all his activities the most poignant were those that brought him into personal contact with families of the volunteers he had met in Spain. In the beginning these were happy occasions with Paul delivering personal messages from the front, but later they became a grim ritual of comforting grieving families. While the many noted scientists, writers, and intellectuals who visited and fought in Spain made the headlines, by far the largest number of British casualties were among the working class, many the same people who had suffered the brunt of Britain's economic depression. Robeson's appearance at the later rallies, especially after the Loyalist defeat, meant a great deal to people in those small towns who were now suffering personal losses on top of years of economic deprivation. In September, just before a Glasgow concert, a mother brought her two young sons (George and Eric Park) to be introduced to Robeson. The boys' father had been killed in Spain. The youngsters showed Paul the autograph book Robeson had signed while visiting the Teruel front. Paul spoke with the boys about their father and told them how sorry he was. Later, at the concert, with tears in his eyes Robeson told the audience about the boys and their father and only then began to sing.[83] Robeson's compassion became almost legendary in these working-class towns. His personal contact with local loved ones in Spain established strong ties between Paul and his working-class audiences, enabling him to offer real solace, which he did with great generosity.

Two of the most difficult and moving of these events were the Welsh National Memorial Meeting held on December 7, 1938, at the Mountain Ash Pavilion at Cynon Valley in South Wales and the final gathering of Britain's International Brigade in January 1939 at the Empress Hall, Earl's Court. South Wales had a long tradition of radical political activism, but the outbreak of civil war in Spain coincided with a period of unrest in South Wales coalfields unrivaled since the General Strike of 1926. Since 1924 these mining communities had endured unremitting economic depression, poverty, unemployment, forced emigration, starvation, and the British government's humiliating "means test" (a test that ensured that no family received unnecessary income from the British government). Having lost any sense of political or economic power, miners showed an increased willingness to participate in militant direct action. Seeing their own problems in a larger context, workers identified their class war and fight for free trade unions with the international anti-Fascist cause. Two months before the outbreak of war in Spain Arthur Horner, the flamboyant miner from Maerdy and president of the South Wales Miners Federation (SWMF), speaking at an anti-Fascist rally in Tonypandy declared that "the fight against fascism is the fight for trade unionism . . . one hundred percent conscious militant trade unionism is the most important safeguard against fascism. . . . Scab unionism is fascism in embryo."[84]

Support for the Spanish Republic in South Wales grew hand in hand with the sharpened sense of class consciousness among miners and their families. Despite their own meager resources the people of South Wales supported Spain generously with material goods and often their lives. "We could go to the door of any unemployed family in the Rhondda," one volunteer recalled, "and need only say we were collecting for Spain and without question or exception, we would be handed a tin of milk or a pound of sugar or whatever they had to give, and this week after week from the same homes." Miners from South Wales accounted for the largest occupational group in the entire International Brigade. Of the 170 volunteers from Wales, 116 of them came from the mining industry and close to 25 percent of them were union officials at the pit level.[85]

The special feeling the people of South Wales had for the Welsh members of the International Brigade was demonstrated in the number of meetings organized to honor the thirty-three men who were killed and to welcome back those who returned. Of these gatherings, the largest, and perhaps most revealing of the support for internationalism which the Spanish struggle had represented, was the memorial meeting at Mountain Ash. Five thousand people gathered on that December day to welcome back the Welsh contingent of the British battalion of the International Brigade as well as to pay tribute to the many who would never return. The audience included not only locals from surrounding mining valleys but Italians, Jews, English, and a hundred from Cardiff's West Indian community. In 1938 shared politics made brothers even of strangers.[86]

Robeson was the only soloist on a program that included speakers Arthur L. Horner; the Reverend H. S. Duncan-Jones, dean of Chichester; and the Rhondda Unity Choir, conducted by George Hall. It was an emotional occasion for all involved. Next to the Soviet Union, Robeson considered Wales to be the place where he experienced the least racial prejudice. In addition, he felt a deep tie to Wales and its love of and appreciation for music. The people of Wales for their part fell first in love with Robeson's voice then later with the man who with such devotion championed their causes. As one native put it, "Robeson's politics were the politics of the miners — fighting for the downtrodden wherever they were and working for peace and freedom throughout the world. In this the Welsh and Robeson were one. Paul Robeson was a living legend in Wales."[87]

Robeson spoke simply and briefly to his audience — "I have waited a long time to come to Wales because I know there are friends here. I am here tonight because as I have said many times before, I feel that in the struggle we are waging for a better life, the artist must do his part. I am one of an oppressed race and am here because these fellows have fought for me and all the world" — and then sang to thunderous applause.[88]

At the National Memorial Meeting held at the Empress Hall on January 8, 1939, the roll for the British battalion of the International Brigade was called for the last time. The gathering drew an audience of over 5,000, with the hundreds unable to get seating left standing outside the building. Bereaved family and friends gave mute witness to losses endured. Amid a silence both respectful and chilling, the 412 survivors, some missing limbs and others maimed, marched into the darkened hall bearing flags of the nations represented by their dead comrades. Searchlights picked them out as they marched in and the final roll was called.[89]

The Communist Isabel Brown, a member of the National Joint Committee for Spanish Relief (NJCSR) and a talented and tireless fund-raiser, appealed for money, this time for the families of the dead. Because the Roman Catholic Church supported Franco over the "godless Communist-led" Republican forces, it was ironic that it was a Catholic priest from Dublin who expressed the bitterness most people felt toward those powerful countries and institutions that complacently sat back and let Spain flounder; his speech drew thunderous applause.[90] CPGB chairman Harry Pollitt, as well as Philip Jordan, Ellen Wilkinson, and Wilfred Roberts (also a member of Parliament), spoke emotionally of the suffering endured and the need to continue the fight. Pollitt, in a gesture that would soon prove bitterly ironic, assured the audience of the continued support of the Communist Party, reiterating its pledge to continue "to fight for the principle for which these men have laid down their lives [and to] stand by the struggles of the Spanish people until the cause of peace and democracy has triumphed." Robeson sang; the drums rolled; and the final reveille was sounded.[91]

Robeson's crusading took a new shape after this final gathering of the International Brigade, finding expression in relief rallies for Spanish refugees, charitable affairs, and peace rallies. Early in 1939, he, along with 150 ranking U.S. musicians, signed a letter to President Roosevelt, urging him to lift the U.S. arms embargo against Loyalist Spain, as it served only "to aid the forces of aggression and international lawlessness."[92] In February Paul sang at London's Comedy Club for the annual dinner (attended by nearly all Britain's notable left-wingers) of the Society for Cultural Relations between the Peoples of the British Commonwealth and the USSR. In April he participated in the weeklong peace festival, "Music for the People," held at the Royal Albert Hall, an event that like the rallies for Spain a year earlier drew a varied crowd and featured a program that included Basque children, the Rhondda Valley Choir — the best of the Welsh choirs — the dean of Canterbury, Christian groups, and trade unionists, with Robeson the main attraction.[93] Many reviewers found the Albert Hall festival, intended to portray the historical movement of people toward freedom and democracy, burdensome and disjointed, but Robeson's singing, described by one as filling "the gallery's furthest cranny like a rushing mighty wind," disappointed no one.[94]

In January Robeson began a concert tour of Britain that included twenty-five appearances covering the length of England and extending throughout the British Isles. By 1939 his reputation, not only as a performer but, more important, as a human being of exceptional warmth and feeling, preceded him wherever he went. Stories documenting his compassion were legion. In Sheffield, newspaper announcements before an upcoming appearance recounted an incident that had occurred five years earlier in 1934. A dying boy had been comforted by Robeson's recitation of Blake's "Little Black Boy," which he heard from his hospital bed on a radio broadcast. By the time Robeson performed in Sheffield, three weeks later, the young boy had died. The dead boy's brother told Robeson what had happened and asked him to recite the poem again during the concert. Paul did not have a copy of the poem with him, nor had he committed it to memory. And so, as the *South Wales Evening Post* reported, "wishing to accede to the pathetic request [Robeson] dashed by car to the public library." Finding it closed, "he knocked up the caretaker, persuaded him to let him have the book from the reference department and sped back to the hall just in time to read the verse as an encore."[95]

Robeson sang almost exclusively the fare that had made him famous: black work songs, spirituals, and folk songs interspersed with Russian, Spanish, Mexican, English, and Scottish folk songs and readings of Blake's "Black Boy." "If there is one thing I am proud of," Robeson said in a June 1939 interview, "it's that I have been able to do something, along with others, towards giving this Negro American folk song its rightful place in the world."[96] Robeson had come home at last, to the music that was his birthright, to people with whom he felt at ease, and he relished every moment.

Not even the rainy bleak winter could dull the ardor of Robeson fans. Wherever he went people were overjoyed to have their Paul, this "gentle giant," resting easily against a piano among them; for many, seeing him for the first time was the occasion of a lifetime, and they arrived "in immaculate evening dress."[97] Robeson performed to packed halls. In town after town he was met by hordes of autograph seekers crying wildly "It's Paul Robeson!" and honored with civic awards, receptions, and whatever special tokens of welcome each town could devise. At Colston Hall, in Bristol, Robeson signed autographs for a full thirty-five minutes after performing.[98] In Wolverhampton fans "and autograph hunters swarmed like flies around the giant figure . . . [and] dodged the police, who tried to clear a way for him." They crowded the hotel entrance and were thwarted once again, but only briefly. After Paul had finished registering, a porter followed him to his room "with a double armful of autograph books, which he [Robeson] quickly signed and sent downstairs again to their clamorous owners."[99] In Halifax the mayor officially welcomed Robeson with the comment that he doubted "if there had ever [before] been a man of such world wide reputation" visiting their town.[100]

Robeson performed simply, much as he had in the early London days, walking onto the stage with his famous slow stride accompanied by Larry Brown, looking, as one reviewer put it, "like the Prime Minister to an African Chief." Always Robeson appeared surprised by the "frenzied clapping" that time and again succeeded in transforming the international celebrity into "a shy boyish giant."[101] Reviewers groped for words to describe his concerts, which consistently left audiences determined "to tax the singer's musical endurance" with repeated requests for encores.[102] Robeson responded generously, in Aberdeen singing "at least double the number of songs as encores as were printed in the programme," and in Hull thoughtfully performing the encore "Scandalize My Name" "exclusively to the small company [seated] under the organ behind the singer's back," who had been unable to see him for the main concert.[103] The *Stafford Sentinel* compared him to Chaliapin; in Belfast he was likened to the great Irish tenor John McCormack; and in Coventry reviewers noted that only the great Gracie Fields could compete with his audience appeal.[104] "If you have only heard Paul Robeson sing on a record or in a film you have only experienced half of his art," wrote the critic for the *Cambridge Daily News*. "The other half, that mysterious something called personality, was much in evidence at the concert. . . . His friendly smile, his magnificent yet easy stage presence, and his expressiveness of face and voice, combined to make us aware of something more than just a wonderful voice."[105]

Robeson thrilled audiences with songs like "Loch Lomond," "seldom sung with such beauty of voice and expression," Russian folk and lyrical pieces like Moussorgsky's song about an orphan crying for bread under the old regime, and popular tunes like "My Curly-Headed Baby." But, as always, it was his impassioned rendering of Negro spirituals and folk songs like "Go Down, Moses," the poignant "Sometimes I Feel Like a Motherless Chile," and lighter pieces like "Joshua Fit de Battle ob Jericho" and "Lil David," for which Larry Brown joined in the singing, that most touched audiences.[106]

Robeson's energy never flagged, even though the tour was long and arduous. It would be Robeson's last British tour until well after the war, but no one, not even Paul, could have hoped for a more satisfying finale. Professionally he had never been in better form; personally, never happier. He had reason to be pleased. His achievement, which was summed up by the humorous quip of one reviewer who observed, "There is probably only one man in the world who could pack the Birmingham Town Hall with people and then sing 'Swanee River' to them," was indeed stunning.[107] Within the space of ten years Robeson had succeeded in bringing black folk music and spirituals to all parts of the British Isles. He not only popularized this musical form, once considered child-ish and second-rate, but elevated it to the level of art. And, finally, by virtue of his personal charisma and that elusive emotionally charged quality he brought to his performing, Robeson established between himself and the British, Welsh, Irish, and Scottish working classes a bond that would endure a lifetime.

18

Going Home

1939

There can be no greater tragedy than to forget one's origins and
finish despised and hated by the people among whom one grew up. To have
that happen would be the sort of thing to make me rise from my grave.
Paul Robeson, handwritten note, 1936

I am a citizen of the world as well as a singer, and I have the right
to say what I think.
Paul Robeson, January 23, 1939

In late May 1939 Paul Robeson and Larry Brown arrived in New York, according to press reports, to "rest and relax" and visit with family and friends but, in
fact, they were also there to get a feeling for the reception they would receive if
they returned permanently in the fall. Essie and Paul had been considering the
idea for some time. Both were discouraged and deeply disappointed by the
British government's policy of nonintervention and appeasement. "The Chamberlain government is going to sell out France, and are very quickly moving
toward an alliance with Germany, —even an open alliance," Essie wrote to
Robert Rockmore in March 1938. "And what makes us so sick at the stomach is,
that Labour is going to help Chamberlain do it. The bastards. Which means the
French, the Austrians, the Spaniards, the Czechs, the Jews are all definitely left
high and dry, deserted, and facing Italy, Germany and England, all on the
rampage. . . . Well, we are sick at the stomach, and simply can't stand by . . . so we
gotta go."[1]

Robeson had last been in the United States at the end of 1935 to play the role
of Joe in the film version of *Show Boat*. In the interim, his sense of himself and his
place in the world had changed dramatically. He had acknowledged not only

that England was *not* the racial paradise he once imagined it to be but also that the British government was unwilling to defend basic democratic values. The Soviet Union, however, had won what would prove to be his unyielding loyalty, primarily because of its racial liberality, its willingness to fight the forces of fascism, and the way it appeared to have lifted up its own "backward races." The fact that conservative forces in Britain — those same forces that had abandoned the countless unemployed in Britain's depressed areas — were so ardently anti-Bolshevik confirmed for Robeson that he was on the right path. He no longer identified with, nor aspired to identify with, the elite of Britain's upper class. Instead, he found the kinship and acceptance that had for so long eluded him among Britain's poor and working classes — Cardiff seamen, Welsh miners, railway men, dockworkers, and textile workers. And, finally, he had transformed himself from a performer focused on his personal and professional development to a people's artist determined to use his art, his charisma, and any other gifts at his disposal to fight for causes he believed in.

Ironically, it was the bond Robeson felt with Britain's working classes that led him to take a new look at America. "The miners of Wales, who gave support to the anti-fascist movement, welcomed me when I came to sing in behalf of aid to Spain and invited me into their union halls and into their homes," Robeson wrote in his autobiography. "[They] made it clear that there was a closer bond between us than the general struggle to preserve democracy from its fascist foes. At the heart of that conflict, they pointed out, was a class division, and although I was famous and wealthy, the fact was I came from a working-class people like themselves and therefore, they said, my place was with them in the ranks of Labor."[2] Robeson's contact with Welsh miners solidified his growing conviction that at heart the racial question was a class question and that the oppression of any people limited the freedom of all. By 1936 Robeson made it a point to mention in interviews that he was the son of a former slave and the product of a working-class family. Most American blacks, he later wrote, "were working people like these English workers, like the Welsh miners I knew so well. I tied this all together. I saw the same British aristocracy oppressing white English, Welsh, and Scotch workers and African and West Indian seamen, and the whole of my people in these lands."[3] Looking back on this period in his life Robeson said, "Spain — the anti-fascist struggle and all that I learned in it — brought me back to America. For another year I remained in Britain, and the more I became part of the Labor movement the more I came to realize that my home should be in America."[4]

The *Normandie* docked promptly at 8:45 a.m., and Robeson's attorney, Robert Rockmore, was waiting at the dock. Mrs. Goode had also planned to meet the pair, but she arrived late and missed Robeson and Brown completely. Rockmore seized the opportunity, whisked Robeson off in a cab, and spent several hours in conference with him before taking him to lunch.[5]

A year earlier Rockmore had written Brown that he and Robeson needed to reestablish themselves in the United States. "He [Robeson] has been away so long that I am afraid he may lose his so-called American audience, which, as you know, at best is a very fickle one." After living for over ten years in England, Robeson was indeed more a British than an American star. In America, even among blacks (some of whom he had alienated by criticizing them from the other side of the Atlantic), his popularity did not compare with what he enjoyed in England. In the vote for candidates for the NAACP's 1940 Spingarn Medal, for example, Robeson placed only tenth out of the eleven names submitted.[6]

Now, in May 1939, Rockmore had more to worry about than the fickleness of Robeson's audience. What especially concerned him was Robeson's stepped-up and widely publicized political involvements. Since 1936 the *Daily Worker* had given consistent and glowing coverage of the activities not only of Robeson but of his wife and son as well, and during this short trip to America the paper would feature almost daily articles on Robeson.[7] Fred Schang said that Rockmore felt Robeson "was going overboard" and was "in over his head" politically. "Even this early, Rockmore knew politics could undo everything. It was one thing to advocate a cause but quite another to lose your audience and career for that cause. People didn't come to concerts to hear Paul give speeches; they came to hear him sing. Rockmore felt strongly that Paul's politics would cause him trouble and soon, and said as much to Paul."[8]

Judging from his press interviews, each tempered and tailored to fit the particular audience he was addressing, Robeson heeded Rockmore's warnings and may even have been coached by him. Although Schang was already making plans for a concert tour and Rockmore was finalizing arrangements for Robeson to star in Roark Bradford's stage portrayal of the great black hero John Henry, Robeson never cited professional or financial considerations as among his reasons for returning home. With the *Daily Worker*'s black reporter Eugene Gordon, Robeson suggested his reasons were political: "In my travels in many countries in Europe, particularly in Spain, and having been close to the struggles in China, Ethiopia and the West Indies, I have seen and recognized the essential unity of this international fight for democracy and against fascism. . . . Having helped on many fronts, I feel it is now time for me to return to the place of my origin — to those roots, which though embedded in Negro life are essentially American."[9]

In interviews with reporters from the black weeklies Robeson now concurred with what writers like Kelly Miller and Joel Rogers had been saying for years and frankly admitted his disappointment with white Britain's racial attitudes. "I have the boy in a Soviet school in London not because I am a Communist," Robeson told the *Amsterdam News*, "but because there is no prejudice . . . there [in the Soviet school]." And in the *Chicago Defender* he explained, "The boy gets a cultural advantage in that school that he would not have in an American or British school. . . . My boy is already interested in aviation engineering. You could imagine what chance a Negro aviation engineer would have in the United States or England."[10]

On the subject of American racial prejudice Robeson also appeared to have adopted a less confrontational stance. No longer railing at the barbarism of white America or the pitiful inferiority complexes of American blacks, he said that he anticipated little difficulty because he had come to a new understanding of race prejudice. "I've learned that my people are not the only ones oppressed. That it is the same for Jews or Chinese as for Negroes," Robeson said in a July interview published in all the major black weeklies. "I've found that where forces have been the same, whether people weave, build, pick cotton, or dig in the mines, they understand each other in the common language of work, suffering and protest. . . . I feel closer to my country than ever. There is no longer a feeling of lonesome isolation. Instead — peace. I return without fearing prejudice that once bothered me. It does not hurt or anger me now, for I know that people practice cruel bigotry in their ignorance, not maliciously." To illustrate just how much he had "changed inside," Robeson recounted an incident that occurred shortly after his arrival in New York. The scenario was all too familiar: upon entering an upscale hotel, Robeson was asked to ride the service elevator. "Several years back I would have smarted at this insult and carried the hurt for a long time. Now — no — I was just amused and explained . . . that I didn't belong with the freight . . . as I was the guest of honor at the tea, my hosts might be surprised to see me arrive with the supplies."[11]

The touchy issues of Robeson's politics, racial sensitivities, and history of lecturing fellow blacks temporarily handled, Robeson would test his "fickle" American following with a summer stock revival of an old chestnut, O'Neill's *Emperor Jones* at the Ridgeway Theater in White Plains, New York. For this production the word "nigger," at Robeson's insistence ("Either that or I won't play in it," Robeson said), would be totally expunged from the script. The play, then, would be his trial balloon, Robeson's audition in America after a decade's absence.[12]

Opening night drew a flashy crowd of the first families of White Plains, with a sprinkling of Broadwayites led by the faithful Carl Van Vechten.[13] It was a friendly, partisan group — all genuinely glad to have Robeson back. Reviews abounded with superlatives, and the play drew packed houses for the remainder of its weeklong run. Directed by Harold ("Gig") McGhee (with whom Robeson had worked in the 1924 *Emperor Jones*) and flanked by a seasoned and talented supporting cast (Eustace Watt as Smithers, dancer and choreographer Asadata Dafora as the witch doctor, and Frank Wilson playing the parts of Jeff, Lem, and the native chief), the production showed Robeson at his best. "Brilliant in form . . . still capable of holding an audience in the grip of strong emotion . . . an artist of tremendous almost superhuman skill," said the *World Telegram*'s Sidney Whipple, and the *Post*'s Vernon Rice: "Power is in his voice and . . . the eloquence with which that body speaks . . . has more beauty and poetry than thousands of words a playwright might have given him to say."[14]

Jones earned Robeson the actor the applause he sought. But old friends panned his personal performance in the weeks that followed. All but a select few found it impossible to contact Robeson. Paul gave as his summer address Gig McGhee's apartment in the Village but he was seldom there and made it a point to keep his precise whereabouts as vague as possible. Walter White, the Van Vechtens, and others soon interpreted Robeson's elusiveness as deliberate.

Once again White found himself asked to play the role of contact person for Robeson when he himself knew little more about Robeson's arrangements than what he read in the papers. Michael Novik, director of New York City's Municipal Broadcasting System (MNYC) asked White in May to approach Robeson about performing along with several other noted black artists in a radio broadcast celebrating MNYC's fifteenth anniversary. White's initial efforts to contact Robeson failed. In what had by now become a tiresome game of trying to catch the dodging Robeson, White took the circuitous route of contacting Essie in London, as she could at least be depended on to read her incoming mail. (White probably knew better than to try contacting Fred Schang, who had been told by Rockmore to stay clear of White and other people making requests for concerts that did not pay. "Paul will just give the money away," Rockmore told Schang. "If that's what he wants to do that's Ok, but let him do all the arranging.") Essie did respond, but her forwarding of White's letter to Paul left White in the same predicament that had prompted him to contact her in the first place.[15] (Alexander Woollcott, who wanted to speak with Robeson about Hamilton College's plans to award Robeson an honorary degree, fared much better. Woollcott contacted Essie, Essie cabled Paul, and Paul responded to Woollcott by telegram.) A month later in June, Novik, who still had heard nothing, contacted White only to discover that he had not yet caught up with Robeson. White's response to Novik — "I don't know what the chances are. . . . Write him up at the Ridgeway Theater" — spelled out what insiders already knew: Walter White no longer had any special access to Robeson.[16]

The Van Vechtens were angry with Paul, who had also failed to contact them.

Neither Carlo nor Fania appreciated being overlooked. "[Robeson is] weak, selfish, indulgent, lazy—really if it were not for his meager talent and his great charm he would just be the traditional 'lowdown worthless nigger,'" Fania raged in a letter to her husband at the end of the summer. Van Vechten replied the following day: "The point is about Paul that he only wants to talk about himself and how he's improving and how he is working on new songs and he can't talk to his old friends because they've heard this story so long." Essie also heard from the couple and hastily dashed off a letter of apology and explanation. It would not do. "There is no word from Paul that HE is sorry," Carl reminded his wife. "It's pretty obvious that Paul doesn't want to see *us* very much, or *most* of his old friends."[17]

Robeson's elusiveness may well have been, as Fania Marinoff suggested, the result of self-absorption. He had behaved much the same way on other visits to the United States, and over the years a number of people close to him said he could be "careless about friends." Fredda Brilliant, Herbert Marshall's wife, said that while Essie cared for people in particular, Robeson was concerned about "humanity" and could be thoughtless to individuals around him. Sculptor Antonio Salemme said the same, but more bluntly. Salemme recalled that he and Robeson had arranged to meet in Paris in 1933. Robeson never showed up, nor did he later apologize or offer any explanation. A short time later Salemme ran into Larry Brown and asked him what happened. Larry hemmed and hawed. Finally, Salemme interrupted: "Tell Paul he's a horse's ass." Salemme never saw or heard from Robeson again.[18]

It may also have been that Paul, like Larry Brown who never liked or trusted Carl Van Vechten, considered the Whites and the Van Vechtens Essie's friends rather than his. Robeson's manner, the way he had of making people feel they were important, led many to believe Paul felt much closer to them than he actually did. Whether Robeson was self-absorbed or simply had elected to spend the short amount of time he had in the United States with people who shared his political commitments, Walter White and the Van Vechtens were no longer part of his inner circle. Robeson now found his kindred spirits in Harlem, among an active and effective coalition of Communists and fellow travelers—Benjamin Davis Jr., James Ford, James Ashford, Manning Johnson, Abner Berry, Langston Hughes, Carlton Moss, Louise Thompson, Bonita Williams, Audley Moore, Max Yergan, and Adam Clayton Powell Jr.—many of whom had been waging war for over a decade on behalf of civil rights. In later years, two of these men— Ben Davis Jr. and Max Yergan—would exercise a decisive influence in Robeson's life: Davis as Robeson's closest friend and political ally and Yergan as Robeson's self-appointed political manager.[19]

Robeson had left Harlem and the United States in 1928, just as the "Negro vogue" began to wane and on the eve of the Great Depression. While the Depression wrecked havoc on people's lives throughout the country, it crippled Harlem. Within months of the stock market crash there were breadlines in Harlem that would last for years. Communist recruitment efforts in Harlem, which had failed miserably during the twenties, took on new life during the Depression years. Responding to a massive rise in unemployment, evictions, bank and business failures, and loss of family savings, the Party took direct action on a grass-roots level. It formed Councils of the Unemployed to fight for work and wage improvements (on March 6, 1930, the Upper Harlem Council of the Unemployed held an "International Day of Unemployment" demonstration in Union Square), organized boycotts to protest job discrimination, battled lynchings and police brutality, supported and ran tenant and relief organizations, held interracial dances at the Rockland Palace for CPUSA black-white unity, devised strategies to deal with evictions for nonpayment of rent, exerted a strong influence in local trade unions, and through its legal arm, the International Labor Defense (ILD), made the defense of blacks and their civil rights a key Party issue. With one out of every two blacks in New York out of work, the Communist Party's relentless battling for bread-and-butter issues won community support. More and more Harlem blacks listened as Party members admonished, often harshly, local black organizations like the NAACP, the Urban League, and Garvey's UNIA for their allegiance to the white capitalist conspiracy.[20]

More than anything else, it had been its efforts on behalf of the Scottsboro Boys that earned the Communist Party credibility and respect in Harlem. The Party, acting through the ILD, rushed in as soon as indictments were issued to defend nine black youths accused of raping two white girls near Scottsboro, Alabama.[21] In a battle that lasted for years, the Scottsboro case provided almost unlimited propagandistic possibilities, which the Party eagerly exploited, primarily at the expense of the NAACP. That organization's unwillingness to get involved until it was reasonably sure the boys were innocent the CPU attributed to the NAACP's middle-class bias, a judgment that many working-class blacks shared. In the initial phases of the Scottsboro case, William Patterson, Robeson's friend from the Harlem "striver" days, had worked as a Party organizer in Harlem and several years later Patterson became national secretary of the ILD. He played a key organizational and strategic role both in the unfolding court drama and in projecting the Communist Party as a forceful and meaningful presence in black life. When Robeson and he were in the Soviet Union in 1934 (Robeson was on his first visit; Patterson was there recuperating from a serious illness) they had talked not just about the case itself but also of its larger implications in terms of the racial and economic exploitation of American blacks, colonials, and working masses around the world. Shortly after returning to England in 1934 Robeson had publicly criticized the NAACP (and, by implication, his old friend Walter White) and defended the Party's handling of the Scottsboro case.[22]

The Party's other high profile court case of the 1930s was less spectacular but widely followed: the defense of Angelo Herndon, a nineteen-year-old black Communist charged in June 1932 with "attempting to incite insurrection" because of his activities working for the Party in Atlanta. In this instance, Benjamin Davis Jr., a young black southern-born lawyer, read about the case and offered to defend Herndon for no fee. Davis contacted the ILD, in whose hands Herndon had placed his defense, and the organization agreed to let Davis serve as counsel. The trial ended on January 18, 1933, with the all-white jury finding Herndon guilty and sentencing him to an eighteen-to-twenty-year prison term. Davis continued to fight on Herndon's behalf, and in 1937 the Georgia verdict was reversed on appeal when the Supreme Court declared Georgia's insurrection law unconstitutional.[23]

Robeson and Davis had first met sometime in the early twenties, but the two men had not talked with each other at length for nearly a decade. Both lawyers and former all-Americans (Davis at Amherst College), they had much in common. A gifted orator and a writer graced with both toughness and the charm of a southern politician, Davis had been practicing law for only six months when he decided to take on the Angelo Herndon case. It was a decision that marked, as Davis put it, the "real beginning of the interconnection between my personal desire for dignity and equal rights and the aspirations of the masses of the people for first-class citizenship." By the time the case was concluded in 1937, Davis had abandoned whatever wealth and prestige he might have been able to earn practicing law and committed himself to the Communist Party, which he saw as the only organization actually willing to work for the rights of American blacks.[24]

Although Robeson was not directly involved with either the Scottsboro or the Angelo Herndon campaigns, he did talk at length with both Patterson and Davis about the cases and the Communist Party's continuing battle for civil rights for American blacks.[25]

It takes little imagination to understand why Robeson was far more interested in talking with Davis and other Harlem activists than with the Van Vechtens or Walter White. The life and work of these activists — their energetic campaigning on behalf of international causes and, on the home front, for equality and opportunity for blacks — inspired Robeson and made him feel almost instantly at home. There was no doubt in Robeson's mind that he could carry on his "work" — both political and professional — in the United States as effectively as he had in England, perhaps even more so.[26] It was an exhilarating discovery, and in June Paul cabled Essie: "Great Possibilities Feel at Home Here Love It."[27]

Robeson spent his time visiting family and friends, exchanging views with political allies, singing for various political causes, and lending his support to Harlem's invigorated artistic community. More than 1,500 people had jammed the Mother AME Zion Church for Robeson's concert in July, held as a continuation of the celebration of his brother Ben's reappointment three weeks earlier. Harlemites cheered him, clamored for encores, and inundated him with requests for autographs: it was a warm and gratifying welcome home.[28] That same month Robeson performed in Greenwich Village at a concert to benefit the Spanish Refugee Relief Campaign (later to be labeled a subversive group by the FBI, but in 1939 still attracting mainstream support). Sponsored by Mayor Fiorello H. La Guardia and staged as part of the Second Annual Village Fair, its aim was to raise funds to transport the nearly half-million Spanish Republicans still in concentration camps in southern France to new settlements provided for them by the Mexican government. Joined by celebrities Bill ("Bojangles") Robinson, Helen Hayes, Gypsy Rose Lee, Richmond Barthé, Orson Welles, Sam Jaffe, Jo Davidson, Al Jolson, and Eddie Dowling, Robeson proved as apt a fund-raiser in the United States as he had been in England. Under the able hand of auctioneer Vincent Sheean (who a short time later would oppose Robeson on the issue of the Soviet invasion of Finland), Robeson's autograph sold for a whopping twenty-five dollars. Later, in the grand ballroom of the Roosevelt Hotel, Robeson spoke along with the French Communist poet and writer Louis Aragon at a symposium, "Spanish Culture in Exile," sponsored by the Negro Peoples Committee, the Spanish Intellectual Aid Committee, and the Musicians Committee—all part of the larger Spanish Refugee Relief Campaign. In his remarks Robeson emphasized the "need for close, united action on the part of all people if freedom and liberty are to remain safeguarded," and ended with the simple statement: "And so, I'm coming home again to join in the fight." The high point of the three-hour program was a Robeson concert that included folk and work songs of the people of Spain, America, and the Soviet Union, all performed in their original languages.[29]

Perhaps one of Robeson's most exciting discoveries that summer was Harlem's revitalized theater and art scene: it was almost precisely the type of theater and artistic community Robeson had for years dreamed of creating in England. Works Projects Administration (WPA) arts projects, fully functional by 1936, had dramatically altered the world of Harlem's black artists, providing them with something they had never had before: financial support that eliminated humiliating relations with white patrons, booking agents, and producers. The project included a Federal Negro Theatre that employed 350 people, put on sixteen plays, and gave playwrights, actors, directors, and technicians the opportunity to practice their craft; a Federal Writers Project that studied the history of New York blacks and the cultural, political, and economic life of Harlem residents; a Harlem Community Art Center that provided studio space for Harlem's best-known artists and offered art classes free of charge; a music project that sponsored orchestras, bands, and music appreciation classes; a puppet show; and an African dance troupe.[30]

Many of the people most intimately connected with the Negro Theatre Project were friends of Paul's or people with whom he had previously performed. As administrator of the project, the distinguished and highly respected actress Rose McClendon (who had played opposite Robeson in *Roseanne*) did much of the initial planning and served as a guiding light until her death in 1936. It was McClendon who initiated and pushed the idea of establishing separate groups of blacks to produce, direct, and act in plays concerned with black themes. She envisioned a permanent "Negro Theater" that would produce black plays and feature not just "an isolated Paul, or an occasional Bledsoe or Gilpin, but a long line of first rate [black] actors." Toward this end, she worked tirelessly despite the fact that she was seriously ill. Carlton Moss, who Robeson knew from his early days in Harlem, was a managing supervisor for the theater. Frank Wilson, who had played the leading role in the original *Porgy,* produced the Negro Theatre's first play, *Walk Together Children,* at the Lafayette. Here, in Harlem, Robeson had found theater that provided work for all talented actors regardless of race, theater for "the people," and theater priced so that those people could actually attend. Tickets at the Lafayette (situated right in the heart of Harlem) started at twenty-five cents with the best seats in the house priced at one dollar.[31]

WPA projects, however, were already under fire at the time of Paul's visit. Ever since the projects had begun operation, congressional conservatives led by Texas Representative Martin Dies, chairman of the notorious Special Committee to Investigate Un-American Activities, attacked them, and periodic layoffs and budget cuts were the result. "We were too damned liberal for them," said world-renowned choral director and head of Community Relations at Lincoln Center, Leonard de Paur. At the time de Paur was just beginning his career and the opportunity provided by the WPA to work as musical director of the Negro Unit of the Federal Theatre Project proved pivotal in his development. "Our plays were realistic and showed what it was really like in the Depression," de Paur remembered. "We did 'Triple A Plowed Under,' produced by the Living Newspaper, and the play *Turpentine,* which showed quite movingly the plight of southern blacks. They didn't like that kind of honesty. In fact, they were offended by it. And, I'm sure Dies and his committee members weren't happy to see blacks and whites working together, either. To Dies, a forerunner of McCarthy, we were subversives."[32]

The arts projects could hardly have asked for a more staunch supporter than Robeson, and during his summer visit Paul did everything he could to fight for continued funding for the enterprise. De Paur, for one, was grateful for Robeson's support. "At the time I was involved with the Hall Johnson Choir. We were engaged to sing at the Ford Exhibit at the World's Fair. Paul came to rehearsals specifically to show his support and give us a morale boost."[33]

In July Robeson appeared as a guest of honor at a reception sponsored by the Greater New York Committee for Better Negro Films. Robeson, Gwendolyn Bennett (director of the Harlem Community Art Center and chairman of the committee), and Max Yergan (honorary chairman) all spoke at the event, which was held to garner support for the 200 black actors who had just received their pink slips from the WPA's Federal Theatre Project.[34] Although Robeson agreed to very few interviews that summer, on two separate occasions he spoke out on behalf of the WPA Theatre Project and voiced his personal commitment to fight for continued funding.

By the end of the summer Robeson had made up his mind to move back to the United States and in August he returned to England to settle affairs there and make what would be his last British film, *The Proud Valley.* For almost two years Robeson had refused all film contracts—British and American—adamant that he would not act "in plays and films that cut against the very people and ideas [he] wanted to help" and determined to find "somewhere to work that would tie me up with the things I believed in" or stop working altogether.[35] Herbert Marshall, one of the few people whose assessment of a drama or film script Robeson could rely on, convinced both Essie and Paul that his new script—*David and Goliath* (later retitled *The Proud Valley*)—was the "work" Paul had been waiting for.[36]

Paul and Essie first met Marshall and Fredda Brilliant in Moscow in 1934, and over the years they had become close friends. In the late thirties the couple lived about two minutes from the Robesons' home at 2 St. Albans Villa on Highgate Road, where they were frequent visitors and enjoyed the distinction, as Essie once put it to Fredda, of being "the only two people who could come by and knock on the Robeson door anytime. Everyone else had to make an appointment."[37]

Brilliant, a Polish sculptor, had grown up in Australia and moved to the Soviet Union, where she met and married Herbert Marshall. It was her work that took her to the Soviet Union: she had been unable to support herself as an artist in either Australia or the United States. Brilliant had particularly warm feelings for Essie who on more than one occasion had helped her and Marshall out financially. When Essie learned, for example, that the couple was having difficulty saving enough money to move to England she came up with an idea: "She knew that we had just got married and didn't have much money. 'We're changing our dollars here,' she told us, 'and we're getting very little money in return from the government. You know what, I will give you some money, the same dollars for the same rubles as I get from the Government. I'll give you the dollars in England and you give me the rubles here.' With Essie helping us we made about eight times the amount of money we gave her."[38]

Once Marshall and Brilliant had arrived in London, Essie continued to assist them. " 'Fredda, it takes several years in a country to learn where you should or shouldn't go shopping, who you should meet, and all of that,' she told me. 'I suffered a lot when we first moved here,' she said. 'There's no need for you to suffer too.' And so she told me where to shop, what hairdresser to go to, what doctor to see — in fact, she gave me the name of her own doctor."[39]

Later, after the couple had settled, Essie said to Brilliant, "You know, you need to do something to get your work known in England. I have an idea. Why don't you do a sculpture of Paul? That will certainly get you the publicity you need to get started." Brilliant added, "Now Paul never said to me, how about making a sculpture of me; it will help you. It was Essie who thought of that. She must have been thinking a long time beforehand about what she could do to help."[40]

Both the Robesons liked and admired Herbert Marshall. Robeson (this according to Marshall) felt that Marshall understood his racial sensitivities because he himself had experienced snubbing and exclusion as an "inferior" cockney.[41] Marshall's political credentials (a member of the CPGB, he was one of Robeson's earliest political mentors, guiding him through Moscow on his first visit to the Soviet Union and, in the process, introducing him to Soviet culture and political ideology) and his professional accomplishments (his transformation of Unity Theatre's unskilled worker-actors into critically acclaimed theatrical troupes, for example) likewise impressed Robeson and gave him confidence in this new undertaking.

Essie had worked with Marshall on the script during the summer, and when Robeson returned he also helped Marshall rework sections of the story. Writer Louis Golding and Jack Jones, a former miner and the author of *Rhondda Roundabout* who had a bit part in the film, revised the script further and they were still working on it when filming began in August.[42] The film's director, Pen Tennyson, the twenty-seven-year-old great-grandson of the poet, made more revisions to the script and retitled it *The Proud Valley.*

Michael Balcon's inventive and personally controlled Ealing Studio in London's western suburbs produced the film. The music, arranged by Ernest Irving, included authentic Welsh songs: "Land of My Fathers," "All Through the

Night," and "Ton y botel." Supporting actors, nearly all newcomers to film, were drawn almost exclusively from the ranks of South Wales radio artists. Among them, Rachel Thomas (Mrs. Parry) would be Tennyson's most impressive "discovery." Thomas, who had no previous acting experience, was in real life a thirty-five-year-old mother and the wife of a Welsh schoolteacher (she first read for the role in her own front parlor in Cardiff). She earned rave reviews for her acting as well as for her singing of the Welsh prayer, "Yn y Drfroedd," which unfailingly reduced Robeson to tears.

Proud Valley is the story of David Goliath (Robeson), a gentle giant and one of Cardiff's many unemployed and wandering black seamen. Hoping to find a job in one of the valleys, he travels to the Welsh countryside. On his way David befriends Bert (Edward Rigby) who tells him about "a coloured bloke [who] used to work in the Glen Colliery. Blackie Ellis they called him." Bert's chance remark persuades David that perhaps, despite the Depression, not all collieries operated a color bar.

After arriving in the mining village of Blaendy, David and Bert busk in the street for money and stop to listen to a Welsh choir rehearsing a chorus from *Elijah* for the National Eisteddfod.[43] The choirmaster, mine worker Dick Parry (Edward Chapman), hears David singing along with the choir as they practice. Struck by his fine voice, badly in need of a bass (as theirs had failed to show up), and eager to win the competition, Parry takes David home to meet his wife. "He's got a bottom base like an organ," he tells her. "The finest I ever heard in these valleys. It floated in that hall like thunder from the distance." Dick invites David to board at their home and promises to find him a job in the colliery and a place in the choir.

David's new job is not without its problems. At first, some of the miners object to the presence of a black man. Miner Seth Jones (Clifford Evans) makes it clear from the outset that he resents David's employment. "This fellow is a black man to work down the pit," he complains aloud. "Well, what about it?" asks David angrily. Parry steps in to defend his new friend: "Damn and blast it, man, aren't we all black down that pit?" In time David's competence and hard work earn him the respect of the other miners.

David enjoys the Parry family and looks forward to performing with the Blaendy Male Voice Choir at the coming Eisteddfod. But on the day of the Eisteddfod Dick Parry is killed in a pit disaster. David makes a heroic but unsuccessful effort to save his friend, trapped in a cave-in after an explosion, and later poignantly sings "Deep River" in memory of him.[44]

The mine owners decide that the explosion has rendered the pit unworkable and shut the mine down. David remains with the Parry family, doing what he can to help them, as poverty and starvation stalk the village. Finally, he and three other miners are chosen by the workers to go to London to represent them to the owners. The four men walk to London in a manner reminiscent of the great hunger marches of the early thirties (with David's fine voice earning them coins for food), arrive just as war breaks out, and persuade the owners that coal is now as necessary as munitions.[45] The pit is opened, but there is another explosion and David is killed when he volunteers to sacrifice his own life to save the life of Dick's son Emlyn (Simon Lack) by lighting the short fuse that will blast a hole in the mine wall and free Emlyn and the other miners. "Your father was my friend," David explains before he dies. "He took me in, gave me food and shelter, found me work. What kind of a man would I be if I left now when things are bad?"

Proud Valley had great meaning for Robeson. Not only did it feature a heroic black protagonist, it also dealt with real people and their brave effort to survive. The film would dramatize for all the world to see the result of mine owners' greed and the unconscionable apathy of the British government. Robeson had a deep personal attachment to the people in the mining villages of South Wales and in some way this film would be a tribute to them. The people of the Rhondda Valley, where parts of the film were shot, like those in other depressed British mining regions, had lived *Proud Valley*'s story of economic depression, poverty, unemployment, forced emigration, starvation, and the British government's humiliating "means test." The people of South Wales supported with material goods and often their lives political causes close to Robeson's heart. South Wales had a long tradition of radical political activism, but the outbreak of war in Spain coincided with a period of social unrest and political activity in the South Wales coalfield unrivaled since the General Strike of 1926. Spanish Aid Committees became a popular front in Welsh mining towns and villages, unofficially uniting not only the working class but all those hostile to fascism. Robeson remembered well the heavy losses families in this region endured during the Spanish Civil War: South Wales miners had accounted for the largest regional occupational group in the entire International Brigade. Of the 170 volunteers from Wales, 116 of them came from the mining industry and close to 25 percent of them were union officials at the pit level.[46] Membership in the Communist Party grew also, and by the mid-1930s the Party had become firmly rooted in the Cynon Valley and other coalfield towns and villages. In some, known as "little Moscows" (with people like Harry Pollitt and Arthur Horner affectionately dubbed "little Stalins"), the Communist Party had supplanted the Labour Party.

But Robeson was drawn to the Welsh for reasons other than the identification he felt with their politics, their economic plight, and their generous fighting spirit. He himself may not yet have seen the mines and mine workers close-up, but he did so now as part of preparing for the role of David and then later during the filming of location shots when he stayed with a miner's family in the Abader Valley. Marshall and Brilliant, who had interviewed miners as part of their research, saw to it that Paul visited mines in the Rhondda Valley. "We all wore miner's helmets and went down," Brilliant recalled. "We went way down into the mine shaft; we did this several times in preparation for the film. To reach the mine itself, you had to crawl through a space that was only three feet high. It was much too small for Paul—who was massive, overweight in fact, and towered over the Welsh miners—to fit through. I was smaller, so I crawled in on my belly and into that mine. And the things I saw there—when I came out I told Paul all about it."[47]

Miners coming up in the cages when their shifts were done were black with coal dust, "pitch black devils. . . . For a second the cage looked like a prison full of Negroes," said one observer in the early 1930s.[48] A longtime veteran of the mines remembered "the men—among them, my father—returning home, walking very slowly and very black they were, covered with coal dust. There was a bucket of water waiting and the men bathed outdoors, changing quite suddenly from black to white—quite a transformation. There was coal dust everywhere. Especially the slag—coal dust that was mixed with dirt taken from the pit and piled in great heaps. It was everywhere. Virtually all of the Rhondda Valley was one big slag heap set along the mountain side. The slag heaps caused landslides that destroyed homes in the Valley—in all a horrendous and total disaster."[49] One of Robeson's earliest and most vivid childhood memories was of his father—also a proud man, also crushed and humbled by circumstance—returning home from his work as an ash hauler. Robeson's father was also caked in dust—white ash, rather than coal black. And, in the back of the Robeson's home were the ashes, piled like slag, in ugly heaps.

As much as South Wales is known for its mining, it is equally known for its love of music and its world-renowned male choirs. Outsiders often assume that this passion for singing had only to do the Eisteddfod and winning the competition and a financial prize. "This is not so," commented one observer. "Most of these choirs cannot afford to sing at the Eisteddfod, and few of them make much money. They sing for the joy of singing. . . . 'If I get depressed I sing to myself,' said one man to me. 'But that only makes me worse! If I meet three or four other men and can harmonize my voice with theirs I soon find that my mood changes. I forget my worries—for a time!'"[50]

One resident of Barrow-in-Furness, Cumbria, recalled that "people in Wales wanted him [Robeson] to open the Eisteddfod but some said he would want too much money, but when he was asked he shook his head and said all he wanted was a Welsh hymnbook. He said Welsh hymns were the closest thing to negro spirituals."[51] For the Welsh, as for Robeson, the habit of singing had its roots in pain and privation. Singing—whether spirituals (which were also sung by Welsh choirs, most likely first introduced to the Welsh by the Fisk Jubilee Singers) or Welsh hymns—was for both Robeson and the Welsh miners, a spiritual survival tool, a means of enduring in an unforgiving and often unkind world.

The Proud Valley would earn good reviews but suffered when compared with *The Stars Look Down* (also released in 1940, about one month before *The Proud Valley*) and the later classic portrayal of life in a Welsh mining town, *How Green Was My Valley* (1941). Critics applauded *The Proud Valley's* portrayal of "that terrible monster, the pit, which devours those who go to it for their livelihood and kills by starvation those who stay away" and praised Robeson's performance, in particular his breathtaking singing. "For its music alone everything else could be forgiven," said one critic, and another, "Some of the loveliest singing I have ever heard in a film."[52] But more than one reviewer criticized Robeson's role, which "hardly exploited" his talents and called upon him "only to display benign resignation."[53] Reviewers also complained that the film's plot, especially at the end, was "patchy and sentimental" and "full of improbabilities," and some found the dialogue "frankly bad."

And it was. When the filming began in August, the writers who were reworking Marshall's screenplay still had not settled on an ending. The original script had the miners themselves taking over the abandoned pit, but censors insisted on a less radical ending. A miraculous reconciliation with the British government and a reopening of the mines were out of the question. Still, something had to happen. The problem was unexpectedly settled by an event that made the matter of the film's ending seem trivial. On August 23, about two weeks into the filming, the world learned that the Soviet Union had entered into a nonaggression pact with Nazi Germany. The most bitter ideological enemies had suddenly, overnight, become allies. The pact's secret provisions, easily guessed and soon carried out, divided Poland between the two powers and allowed Russia to assume control over the Baltic states and take Bessarabia from Romania. The Polish situation made England and France's entry into the war inevitable, and on September 3, 1939, two days after the Germans invaded Poland, Britain and France declared war on Germany.

For the film's writers the news provided the perfect solution to their dilemma: the mines reopen—not because the owners had relented but because the necessities of war demanded it. And, indeed, a montage of patriotic and anti-Fascist images—miners, flags, coal-hoppers working feverishly in behalf of the war effort—concludes the film, with the camera gradually pulling back from scenes of mine workers and their families to the rolling hills and seashore of Wales, with Robeson's moving rendering of "Wales" in the background (he would sing the same song in 1956 after his passport had been revoked, as a conclusion to a radio program broadcast by telephone for the Welsh miners). The new ending, however, contributed to what one critic called *The Proud Valley*'s fudging of the main political issues. It blunted the original thrust of the movie — oppressed workers fighting capitalistic greed — by naming Hitler as *the* enemy. In addition, while the effects of the British government's intransigence are well documented, the film makes little mention of organized action (such as the miners' union or group-initiated protests) on the part of the miners, primarily because censors objected to overt references to unions. The music — Robeson's singing and the Welsh choir's — is perhaps the one exception to this. The choir boasts that "you can't stop us singing" and members are correct. In *The Proud Valley* choral singing became one way of suggesting solidarity and, by implication, union solidarity.[54]

The Proud Valley would be one of the few films Robeson never later complained about, one of the few of which he was truly proud. It stands apart from other British films of the period in that it features believable working-class characters — not caricatures. David Goliath is perhaps the fullest, most realistic character Robeson ever played on film. One need only compare the role with any of the roles played by blacks in the American film classic, *Gone with the Wind,* which premiered in 1939, to get a sense of what a radical departure in the history of black portraiture in film the role of David Goliath represented.

And, as was the case with Robeson's other films, the public flocked to *The Proud Valley.* "As a child I saw *Sanders of the River, Song of Freedom,* and *The Proud Valley,*" recalled one South Yorkshire native. "Paul Robeson had a very commanding presence. I think many cinemagoers went to hear him sing rather than the simply awful dialogue and storylines of his films. As a child I was impressed by the sheer goodness of the man, which shone through his screen roles." "He was unforgettable in his films, enjoyed by all," said Ruby Stuart of West Huntspill, Somerset. "We could enjoy the films and come away feeling the impact of a performance far deeper than mere entertainment. His physical presence, a commanding physique, conveyed a gentleness and dignity that invited trust. Add to this a magnificent voice, with such understanding and depth of feeling, and there you have an outstanding man of his age, not just a twinkling star."[55]

With the signing of the Soviet–German nonaggression pact, overnight Britain's popular-front alliance of workers, leftists, anti-Fascists, and Party members shattered, as most fellow travelers solidly backed the war effort and Communist Party members and die-hard sympathizers found themselves forced to justify their contradictory anti-Fascist commitments and Party ties. At the time, Robeson made no comment whatsoever in England concerning the Soviet Union's sudden shift in policy, undoubtedly because he, like others in his position, did not know what it meant. British Party members received no explanation from Moscow and in the absence of any official word were left to guess at the Soviet government's aims and motives. The leadership of Britain's Communist Party regarded Hitler as a far greater threat than Chamberlain and assumed, pact or no pact, that the Soviet government did as well. Thus, when Germany invaded Poland, the Party's Central Committee in London confidently reaffirmed its support of all efforts to vanquish fascism.[56] Harry Pollitt, the British Party's general secretary and one of its most articulate, loyal, and outspoken members, hastily prepared a pamphlet backing Britain's entry into the war. But the ink was barely dry on Pollitt's "How to Win the War" when it became clear that Stalin's policy was anything but anti-Fascist. As Russia's invasion of Poland on September 17 dramatically confirmed, the Soviet Union had adopted a position of benevolent neutrality toward Germany and direct participation in the dismemberment of Poland.

British Party members were stunned. The September 20 edition of the *Daily Worker* hobbled to press with the lame report: "Red Army Takes Bread to Starving Peasants."[57] Heads began to roll, as instructions finally arrived from the Comintern, and Pollitt's was among the first to go. However well intentioned, he had made a serious error, and it cost him his position as secretary of the Central Committee. Others, including the *Daily Worker*'s editor, J. R. Campbell, were also stripped of their posts and sent packing.[58]

The British public made clear its disapproval of Soviet policy in August and would do so more vehemently in September when Britain and France entered the war. General mobilization began on September 2 and a million children were removed from what the military regarded as danger zones. At 11:15 a.m. on Sunday morning, September 3, Prime Minister Neville Chamberlain spoke on the radio, urging Hitler to withdraw his troops from Poland. Almost before he finished speaking the first air-raid sounded. It was a false alarm, but later alarms would not be.[59]

The Soviet Union's attack on Finland in November effectively destroyed any lingering Party credibility among British moderates and liberals. The Communist press described the invasion as an effort to "liberate" the Finns, a defense so patently absurd it convinced no one. Set against the backdrop of five years of militant anti-Fascist popular-front propaganda culminating in Moscow's championing the cause of Spain, such an about-face was impossible to justify, and Party membership diminished rapidly. Veterans of the International Brigade like Tom Wintringham and George Aiken resigned, and fellow travelers absconded as well. Formerly unshakable allies like Victor Gollancz now openly attacked the Party. Not since the early 1920s had hostility toward the Party been so pronounced in England. Angry mobs routinely broke up meetings and assaulted Communist speakers, who, after being rescued by police, were then often arrested for having started the fracas in the first place.[60] Labourites and almost all the people with whom Robeson had shared the platform on behalf of Spain followed the lead of Clement Attlee and denounced the Party, rallied to the colors, and supported the war.[61]

Mercifully, by November Robeson was safely ensconced in the United States, having left England as soon as *The Proud Valley* was completed. His timing could not have been better because it saved him from having to justify what now appeared to be an indefensible allegiance. One wonders how much of the Party's rationalizing Robeson accepted. He kept private notes, explaining (perhaps first to himself) Russian political decisions, in particular the pact, Poland, and Finland, which suggests that he understood full well he would be challenged for remaining loyal.[62]

While Robeson could understand that his decision to maintain his Soviet loyalties would appear illogical, he had made up his mind that no matter how his position might appear to others, he would give the Soviet Union every benefit of the doubt. He looked on the Soviet Union and its people as a friend. He had certainly been the recipient of bigotry in the United States and, on occasion, even in England — but never in the Soviet Union. In addition, the Soviet Union, no fair-weather friend (and Paul had known many), did not disappear or remain silent in the face of racial controversy, but instead proved itself again and again willing to back up its racial rhetoric with action. Why should Robeson not return the favor with a corresponding loyalty? It was a relationship and bond that Robeson could not easily explain, especially to whites. It reached far back to the traumas of Robeson's youth — the Bustill's abandonment of his father after Robeson's mother's death, Robeson's inability as a child to protect and save his father after William lost his pastorate in Princeton. Metaphorically, the Soviet Union was willing to step in and fight for his father, fight for Robeson when Rutgers benched him to avoid a racial confrontation, speak up when Robeson and Brown were denied awards at the Dutch Treat Club, and fight on Robeson's behalf as he struggled to find a role equal to his talent. Robeson did not expect to be able to explain all this to others. And so, on the eve of his departure from England to the United States he said to Joe Andrews, both in jest and with the utmost seriousness, "It's going to take a lot of convincing when I try to explain this one to my friends."[63]

The Robesons, Larry Brown, and Paul Jr., after a three-day delay in Bordeaux caused by uncertain weather conditions, arrived in New York. The S.S. *Washington* had been booked to capacity with passengers who, fearing they would be stranded in England, had frantically purchased tickets only to wait weeks to obtain passage. The *Amsterdam News* gave the Robesons' arrival enthusiastic front-page coverage, describing in detail not only Essie's smart outfit but also the prominent patch on Paul Jr.'s forehead, the result, Paul Jr. admitted, of swinging on a porthole door. Mrs. Goode, Minnie Sumner Patterson, Ethel Gardner, Sam Byrd (*John Henry*'s producer), and the ubiquitous Max Yergan were among those gathered at the dock to greet the Robesons.[64]

Robeson was welcomed back by political allies and friends — Ben Davis, the CPUSA, the establishment black press, and Jewish American and black leaders — and he got right to work rehearsing for Roark Bradford and Jacques Wolfe's *John Henry* — a play that called for a nearly all-black cast and for which Robeson would have some say in the wording of the script. He was particularly excited about *John Henry* because, as he told Ben Davis, "I want to get back to American folk life. I want to work with my people with whom I belong."[65]

Paul dove into his work in the United States, apparently oblivious to England's plight. The Savoy Hotel was being revamped for use as an air-raid shelter and the Robesons' own home would later be damaged by bombs. Still, Robeson would continue to stand with the Soviet Union, even justifying its invasion of Finland. In the United States he found dissension within CPUSA ranks, especially among Jewish Americans, who believed Stalin had betrayed them. But for the time being the vast majority of Americans — both black and white — wanted to stay far away from war in Europe and were unconcerned with Robeson's politics. Even though the *Daily Worker* recorded Robeson's political views in detail, his opinions did not affect his American popularity.

Robeson would enjoy the greatest success of his career during the next five years, saved by the fact that his politics did not affront American sensibilities. For his own part, he tried valiantly to find a middle road, a path that would allow him to stay true to his loyalties and realize his professional aspirations. So while he played the politically and racially charged roles he believed in, like *John Henry*, he also appeared in American staples like the Rudy Vallee radio program. He bought a house in rural Connecticut and, for appearance sake at least, settled into American-style family life. When that picture changed in the postwar years, and America began its head-on assault of the Soviet Union, Robeson would react to criticism of the Soviet Union, regardless of its source, with the same intensity he had in England. As much as he struggled to avoid repeating in his own life the downward trajectory of his father's life, like his father he would ultimately lose the position and status he had worked a lifetime to earn. As for being duped, it was not the Soviet Union that lured him into its web so much as it was his experience of race that gave him no alternative but to side with the people who, from all appearances, were the only ones who truly sided with him.

NOTES

Material from the Robeson Collections (Moorland-Spingarn Library, Howard University) is used by permission of Paul Robeson Jr. and Howard University and is cited in these notes as Robeson Collections (PR Jr.).

All interviews were conducted by Andrew Bunie except where otherwise attributed.

1. PRINCETON

1. Interview with Miki Fisher, Sept. 20, 1978.

2. Larry Brown qtd. in Marie Seton, *Paul Robeson* (London: Dennis Dobson, 1958), 169. For biographical information on Brown, see chapter 5, herein.

3. FBI report (citing *Daily Worker,* Apr. 19, 1977), File 100–12304–72, May 3, 1947.

4. Robeson (hereafter PR) qtd. in *St. Louis Globe Democrat,* Jan. 26, 1946; interview with Saul H. Fisher, Sept. 28, 1978; interview with Miki Fisher, Sept. 20, 1978.

5. Interview with Saul Fisher, Sept. 28, 1978.

6. A fire destroyed the county courthouse and all its records, thus hampering research on the history of Martin County. See *The Formation of North Carolina Counties, 1663–1943* (Raleigh: State Department Publications, Department of Archives and History, 1950), 145; James H. McCallum, M.D., *Martin County during the Civil War* (Williamstown, N.C.: Enterprise, 1971), 3; and *1872–1972 Robersonville Area Centennial Booklet* (available at Robersonville, N.C., Library). It is unclear whether William Robeson's slave name was Roberson or Robeson. In *Here I Stand* (1958; reprint, Boston: Beacon Press, 1971), Robeson suggests that Roberson was his father's ancestral slave name (8). Also, Paul P. Roberson, a white attorney practicing in New York City whose family came from North Carolina and who knew several of Robeson's cousins, indicated (when interviewed by James Clark, Apr. 10, 1975) that his family had owned the Robesons. Other names in Martin County include Robertson, Robason, Roboson, and Roberson.

7. PR, *Here I Stand,* 6, 13. PR supplies a fair amount of information concerning his childhood in his autobiography and political apologia, *Here I Stand.* Written in collaboration with his friend and political ally Lloyd Brown, the book was primarily intended, as PR put it, "to set the record straight" regarding his own political views. It should be understood that he includes autobiographical data only as it explains his later politics. The often idealistic descriptions of his family (in particular, his father), Princeton's black community, and Harlem blacks should be interpreted and weighed in the context of the larger purpose of the book, which was essentially political. See also Kenneth Mostern, *Autobiography and Black Identity Politics: Racialization in Twentieth-Century America* (New York: Cambridge University Press, 1999), 120, 129–33.

8. Anna Bustill Smith, *Reminiscences of Colored People of Princeton, New Jersey* (Princeton Historical Society, 1913), reprinted in *Princeton Recollector,* Feb. 13, 1977, 18–20.

9. Guion Griffis Johnson, *Antebellum North Carolina* (Chapel Hill: University of North Carolina Press, 1937), 3, 535.

10. Jeffrey J. Crow, Paul D. Escott, and Flora J. Hatley, *A History of African Americans in North Carolina* (Raleigh: Department of Cultural Resources, 1992), 3–5, 19–21.

11. Tobacco was one of North Carolina's primary crops and, according to PR, relatives of William Robeson who remained in North Carolina worked in tobacco fields. James Clark, in an interview with Paul Robeson's cousins in North Carolina (Apr. 1975), confirmed they were tobacco farmers. See PR, "For Freedom and Peace" address given in New York, June 19, 1949, pamphlet issued by the Council on African Affairs (CAA), reprinted in *Paul Robeson Speaks: Writings, Speeches, Interviews, 1918–1974,* ed. Philip S. Foner (Secaucus, N.J.: Citadel, 1978), 202.

12. In 1860 North Carolina had 34,658 slave owners; of the state's 85,000 farmers, less than 27,000 owned slaves. Crow, Escott, and Hatley, *History of African Americans,* 51–52.

13. John Hope Franklin, *From Slavery to Freedom,* 5th ed. (New York: Knopf, 1980), 17; Crow, Escott, and Hatley, *History of African Americans,* 7–9. Like enslaved blacks, the activities of free blacks in the South had always been proscribed educationally, legally, and economically, but after 1831 surveillance of free blacks increased, and frequently they were forced to go to court and produce affidavits documenting that they were free.

14. PR, *Here I Stand,* 6; Eslanda Robeson, *Paul Robeson, Negro* (New York: Hayes and Brothers, 1930), 10 (hereafter ER, *PR, Negro*); *Princeton Recollector,* Feb. 13, 1977. Biographer Lloyd Brown contends that William Robeson escaped, along with his younger brother Ezechial, not in 1860 but during the war, in 1862 (*The Young Paul Robeson* [Boulder: Westview Press, 1997], 12–13).

15. Franklin, *From Slavery to Freedom,* 123–27. By 1815 domestic slave trade was a major economic activity in the South; it reached its peak in 1837 but remained a profitable business until the beginning of the Civil War.

16. Interviews with Charles Blockson, Feb. 12, 1986, Aug. 20, 1991, and Apr. 6, 1994; Charles L. Blockson, *Pennsylvania's Black History* (Philadelphia: Portfolio Associates, 1975); idem, *The Underground Railroad* (New York: Berkeley Books, 1989); idem, *Hippocrene Guide to the Underground Railroad* (New York: Hippocrene Books, 1994).

17. Vincent Harding, *There Is a River: The Black Struggle for Freedom in America* (New York: Harcourt Brace Jovanovich, 1981), 196.

18. According to Blockson (interviewed Apr. 6, 1994), white sea captains, some of whom were abolitionists, may have also helped move William up the coast toward Philadelphia.

19. Franklin, *From Slavery to Freedom,* 222–23. Martin County's free blacks numbered about 450 in 1860.

20. Edward T. Jones, ed., *Notable American Women: A Biographical Dictionary* (Cambridge: Harvard University Press, 1971), 3:481–83. Eleanor Flexner, *Century of Struggle* (New York: Atheneum, 1974), 96–97; Lloyd Brown conjectured that William may have been among the many blacks who sought refuge at New Bern, a port at the mouth of the Neuse River, about sixty miles from the Robeson plantation. If so, he may well have volunteered to defend the base from enemy assault (*Young Paul Robeson,* 12–13).

21. Nat Law interview with PR in *The Worker,* Apr. 16, 1944; telephone interview with Paul Robeson Jr., Dec. 5, 1982. There is no official record of William's fighting for the Union army.

22. Robertson Ballard, "Paul Robeson: A Genius with a Soul," *Methodist Times,* June 3, 1929; Horace Mann Bond, *Education for Freedom* ([Lincoln University, Pa.]: Lincoln University, 1976), 219. President of Lincoln University from 1945 to 1957, Bond has written a thoughtful and detailed history of Lincoln, rich in anecdotes as well as scholarly research. On Bond, see Wayne J. Urban, *Black Scholar: Horace Mann Bond, 1904–1972* (Athens: University of Georgia Press, 1992). On Lincoln University, see J. B. Rendall, *A Historical Sketch of Lincoln University* (Philadelphia, 1904), and William D. Johnson, *Lincoln University; or, The Nation's First Pledge of Emancipation* (1867).

23. Andrew E. Murray, "The Founding of Lincoln University," *Journal of Presbyterian History* 51 (1973): 397; Bond, *Education,* 44–68, 488–91. Ashmun Institute was founded primarily in response to the needs of Protestant foreign missionary activity, especially in Liberia. During the period between the opening of the school in 1853 and 1865, the Foreign Board established its first presbytery in Liberia, staffed with three missionaries from the Ashmun Institute.

24. Attributed to Isaac Norton Rendall (president of Lincoln University from 1865 to 1905), in George Johnson, "Biographical Reminiscences of Isaac N. Rendall," qtd. in Bond, *Education,* 351.

25. Urban, *Black Scholar,* 14. During the first half of the nineteenth century Princeton's Theological Seminary, the center of old-school Presbyterian orthodoxy, was a strong supporter of African colonization and, consequently, continually at war with radicals from New England.

26. For Lincoln University's ties with Princeton's Theological Seminary, see Murray, "Founding of Lincoln," 392–410.

27. Bond, *Education,* 262, 279.

28. See Johnson, "Biographical Reminiscences" qtd. in Bond, *Education,* 274; see also 275–77.

29. Bond, *Education,* 287, 258, 5; for Lincoln's refusing the trend toward industrial study, see Urban, *Black Scholar,* 15, 181.

30. Murray, "Founding of Lincoln," 396; Bond, *Education,* 284, 299, 303.

31. John Miller Dickey Notes, Lincoln University, qtd. in Bond, *Education,* 332.

32. Julie Winch, *Philadelphia's Black Elite* (Philadelphia: Temple University Press, 1988), 70–90; *Philadelphia Tribune,* Apr. 27, 1912; Bond, *Education,* 135–42.

33. Bond, *Education,* 344–48.

34. William Still, in undated *Alumni Magazine* (ca. 1884–1886), Lincoln University, qtd. in Bond, *Education,* 340.

35. Bond, *Education,* 356; Urban, *Black Scholar,* 14.

36. Bond, *Education,* 418–24. Webb was convinced that "the students themselves . . . were the best promotional device Lincoln possessed" and used them accordingly (289).

37. *Lancaster Intelligencer,* June 2, 1880, qtd. in Bond, *Education,* 423; *Oxford Press,* June 25, 1873.

38. PR, *Here I Stand,* 9; Bond, *Education,* 422.

39. Bond, *Education,* 411–12. In addition to the six Dickens novels, William Robeson borrowed *Reids's Lectures on Literature,* and a book on astronomy.

40. The presbytery of West Africa had sent the boys to Lincoln to be educated.

41. Dickey qtd. in *Oxford Press,* June 25, 1873.

42. *Oxford Press,* June 25, 1873; Booker T. Washington to Cain Triplett, Poindexter Smith, and John P. Powell, Dec. 12, 1904, *Booker T. Washington Papers,* 8:153–54, qtd. in Louis R. Harlan, *Booker T. Washington: The Wizard of Tuskegee, 1901–1915* (New York: Oxford University Press, 1983), 269.

43. Although the historian Sterling Stuckey contends that William Robeson, "deeply and unashamedly African, clung to his African roots," derived his dignity and sense of self-worth from this heritage, and thus planted the seeds of African nationalism in his son Paul, there is little evidence in either William's or Paul's life to substantiate this claim. Stuckey makes no mention of Lincoln's influence on William Robeson and erroneously claims that William learned to read Greek and Latin not at Lincoln (where both were required subjects) but on his own, "late in life." In truth, Lincoln had a profound effect on William Robeson, teaching him that upward mobility depended on movement away from Africa (Stuckey, *Slave Culture: Nationalist Theory and the Foundation of Black America* [New York: Oxford University Press, 1987], 303–58).

44. Brown, *Young Paul Robeson,* 17; Bond, *Education,* 139; Winch, *Philadelphia's Black Elite,* 6; *Philadelphia Tribune,* June 27, 1914. The *Philadelphia Tribune's* weekly column, "Pencil Pusher Notes," frequently mentioned black aristocrats, including the Bustills. Written by William Carl Bolivar, a native Philadelphian whose memory stretched back to the early 1860s, the column rehearsed both obscure and well-known details of the history of black Philadelphia. On Bolivar, see Roger Lane, *Roots of Violence in Black Philadelphia, 1860–1900* (Cambridge: Harvard University Press, 1986); idem, *William Dorsey's Philadelphia and Ours* (New York: Oxford University Press, 1991), 114; and Willard B. Gatewood, *Aristocrats of Color: The Black Elite, 1880–1920* (1991; reprint, Bloomington: Indiana University Press, Midland Books, 1993), 216.

45. Gatewood, *Aristocrats,* passim; August Meier, "Negro Class Structure and Ideology in the Age of Booker T. Washington," *Phylon* 22 (1962): 263. Sometimes referred to as the "colored aristocracy," the "black 400," the "upper tens," or simply the "old families," small enclaves of the black elite could be found in Detroit, St. Louis, Memphis, Cleveland, Charleston, Boston, and Washington, D.C.

46. Anna Bustill Smith, "The Bustill Family," *Journal of Negro History* 10 (1925): 638; *Philadelphia Tribune,* June 27, 1914. Anna Bustill Smith, self-appointed genealogist of the Bustill family, was born in Harrisburg, Pennsylvania. The daughter of Joseph Cassey Bustill, she was also the cousin of PR's mother, Maria Louisa Bustill.

47. Melvin H. Buxbaum, "Cyrus Bustill Addresses the Blacks of Philadelphia," *William and Mary Quarterly* 29 (1972): 99–108; Winch, *Philadelphia's Black Elite,* 71. According to Buxbaum,

Pryor may well have been pressured by fellow Quakers to free Bustill because Pryor was in technical violation of the Quaker yearly meeting, which, in 1758, took a strong stand against slavery and the purchase of slaves.

48. Smith, "Bustill Family," 638–39; Winch, *Philadelphia's Black Elite,* 5, 6, 71; Bond, *Education,* 139; *Philadelphia Tribune,* June 27, 1914.

49. Smith, "Bustill Family," 639, 638.

50. Ibid., 640–41; *Philadelphia Tribune,* June 27, 1914.

51. Blockson, *The Underground Railroad,* 213; *Philadelphia Tribune,* July 4, 1914; Rayford Logan and Michael Winston, eds., *Dictionary of American Negro Biography* (New York: Norton, 1982), s.v., Mossell, Gertrude; Bond, *Education,* 304; Maria L. Bustill to Robert Vaux, Consolidated School Board of Directors, Sept. 1873, Apr. 1876, Charles Blockson Afro-American Collection, Temple University, Philadelphia.

52. For the Institute for Colored Youth and the Robert Vaux School, see Lane, *Dorsey's Philadelphia,* xiii, 139–40, 150–51, and Harry C. Silcox, "Nineteenth-Century Philadelphia, Black Militant, Octavius V. Catto, 1839–1871," in *African Americans in Pennsylvania, Shifting Historical Perspectives,* ed. Joe William Trotter and Eric Ledell Smith (University Park: Pennsylvania State University Press, 1997), 199, 216. The Institute for Colored Youth is now Cheyney State College, located in Cheyney, Pennsylvania. The Robert Vaux, an all-black primary and grammar school, attracted elite children unable to meet ICY's rigorous standards. The school boasted an additional distinction: the Vaux had black teachers (the only other black school in Philadelphia, the James Forten School, had an all-white staff).

53. Charles Blockson interview, Aug. 20, 1991. (According to Blockson, the saying was that if you were "dark as a brown paper bag, it was too dark.") On color as a stratifier, see E. F. Frazier, *The Negro Family in the United States* (Chicago: University of Chicago Press, 1939), 405–6; and Gatewood, *Aristocrats,* 149–81.

54. W. E. B. Du Bois, *The Philadelphia Negro: A Social Study* (1899; reprint, New York: Schocken Books, 1967), 80; idem, *The Black North in 1901* (New York: Arno, 1969), 29–30; Blockson interview, Aug. 20, 1991.

55. Gatewood, *Aristocrats,* 96–103; Blockson interview, Aug. 20, 1991.

56. On Gertrude Mossell, see Rodger Streitmatter, *Raising Her Voice: African-American Women Journalists Who Changed History* (Lexington: University Press of Kentucky, 1994), 38–44; Monroe A. Majors, *Noted Negro Women: Their Triumphs and Activities* (1893; reprint, Freeport, N.Y.: Books for Libraries, 1971); Martin Dann, ed., *The Black Press, 1827–1890: The Quest for National Identity* (New York: Capricorn, 1971); Dorothy Sterling, ed., *We Are Your Sisters: Black Women in the Nineteenth Century* (New York: Norton, 1984), 435; Logan and Winston, *Dictionary of American Negro Biography,* 457; Lane, *Dorsey's Philadelphia,* 184–87; Mossell obituary, *Philadelphia Tribune,* Jan. 24, 1948. Gertrude Mossell was nearly as important as a journalist as her husband was as a doctor. Early in her career she contributed to the *A.M.E. Review* and the *Christian Recorder* and later wrote for numerous papers and magazines, including *Our Women and Children, New York Age, Philadelphia Times,* and *Ladies' Home Journal.* She is the author of two books: *Little Dansie's One Day at Sabbath School* (1902) and *The Work of Afro-American Women* (1894).

57. Bond, *Education,* 339–50. Nathan Mossell played a key role in the 1886, 1888, and 1893 petitions for Negro faculty at Lincoln. Lincoln did not appoint a Negro to the Board of Trustees until 1929 or a Negro faculty member until 1932, and only in 1945 was a black president appointed (Urban, *Black Scholar,* 14). On Nathan Mossell, see Arthur O. White, "The Black Movement against Jim Crow Education in Lockport, N.Y.," *New York History,* July 1969, 276, 279; Herbert B. Morais, *History of Negroes in Medicine* (New York: Publishers Co., 1977), 80.

58. Smith, *Reminiscences;* Seton, *Paul Robeson,* 16. It would be a mistake to underestimate the extent to which Maria Louisa's upbringing and Quaker heritage affected her values, life choices, and influence on her children. In an attempt to explain his own worldview and political convictions, life-time civil rights leader and political activist Bayard Rustin, also born into a Quaker family in West Chester, Pennsylvania, said, "My activism did not spring from being black. Rather, it is rooted fundamentally in my Quaker upbringing and the values instilled in me by the grand-

parents who reared me. Those values were based on the concept of a single human family and the belief that all members of that family are equal. . . . It is very likely that I would have been involved had I been a white person with the same philosophy" (Bayard Rustin to Joseph Beam, Apr. 21, 1986, Bayard Rustin Papers, quoted in Jervis Anderson, *Bayard Rustin: Troubles I've Seen* [Los Angeles: University of California Press, 1998], 19).

59. *Princeton Recollector,* Feb. 13, 1977; ER, *PR, Negro,* 11.

60. Gatewood, *Aristocrats,* 164–65.

61. Bond, *Education,* 289. Lincoln faculty and administration routinely helped alumni establish themselves.

62. Lefferts A. Loetscher, "New Vitality in Church and Nation," in Arthur S. Link, *The First Presbyterian Church of Princeton: Two Years of History* (Princeton, N.J.: The First Presbyterian Church, 1967), 34–35.

63. Smith, *Reminiscences.*

64. Link, *First Presbyterian Church,* 74–78; Smith, *Reminiscences.* During the time William was still at Lincoln, Princeton's Presbyterian churches (both white and black) devoted considerable time and energy to missionary work in North Africa and other "Heathen lands."

65. Arthur S. Link, *Wilson: The Road to the White House* (Princeton, N.J.: Princeton University Press, 1947), 45–48.

66. Marion Manola Thompson, "The Education of Negroes in New Jersey" (Ph.D. diss., Columbia University, 1941), 160–80, 195–201.

67. U.S. Bureau of the Census, *Negro Population in the U.S., 1790–1915* (New York: Arno Press and New York Times, 1968).

68. Smith, *Reminiscences.* See also Leslie Fishel, "The Nation and the Negro, 1865–1900: A Study of Race Discrimination" (Ph.D. diss., Harvard University, 1943); Thompson, "Education in New Jersey."

69. Patricia Sullivan interview with the Reverend Howard Waxwood, Aug. 27, 1975.

70. V. Lansing Collins, *Princeton — Past and Present* (Princeton, N.J.: Princeton University Press, 1945), 128.

71. Smith, *Reminiscences.*

72. Interview with James Fletcher, Mar. 16, 1976.

73. Smith, *Reminiscences.*

74. PR, *Here I Stand,* 11.

75. Andrew E. Murray, *Presbyterians and the Negro: A History* (Philadelphia: Presbyterian Historical Society [Pres. HS], 1966), 40–41. The poverty of small Negro communities made it difficult for black congregations to support a minister. Other denominations permitted their ministers to engage in secular employment to supplement their incomes, but Presbyterians frowned on this practice.

76. *Princeton Press,* Mar. 21, 1896.

77. William L. Ulyat to *Princetonian,* Mar. 6, 1950, Princeton Historical Society (PHS).

78. *A Princeton Guide — Walks, Drives, and Commentary* (Somerset, N.J.: Middle Atlantic Press, n.d.).

79. Smith, *Reminiscences.*

80. Through the mid-to-late 1890s the Witherspoon Street Church is seldom listed in the *Princeton Press*'s weekly "Church Notices," whereas both Bright Hope Baptist and Mt. Pisgah AME are, along with local white churches. For guest preachers, see *Princeton Press,* May 18, 1894; Apr. 8 and 29, Oct. 28, 1899; Jan. 20 and Mar. 19, 1900.

81. Photostat of Certificate of Record of Birth, State of New Jersey, Bureau of Vital Statistics. The certificate reads "Paul Leroy Robeson." On many occasions, particularly between 1917 and 1932, Robeson refers to himself as Paul Bustill Robeson. (See Ulyat to *Princetonian,* Mar. 6, 1950, PHS.)

82. Interview with Mrs. Raymond Pace Alexander, Apr. 15, 1975. Paul was Maria Louisa's seventh child; two children did not survive infancy.

83. Obituary, Maria L. Robeson, *Princeton Press,* Jan. 23, 1904.

84. PR, *Here I Stand,* 11–12; ER, *PR, Negro,* 11.

85. Records of the New Brunswick Presbytery (NBP), Jan. 30, June 20 and 26, Sept. 18 and 24, Oct. 17, and Nov. 12, 1990 (Pres. HS).

86. Ibid., Jan. 30, 1900.

87. Ibid.

88. Ibid., June 26, 1900.

89. *Trenton Times,* Sept. 20, 1900.

90. *Princeton Press,* Sept. 22, 1900; *Daily Star Gazette* (Trenton), Sept. 25, 1900; records, NBP, Oct. 17, 1900 (Pres. HS).

91. Records, NBP, Oct. 17 and Nov. 12, 1900 (Pres. HS).

92. Ibid.; *Princeton Press,* Nov. 10, 1900. Church members met under the auspices of a white faculty member of Princeton Seminary.

93. Records, NBP, Oct. 17, 1900 (Pres. HS).

94. *Princeton Press,* Nov. 17, 1900. William's salary, as well as his use of the parsonage, would continue, as needed, until May 1, 1901.

95. Brown, *Young Paul Robeson,* 23; *Princeton Press,* June 23, 1900; interview with a member of William's congregation from one of Princeton's old black families who insisted on remaining unnamed, Mar. 29, 1975.

96. Alexander Woollcott, *New York World,* May 20, 1928, and Hearst's *International Cosmopolitan,* July 1933; for blacks at Princeton Seminary, see the autobiography of Matthew Anderson, black graduate of Princeton Seminary, in *Presbyterianism and Its Relation to the Negro* (Philadelphia: John McGill White, 1897), 168–76.

97. Fletcher interview, Mar. 16, 1976. Fletcher, who attended the Witherspoon Street grammar school, became acquainted with the Robesons almost coincidentally with William Robeson's dismissal. He was closest to Ben, although he also knew Paul. Possibly the drinking episodes occurred after William's dismissal, although this is unlikely as William then had limited opportunities to preach.

98. D. Leigh Colvin, *Prohibition in the United States* (New York: George Doran, 1926), 264–66; Jack S. Blocker Jr., *Retreat from Reform: The Prohibition Movement in the United States, 1890–1913* (Westport, Conn.: Greenwood Press, 1976). The temperance movement, represented by groups like the Women's Christian Temperance Union and the Anti-Saloon League, had acquired considerable support by the turn of the century, especially in southern states.

99. *Princeton Press,* 1899–1900, passim.

100. Interview with a member of the Bustill family, allied by marriage, who wishes to remain unnamed. Also, interviews with Clark Foreman (Jan. 9–11, 1975), Marie Seton (Nov. 11, 1974), Revels Cayton (Jan. 16, 1981), and Helen Rosen (Feb. 9, 1981); FBI report, File 100–25857 (summarizes similar remarks made by Robeson concerning his early family life).

101. *Princeton Press,* Feb. 2, 1901, 4.

102. Fletcher interview, Mar. 16, 1976.

103. Interview with Joseph Andrews, Nov. 13–20, 1974; PR qtd. in *Forward* (London), June 11, 1938. See also *Guernsey Evening Press* (London), June 18, 1935; M. H. Halton, "Negro Free When All Men Emancipated," unnamed newspaper (London), 1938, Robeson Collections (PR Jr.). The West Indian Joseph Andrews was Robeson's dresser and close friend for over twenty years (1928–38, 1939–46, and 1958–59). Andrews wrote a short unpublished biography of Robeson (1949) (copy in Boyle/Bunie's possession). Bunie conducted lengthy interviews with Andrews in London. For biographical information on Andrews, see chapter 8, herein.

104. Fletcher interview, Mar. 16, 1976.

105. *Princeton Press,* Jan.–Feb. 1903. For a limited time a column appeared listing people with unpaid bills and taxes; William Robeson was among those listed.

106. Mrs. D. S. Klugh, *Boston Globe,* Mar. 13, 1926.

107. Fletcher interview, Mar. 16, 1976.

108. PR, *Here I Stand,* 12.

109. *Princeton Press,* Feb. 1894 (honor roll), Feb. 1896 (honor roll), June 1896 (honor roll), June 28, 1897 (scholarship prize), and June 1899 (graduation). There is no mention of Reeve's

academic performance after 1899. Robeson's biographer Lloyd Brown claims that Reeve attended Lincoln University and later dropped out. Lincoln University records from 1890 to 1907 list only William Robeson as having attended. There is no mention of Reeve.

110. ER, *PR, Negro*, 15–17; *Princeton Press*, Jan. 23, 1904.

111. Klugh, *Boston Globe*, Mar. 13, 1926. Mrs. Klugh recalled Maria Louisa's death in March 1926 in a speech given (just before a Robeson–Brown concert) to black members of Boston's Civic Music Association.

112. PR, *Here I Stand*, 7.

113. Foreman interview, Jan. 11, 1975; Foreman written memoir, Jan. 11, 1968 (memoir in Foreman's possession in Adjuntas, Puerto Rico; the Robeson Archives in Berlin [Akademie der Kunst] also have a copy of this memoir, but the authors were refused access to it, possibly because of the controversies surrounding Robeson in the United States); Seton interview, Nov. 11, 1974; Cayton interviews, July 16, 1980, and Jan. 16, 1981; FBI Confidential Report for the period Nov. 17–19, 1942 for Internal Security Purposes, New York File, 100–25859, folder 2.

114. Klugh, *Boston Globe*, Mar. 13, 1926. According to Mrs. Klugh, she and her husband took in Marian until "a group of white friends raised money to send her South to school." See also PR, *Here I Stand*, 12, and ER, *PR, Negro*.

115. PR, *Here I Stand*, 14–15; idem, "For Freedom and Peace," in Foner, *Robeson Speaks*, 201–3.

116. Elizabeth Sergeant, "Paul Robeson: Man with His Home in a Rock," *New Republic* 46 (Mar. 3, 1926): 40–43; PR interviewed by Percy Stone, *New York Herald Tribune*, Oct. 17, 1926; Fletcher interview, Mar. 16, 1976.

117. Interview with Uta Hagen, Feb. 23, 1977.

118. PR, *Here I Stand*, 12. Also, Cayton interviews, July 16, 1980, and Jan. 16, 1981; Valerie Oblath interview with Carlton Moss, July 16, 1980.

119. Fletcher interview, Mar. 16, 1976.

120. PR, "For Freedom and Peace," in Foner, *Robeson Speaks*, 202.

121. PR, *Here I Stand*, 13; "Reed" was the family's nickname for Reeve.

122. Ibid.

123. Interview with Herbert Marshall, Sept. 20–21, 1974; Kenneth Nelson interview with Herbert Marshall, Feb. 14, 1975.

124. *Boston Globe*, Mar. 13, 1926.

125. Carter Woodson, *The History of the Negro Church*, 2nd ed. (Washington, D.C.: Associated Publishers, 1921), 195–96; Albert J. Raboteau, *Slave Religion: The Invisible Institution in the Antebellum South* (New York: Oxford University Press, 1978), 207.

126. PR, *Here I Stand*, 16.

127. Ibid., 6.

128. Andrews interview, Nov. 13–20, 1974.

129. Seton interview, Nov. 11, 1974.

130. Foreman interview, Jan. 9–11, 1975.

131. *Princeton Recollector*, Feb. 13, 1977.

2. FATHER AND SON

1. PR, *Here I Stand* (1958; reprint, Boston: Beacon Press, 1971), 9; also Marie Seton, *Paul Robeson* (London: Dennis Dobson, 1958), 18–19.

2. Anna Bustill Smith, *Reminiscences of Colored People of Princeton, New Jersey* (Princeton Historical Society, 1913), reprinted in *Princeton Recollector*, Feb. 13, 1977, 18–20.

3. Kathy Kelly interview with Geraldine Bledsoe, Apr. 1975.

4. PR, *Here I Stand*, 11. Louis P. Gaston, a wealthy Somerville engineer and contractor, helped Paul financially at Rutgers, and Paul often had dinner with the Gastons during his high school years. Classmates of Robeson's confirmed this (Arthur Van Fleet, interviewed May 8, 1975; Margaret Potter Gibbons, interviewed Aug. 27, 1975; Frank E. Barnes, a Somerville contemporary of Paul's, interviewed May 5, 1975), as did Gaston's son, Hugh M. Gaston (interviewed 1975).

5. Interview with James Fletcher, Mar. 16, 1976.

6. Ibid. In 1913 William Robeson Jr. was the only black Princeton graduate of Trenton High School.

7. PR, *Here I Stand*, 16–17; PR, "For Freedom and Peace," address given in New York, June 19, 1949, reprinted in *Paul Robeson Speaks: Writings, Speeches, Interviews, 1918–1974,* ed. Philip S. Foner (Secaucus, N.J.: Citadel, 1978), 202.

8. PR, *Here I Stand*, 17; Margaret Gilman, "Profile of the King of Harlem," *New Yorker,* Sept. 29, 1928, 26–29.

9. PR, *Here I Stand,* 17.

10. Ibid., 6. Eslanda Robeson, *Paul Robeson, Negro* (New York: Hayes and Brothers, 1930), 19 (hereafter ER, *PR, Negro*).

11. PR, *Here I Stand,* 9.

12. Ibid., 18.

13. Kelly–Bledsoe interview, Apr. 1975.

14. Interview with J. Douglas Brown, Mar. 29, 1975.

15. Patricia Julin interview with Van Fleet, May 8, 1975.

16. Seton, *Paul Robeson,* 19.

17. Julin–Van Fleet interview, May 8, 1975. Van Fleet, a white friend of Paul's, said that Paul had been to his home but that he had never been to Paul's.

18. *Unionist Gazette* (Somerville), Apr. 1, 1915.

19. Julin–Van Fleet interview, May 8, 1975.

20. Julin interview with Samuel I. Woldin, May 5, 1975; Woldin, "The Real Paul Robeson in Somerset," *Somerset Messenger Gazette* (3 articles), Sept. 23 and 30, Oct. 7, 1971.

21. PR, *Here I Stand,* 19.

22. Brown interview, Mar. 29, 1975.

23. Interview with Clark Foreman, Jan. 9–11, 1975.

24. Telephone interview with Mrs. James C. Ford, Apr. 12, 1975.

25. Brown interview, Mar. 29, 1975.

26. PR, *Here I Stand,* 18.

27. ER, *PR, Negro,* 19–20.

28. Brown interview, Mar. 29, 1975.

29. PR, *Here I Stand,* 9.

30. John Blassingame, *The Slave Community: Plantation Life in the Antebellum South,* rev. ed. (New York: Oxford University Press, 1979), 130–32; Andrew E. Murray, *Presbyterians and the Negro: A History* (Philadelphia: Presbyterian Historical Society, 1966), 49–50; Taylor Branch, *Parting the Waters* (New York: Simon and Schuster, 1988), 3.

31. PR interviewed by Nat Law, *The Worker,* Apr. 14, 1944.

32. Ibid.

33. Brown interview, Mar. 29, 1975; *Unionist Gazette* (Somerville), Feb. 18, 1915; on immigration, see Andrew Bunie, *Robert L. Vann and the* Pittsburgh Courier (Pittsburgh: University of Pittsburgh Press, 1974), 107–8.

34. *Unionist Gazette,* Feb. 11, Mar. 4, 1915.

35. *Sunday Times* (New Brunswick), Apr. 1, 1934, and *Somerset Messenger Gazette,* Apr. 19, 1972; PR, *Here I Stand,* 15; Brown interview, Mar. 29, 1975.

36. PR, *Here I Stand,* App. A (Ben Robeson, "My Brother Paul"), 112; Charlotte Himber's interview with Ben Robeson in Himber, *Famous in Their Twenties* (New York: Association Press, 1942), tells essentially the same story (94–95).

37. Ben Robeson interview in Himber, *Famous in Their Twenties,* 94–95.

38. *New York Age,* Feb. 25, Mar. 11, 1915; Sept. 28, Feb. 12, 1916, Nov. 9, 1916. See also Himber, *Famous in Their Twenties.*

39. Kelly–Bledsoe interview, Apr. 1975; Brown interview, Mar. 29, 1975.

40. Floyd G. Sheldon, "Broadway Bound," *Pittsburgh Courier,* undated 1932, Robeson Collections (PR Jr.). Sheldon quotes from Sidney Skolsky's *New York Times* article, "Tintype of Paul Robeson."

41. PR, *Here I Stand*, 22.

42. Julin–Van Fleet interview, May 8, 1975.

43. Brown interview, Mar. 29, 1975.

44. Ibid.

45. Julin interview with Margaret Potter Gibbons, Aug. 27, 1975. Born in 1898, the same year as Paul, Potter Gibbons said she "literally grew up with Paul, almost in the same family." She mentioned that biographer Shirley Graham (*Paul Robeson, Citizen of the World* [New York: Julian Messner, 1946]) interviewed her but "passed through very quickly." She said emphatically that Graham "invented the material about Paul's early risings." Biographer Martin Duberman (*Paul Robeson* [New York: Knopf, 1988]) accepts Graham's version without qualification.

46. Miller's reminiscences, *Sunday Times* (New Brunswick), Apr. 1, 1934.

47. Julin–Potter Gibbons interview, Aug. 27, 1975.

48. Brown interview, Mar. 29, 1975.

49. *Unionist Gazette*, Feb. 11, Mar. 4, 1915.

50. Brown interview, Mar. 29, 1975, and Julin–Woldin interview, May 5, 1975; Julin–Potter Gibbons interview, Aug. 27, 1975.

51. PR, *Here I Stand*, 20; Brown interview, Mar. 29, 1975. Ackerman's disciplining of Robeson, despite the protests of some of Paul's classmates to the contrary, may well have been racially motivated. George Hoffman (interviewed Aug. 26, 1975) claimed that Ackerman fought against integrating Somerville's grammar school but lost; the school was integrated in 1916.

52. PR, *Here I Stand*, 20–21.

53. Brown interview, Mar. 29, 1975.

54. PR, *Here I Stand*, 19.

55. Brown interview, Mar. 29, 1975; *Unionist Gazette*, June 4, 1915. On minstrelsy, see Joseph Boskin, *Sambo: The Rise and Demise of an American Jester* (New York: Oxford University Press, 1986); Robert C. Toll, *Blacking Up: The Minstrel Show in Nineteenth-Century America* (New York: Oxford University Press, 1974); David R. Roediger, *The Wages of Whiteness* (New York: Verso, 1991), 115–31; Mel Watkins, *On the Real Side* (New York: Touchstone, 1994), 80–133; Leroi Jones, *Blues People* (New York: Morrow, 1963); Thomas L. Morgan and William Barlow, *From Cakewalks to Concert Halls* (Washington, D.C.: Elliott and Clark, 1972), 13–19; Houston A. Baker Jr., *Modernism and the Harlem Renaissance* (Chicago: University of Chicago Press, 1987), 17–24; Eric Lott, "Blackface and Blackness: The Minstrel Show in American Culture," in *Inside the Minstrel Mask: Readings in Nineteenth-Century Blackface Minstrelsy*, ed. Annemarie Bean, James V. Hatch, and Brook McNamara (Hanover, N.H.: Wesleyan University Press, 1996), 3–32; Lott, *Love and Theft: Blackface Minstrelsy and the American Working Class* (New York: Oxford University Press, 1993), 3–37; and W. T. Lhamon Jr., *Raising Cain: Blackface Performance from Jim Crow to Hip Hop* (Cambridge: Harvard University Press, 1998). At the time minstrel performers, both black and white (black minstrels had began performing in public after the Civil War), blackened up. For many aspiring black artists, minstrelsy provided the only jobs available, but such gainful employment required adopting the stereotyped characters and routines of minstrelsy. Black minstrel star Billy Kersand blackened up to conform to the caricature of the large mouth and large lips; *Ziegfeld Follies* headliner Bert Williams to darken his light skin. Musician and composer Eubie Blake reported that even as late as the early 1920s, black performers were routinely expected "to black up and do low 'darky' comedy" (Al Rose, *Eubie Blake* [New York: Schirmer Books, 1979], 62). See also Tom Fletcher, *The Tom Fletcher Story: 100 Years of the Negro in Show Business* (New York: Burdge, 1954).

56. PR, *Here I Stand*, 19.

57. Ibid., 95.

58. Although the *Unionist Gazette* (Apr. 18, 1915) lists Paul as particpating in the class trip, two classmates (Brown and Van Fleet) say otherwise.

59. Brown interview, Mar. 29, 1975.

60. Julin–Van Fleet interview, May 8, 1975.

61. See Kathleen L. Wolgemuth, "Woodrow Wilson and Federal Segregation," *Journal of Negro History* 44 (Jan. 1959): 158–73. Wolgemuth offers thorough and thoughtful coverage of Wilson

and his cabinet's efforts to segregate the federal government. See also Constance McLaughlin Green, *The Secret City: A History of Race Relations in the Nation's Capital* (Princeton, N.J.: Princeton University Press, 1967), viii, 171–73; Rayford Logan, *Betrayal of the Negro: From Rutherford B. Hayes to Woodrow Wilson* (New York: Collier Books, 1965), 74; William Loren Katz, *Eyewitness: A Living Documentary of the African American Contribution to American History,* rev. ed. (New York: Simon and Schuster, 1995), 351–52. Washington is quoted in Green, *Secret City,* 173; Trotter and Wilson are discussed in Katz, *Eyewitness,* 351–52. See also John Edward Hasse, *Beyond Category: The Life and Genius of Duke Ellington* (New York: Da Capo, 1995), 26–29.

62. Fletcher interview, Mar. 16, 1976; *Philadelphia Tribune,* Dec. 12, 1914. See also *Somerset Messenger,* Dec. 15, 1914.

63. Barbara Kleinhaus interview with Donald Moore (Christine Moore's nephew), Aug. 2, 1975.

64. Valerie Oblath interview with Carlton Moss, July 16, 1980.

65. Kelly–Bledsoe interview, Apr. 1975; Kleinhaus–Moore interview, Aug. 2, 1975.

66. PR, *Here I Stand,* 22–23. See also PR, "My Father Was a Slave," *Forward* (London), June 11, 1938, in which Robeson claims he began working at Narragansett at the age of twelve; Ben Robeson interview in Himber, *Famous in Their Twenties,* 93.

67. Maury Klein, "Summering at the Pier," *American History Illustrated* 13 (Jan. 1979): 33–43.

68. Interview with Margaret Upshur, Oct. 18, 1975.

69. Louis Harlan, *Booker T. Washington: The Making of a Black Leader, 1865–1901* (New York: Oxford University Press, 1972), 78–80. Oscar C. Brown, father of the musician Oscar Brown, earned money for his schooling at Howard by working summers at the Imperial Hotel in Narragansett. See Oscar C. Brown, *By a Thread* (New York: Vantage, 1983), 25.

70. Klein, "Summering," 39.

71. PR, *Here I Stand,* 23.

72. Ibid.

73. Edward Lawson, "Robey Comes Home," *Anthologist* (Rutgers University), Jan. 1932, 22–23; Fletcher interview, Mar. 16, 1976.

74. PR, *Here I Stand,* 24–25.

75. Himber, *Famous in Their Twenties,* 92–93.

76. See also Gene Robinson, *Rutgers Daily Targum,* Apr. 10, 1973.

77. PR, *Here I Stand,* 25.

78. *New York Amsterdam News,* Mar. 27, 1939; *Pittsburgh Courier,* June 10, 1939.

79. Julin–Van Fleet interview, May 8, 1975. According to Van Fleet, Robeson spoke about the life of the Negro. Van Fleet spoke also. R. Anna Miller coached them both.

3. ROBESON OF RUTGERS

1. William H. Demarest, *A History of Rutgers College, 1766–1924* (New Brunswick, N.J., 1924), 501–50.

2. See above, chapter 2, n. 4.

3. PR qtd. in *News Review,* June 1, 1939; John M. Carroll, *Fritz Pollard: Pioneer in Racial Advancement* (Urbana: University of Illinois Press, 1992), 59; *Daily Home News* (New Brunswick), Sept. 2, 3, 7, 1919. In 1919 approximately twenty-five race riots broke out in cities across the country. New Brunswick papers chronicled the mistreatment of blacks locally.

4. Patricia Sullivan interviews with Malcolm Pitt, May 30, 1975, and Dec. 6, 1976 (telephone). During his freshman year Paul filled out a form (filled out yearly, presumably for yearbook purposes) on which he listed Malcolm Pitt as one of his best friends. Like J. Douglas Brown (Somerville High School classmate), Pitt was a scholar, not an athlete. Pitt later became head of Hartford Seminary and Brown was dean of Princeton University.

5. Interview with Steve White, Sept. 15, 1975.

6. Robeson transcript, Rutgers University; Sullivan–Pitt interview, May 30, 1975.

7. Benjamin G. Rader, *American Sports* (Englewood Cliffs, N.J.: Prentice-Hall, 1983), 140–41. See also John Richards Betts, *America's Sporting Heritage, 1850–1950* (Reading, Mass.: Addison-Wesley, 1974).

8. Rader, *American Sports*, 140–41. By 1914 over 450 colleges and 6,000 secondary schools were playing the sport.

9. Richard P. McCormick, *Rutgers: A Bicentennial History* (New Brunswick, N.J.: Rutgers University Press, 1966), 163. By 1910 Rutgers alumni had formed fourteen clubs in localities across the country, from Boston to southern California.

10. Patricia Julin interview with Kenneth Rendall (Rutgers football teammate), Oct. 2, 1975; McCormick, *Rutgers*, 163. The *Rutgers Alumni Quarterly* began publication in October 1914.

11. McCormick, *Rutgers*, 161.

12. White interview, Sept. 15, 1975. See also Harry J. Rockafeller, "Foster Sanford," in *Aloud to Alma Mater*, ed. George Lukac (New Brunswick, N.J.: Rutgers University Press, 1966), 107–8.

13. Larry Pitt, *Football at Rutgers: A History, 1869–1969* (New Brunswick, N.J.: Rutgers University Press, 1972), 27–50; Rockafeller, "Foster Sanford," 107–12.

14. White interview, Sept. 15, 1975; interview with John Wittpenn, Aug. 28, 1975.

15. White interview, Sept. 15, 1975; interview with Robert Nash, Oct. 12, 1975.

16. White interview, Sept. 15, 1975; Nash interview, Oct. 12, 1975; Wittpenn interview, Aug. 28, 1975.

17. Interview with J. Douglas Brown, Mar. 29, 1975.

18. Earl Schenck Miers, "Paul Robeson — Made in America," *Nation*, May 27, 1950, 523. See also Miers's fictionalized version of Robeson's life, *Big Ben: A Novel* (Philadelphia: Westminster, 1942), xii, 17–18. Miers, a Rutgers graduate, interviewed Robeson as part of his research for the novel.

19. White interview, Sept. 15, 1975.

20. Arthur Ashe Jr., *A Hard Road to Glory: A History of the African-American Athlete, 1619–1981* (New York: Warner, 1988), 90–94, 173–74. According to Ashe, there was no quota system per se, but it was seldom that more than one black played for the same team. When they did, both players were starters. In 1915 six blacks played on white college teams: Frederick ("Fritz") Pollard, Brown; Gideon Smith, Michigan State; Joseph Trigg, Syracuse; Edwin Morrison and William F. Brown, Tufts; and Paul Robeson, Rutgers. From 1889 to 1920 only sixty-six blacks played collegiate football. There were also a number of blacks who attended white colleges and played athletics, but did not graduate. See Carroll, *Fritz Pollard*, 41–56; see also Robert A. Bellinger, "African Americans in White Colleges and Universities, 1890–1919," dissertation in progress, Boston College.

21. See Randy Roberts, *Papa Jack: Jack Johnson and the Era of White Hopes* (New York: Free Press, 1983); see also Eslanda Robeson, *Paul Robeson, Negro* (New York: Hayes and Brothers, 1930), 30 (hereafter ER, *PR, Negro*).

22. White interview, Sept. 15, 1975.

23. Robert Van Gelder, "Robeson Remembers: An Interview with the Star of *Othello*, Partly about His Past," *New York Times*, Jan. 16, 1944, sec. 2; also ER, *PR, Negro*, 31–32, and *Rutgers Alumni Quarterly*, Nov. 1930, 44.

24. Van Gelder, "Robeson Remembers," 1.

25. Interviews with Revels Cayton, July 16, 1980, and Jan. 16, 1981; see also M. H. Halton, "Negro Free When All Men Emancipated," unnamed newspaper, 1938, Robeson Collections (PR Jr.), and Miers, *Big Ben*, 93–106. Miers devotes a number of pages to Paul's summer job working at the brickyard and erroneously portrays the teenage Robeson as a union crusader fighting injustice, in this case an unfair foreman.

26. Van Gelder, "Robeson Remembers," 7; ER, *PR, Negro*, 32.

27. Julin interview with William Feitner, Aug. 27, 1975.

28. Harry Kipke qtd. in *Baltimore Afro-American*, Nov. 16, 1935; Nash interview, Oct. 12, 1975. See also Thomas G. Smith, "Outside the Pale: The Exclusion of Blacks from the National Football League, 1934–1946," *Journal of Sport History* 15, no. 3 (1988): 255–81.

29. "Fritz," *Brown Alumni Quarterly*, Oct. 1970, 31; Carlo Nesfield, "Pride against Prejudice," *Black Sports*, Nov. 1971, 30; Carroll, *Fritz Pollard*, chap. 2, "The Tramp Athlete," 41–56, 61–62; interview with Frederick Douglass Pollard, Sept. 16, 1974.

30. Nash interview, Oct. 12, 1975.

31. Ibid.

32. Julin–Rendall interview, Oct. 2, 1975.

33. Harry Rockafeller to Andrew Bunie, Mar. 10, 1975.

34. Nash interview, Oct. 12, 1975.

35. White interview, Sept. 15, 1975; Wittpenn interview, Aug. 28, 1975.

36. Wittpenn interview, Aug. 28, 1975.

37. White interview, Sept. 15, 1975.

38. *New York Times,* Nov. 7, 1915.

39. Ronald Dean Brown interview with Harry Rockafeller, *Rutgers Daily Targum,* Apr. 10, 1973; Julin–Feitner interview, Aug. 27, 1975.

40. Sullivan–Pitt interview, May 30, 1975.

41. Edward Lawson, "Robey Comes Home," *Anthologist* (Rutgers University), Jan. 1932, 22–23; Julin–Rendall interview, Oct. 2, 1975; Sullivan–Pitt interview, May 30, 1975; PR, *Here I Stand* (1958; Boston: Beacon Press, 1971), 19; Miers, *Big Ben,* 65. Miers claims that because of the dance that followed Glee Club performances, Robeson never asked to be admitted to Rutgers's Glee Club.

42. Andrew S. Eschenfelder to Bunie, Mar. 24, 1975, and telephone interview, Apr. 6, 1975.

43. Sullivan–Pitt interview, May 30, 1975.

44. Wittpenn interview, Aug. 28, 1975.

45. Telephone interview with Pitt, May 14, 1975; Sullivan–Pitt interview, May 30, 1975.

46. Brown–Rockafeller interview, *Rutgers Daily Targum,* Apr. 10, 1973.

47. Marcia Graham Synnot, *The Half-Open Door: Discrimination and Admissions at Harvard, Yale, and Princeton, 1900–1960* (Westport, Conn.: Greenwood Press, 1979), 173–221; see also Steven Steinberg, *The Academic Melting Pot: Catholics and Jews in American Higher Education* (New York: McGraw-Hill, 1974), 5–31.

48. Telephone interview with Rendall, Oct. 2, 1975.

49. Ibid.

50. John Higham, *Strangers in the Land: Patterns in American Nativism, 1860–1925* (New Brunswick, N.J.: Rutgers University Press, 1955), 66–67; Leonard Dinnerstein, *The Leo Frank Case* (Athens: University of Georgia Press, 1987), 134; Lucy Dawidowicz, *The Jewish Presence: Essays on Identity and History* (New York: Holt, Rinehart and Winston, 1977), 127; McCormick, *Rutgers,* 160–61.

51. Interview with Miki Fisher, Sept. 13, 1978.

52. See chapter 2.

53. White interview, Sept. 15, 1975.

54. Lawrence W. Pitt (professor of educational policy sciences, dean of the College of New Jersey, Union, N.J.) to Bunie, June 22, 1977. Pitt obtained the information from Bill Miller and Harmony Coppola of the Rutgers University Archives (assorted Paul Robeson–related material).

55. Julin interview with M. Harold Higgins, Aug. 27, 1975.

56. Sullivan–Pitt interview, May 30, 1975.

57. White interview, Sept. 15, 1975.

58. See, for example, *New York Age,* Feb. 25, Mar. 11, 1915; Feb. 12, Sept. 28, Oct. 12, Nov. 9, 1916.

59. PR interview with Percy N. Stone, *New York Herald Tribune,* Oct. 17, 1926; also ER, *PR, Negro,* 23.

60. *New York Times,* Oct. 28, 1915.

61. *New York Age,* Feb. 17, 1916.

62. Pollard interview, Sept. 16, 1974. See also Carroll, *Fritz Pollard,* 58.

63. Interview with Joe Nelson, Jan. 15, 1983.

64. Interviews with Bertha Reckling Bunt, Dec. 6, 1974, and with Margaret Upshur Kennerly, Oct. 18, 1975.

65. Nash interview, Oct. 12, 1975.

66. Demarest, *History of Rutgers,* 531–32.

67. White interview, Sept. 15, 1975; Julin–Feitner interview, Aug. 27, 1975. Player Kenneth Ren-

dall, however, in a telephone interview (Oct. 2, 1978) claimed most of the negotiating had taken place beforehand and that everyone knew well in advance Robeson would not be in the lineup.

68. Julin–Feitner interview, Aug. 27, 1975. See also Miers, *Big Ben,* 126–27.

69. White interview, Sept. 15, 1975.

70. Wittpenn interview, Aug. 28, 1975; ER, *PR, Negro,* 34; Lawson, "Robey Comes Home," 22.

71. PR interviewed by George C. Carens, *Boston Traveler,* Aug. 14, 1942.

72. Interview with Angus Cameron, Feb. 10, 1977.

73. White interview, Sept. 15, 1975. According to Kingsley Martin, Paul, reminiscing about his football days, described himself as "naturally lazy and difficult to arouse." He said that on occasion "one of the other men on his own team would give him a sly kick to engage him. 'Of course, he's yellow, you know.' They would make sure that [Paul] had heard them talking about him." That kind of comment usually got Paul going (Kingsley Martin, ed., *New Statesman Years, 1931–1945* [Chicago: Henry Regnery, 1968], 126–27).

74. In 1919 Rutgers alumnus James Carr, a Phi Beta Kappa and Rutgers's first black graduate (1892), at the time district attorney and assistant corporate counsel in New York City, irate over a similar incident that occurred in June 1919 when Penn State bowed to pressure from the Naval Academy and benched its black athlete, wrote to Rutgers College president William Demarest to voice the first formal opposition to the now three-year-old Washington and Lee incident. "I am deeply moved at the injustice done a student of Rutgers . . . one of the best athletes ever developed at Rutgers — who, because guilty of a skin not colored as their own, was excluded from the honorable field of athletic encounter, as one inferior," Carr wrote. "Can you imagine his [Robeson's] thoughts and feelings when, in contemplative mood, he reflects in the years to come that his Alma Mater faltered and quailed when the test came, and that she preferred the holding of an athletic game to the maintenance of honor and principle?" Carr concluded: "The Trustees and Faculty of Rutgers College should disavow the action of the athletic manager who dishonored her ancient traditions by denying to one of her students . . . equality of opportunity and privilege" (Carr to Demarest, June 6, 1919, Class of 1892, Special Collections, Rutgers University Library).

75. In his autobiography (*Here I Stand,* 27–28), Robeson says nothing about his football career at Rutgers.

76. Pollard interview, Sept. 16, 1974. Also telephone interview with Wallace Wade, Dec. 3, 1964; and Frederick William Marvel Scrapbook, Brown University Athletic Scrapbooks, vol. 8, Brown University.

77. Frank Hathorn, *New York World,* Dec. 28, 1919.

78. The *New York Times* postseason survey did not rank Rutgers in its roster of top fifteen teams in the East but did include Brown University (3rd) and Washington and Lee (14th). Fritz Pollard won first team selection in the all-eastern pollings, but no one from Rutgers was chosen.

79. *Rutgers Targum,* Apr. 1918.

80. Yearbook form, Rutgers University.

81. Telephone interview with Pitt, May 14, 1974.

82. Lloyd Brown (*The Young Paul Robeson* [Boulder: Westview Press, 1997], 67) claims that Robeson first met Neale in the spring of 1916 in Freehold. Robeson was there to address the local YMCA, and after that meeting he visited a local Sunday school where he met Geraldine Neale; Kathy Kelly interview with Geraldine Neale Bledsoe, May 1975.

83. Kelly–Bledsoe interview, May 1975.

84. *New York Times,* Aug. 25, 1917.

85. Ibid., Oct. 14, 1917.

86. Charles Taylor, *New York Tribune,* Oct. 28, 1917.

87. On coon song euphemisms, see William H. Wiggins Jr., "Boxing Sambo Twins: Racial Stereotypes in Jack Johnson and Joe Louis Newspaper Cartoons, 1908 to 1938," *Journal of Sport History* 15, no. 3 (1988): 246. Interview with Roland Tailby, June 11, 1978.

88. Interview with Pare Lorentz, Dec. 27, 1974.

89. Heywood Broun, "It Seems to Me," *Cincinnati Post,* Oct. 2, 1929. This was one of the few times Robeson openly discussed foul play on the part of whites.

90. Rendall interview, Oct. 2, 1975.

91. *New York Times,* Nov. 25, 1917.

92. Louis Lee Arms, *New York Sunday Tribune,* Nov. 25, 1917.

93. Lester Walton, *New York Age,* Nov. 29, 1917.

94. Valerie Oblath interview with Carlton Moss, July 16, 1980; Robert Macieski telephone interview with Moss, June 16, 1980. Robeson was also a member of the black fraternity Alpha Phi Alpha. The stereotype was that dark-skinned and athletic blacks were members of the fraternity Omega Psi Phi and that prospective professionals were members of Alpha Phi Alpha.

95. Oblath–Moss interview, July 16, 1981.

96. Ibid.

97. PR, "Review of the 1917 Football Season," *Rutgers Alumni Quarterly,* January 1918, reprinted in Lukac, *Aloud to Alma Mater,* 120–27; *Quarterly* editors prefaced Robeson's article with a note that filled in the gap.

98. Unnamed newspaper, Providence, R.I., 23, Robeson Collections (PR Jr.).

99. Marie Seton, *Paul Robeson* (London: Dennis Dobson, 1958), 23.

100. Edwin R. Embree, *Thirteen against the Odds* (New York: Viking, 1944), 253.

101. Kelly–Bledsoe interview, May 1975; William Robeson's obituary in the *Somerset Messenger* included a large photo, taking up about a third of the page (May 22, 1918); *Daily Home News* (Somerville), May 21, 22, 1918. The funeral was delayed until May 26 to allow Ben time to return home from Camp Taylor, Louisville, Ky., where he was in army training.

102. Kelly–Bledsoe interview, May 1975; *Daily Home News* (Somerville), May 21, 1918.

103. Interview with Helen Rosen, Feb. 9, 1981. Rosen, a close friend of Paul's in later years, repeatedly used the word "goaded" to describe William's dealings with Paul.

104. PR, *Here I Stand,* 1; "I have often remarked on the happy relationship between you two," wrote an acquaintance to Paul shortly after the death of William Robeson ("Lawrence" to PR, May 20, 1918, Robeson Collections [PR Jr.]).

105. PR qtd. in Seton, *Paul Robeson,* 18–19.

106. Interview with unnamed Bustill relative, June 12, 1975; interview with Charles Blockson, Aug. 30, 1991; interview with Julia Porter, Sept. 2, 1991.

107. PR, *Here I Stand,* 8.

108. Ibid., 8–9.

109. Ibid., 8.

110. *Daily Home News* (New Brunswick), June 13, 1918; also Shirley Graham, *Paul Robeson, Citizen of the World* (New York: Julian Messner, 1946), 93; Seton, *Paul Robeson,* 22.

111. Nelson interview, Jan. 15, 1983.

112. Ibid.

113. McCormick, *Rutgers,* 165.

114. Ibid., 166; *Rutgers Targum,* Oct. 1918.

115. McCormick, *Rutgers,* 166.

116. *Rutgers Targum,* Nov. 1918.

117. David Levering Lewis, *W.E.B. Du Bois: Biography of a Race, 1868–1919* (New York: Henry Holt, 1993), 555–57, 560; "Close Ranks," *W.E.B. Du Bois: A Reader,* ed. David Levering Lewis (New York: Henry Holt, 1995), 697; see also pp. 331, 341, 342, 540–42; *Somerset Messenger,* Apr. 17, 1918.

118. McCormick, *Rutgers,* 166.

119. Walter Camp, "Industrial Athletics: How the Sports for Sailors and Soldiers Are Developing into Civilian Athletics," *Outlook* 122 (1919): 253, reprinted in S. W. Pope, *Patriotic Games: Sporting Traditions in American Imagination, 1876–1926* (New York: Oxford University Press, 1997), 150. Walter Chauncy Camp, author of nearly thirty books and more than 200 magazine and newspaper articles, personally helped put order into a game formerly known only for its brute physicality. Camp shaped modern football's rules and introduced the concepts of the eleven-man slide, downs and yards gained, and a new points-scoring system.

120. *Rutgers Alumni Quarterly,* Jan. 1919.

121. PR qtd. in *Boston Evening Globe,* Mar. 13, 1926; Julin interview with Arthur Van Fleet, May 8, 1975.

122. Julin–Feitner interview, Aug. 27, 1975.

123. *Rutgers Targum,* June 1919, 537.

124. Wittpenn interview, Aug. 28, 1975.

125. *Rutgers Targum,* June 1919, 547.

126. Eschenfelder interview, Mar. 24, 1975.

127. Interview with Rev. Calvin G. Meury (class of 1920), May 14, 1975; *New York Times,* Jan. 8, 20, 1918. In the 1916–17 season Rutgers was beaten twice by Princeton in two close games (28 to 21 and 22 to 20). In the 1917–18 season Rutgers posted five wins and three losses.

128. Meury interview, May 14, 1975.

129. Julin–Van Fleet, May 8, 1975.

130. *Daily Home News,* June 5, 15, 1919. According to one classmate, the Skull and Cap Award was "the most important of all honors as it was given only to those seniors exemplifying excellence in all facets of Rutgers life" (Sullivan–Pitt interview, May 30, 1975). During his four years at Rutgers Robeson won every oratory contest he entered (*Rutgers Targum,* Apr. 1919, 515).

131. Earl Schenck Miers, *The Trouble Bush* (Chicago: Rand McNally, 1966), 148–49.

132. David Kelly (class of 1920) to Bunie, May 30, 1975; Anton Ward to Bunie, May 17, 1975.

133. *Rutgers Targum,* Apr. 1919, 515; Robeson transcript, Rutgers University.

134. Lawson, "Robey Comes Home," 23; Robeson's senior thesis is reprinted in *Paul Robeson Speaks: Writings, Speeches, Interviews, 1918–1974,* ed. Philip S. Foner (Secaucus, N.J.: Citadel, 1978), 53–65.

135. Robeson refers to civil rights cases dealing with blacks that occurred in the 1870s and 1880s, but he makes no mention of the Supreme Court's 1896 upholding of the "separate but equal" doctrine set forth in *Plessy v. Ferguson.* Similarly, while he cites cases involving prejudicial treatment of Chinese and Japanese (*Yick Wo v. Hopkins,* 1886, and *U.S. v. Wong Kim Ark,* 1898), he is silent about the Chinese Exclusion Acts (beginning in 1882) and the anti-Japanese sentiment in California that culminated with the "Gentlemen's Agreement" in San Francisco's schools. See Peter Irons, *Justice at War: The Story of the Japanese American Internment Cases* (Berkeley: University of California Press, 1983), 125.

136. Francis E. Lyons, "Prophecy of the Class of 1919," *Rutgers Targum,* June 1919, 563.

137. ER, *PR, Negro,* 36–37.

138. "The New Idealism," *Rutgers Targum,* June 1919, 570–71, reprinted in Foner, *Robeson Speaks,* 62–65. The speech was delivered on June 10, 1919.

139. *Sunday Times,* June 8, 1930, 12.

4. HARLEM

1. PR interviewed by Rev. Robertson Ballard, "Genius with a Soul," *Methodist Times,* Jan. 3, 1929; PR, "From My Father's Parsonage to My 'Ole' Man River' Stage Triumph," *Sunday Sun* (London), Jan. 13, 1929; Charlotte Himber interview with Ben Robeson, in *Famous in Their Twenties* (New York: Association Press, 1942).

2. Interview with John Wittpenn, Aug. 28, 1975; interview with Robert Nash, Oct. 12, 1975.

3. Blacks had been steadily migrating north since the end of the Civil War. By 1870 and 1890 their numbers averaged over 40,000 per decade, but in the decades that followed, these figures more than doubled. Between 1890 and 1910 the black population of New Jersey, Pennsylvania, and Illinois increased two and a half times, and that of New York tripled, as a total of over 200,000 Negroes left the South. On Harlem, see David Levering Lewis, *When Harlem Was in Vogue* (1979; reprint, New York: Vintage, 1982); Jervis Anderson, *This Was Harlem, 1900–1950* (New York: Farrar, Straus and Giroux, 1982); James W. Johnson, *Black Manhattan* (1930; reprint, New York: Atheneum, 1968); and Gilbert Osofsky, *Harlem, the Making of a Ghetto: Negro New York, 1890–1930,* 2d ed. (New York: Harper and Row, 1971).

4. *New York Times,* Feb. 18, 1919. On James Reese Europe, see Reid Badger, *A Life in Ragtime: A Biography of James Reese Europe* (New York: Oxford University Press, 1995); Lewis, *When Harlem Was in Vogue,* 31–34; Anderson, *This Was Harlem,* 75–78.

5. *New York Times,* Feb. 18, 1919. For the 369th Negro Regiment, see Arthur W. Little, *From Harlem to the Rhine* (New York: Covici Friede, 1936); Charles H. Williams, *Negro Soldiers in*

World War I: The Human Side (1923; reprint, New York: AMS Press, 1979); Jack D. Foner, *Blacks and the Military in American History* (New York: Praeger, 1974); Florette Henri, *Bitter Victory: A History of Black Soldiers in World War I* (New York: Doubleday, 1970), 103–7; Lewis, *When Harlem Was in Vogue*, 3–6; Anderson, *This Was Harlem*, 118.

6. W. E. B. Du Bois, "Close Ranks," *Crisis,* July 1918; idem, *Crisis,* Aug. 1918. On Du Bois's view on black soldiers in World War I, see David Levering Lewis, *W.E.B. Du Bois: Biography of a Race, 1868–1919* (New York: Henry Holt, 1993), 528–36, 542–43, 552–60, 569–74.

7. William M. Tuttle Jr., *Race Riot: Chicago in the Red Summer of 1919* (New York: Atheneum, 1970), 3–31; John Hope Franklin, *From Slavery to Freedom,* 5th ed. (New York: Knopf, 1980), 345–47.

8. *Daily Home News* (New Brunswick), June 5, 1919; *Standard Union* (Brooklyn), July 17, 1919. Paul was one of four speakers. Musician, writer, and radiologist Rudolph ("Bud") Fisher was another. May Edward Chinn, at the time a college student studying music, played the piano. Paul became friends with Fisher and Chinn, both of whom accompanied him on the piano at small recitals throughout the early 1920s. This occasion may have been where Paul first met Fisher and Chinn. For Longview riots, see Tuttle, *Race Riot,* 25–29.

9. Claude McKay, "If We Must Die," in *Selected Poems of Claude McKay* (Boston: Twayne, 1953).

10. See Arthur P. Davis, "Growing Up in the New Negro Renaissance," in *Cavalcade: Negro American Writing from 1760 to the Present,* ed. Arthur P. Davis and Saunders Redding (Boston: Houghton Mifflin, 1971), 429.

11. Claude McKay, *Harlem: The Negro Metropolis* (New York: Harcourt Brace Jovanovich, 1968), 21.

12. Rudolph Fisher, "City of Refuge" (*Atlantic Monthly,* 1925), reprinted in *Norton Anthology of African American Literature,* ed. Henry Louis Gates and Nellie Y. McKay (New York: Norton, 1997), 1177.

13. Hazel Schultz interview with Clarence Muse, Nov. 15, 1975.

14. PR, "My Father Was a Slave," *Forward* (London), June 11, 1938.

15. Ibid.; PR, "What Harlem Means to Me," *People's Voice,* July 26, 1947; PR interviewed by Haemi Scheien, "Paul Robeson Becomes an Amateur," *Drama,* July 1938, 154.

16. Robeson speech to the Women's Republican Club, *Boston Evening Globe,* Mar. 13, 1926; PR, "My Father Was a Slave"; George Davis, "A Healing Hand in Harlem," *New York Times Magazine,* Apr. 22, 1979, 42; Ruth Edmonds Hill, ed., *The Black Women Oral History Project* (Westport, Conn.: Meckler, 1991), 2:461–62, 510; Lloyd L. Brown, *The Young Paul Robeson* (Boulder: Westview Press, 1997), 107; Schultz–Muse interview, Nov. 19, 1975; Boyle interview with Rudolph Fisher scholar John McCluskey Jr., Sept. 22, 1997 (Fisher's widow, Jane Ryder Fisher, recounted this story to McCluskey).

17. PR to Dean Harlan Stone, Jan. 11, 1923, Harlan Fiske Stone Collection, Columbia University.

18. Telephone interview with M. Harold Higgins, May 2, 1975.

19. Robeson attended New York University from Oct. 3, 1919, to Jan. 3, 1920, and received credit for those courses (PR to Stone, Jan. 11, 1923, Stone Collection).

20. William O. Douglas, *Go East, Young Man* (New York: Delta, 1974), 146.

21. Shelton H. Bishop, "A History of St. Philip's Church in New York City," *Historical Magazine of the Protestant Episcopal Church* 15 (Dec. 1946): 298–317; *New York Age,* June 12, 1920. See also Anderson, *This Was Harlem,* 6–7, 23; and Osofsky, *Harlem,* 115–17.

22. *New York Age,* Feb. 7, 1920; PR interviewed by Floyd Calvin, *Pittsburgh Courier,* Jan. 8, 1927; Arthur Ashe Jr., *A Hard Road to Glory: A History of the African-American Athlete, 1619–1981* (New York: Warner, 1988), 106–7. The Leondi Big Five, organized in 1913, dominated the black basketball world until 1924.

23. Euline W. Brock, "Thomas W. Cardozo: Fallible Black Reconstruction Leader," *Journal of Southern History* 47 (1981): 186; Richard Bardolph, *The Negro Vanguard* (New York: Vintage, 1961), 93; Willard B. Gatewood, *Aristocrats of Color: The Black Elite, 1880–1920* (1991; reprint, Bloomington: Indiana University Press, Midland Books, 1993), 249, 254–55, 288; Edmund L.

Drago, *Initiative, Paternalism, and Race Relations: Charleston's Avery Normal Institute* (Athens: University of Georgia Press, 1990), 8, 20, 39, 46–48, 59, 61, 68–69; interview with Elizabeth Barker (Eslanda's cousin), Dec. 8, 1976, *The Black Women Oral History Project*, 2:122–22, 128–30.

24. Drago, *Initiative*, 39.

25. Ibid., 54. A high school in Washington is named after Francis Cardozo (ER obituary, *Daily Worker*, Dec. 19, 1965).

26. Interview with Barker, *Black Women Project*, 2:122–23.

27. Pearl S. Buck with Eslanda Robeson, *American Argument* (New York: John Day, 1949), 19. According to Essie, when she married Paul these same relatives said, "Like mother, like daughter." Pearl Buck and Eslanda Robeson first met in the early 1930s. Both Robesons had admired *The Good Earth* before meeting Buck, and Essie said that the book helped convince her to pursue a career as a writer. Buck's passionate commitment to civil rights for blacks and equal rights for women gave Buck and Essie much in common. In 1948 the two collaborated on *American Argument*, a book recording conversations between the two women that took place over several days in 1948. In the book Buck and Robeson shared views on subjects ranging from their childhoods and upbringings to family life, politics, and world peace. On many matters, such as American race relations, they were in complete agreement; on others, in particular the issue of Communism, they diverged sharply. For Buck, see Peter Conn, *Pearl S. Buck: A Cultural Biography* (New York: Cambridge University Press, 1996).

28. Buck with ER, *American Argument*, 8, see also 9; ER speech at a meeting at Riversdale Plaza, New York City, for the victims of the Smith Act, Oct. 1951 (Robeson Archives, Akademie der Kunste, Berlin [RA]); see also ER obituary, *Daily Worker*, Dec. 19, 1965; ER, "The Freedom Family," Oct. 1951 (Robeson Archives, Akademie der Kunste, Berlin [RA]).

29. ER, "Freedom Family."

30. Interview with Marie Seton, Nov. 11, 1974. On women's suffrage, see *Crusade for Justice: The Autobiography of Ida B. Wells*, ed. A. M. Duster (Chicago: University of Chicago Press, 1970), 345–53, and Harold Foote Gosnell, *Negro Politics in Chicago* (Chicago: University of Chicago Press, 1976), 25–26. While white suffragettes rallied around people like Susan B. Anthony, black women looked to figures like Ida B. Wells, who in Chicago in 1914 led the fight for women's suffrage, this despite opposition from black men who, like their white counterparts, insisted women belonged in the home. Essie's mother, in Chicago at the time, may well have been one of these pioneering female organizers.

31. Seton interview, Nov. 11, 1974.

32. Interview with Barker, Mar. 12, 1975.

33. Buck with ER, *American Argument*, 19.

34. Ibid., 6–7.

35. Ibid., 11.

36. Ibid., 13.

37. Ibid.; ER obituary, *Daily Worker*, Dec. 19, 1965.

38. Buck with ER, *American Argument*, 13.

39. Ibid., 13–14.

40. Seton interview, Nov. 11, 1974; Patricia Sullivan interview with Malcolm Pitt, May 30, 1975.

41. Buck with ER, *American Argument*, 14.

42. Ibid.; see also Medical Surgical Report of the Presbyterian Hospital in the City of New York, vol. 1, Oct. 1918, from the article, "A Pathologist," undated, in Robeson Collections (PR Jr.).

43. Transcript from Teachers College, Columbia University, in Hartford Seminary Records.

44. Buck with ER, *American Argument*, 15.

45. Osofsky, *Harlem*, 111.

46. Interview with William Patterson, Jan. 20, 1975. Patterson tells essentially the same story in Patterson, *The Man Who Cried Genocide: An Autobiography* (New York: International Publishers, 1971), 53.

47. Patterson interview, Jan. 20, 1975; see also Patterson, *Man Who Cried Genocide*, 53–54, and

Marie Seton, *Paul Robeson* (London: Dennis Dobson, 1958), 24. Seton suggests that, because Essie was two years older than Paul, she seemed to him "much more adept . . . at handling the harsh realities of New York's competitive society" (24).

48. Interview with ER, *Amsterdam News,* Aug. 6, 1938. Many people have taken credit for introducing the couple. Essie herself tells several versions of how they first met.

49. Barker interview, Mar. 12, 1975.

50. Interview with Mary Braggiotti (ER's cousin), *New York Post,* Aug. 22, 1945.

51. Buck with ER, *American Argument,* 22.

52. Ibid., 22, 25.

53. Barker interview, Mar. 12, 1975.

54. PR interviewed by Percy Stone, *New York Herald Tribune,* Oct. 17, 1927; souvenir program of the Theatre Guild's production of *Othello,* MW Box 15, *Othello* File, Theatre Guild Papers, Yale University. For other versions of the story, see Seton, *Paul Robeson,* 23; PR, "An Actor's Wanderings and Hopes," *Messenger* 6 (Oct. 1924): 32; PR interview, *Evening News* (London), reprinted in *Baltimore Afro-American,* Sept. 22, 1928.

55. Johnson, *Black Manhattan,* 175.

56. *New York Age,* June 19, 1920.

57. "The excellent acting and producing abilities of the Guild were worthy of a better constructed vehicle," said the *New York Age,* June 19, 1920.

58. Arthur Gelb and Barbara Gelb, *O'Neill* (New York: Harper and Row, 1962), 445; Louis Sheaffer, *O'Neill, Son and Artist* (Boston: Little, Brown, 1973), 33. Initially there was some controversy among the Provincetowners as to whether a white man in blackface should perform the role. In the end the pro-Negro advocates won, and Gilpin was given the part. For O'Neill as boxing fan, see Gelb and Gelb, *O'Neill,* 463. O'Neill saw the Dempsey–Firpo fight.

59. None of O'Neill's biographers recorded any incident like that described by Robeson. PR interviewed by Percy Stone, *New York Herald Tribune,* Oct. 17, 1926; see also PR, "From My Father's Parsonage"; Ballard, "Paul Robeson: Genius with a Soul."

60. See Rayford Logan and Michael R. Winston, eds., *Dictionary of American Negro Biography* (New York: Norton, 1982); Loften Mitchell, *Black Drama: The Story of the American Negro in the Theatre* (New York: Hawthorn, 1967), 50, 69, 75–76, 84–85; Bruce Kellner, ed., *The Harlem Renaissance: An Historical Dictionary for the Era* (New York: Metheun, 1987), 137–38; Moss Hart, *Act One: An Autobiography* (New York: Signet, 1959), 86–93; *New York Herald Tribune,* Mar. 13, 1921; *Amsterdam News,* Jan. 17, 1923.

61. Heywood Broun, *New York Herald Tribune,* Nov. 4, 1920; Alexander Woollcott, *New York Times,* Nov. 7, 1920; Gelb and Gelb, *O'Neill,* 446–48; Sheaffer, *O'Neill,* 33.

62. Interview with Antonio Salemme, Sept. 7, 1976.

63. *Daily Home News* (Somerville), Oct. 4, 1920; *Philadelphia Tribune,* Oct. 11, 1919; see also *New York Age,* Oct. 25, 1919.

64. John M. Carroll, *Fritz Pollard: Pioneer in Racial Advancement* (Urbana: University of Illinois Press, 1992), 141–45.

65. Interview with Fritz Pollard, Sept. 16, 1974.

66. Carroll, *Fritz Pollard,* 141. As a result of the Lincoln debacle, Pollard came under considerable fire. The *Philadelphia Tribune* charged that he had been absent from team practices and games "over two thirds of the time" (Dec. 25, 1920).

67. Carroll, *Fritz Pollard,* 147.

68. James Weldon Johnson, *New York Age,* Feb. 26, 1921.

69. *New York Herald Tribune,* Mar. 13, 1921.

70. Torrey Ford, ibid., Mar. 7, 1921. At O'Neill's suggestion recipients agreed to decline their invitations should Gilpin not be invited to the dinner.

71. *New York Herald Tribune,* Mar. 13, 1921.

72. Gilpin qtd. in Gelb and Gelb, *O'Neill,* 448.

73. Gilpin interviewed by Ford, *New York Herald Tribune,* Mar. 13, 1921; Mitchell, *Black Drama,* 50, 69, 75, 76, 84–85; Edith Isaacs, *The Negro in the American Theatre* (New York: Theatre

Arts, 1947), 61–63; *Amsterdam News*, Jan. 17, 1923, 5; Sheaffer, *O'Neill*, 35–37; Hart, *Act One*, 86–93; Logan and Winston, *Dictionary of American Negro Biography*, 261–62; "Eugene O'Neill Returns after Twelve Years," *New York Times*, Sept. 15, 1946, qtd. in Sheaffer, *O'Neill*, 37. We are grateful to Louis Sheaffer for the comparison of the careers of Wolheim and Gilpin (80).

74. *New York Age*, Mar. 26, 1921.

75. PR, "From My Father's Parsonage"; Ballard, "Paul Robeson: Genius with a Soul."

76. Barker interview, Mar. 12, 1975.

77. Sullivan interview with Mrs. George (Louise) Hayes, May 22, 1976. Mrs. Hayes said she drove Paul to Howard's Minor Hall to see Gerry.

78. Kelly interview with Geraldine Neale Bledsoe, April 1975.

79. Buck with ER, *American Argument*, 26.

80. Ibid.

81. Martin B. Duberman, *Paul Robeson* (New York: Knopf, 1988), 40; Barker interview, Mar. 12, 1975.

82. Even as late as 1949 Essie reflected this attitude. In her conversations with Pearl Buck (*American Argument*), Buck asks Essie if she thinks people should marry young. Essie responded: "I think the Africans have the final answer to that: people should sleep together, make a home together, when the feeling comes. When they feel very strongly the urge to do so, that is the time."

83. Buck with ER, *American Argument*, 26–27.

84. Ibid., 64; Nash interview, Oct. 12, 1975. Robeson was recruited by Pollard to replace Nash, who had left to play for the Buffalo All-Americans.

85. Nash interview, Oct. 12, 1975.

86. Ibid.

87. Telephone interview with Scotty Bierce, Sept. 30, 1975.

88. See *Yale Daily News*, Dec. 6, 1921, and *New York Times*, Dec. 4, 1921, report on the first professional contest played in New York City between Jim Thorpe's Cleveland Tigers and Charlie Brickley's Giants.

89. On the racial situation in professional football, see Henry March, *Pro-Football: Its "Ups" and "Downs"* (New York, 1934), 151–53.

90. Pollard interview, Sept. 16, 1974.

91. Ran Rapoport, "Fritz Pollard Remembers," *Los Angeles Times*, July 6, 1976.

92. *Akron Press*, Oct. 17, 1921.

93. Pollard interview, Sept. 16, 1974.

94. Ibid.

95. *Akron Times*, Oct. 25, 1921, and *Akron Evening Times*, Oct. 4, 1975.

96. No team had scored against the Pros since Nov. 14, 1920; the team had compiled a remarkable string of twelve consecutive games without a defeat (Carroll, *Fritz Pollard*, 148).

97. *Akron Press*, Oct. 24, 1921.

98. Carroll, *Fritz Pollard*, 148–49.

99. *Akron Evening Times*, Nov. 23, 1921. Corcoran was a new player, recruited by Pollard from the Cleveland Tigers (Carroll, *Fritz Pollard*, 148–49).

100. *Akron Evening Times*, Dec. 4 and 9, 1921; Nash interview, Oct. 12, 1975.

101. *Official Guide to the Railways and Steam Navigation Lines of the U.S.* (1920), 425, 1,007. According to Columbia classmates Milton Rettenberg (Rettenberg to Bunie, Jan. 10, 1976) and M. Harold Higgins (interviewed Jan. 16, 1976), Paul copied notes for classes he missed from classmates.

102. Buck with ER, *American Argument*, 65.

103. Interview with Dame Rebecca West, Nov. 13, 1974.

104. Allen Woll, *Black Musical Theatre: From Coontown to Dreamgirls* (Baton Rouge: Louisiana State University Press, 1989), 58–75.

105. Johnson, *Black Manhattan*, 188. *Shuffle Along* ran for 504 performances with gross receipts of $13,000 (*Variety*, Nov. 25, 1921). Despite its location only a few blocks west of the Negro section of San Juan Hill, *Shuffle Along*'s audiences were almost entirely white (90 percent, accord-

ing to *Variety*); black patrons were not, however, relegated to balcony seats (*Variety,* May 27 and Dec. 9, 1921).

106. Johnson, *Black Manhattan,* 188–89; *New York Age,* Nov. 19, 1921; Al Rose, *Eubie Blake* (New York: Macmillan, 1979), 59; Robert Kimball and William Bolcom, *Reminiscing with Sissle and Blake* (New York: Viking, 1973), 110–11.

107. Rose, *Eubie Blake,* 69–83; Ethan Mordden, *Make Believe: The Broadway Musical in the 1920s* (New York: Oxford University Press, 1977), 138–39; Reid Badger, *A Life in Ragtime: A Biography of James Reese Europe* (New York: Oxford University Press, 1995), 135.

108. Lucien White, *New York Age,* Nov. 19, 1921; ibid., July 30, 1921. According to Noble Sissle, the great black tenor Roland Hayes, at that point still trying to establish a name for himself, sang for a short time with the Harmony Kings when they performed with Lieutenant James Reese Europe's 369th U.S. Infantry Band in Chicago in 1919 (see Badger, *A Life in Ragtime,* 208).

109. Interview with Eubie Blake, Jan. 18, 1977.

110. Interviews with Ivan Browning, Feb. 1, Apr. 15, 1977.

111. Blake interview, Jan. 18, 1977.

112. Ibid.

113. Ibid.

114. PR qtd. in *New York World,* May 3, 1925.

115. Browning interview, Feb. 1, 1977.

5. BEGINNINGS OF A CAREER

1. *The City of Refuge: The Collected Stories of Rudolph Fisher,* ed. John McCluskey Jr. (Columbia: University of Missouri Press, 1987), xi; Boyle telephone interview with McCluskey, Sept. 22, 1997. McCluskey heard this story from Francis (Frank) Turner, whom he interviewed in February 1984.

2. Heywood Broun's review was reprinted in *New York Age,* Apr. 4, 1922. Marie Seton agreed that the central point of the play was never clear (*Paul Robeson* [London: Dennis Dobson, 1958], 58).

3. Program, *Taboo,* Sam Harris Theater, n.d.; *New York Age,* Apr. 15, 1922. Dora Cole Norman was the sister of musician and composer Bob Cole, who helped blaze the trail for blacks in musical comedy before World War I. According to James Weldon Johnson, an outstanding feature of the New York production was an African dance done by C. Kamba Simango. On Simango, see James Weldon Johnson, *Black Manhattan* (1930; reprint, New York: Atheneum, 1968), 192–93; Jeffrey Green, "The Negro Renaissance and England," in *Black Music and the Harlem Renaissance,* ed. Samuel A. Floyd Jr. (Knoxville: University of Tennessee Press, 1993), 163.

4. *New York Age,* Apr. 15, 1922. See also Alexander Woollcott's comment on audience segregation, *New York Times,* Apr. 9, 1922, sec. 7, 1.

5. Alexander Woollcott, *New York Sun,* Apr. 15, 1922; Robert Benchley, *Life,* Apr. 20, 1922; Burns Mantle, "Blaming the Director," *New York News,* Apr. 15, 1922; Lucien White, *New York Age,* Apr. 15, 1922; Charles Darnton, " 'Taboo' Casts Voodoo Spell," *Evening World,* Apr. 15, 1922; Seton, *Paul Robeson,* 24.

6. According to Langston Hughes, in *The Big Sea* (New York: Hill and Wang, 1940), Fisher performed with Robeson during his college days (241); telephone interview with May Chinn. See also George Davis, "A Healing Hand in Harlem," *New York Times Magazine,* Apr. 22, 1979, 40–59. Paul and May Chinn gave recitals at Mme. C. J. Walker's house on 136th Street.

7. St. Christopher Club show, June 11 and 12, 1920.

8. PR to Harlan Stone, Sept. 8, 1920, Harlan Fiske Stone Collection, Columbia University.

9. PR to Stone, Mar. 22, 1922, Stone Collection.

10. Robeson graduated from Columbia Law School in 1923. Lawrence Bruser (assistant to Dean Kimball, Columbia University) to Lloyd Brown, Feb. 17, 1975, Robeson Collections (PR Jr.).

11. BBC interview with PR, 1958.

12. Martin Luther King's biographer Taylor Branch's description of King's assessment of law as a profession (a view shared by many of King's Morehouse College classmates) is instructive: The

perception was "that idealists must look to the law, breadwinners to church. . . . This stark cultural reversal was part of the natural landscape for Negroes" (Taylor Branch, *Parting the Waters* [New York: Simon and Schuster, 1988], 60–61).

13. Seton, *Paul Robeson,* 24. On Robeson attributing his success to luck, see also PR, "An Actor's Wanderings and Hopes," *Messenger* 6 (Oct. 1924): 32; William P. Frank interview with PR, *Every Evening* (Wilmington, Del.), Oct. 4, 1926; Percy Stone interview with PR, *New York Herald Tribune,* Oct. 17, 1926; and PR interview, *London Evening News* and *African World,* reprinted in *Baltimore Afro-American,* Oct. 17, 1926.

14. Eslanda Robeson, ms. of *Paul Robeson, Negro,* Robeson Collections (PR Jr.).

15. Frank C. Taylor with Gerald Cook, *Alberta Hunter: A Celebration in Blues* (New York: McGraw Hill, 1987), 98–101, 104.

16. Marie Seton, "Lawrence Brown: Musician Who Honors Music," *Freedom,* Apr. 1952; Ethel Waters with Charles Samuels, *His Eye Is on the Sparrow* (New York: Bantam, 1952), 261; Marian Anderson, *My Lord What a Morning* (New York: Viking, 1956), 121–29. On Britain's black community, see Green, "Negro Renaissance," 151–71; idem, "Conversation with Leslie Thompson: Trumpet Player from the West Indies," *Black Perspective in Music* 12, no. 3 (1984): 112, 119, 120; idem, "Roland Hayes in London, 1921," ibid. 10, no. 1 (1982): 29–41; Edward Scobie, *Black Britannia* (Chicago: Johnson, 1972), 141–72; James Walvin, *Black and White: The Negro and English Society, 1555–1945* (London: Allen Lane, Penguin Press, 1973), 202–15.

17. Seton, *Paul Robeson,* 10; *New York Age,* May 19, 1923.

18. Margot Peters, *Mrs. Pat* (New York: Knopf, 1984), 84; Seton, *Paul Robeson,* 10.

19. BBC program, Aug. 8, 1959; Seton, *Paul Robeson,* 12, 13; *Empire News* (Glover), Aug. 31, 1930.

20. PR to ER, Aug. 23, 1922; July 1922; Aug. 22, 1922, Robeson Collections (PR Jr.).

21. PR to ER, 1923, Robeson Collections (PR Jr.).

22. The event was sponsored by Mr. and Mrs. Cary Blackburn, undated, unnamed paper, Nov. 1922, Robeson Collections (PR Jr.).

23. *New York Herald Tribune,* undated.

24. *Milwaukee Journal,* Oct. 10 and 17, 1922.

25. Interview with Fritz Pollard, Sept. 16, 1974. In the contest with the Green Bay Blues, Pollard was knocked unconscious, and Robeson was also injured (*Milwaukee Journal,* Oct. 25, 1922).

26. *Milwaukee Journal,* Nov. 9, 1922.

27. *Milwaukee Evening Sentinel,* Nov. 20, 1922; Pollard interview, Sept. 17, 1974; John M. Carroll, *Fritz Pollard: Pioneer in Racial Advancement* (Urbana: University of Illinois Press, 1992), 154; *Canton Daily News,* Dec. 4, 1922.

28. Pollard interview, Sept. 17, 1974; *Chicago Defender,* Dec. 16, 1922.

29. Alexander Woollcott, *While Rome Burns* (New York: Grosset and Dunlap, 1935), 127.

30. Ocania Chalk, *Pioneers of Black Sport: The Early Days of Black Professional Athletes in Baseball, Basketball, Boxing, and Football* (New York: Dodd and Mead, 1975), 163; Jerome Beatty, "America's #1 Negro," *American Magazine* 137 (1944): 28–29, 142–44. See also *Daily Worker,* Apr. 10, 1944; *Amsterdam News,* Jan. 24, 1923.

31. Beatty, "America's #1 Negro," 28–29, 142–44. According to one source, even during Robeson's college days rumors circulated to the effect that Robeson intended "to take up boxing after his graduation" (Edward Lawson, "Robey Comes Home," *Anthologist* [Rutgers University], Jan. 1932, 22).

32. That classmate was the later Supreme Court justice, William O. Douglas; see William O. Douglas, *Go East, Young Man* (New York: Delta, 1974), 138.

33. PR to William P. Harrison, Jan. 16, 1923, Robeson Papers, Rutgers University Archives; *Daily Home News* (New Brunswick), Jan. 8, 1923 (includes Perry's Oct. 17, 1922, *New York Herald Tribune* article, Robeson's response, and Perry's retraction/apology); PR qtd. in Lawson, "Robey Comes Home," 22; see also *New York World,* Jan. 29, 1923 (story by George Daly in "Sport Talk"); and *Amsterdam News,* Jan. 24, 1923.

34. "If I am not mistaken," fan Adolph Howell wrote, "Robeson played at least half of the

game against the Chicago Defenders on New Year's Eve and has never been seen in the uniform of the Commonwealth since" (*Amsterdam News,* undated, 1923).

35. Augustin Duncan to Eugene O'Neill, Feb. 23, 1923; PR to Otto Kahn, Feb. 1923; Kahn to PR, Mar. 12, 1923, William Seymour Theatre Collection, Otto Kahn Papers, Princeton University. Nothing came of this initial request although Essie would later successfully appeal to Kahn.

36. Interviews with Eubie Blake, Jan. 18, 1977, and I. Harold Browning, Feb. 1, 1977; *Variety,* July 21, 1922; *Amsterdam News,* Mar. 21, May 16, 1923. Although biographer Martin Duberman (*Paul Robeson* [New York: Knopf, 1988], 52) cites 1923 as the year Robeson performed in *Plantation Revue,* Robeson's own comments about the experience (*People's Voice,* July 26, 1947) indicate that he performed in the chorus sometime in 1922 while the show was still at the Plantation Room and before July 1922 when it moved to the Forty-eighth Street Theatre. On *Plantation Revue,* see Allen Woll, *Black Musical Theatre: From Coontown to Dreamgirls* (Baton Rouge: Louisiana State University Press, 1989), 82–83, 95–98; Bruce Kellner, ed., *"Keep-a-Inchin' Along": Selected Writings of Carl Van Vechten about Black Arts and Letters* (Westport, Conn.: Greenwood Press, 1979), 156; Ethan Mordden, *Make Believe: The Broadway Musical in the 1920s* (New York: Oxford Press, 1997), 138, 139; Robert Kimball and William Bolcom, *Reminiscing with Sissle and Blake* (New York: Viking, 1973), 116; Louis A. Erenberg, *Steppin' Out: New York Nightlife and the Transformation of American Culture* (Westport, Conn.: Greenwood Press, 1981), 254–55; and Waters and Samuels, *His Eye Is on the Sparrow,* 225–26. On producer Lew Leslie, see Woll, *Black Musical Theatre,* 94–113.

37. Interview with William Patterson, Jan. 20, 1975. Paul's close friend Ben Davis said much the same concerning the difficulties of Negro lawyers. See Benjamin J. Davis, *Communist Council-man from Harlem: Autobiographical Notes Written in a Federal Penitentiary* (New York: International Publishers, 1969), 45. For the NAACP and white lawyers, see J. Clay Smith Jr., *Emancipation: The Making of the Black Lawyer, 1844–1944* (Philadelphia: University of Pennsylvania Press, 1993), 16.

38. William L. Patterson, *The Man Who Cried Genocide: An Autobiography* (New York: International Publishers, 1971), 54–55; Patterson interview, Jan. 20, 1975; on black lawyers and politics, see Smith, *Emancipation,* 400–401.

39. Robeson's law school grades, Columbia University, Law Archives; interview with Steve White, Sept. 15, 1975.

40. Eslanda Robeson, *Paul Robeson, Negro* (New York: Hayes and Brothers, 1930), 73–74 (hereafter ER, *PR, Negro*).

41. Robeson biographer Martin Duberman, relying primarily on writings by Essie and personal interviews, claims that Robeson did indeed write a brief on the Gould case and that the brief was used in court (Duberman, *Paul Robeson,* 54–55). For the Gould case, see *New York Times,* Dec. 23, 1928. The case involved some fifty defendants, with an estate of $80 million at stake. It received almost daily reportage in the *Times* in 1923, the last year of litigation.

42. Federal Bureau of Investigation records indicate that, although Robeson applied for the New York Bar exam, he failed to take the test (FBI report, File 100–12304–136, 137, 138; June 23 and 28, 1949); telephone interview with M. Harold Higgins, May 2, 1975.

43. Interview with Antonio Salemme, Sept. 7, 1976; Paul on several occasions talked about stenographers in the white firm who were unwilling to take dictation from a black man (*Journal News* [Ithaca, N.Y.], Apr. 23, 1926).

44. ER, *PR, Negro,* 75. (Essie's biography of her husband was written in 1929, during a period of severe marital difficulties and reflects the hurt and bitterness she felt at that time.) Ben Robeson, "My Brother, Paul," App. A, in PR, *Here I Stand* (1958; reprint, Boston: Beacon Press, 1971), 113; interview with Joe Andrews, Nov. 13–20, 1974.

45. Interview with Clara Rockmore, Sept. 15, 1980; interview with Helen Rosen, Feb. 9, 1981; telephone interview with Mrs. E. B. Marques, Feb. 14, 1979.

46. Marques interview, Feb. 14, 1979.

47. Ibid.

48. ER Diary, Robeson Collections (PR Jr.).

49. Gilpin interviewed by Torrey Ford, *New York Tribune,* Mar. 13, 1921; O'Neill quotes and

undated letter ca. June 1923, in Louis Sheaffer, *O'Neill, Son and Artist* (Boston: Little, Brown, 1973), 35, 37; interview with Leigh Whipper, Dec. 10–11, 1974.

50. Brooks Atkinson, *Broadway* (New York: Macmillan, 1970), 193, 198.

51. Ibid., 160.

52. Sheaffer, *O'Neill*, 135; *Brooklyn Eagle*, Feb. 25, 1924 (Sheaffer says in notes that Kahn gave $5,000); *New York American*, Mar. 14, 1924; *New York Telegraph*, Mar. 1, 1924.

53. *New York American*, Mar. 15, 1924, 3; see also *New York Herald*, Mar. 17, 1924. The Board of Directors of the Federation of Women's Clubs of New York condemned the play (*New York Telegraph*, Mar. 20, 1924).

54. O'Neill's statement to the press, Mar. 19, 1924, quoted in Arthur Gelb and Barbara Gelb, *O'Neill* (New York: Harper and Row, 1962), 550.

55. *Tampa Tribune*, Feb. 23, 1924; *Greensboro Daily News*, Feb. 23, 1924; *North Carolina Herald Age*, Feb. 24, 1924; *Birmingham Age-Herald*, Mar. 16, 1924 (NAACP Papers, Folder Mar. 24, 1924, Box C-299).

56. *New York Telegraph*, Mar. 17, 1924; *New York American*, Mar. 15, 1924 (NAACP Papers, Folder Mar. 24, 1924, Box C-299); *New York Telegraph*, Feb. 24, 1924.

57. *Philadelphia Tribune*, Mar. 15, 1924.

58. Whipper interview, Dec. 10–11, 1974; Bruce Kellner, ed., *The Harlem Renaissance: An Historical Dictionary for the Era* (New York: Methuen, 1987), 383.

59. J. W. Johnson, NAACP Papers, Folder Mar. 3–21, 1924, Box C-299.

60. W. E. B. Du Bois, "The Negro and Our Stage," *Provincetown Playbill* 4 (1923–24): 2; see also *New York Sunday World*, May 4, 1924.

61. Interview with Walter Abel, Feb. 5, 1975.

62. Sheaffer, *O'Neill*, 140; Sheaffer interview with James Light, May 21, 1960.

63. Abel interview, Feb. 5, 1975.

64. *New York Times*, Mar. 19, 1924. Gilpin starred with Rose McClendon and an all-black cast at the Schubert-Riviera on Broadway and Ninety-seventh Street. Lester Walton gave the all-black production a favorable review, but the *Messenger*'s Theophilus Lewis lambasted Gilpin ("dumbell acting that made the author's portraits look like caricatures"). Walton, *New York Age*, Mar 15, 1924; Lewis, *Messenger* 6 (March 1924).

65. Loften Mitchell, *Black Drama: The Story of the American Negro in the Theatre* (New York: Hawthorn, 1967); *New York Age*, Mar. 29, 1924. In 1935 McClendon and actor Dick Campbell organized the Negro People's Theatre, which produced a black version of Clifford Odets's *Waiting for Lefty*. In 1937, after McClendon's death, Dick Campbell founded the Rose McClendon Players, a group dedicated to training blacks in all aspects of theater.

66. *Philadelphia Tribune*, Mar. 29, 1924; on black theater groups, see Sister M. Francesca Thompson, O.S.F., "The Lafayette Players, 1917–1932," in *The Theater of Black Americans*, ed. Errol Hill, vol. 2 (Englewood Cliffs, N.J.: Prentice-Hall, 1980), 13–32, and Mitchell, *Black Drama*. The contribution of theater groups like the Lafayette Players cannot be overestimated. Frequently criticized as a poor imitation of white theater, the Lafayette Players gave aspiring black actors like Charles Gilpin, Clarence Muse, Evelyn Preer, Andrew Bishop, Lawrence Chenault, Evelyn Ellis, Inez Clough, Laura Bowman, and "Dooley" Wilson an opportunity to play serious dramatic roles. Charles Gilpin, for example, would have had little chance to develop the acting technique he displayed in *The Emperor Jones* had it not been for his training with the Lafayette Players.

67. James Weldon Johnson, "The Dilemma of the Negro Author," *New York Age*, Jan. 7, 1922; Mitchell, *Black Drama*, 84.

68. Sheaffer, *O'Neill*, 140.

69. Lester Walton, *New York Age*, undated, Robeson Collections (PR Jr.).

70. George Jean Nathan, *American Mercury*, July 1924; interview with Mrs. James (Patti) Light, Apr. 9 and 26, 1975.

71. PR qtd. in *Opportunity*, Dec. 19, 1924, 370; ER, "Notes on Theater and Cinema from a Professional Standpoint," Robeson Archives, Akademie der Kunst, Berlin (RA); ER, *PR, Negro*, 80.

72. Seton, *Paul Robeson*, 24.

73. *Pittsburgh Courier*, May 24, 1924; Andrews interview, Nov. 13–20, 1974; *New York Herald Tribune*, May 7, 1924. See also *New York World*, May 7, 1924.

74. *New York World*, May 7, 1924; Alexander Woollcott, *New York Sun*, May 8, 1924; *New York Telegram and Evening Mail*, May 7, 1924; Frank Vreeland, *New York Herald Tribune*, May 7, 1924.

75. Interview with harpist Marietta Ritter, Feb. 5, 1975; Ritter saw each evening's performance of *The Emperor Jones*. Frank Vreeland, *New York Evening Post*, May 7, 1924.

76. *New York Telegram and Evening Mail*, May 7, 1924; Gelb and Gelb, *O'Neill*, 450; Gilpin qtd. in Sheaffer, *O'Neill*, 37; *Pittsburgh Courier*, May 24, 1924; Sheaffer, *O'Neill*, 157. At the end of his life O'Neill wrote, "there have only been three actors in my plays who managed to realize their characters . . . as I originally saw them" and named Gilpin in *The Emperor Jones*, Wolheim in *The Hairy Ape*, and Huston in *Desire under the Elms*.

77. *New York American*, Mar. 2, 1924.

78. Sheaffer, *O'Neill*, 142.

79. Hart Crane to Charlotte and Richard Rychtarick, Mar. 5, 1924, qtd. in Sheaffer, *O'Neill*, 143; Sheaffer interview with Jimmy Light, May 21, 1960.

80. Sheaffer–Light interview, May 21, 1960; Gelb and Gelb, *O'Neill*, 553–54.

81. Interviews with Patti Light, Apr. 26, 1975, and Walter Abel, Feb. 5, 1975.

82. O'Neill qtd. in Gelb and Gelb, *O'Neill*, 555.

83. Heywood Broun, *New York World*, May 16, 1924; Burns Mantle, *Pittsburgh Times*, May 25, 1924; Percy Hammond, *New York Herald Tribune*, May 17, 1924.

84. Theophilus Lewis, *Messenger* 6 (July 1924): 223; Johnson, *Black Manhattan*, 196; Mitchell, *Black Drama*, 83; A. B. Budd, *New York Afro-American*, May 23, 1924.

85. Whipper interview, Dec. 10 and 11, 1974.

86. Johnson, *Black Manhattan*, 195.

87. Barry Singer, *Black and Blue: The Life and Lyrics of Andy Razaf* (New York: Schirmer Books, 1992), xviii; Hughes, *Big Sea*, 225.

88. Gelb and Gelb, *O'Neill*, 557.

89. See *Variety*, Aug. 6, 1924; clipping from Cincinnati, Ohio, *Billboard*, Aug. 9, 1924; *Philadelphia Tribune*, Nov. 22, 1924. *New York American*, Dec. 18, 1924.

90. MacGowan qtd. in Gelb and Gelb, *O'Neill*, 551.

91. Abel interview, Feb. 5, 1975.

92. ER, *PR, Negro*, 76, 78.

93. *New York Age*, July 26, 1924.

94. *New York Herald Tribune*, July 26, 1924.

95. *Opportunity*, Dec. 24, 1924, 368–70.

96. PR qtd. in Allan Sutton, "Paul Robeson, the Actor, Lived His Roles with Rare Passion," *Rutgers Daily Targum*, Apr. 10, 1973. Receipt for salary to PR, signed by M. Eleanor Fitzgerald, Robeson Collections (PR Jr.).

97. PR qtd. in Seton, *Paul Robeson*, 34.

98. ER Diary, Oct. 17, 1924, Robeson Collections (PR Jr.). On Micheaux, see Henry T. Sampson, *Blacks in Black and White: A Sourcebook on Black Films* (Metuchen, N.J.: Scarecrow Press, 1977), 42–55; Daniel J. Leab, *From Sambo to Superspade: The Black Experience in Motion Pictures* (Boston: Houghton Mifflin, 1975); and Thomas Cripps, *Slow Fade to Black* (New York: Oxford University Press, 1977).

99. *Chicago Defender*, Apr. 2, 1921. Micheaux's most controversial film, *Within Our Gates*, premiered in Chicago's Peking Theatre at the end of the summer of 1919. The most powerful segment in the film deals with an old southern story, a rape and a lynching. What is remarkable about Micheaux's work is that for the first time this "old story" is told from a black point of view. A greedy white farmer is killed by his brother, and an innocent black man and his wife are lynched for the crime. The crowd of onlookers features not the usual white cracker, beer-drinking men but, instead, young and old men, women and children, all eager to see this helpless couple hang and burn. A twist is added to the plot when the guilty brother attempts to rape a young black woman.

The scene has unmistakable echoes of the rape scene in *Birth of a Nation,* but with one significant difference: it sets the record straight as to who rapes whom. In Micheaux's rendering the murderer and lecher is a white man who, as he attacks the young black woman, discovers that she is his own illegitimate daughter. The choice of Chicago — recently rocked by the worst race riot in the city's history — for the film's premiere doomed it. Most vociferous in their criticism were Chicago blacks, who were clearly frightened that the film would only spark more anger and reprisals. Other cities demanded that Micheaux edit out parts before the film could be shown. The film disappeared, and seventy years later resurfaced as a 35-mm print with Spanish subtitles, *La Negra.* For more on Micheaux, see Jane Gaines, "Fire and Desire: Race Melodrama and Oscar Micheaux," in *Black American Cinema,* ed. Manthia Diawara (London: Routledge, 1993), 49–70; Thomas Cripps, "Oscar Micheaux: The Story Continues," in ibid., 71–79; J. Ronald Green, "'Twoness' in the Style of Oscar Micheaux," in ibid., 26–47; *Midnight Ramble,* American Experience video, Northern Lights Productions, 1994; *Black Shadows on a Silver Screen,* video, Post-Newsweek Television, Ray Hubbard, prod., 1975.

100. According to Cripps's *Slow Fade,* there are two versions of the film, a 1924 copy and a 1925 edited version. The only extant version of the film is in the Eastman Kodak print done in 1924. To judge from Cripps's discussion of the later edited version (which bears little resemblance to the Eastman Kodak version), we assume that the Eastman Kodak version is the first, unedited print of Micheaux's film.

101. Cripps, *Slow Fade,* 192; Richard Dyer, *Heavenly Bodies: Film Stars and Society* (London: Macmillan, 1986), 109–15.

102. Cripps, *Slow Fade,* 192; *Amsterdam News,* Dec. 23, 1925.

103. During his years in England, Robeson never mentions the film, nor does Essie in her 1930 biography.

6. CONCERT STAGE

1. Nathan Huggins interview with Eubie Blake, qtd. in Nathan Huggins, *Voices from the Harlem Renaissance* (New York: Oxford University Press, 1976), 339; Rudolph Fisher, "The Caucasian Storms Harlem" (1925), in *The Norton Anthology of African American Literature,* ed. Henry Louis Gates and Nellie W. McKay (New York: Norton, 1997), 1187.

2. Langston Hughes, *The Big Sea* (New York: Hill and Wang, 1940), 228.

3. Allen Woll, *Black Musical Theatre: From Coontown to Dreamgirls* (Baton Rouge: Louisiana State University Press, 1989), 76–113; Theophilus Lewis, *Messenger* 8 (Sept. 1926): 278.

4. PR qtd. in *Messenger* 7 (1925): 32. In March the *Survey Graphic* published its own special issue on the subject of race, edited by Alain Locke. Subtitled "Harlem: Mecca of the New Negro," the issue featured a wide variety of articles, poems, and stories by black writers. Locke's *The New Negro,* published eight months later, included many of the *Survey Graphic* pieces as well as much new material.

5. See Woll, *Black Musical Theatre,* 1–58; David Levering Lewis, *When Harlem Was in Vogue* (1979; reprint, New York: Vintage, 1982), 29–34; Samuel A. Floyd Jr., *The Power of Black Music: Interpreting Its History from Africa to the United States* (New York: Oxford University Press, 1995), 100–110; Houston Baker Jr., *Modernism and the Harlem Renaissance* (Chicago: University of Chicago Press, 1987), 111 n. 30.

6. A. P. Randolph, *Messenger* 6 (Jan. 1924): 21; *New York Age,* Dec. 12, 1923.

7. James Weldon Johnson, *The Book of Negro American Poetry* (New York: Harcourt and Brace, 1922), vii. See also Alain Locke, ed., *The New Negro* (1925; reprint, New York: Atheneum, 1968) and *The Negro and His Music* (1936; reprint, Port Washington, N.Y.: Kennikat Press, 1968); Randolph, *Messenger* 6 (Jan 1924): 21; Douglas Gordon, *Richmond Times Dispatch,* Oct. 25, 1924.

8. Edwin R. Embree, "Paul Robeson, the Voice of Freedom," *Thirteen against the Odds* (New York: Viking, 1944), 253–55; ER Diary, Mar. 1925, Robeson Collections (PR Jr.); Carl Van Vechten to PR, Mar. 30, 1925, Robeson Collections (PR Jr.); interview with Marie Seton, Nov. 11, 1974. Van Vechten did help with arrangements, but so did many others.

9. Brown qtd. in Marie Seton, *Paul Robeson* (London: Dennis Dobson, 1958), 34–35.

10. Interview with I. Harold Browning, Feb. 3, 1979.

11. See James Weldon Johnson and J. Rosamond Johnson, eds., *The Book of American Negro Spirituals* (New York: Viking, 1925), 21–23. Several of Brown's solo arrangements were published in the early 1920s: "Steal Away" (Winthrop Rogers, London, 1922); "Five Negro Melodies for Cello" (Schott, London, 1923); "Five Spirituals for Voice and Piano" (Schott, 1924); "Two Songs for Male Quartet" (Boosey, 1924), cited in Locke, *The New Negro*, 437. Johnson and Johnson included many of Brown's arrangements in their *Book of American Negro Spirituals* ("Git on Board Little Children," "You May Bury Me in de Eas'," "Joshua Fit de Battle ob Jericho," "Dere's No Hidin' Place Down Dere," and "I Got a Home in a-dat Rock"). PR qtd. in *Detroit Evening Times*, Jan. 20, 1926.

12. Marie Seton conjectured that Brown trusted her because she was a British rather than an American white woman. Seton interview, Nov. 11, 1974, and interview with Revels Cayton, July 16, 1980; Curtis McDougall interview with PR, Sept. 17, 1952, Progressive Party Collection, University of Iowa, Box 49; Ethel Waters with Charles Samuels, *His Eye Is on the Sparrow* (New York: Bantam, 1951), 239–42; Carl Van Vechten to ER, n.d., 1925, Robeson Collections (PR Jr.); ER to Van Vechten, Sept. 28, 1925, Yale University.

13. Brown obituary, *New York Daily World*, Dec. 27, 1972. When Hayes and Brown first arrived in London in 1920, they were introduced to African-born actor turned journalist Duse Mohammed (later Duse Mohammed Ali) who found them a place to stay and arranged initial contacts. Roger Quilter assisted them materially and helped them make contacts in musical circles. See MacKinley Helm, *Angel Mo' and Her Son, Roland Hayes* (Boston: Little, Brown, 1942), 128; Jeffrey P. Green, "The Negro Renaissance and England," in *Black Music in the Harlem Renaissance*, ed. Samuel A. Floyd Jr. (Knoxville: University of Tennessee Press, 1993), 155; Trevor Hold, *The Walled-In Garden: A Study of the Songs of Walter Quilter* (Ricksmansworth, Eng.: Triad Press, 1978). On conjectures concerning Brown's contact with West Indian and African musicians and music, see Green, "Negro Renaissance," 151–71; idem, "Conversation with Leslie Thompson: Trumpet Player from the West Indies," *Black Perspective in Music* 12, no. 3 (1984): 112–20; and idem, "Roland Hayes in London, 1921," ibid. 10, no. 1 (1982): 29–41.

14. Seton interview, Nov. 11, 1974; Cayton interview, July 16, 1980.

15. See Edward E. Waldron, *Walter White and the Harlem Renaissance* (Port Washington, N.Y.: National University Publishers, 1978).

16. Eslanda Robeson, *Paul Robeson, Negro* (New York: Hayes and Brothers, 1930), 101 (hereafter ER, *PR, Negro*). See also White to Hayes, NAACP Papers, May–June, 1924, Box C-91.

17. Alexander Woollcott, *New York Sun*, May 8, 1924; idem, "Colossal Bronze," *While Rome Burns* (New York: Viking, 1934), 128; "The Reminiscences of Mildred Gilman," Oral History Research Office, Columbia University, 1973 (interviewed by Pauline Madov, Dec. 1969). Fred Schang, the founder and president of Columbia Artists Management, Inc., from 1930 until his retirement in 1963, booked Robeson's American concerts from the early 1930s until 1949. Schang knew Woollcott through the *New York Herald Tribune* where Schang worked in the drama department from 1915 to 1917, and confirmed that both Broun and Woollcott promoted Robeson (interview with Schang, Oct. 25, 1978). See also Howard Teichmann, *Smart Aleck* (New York: Morrow, 1976), 87, and Richard O'Connor, *Heywood Broun, a Biography* (New York: Putnam's, 1975), 143. Teichmann cites Woollcott's insistence that Robeson develop his singing voice as a turning point in Robeson's career. Similarly, Richard O'Connor claims that the combined prodding of Woollcott, Broun, and Essie convinced Paul to abandon law and pursue a concert career.

18. According to Nathan Huggins (cited in Waldron, *White and the Harlem Renaissance*), White first introduced Van Vechten to black social circles. See also Waters and Samuels, *His Eye Is on the Sparrow*, 241. By his own admission, Van Vechten spent "most of the twenties intoxicated by gin and sidecars," piloting other well-lubricated whites through Harlem's clubs and night spots. Carl Van Vechten, Oral History, Columbia University, qtd. in Lewis, *When Harlem Was in Vogue*, 182. See also Bruce Kellner, *Carl Van Vechten and the Irreverent Decades* (Norman: University of Oklahoma Press, 1968); George Schuyler, "The Van Vechten Revolution," *Phylon* 11 (1950):

362–69; Mark Helbling, "Carl Van Vechten and the Harlem Renaissance," *Negro (Black) American Literary Forum,* July 1976, 39–46; and Leon Coleman, *Carl Van Vechten and the Harlem Renaissance: A Critical Assessment* (New York: Garland, 1998).

19. Interviews with Paul Robeson Jr., Dec. 5, 1982; William Patterson, Jan. 20, 1975; Glenway Wescott, Nov. 28, 1975; and Mildred Gilman, Sept. 16, 1974; Patricia Sullivan interviews with Mrs. George (Louise) Hayes, Mar. 22, 1976, and Malcolm Pitt, May 3, 1975. See also *New York Times* obituary, Eslanda Robeson, Dec. 14, 1965, and ER–Carl Van Vechten correspondence, Yale University Library and Robeson Collections (PR Jr.).

20. Sullivan–Hayes interview, May 22, 1976.

21. For Europe's funeral, see *Washington Bee,* June 14, 1919; *Chicago Defender,* May 24, 1919; and Reid Badger, *A Life in Ragtime: A Biography of James Reese Europe* (New York: Oxford University Press, 1995), 219. Robeson's singing engagements are covered in *Boston Evening Globe,* Mar. 13, 1926; *Detroit Evening Times,* Jan. 20, 1926; Seton, *Paul Robeson,* 12–13; Program Note, Copley Plaza, Boston, Nov. 2, 1924; his radio appearances, press release, WGBS Radio Station, Apr. 4 and 11, 1924, Gimbel Brothers; *New York American,* Dec. 19, 1924; and *Milwaukee Sentinel,* June 29, 1924; interview with Walter Abel, Feb. 5, 1975; Brooks Atkinson, *Broadway* (New York: Macmillan, 1970), 159–60.

22. ER, *PR, Negro,* 99–100; Heywood Broun, "It Seems to Me," *New York World,* Apr. 18, 1925.

23. W. E. B. Du Bois, *The Souls of Black Folk* (New York: Fawcett, 1961), 183.

24. On the spirituals, see James Weldon Johnson and J. Rosamond Johnson, *The Books of American Negro Spirituals,* 2 vols. in 1 (*The Book of American Negro Spirituals* [1925] and *The Second Book of Negro American Spirituals* [1926]; 1969; reprint, New York: Da Capo, 1977); W. E. B. Du Bois, "Of the Sorrow Songs," *Souls of Black Folk,* 181–90; Alain Locke, "The Negro Spirituals," in *The New Negro*; Lawrence Levine, *Black Culture and Consciousness* (New York: Oxford University Press, 1977); Zora Neale Hurston, "Spirituals and Neo-Spirituals," in *Voices from the Harlem Renaissance,* ed. Nathan I. Huggins (New York: Oxford University Press, 1976), 344–47; John Lovell Jr., *Black Song: The Forge and the Flame* (New York: Macmillan, 1972); Richard Newman, *Go Down Moses: Celebrating the African-American Spiritual* (New York: Clarkson Potter, 1998); Willis Lawrence James, *Stars in de Elements: A Study of Negro Folk Music,* special issue of *Black Music: A Journal of Theomusicology* 9, no. 1 and 2 (1995); and Jon Spencer, *The R. Nathaniel Dett Reader: Essays on Black Sacred Music,* special issue of ibid. 5, no. 2 (1991).

25. Levine, *Black Culture and Black Consciousness,* 45.

26. Ibid., 50.

27. Ibid., 24.

28. Ibid.

29. ER, *PR, Negro,* 101; Johnson and Johnson, *Books of American Negro Spirituals,* 29.

30. ER, *PR, Negro,* 101; Abel interview, Feb. 5, 1975.

31. Elizabeth Sergeant, "Paul Robeson: Man with His Home in a Rock," *New Republic* 46 (Mar. 3, 1926): 40–43; *New York Evening Post,* Apr. 20, 1925.

32. Program, Provincetown Playhouse, New York, Apr. 19, 1925.

33. Newman, *Go Down, Moses,* 9; Gwendolyn Sims Warren, *Every Time I Feel the Spirit* (New York: Henry Holt, 1997), 34.

34. PR, *Here I Stand* (1958; reprint, Boston: Beacon Press, 1971), 6–27; Edgar G. Brown, *New York News,* Apr. 25, 1925. See also Lucien White, *New York Age,* May 9, 1925, and H. C., "Paul Robeson's Musical Debut," *Musical America* 42 (Apr. 25, 1925): 39.

35. Program, Provincetown Playhouse, New York, Apr. 19, 1925; Newman, *Go Down Moses,* 48, 106, 213; Warren, *Every Time I Feel the Spirit,* 84; Johnson and Johnson, *Books of American Negro Spirituals*; interview with Mrs. Walter Abel, Feb. 5, 1975.

36. Edgar G. Brown, *New York News,* Apr. 25, 1925; Lucien White, *New York Age,* May 9, 1925; H. C., "Paul Robeson's Musical Debut," *Musical America* 42 (Apr. 25, 1925): 39.

37. The reviewer for the *New York Post* reported "a thrill as exquisite as the revelation of Chaliapin singing Moussorgsky" (Apr. 25, 1925).

38. A. S., *New York World,* Apr. 20, 1925; *New York Times,* Apr. 20, 1925; on Brown's performance see *New York Evening Post,* Apr. 20, 1925; *New Yorker,* Apr. 25, 1925.

39. Abel interview, Feb. 5, 1975. See also *New York Age,* Sept. 10, 1925, 225.

40. Lucien White, *New York Age,* May 9, 1925; Mark Whitman, *Amsterdam News,* May 6, 1925.

41. Gilman interview, Sept. 16, 1974; Carl Van Vechten, "Moanin' wid a Sword in Ma Han'," *Vanity Fair,* Feb. 1926. By January 1926 Van Vechten would write elatedly to Essie, "Many people in the West I know have Paul's records" (Van Vechten to ER, Jan. 11, 1926, Robeson Collections [PR Jr.]).

42. James P. Pond to PR (2 letters), May 29, 1925, Robeson Collections (PR Jr.); interview with Leigh Whipper, Dec. 10 and 11, 1974; Waldron, *White and the Harlem Renaissance,* 162. White was instrumental in getting Victor's Clifford Cairns and Robeson and Brown together. On September 25, 1925, "Steal Away," "Were You There," "Joshua Fit de Battle ob Jericho," and "By and By" (the latter two recorded with Brown) were released; "Were You There" and "Steal Away" sold 14,243; "Joshua Fit de Battle ob Jericho" and "By and By," 16,380; "Water Boy" and "Li'l Gal," 13,362; "Sometimes I Feel Like a Motherless Child" and "On My Journey," 11,048. Victor Talking Machine Company, Statement of Royalty due on Selections by Paul Robeson for period ending May 31, 1928, Robeson Collections (PR Jr.).

For early Robeson recordings, see *A Lonesome Road,* London: (Living Era) Academy Sound and Vision, 1984, from the Jennings and Daly Collection and Robert Parker Collection (recordings from 1926 to 1932), includes "Steal Away" (1925), "Water Boy" (1926), and "Li'l Gal" (1926); *Paul Robeson: Spirituals/Folksongs/Hymns,* Sparrows Green, Wadhurst, E. Sussex, England: (Pearl) Pavilion Records, Ltd. (n.d.) from the collection of Timothy Massey (recordings from 1927 to 1936), includes "Down in Lovers' Lane" (1927), "Witness" (1927), "Scandalize My Name" (1927), and "Sinner Please Doan' Let This Harvest Pass" (1927); *Paul Robeson,* Sparrows Green, Wadhurst, E. Sussex, England: (Pearl) Pavilion Records, Ltd. (n.d.), from the collection of Timothy Massey (recordings from 1925 to 1938), includes "Water Boy" (1925), "Deep River" (1926), and "Swing Lo, Sweet Chariot" (1926).

43. Hughes, *Big Sea,* 225.

44. Ibid.

45. Ibid.

46. *New York Age,* May 9, 1925.

47. James Weldon Johnson qtd. in *Pittsburgh Courier,* May 10, 1925. See also *Philadelphia Tribune,* May 21, 1925; *Amsterdam News,* May 6, 1925; *New York Age,* May 6, 1925; *New York Sun,* Apr. 30, 1925, and *New York World,* Apr. 30, 1925; Mallon and Cobb qtd. in Lucien White, "In the Realm of Music," *New York Age,* May 9, 1925.

48. *Amsterdam News,* May 6, 1925. Sculptor Antonio Salemme said that Paul never mentioned the incident to him (interview with Salemme, Sept. 7, 1976). Many other friends said the same.

49. PR, *Here I Stand,* 20 (PR's italics).

50. *New York Age,* Apr. 30, 1927; *Zit's,* July 3, 1927; *New York Times,* Aug. 11, 1927; Sullivan–Pitt interview, Dec. 6, 1976; Mildred Lovell interview with PR, 1927, undated newspaper.

51. Interview with Marc Connelly, Aug. 4, 1976; letter from Lowell Thomas to Bunie, Dec. 17, 1976; *New York World,* Aug. 5, 1975; O'Connor, *Heywood Broun,* 89.

52. White to James Weldon Johnson, Aug. 19, 1924, NAACP Papers, Administrative File, Box C-77, File 1923–25.

53. NAACP Papers, Administrative File, Box C-77, Special Correspondence, Walter White, File 1923–25 (White did not sue but instead settled the matter with the hotel manager); interview with John Wolforth, Oct. 5, 1974.

54. Hughes, *Big Sea,* 227; ER Diaries, 1924 and 1925, Robeson Collections (PR Jr.); Gilman interview, Sept. 16, 1974.

55. Hughes, *Big Sea,* 251; Lewis, *When Harlem Was in Vogue,* 182–85; Oral History, Carl Van Vechten, Columbia University. See also Kellner, *Carl Van Vechten and the Irreverent Decade,* 196, 201, 204.

56. ER Diary July 10, 1925, Robeson Collections (PR Jr.). O'Neill biographer Louis Sheaffer also mentions this evening. O'Neill apparently had been on the wagon for the two previous

months, and "his next few days [after the Robeson extravaganza] were a blur of drinking at his hotel" (Sheaffer, *O'Neill, Son and Artist* [Boston: Little, Brown, 1973], 182).

57. See ER Diaries, Aug.–Sept. 1924, Robeson Collections (PR Jr.).

58. Wescott interview, Nov. 28, 1975; Salemme interview, Sept. 7, 1976; Abel interview, Feb. 5, 1975. Essie told Wescott that Salemme was a "bad connection" for Paul.

59. Salemme interview, Sept. 7, 1976.

60. Frequenters included IWW hero William Haywood, writers Walter Lippmann and Frank Harris, radical journalist John Reed, scene designer Robert Edmond Jones, poets Edward Arlington Robinson and Ridgely Torrence, artists Marsden Hartley and Andrew Dasbury, and anarchist-feminists Emma Goldman and Margaret Sanger.

61. Edmund Wilson, "The Road to Greenwich Village," *The Shores of Light* (Boston: Northeastern University Press, 1985), 81.

62. Waters and Samuels, *His Eye Is on the Sparrow,* 238.

63. Salemme interview, Sept. 7, 1976.

64. Ibid.

65. Ibid.

66. Ibid.

67. Gilman interview, Sept. 16, 1974.

68. Salemme interview, Sept. 7, 1976.

69. Abel interview, Feb. 5, 1975.

70. Patti Light interview, Apr. 26, 1975; Gilman interview, Sept. 16, 1974.

71. Salemme interview, Sept. 7, 1976; Patti Light interview, Apr. 26, 1975.

72. Interviews with William Patterson (Jan. 20, 1975), Revels Cayton (July 16, 1980), and Joe Andrews (Nov. 13–20, 1974). This story is also recounted in Woollcott, "Colossal Bronze," *While Rome Burns,* 124.

73. Langston Hughes, "Ambassador to the World," *New York Herald Tribune,* June 29, 1930; Wescott interview, Nov. 28, 1975.

74. Wescott interview, Nov. 28, 1975.

75. Salemme interview, Sept. 7, 1976.

76. Gilman interview, Sept. 16, 1974.

77. Salemme interview, Sept. 7, 1976.

78. Wescott interview, Nov. 28, 1975.

79. Gilman interview, Sept. 16, 1976; interview with John Wittpenn, Aug. 28, 1975; Wescott interview, Nov. 28, 1975.

80. Memorandum of Agreement signed between Paul Robeson and Lawrence Brown, July 31, 1925, Robeson Collections (PR Jr.).

81. ER to Otto Kahn, n.d. but filed June 25, 1925, Princeton University. See also Van Vechten to Blanche Knopf, June 30, 1925, University of Texas, and Van Vechten to Ettie Stettheimer, June 18, 1925, New York Public Library.

82. *Amsterdam News,* Aug. 5, 1925.

83. *Gentlewoman* (London) 71 (Sept. 19, 1925); John Shand, "The Emperor Jones," *New Statesman* 25 (Sept. 19, 1925): 629; *Daily Sketch* (London), Sept. 11, 1925; Cicely Hamilton, *Time and Tide* (London) 6 (Sept. 25, 1925): 938–39. See also Seton, *Paul Robeson,* 39. Seton said British audiences found the steady beating of the tom-tom almost unbearable. " 'Their nerves were frayed.' . . . Here and there hysterical laughter sprang up from the audience and as suddenly subsided." A few reviewers lauded the play as "deep tragedy," "a great play to read and a great play to watch," but most saw little to recommend. See Ivor Brown, *Saturday Review* 140 (Sept. 19, 1925); *Daily Mirror* (London), Sept. 25, 1925, 34; and *Theatre World and Illustrated Stage Review* 2 (Oct. 1925): 12–13.

84. Shand, "The Emperor Jones," 629; *Daily Sketch,* Sept. 11, 1925; *Star* (London), Sept. 11, 1925.

85. *Weekly Dispatch* (London), Sept. 11, 1925; *Tatler,* Sept. 30, 1925, 599; Cicely Hamilton, *Time and Tide* 6 (Sept. 25, 1925): 938–39; and *Star,* Sept. 11, 1925.

86. PR qtd. in *Star,* Sept. 11, 1925.

87. *Gentlewoman* 71 (Sept. 19, 1925). See also *Daily Sketch,* Sept. 11, 1925.

88. PR qtd. in *Star,* Sept. 11, 1925; Reginald Pound interview with PR, *Reynold's Newspaper,* Sept. 20, 1925.

89. Abel interview, Feb. 5, 1975; Pound–PR interview, *Reynold's Newspaper,* Sept. 20, 1925.

90. ER to Van Vechten, Sept. 7, 1925, Yale University. See also ER Diary, Aug. 13, 14, 15, 1925, Robeson Collections (PR Jr.); ER, *PR, Negro,* 109–11; Patti Light interview, Apr. 26, 1975.

91. ER, *PR, Negro,* 105–6, 109–10; ER Diary, Aug. 22, 1925, Robeson Collections (PR Jr.); Paul Robeson Jr., "Paul Robeson's Legacy," *Common Quest* 2, no. 1 (1997): 4; Emma Goldman, *Living My Life* (1931; reprint, New York: Dover 1970), 2:980; Henry S. Robinson, "In Retrospect: J. Turner Layton, Musical Ambassador to London," *Black Perspective in Music* 12, no. 2 (1984): 235–43. Layton and Johnson maintained their partnership until 1935 and together sold more than 10 million records (Peter Gammond, *The Oxford Companion to Popular Music* [Oxford: Oxford University Press, 1991], 333).

92. Janet Hobhouse, *Everybody Who Was Anybody: A Biography of Gertrude Stein* (New York: Putnam's, 1975), 140; James R. Mellow, *Charmed Circle: Gertrude Stein and Company* (New York: Avon Books, 1974), 340–74. White artists vacationing or working in Paris made these ritual contacts as a matter of course; ER, *PR, Negro,* 105–6; Gertrude Stein, *The Autobiography of Alice B. Toklas* (New York: Harcourt, Brace, 1933), 238.

93. Claude McKay, *A Long Way from Home* (New York: Furman, 1937), 265. See also Wayne F. Cooper, *Claude McKay: Rebel Sojourner in the Harlem Renaissance* (Baton Rouge: Louisiana State University Press, 1987), 207.

94. Arthur Mizener, *Far Side of Paradise: A Biography of F. Scott Fitzgerald* (Boston: Houghton, Mifflin, 1951), 202; Max Eastman, *Love and Revolution* (New York: Random House, 1964).

95. West interview, Nov. 13, 1974; ER, *PR, Negro,* 120.

96. West interview, Nov. 13, 1974; ER, *PR, Negro,* 120.

97. ER, *PR, Negro,* 113.

98. Cooper, *Claude McKay,* 227.

99. Eastman, *Love and Revolution,* 468; McKay, *Long Way from Home,* 265.

100. McKay, *Long Way from Home,* 256.

101. Wescott interview, Nov. 28, 1975.

102. ER qtd. in McKay, *Long Way from Home,* 267–68.

103. Eastman, *Love and Revolution,* 468–69; Wescott interview, Nov. 28, 1975.

104. Wescott interview, Nov. 28, 1975; Schang interview, Oct. 25, 1978.

105. Thanks to Essie, the *Pittsburgh Courier* headlined Paul's London performance: "Robeson Wins Praise of Critics in London: Hailed as Black Chaliapin in European Triumph of *The Emperor Jones* — Takes 12 Curtain Calls as Audience Applauds" (undated, 1925). See also *Amsterdam News,* Oct. 28, 1925; *Opportunity,* Nov. 1925, 346–48.

7. TOURING AMERICA

1. On the minstrel mask, see Houston Baker Jr., *Modernism and the Harlem Renaissance* (Chicago: University of Chicago Press, 1987), 17–24. On the long-term effects of minstrelsy, especially for black entertainers, who bore the burden of working within minstrelsy's distorted standard, see Mel Watkins, *On the Real Side* (New York: Touchstone, 1994), 80–133, and Eric Lott, *Love and Theft: Blackface Minstrelsy and the American Working Class* (New York: Oxford University Press, 1993), 3–37. See also Paul Burgett, "Vindication as a Thematic Principle in the Writings of Alain Locke on the Music of Black Americans," in *Black Music in the Harlem Renaissance,* ed. Samuel A. Floyd Jr. (Knoxville: University of Tennessee Press, 1993), 29–40.

2. *New York Post,* Jan. 6, 1926.

3. Ibid.; Grena Bennett, *New York American,* Jan. 6, 1926; *New York Telegram,* Jan. 6, 1926.

4. *New York Post,* Jan. 6, 1926; *Register* (Hotel, Pa.), Jan. 19, 1926.

5. Typical programs of this period included "I Know de Lord's Laid His Hand on Me," "Sometimes I Feel Like a Motherless Child," "Water Boy," "Scandalize My Name," "I'll Hear the Trumpet Soon," "I Got a Home in-a-dat Rock," "Every Time I Feel de Spirit," "Little David," "Stan' Still Jordan," "Git on Board, Little Children," "By and By," "Oh Gimme Yo' Hand," "Were

You There," "My Way's Cloudy," "Nobody Knows de Trouble," "Joshua Fit de Battle ob Jericho" (Program, concert at Carnegie Music Hall, Pittsburgh, Jan. 27, 1926).

6. PR qtd. in *Detroit News,* Jan. 21, 1926.

7. Ibid.; Cyril Player, *Detroit News,* Jan. 24, 1926; Clifford Epstein, *Detroit News,* Jan. 29, 1926. See also Charlotte M. Tarsney, *Detroit Free Press,* Jan. 29, 1926.

8. *New York Sun,* May 4, 1925; Harvey Gaul, *Pittsburgh Post,* Jan. 28, 1926; Burt McMurtrie, *Pittsburgh Press,* Jan. 28, 1926; Glenn Dillard Gunn, *Chicago Herald Examiner,* Feb. 11, 1926; Edward Moore, *Chicago Daily Tribune,* Feb. 11, 1926; Clifford Epstein, *Detroit News,* Jan 29, 1926; *Pittsburgh Chronicle Telegraph,* Jan. 28, 1926; Karleton Hackett, *Chicago Evening Post,* Feb. 11, 1926; Ralph Holmes, *Detroit Evening Times,* Jan. 29, 1926. For the first time, Larry Brown earned less than laudatory comment: Burton Davis, the critic from the *Morning Telegraph,* complained that Brown's voice, "about half the size of Robeson . . . suffers in comparison with Robeson's great pipe organ" (Dec. 19, 1926).

9. Patricia Sullivan interview with Malcolm Pitt, May 30, 1975; telephone interviews with Malcolm Pitt, May 14, 1975, and Dec. 6, 1976.

10. If the situation annoyed Paul, he kept his chagrin well hidden and at the end of the concert good-naturedly agreed to an interview with the student representative of "The Newsiest High School Paper in Iowa," *Purple and Grey* (Burlington), Feb. 22, 1926; ER to Carl Van Vechten and Fania Marinoff, Feb. 15, 1926, from Green Bay, Wisc., Yale University; Eslanda Robeson, *Paul Robeson, Negro* (New York: Hayes and Brothers, 1930), 123 (hereafter ER, *PR, Negro*); Glenn Dillard Gunn, *Chicago Herald Examiner,* Feb. 11, 1926; press releases, NAACP Papers, released on Feb. 19, 1926.

11. ER to Van Vechten and Marinoff, Feb. 15, 1926, Yale University.

12. Ibid.

13. ER, *PR, Negro,* 124.

14. Ibid., 127; *Boston Transcript,* Mar. 15, 1926. Canceled concerts: one at New York's Town Hall; the other, a benefit for the Manassas (Va.) Industrial School for Colored Youth, also in New York (*New York Telegram,* Apr. 17, 1926; *New York Times,* Apr. 5, 1926; *Musical Leader,* Apr. 8, 1926).

15. James Pond to PR (two letters), May 29, 1925, Robeson Collections (PR Jr.); Victor Talking Machine Company, Statement of Royalty due on Selections by Paul Robeson for period ending May 31, 1928, Robeson Collections (PR Jr.); interview with Antonio Salemme, Sept. 7, 1976.

16. Floyd Calvin interview with PR, *Pittsburgh Courier,* Jan. 8, 1927; Royalty Statement up to May 31, 1926, Victor Talking Machine Co., Robeson Collections (PR Jr.); Edwin R. Embree, *Brown Americans: The Story of a Tenth of the Nation* (New York: Viking, 1945); ER, *PR, Negro,* 131. See also *Musical Leader,* Oct. 20, 1927.

17. Interview with Reginald Boardman, Oct. 20, 1981.

18. ER to Van Vechten and Marinoff, July 26, 1926, Yale University.

19. Ibid.

20. Salemme interview, Sept. 7, 1976; ER Diary, May 8, 23, 30, June 4–15, 1926, Robeson Collections (PR Jr.); interviews with Revels Cayton (July 16, 1980), Helen Rosen (Feb. 9, 1981), and Joe Andrews (Nov. 13–20, 1974); ER, *PR, Negro,* 136.

21. Interview with Mildred Gilman, Sept. 16, 1974; ER, *PR, Negro,* 136.

22. Percy Stone interview with PR, *New York Herald Tribune,* Oct. 17, 1927. For Walter White's recommendation, see White to Juilliard Foundation, New York, Jan. 6, 1927, NAACP Papers, File Jan. 1–7, 1927, Box C-96.

23. Donald Friede, *The Mechanical Angel: His Adventures and Enterprises in the Glittering 20's* (New York: Knopf, 1948), 39; Fredi Washington had been part of the famed *Shuffle Along* dance group and, at the time, worked at Club Alhambra on Seventh Avenue at 126th Street.

24. Friede, *Mechanical Angel,* 39.

25. Jim Tully tells a similar story, or another version of the same story. Liveright and Robeson were to meet at the door of a well-known New York restaurant, reportedly the Cafe des Beaux Arts, but upon arrival were greeted "with the polite, nevertheless firm information that there was

not a single table to be had in the entire establishment, although it is said a number of waiters idly strolled about the premises" (Tully qtd. in *Brooklyn Eagle,* Oct. 17, 1926).

26. Friede, *Mechanical Angel,* 40.

27. Burton Davis, *Morning Telegraph;* Arthur Pollock, *Brooklyn Daily Eagle;* E. W. Osborn, *New York World;* Burns Mantle, *New York News* (all Oct. 7, 1926). Percy Hammond, writing for *Variety,* concluded that Washington fell "very short of the mark in some of the high dramatic spots when a truly big actress would have made much of the opportunities" (Oct. 13, 1926).

28. George Jean Nathan, *American Mercury,* Feb. 1927, 502.

29. Burton Davis, *Morning Telegraph,* Oct. 7, 1926; Alexander Woollcott, *New York World,* Oct. 7, 1926; Robert Benchley, *Life,* Oct. 28, 1926, 19. An antiracist throughout his career, Benchley often used his column to protest intolerance. In 1921 he came to the defense of Charles Gilpin when he was denied an invitation to the Drama League's dinner, and in 1924 spoke out in behalf of Robeson and Mary Blair when controversy plagued the opening of *All God's Chillun.* See Billy Altman, *Laughter's Gentle Soul* (New York: Norton, 1997), 195–96.

30. George Schuyler, "Young Black Joe on Broadway," *Messenger* 8 (Nov. 1926). Theophilus Lewis called "Professor Tully . . . one of a long line of authors who can see blacks only in the extremes of 'angel' or 'devil' " (ibid.); *Baltimore Afro-American,* Nov. 13, 1926; see also *Amsterdam News,* Oct. 13, 1926.

31. On Van Vechten's *Nigger Heaven* see Joel Roger's comments in *Messenger* 9 (Feb. 1927): 47: "If being in a place where the chief excuse for one's existence is to furnish a living for exploiters, white and colored, is heaven, then Harlem is 'Negro Heaven.' When Carl Van Vechten says 'Nigger Heaven' what he really means is 'Van Vechten Heaven,' since Harlem furnishes a release of soul for white people of the lewd cow-like sort, 'fed up' with the monotony and Arctic whiteness, spiritual and physical, in their own group"; Langston Hughes, *The Big Sea* (New York: Hill and Wang, 1940), 268–69.

32. Telegram from PR to Carl Van Vechten, Aug. 12, 1926, Yale University. In an interview with a reporter from the *Wilmington* (Del.) *Press,* Robeson said *Nigger Heaven* was "excellently written and judicially presents life in Harlem"; *Fire!* folded after its premiere issue. According to Langston Hughes, Du Bois "roasted the publication"; the *Baltimore Afro-American's* Leon Graves "just tossed the first issue of *Fire!* into the fire"; and white critics, with the exception of *Bookman,* ignored it entirely (Hughes, *Big Sea,* 237).

33. Wayne Cooper interview with Bruce Nugent as told to authors, May 20, 1990.

34. George Schuyler, *Messenger* 8 (Nov. 1926): 333–34.

35. PR interview with Floyd Calvin, *Pittsburgh Courier,* Jan. 8, 1927; interviews with Antonio Salemme (Sept. 7, 1976), Patti Light (Apr. 26, 1875), Ivan Browning (Apr. 15, 1977), and Leigh Whipper (Dec. 10 and 11, 1974).

36. On white managers, see Browning interviews (Feb. 1 and Apr. 15, 1977) and Whipper interview (Dec. 10 and 11, 1974).

37. *Morning Telegraph,* Dec. 19, 1926.

38. Burton Davis, *Morning Telegraph,* Dec. 19, 1926.

39. *Worcester Telegram,* Jan. 10, 1927.

40. Interviews with Fred Schang, Oct. 25, 1978, Oct. 20, 1974.

41. Brown quoted by Revels Clayton, interviewed on July 16, 1981. Robeson was not the first black performer to run into the segregated seating problem. Roland Hayes, who blazed this trail one year earlier, learned southern racial mores the hard way on tour. Hayes had stipulated he would perform only for integrated audiences but found this requirement almost impossible to enforce in the South. In Atlanta, his native state and the first of his concert stops, theater managers "integrated" the audience by vertically dividing the concert hall in two, one half for black patrons and the other for whites — hardly the "integration" Hayes had intended. In Washington, D.C., and Baltimore, Hayes likewise received assurances, first by letter and then by telegram, that the seating would be integrated but on arrival in both cities he was informed the audience would be segregated. Faced with the dilemma of honoring his contract or refusing to perform, Hayes chose to sing because breaking his contract would lend credence to the stereotype of blacks as irresponsible. His decision exposed him to heavy fire from the black weeklies as well as the National Race Congress, the

NAACP, and a large committee of black ministers, all of whom urged him to refuse to appear. See Joel Rogers, "Roland Hayes' Dilemma," *Messenger* 8 (March 1926): 82; also (Feb. 1926): 47–48.

42. *Wichita Eagle,* Jan. 27, 1927, Kansas State Historical Society, Topeka.

43. "The Reminiscences of Roy Wilkins," Oral History Research Office, Columbia University, 1962, 23–25 (interview conducted by William Ingersoll, 1960). Also, Roy Wilkins, *Standing Fast* (New York: Viking, 1982), 71–72.

44. "Reminiscences of Roy Wilkins"; *Kansas City Times,* Jan. 26, 1927.

45. *Kansas City Call,* Feb. 25, 1927. Although Larry Brown almost always earned fine reviews, Bacote was not the only one to speak in less than flattering terms about his musicianship. Among others, John Hammond, a Columbia Records executive who first met Robeson in the early 1930s, described Brown as a "charming man" but a "terrible accompanist, technically. His duets were lovely, but I was a purist and what he wrote was music for white folks" (interview with John Hammond, Mar. 17, 1977).

46. Letters from J. F. Watkins and Charles A. Starks, *Kansas City Call,* Feb. 25, 1927.

47. *Columbus Citizen,* Mar. 13, 1927; *Ohio State Journal,* Mar. 13, 1927.

48. *Variety,* Feb. 2, 1927. John McCormack headed the list at $5,000, followed by Fritz Kreisler ($4,750) and Feodor Chaliapin ($4,000). Robeson was the last name on the list at $1,250 (figures based on guaranteed fees per performance in cities of 390,000); *New York Herald Tribune,* Sept. 4, 1927 (other blacks named in the proposed Bar Harbor project include Ethel Waters, Florence Mills, and boxer Harry Wills); Lester A. Walton, *New York Evening World,* Sept. 11, 1927.

49. Frank B. Lenz in an interview with PR, "When Robeson Sings," *Association Men* (YMCA publication), July 1927, 495–96.

50. Jack Foster, *Denver Evening News,* Oct. 1, 1927.

51. *New York Evening Sun,* Oct. 1927, and contract with Walter Varney, dated Sept. 1927, Robeson Collections (PR Jr.); PR to ER, Oct. 16, 1927, Robeson Collections (PR Jr.).

52. Thurston McCauley, *New York Sun,* Nov. 22, 1927; *Baltimore Afro-American,* Nov. 19, 1927. See also *Le Presse,* Nov. 1, 1927; *Comedia,* Oct. 31, 1927; *Courier Musical,* Dec. 1927; *Daily Mail* (London), Oct. 31, 1927.

53. McCauley, *New York Sun,* Nov. 22, 1927; see also *Baltimore Afro-American,* Nov. 19, 1927. See *Philadelphia Tribune,* Nov. 12, 1927; *Amsterdam News,* Nov. 17, 1927; *New York Age,* Nov. 17, 1927.

54. Pearl Buck with Eslanda Goode Robeson, *An American Argument* (New York: John Day Co., 1963), 5–6; PR to ER, Dec. 10 and 12, 1927, Robeson Collections (PR Jr.).

55. PR to ER, Dec. 12, 1927, Robeson Collections (PR Jr.).

56. ER, *PR, Negro,* 136.

8. SHOW BOAT

1. ER to Carl Van Vechten, Nov. 16, 1925 (from France), Yale University.

2. Phyllis Rose, *Jazz Cleopatra: Josephine Baker in Her Time* (New York: Doubleday, 1989), 8, 61–62, 79–80; Tyler Stovall, *Paris Noir: African Americans in the City of Light* (Boston: Houghton Mifflin, 1996), 52, 53–54, 70, 151, 170; William Marion Cook, "Deplores 'High Yellow Reviews,'" *Chicago Tribune* (Paris edition), Nov. 18, 1925 (clipping file, James Weldon Johnson Collection, Beinecke, Yale University), qtd. in Rose, *Jazz Cleopatra,* 79–80. Cook, a violin prodigy, studied at Oberlin Conservatory of Music, at the age of fifteen in Berlin, and for a brief time with the Czech composer Antonin Dvorak. At the age of twenty-five he made his solo debut at New York's Carnegie Hall but was so distraught when critics called him "the world's greatest Negro violinist" ("I am the world's greatest violinist," Cook snapped) that he vowed never to play the violin again. Concentrating on popular music, he went on to become a composer and conductor of unusual originality and skill. On Cook, see Loften Mitchell, *Black Drama: The Story of the American Negro in the Theatre* (New York: Hawthorn, 1967), 47, 49, 50, 61; Rayford W. Logan and Michael R. Winston, eds., *Dictionary of American Negro Biography* (New York: Norton, 1982), 127; Edward Kennedy (Duke) Ellington, *Music Is My Mistress* (1973; reprint, New York: Da Capo Press, 1976), 97; Sidney Bechet, *Treat It Gentle* (1960; reprint, New York: Da Capo Press, 1975), 125; and Thomas L. Morgan and William Barlow, *From Cakewalks to Concert Halls* (Washington, D.C.: Elliot and Clark, 1992), 62–64.

3. "The Tangled Affairs of Paul Robeson," *Equity,* Sept. 1928; Fania Marinoff to Van Vechten, Feb. 29, 1928, Carl Van Vechten Papers, New York Public Library.

4. Black critics objected to *Porgy*'s racist stereotypes and liberal use of the word "nigger." See Mitchell, *Black Drama,* 86, 98–99; *New York Times,* Oct. 16, 1927; *Porgy,* act 1, in DuBose Heyward and Dorothy Heyward, "Porgy," *Famous Plays of the 1920s,* ed. Kenneth MacGowan (New York: Dell, 1967); *New York Times,* Mar. 1, 1928. Only four other musicals in New York stage history had enjoyed a longer run; see Columbia Records, *Show Boat,* AG 55, mono; also, Burns Mantle, *Best Plays of 1928–1929* (New York: Dodd and Mead, 1929).

5. PR to Larry Brown, Apr. 10 and 19, 1928, Lawrence Brown Papers, Schomburg Collection, New York Public Library.

6. *Observer* (London), Apr. 15, 1928; *Sunday News* (London), Apr. 27, 1928; Frank C. Taylor with Gerald Cook, *Alberta Hunter: A Celebration in Blues* (New York: McGraw Hill, 1987), 101; *Evening Standard* (London), May 4, 1928; *Daily Mail* (London), May 2, 1928. In addition to "Ol' Man River," the musical featured "My Bill," "Life upon the Wicked Stage," and "Can't Help Lovin' Dat' Man." See also Miles Kreuger, *Show Boat: The Story of a Classic American Musical* (New York: Da Capo Press, 1977).

7. Alexander Woollcott, "Colossal Bronze," *While Rome Burns* (New York: Viking, 1974), 123–25; Kreuger, *Show Boat,* 20; *Sunday Graphic* (London), May 6, 1928; *Observer* (London), May 6, 1928; *Referee,* June 5, 1928; *Morning Post* (London), May 4, 1928; James Agate, *Sunday Times,* May 7, 1928.

8. Kern initially offered the role to Robeson, but repeated construction delays on the resplendent new Ziegfeld Theatre plagued efforts to get the show under way, and by December 1927, when rehearsals were finally ready to begin, Robeson was in Europe. Baritone Jules Bledsoe played the part instead (Whitney Balliet, "Our Local Correspondents," *New Yorker,* Oct. 31, 1977, 104). ER to Van Vechten, June 14, 1928, Yale University.

9. For his insights on Kern's "Ol' Man River" we are grateful to Richard Dyer, "Paul Robeson: Crossing Over," in Dyer, *Heavenly Bodies: Film Stars and Society* (London: Macmillan, 1986), 79, 104–6.

10. Nat Hentoff, *Listen to the Stories: Nat Hentoff on Jazz and Country Music* (New York: HarperCollins, 1995), 51; Pete Hamill, *Why Sinatra Matters* (Boston: Little, Brown, 1998), 116; PR qtd. in *North Mail and Newcastle Chronicle,* Mar. 1, 1939.

11. It is possible that Robeson initially did sing "Niggers all work" but if he did, he soon changed the words. Joel Rogers, writing for the *Amsterdam News,* said that he had heard from black Americans who saw the show that the word "nigger" was "perhaps the most frequent one in the play." Rogers, however, after seeing the show for himself gave it a good review and never mentioned the use of the word (Rogers, *Amsterdam News,* Oct. 3, 1928). Similarly, Alberta Hunter specifically states that Robeson eliminated the word "nigger" from the song (Taylor and Cook, *Alberta Hunter,* 101). In England, however, the word "nigger" was used frequently as a synonym for black and carried no racist connotations. And we did find one recording, made in 1930, in which Robeson sings "Ol' Man River" with the original lyrics ("Niggers all work") intact. Recorded in 1930 (Mat. Bb20084; HMV B 3653) in *Paul Robeson,* (Pearl) Pavilion Records, Ltd., Sparrows Green, Wadhurst, E. Sussex, England, GEMM CD 9356.

12. Recording with Paul Whiteman and his orchestra, Jan. 3, 1928, *Paul Robeson,* Pavilion Records, Ltd., Sparrows Green, Wadhurst, E. Sussex, England, PAST CD 7009; recording with London *Show Boat* cast, May 5, 1928, *Paul Robeson Sings Ol' Man River and Other Favorites Recorded 1928–1939,* 1985 EMI Records, Ltd., U.K., and 1987 Angel Records (Capitol Records, Inc.), 1750 N. Vine Street, Hollywood, CDC-7 47839 2.

13. *Observer,* May 6, 1928; interview with Joe Andrews, Nov. 13–20, 1974.

14. Alberta Hunter qtd. in Taylor and Cook, *Alberta Hunter,* 102; telephone interview with Bernard Sarron, Nov. 2, 1974; ER to Van Vechten, June 14, 1928, Yale University.

15. *Variety,* Oct. 17, 1928; *Amsterdam News,* July 4, 1928; Whitney Balliet, "Our Local Correspondents," *New Yorker,* Oct. 31, 1977; Taylor and Cook, *Alberta Hunter,* 104.

16. Marie Seton, *Paul Robeson* (London: Dennis Dobson, 1958), 42; ER to Van Vechten, June 14, 1928, Yale University.

17. *Evening Standard,* July 4, 1928; *Evening News* (London), July 6, 1928.

18. ER to Van Vechten, June 14, 1928, Yale University; *Evening Standard,* July 4, 1928. Robeson's special matinee performances at Drury Lane, touted as "among the great social and popular events of [the] season," proved quite lucrative as well, earning Robeson £450 and, three weeks later, £675 (*Evening Standard,* Apr. 29, 1929).

19. *Evening News,* July 6, 1928; *Daily Sketch* (London), July 4, 1928. Chaliapin performed *Boris Godunov* in London on July 4, 1928 (*People* [London], July 8, 1928).

20. *Amsterdam News,* Sept. 15, 1928; James Douglas, *Daily Express* (London), July 5, 1928.

21. Black Americans had been performing in England — albeit in small numbers — since the turn of the century. In 1903 Bert Williams and George Walker headed a cast of some ninety performers in a London production of *In Dahomey;* between 1904 and 1925 the black impresario and singer Will Garland produced numerous other black revues — *Darktown Entertainers, Some Revue, Coloured Society, Down South, Creole Carols,* and *Coloured Lights;* and various black instrumental and vocal groups — the Four Black Diamonds, the Exposition Four, the Royal Southern Singers, the Versatile Four, and Will Marion Cook's Southern Syncopated Orchestra — played in London. On black entertainers in England before 1922 see Jeffrey P. Green, "The Negro Renaissance and England," in *Black Music in the Harlem Renaissance,* ed. Samuel A. Floyd Jr. (Knoxville: University of Tennessee Press, 1993), 153–63, and Stephen Bourne, *Black in the British Frame: Black People in British Film and Television, 1896–1996* (London: Cassell, 1998), 1–12, 43 n. 50. On Will Garland see Rainer Lotz, "Will Garland and His Negro Operetta Company," in *Under the Imperial Carpet,* ed. Rainer Lotz and Ian Pegg (Crawley, Sussex, Eng.: Rabbit Press, 1986), 130–44; see also Ray Funk, "Three Afro-American Singing Groups," in ibid., 145–55.

22. James Walvin, *Black and White: The Negro and English Society, 1555–1945* (London: Allen Lane, Penguin Press, 1973), 203–15; Edward Scobie, *Black Britannia: A History of Blacks in Britain* (Chicago: Johnson, 1972), 174–93; Joel Rogers, "The Critic," *Messenger* 8 (Jan. 1926): 12; *New York Age,* Apr. 7, 1923. On the feeling among British entertainers that American blacks were taking their jobs, see the *New York Age,* May 19, 1922.

23. Seton, *Paul Robeson,* 38.

24. *Kent and Sussex Courier,* May 17, 1929; Richard Hough, *Mountbatten: Hero out of Time* (London: Weidenfeld and Nicolson, 1980), 104; Allen Woll, *Black Musical Theatre: From Coontown to Dreamgirls* (Baton Rouge: Louisiana State University Press, 1989), 123; Ivan H. Browning qtd. in Taylor and Cook, *Alberta Hunter,* 107; on the "Negro vogue" in England, see Green, "Negro Renaissance," 153–63.

25. Rogers, "The Critic," *Messenger* 8 (Jan. 1926): 12; *New York Age,* Apr. 7, 1923.

26. PR interviewed by Floyd Calvin, *Pittsburgh Courier,* Jan. 8, 1927.

27. Rich Ruda interviews with J. Murray-Brown, June 2, 1975, and with Yusuf Dadoo, Feb. 24, 1974; interview with C. L. R. James, May 8, 1975; Hannen Swaffer, *Bystander,* Apr. 24, 1929. Marie Seton confirmed this "colonial mentality," noting that the first gifted Indian performer did not appear in London until the 1950s (Seton interview, Nov. 11, 1974).

28. *Daily Sketch* and *Daily Telegraph* (London), June 16, 1928. The guest lists were impressive (the duchess of Marlborough, Mrs. Samuel Courtauld, Mrs. Phipps, and Lord Arlington), and for both occasions Robeson was paid handsomely: the Lord Beaverbrook recitals earned Paul £84, 10s. for each of his four successive appearances. For Lady Ravonsdale, see *Daily Sketch* and *Daily Telegraph,* June 16, 1928; for Lord Beaverbrook, see A. P. Taylor, *Beaverbrook* (New York: Simon and Schuster, 1972), 311–12; ER to Van Vechten, July 8, 1928, Yale University; Marie Burke to Bunie, Feb. 22, 1976.

29. Andrews acted as Robeson's dresser during the years 1928–1939, 1939–1946, and 1958–59.

30. Andrews interview, Nov. 13–20, 1974.

31. Ibid.

32. "Paul respected my judgment," Andrews said. "He asked my opinion and gradually developed respect for what I had to say, and most important, he trusted me" (ibid.).

33. *Amsterdam News,* Sept. 19, 1928; O. O. McIntyre, "New York Day by Day," clipping from *Bay City* (Mich.) *Times,* Dec. 11, 1928; ER to Van Vechten, July 8, 1928, Yale University.

34. Andrews interview, Nov. 13–20, 1974.

35. *Sunday Sun* (London), undated, 1929.

36. PR interviewed by Floyd Calvin, *Pittsburgh Courier,* Jan. 8, 1927.

37. Andrews interview, Nov. 13–20, 1974. On the racial ease he himself felt in England, drama critic Joel A. Rogers wrote, "The English . . . are marvelously polite. All of the time I was in England I never met a single discourteous person. After a lifetime among white Americans . . . I found myself so much out of place among these amiable people that I was positively uneasy" (Rogers, "The Critic," 12).

38. For the Equity controversy, see "Tangled Affairs of Paul Robeson"; *Amsterdam News,* Sept. 12 and 19, 1928; *Variety,* Oct. 17, 1928; *New York World,* Sept. 15, 18, 25, and Oct. 4, 1928; *Times,* Oct. 4, 1928; *Star* (London), Oct. 3, 1928.

39. "Tangled Affairs of Paul Robeson."

40. *Amsterdam News,* Sept. 12, 1928.

41. On Swaffer see Jean Nicol, *Meet Me at the Savoy* (London: Museum Press Ltd., 1952), 25, 46–47; Anne Chisolm and Michael Davie, *Lord Beaverbrook: A Life* (New York: Knopf, 1993), 212, 363.

42. Hannen Swaffer qtd. in *Amsterdam News,* Sept. 12, 1928.

43. PR qtd. in ibid., Oct. 24, 1928.

44. *Variety* (London), Oct. 17, 1928. Also in *Amsterdam News,* Oct. 24, 1928, reprinted from *London Express;* ER to Carlo and Fania, Oct. 17, 1928, Yale University.

45. "Tangled Affairs of Paul Robeson."

46. Langston Hughes, *The Big Sea* (New York: Hill and Wang, 1940), 255; on Nora Holt, see Bruce Kellner, ed., *The Harlem Renaissance: An Historical Dictionary for the Era* (New York: Methuen, 1987), 172–73.

47. "Tangled Affairs of Paul Robeson."

48. Walter White to PR, Sept. 20, 1928, NAACP Papers, File Sept. 7–27, 1928, Box C-96.

49. Walter White to PR, NAACP Papers, File Jan. 23–27, 1929, Box C-96; *Amsterdam News,* Sept. 19, 1928, 1–2.

50. White believed that Robeson's British successes would contribute to improved race relations and "provide an important means of breaking down the color barrier in England and its colonial possessions, and of familiarizing the English masses with Negroes" (NAACP Papers, File Aug. 24–Sept. 17, 1928; 9-page draft by White, "The Color Line in Europe," sent to Annals of the American Academy, Sept. 11, 1928).

51. *Amsterdam News,* Oct. 24, 1928 (from *Sunday Express*). The success of "Ol' Man River" confirms the show's dependence on Paul and his singing. By the end of the summer "Ol' Man River" was a best-seller, recorded by almost every British record company (*Sunday Dispatch,* Oct. 4, 1928).

52. In a letter printed in the "Cast and Forecast" column of the *New York World,* Ziegfeld stated that Equity's decision on the matter should be governed by the number of persons engaged to play in the second company of *Show Boat.* Surely a production employing 150 actors was deserving of more consideration than a revue whose cast might only number ten. Frank Gillmore, executive secretary of Actors' Equity, however, would not move from his position, and while expressing "considerable regret" over Ziegfeld's letter, remained adamant that "fair is fair." Robeson had signed a contract to appear in the Reagan revue (*New York World,* Sept. 21, 1928).

53. *Times,* Oct. 3, 1928, par. 2B, lines 21–24. The injunction was denied, and *Show Boat* continued uninterrupted. A year later an order for damages was awarded in favor of the plaintiffs. Robeson agreed to pay Reagan £1,600 in three installments between July 31, 1929, and January 1, 1930 (copy of order in High Court of Justice, Kings Bench Division, 1928, R. no. 1936, dated July 5, 1929).

54. *Amsterdam News,* Sept. 19, 1928, 1–2.

55. Ibid., Oct. 24, 1929. White to ER and PR, NAACP Papers, undated, ca. 1928–29.

56. Interview with Leigh Whipper, Dec. 10, 1974.

57. Joel Rogers, *Amsterdam News,* Oct 6, 1928; *Pittsburgh Courier,* Oct. 6, 1928. See also *Philadelphia Tribune,* Sept. 27, 1928.

58. *Vogue,* Nov. 20, 1928.

59. Ivan Browning, "European Notes," *Amsterdam News,* Dec. 26, 1928. See also Van Vechten to Gertrude Stein, Nov. 27, 1928, in *Letters of Gertrude Stein and Carl Van Vechten,* ed. Edward Burns (New York: Columbia University Press, 1986), 106.

60. White to ER and PR, NAACP Papers, undated, ca 1928–29.

9. THE TOAST OF ENGLAND

1. Interview with Walter Abel, Feb. 5, 1975.

2. *Era* (London), Jan. 23, 1929; Abel interview, Feb. 5, 1975.

3. Interview with Dorothy West, Oct. 27, 1981. West was among the group of writers who went to the Soviet Union in 1931 to write the screenplay for a movie about blacks in Alabama. On West, see Bruce Kellner, ed., *The Harlem Renaissance: An Historical Dictionary for the Era* (New York: Metheun, 1987), 282; *Time,* July 24, 1995; West interview with Genii Guinier, May 6, 1978, in *The Black Women Oral History Project,* ed. Ruth Edmonds Hill (Westport, Conn.: Meckler, 1991), 10:145–223. On white servants in black households, see Willard B. Gatewood, *Aristocrats of Color: The Black Elite, 1880–1920* (Bloomington: Indiana University Press, 1993), 8, 196. Historically, elite black American families, like their white counterparts, employed one or more servants. In Charleston and other parts of the South servants were likely to be black. In the North and Midwest they were likely to be white, often Scandinavian or German immigrants.

4. Abel interview, Feb. 5, 1975.

5. Interview with Patti Light, Apr. 26, 1975.

6. Eslanda Robeson, *Paul Robeson, Negro* (New York: Hayes and Brothers, 1930), 166 (hereafter ER, *PR, Negro*).

7. *New York Times,* Mar. 4, 1928; Phyllis Rose, *Jazz Cleopatra: Josephine Baker in Her Time* (New York: Doubleday, 1989), 123–32. In 1933 conservative critics' distaste for jazz would take the form of law in Germany and by 1935 jazz would be banned from German radio.

8. *Die Stunde* (Vienna), Apr. 11, 1929; Program, Vienna Concert House, Apr. 9, 1929; ER Log, 1929 European Tour, Robeson Collections (PR Jr.).

9. The Budapest concert took place on April 12; the Prague concert on April 19 at Plodinova Bursa (ER Log, 1929 European Tour, Robeson Collections [PR Jr.]); *Pesti Napolo* (Budapest), Apr. 13, 1929; *Orai Ujsag* (Budapest), Apr. 14, 1929. See also Henri de la Tour, *Amsterdam News,* May 7, 1930.

10. *Orai Ujsag,* Apr. 14, 1929; interview with Joe Andrews, Nov. 13–20, 1974; ER Log, 1929 European Tour, Robeson Collections (PR Jr.).

11. *Royal Albert Hall 1984 Compendium* (Royal Albert Hall, Kensington Gore, London, 1984), 17–19; Michael Bonavia, *London before I Forget* (London: Self-Publishing Association, 1990), 57 (our italics).

12. R.H.L., *Daily Telegraph* (London), Apr. 29, 1929.

13. Marie Seton, *Paul Robeson* (London: Dennis Dobson, 1958), 49–50.

14. Andrews interview, Nov. 13–20, 1974; *Daily Express* (London), reprinted in *Amsterdam News,* June 5, 1929; *Interstate Tatler,* undated, 1930; *Ceylon Morning Leader,* Sept. 13, 1920.

15. *Daily Express,* Apr. 29, 1929; *Daily Telegraph,* Apr. 29, 1929; R.C., *Daily Mail* (London), Apr. 29, 1929.

16. ER to Otto Kahn, Jan. 21, 1929, Princeton University; ER to Larry Brown, Feb. 15, 1929, Lawrence Brown Papers, Schomburg Collection, New York Public Library; Bledsoe's repertoire in *Amsterdam News,* July 28, 1929.

17. Andrews interview, Nov. 13–20, 1974. In 1926 Sissle fought British union efforts to keep him and Florence Mills out of England. He won and scored a spectacular success in London with his interpretations of such masterpieces as "Love Will Find a Way."

18. ER to Kahn, Jan. 21, 1929, Princeton University. The tour was part of Powell's Celebrity Concert Series. On Powell, see "F. C. Coppicus Gives Interesting Account of His Trip Abroad," *Musical Courier,* Sept. 21, 1929.

19. Robeson's radio appearances were covered in *Saturday Review* (London), Sept. 28, 1929; *Encore* (London), Mar. 27, 1930; *Stage* (London), Mar. 22, 1930. On the significance of radio, see

Ross McKibben, *Classes and Cultures: England, 1918–1951* (New York: Oxford University Press, 1998), 402–3.

20. *Kent and Sussex Courier,* May 14, 1929; *Evening News* (London), June 20, 1929; *Eastbourne Gazette,* July 24 1929; interview with Nancy Fenn (who lived in the British provinces at the time), Feb. 29, 1980.

21. On race relations in England, see K. L. Little, *The Relations of White and Coloured People in Great Britain* (Malvern, Eng.: Playhouse Press, 1946), 1–8; Edward Scobie, *Black Britannia* (Chicago: Johnson, 1972), 153–73; and James Walvin, *Black and White: The Negro and English Society, 1555–1945* (London: Allen Lane, Penguin Press, 1973), 202–19.

22. Little, *Relations,* 2; PR interviewed in *Ceylon Morning Leader,* Aug. 14, 1929. "I was never up against it [the color bar]," Robeson said. "The color problem exists only with illiterate English people."

23. Roi Ottley, *The Lonely Warrior* (Chicago: Regency, 1955), 287. Louis Drysdale trained Florence Mills in London and assisted others, including George Robert Garner and Ethel Waters. On Drysdale, see Eileen Southern, *The Music of Black Americans* (New York: Norton, 1971), 143; Ethel Waters with Charles Samuels, *His Eye Is on the Sparrow* (New York: Bantam, 1952), 198; and Jeffrey P. Green, "The Harlem Renaissance and England," in *Black Music in the Harlem Renaissance,* ed. Samuel A. Floyd Jr. (Knoxville: University of Tennessee Press, 1993), 159.

24. *Daily Express,* qtd. in Ottley, *The Lonely Warrior,* 279; for protests, see 282.

25. The heiress Nancy Cunard's lover, black musician Henry Crowder, for example, also in summer 1929; see Anne Chisholm, *Nancy Cunard* (New York: Knopf, 1979), 195. While Crowder's slights may not have been as widely written about in the newspapers as was the Abbott incident, they were certainly talked about and discussed with great relish in London artistic and theatrical circles.

26. According to *Amsterdam News,* however, which reprinted its story from the Paris edition of the *New York Herald,* Robeson was not refused admittance. "It seemed that a man who owed the Savoy a considerable sum of money was told he must pay or he would not be served." That man was Robeson's host and because he could not or would not pay he was not served, nor was Robeson. According to this informant (J. S. Kaufman), Robeson did not return to the hotel because within the next few days he had sailed for New York (*Amsterdam News,* Apr. 2, 1930).

27. Seton, *Paul Robeson,* 51. Andre Van Gyseghem said that Paul and Forbes "were great friends then" (interview with Van Gyseghem, Nov. 4, 1974); PR letter qtd. in *Manchester Guardian,* Oct. 23, 1929.

28. Goode and Henschel mentioned in unnamed paper, 1929, possibly the *Manchester Guardian;* see *Manchester Guardian,* Oct. 23, 1929. Marley listed other instances in which distinguished colored men had been requested to leave dance halls and predicted that continued racial prejudice in England would have repercussions in other parts of the world and throughout the British Empire. Marley expected backing from the prime minister, as in the past MacDonald had gone out of his way to be gracious to Robeson, entertaining him along with Labour MPs at the House of Commons, but in this case MacDonald said that there was nothing he or the government could do.

29. "The Colour Bar in England," *Manchester Guardian,* Oct. 23, 1929; *Liverpool Post,* Oct. 30, 1929; *New Leader* (London), Oct. 25, 1929; John Edward Hasse, *Beyond Category: The Life and Genius of Duke Ellington* (New York: Da Capo Press, 1995), 170.

30. *Amsterdam News,* Oct. 16, 1929. Paul and Essie sailed for the United States on Oct. 19; Andrews interview, Nov. 13–20, 1974; *New York Mirror,* Oct. 29, 1929; *New York World,* Oct. 29, 1929; *New York Herald Tribune,* Oct. 29, 1929; *New York News,* Oct. 29, 1929; *New York Contender,* Oct. 28, 1929.

31. The two incidents barely caused a ripple among whites in America. Robeson's slight was treated as a news item, a simple middle-page announcement by *Time,* which commented that Robeson "handled the situation with grace and dignity" (*Time,* Nov. 19, 1929); Kelly Miller, *Amsterdam News,* Dec. 18, 1929; Abbott qtd. in Ottley, *The Lonely Warrior,* 283; see also 267–90; and Joel A. Rogers, *Messenger* 8 (Jan. 1926): 12.

32. PR Diary, Nov. 8, 1929, Robeson Collections (PR Jr.).

33. *Musical Courier*, Sept. 2, 1929, 25. According to Coppicus, it was *he* who initiated arrangements with Robeson while on a visit to Europe where he first met him. "On being introduced to him I said: 'I am pleased to meet you, Mr. Robeson, and I hereby engage you for the United States and Canada.' He [Robeson] looked at me in amazement, but I went on and told him I would sign a contract that was fair."

Although approximately 300 blacks attended Robeson's opening concert at Carnegie Hall, Nannie H. Burroughs, writing for the Associated Negro Press, chastised fellow blacks for not coming out in larger numbers to support Robeson. "New York Negroes should have stormed Carnegie Hall, even though they could not have gotten in, and even though it was not Roland Hayes" (*Philadelphia Tribune*, Nov. 21, 1929). For reviews of the first New York concert, see Oscar Thompson, *New York Evening Post*, Nov. 6, 1929; *Daily Eagle*, Nov. 6, 1929; *New York Evening Sun*, Nov. 6, 1929; *New York Herald Tribune*, Nov. 6, 1929; Noel Strauss, *New York Evening World*, Nov. 6, 1929; Charles D. Isaacson, *New York Telegram*, Nov. 6 and 7, 1929; Pitts Sanborn, *New York Telegram*, Nov. 6, 1929; for the second New York concert: *New York Times*, Nov. 11, 1929, and *Musical Courier*, Nov. 16, 1929, 6; for reviews of other concerts: *Musical Courier*, Sept. 2, 1929, 25.; *Worcester Telegram*, Dec. 9, 1929; *Columbus Dispatch*, Dec. 1, 1929; *Toronto Daily Star*, Nov. 22, 1929; *Evening Telegraph* (Toronto), Nov. 22, 1929; William R. Mitchell, *Pittsburgh Press*, Dec. 4, 1929; *Chicago Daily News*, Dec. 11, 1929.

34. Editorial, *Morgantown* [West Virginia] *Post*, Dec. 13, 1929. Robeson mentions having dined at Beaverbrook's table in an interview with R. E. Knowlls of the *Toronto Daily Star* (Nov. 21, 1929). Beaverbrook attended the London opening of *Porgy* as a guest of the Robesons (*Interstate Tatler*, May 10, 1929).

35. PR interviewed by Roy Wilkins, *Kansas City Call*, Feb. 13, 1931; PR Diary, Nov. 8, 1929, Robeson Collections (PR Jr.); *Newark Evening News*, Nov. 20, 1929; interview with Steve White, Sept. 15, 1975.

36. Maurice Browne, *Too Late to Lament* (Bloomington: Indiana University Press, 1956), 318.

37. Ibid., 323.

38. *Era*, Feb. 19, 1930; Andrews interview, Nov. 13–20, 1974.

39. Kahn to PR, Dec. 21, 1928, Robeson Collections (PR Jr.); ER to Kahn, Jan. 21, 1929, Princeton University; Kahn to ER, Feb. 1, 1929, Robeson Collections (PR Jr.); ER to Otto Kahn, Oct. 7, 1929, Princeton University.

40. For a historical overview of black Shakespearean actors see Errol Hill, *Shakespeare in Sable* (Amherst: University of Massachusetts Press, 1984). Neil Porter, a critic and Shakespearean actor who had been at the Old Vic from 1924 to 1927, expressed the sentiments of many when he pleaded in a letter to the *Daily Telegraph* (May 30, 1930) that the subject at last be dropped: "The question of Othello's colour has been so discussed that one hesitates to add another word to what has been said. After all, is it so very important? . . . In the present instance surely the point is this. Mr. Robeson is a Negro actor, and a magnificent actor, whatever his race. But being a Negro the parts for which he is suited are singularly few. Are we never to see him?"

41. Once Robeson accepted the role, Maurice Browne immediately announced the news to the press, which in turn surmised that casting the sure-selling name of Robeson was proof that even the indomitable theater magnate was beginning to feel the pinch of London's theater slump (*New York American*, Sept. 6, 1929). Although it is possible that Browne, who had failed to score a hit since *Journey's End* and in the interim suffered several financial reversals, had overextended himself, Browne denied these accusations and insisted that "the production, planned at least a year earlier, was not a 'remedy' for a 'desperate' situation." See "Shakespeare in the Slump," *Time and Tide*, May 15, 1930; also *Everyman*, May 24, 1930; *Pearson's Weekly*, Apr. 5, 1930, 1100–101.

42. *Pearson's Weekly*, Apr. 5, 1930, 1100–101; PR qtd. in *Morning Post* (London), May 21, 1930, and *Observer* (London), May 18, 1930.

43. PR qtd. in *Pearson's Weekly*, Apr. 5, 1930, 1101; in *Daily Express*, Mar. 7, 1930; in *Daily Herald* (London), May 7, 1930; and in *Observer*, May 18, 1930.

44. *Era*, Feb. 19, 1930; Walter White to ER and PR, Mar. 27, 1930; Apr. 9 and 22, 1930; ER to White, Mar. 28, 1930, NAACP Papers, Box C-98; Andrews interview, Nov. 13–20, 1974; *Zit's*, May 31, 1930; *Time*, June 22, 1930.

45. *Dundee Evening Telegram,* May 4, 1930; *Edinburgh Evening Dispatch,* Mar. 8, 1930; *Bristol Evening World,* Feb. 26, 1930.

46. PR qtd. by Macpherson in "A Negro Film Union — Why Not?" in *Negro: An Anthology,* ed. Nancy Cunard (New York: Frederick Ungar, 1970), 206; Peter Noble, *The Negro in Films* (London: Skelton Robinson, 1948), 144; Barbara Guest, *Herself Defined: The Poet H.D. and Her World* (New York: Doubleday, 1984), 196–98; *Evening Standard* (London), June 12, 1930; see also ER to Kenneth Macpherson, Feb. 19, 1938, Robeson Collections (PR Jr.); *Aberdeen Evening Express,* Apr. 1, 1930; PR interviewed by R.H., *Manchester Guardian,* May 1930.

47. *Borderline* (Pool Films, 1930), International Museum of Photography at George Eastman House, 5–35 passim. Pool Productions was a publishing enterprise formed in 1926 in Territet, Switzerland, by three close friends — Winifred Bryhers, Kenneth Macpherson, and the poet H.D. (Hilda Doolittle). It published the journal *Close-Up* for six and a half years as well as numerous books on film and film production. *Borderline*'s producer Kenneth Macpherson was particularly influenced by the Russian film giant Sergei Eisenstein, whom he first met in 1929. The montage sequences of *Borderline,* for example, were based on Eisenstein's film theories. *Close-Up* published many of the first translations of Eisenstein's ideas. In addition, the journal devoted an entire issue (Aug. 1929) to the Negro in film. On the journal *Close-Up,* see Anne Friedberg, "Writing about Cinema: 'Close-Up,' 1927–1933" (Ph.D. diss., New York University, 1983), esp. 144–45, 157. On *Borderline,* see ibid., 60, 152–53; Thomas Cripps, *Slow Fade to Black: The Negro in American Film* (New York: Oxford University Press, 1977), 208–10; and Richard Dyer, *Heavenly Bodies: Film Stars and Society* (London: Macmillan, 1986), 130–32.

48. Clive MacManus, *Evening Standard,* Oct. 20, 1930; *Weekend Review,* Oct, 18, 1930; *Bioscope,* Oct. 25, 1930; *Studio Cines, Le Veu de Cataluyna, La Nau, La Publicat,* Jan. 3, 1931; *Today's Cinema,* Oct. 14, 1930; *Manchester Guardian,* Oct. 14, 1930; and C. A. Lejeune, *Observer,* Oct. 14, 1930.

49. According to a report in the *Detroit Free Press* (Dec. 1, 1929), Max Reinhardt, the director-genius and owner of the Deutsches Theater, had approached Robeson after his 1929 concert in Vienna and invited him to come back in the spring of 1930 to perform again in Vienna and in Germany as well. ER qtd. in Martin Duberman, *Paul Robeson* (New York: Knopf, 1988), 132; Light interview, Apr. 26, 1975. Sol Hurok qtd. in Otto Friedrich, *Before the Deluge: A Portrait of Berlin in the 1920s* (New York: Harper Collins, Harper Perennial, 1995), 11. On Berlin and decadence between the wars, see ibid., 128–32; Anton Gill, *A Dance between the Flames: Berlin between the Wars* (New York: Carroll and Graf, 1993); Peter Gay, *Weimar Culture: The Outsider as Insider* (New York: Harper and Row, 1968), 128–32; Wolfgang Von Eckhardt and Sander L. Gilman, *Bertolt Brecht's Berlin* (Garden City, N.Y.: Doubleday, 1975), 33–39. Within a few years (in 1933), the Jewish Max Reinhardt would be forced into exile when the Nazis assumed power.

50. *Daily Times* (Beaver, Pa.), Apr. 2, 1930; *New York Times,* May 25, 1930; Eugene O'Neill to ER, Apr. 19, 1930, Robeson Collections (PR Jr.).

51. Andrews interview, Nov. 13–20, 1974; ER, *PR, Negro,* 165.

52. Interview with Peggy Ashcroft, Nov. 2, 1974.

53. *Daily News Chronicle* (London), May 21, 1930; *Daily Express,* May 21, 1930.

54. Interview with Dame Sybil Thorndike, Nov. 6, 1974; on Thorndike, see Sheridan Morely, *Sybil Thorndike: A Life in Theatre* (London: Weidenfeld and Nicolson, 1977).

55. Browne, *Too Late to Lament,* 323; Ashcroft interview, Nov. 2, 1974.

56. Ashcroft interview, Nov. 2, 1974; Thorndike interview, Nov. 6, 1974.

57. Ashcroft interview, Nov. 2, 1974; PR quoted in *Star* (London), May 21, 1930; PR interviewed by Robert van Gelder, *New York Times,* Jan. 16, 1944.

58. Andrews interview, Nov. 13–20, 1974.

59. PR qtd. in John J. Hutchens, "Paul Robeson," *Theatre Arts,* Oct. 1944; *Glasgow Standard,* May 21, 1930; Browne, *Too Late to Lament,* 323; Ashcroft interview, Nov. 2, 1974; Andrews interview, Nov. 13–20, 1974; *Sunday Express* (London), May 25, 1930.

60. PR interviewed by Hannen Swaffer, *Sunday Express,* May 25, 1930; PR qtd. in *Glasgow Evening Standard,* May 21, 1930. See also *New York Herald Tribune,* May 21, 1930.

61. Jacob Epstein completed his sculpture of Robeson in 1928 while he was in New York working on busts of Franz Boaz and John Dewey. The bronze-painted head mounted on a two-

inch, slightly truncated base has great dignity and an arresting vitality; see *Epstein: An Autobiography* (New York: Dalton, 1955), 62, 128–31. Carl Van Vechten photographed the Robeson bust on Mar. 14, 1935; see "A Collection of Photographs Taken by Carl Van Vechten," Goldfarb Library, Brandeis University. *Sheffield Independent,* May 21, 1930; *Daily Sketch* (London), May 21, 1930; Hannen Swaffer, *Daily Express,* June 7, 1930.

62. John Miller, *Ralph Richardson: The Authorized Biography* (London: Sidgwick and Jackson, 1995), 34–35; Ivor Brown, *Observer,* May 25, 1930; A. E. Wilson, *Star,* May 20, 1930; E. A. Baughan, *Daily News Chronicle,* May 20, 1930. The Savoy's orchestra pit was covered over with steps and behind these were more steps leading to the proscenium arch through which was the inner stage.

63. *Daily Express,* May 7, 1930; Ashcroft interview, Nov. 2, 1974; *Daily News Chronicle,* May 20, 1930. See also A. E. Wilson, *Star,* May 20, 1930. Most reviewers complained about Van Volkenburg's cuts. See *Jewish Chronicle* (London), May 23, 1930; G. W. Bishop, *New York Times,* May 20, 1930; G. W. B., *Era,* May 21, 1930; and Ivor Brown, *Observer,* May 25, 1930.

64. L.D., *Daily Sketch,* May 20, 1930; I. B., *Manchester Guardian,* May 20, 1930; G. W. Bishop, *New York Times,* May 20, 1930.

65. G. W. Bishop, *New York Times,* May 20, 1930; *Oxford Mail,* May 20, 1930.

66. *Manchester Dispatch,* May 20, 1930; *Bristol Times,* May 20, 1930; *Sunday Express,* May 25, 1930; *Birmingham Post,* undated, 1930; *Daily News Chronicle,* May 20, 1930; *Evening News,* May 29, 1930; C. B. Purdom, "At the Theatre: Paul Robeson as Othello," *Everyman* 3 (May 29, 1930): 561; *Evening News,* May 20, 1930; *Daily Mail,* May 20, 1930; *Manchester Guardian,* May 20, 1930; *Daily News Chronicle,* May 20, 1930; *West Africa,* May 24, 1930; *Sunday Pictorial,* May 28, 1930.

67. James Agate, *Sunday Times,* May 26, 1930. On Agate as a racist see Michael Billington, *Peggy Ashcroft* (London: John and Murray, 1988), 41; on Agate as a "much-feared" man see Richard Collier, *Make-Believe: The Magic of International Theatre* (New York: Dodd, Mead, 1986), 143–44. A prolific writer, Agate wrote a racy, entertaining one-volume autobiography entitled *Ego 6.*

68. Agate, *Sunday Times,* May 28, 1930.

69. Ibid.

70. *Sporting Times,* May 20, 1930; George Warrington, *Country Life* (London), May 31, 1930 (Warrington attributed Robeson's lack of authority to his "own charm and personal modesty. It is possible that he is afraid that his assumption of arrogance might be mistaken for the insolent assumptions of the less educated of his race"); *Sunday Pictorial,* May 28, 1930; *Graphic,* May 31, 1930; Ivor Browne, "Our Captious Critic," *Illustrated Sporting and Dramatic News,* June 7, 1930; M. Wilson Disher, *Scotsman,* May 31, 1930; Browne, *Too Late to Lament,* 323.

71. *Reynold's Newspaper,* May 25, 1930.

72. Disher, *Scotsman,* May 31, 1930.

73. Ivor Browne, "Our Captious Critic"; John Dover Wilson, "A Life with Shakespeare," broadcast on May 24, 1967, with John Gray of BBC asking Wilson questions; *Listener,* Mar. 30, 1967, 428.

74. Thorndike interview, Nov. 6, 1974.

75. *Variety,* May 28, 1930; *Morning Post,* June 18, 1930.

10. UNCOUPLINGS

1. *Daily News Chronicle* (London), Feb. 28, 1930; interview with Rebecca West, Nov. 13, 1974; interview with Joe Andrews, Nov. 13–20, 1974. According to Essie, she began work on the biography in January 1929 after being approached by the London office of Doubleday and Doran (ER to Otto Kahn, Jan. 21, 1929, Princeton University). Whether such an overture was actually made is unclear. It should be noted that Essie's primary purpose in writing to Kahn was to reassure him that she and Paul would pay back their loan of $5,000.

2. ER to Carl Van Vechten, June 20, 1929, Yale University.

3. Eslanda Robeson, *Paul Robeson, Negro* (New York: Hayes and Brothers, 1930), 42 (hereafter ER, *PR, Negro*); interview with Glenway Wescott, Nov. 28, 1975.

4. ER, *PR, Negro,* 73, 74, 75, 76, 87, 154–56, 171, 72, 80, 83, 105, 142.

5. Ibid., 75–76, 86.

6. Ibid., 144, 72–73.

7. Ibid., 149, 166, 111, 112, 127–28, 156.

8. Andrews interview, Nov. 13–20, 1974; ER, *PR, Negro,* 120–21.

9. ER, *PR, Negro,* 112–14.

10. Ibid., 152. According to Robeson's biographer Martin Duberman, the woman identified as Marion Griffin in the American version of Essie's biography of Paul and Martha Sampson in the English version of the book was in fact Martha Gruening, the sister of Ernest Gruening, later senator from Alaska. Essie changed the name to pseudonyms when Gruening, who apparently had second thoughts about being quoted, threatened legal action (Martin Duberman, *Paul Robeson* [New York: Knopf, 1988], 613 n. 33).

11. W. Keith, *Star* (London), May 20, 1930; *Glasgow News,* May 19, 1930.

12. ER to Walter White, May 29, 1930, NAACP Papers, Box C-98. Essie's letter to White included clippings of British reviews of the book. Harper and Brothers, the book's U.S. distributors, asked for White's comments, but White begged off. "It would be embarrassing for me . . . in view of the paragraph in the book referring to Mrs. White and myself," he explained. On July 17 Harper's publicity agent Ramon Herdman asked White what he thought of a "Paul Robeson Night" as a promotion effort for the book. Again White indicated he wanted no part of any publicity effort in behalf of the biography (Ramon Herdman, Publicity Dept., Harper to White, Aug. 17, 1930, and White to Herdman, Aug. 18, 1930, NAACP Papers, Box C-99). See also Langston Hughes, "Ambassador to the World," *New York Herald Tribune,* June 19, 1930.

13. Stark Young, *New Republic* 63 (Aug. 6, 1930): 345–46.

14. Andrews interview, Nov. 13–20, 1974; PR, "From My Father's Parsonage to My Own 'Ole Man River' Stage Triumph," *Sunday Sun* (London), Jan. 13, 1929; Rev. Robertson Ballard, "Paul Robeson: A Genius with a Soul," *Methodist Times,* Jan. 3, 1929.

15. *The Diaries of Sir Robert Bruce Lockhart,* vol. 1, *1925–1938,* ed. Kenneth Young (London: Macmillan, 1973), 18 (Bruce Lockhart edited the column "Londoner's Diary" in the *Evening Standard* from 1928 to 1937); Ethel E. Mannin, *Confessions and Impressions* (London: Jarrols, 1930), 158; interview with Dorothy West, Oct. 27, 1981; ER to Carlo and Fania, Dec. 19, 1930, Yale University.

16. ER, *PR, Negro,* 161; Wescott interview, Nov. 28, 1975 (in letters Paul almost never refers to Pauli by name); interview with Mildred Gilman, Sept. 16, 1974; Heywood Hale Broun, *Whose Little Boy Are You? A Memoir of the Broun Family* (New York: St. Martins / Marek, 1983), 53–61.

17. Patricia Sullivan interview with Malcolm Pitt, May 20, 1975.

18. PR interviewed by W. R. Titterton, *Daily Herald* (London), Aug. 11, 1930.

19. ER, *PR, Negro,* 157–61.

20. PR qtd. in *Daily Express* (London), June 4, 1930; *Zit's,* July 12, 1930; *Paris Tribune* article reprinted in J. A. Rogers, "With Our Performers in Europe," *Amsterdam News,* July 23, 1930.

21. *Zit's,* July 12, 1930; *Morning Post,* July 3, 1930; *Musical Opinion,* Sept. 1930, 1063; *Era,* May 21, 1930. Marian Anderson had already sung some of Quilter's pieces (Quilter accompanied her) at Wigmore Hall on June 15, 1929. See *Philadelphia Tribune,* July 24, 1928; PR qtd. in *Glasgow Herald,* Feb. 15, 1930; *Yorkshire Herald,* Feb. 14, 1930.

22. ER, *PR, Negro,* 165. Also interviews with Andrews (Nov. 13–20, 1974), Wescott (Nov. 28, 1975), and Dorothy West (Oct. 27, 1981).

23. Interviews with Rebecca West, Nov. 13, 1974, and Reginald Boardman, Oct. 20, 1981.

24. Wescott interview, Nov. 28, 1975.

25. PR qtd. in *Era,* Feb. 19, 1930; *Musical Standard,* Mar. 22, 1930. See also *Observer* (London), Feb. 16, 1930.

26. PR qtd. in *Yorkshire Herald,* Feb. 14, 1930; *Glasgow Herald,* Feb. 15, 1930; *Sheffield Daily Telegraph,* Mar. 14, 1930.

27. PR qtd. in *Yorkshire Herald,* Feb. 14, 1930; *Glasgow Herald,* Feb. 15, 1930; *Era,* Feb. 19, 1930; also *Musical Standard,* Mar. 22, 1930.

28. *Times,* Sept. 4, 1930; *Daily Sketch* (London), Sept. 3, 1930.

29. *Evening Standard* (London), Sept. 26, 1930. On lieder, see also *Times,* Sept. 4, 1930, and *Daily Sketch,* Sept. 3, 1930.

30. *Glasgow Herald,* Sept. 16, 1930; *Sheffield Independent,* Oct. 28, 1930; *Bradford Telegraph,* Nov. 11, 1930.

31. Wescott interview, Nov. 28, 1975.

32. PR to ER, Sept. 29, 1930, Robeson Collections (PR Jr.).

33. ER Diary, Oct. 1930, Robeson Collections (PR Jr.).

34. Interviews with Peggy Ashcroft (Nov. 2, 1974) and Andrews (Nov. 13–20, 1974). See also Gary O'Connor, *The Secret Woman: A Life of Peggy Ashcroft* (London: Weidenfeld and Nicolson, 1977), 18–23, and Michael Billington, *Peggy Ashcroft* (London: John Murray, 1988), 41–42.

35. *New York World,* undated; *New York Herald Tribune,* undated; *New York Times,* Jan. 11, 1931; *Evening Post,* undated.

36. *New York Age,* undated, 1931 (*Age* critics did not comment on the quality of Robeson's lieder); *New York Times,* Jan. 11, 1931.

37. *Minneapolis Journal,* Feb. 12, 1931; *San Francisco News,* Feb. 24, 1931; *Denver Post,* Mar. 10, 1931.

38. Andrews interview, Nov. 13–20, 1974; Nannie H. Burroughs (Associated Negro Press), *Philadelphia Tribune,* Nov. 21, 1929.

39. *New Bedford* [Mass.] *Mercury,* Aug. 16, 1932; *Pittsburgh Courier,* Feb. 20, 1931; *Kansas City Call,* Feb. 12, 1931; *Kansas City Times,* Feb. 20, 1931.

40. *Advocate* (Portland, Ore.), Mar. 21, 1931.

41. Unnamed paper, Apr. 5, 1931, Robeson Collections (PR Jr.).

42. *New York Herald,* Jan. 11, May 23, 1931; Associated Negro Press (ANP), May 21, 1931.

43. On Bledsoe, see Lynette G. Geary, "Jules Bledsoe: The Original 'Ol' Man River,'" *Black Perspective in Music* 17 (1989): 27–34.

44. Interviews with John Sherman (Robert Rockmore's nephew), Mar. 4, 1998, and John Rockmore (Robert Rockmore's brother), Mar. 6, 1998; Arthur Gelb and Barbara Gelb, *O'Neill* (New York: Harper and Row, 1962), 642; Louis Sheaffer, *O'Neill, Son and Artist* (Boston: Little, Brown, 1973), 262, 266; Allen Woll, *Black Musical Theatre: From Coontown to Dreamgirls* (Baton Rouge: Louisiana State University Press, 1989), 157–58.

45. *Evening News* (London), May 2, 1931. See also *Daily News Chronicle,* May 6, 1931; *Evening Times* (Bristol), May 6, 1931; *Glasgow Daily Record,* May 4, 1931.

46. See Noreen Branson and Margot Heinemann, *Britain in the Nineteen Thirties* (London: Panther, 1973), 30–35; *South Wales Echo,* May 6, 1931; *Manchester Evening Chronicle,* May 8, 1931. In Britain unemployment reached an all-time record figure of just under 3 million (23 percent of all insured workers) in 1933. In 1931 figures were as high as 2.7 million. Nearly one in five of the unemployed had been out of work for more than six consecutive months. Unemployment benefits at the time were enough to keep a family from outright starvation, but not much more. The hated "means test" (which forced unemployed laborers to endure a humiliating investigation of their economic status in order to receive unemployment benefits that they had paid for in years of labor) was put into effect in November 1931.

47. *New York Herald,* Jan. 11, 1931. See also B. H., "London Stage, Song, and Show," *West Africa* (London) 14, no. 701 (July 1930): 857. O'Neill had decided almost a year before that any rewriting of the part for Robeson would be unnecessary, and he said as much in a letter to Essie (O'Neill to ER, Apr. 10, 1930, Robeson Collections [PR Jr.]). On the universality of the role, see *Manchester Evening Chronicle,* May 8, 1931; *South Wales Echo,* May 6, 1931; PR qtd. in *South Wales Echo,* May 6, 1931.

48. *Daily Sketch,* May 7, 1931.

49. *Era,* May 13, 1931; *Yorkshire Daily Post,* May 12, 1931; *Daily Mail* (London), May 12, 1931.

50. R.S.P., *Daily Herald,* May 12, 1931; J.S., *Manchester Guardian,* May 12, 1931; *New Age* (London), May 12, 1931; *Sun Dispatch,* May 13, 1931; *Manchester Dispatch,* May 12, 1931; *Yorkshire Observer* (Leeds), May 12, 1931; *Morning Post* (London), May 12, 1931.

51. T, *Punch* 153 (May 20, 1931): 554; A. E. Wilson, *Star,* May 21, 1931; *Daily Express,* May 17, 1931; Alan Parsons, *Daily Mail,* May 12, 1931; *Observer* (London), May 17, 1931; *Frazier's,* May 23, 1931.

52. "Hairy Ape or Bronze Ajax?" *New Statesman and Nation,* May 23, 1931, 461–62; *Morning Post,* May 12, 1931. See Paul Banks, *New York Age,* May 21, 1931; *Star,* May 12, 1931. "You will see Robeson's Hairy Ape not O'Neill's Hairy Ape, who was a white man," said the *Daily Express,* May 12, 1931.

53. *Burton Evening Gazette,* May 16, 1931; *Evening Standard,* May 22 and 18, 1931; *Daily Mail,* May 20, 1931; *Star,* May 18, 1931; PR qtd. in *Era,* May 24, 1931.

54. ER to Carlo and Fania, May 23, 1931, Yale University.

55. *New York News and Harlem Home Journal,* Apr. 11, 1931; *Daily Mirror* (London), May 13, 1931.

56. For a historical overview of British racism, see James Walvin, *Black and White: The Negro and English Society, 1555–1945* (London: Allen Lane, Penguin Press, 1973), 159–76; Edward Scobie, *Black Britannia* (Chicago: Johnson, 1972), 153–73, 176; and Winthrop Jordan, *Black over White* (New York: Norton, 1968), 3–43. See also David Killingray, *Africans in Britain* (Ilford, Eng.: Frank Cass, 1994).

57. Interview with Patti Light, Apr. 26, 1975.

58. When the black actor Ira Aldridge in the early years of his career in England married a white English woman (1825), he was shunned for an entire year in London and forced to try his luck in the English provinces. The specter came to haunt him again in 1847 when the news broke that an Irish woman (not his wife) had given birth to his son. For ten years Aldridge was again shut out from London theaters. See Scobie, *Black Britannia,* 131–34.

59. Andrews interview, Nov. 13–20, 1974; PR qtd. in *Eastern Daily Press,* Aug. 29, 1931.

60. ER to Carlo and Fania, Sept. 6, July 13, and Dec. 20, 1931, Yale University.

61. See David L. Lewis, *When Harlem Was in Vogue* (1979; reprint, New York: Vintage, 1982), 76; Alain Locke to Charlotte Osgood Mason, May 22, 1931, Locke Papers, Box 56, Yale University.

62. Interview with Wescott, Nov. 28, 1975.

63. *Daily Express,* Nov. 19, 1931.

64. ER to Carlo and Fania, May 23, 1931, Yale University.

65. ER Diary, Oct. 5 and 7, 1931, Robeson Collections (PR Jr.); Andrews interview, Nov. 13–20, 1974.

66. Thorndike interview, Nov. 6, 1974; *Daily Sketch,* Nov. 23, 1931.

67. *Daily Herald,* Dec. 14, 1931.

11. COMING OF AGE

1. *Des Moines Register,* Feb. 5, 1932. In 1932 Robeson referred to the blues as "vulgarized rhythms" (*Daily Telegraph* [Sheffield], Mar. 14, 1930), but by 1934 he had apparently changed his mind as he recorded "St. Louis Blues" in February of that year. See Brian Rust, *The Complete Entertainment Discography from the Mid-1890s to 1942* (New Rochelle, N.Y.: Arlington House, 1973), 555 (HMVB-8219, Vic 24653).

2. ER qtd.in *Evening Standard* (London), Apr. 11, 1932.

3. Edna Ferber to Alexander Woollcott, Feb. 19, 1933, Ferber Collection, Houghton Library, Harvard University; *New York World Telegram,* July 3, 1932; *People,* Oct. 23, 1932. Concerning his rendering of the song, Robeson recalled: "Mr. Ziegfeld was afraid my interpretation wouldn't be liked here as it would be too quiet for Broadway audiences" (PR interviewed by Karl K. Kitchen, *New York Sun,* June 16, 1932).

4. Ferber to Woollcott, Feb. 19, 1933, Ferber Collection, Houghton Library, Harvard University.

5. Maurice Dancer, *Pittsburgh Courier,* May 28, 1932; Brooks Atkinson, *New York Times,* May 20, 1932; Percy Hammond, *New York Herald Tribune,* May 20, 1932; Robert Garland, *New York World Telegram,* May 20, 1932. *Show Boat* was one of very few Broadway productions to make it through New York's summer heat and financial doldrums (Kaufman/Ryskind/Gershwin's Pulitzer Prize-winning musical satire *Of Thee I Sing* and the musical comedy *Face the Music* also

survived), but it did so only by a whisker. Even with the financial propping of tycoon A. C. Blumenthal, money was so tight that cast members were frequently forced to take salary cuts.

6. *Daily Mirror,* May 2, 1932. On Cunard, see Anne Chisholm, *Nancy Cunard* (New York: Knopf, 1979).

7. PR qtd. in *Amsterdam News,* May 4, 1932.

8. Chisholm, *Nancy Cunard,* 258; interview with Antonio Salemme, Sept. 7, 1976; interview with Joe Andrews, Nov. 13–20, 1974.

9. Cunard qtd. in *New York Age,* May 7, 1932; *Daily Mirror,* May 7, 1932.

10. *People,* May 29, 1932.

11. On Edwina Mountbatten, see Alden Hatch, *The Mountbattens* (London: Allen Publishers, 1965); Richard Hough, *Mountbatten: Hero Out of Time* (London: Weidenfeld and Nicolson, 1980), 94–95; Philip Ziegler, *Mountbatten* (New York: Knopf, 1985), 114–15.

12. *Times* (London), July 1921; Hough, *Mountbatten,* 94–95; Hatch, *The Mountbattens,* 221; Ziegler, *Mountbatten,* 114–15. Mountbatten's biographer Philip Ziegler had access to the family papers, including Edwina's diary. In 1932 Edwina made an entry that stated emphatically that she had never met Robeson (114). If that was the case, she had met him by the following year. Film director John Krimsky, who had an appointment to talk with Robeson at the Dorchester House concerning the film version of *The Emperor Jones,* distinctly recalled Lord and Lady Mountbatten as being among the guests Robeson was entertaining (John Krimsky, "The Emperor Jones — Robeson and O'Neill on Film," *Connecticut Review,* Apr. 1974, 94–98).

13. Bricktop with Jim Haskins, *Bricktop* (New York: Atheneum, 1983), 128–29.

14. ER to Carl Van Vechten and Fania Marinoff, Mar. 20, Feb. 4, 1931, Yale University.

15. Paul Robeson Jr. qtd. in *Paul Robeson: Here I Stand* (127-minute documentary), American Masters Production, a coproduction of Thirteen/WNET and Menair International (New York: Fox Lorber Associates, 1999); ER to Carl Van Vechten, July 13, 1932, Yale University.

16. ER qtd. in *New York Times,* June 26, 1932.

17. ER qtd. in *Pittsburgh Courier,* June 30, 1932.

18. PR qtd. in *Pittsburgh Courier,* June 30, 1932; *New York Age,* July 3, 1932.

19. *New York Times,* Aug. 1, 1932; PR qtd. in "I Broke the Colour Bar," unnamed English paper, May 13, 1933.

20. PR qtd. in "I Broke the Colour Bar." See also Hannen Swaffer, *People,* Oct. 23, 1932.

21. ER to Carl Van Vechten and Fania Marinoff, June 13, 1932, Yale University; Andrews interview, Nov. 13–20, 1974.

22. Lawrence Studios to Walter White, Apr. 21, 1932, NAACP Papers, Box C-102; White described Haywood's play as "another *Green Pastures*" (White to Zora Neale Hurston, May 31, 1932, NAACP Papers, Box C-102; White to PR, Aug. 15, 1932, NAACP Papers, Box C-102); Alexander Woollcott, "Ol' Man River — in Person," *Cosmopolitan,* July 1933 (also in idem, *While Rome Burns* [New York: Viking, 1934]); "Woollcott to PR," Robeson Collections (PR Jr.).

23. White to PR, Mar. 14 and Aug. 15, 1932, NAACP Papers, Box C-102.

24. White to Woollcott, Aug. 15, 1932, NAACP Papers, Box C-103.

25. PR to Florenz Ziegfeld, July 1, 1932 (Billy Rose Theater Collection, New York Public Library for the Performing Arts). Robeson gave notice on July 1 that he would leave *Show Boat* in September. See also *Pittsburgh Courier,* Sept. 10, 1932; *New York World Telegram,* Aug. 31, 1932.

26. Interview with Herbert Marshall, Sept. 20–21, 1974.

27. *Pittsburgh Courier,* June 30, 1932; *New York Age,* July 3, 1932; C. L. R. James, "Paul Robeson: Black Star (A Friend's Recollections)," *Black World* 20 (Nov. 1970): 106–15; interview with C. L. R. James, May 8, 1975. On James, see Paul Buhle, *C. L. R. James: The Artist as Revolutionary* (New York: Verso, 1988), 56–57.

28. Interviews with Marie Seton (Nov. 11, 1974); C. L. R. James (May 8, 1975); Rebecca West (Nov. 13, 1974); and Andrews (Nov. 13–20, 1974). On Hutchinson, see Peter Gammond, *The Oxford Companion to Popular Music* (Oxford: Oxford University Press, 1991), 280.

29. Andrews, whose information on Jackson has proven in almost all instances accurate, consistently referred to her as Olivia. One must assume then that this is what Paul (and perhaps other intimates) called her. In general, the available biographical information on Olivia Jackson is

scanty to the point of being almost nonexistent. A few letters between Jackson and Larry Brown, John Payne, and Robert Rockmore exist. No birth or death certificate has been located, which suggests Jackson was born and died outside of England. Although Andrews thought she had been presented at court, we have been unable to verify this.

30. Virginia Lloyd interviewed on *Paul Robeson: Here I Stand* (documentary).

31. Andrews interview, Nov. 13–20, 1974.

32. Ibid. Martin Duberman (*Paul Robeson* [New York: Knopf, 1988], 163) contends that Jackson married a Russian aristocrat residing in France, Prince Chervachidze, but Jackson's marriage certificate indicates that she married Maurice Russell Goudey on April 27, 1933, at the parish church of West Tarring, Sussex. (Yolande Olive Jackson and Maurice Goudey, General Register Office, London). Goudey, a composer and the son of a sanitation engineer (William Henry Russell Goudey) was at the time of their marriage living in Paris.

33. Evelyn Waugh, *Decline and Fall* (1928; reprint, Boston: Little, Brown, 1956). The few references Waugh makes to Robeson in his diaries are all unflattering—if not confirmation that Chokey was a take off of Robeson, at least evidence that Waugh's private assessment of Robeson was at variance with what he presented in Paul's presence. See *Diaries of Evelyn Waugh*, ed. Michael Davie (London: Weidenfeld and Nicolson, 1976): Sept. 15, 1925— "The party was given in honour of a negro [Robeson] who is acting in a play called *Emperor Jones,* but he had a fit in the dressing room and would not come" (221); May 26, 1930— "I saw the last two acts of Robeson's *Othello.* Hopeless production but I like his great black booby face. It seemed to make all the silly stuff with the handkerchief quite convincing" (311); June 11, 1930—"Cocktails Sachie Sitwell. Dined Richard and Elizabeth. Small party afterwards. Paul Robeson passed out" (314).

34. Interviews with Andrews (Nov. 13–20, 1974), Seton (Nov. 11, 1974), and Miki Fisher (Sept. 13, 1978). Seton confirmed that Paul was very depressed, alarmingly so. Miki Fisher said that Paul later described it as "a very morbid depression" that lasted in its most intense phase for six weeks.

35. Joel Rogers interview with ER, *Pittsburgh Courier,* Oct. 26, 1932.

36. Interview with Rudolph Dunbar, Oct. 31, 1974.

37. PR interviewed by Hannen Swaffer, *People,* Oct. 23, 1932; Wilson Disher, *Sunday Referee,* Oct. 30, 1932.

38. *Manchester Guardian,* Nov. 14, 1932.

39. Fisher interview, Sept. 13, 1978. Also Andrews interview, Nov. 13–20, 1974.

40. Interview with Revels Cayton, July 16, 1980.

41. Andrews interview, Nov. 13–20, 1974.

42. Ibid.

43. *Manchester Guardian,* Nov. 14, 1932.

44. Cayton interview, July 16, 1980.

45. Ibid.

46. Interview with Diane Loesser, Jan. 8, 1982; Paul Robeson Jr. said the same in the 1999 documentary *Paul Robeson: Here I Stand.*

12. THE EMPEROR AND SCREEN IMAGES

1. Interview with John Krimsky, Dec. 5, 1974; John Krimsky, "The Emperor Jones—Robeson and O'Neill on Film," *Connecticut Review,* Apr. 1974, 95–96.

2. Krimsky interview, Dec. 5, 1974; Krimsky, "The Emperor Jones," 95–96.

3. Interviews with John Sherman (Rockmore's nephew), Mar. 4, 1998, and John Rockmore (Robert Rockmore's brother), Mar. 6, 1998; Max Jones and John Chilton, *Louis: The Louis Armstrong Story, 1900–1971* (1971; London, 1988), 16–17. Himself an art collector, show investor, and advocate of black causes, Rockmore brought an understanding of the arts as well as legal expertise to his relationship with Robeson and remained close friends with Robeson throughout his life.

4. Krimsky interview, Dec. 5, 1974; agreement between Robeson and Cochran and Krimsky, Feb. 24, 1933, Robeson Collections (PR Jr.). See also Mortimer Franklin, "Art in Astoria," *Screenland* 27 (Oct. 1933).

5. *G.K.'s Weekly,* Mar. 23, 1933; telephone interview with Roland Adam, Nov. 4, 1974; *New York Sun,* May 10, 1933; Marie Seton, *Paul Robeson* (London: Dennis Dobson, 1958), 61; see also 60 for the Embassy Theatre.

6. PR qtd. in Seton, *Paul Robeson,* 61.

7. Interview with Andre Van Gyseghem, Nov. 4, 1974.

8. Ibid.; Seton, *Paul Robeson,* 62; Adam interview, Nov. 4, 1974.

9. T, *Punch,* Mar. 22, 1933.

10. Ibid.; *Morning Post* (London), Mar. 23, 1933; *Weekend Review* (London), Mar. 18, 1933. See also *Sunday Times* (London), Mar. 19, 1933, and *Daily News Chronicle* (London), Mar. 14, 1933; C. B. Purdom, *Everyman* 9, no. 217 (Mar. 25, 1933): 361.

11. West letter to Woollcott qtd. in Seton, *Paul Robeson,* 131 (also cited in Alexander Woollcott, *While Rome Burns* [New York: Viking, 1934], 131); *Nottingham Journal,* Mar. 15, 1933; *Sunday Times,* Mar. 19, 1933; Ivor Browne, *Weekend Review,* Mar. 18, 1933; A. E. Wilson, *Star* (London), Mar. 14, 1933; *Manchester Guardian,* Mar. 15, 1933; S. R. L., *Morning Post,* May 14, 1933.

12. Interview with Dame Sybil Thorndike, Nov. 6, 1974.

13. Adam interview, Nov. 4, 1974. According to Adam, "the top price [at the Piccadilly] was to be seven and sixpence, old money, tops." Seton (interviewed Nov. 11, 1974) claimed that Robeson did not ask for an increase in salary, even though when plays moved to the West End actors' salaries generally went up.

14. Krimsky, "Emperor Jones," 94; *Village Voice,* June 24, 1971; Franklin, "Art in Astoria," 84; Thomas Cripps, *Slow Fade to Black* (New York: Oxford University Press, 1977), 205–6; Donald Clarke, *Wishing on the Moon: The Life and Times of Billie Holiday* (New York: Penguin, 1994), 83. *Maedchen in Uniform* was banned in thirteen states including New York. Krimsky and Cochran finally convinced Eleanor Roosevelt to see the film and she, in turn, pressed to have bans on the film lifted. Within two years the film had grossed $1.2 million (Krimsky and Cochran had paid $8,000 for the rights to the film), and this during the Depression years. Dudley Murphy also directed *Ballet Mechanique.* See also *Boston Globe,* May 5, 1974, and *Boston Herald American,* May 11, 1974.

15. Interview with Joe Andrews, Nov. 13–20, 1974; *New York Sun,* May 10, 1933; Krimsky interview, Dec. 5, 1974. Essie accompanied Paul, although the two did not share living quarters — Essie stayed with friends. (According to the *Amsterdam News* [May 17, 1933], Paul Jr. stayed in Switzerland with his uncle John Goode.) Essie helped Paul with his lines on the set, but she also pursued her own projects, which included possibly enrolling in the American Academy of Arts or George Pierce's course in playwriting at Yale. See ER to Larry Brown, Dec. 24, 1932, Lawrence Brown Papers, Schomburg Collection, New York Public Library; ER Diary, Dec. 15 and 25, 1932, Robeson Collections (PR Jr.); ER interview with Ted Poston, *Amsterdam News,* Feb. 8, 1933.

16. Krimsky interview, Dec. 5, 1974; interview with Dorothy Fletcher Cochran (Gifford Cochran's wife), June 23, 1975. Dorothy Cochran assisted Heyward and Murphy as they reworked the script and worked as script girl to cutters and cameramen.

17. Krimsky, "Emperor Jones," 98; Krimsky interview, Dec. 5, 1974; "Jungle in Astoria," *New Yorker* 9, no. 21 (July 22, 1933): 10; Helen Ludlam, "The Black Napoleon," *Picture Play* 39, no. 2 (Oct. 1933): 65.

18. Krimsky interview, Dec. 5, 1974; "Jungle in Astoria," 10; Krimsky, "Emperor Jones," 97; interview with Fritz Pollard, Sept. 16, 1974.

19. Krimsky interview, Dec. 5, 1974.

20. Ibid.

21. Dorothy Cochran interview, June 23, 1975.

22. Pollard interview, Sept. 16, 1974.

23. PR qtd. in *Star,* Aug. 3, 1933.

24. Krimsky interview, Dec. 5, 1974; Krimsky, "Emperor Jones," 98; *Amsterdam News,* July 25, 1933. According to the *Amsterdam News,* because the lighter-skinned Chief Manoedi "reflected the culture of the better class of Africans met in Africa," he was able to convince producers that he be darkened only for the ceremonial scenes; for other scenes he would appear "as is."

25. Richard Dyer, *Heavenly Bodies: Film Star and Society* (London: Macmillan, 1986), 100–103.

26. Krimsky interview, Dec. 5, 1974.

27. John Krimsky and Gifford Cochran, *The Emperor Jones,* screenplay by DuBose Heyward, 1933; The Emperor Jones, 1933, black and white, 72 minutes, Krimsky, Gifford Cochran Productions, 1933, Janus Films, Home Vision, ROB 010.

Dating back to 1916, black-made films were shown only in the ghettos and most reflected to varying degrees black Americans' internalization of white racial values. Films like the Colored Players' *Scar of Shame* and Micheaux's *God's Step Children,* for example, recount the efforts of dark-skinned blacks to improve their stature by marrying fair-skinned upper-class blacks, their rejection, and their ensuing self-destruction. White films featuring blacks invariably portrayed only black stereotypes. But in *The Emperor Jones,* Brutus dies *not* because he is black or inferior but because he is consumed by ambition and greed. For Jones, the black–white issue is irrelevant. He wants desperately to get ahead, but in the end his conscience catches up with him and destroys him. See Norman Kagan, *Village Voice,* July 1, 1971.

28. Krimsky qtd. in *News-Times,* Dec. 9, 1973.

29. Although the Roosevelt catered almost entirely to an uptown black clientele, it generally featured lily-white Hollywood films.

30. *Amsterdam News,* Sept. 20, 1933. Among the celebrities in attendance for the opening were Jack Johnson, Bill Robinson, Fredi Washington, and Frank Wilson. See also *Amsterdam News,* Sept. 27, 1933; *Pittsburgh Courier,* Oct. 21, 1933. The Emperor Jones closed at the Rivoli on Oct. 21, 1933.

31. This source wishes to remain annoymous; interview conducted Apr. 14, 1978.

32. Walter C. Daniel, "The Green Pastures: The Washington Performance," *Negro History Bulletin* 42 (Apr. 1979): 42–43.

33. Wanda Hale, *New York Daily News,* Sept. 20, 1933; Mordaunt Hall, *New York Times,* Sept. 20, 1933; William Troy, "Films — Cinema Minus," *Nation* 127, no. 3562 (Oct. 11, 1933): 419; Regina Crewe, *New York American,* Sept. 20, 1933; Thornton Delaney, *New York Evening Post,* Sept. 20, 1933; Richard Watts, *New York Herald Tribune,* Sept. 20, 1933; "The Emperor Jones," *Close Up,* Dec. 1933, 351–52.

34. In his biography of O'Neill, Louis Sheaffer maintains that O'Neill did not think much of the film, especially after "others had tinkered with Heywood's script to make it flashier, more exciting" (Sheaffer, *O'Neill: Son and Artist* [Boston: Little, Brown, 1973], 414). Krimsky took issue with Sheaffer on this point, arguing that O'Neill felt "that *Jones* was produced with more artistry, honesty and talent than any of his other plays that had been made into film" (Krimsky to Sheaffer, Oct. 10, 1974, Krimsky Papers, Roxbury, Conn.).

35. See *Pittsburgh Courier,* Sept. 23, 1933, and *Amsterdam News,* Sept. 20, 1933. The baritone Lawrence Tibbett starred in an operatic version of *The Emperor Jones* that opened at the Metropolitan early in 1933 and closed in February after six performances, grossing an estimated $70,000 (*New York Times,* Feb. 12, 1933). Many blacks, among them Walter White, criticized Tibbett for playing the part in blackface (see Harry Keelan, *Opportunity,* 1933; *Afro-American,* Feb. 11, 1933). Later that year, in July, soprano Caterina Jarboro and baritone Jules Bledsoe broke ground in the roles of Aida and Amonasro in the Chicago Opera Company's production of *Aida* at New York's Hippodrome Theatre. Robeson was among the many celebrities in attendance for the gala opening night performance (*Amsterdam News,* July 26, 1933).

36. In two instances at least, White begged off. Murphy wrote to him in October inviting him to a private showing of the film and asking his assistance in stemming "some adverse criticism . . . from some of the editors of colored papers." White replied, "Unfortunately your letter comes just as I am leaving for Washington," and promised to phone him when he returned, which he never did (Dudley Murphy to Walter White, Oct. 6, 1933; White to Murphy, Oct. 9, 1933, NAACP Papers, Box C-303). White made one halting defense of the film when he answered Louis Lautier's (*Pittsburgh Courier*) denunciation of the film and its use of the word "nigger." But White's arguments lacked verve and were of necessity qualified because, as he himself said, he had not yet

seen the film (Lautier to White, telegram, Sept. 9, 1933, White to Lautier, Sept. 19, 1933, NAACP Papers, Box C-303).

37. Krimsky interview, Dec. 5, 1974; *Pittsburgh Courier,* Oct. 7, 1933; Joel Rogers, *Amsterdam News,* Sept. 25, 1933.

38. Theophilus Lewis, *Amsterdam News,* Oct. 11 and Nov. 8, 1933; Romeo Dougherty, *Amsterdam News,* Oct. 4, 1933.

39. *Variety,* Sept. 26, 1933; Ted Poston, *Amsterdam News,* Sept. 27, 1933.

40. *Amsterdam News,* Oct. 11, 1933.

41. *Pittsburgh Courier,* Sept. 21, 1933.

42. Frank Durham, *DuBose Heyward: The Man Who Wrote "Porgy"* (Columbia: University of South Carolina Press, 1954), 99; Krimsky interview, Dec. 5, 1974; Krimsky qtd. in *News-Times,* Dec. 9, 1973; Norman Kagan in the *Village Voice* (July 1, 1971) cited a much lower figure for production costs: $280,000.

43. Two days before sailing for England, Robeson did agree to a brief interview with William Lundell (ms., July 25, 1933, Robeson Collections [PR Jr.]), but in general he had little to say to the press. PR qtd. in *Daily Express* (London), Aug. 3, 1933.

44. PR qtd. in *New York World-Telegram,* Aug. 30, 1933.

45. H. De La Tour, "Our Performers Abroad," *Amsterdam News,* Aug. 23, 1933.

46. "Sing Paul, Sing," *Amsterdam News,* Sept. 2, 1933.

47. Walter White, *A Man Called White* (Bloomington: Indiana University Press, 1948), 141.

48. Andrews interview, Nov. 13–20, 1974; *Pittsburgh Courier,* Feb. 6 and 13, 1932.

49. John Chilton, *Billie's Blues: The Billie Holiday Story, 1933–1959* (New York: Da Capo Press, 1975), 21; Jimmy Breslin, *Damon Runyan* (New York: Ticknor and Fields, 1991), 333–34.

50. ER interviewed by Ted Poston, *Amsterdam News,* Feb. 8, 1933. Neither Essie's play, *Uncle Tom's Cabin,* a parody involving a black jazz band touring Europe, nor her novel, *Black Progress,* was ever published.

51. James Baldwin, Introduction, *Nobody Knows My Name* (1961; reprint, New York: Vintage, 1993), xi–xii.

52. Robeson sold 36,284 records in Britain from June 30, 1933, to Dec. 31, 1933 (Gramophone Company, Robeson Collections [PR Jr.]); *People,* Jan. 4, 1934; *Stage,* Jan. 1, 1934. See also *North Mail* (Newcastle-on-Tyne), Jan. 2, 1934; *Daily Telegraph* (London), Jan. 3, 1934; *Sunday Express* (London), Jan. 7, 1934.

53. PR, "Paul Robeson on My Dark Race," *Forum,* March 1934, 5; *Glasgow Evening News,* Jan. 3, 1934; PR interviewed by William Lundell, *Screenland,* Oct. 1933; Andrews interview, Nov. 13–20, 1974.

54. *Cambridge Daily News,* Mar. 31, 1934; Franklin, "Art in Astoria"; PR, "The Culture of the Negro," *Spectator* (London), June 15, 1934, 916–17. Robeson's registration card shows him enrolled in two courses, phonetics and Swahili, 1933–34 term. Robeson's notes for 1934, between 8,000 and 10,000 words, are in the Robeson Collections (PR Jr.).

55. Robeson Archives, Akademie der Kunst, Berlin; *Lancashire Evening News,* Jan. 24, 1934; *Cambridge Daily News,* Mar. 31, 1934.

56. Other black performers sang Stephen Foster's songs, among them the Fisk University Jubilee Singers, W. C. Handy, and Marian Anderson. On Stephen Foster and the cultural significance of his music, see Ken Emerson, *Doo-Dah! Stephen Foster and the Rise of American Popular Culture* (New York: Da Capo Press, 1998), and William W. Austin, *"Susanna," "Jeanie," and "The Old Folks at Home": The Songs of Stephen C. Foster from His Time to Ours,* 2nd ed. (Urbana: University of Illinois Press, 1989); Paul Robeson Jr. qtd. in *Paul Robeson: Here I Stand* (127-minute documentary), American Masters Production, a coproduction of Thirteen/WNET and Menair International (New York: Fox Lorber Associates, 1999).

57. Andrews interview, Nov. 13–20, 1974; Paul Robeson Jr. qtd. in *Paul Robeson: Here I Stand* (documentary).

58. *Sheffield Independent,* Jan. 23. 1934; PR, *Here I Stand* (1958; reprint, Boston: Beacon Press, 1971), 54; *Esquire News,* Jan. 14, 1934; Charles E. Payne interview with Jan Carew, March 1985, in

"Paul Robeson: A Psychobiographical Study of the Emotional Development of a Controversial Protest Leader" (Ph.D. diss., Northwestern University, 1987), 153, 354.

59. Lawrence Brown, qtd. in Seton, *Paul Robeson*, 73–74.

60. *Sheffield Telegraph*, Jan. 24, 1934; *Lancashire Evening News*, Jan. 24, 1934; unnamed Huddersfield newspaper clipping, Apr. 13, 1934. There is some discrepancy in newspaper accounts as to whether it was a dying young boy or a dying father who heard Robeson's New Year recitation. We have cited it as a dying boy because this is the story given in the majority of newspapers cited.

61. Introductory remarks taken from a 1939 recording of Robeson reading the poem: *Paul Robeson: Big Fella*, 1994 Conifer Records, Ltd.; William Blake, "The Little Black Boy," in *The Poetry and Prose of William Blake*, ed. David V. Erdman (Garden City, N.Y.: Doubleday, 1970), 90. Like many other great Romantic poets, Blake spoke out for the abolition of slavery and against what Wordsworth called in "The Prelude," "the Traffickers in Negro blood" (10:202–27). See David V. Erdman, *Blake: Prophet against Empire*, rev. ed. (Garden City, N.Y.: Doubleday, 1969), and Patrick Brantlinger, *Rule of Darkness: British Literature and Imperialism, 1830–1914* (Ithaca: Cornell University Press, 1988), 173–79. We are grateful to John Mahoney of Boston College for his insights concerning Blake and this particular poem.

62. PR, "Culture of the Negro."

63. *Esquire News*, Jan. 14, 1934.

64. Graduate course offerings for 1934 included "The Functional Analysis of Primitive Cultures" (Malinowski) and "The Ethnology of Africa" (Richards). For Department of Anthropology course offerings, see *The Calendar of the London School of Economics and Political Science (University of London) for the Fortieth Session, 1934–1935* (London, 1934), Introduction, 4–5.

65. Raymond Firth to Rich Ruda, Jan. 20, 1975; Rich Ruda interview with Peter Prince of Greece, Mar. 8, 1975.

66. During his lifetime, Wallace wrote 170 books, nearly all best-sellers. He wrote so quickly that his latest work was jokingly referred to as the "Weekly Wallace," later amended to the "Midday Wallace." See Margaret Lane, *Edgar Wallace: The Biography of a Phenomenon* (New York: Doubleday, 1936), 286. After seeing *Show Boat* in 1928, Wallace contacted Robeson, indicating he wanted to write a play with Robeson the star and even offering to invest in the proposed production. The project never materialized, however (Barry O'Brien to PR, Aug. 13, 1928, and Edgar Wallace to PR, Aug. 18, 1928, Robeson Collections [PR Jr.]).

67. Leslie Banks, "Britain Puts Her Empire on Screen at Last," *Film Pictorial*, Apr. 6, 1935, 42–43. Hugh Castle, "Stranded among the Cannibals," *Answers* (London), June 24, 1934; Paul Tabori, *Alexander Korda* (London, 1959), 156; Karol Kulik, *Alexander Korda: The Man Who Made Miracles* (New Rochelle, N.Y., 1975), 136; contract dated June 25, 1934, Robeson Collections (PR Jr.). On Western stereotypes of Africa, see Jan Nederveen Pieterse, *White on Black: Images of Africa and Blacks in Popular Western Culture* (New Haven: Yale University Press, 1992), 9–122; Edward W. Said, *Culture and Imperialism* (New York: Vintage, 1994); Anne McClintock, *Imperial Leather: Race, Gender and Sexuality in the Colonial Contest* (New York: Routledge, 1995), 2–74; Kenneth M. Cameron, "Paul Robeson, Eddie Murphy, and the Film Text of 'Africa,'" *Text and Performance Quarterly* 10, no. 4 (Oct. 1990): 282–93.

68. On McKinney, see Darlene Clark Hine, ed., *Black Women in America: An Historical Encyclopedia*, vol. 2 (New York: Carlson Publishing, 1993), 772–73; Henry T. Sampson, *Blacks in Black and White: A Sourcebook on Black Films*, 2nd ed. (Metuchen, N.J.: Scarecrow Press, 1995), 540–42; Bruce Kellner, ed., *The Harlem Renaissance: An Historical Dictionary for the Era* (New York: Metheun, 1987), 232; Cripps, *Slow Fade to Black*, 250.

69. PR interview, *Evening Standard* (London), Nov. 4, 1938; "British Film News," *Today's Cinema News and Property Gazette* 8, no. 2797 (Sept. 5, 1934): 26; *Picturegoer*, Sept. 28, 1934.

70. PR interview, *Evening Standard*, Nov. 4, 1938; "British Film News," 26; *Picturegoer*, Sept. 28, 1934. On black extras, see Stephen Bourne, *Black in the British Frame: Black People in British Film and Television, 1896–1996* (London: Cassell, 1998), 43–56. Bourne includes interviews with blacks who played bit parts and supporting roles in Robeson films, including Anthony Papafio, the child of a West African seaman and his white wife; Napoleon Florent, a professional actor who

played one of King Mofolaba's henchmen in *Sanders;* Ernest Marke, an extra in *Sanders;* and the Cozier family from London's East End.

71. PR interview, *Evening Standard,* Nov. 4, 1938; "British Film News," 26; *Picturegoer,* Sept. 28, 1934; also interview with C. L. R. James, May 8, 1975; Paul Tabori, *Alexander Korda,* 157; Jeremy Murray-Brown, *Kenyatta* (New York: Dalton, 1973), 6, 214, 216; *Observer,* July 29, 1934; PR qtd. in *Spectator,* June 15, 1934, 916–17; PR, "I Want to Be an African," in E. G. Cousins, *What I Want from Life* (London, 1934), 71–77, included in *Paul Robeson Speaks: Writings, Speeches, Interviews, 1918–1974,* ed. Philip S. Foner (Secaucus, N.J.: Citadel, 1978), 88–91.

72. *Manchester Guardian,* Oct. 10, 1934; *Picturegoer,* Sept. 8, 1934; *Film Weekly,* Sept. 21, 1934; Andrews interview, Nov. 13–20, 1974; Peter Noble, *The Negro in Films* (London: Skelton Robinson, 1948); James interview, May 8, 1974.

73. Andrews interview, Nov. 13–20, 1974; Murray-Brown, *Kenyatta,* 180–83, 195, 217; interview with Lord Fenner Brockway, Nov. 19, 1974. See Jomo Kenyatta, *Facing Mount Kenya* (London, 1935); Guy Arnold, *Kenyatta and the Politics of Kenya* (London: J. M. Dent and Sons, 1974), 28; George Delf, *Jomo Kenyatta: Towards Truth about "The Light of Kenya"* (New York: Doubleday, 1961), 91–96. Prince Peter held an undergraduate degree from Columbia University and attended Malinowski's seminar with Kenyatta.

74. Brockway interview, Nov. 19, 1974; Rich Ruda interview with J. Murray-Brown, June 2, 1975; Murray-Brown, *Kenyatta,* 214; Andrews interview, Nov. 13–20, 1974.

In his biography, Murray-Brown portrays Kenyatta as a "dissimulator," not averse to using people when necessary during these early years in London. C. L. R. James said the same: "Kenyatta owed money to everyone, and he may well have tried to get Robeson to help him out financially" (James interview, May 8, 1974). Prince Peter, a friend of Kenyatta's, said that Kenyatta stayed with his parents for a month in France and that he later got Kenyatta a scholarship to the International School in Denmark for a summer of study (Ruda–Prince Peter of Greece interview, Mar. 18, 1975. Prince Peter was the grandson of George I of Greece and the son of Prince George of Greece and Denmark). In *Kenyatta and the Politics of Kenya,* Guy Arnold claims that Kenyatta shared a flat with Robeson in 1933.

75. *Observer,* July 29, 1934; PR qtd. in *Spectator,* June 15, 1934, 916–17; PR, "I Want to Be an African."

76. PR qtd. in *Spectator,* June 15, 1934, 916–17; PR, "I Want to Be an African."

77. John F. Szwed, "An American Anthropological Dilemma: The Politics of Afro-American Culture," in *Reinventing Anthropology,* ed. Dell Hymes (New York: Vintage, 1974), 153–81; Gunnar Myrdal, *An American Dilemma* (New York: Harper and Brothers, 1944), 928–29.

78. *London Illustrated News,* Sept. 19, 1934; *Manchester Guardian,* Oct. 10, 1934.

79. Tabori, *Alexander Korda,* 157–58. Despite the fact that the handshake between a white man and a black one would not have occurred in real life, this "became the most moving, though too self-consciously 'poignant,' scene in Sanders" (Kulik, *Alexander Korda: The Man Who Made Miracles,* 136; see also 5).

80. *Sanders of the River,* black and white, 1935, Distributed by Timeless Video Inc., P.O. Box 16354, North Hollywood, CA 91615–6354, no. 5041.

81. Murray-Brown, *Kenyatta,* 217. According to Murray-Brown, Kenyatta never mentioned his appearance in *Sanders,* but neither did he protest about his role. In fact, when work was completed, Kenyatta was among those whose name was inscribed on a gold cigarette case presented to Korda "with deep admiration and gratitude."

82. See Eslanda Robeson, *African Journey* (New York: John Day, 1945), 13, and PR, *Here I Stand,* 33. Both Essie and Paul talk in these books about how little they learned about Africa in the United States; Andrews interview, Nov. 13–20, 1974.

83. Flora Robson, interviewed in *Paul Robeson* (BBC television, tx26, Nov. 1978); qtd. in Bourne, *Black in the British Frame,* 17.

84. Interview with Hugh Scotland, Nov. 2, 1974. The situation was so difficult that in the 1920s various student welfare organizations—the East and West Friendship Council, the League of Colored Peoples, the West African Students' Union—were founded specifically to offer support

to students facing British race prejudice. See Edward Scobie, *Black Britannia* (Chicago: Johnson, 1972), 142–43.

85. PR qtd. in *Tid-Bits,* May 27, 1933. See also D. F. Karaka, "Colour Bar," *Daily Herald,* Apr. 10, 1934.

86. James Baldwin, "Princes and Powers," in *Nobody Knows My Name* (1961; reprint, New York: Vintage, 1993), 19–21.

87. Interviews with James (May 8, 1975) and Brockway (Nov. 19, 1974).

88. *Sanders of the River* publicity book, British-Lion, n.d., 3, Robeson Collections (PR Jr.); Cripps, *Slow Fade to Black;* PR qtd. in *Observer,* July 28, 1934.

89. Imanuel Geiss, *The Pan African Movement* (1968; London: Metheun, 1974), 340–47. Membership of the League of Coloured Peoples (LCP) was largely West Indian with some African and African American representation.

90. *West Africa,* Dec. 22, 1934; *Manchester Guardian,* Dec. 14, 1934; *Norfolk Journal,* Jan. 5, 1935; *Daily Mail,* Dec. 14, 1934; *Times of Malaysia,* Dec. 14, 1934. The other speaker that evening was W. G. Ballinger, who described industrial conditions and the lot of the African worker in South Africa.

91. PR qtd. in *Manchester Guardian,* Dec. 14, 1934; *Norfolk Journal,* Jan. 5, 1935. The *Manchester Guardian* noted a sadness about Robeson as he made the announcement and titled his remarks "Robeson's Lament."

92. *Star,* Dec. 15, 1934. Letter to *Star,* signed D. Y. Dev., Cambridge-terrace, W.2.

93. PR, *Here I Stand,* 33; PR, "Paul Robeson on My Dark Race," *Forum,* March 1934, 5–7.

13. THE SEARCH FOR HOME

1. PR, *Here I Stand* (1958; Boston: Beacon Press, 1971), 33; Marie Seton, *Paul Robeson* (London: Dennis Dobson, 1958), 78; interviews with Marie Seton (Nov. 11, 1974) and Joe Andrews (Nov. 13–20, 1974).

2. Seton interview, Nov. 11, 1974; Ken Nelson interview with Herbert Marshall, Feb. 14, 1975. Sergei Eisenstein, in his autobiography, also recalled Paul's wanting "to enter, for one year of his life, into the primeval state of one of the most primitive peoples in Africa. He wished to submerge himself completely in their customs, morals, languages and thinking." See *Immoral Memories: An Autobiography of Sergei Eisenstein,* trans. Herbert Marshall (Boston: Houghton Mifflin, 1983), 212.

3. Andrews interview, Nov. 13–20, 1974.

4. Seton kept Eisenstein well supplied with books unavailable in the Soviet Union and frankly admitted her infatuation with the charismatic film genius. Seton, *Paul Robeson,* 55–57; Seton interview, Nov. 11, 1974; interview with Herbert Marshall, Sept. 20–21, 1974; Rachel Low, *Films of Comment and Persuasion of the 1930s: The History of British Film, 1929–1939* (London: George Allen and Unwin, 1979), 110; Marie Seton, *Sergei M. Eisenstein* (London: Dennis Dobson, 1978), 13.

5. Sergei Eisenstein to PR, undated, 1934, Robeson Collections (PR Jr.).

6. Seton, *Paul Robeson,* 79–80.

7. Andrews interview, Nov. 13–20, 1974.

8. Ibid.; ER Diary, May 15, July 27 and 30, 1931, Robeson Collections (PR Jr.); *New York Post,* Jan. 28, 1932; PR interviewed by Sulamith Ish-Kishor, *Jewish Tribune,* July 22, 1927; Roy Wilkins–PR interview, *Kansas City Times,* Feb. 9, 1931; G.W.B., *Observer* (London), May 1931. See also *Newark Evening News,* Aug. 16, 1933; C.A.L., *Observer,* July 29, 1934; *Daily Gleaner* (Jamaica, BWI), Dec. 17, 1932; *New York Post,* Jan. 18, 1932; and *Film Pictorial,* Jan. 27, 1934. For Russian pieces, see programs of Robeson's concerts, 1931–1936, Robeson Collections (PR Jr.). Some of the programs state specifically that the songs were sung in Russian.

Many other blacks saw likenesses between the experiences of American blacks and Russian serfs. As early as 1919 the great jazz musician and conductor James Reese Europe advised aspiring black musicians, "If we try to copy whites we will make bad copies. . . . Our musicians do their best work when using Negro material. . . . The music of our race springs from the soil, and this is true with no other noble race, except possibly the Russians" (qtd. in Gerald Early, *The Culture of*

Bruising: Essays on Prizefighting, Literature, and Modern American Culture [Hopewell, N.J.: Ecco Press, 1994], 190).

9. Van Gyseghem covered such topics as the training of Russian actors, state promotion of the arts, Russian children's theater, the Jewish State Theatre, national minority theaters, the great Russian producers (Vsevolod, Meyerhold, and Stanislavski), the Moscow Art Theatre, the Maly Theatre, and the Kamerny Theatre. Many of these articles were later published in Van Gyseghem, *Theatre in Soviet Russia* (London: Faber and Faber, 1943).

10. Russia evoked feelings of unease among many British, not because it constituted a military threat but because the idea of communism challenged the established order, especially given the Soviet Union's apparent immunity from the economic crisis plaguing the entire capitalist world. Most British newspapers saw it as their duty to combat socialist ideas and so they suppressed news of any genuine achievement in the Soviet Union, reporting that Stalin's Five-Year Plan was a failure brought about by a regime on its last legs. See Noreen Branson and Margot Heinemann, *Britain in the Nineteen Thirties* (London: Panther, 1973), 32–34.

11. *Moscow Daily News,* undated.

12. See the article on semiliterate peasant girls studying engineering at night while working days at a Moscow ball-bearing plant (*Moscow Daily News,* May 19, 1937). For a very detailed analysis of Soviet policy in regard to its national minority population, see Terry D. Martin, "An Affirmative Action Empire: Ethnicity and the Soviet State, 1922–1938" (Ph.D. diss., University of Chicago, 1996).

13. Fenner Brockway said the East African referred to in Robeson's autobiography was Kenyatta (interview Nov. 19, 1974). See PR, *Here I Stand,* 35–36.

14. Claude McKay, *A Long Way from Home* (New York: Furman, 1937), 168; William Patterson, *The Man Who Cried Genocide: An Autobiography* (New York: International Publishers, 1971), 112; Henry Lee Moon, "A Negro Looks at Soviet Russia," *Nation* 138, no. 3582 (June 28, 1934): 244–46; Langston Hughes, "Moscow and Me: A Noted American Writer Relates His Experiences," *International Literature,* no. 3 (July 1933): 60–66, and *I Wonder as I Wander: An Autobiographical Journey* (New York: Hill and Wang, 1956), 69–237 (our italics); on blacks visiting and immigrating to the Soviet Union during this period, see Allison Blakely, *Russia and the Negro* (Washington, D.C.: Howard University Press, 1986). For a general study of American and European "pilgrimages" to the Soviet Union, see Sylvia R. Margulies, *The Pilgrimage to Russia: The Soviet Union and the Treatment of Foreigners, 1924–1937* (Madison: University of Wisconsin Press, 1968).

15. See Homer Smith, *Black Man in Red Russia* (Chicago: Johnson, 1964). According to Smith, the racial commingling of American blacks with white Russians was not only tolerated but encouraged. Smith married a white Russian woman as did other blacks who lived in the Soviet Union. Although Smith's reminiscences are hardly sympathetic to the USSR, he gives the Soviets their due in regard to their treatment of blacks.

16. Louise Thompson to Louise ("Mother") Thompson, July 14, 1932, and Matt Crawford to Evelyn Crawford, Sept. 21, 1932; both in Arnold Rampersand, *The Life of Langston Hughes,* vol. 1, *1902–1941* (New York: Oxford University Press, 1986), 246, 251–52.

17. As John Goode put it to Ben Davis, "There is always work in the Soviet Union" (*Daily Worker,* Mar. 2, 1937); see also ER to Mrs. Goode, Jan. 5, 1935, Robeson Collections (PR Jr.). On John Goode, see *Amsterdam News,* Mar. 6, 1937, and *Pittsburgh Courier,* June 3, 1933; on Frank Goode, see *Amsterdam News,* Mar. 6, 1937. In the West the circus was considered on a par with cheap, sideshow entertainment, but in the Soviet Union it was regarded as a respectable well-paying professional venue. Russia's State Circus Association included more than 100 individual groups, together employing more than 3,000 performers. See Eugene Gordon, *Moscow Daily News,* Apr. 8, 1936.

18. John Goode to Mrs. Goode, July 30, 1935, Folder M, John Goode and Frank Goode, Robeson Collections (PR Jr.).

19. Seton, *Paul Robeson,* 55–57; Seton interview, Nov. 11, 1974, and Marshall interview, Sept. 20–21, 1974.

20. PR interview, *Berliner Zeitung,* June 21, 1960 (a condensed version of a more lengthy

interview with Klaus Ulrich in *Neues Deutschland*); Vern Smith–PR interview, *Daily Worker,* Jan. 15, 1935; Seton's account in *Paul Robeson,* 70–73.

21. *Chicago Defender,* Jan. 12, 1935; *Moscow Daily News,* Dec. 24, 1934; see also Seton, *Paul Robeson,* 85.

22. David Caute, *The Fellow Travellers,* rev. ed. (New Haven: Yale University Press, 1988), 11; Margulies, *The Pilgrimage to Russia,* 32–37, 58–63, 79–95.

23. Despite his reputation as an international star, Robeson had only twice performed in mainland Europe. As a recording artist, Robeson was best known in Britain where he had sold over 50,000 records between July and December 1934. He also enjoyed considerable popularity in the British colonies of India and Australia where he sold approximately 2,900 and 2,000 recordings respectively. "Overseas," including Holland, South Africa, Egypt, and Switzerland, the total was just under 4,000. In Germany he sold 800 records. Record sales for Sweden totaled 472, Denmark 415, France 133, Austria 42. The lowest sales were in Italy, Spain, Hungary, and Czechoslovakia — all in the single numbers (Gramophone Company, "Statement of Records Sold and Property Earned," June 30, 1934–Dec. 31, 1934, Robeson Collections [PR Jr.]). Sales were substantially the same for the first six months of 1935; John Hammond with Irving Townsend, *On Record* (New York: Ridge Press, 1977), 154. On the Soviet Union's chronic shortages of food and consumer goods, see Sheila Fitzpatrick, *Everyday Stalinism: Ordinary Life in Extraordinary Times: Soviet Russia in the 1930s* (New York: Oxford University Press, 1999), 43–50.

24. *Moscow Daily News,* Dec. 24, 1934; *Times,* Jan. 2, 1935; *Pittsburgh Courier,* Jan. 19, 1935.

25. For PR's "skepticism," see Chen Leyda, *Footnote to History,* ed. Sally Barnes (New York: Dance Horizons, 1984), 196–97.

26. *Chicago Defender,* Jan. 12, 1935; Seton, *Paul Robeson,* 88–89; ER Diary, Dec. 24 and 25, 1934, Robeson Collections (PR Jr.).

27. Marshall interview, Sept. 20–21, 1974. Clara Rockmore (interviewed Sept. 15, 1980) said that even as late as the 1950s Robeson used an interpreter (Victor Gorakhov). For PR's lack of confidence see Leyda, *Footnote to History,* 196.

28. Seton, *Paul Robeson,* 89.

29. *Moscow Daily News,* Sept. 7, 1934.

30. On Stalin's huge construction efforts, see Timothy J. Colton, *Moscow: Governing the Socialist Metropolis* (Cambridge: Harvard University Press, Belknap Press, 1995), 249–91. On the city's optimistic spirit, see Fitzpatrick, *Everyday Stalinism,* 42, 68–88.

31. *Moscow Daily News,* Jan. 31, 1935.

32. *Daily Worker,* Sept. 13, 1934.

33. The activities of the Children's Theatre were reported regularly in the *Moscow Daily News.* In January the newspaper featured a photo of Paul and Essie standing with Natalia Satz, director of the Central Children's Theatre of Moscow, watching the games in the foyer of the theater (*Moscow Daily News,* Jan. 10, 1935); Paul Robeson, "Why I Left My Son in Moscow," *Russia Today,* Feb. 1938; Shirley Graham, *Paul Robeson: Citizen of the World* (New York: Julian Messner, 1946), 225–26.

34. Interview with Helen Rosen, Feb. 9, 1981; Marshall interview, Sept. 20–21, 1974.

35. *Moscow Daily News,* Jan. 10, 1935.

36. *Moscow Daily News,* Jan. 10 and May 19, 1937.

37. Nelson–Marshall interview, Feb. 14, 1975; Marshall interview, Sept. 20–21, 1974.

38. Both Fredda Brilliant, in her biographical sketch, and Marie Seton, in her writings on Russia, stress that during the 1930s foreign-born students and artists in Russia were welcomed with open arms. See also Anna Strong, *I Change Worlds: The Remaking of an American* (New York: Henry Holt, 1935). A white American, originally from the Midwest, Strong took up residence in Russia and was prominent in founding the *Moscow Daily News* in 1930. She was a prolific writer and spent most of her life extolling the virtues of communism until 1949 when she was expelled from the Party.

39. Nelson–Marshall interview, Feb. 14, 1975; John Morocco interview with Ivor Montague, Mar. 13, 1975; Herbert Marshall, ms. autobiography, Southern Illinois University, Carbondale; *Hampstead and St. John's Wood News and Advertiser,* June 1, 1939.

40. Herbert Marshall, "Eisenstein and Others . . . ," *Listener* 89 (May 29, 1973).

41. Herbert Marshall, ms. autobiography.

42. Patterson, *Man Who Cried Genocide,* passim; *New York Times,* Sept. 8, 1932.

43. Interview with William Patterson, Jan. 20, 1975. Herbert Marshall confirmed that Robeson and Patterson met in Russia and "talked quite a bit with each other, going at it for long periods of time" (Nelson–Marshall interview, Feb. 14, 1975; Marshall interview, Sept. 20–21, 1974).

44. The *Pittsburgh Courier,* for example, reported on Feb. 16, 1933, that nine whites had been expelled from the Party because of alleged race prejudice. Charges included refusal to eat with blacks, refusal to dance with blacks, name calling, referring to Negroes as "dumb, cowardly and unorganizable," and refusal to admit Negroes to social affairs.

45. See Robert Robinson, *Black on Red* (Washington, D.C.: Acropolis, 1988).

46. See Eisenstein, *Immoral Memories;* Seton, *Eisenstein,* 7; and Ronald Bergan, *Sergei Eisenstein: A Life in Conflict* (New York: Overlook Press, 1977).

47. ER Diary, Dec. 25 and Dec. 23, 1934, Robeson Collections (PR Jr.); Seton, *Eisenstein,* 327; Eisenstein, *Immoral Memories,* 213.

48. Marshall interview, Sept. 20–21, 1974; Seton, *Paul Robeson,* 86–87; Seton, *Eisenstein,* 316–17.

49. See Herbert Marshall, introduction to Eisenstein's autobiography (*Immoral Memories*); Seton, *Eisenstein,* 329–52; Bergan, *Eisenstein,* 269–75; David Bordwell, *The Cinema of Eisenstein* (Cambridge: Harvard University Press, 1995), 24–25. On the effects of political changes on the Soviet film industry during the 1930s see Peter Keney, "Soviet Cinema in the Age of Stalin," in *Stalinism and the Soviet Cinema,* ed. Richard Taylor and Derek Spring (New York: Routledge, 1993), 55–67. Despite Eisenstein's past successes, his political position was such that his future career hinged upon his ability to get himself back in favor with Stalin as soon as possible.

50. William E. Kon interview with PR, "Paul Robeson Is Pro-Soviet," *Soviet Russia Today,* Nov. 1935, 4–5.

51. Marshall interview, Sept, 20–21, 1974.

52. On Robeson and the English weather, see *Picturegoer Weekly,* Oct. 26, 1935; ER Diary, Jan. 6, 1935, Robeson Collections (PR Jr.); Seton, *Paul Robeson,* 87–88.

53. *Moscow Daily News,* Jan. 10, 1935.

54. Julia Dorne interview with PR, "I Breathe Freely," *New Theatre,* July 1935.

55. Vern Smith–Robeson interview, *Daily Worker,* Jan. 15, 1935.

14. FILM AND ITS LIMITS

1. On Ballinger, see Les Switzer, "Moderate and Militant Voices in the African Nationalist Press during the 1920s," in *South Africa's Alternative Press: Voices of Protest and Resistance, 1880–1990,* ed. Switzer (Cambridge: Cambridge University Press, 1997), 152–54; *Argus,* Jan. 29 and Feb. 2, 1935; *Daily New Chronicle* (London), Feb. 18, 1935; *Southampton Echo,* Feb. 5, 1935. The rumors suggested that Robeson might "go native," an expression mentioned or alluded to by imperialist romancers from Kipling to Henry Rider Haggard. Joseph Conrad in *Heart of Darkness* describes this "regression" as the ultimate atrocity (Kurtz is "tropenkollered" or "maddened by the tropics") — the betrayal by a white European of the ideals of civilization he is supposedly bringing to the untamed jungle. (See Patrick Brantlinger, *Rule of Darkness* [Ithaca: Cornell University Press, 1988], 192–93, 229–31.) An anonymous black South African, writing in the *Cape Times* (Jan. 2, 1935) commended Robeson's plan to visit South Africa but called it "mischievous" of Ballinger to suggest Robeson's intentions were political. "Mr. Ballinger has no status as a representative of the 'race' either here or abroad . . . and at most can claim to speak only for white organizations interested in the non-Europeans. . . . Anyone who suggests even inferentially, that a man of Robeson's calibre would have either the time or the stupidity to come all the way to South Africa in order that he might be challenged for his 'pass' by a Transvaal policeman . . . either just does not know what he is talking about, or else is naturally reckless in his statements."

2. *Daily Herald* (London), Jan. 21 and Feb. 5, 1935; *Cape Times,* Feb. 2, 1935; *Argus,* Jan. 29 and Feb. 2, 1935; *Liverpool Post,* Jan. 31, 1935; *Sunday Times* (Johannesburg), Feb. 3, 1935; *Nottingham Guardian,* Jan. 31, 1935; for Harold Holt's statement, see *Daily News Chronicle,*

Feb. 18, 1935; see also *Southampton Echo,* Feb. 5, 1935; *Daily Mail* (London), Jan. 31, 1935; *Birmingham Gazette,* Mar. 20, 1935; *West Africa,* Feb. 2, 1935; and *Evening News* (London), Jan. 30, 1935.

3. Padmore quote cited in Kent Worcester, *C. L. R. James: A Political Biography* (New York: State University of New York Press, 1996), 31. See also C. L. R. James, "The Black Scholar Interview," *Black Scholar,* May 1970.

4. On Ethiopia, see George W. Baer, *The Coming of the Italian-Ethiopian War* (Cambridge: Harvard University Press, 1967); Thomas M. Coffey, *Lion by the Tail: The Story of the Italian-Ethiopian War* (New York: Viking, 1974); Angelo Del Boca, *The Ethiopian War, 1935–1941,* trans. P. D. Cummins (Chicago: University of Chicago Press, 1969); Pietro Badoglio, *The War in Abyssinia* (New York: Putnam, 1937); and S. K. Asante, *The Pan-American Protest: West Africa and the Italo-Ethiopian Crisis* (London: Longman, 1977).

5. Imanuel Geiss, *The Pan-African Movement,* trans. Ann Keep (1968; London: Methuen, 1974), 280–97, 340–56; Peter Fryer, *Staying Power: Black People in Britain since 1504* (Atlantic Highlands, N.J.: Humanities Press, 1984), 324–45; James Walvin, *Black and White: The Negro in English Society, 1555–1945* (London: Allen Lane, Penguin Press, 1973), 202–12; Hakim Adi, "West African Students in Britain, 1900–1960: The Politics of Exile," in *Africans in Britain,* ed. David Killingray (London: Frank Cass, 1994), 107–28; Ron Ramdin, *The Making of the Black Working Class in Britain* (Aldershot, Eng.: Gower Publishing, 1987), 100–115; Edward Scobie, *Black Britannia* (Chicago: Johnson, 1972), 141–52; Paul Buhle, *C. L. R. James: The Artist as Revolutionary* (New York: Verso, 1988), 53–57; Worcester, *C. L. R. James,* 30–33; C. L. R. James, "Abyssinia and the Imperialists," *Keys* (Jan.–Mar. 1936): 32–41; Philip Garique, "The West African Students' Union: A Study in Culture Contact," *Africa: Journal of the International African Institute* 23, no. 1 (1953): 55–69. On the 1924 British Empire Exhibitions, see Robert Graves and Alan Hodge, *The Long Week-End: A Social History of Great Britain, 1918–1939,* 2nd. ed. (New York: Norton, 1963), 176–77.

6. On Max Yergan, see David H. Anthony, "Max Yergan and South Africa: A Transatlantic Interaction," in *Imagining Home: Class, Culture, and Nationalism in the African Diaspora,* ed. Sidney Lemelle and Robin D. G. Kelley (New York: Verso, 1994), 185–206.

7. *Manchester Evening News,* Jan. 31, 1935.

8. *Neath Guardian,* Apr. 5, 1935; *Herald of Wales,* Apr. 6, 1935; *Northern Whig and Belfast Post,* Feb. 18, 1935; unnamed Belfast paper, Feb. 18, 1935; *Sheffield Telegraph,* Feb. 2, 1935.

9. *Neath Guardian,* Apr. 5, 1935; *Belfast Newsletter,* Feb. 18, 1935; *Sheffield Telegraph,* Feb. 2, 1935; *Glasgow Evening News,* Jan. 31, 1935; *Gloucestershire Echo,* Mar. 29, 1935; *Birmingham Post,* Mar. 21, 1935; *Manchester Evening News,* Jan. 31, 1935.

10. Miscellaneous advertisements and publicity releases for *Sanders of the River.* See also Charles L. Blockson, Afro-American Collection, Temple University, Philadelphia. *Sanders* opened in a double bill with the premiere of Walt Disney's *Mickey Mouse,* at first glance an incongruous, almost humorous combination. In fact, the two films had much in common. Both promised novelty and both made innovative use of the film medium. In the United States, between 1932 and 1939, Walt Disney won every Academy Award for cartoon shorts. For a discussion of European colonialism, racism, and enchantment with African exotica, see Phyllis Rose's biography of Josephine Baker, *Jazz Cleopatra* (New York: Doubleday, 1989), 33–40; Anne McClintock, *Imperial Leather: Race and Gender in the Colonial Contest* (New York: Routledge, 1995); Lemke Sieglinde, *Primitivist Modernism: Black Culture and the Origins of Transatlantic Modernism* (New York: Oxford University Press, 1998), 95–116; and Jan Nederveen Pieterse, *White on Black: Images of Africa and Blacks in Popular Western Culture* (New Haven: Yale University Press, 1992).

11. *Observer* (London) and *Daily Mail,* May 25, 1935; *Harper's Bazaar* (London), March 1935.

12. *Western Mail,* Apr. 3, 1935, and *Daily Sketch* (London), Apr. 3, 1935.

13. *Daily Mirror* (London), Apr. 5, 1935.

14. *Daily Mirror,* Apr. 5, 1935; *Tatler,* Apr. 10, 1935. In July Robeson sang for a private party at Dudley House, Park Lane, given by the Hon. Sir John and Lady Ward. The duke and duchess of

York were among the notables attending. Among this audience, "The Canoe Song" was a favorite (*Sunday Times,* July 13, 1935).

15. *Spectator* (London), Apr. 5, 1935; *Reynold's Newspaper,* Apr. 4, 1935.

16. *Irish Independent,* Apr. 3, 1935; *Film World,* Apr. 13, 1935; *Film Weekly,* Mar. 12, 1935; *Daily Sketch,* Apr. 10, 1935; James Agate, "The Cinema: Lighted Africa," *Tatler,* no. 1764 (Apr. 17, 1935).

17. *Daily Telegraph* (London), Apr. 8, 1935; *Nottingham Journal,* Apr. 3, 1935; *Film Weekly,* Mar. 12, 1935; Michael Orde, *Illustrated London News,* Apr. 20, 1935.

18. *Reynold's Newspaper,* Apr. 4, 1935; *Film Weekly,* Mar. 12, 1935; *Lady,* Apr. 11, 1935. See also *Punch* 188 (Apr. 24, 1935): 454; *Spectator,* Apr. 5, 1935; Agate, "The Cinema: Lighted Africa."

19. *Daily Mirror,* Apr. 5, 1935; Marie Seton, *Paul Robeson* (London: Dennis Dobson, 1958), 97; interview with Seton, Nov. 11, 1974.

20. *Daily Express* (London), Sept. 18, 1937.

21. Interviews with Joe Andrews (Nov. 13–20, 1974), Revels Cayton (July 16, 1980), John Abt (Mar. 5, 1975), and Miki Fisher (Sept. 20, 1978).

22. Thus it is likely that Robeson, elaborating on the *Daily Mirror's* story in an attempt to explain himself, led Marie Seton to conclude that he had indeed stormed out in protest after seeing the film. Papers that reviewed the premiere but made no mention of Robeson's leaving the theater include *Tatler,* Apr. 10, 1935; *Western Mail* (Cardiff), Apr. 5, 1935; and *Evening News* (London), July 4, 1935.

23. Rich Ruda interview with Yusuf Dadoo, Feb. 24, 1975; *The Black Man: A Monthly Magazine of Negro Thought and Opinion* 2, no. 5 (January 1937).

24. Interview with C. L. R. James, May 8, 1975. *Daily Mail* (Apr. 8, 1935) reported on two cuts made during the final edits: one a love song to be sung by Bosambo to his bride and the other, a dialogue between natives as they gazed at the Union Jack: " 'What's that?' asked one chief. 'That,' replied a native soldier on sentry duty, 'is the law.' " Korda explained: "Film making would be easy if we had only cut out what is bad. It is difficult because we must cut what is not in harmony with our theme, and sometimes we have to cut the best things we have done."

25. *Amsterdam News,* July 20, 1935; Eslanda Robeson qtd. in *Amsterdam News,* Oct. 5, 1935; Howard Barnes, *New York Herald Tribune,* June 27, 1935; *New Masses* 16 (July 1935): 28–29. In her *African Journey* (New York: John Day, 1945), Eslanda Robeson expressed a different viewpoint on *Sanders:* "I blush with shame for the mental picture my fellow Negroes in American have of our African brothers: wild black savages in leopard skins, waving spears and eating raw meat. And we, with films like *Sanders of the River,* unwittingly helping to perpetuate this misconception" (48). Later, the *Amsterdam News* changed its tune (Jan. 11, 1936) and called *Sanders* "that plea for imperialism." From 1929 to 1935 Stepin Fetchit (Lincoln Perry), the best known, most successful black actor of the time, played in twenty-six films, including the role of Joe in the 1929 *Show Boat* film. He was the first black actor ever to receive feature billing and special scenes were often written into pictures specifically for him. On Perry, see Donald Bogle, *Toms, Coons, Mulattoes, Mammies, and Bucks* (New York: Continuum, 1994), 38–44; Henry T. Sampson, *Blacks in Black and White: A Source Book on Blacks in Films,* 2nd ed. (Metuchen, N.J.: Scarecrow Press, 1995), 555; Thomas Cripps, *Slow Fade to Black: The Negro in American Film, 1900–1942* (New York: Oxford University Press, 1977), 105–9, 266–67, 272–76, 193–94.

26. On Western paradigms, see Pieterse, *White on Black,* 9–122; Edward W. Said, *Culture and Imperialism* (New York: Vintage, 1994); McClintock, *Imperial Leather;* and Amiri Baraka, "Paul Robeson and the Theater," in *Black Renaissance/Renaissance Noire* 2, no. 1 (Fall–Winter 1998): 26–27. On *Old Bones of the River,* see Marcia Landy, *British Film Genres: Cinema and Society, 1930–1960* (Princeton, N.J.: Princeton University Press, 1991), 102–4; Kenneth M. Cameron, *Africa on Film: Beyond Black and White* (New York: Continuum, 1994), 89–90; Cripps, *Slow Fade to Black,* 314–15, 320; Stephen Bourne, *Black in the British Frame: Black People in British Film and Television, 1896–1996* (London: Cassell, 1998), 46, 56–58, 85; James Baldwin, *The Devil Finds Work* (New York: Dial, 1976), 100. *Old Bones of the River* burlesqued not only *Sanders* but the missionary-imperialist premises of African exploitation as well. The opening title reads: "Darkest Africa" where "a handful of Englishmen" try "teaching the black man to play the white man."

27. See Ben Davis interview with PR, *Daily Worker,* May 10, 1936; *Pittsburgh Courier,* Aug. 13, 1949. See also Tom O'Connor interview with PR, *PM,* Sept. 22, 1942; Ross Parmeter interview with PR, *New York Times,* Apr. 19, 1942; and *Pittsburgh Courier,* Mar. 12, 1960, 2.

28. PR qtd. in *Afro,* Oct. 14, 1935; *Amsterdam News,* Oct. 5, 1935.

29. On the British public and films, see Leslie Halliwell, *Seats in All Parts: Half a Lifetime at the Movies* (New York: Charles Scribner's Sons, 1985); *Evening News* (London), Apr. 2, 1935; *Sunday Times* (London), Apr. 7, 1937; see also *The Picture Show,* Mar. 23, 1935; *Film World,* Apr. 13, 1935; Leslie Banks, "Britain Puts Their Empire on the Screen at Last," *Film Pictorial,* Apr. 6, 1935, 42–43.

30. Jeffrey Richards, *The Age of the Dream Palace: Cinema and Society in Britain, 1930–1939* (London: Routledge and Kegan Paul, 1985), 11; Graves and Hodge, *The Long Week-End,* 133–42; Halliwell, *Seats in All Parts,* 1–14, 23, 26–27, 33, 53; Andrews interview, Nov. 13–20, 1974.

31. *Amsterdam News,* Jan. 11 and Dec. 12, 1936; *Daily Herald,* Sept. 9, 1935; *Evening News* (London), Jan. 25, 1937; Karol Kulik, *Alexander Korda: The Man Who Made Miracles* (New Rochelle, N.Y., 1975), 136–37; the incident in Australia is reported in "Darwin, North Australia," unnamed paper, Feb. 12, 1937.

32. *Evening News* (London), Jan. 25, 1937; *Daily Herald,* Sept. 9, 1935; *Sunday Times* (London), Apr. 7, 1937; see also *The Picture Show,* Mar. 23, 1935; *Film World,* Apr. 13, 1935; Banks, "Britain Puts Their Empire on the Screen," 42–43; Richards, *Age of the Dream Palace,* 11.

33. Landy, *British Film Genres,* 97.

34. *Daily Telegraph,* Apr. 8, 1935; A. E. Wilson, *Star,* Apr. 8, 1935; M. Wilson Disher, *Daily Mail,* Apr. 8, 1935; *Daily Sketch,* Apr. 7, 1935. See also I.B., *Manchester Guardian,* Apr. 9, 1935; Ivor Brown, *Observer,* Apr. 14, 1935; *Evening Standard* (London), Apr. 8, 1935.

35. J.C., *Daily Sketch,* Apr. 8, 1935; also Ivor Brown, *Observer,* Apr. 14, 1935. According to the *Observer,* Apr. 7, 1935, the play was sold out as soon as it was announced Robeson would play the lead. See also S.W., *Evening Standard,* Apr. 8, 1935.

36. Alex Bloom interview with George Sklar, Jan. 3, 1975; interview with Leigh Whipper, Dec. 10 and 11, 1974.

37. Interview with Andre Van Gyseghem, Nov. 4, 1974.

38. Ibid.

39. William E. Kon interview with PR, "Paul Robeson Is Pro-Soviet," *Soviet Russia Today,* Nov. 1935, 4–5; Van Gyseghem interview, Nov. 4, 1974; telephone interview with Roland Adam, Nov. 4, 1974; See also Seton, *Paul Robeson,* 100.

40. *Era* (London), May 8,1935; *Daily Mail,* May 7, 1935.

41. *Stevedore,* act 3, sc. 2.

42. *Observer,* May 12, 1935; *Stevedore,* act 3, sc. 1.

43. James Agate, *Sunday Times,* May 12, 1935; *Daily Herald,* May 10, 1935. The 1935 Silver Jubilee was a huge royal extravaganza, complete with a state procession to St. Paul's Cathedral that included foreign dignitaries and representatives of all the ministers of the Crown.

44. *Jewish Chronicle* (London), May 10, 1935; *Evening News* (London), May 7, 1935.

45. *Jewish Chronicle,* May 10, 1935; *World Jewry,* May 10, 1935; *New English Weekly* 7, no. 5 (May 16, 1935): 93; "London Theatres," *Stage,* no. 2823 (May 9, 1935): 10; *Evening News* (London), May 7, 1935; *New English News,* May 16, 1935; J. T. Grien, *Daily Sketch,* May 22, 1935.

46. *Observer* (London), May 12, 1935.

47. Hannen Swaffer, "I Saw in America: A Night with the Negroes," *Daily Herald* (London), Aug. 18, 1934; *Daily Sketch,* May 22, 1935; *New Statesman and Nation,* May 18, 1935; *Daily Mail,* May 7, 1935; Leslie Rees, *Era,* May 8, 1935; *New English Weekly,* May 16, 1935. See also *Jewish Chronicle,* May 10, 1935; Bloom–Sklar interview, Jan. 3, 1975.

48. Tour flyer, Harold Holt Celebrity Series, June 23–Sept. 22, 1935. The original *Show Boat,* a silent film, cast Laura La Plante and Joseph Schildkraut as the stars with Stepin Fetchit in the part of Joe.

49. ER, undated ms., 4, Robeson Collections (PR Jr.).

50. ER to Mrs. Goode, Sept. 4, 1935, Robeson Collections (PR Jr.); PR interview with Marguerite Tazelaar, *New York Herald Tribune,* Oct. 27, 1935; Paul Robeson Jr. qtd. in *Paul Robe-*

son: Here I Stand (127-minute documentary), American Masters Production, a coproduction of Thirteen/WNET and Menair International (New York: Fox Lorber Associates, 1999).

51. Cable, Carl Laemmle Jr. to Universal Pictures Corp., Sept. 20, 1935; agreement between Universal Pictures Corporation and PR, Sept. 21, 1935; Robeson's contract with Universal stated that location work outside of California would require "the approval of Mr. Robeson who has no wish to go to the Southern states" (Robeson Collections [PR Jr.]).

52. Walter White to PR, Sept. 27, 1935, NAACP Papers, File Sept. 20–29, 1935, Box C-107.

53. PR qtd. in "I Breathe Freely," Julia Dorn interview with PR, *New Theatre,* July 1953.

54. White to Eugene Martin, NAACP Papers, File Oct. 15–Nov. 16, 1935, Box C-107.

55. White to PR, Sept. 27, 1935.

56. ER to White, Nov. 24, 1935, NAACP Papers, File Nov. 26–Dec. 12, 1935, Box C-107.

57. Program from Portland concert; *Portland News Telegram,* Nov. 12, 1935.

58. *Picturegoer Weekly,* Jan. 2, 1937; *Evening Chronicle,* June 18, 1936; *New York Evening Journal,* May 9, 1936.

59. *Show Boat,* mimeographed script, seq. B-15, p. B-10, and mimeographed script, seq. F-4, p. F-2.

60. Bernice Patton, on location for the *Pittsburgh Courier,* reported that Paul mingled easily and often with the production's 250 black extras and Hollywood moguls took note of his generally cooperative attitude, "his modest dignity and culture." Patton reported that Robeson so impressed producers that the paper sent scouts to colleges — the University of Southern California and the University of California — in search of other similarly talented (and well-behaved) blacks. "Robeson returning from Europe to star in pictures means thousands of colored people will [receive] bit parts that will bring to the celluloid many talented artists who have not yet been discovered" (*Pittsburgh Courier,* June 10, 1936).

61. Sidney S. Kalshy, *Hollywood Citizen News,* Jan. 7, 1936; *Referee* (London), Mar. 8, 1936; ER, undated ms., 4 (Robeson Collections [PR Jr.]).

62. *Cinema,* June 3, 1936; *New York Herald Tribune,* May 15, 1936.

63. Howard Barnes, *New York Herald Tribune,* May 15, 1936; *New York Daily Mirror* and *Hollywood Register,* Apr. 27, 1936. See also Frank S. Nugent, *New York Times,* May 16, 1936; *Los Angeles Times,* May 12, 1936.

64. *Sunday Pictorial,* June 14, 1936; *Manchester Guardian,* June 11, 1936.

65. *Saturday Review* (London), June 23, 1936.

66. *Tatler,* June 17, 1936.

67. *Daily Film Renter,* June 8, 1936.

68. PR, *Here I Stand* (1958; reprint, Boston: Beacon Press, 1971), 31.

15. AFRICAN JOURNEYS

1. Ronald Bergan, *Sergei Eisenstein: A Life in Conflict* (New York: Overlook Press, 1999), 260–75.

2. On socialist realism, see Sheila Fitzpatrick, *Everyday Stalinism: Ordinary Life in Extraordinary Times: Soviet Russia in the 1930s* (New York: Oxford University Press, 1999), 9; Bergan, *Eisenstein,* 247–48; James van Geldern and Richard Stite, eds. *Mass Culture in Soviet Russia* (Bloomington: Indiana University Press, 1995), xvii–xxi; Robert C. Tucker, *Stalin in Power: The Revolution from Above, 1928–1941* (New York: Norton, 1990), 554–60.

3. Stalin had a passion for films and a deep appreciation of their potential influence on the public. He had his own projection room where he previewed films before they reached the public. Tucker, *Stalin in Power,* 556; Bergan, *Eisenstein,* 247.

4. C. L. R. James, "Paul Robeson: Black Star (A Friend's Recollections)," *Black World* 20 (Nov. 1970): 107.

5. Interview with C. L. R. James, May 8, 1975; H.G., *Observer* (London), Oct. 20, 1935; James, "Robeson: Black Star," 107.

6. James interview, May 8, 1975; James, "Robeson: Black Star," 106–7.

7. George Lamming, *The Pleasures of Exile* (London: Allison and Busby, 1984), 47; C. L. R.

James, *Beyond a Boundary* (1963; reprint, New York: Pantheon, 1983), quoted in *The C. L. R. James Reader,* ed. Anna Grimshaw (Oxford: Blackwell, 1992), 2. On James, see Paul Buhle, *C. L. R. James: The Artist as Revolutionary* (New York: Verso, 1988); Kent Worcester, *C. L. R. James: A Political Biography* (Albany: State University of New York Press, 1966); *Special Delivery: The Letters of C. L. R. James to Constance Webb, 1939–1948,* ed. Anna Grimshaw (Oxford: Blackwell, 1966); C. L. R. James, *Spheres of Existence: Selected Writings* (London: Allison and Busby, 1980); Frederick Warburg [James's publisher], *An Occupation for Gentlemen* (London: Hutchinson, 1959), 214–15; Peter Fryer, *Staying Power: Black People in Britain since 1504* (Atlantic Highlands, N.J.: Humanities Press, 1984), 334–38.

8. On James and cricket, see James's semiautobiographical *Beyond a Boundary* (1963), a fusion of anecdote, report, analysis, and comment on the connections and relations between sports and politics. See also James interview, May 8, 1975, and Buhle, *C. L. R. James,* 15–16, 18–19.

9. James would later publish his findings in the scholarly 1938 publication, *The Black Jacobins: Toussaint L'Ouverture and the San Domingo Revolution* (London: Seeker and Warburg, 1938).

10. On reaction to Ethiopia in the United States, see Joseph E. Harris, *African-American Reactions to the War in Ethiopia 1936–1941* (Baton Rouge: Louisiana State University Press, 1994); Andrew Bunie, *Robert L. Vann of the "Pittsburgh Courier"* (Pittsburgh: University of Pittsburgh Press, 1974), 244–48; Roi Ottley, *"New World A-Coming": Inside Black America* (Boston: Houghton Mifflin, 1943), 106–12; and Mark Naison, *Communists in Harlem during the Depression* (Urbana: University of Illinois Press, 1983), 138–40, 155–58, 174–76.

11. James, "Robeson: Black Star," 106–15; James interview, May 8, 1975.

12. Ibid.

13. Ibid.

14. James interview, May 8, 1975.

15. *Times* (London), Mar. 17, 1936; *Daily Herald* (London), Mar. 17, 1936; *Evening News* (London), Mar. 17, 1936.

16. *Observer,* Mar. 22, 1936; James, "Robeson: Black Star," 106–15.

17. *Times,* Mar. 17, 1936.

18. Ibid.; G.W.B., *Sunday Times,* Mar. 22, 1936.

19. *Era* (London), Mar. 18, 1936.

20. W.A.D., *Daily Telegraph* (London), Mar. 17, 1936.

21. PR qtd. in *Film Weekly,* Sept. 19, 1936.

22. *Evening News* (Edinburgh), Feb. 13, 1936. Elisabeth Welch had a long career in England on stage and in clubs. On Welch, see Bruce Kellner, ed., *The Harlem Renaissance: An Historical Dictionary for the Era* (New York: Methuen, 1987), 381; Brian Rust, *Elisabeth Welch,* World Records Album, SH328, 1979; Peter Gammond, *The Oxford Companion to Popular Music* (New York: Oxford University Press, 1991), 602.

23. At the end of the scene where John Zinga tries to explain to his wife why he wants to go to Africa, Robeson and Welch kiss. This is probably one of the first times a black couple did this on film. *Song Of Freedom* (1937, USA), with Paul Robeson, Elisabeth Welch, Ecce Homo Toto, and George Mozart. Reel Images, Box 137-M, Monroe, Conn., no. 559; Stephen Burne, *Black in the British Frame* (London: Cassell, 1998), 24.

24. *Song of Freedom.*

25. Eslanda Robeson, *African Journey* (New York: John Day, 1945). References that follow related to ER's trip to Africa are all taken from *African Journal* unless otherwise stated. The material presented in *African Journey* represents Essie's fieldwork for her doctoral dissertation, which she never completed. See also Robert Shaffer, "Out of the Shadows: The Political Writings of Eslanda Goode Robeson," paper presented at conference commemorating the centennial birth of Paul Robeson, Long Island University, Brooklyn, New York, Feb. 1998.

26. *Evening Standard* (London), Feb. 19, 1936; see also *Daily Herald,* Feb. 11, 1936.

27. *Pittsburgh Courier,* Jan. 2, 1937; PR interview with Elliseve Sayers, *Answers,* Apr. 4, 1939.

28. ER and PR to PR Jr., Sept. 14, 1935 (Essie wrote the letter; Paul signed it), Robeson Collections (PR Jr.).

29. ER to Mrs. Goode, Feb. 14 and July 23, 1935, Robeson Collections (PR Jr.).

30. ER, *African Journey,* 19.

31. Ibid., 18.

32. For information of Yergan's years in South Africa we are particularly indebted to David H. Anthony's article, "Max Yergan and South Africa: A Transatlantic Interaction" in *Imagining Home: Class, Culture, and Nationalism in the African Diaspora,* ed. Sidney J. Lemelle and Robin D. G. Kelley (New York: Verso, 1994), 185–206.

33. ER, *African Journey,* 77, 50–51.

34. Ibid., 136–37; interview with Marie Seton, Nov. 11, 1974.

35. Seton interview, Nov. 11, 1974, and interview with Joe Andrews, Nov. 13–20, 1974.

36. Elisabeth Welch was clothed in plain gingham dresses rather than the sarong worn by McKinney; she was wholesome rather than sophisticated, a "natural" wife and mother.

37. *Daily Express* (London), Sept. 15, 1936. According to *Film Renter* (Aug. 17, 1936), editors "worked in close cooperation with . . . Robeson . . . to ensure that the story and Robeson's personality should be kept to the fore."

38. *Daily Express,* Sept. 15, 1936.

39. *Film Weekly,* May 23, 1936, 17.

40. The trade show program was a publicity device promoting British-Lion. Other films presented included *Hearts in Bondage, The Happy Emily, Federal Agent,* and *The Lawless Nineties; Cinema,* Aug. 5, 1936.

41. *New Statesman and Nation,* Sept. 26, 1936. Other Robeson songs included "Song of Freedom," "Sleepy River," and "Stepping Stones."

42. Guy Morgan, *Daily Express,* Sept. 15, 1936; G.G.W., unnamed paper, Sept. 10, 1936; *Observer,* Sept. 20, 1936.

43. George Campbell, "What Paul Robeson Could Do," *Bystander,* Sept. 30, 1936.

44. Louis Lautier, *Pittsburgh Courier,* May 20, 1937; Dan Burley, *Amsterdam News,* July 16, 1938.

45. Prologue to *My Song Goes Forth;* Joseph Best to PR, Feb. 18, 1944, and revisions to Best ms., Robeson Collections (PR Jr.).

46. "My Song Goes Forth," U.K., 1935, Coronel Pictures Ltd. Produced by Gilbert Church, written by Joseph Best. 35 mm, 40 min. Available at the Library of Congress.

47. Ibid.

48. Ibid. The *Daily Worker* (Apr. 12, 1937) berated the film as bereft of a "really militant spirit" and unwilling to examine the machinery underlying the South African system.

49. Best to PR, Feb. 18, 1944, Robeson Collections (PR Jr.).

50. PR refers to this brief trip in his Notes for 1938, Robeson Collections (PR Jr.) and in "Why I Left My Son in Moscow," *Russia Today,* Feb. 1938; see also Contract between Paul Robeson and the State Philharmony, signed Aug. 13, 1936, Robeson Collections (PR Jr.). The contract contained several stringent restrictions, among them that all money earned must be spent inside the Soviet Union.

51. Michael Balcon (the "man with $1,000,000 a year to spend") had already done a host of Empire films including *Rhodes of Africa* and *Forever England* (the only British film done with official naval cooperation), and was working on *The Great Barrier* (the story of the building of the Canadian Pacific Railway) and *Soldiers Three* — a film version of the Rudyard Kipling story; its filming enjoyed the full cooperation of the British army (*Morning Post* [London], Dec. 10, 1936).

52. *Morning Post,* Dec. 10, 1936.

53. Ibid.

54. *Magazine Program,* Dec. 19, 1936.

55. *News of the World,* Nov. 28, 1936.

56. *Cumberland Echo,* Dec. 27, 1936.

57. Ibid.; *Picturegoer,* Nov. 11, 1936; *Evening Standard,* Apr. 30, 1936.

58. *King Solomon's Mines* came off the press in 1885, only six months after European powers met in Berlin to set the rules for dividing up Africa. The book was an instant success: in its first year alone it sold 31,000 copies in Britain and went through thirteen U.S. editions. The novel was filmed five times and was also standard reading in schools in Britain and English-speaking Africa.

See William Minter, *King Solomon's Mines Revisited: Western Interest and the Burdened History of Southern Africa* (New York: Basic Books, 1986), 3–4; Kenneth M. Cameron, *Africa on Film: Beyond Black and White* (New York: Continuum, 1994), 17–30. On *King Solomon's Mines* and racial and exotic wish fulfillment, see Anne McClintock, *Imperial Leather: Race, Gender and Sexuality in the Colonial Conquest* (New York: Routledge, 1995), 1–17.

59. The term "white hunter," although not coined by Haggard became permanently identified with the character Allan Quatermain. In fact, the term dates from a safari company's 1908 brochure, used to assure white clients that a *white* professional would guide them in the field and run the safari. See Cameron, *Africa on Film*, 23.

60. *New York Times Film Review*, Aug. 13, 1937.

61. *Sunday Chronicle*, July 25, 1937; *Daily Herald*, July 23, 1937; *New York Times Film Review*, Aug. 13, 1937.

62. *Film Pictorial*, Nov. 28, 1936. Songs were "The Song of the Mountains," "Kukuanna Song," and "Trek Song."

63. Basil Wright, *Spectator*, July 30, 1937, 203; *Sunday Dispatch*, July 27, 1937.

64. Interviews with Charles Blockson (Feb. 12, 1986, Aug. 30, 1991) and Paul Robeson Jr. (Dec. 1982, Feb. 1996).

65. *Picturegoer*, Oct. 31, 1936.

66. ER, *African Journey*, 72, 56–57.

67. *Film Pictorial*, undated, Robeson Collections (PR Jr.).

68. *Daily Express* (Glasgow), Dec. 3, 1936.

69. Robeson sang "Lazin'," "Roll Up Sailorman," and "You Didn't Orta Do Such Things."

70. *Kinematograph*, June 10, 1937.

71. Fenn Sherie to James Elder Wills, Oct. 14, 1936, Robeson Collections (PR Jr.).

72. *Kinematograph*, June 10, 1937.

16. RUSSIAN ROMANCE

1. See PR, "Bonds of Brotherhood," *Jewish Life*, Nov. 1954. The article originally appeared in the tercentenary anniversary edition of *Jewish Life*, and is reprinted in *Paul Robeson Speaks: Writings, Speeches, Interviews, 1918–1974*, ed. Philip S. Foner (Secaucus, N.J.: Citadel, 1978), 390–93; interview with Miki Fisher, Sept. 20, 1978; PR, "Here's My Story," *Freedom*, May 1952; see also Paul Robeson Jr., "Paul Robeson's Legacy," *Common Quest* 2, no.1 (Summer 1997): 4.

2. For Miskend, see chap. 3. On blacks in the Yiddish and Jewish press, see Hasia Diner, *In the Almost Promised Land: American Jews and Blacks, 1915–1935* (1977; reprint, Baltimore: Johns Hopkins University Press, 1995), 35–66; idem, "Drawn Together by Self Interest: Jewish Representation of Race Relations in the Early Twentieth Century," in *African Americans and Jews in the Twentieth Century*, ed. V. P. Franklin (Columbia: University of Missouri Press, 1998), 27–39; *Jewish Transcript*, Nov. 22, 1935; *Jewish Life*, Nov. 1954. Interviews with Marie Seton (Nov. 11, 1974); Miki Fisher (Sept. 20, 1978); John Rockmore (Mar. 6, 1998); and Clara Rockmore (Sept. 15, 1980); Paul Robeson Jr., "Paul Robeson's Legacy," 4.

3. PR interviewed by Sulamith Ish-Kishor, *Jewish Tribune*, July 22, 1927.

4. PR qtd. in interview with Marguerite Tazelaar, *New York Herald Tribune*, Oct. 27, 1953; Marie Seton, *Paul Robeson* (London: Dennis Dobson, 1958), 61–64, 66–69; Seton interview, Nov. 11, 1974.

5. Interview with Hans Ernst Meier, Dec. 12, 1982. Meier's autobiography, *Kontraste-Konflike* (1979), is based on interviews with members of the Akademie der Kunste staff. In 1936 Robeson also became a patron of Great Britain's "Free German League of Culture," whose members included Sybil Thorndike, E. M. Forster, J. B. Priestly, Ralph Vaughn Williams, and Alan Bush.

6. PR interview with Nathan Krems, *Jewish Transcript*, Nov. 22, 1935; Richard Bak, *Joe Louis: The Great Black Hope* (New York: Da Capo Press, 1998), 114–24; Chris Mead, *Champion: Joe Louis, Black Hero in White America* (New York: Scribner's, 1985). Robeson, like blacks throughout the world, was ecstatic when on June 22, 1938, before a crowd of over 70,000 in a rematch at Yankee Stadium, "billed everywhere as a struggle between American democracy and Nazi fascism," Louis pummeled Schmeling in the first round.

7. Eighteen black athletes represented the United States in the 1936 Olympics. Jesse Owens, Eulace Peacock, and Ralph Metcalfe said they were participating because their victories would serve to repudiate Nazi racial theories. See *Chicago Defender*, Dec. 14, 1935.

8. Interview with Joe Andrews, Nov. 13–20, 1974; alternate games — "the People's Olympics" — scheduled to take place from June 19 to June 26 in Barcelona were canceled at the last minute because on June 19, reactionary forces, led by General Francisco Franco, plunged Spain into Civil War.

9. William J. Baker, *Jesse Owens: An American Life* (New York: Free Press–Macmillan, 1986), 123.

10. ER to Carl Van Vechten, Apr. 27, 1936, Yale University; Sidney Webb and Beatrice Webb, *Soviet Communism: A New Civilisation?* (London, 1936); PR, "Why I Left My Son in Moscow," *Russia Today*, Feb. 1938.

11. PR, "National Cultures in the Soviet Union," *Left Review* 3, no. 10 (Nov. 1938): 579.

12. PR, "Why I Left My Son in Moscow"; *Amsterdam News*, Dec. 26, 1936.

13. PR, Notes, 1938; ER Diary, Jan. 1935; ER to Mrs. Goode, Feb. 6 and 14, Aug. 23, 1935, Robeson Collections (PR Jr.).

14. PR interview with Derek Tangye, *Daily Mirror* (London) Apr. 11, 1938; for other versions of the story see *Black Dispatch*, Oct. 29, 1937, and *Reynold's Newspaper* (London), Oct. 10, 1937. Close friends include Marie Seton, Joe Andrews, and Revels Cayton.

15. Peggy Dennis, *The Autobiography of an American Communist, 1925–1975* (Westport, Conn.: Lawrence Hill, Creative Books, 1977), 120.

16. *Moscow Daily News*, Jan. 9, May 1, June 3, 1936.

17. Ibid., Jan. 9, 1936.

18. ER to Carl Van Vechten, postcard, Feb. 9, 1937, Yale University.

19. Chatwood Hall, *Black Dispatch*, Feb. 18, 1937; Sergei Eisenstein review of Robeson's Moscow concert, *Workers' Moscow (Rabochaya Moskva)*, Dec. 20, 1936.

20. Hall, *Black Dispatch*, Feb. 18, 1937.

21. PR qtd. in ibid.

22. A. Constant Smith, *Moscow Daily News*, Dec. 30, 1936; see also Sender Garlin, *Daily Worker*, Dec. 17, 1936.

23. William Patterson, "Revolutionäre Negerlieder anlässlich der Paul Robeson Konzerte," *Deutsche Zentral Zeitung*, Dec. 22, 1936.

24. Eisenstein, *Workers' Moscow*, Dec. 20, 1936.

25. PR, "Why I Left My Son in Moscow."

26. *Pravda, Izvestya*, and the *Moscow Daily News* had given the new constitution extensive coverage and covered in detail the discussions that took place among the Russian population before the constitution was approved. In all, 527,000 meetings were held with 36.5 million Russians attending.

27. Sidney Webb qtd. in *Moscow Daily News*, Oct. 7, 1936; PR qtd. in *Sunday Worker*, Feb. 7, 1937. See also PR, "National Culture and the Soviet Union."

28. Interview with George Padmore, May 20, 1975. See also George Padmore, *Pan-Africanism or Communism* (New York: Anchor Books, Doubleday, 1971); idem, *Africa: Britain's Third Empire* (London: Dennis Dobson, 1949).

29. Interview with Lord Fenner Brockway, Nov. 19, 1974.

30. Interview with C. L. R. James, May 8, 1975.

31. *Sunday Worker*, Feb. 7, 1937; abridged version in *Negro Worker*, March 1937, 12–13. The *Crisis* editorial urged "Colored people who are poor, landless and disfranchised" to "cut through all the headlines about Spain and remember . . . the war is between the Spanish people, poor, landless and disenfranchised, and the army which is controlled by those who want to keep the Spanish people poor, landless and disenfranchised" (*Crisis*, Nov. 1936, 337).

32. There is a wealth of material on the show trials and Stalin's purges. The following were particularly helpful: Robert Conquest, *The Great Terror: A Reassessment* (New York: Oxford University Press, 1990); Robert C. Tucker, *Stalin in Power: The Revolution from Above, 1928–1941* (New York: Norton, 1990); Dmitri Volkogonov, *Stalin: Triumph and Tragedy* (London: Weiden-

feld and Nicolson, 1991); and Sheila Fitzpatrick, *Everyday Stalinism: Ordinary Life in Extraordinary Times: Soviet Russia in the 1930s* (Oxford: Oxford University Press, 1999); Joseph E. Davies, *Mission to Moscow* (London, 1942), 38–39; David Caute, *The Fellow Travellers,* rev. ed. (New Haven: Yale University Press, 1988), 123–29.

33. Conquest, *The Great Terror,* 91.

34. "Letter of an Old Bolshevik," in Boris I. Nicolaevsky, *Power and the Soviet Elite* (New York, 1965), 416.

35. D. N. Pritt, *From Right to Left* (London, 1966), 106–11, and Walter Duranty, *The Kremlin and the People* (London, 1942), 37; both qtd. in Conquest, *The Great Terror,* 467, 37.

36. PR interviewed by Ben Davis Jr., *Sunday Worker,* May 10, 1936.

37. Interview with Revels Cayton, Jan. 16, 1981.

38. Fitzpatrick, *Everyday Stalinism,* 67–75.

39. Langston Hughes, *New Masses* 14, no. 7 (Feb. 12, 1935): 18–20; idem, *I Wonder as I Wander* (New York: Hill and Wang, 1956), 212.

40. Interview with Fred Schang, Oct. 25, 1978.

41. *Film Pictorial,* May 10, 1937.

42. R. W. Merguson interview with PR in Cairo for the *Pittsburgh Courier,* May 1, 1937; *California Eagle,* May 21, 1937.

43. PR qtd. in *Film Pictorial,* May 10, 1937; Jan Nederveen Pieterse, *White on Black: Images of Africa in Popular Western Culture* (New Haven: Yale University Press, 1992), 110.

44. *Northampton Telegraph,* Jan. 1, 1937. See also *Era* (London), Sept. 23, 1936; *Daily News Chronicle* (London), Jan. 5, 1937; *Daily Sketch* (London), Nov. 23, 1936.

45. Producer Walter Futter qtd. in *Golden Green Gazette,* Jan. 8, 1937. See also Rudolph Dunbar, reporting for the *Amsterdam News,* Jan. 9, 1937.

46. *Golden Green Gazette,* Jan. 8, 1937; on Princess Kouka, see also *Evening Standard* (London), Dec. 12, 1936; *Morning Post* (London), Nov. 23, 1936; and *Evening News* (London), Dec. 22, 1936.

47. Andrews interview, Nov. 13–20, 1974; *Le Journal d'Egypte,* Feb. 4, 1937; *La Bourse Egyptienne Mercredi,* Feb. 3, 1937; and *Egyptian Gazette,* Feb. 6, 1937.

48. R. W. Merguson for the *Pittsburgh Courier,* May 1, 1937; Andrew Bunie, *Robert L. Vann of the Pittsburgh Courier* (Pittsburgh: University of Pittsburgh Press, 1974), 248; Fay Jackson for the Associated Negro Press (ANP), *California Eagle,* May 21, 1937.

49. *The Odyssey of Paul Robeson,* Omega Classics, 1992, OCD 3007, liner notes by Paul Robeson Jr.

50. *Times* (London), Nov. 1, 1937. For other reviews, see *Daily News* (London), Aug. 17, 1938; *New York Journal,* Aug. 17, 1938; *New York Herald Tribune,* Aug. 17, 1938.

51. Ralph Matthews, *Baltimore Afro-American,* Aug. 20, 1938.

52. For Robeson's itinerary, see Chatwood Hall for the ANP, *California Eagle,* Oct. 7, 1937.

53. Chatwood Hall, ANP, *Black Dispatch,* Oct. 29, 1937; see also *New York Herald Tribune,* Jan. 10, 1937, and *Amsterdam News,* Dec. 26, 1936.

54. Hall, *Black Dispatch,* Oct. 29, 1937; PR Jr. qtd. in *Daily Worker,* Apr. 26, 1938, p. 7, cols. 2–5.

55. Hall, *Black Dispatch,* Oct. 29, 1937; *Daily Worker* (London), June 28, 1937, and Jan. 24, 1938.

56. See James K. Hopkins, *Into the Heart of the Fire: The British in the Spanish Civil War* (Stanford: Stanford University Press, 1998), 20–44. For histories of the CPGB, see Henry Pelling, *The British Communist Party: A Historical Profile* (London: A. and C. Black, 1958), and *A Short History of the Labour Party* (London: Macmillan, 1961); James Jupp, *The Radical Left in Britain, 1931–1941* (London: Frank Cass, 1982); Keith Layhourn and Dylan Murphy , *Under the Red Flag: A History of Communism in Britain, 1849–1991* (London: Sutton, 1999); Hugo Dewar, *Communist Politics in Britain* (London: Pluto Press, 1976); Ben Pimlott, *Labour and the Left in the 1930s* (Cambridge: Cambridge University Press, 1977); Nina Fishman, *The British Communist Party and the Trade Unions, 1933–1945* (London: Ashgate Publishing, 1995); Jon Clark, Margot Heine-

mann, David Margolies, and Carole Snee, eds., *Culture and Crisis in Great Britain in the Thirties* (London: Lawrence and Wishart, 1979).

57. Hopkins, *Into the Heart of the Fire*, 20–44 ("exciting" and "spree" on 21); Robert Graves and Alan Hodge, *The Long Week-End: A Social History of Great Britain, 1918–1939,* 2nd ed. (New York: Norton, 1963), 259. The British historian Noel Annan, himself a teenager during the thirties, remembered asking his father what could be done to find work for the unemployed. "Nothing," his father answered. Annan was unwilling to accept this: "Like my contemporaries, Conservative and Labour alike, [I] believed that the state could engineer employment. How else could it be done? And thus came the swing to collectivism from which hardly any of us dissented" (Annan, *Our Age: English Intellectuals between the Wars: A Group Portrait* [New York: Random House, 1990], 173).

58. Paul Robeson Jr. and Martha Edwards qtd. in *Paul Robeson: Here I Stand* (127-minute documentary), American Masters Production, a co-production of Thirteen/WNET and Menair International (New York: Fox Lorber Associates, Inc., 1999).

59. PR, "National Cultures and the Soviet Union."

60. Henry Felix Srebrnik, *London Jews and British Communism, 1935–1945* (Ilford, Eng.: Vallentine Mitchell, 1995), 53–102; Hopkins, *Into the Heart of the Fire*, 143–46.

61. See *Daily Worker* (London), June 12, 1937, for a listing of the many small fund-raisers occurring throughout Britain.

62. Founded in 1936, the Left Book Club was designed specifically to facilitate sales of anti-Fascist and socialist publications. With a monthly selection chosen by a committee of three (Victor Gollancz, Harold Laski, and John Strachey), subscribers were offered books at significantly lower than retail prices. The club proved a phenomenal success, astounding even its most ardent supporters and testifying to the reading public's heightened interest in understanding world events from a leftist perspective. By the end of 1937 monthly sales had soared to a peak of 50,000, and local clubs devoted to discussing the books and related issues had sprung up all over Britain. See Stuart Samuels, "The Left Book Club," *Journal of Contemporary History* 1, no. 2 (1966): 65–86.

63. Interview with Herbert Marshall, Sept. 20–22, 1974.

64. Of the events publicized as drawing cards, the two most widely touted were the auctioning of a Guernica sketch donated by Picasso and the broadcast from Moscow by Paul Robeson.

65. *Daily Herald,* June 19, 1937; *Manchester Guardian,* June 22, 1937.

66. *Manchester Guardian,* June 22, 1937.

67. *Daily News Chronicle,* June 24, 1937; *Daily Mirror,* June 25, 1937. Robeson said the Soviets could not have been more cooperative and helpful. "In Moscow I was given every possible help to make my broadcast at the exact time when the organisers of the meeting wanted it" (*Daily Worker* [London], June 25, 1937).

68. *Daily Mirror,* June 25, 1937; *Nottingham Journal,* June 25, 1937.

69. PR qtd. in *Daily Mirror* and *Daily Worker,* June 25, 1937. For accounts of jamming, see *Manchester Guardian,* June 25, 1937; *Daily Worker,* June 25, 1937; and *Daily News Chronicle,* June 19, 1937.

70. *Daily Worker,* June 26, 1937.

71. Ibid., Nov. 4, 1937; also *Washington Tribune,* Dec. 4, 1937. Three-page typed ms. of speech given June 24, 1937, in Robeson Collections (PR Jr.).

72. *Daily News Chronicle,* June 25, 1937; Andrews interview, Nov. 13–20, 1974.

17. THE WORLD SCENE

1. *Liverpool Express,* Nov. 24, 1932.

2. Hannen Swaffer, *Daily Herald* (London), Dec. 20, 1937. Republican forces began the campaign to capture the small city of Teruel on Dec. 17, 1937, during the worst winter Spain had experienced in years. The city was in Republican hands by the new year. The Nationalists mounted a counter offensive, however, and by February had won the city back.

3. In 1939 the Labour Party expelled Stafford Cripps for repeatedly appearing on the same

platform as Communists. Bevan and Strauss were allowed to remain but only on the condition that they agreed not to appear publicly with Communist Party members. See Jonathan Schneer, *Labour's Conscience: The Labour Left, 1945–1951* (Boston: Unwin Hyman, 1988), 8–9, and James Jupp, *The Radical Left in Britain, 1931–1941* (London: Frank Cass, 1982), 44–84 passim.

4. On volunteers and the Spanish Civil War, see Jim Fyrth, *The Signal Was Spain: The Spanish Aid Movement in Britain 1936–1939* (New York: St. Martin's Press, 1986); Tom Buchanan, *The Spanish Civil War and the British Labour Movement* (Cambridge: Cambridge University Press, 1991) and *Britain and the Spanish War* (Cambridge: Cambridge University Press, 1997); Bill Alexander, *British Volunteers for Liberty, 1936–1939* (London: Lawrence and Wishart, 1982); James Yates, *Mississippi to Madrid: Memoir of a Black American in the Abraham Lincoln Brigade* (Seattle: Open Hand, 1989); Danny Duncan Callum, ed., *African Americans in the Spanish Civil War: This Ain't Ethiopia, But It'll Do* (a project of the Abraham Lincoln Brigade Archives, Waltham, Mass.) (New York: Macmillan, 1992); and James K. Hopkins, *Into the Heart of the Fire: The British in the Spanish Civil War* (Stanford: Stanford University Press, 1998). On Jews in the International Brigades, see Albert Prago, "Jews in the International Brigades" in *Our Fight,* ed. Alvah Bessie and Albert Prago (New York: Monthly Review Press, 1987), 94–103; Henry Srebrnik, "Jewish Community Activism in London on Behalf of the Spanish Republic," *Michigan Academician* (Spring 1994): 371–81, and *London Jews and British Communism, 1935–1945* (Ilford, Eng.: Vallentine Mitchell, 1995).

5. Atlee quoted in *Daily News Chronicle* (London), Dec. 20, 1937; Wilkinson qtd. by Hannen Swaffer, *Daily Herald* (London), Dec. 20, 1937.

6. *Daily Mail* (London), Dec. 20, 1937.

7. ER to William Patterson, March 1938, and ER Diary 1938, Robeson Collections (PR Jr.).

8. ER Diary, Jan. 21, 1938, Robeson Collections (PR Jr.). Sections of the diary are excerpted in "Journey into Spain," in *The Heart of Spain,* ed. Alvah Bessie (New York: Veterans of the Abraham Lincoln Brigade, 1952), 245–48.

9. ER Diary, Jan. 20, 1938, Robeson Collections (PR Jr.). It was not easy, even for Americans, to get permission to go to Spain in 1937. In most cases, the Paris office of the American embassy would simply stamp "Not Valid for Travel in Spain" across U.S. passports.

The U.S. State Department's file on Robeson for January 1938 reports his arrival in Barcelona and quotes the following statement made in a Madrid interview: "Spain is for me one more fatherland since its people do not wish to perceive differences of classes or of color. I have sung in London to raise funds for Spain" (Walter C. Thurston, U.S. Embassy, Barcelona, to U.S. Secretary of State, Jan. 28, 1938, National Archives, State Decimal File, 1930–1939, 852.00/7363). The Public Records Office in London had also had a file on Robeson but it has been thrown out with all documents dealing with passport matters that were deemed unimportant and were subject to a thirty-year holding period (Martin Daly to Bunie, Jan. 22, 1975).

10. *Daily Express* (London), Jan. 22, 1938.

11. Charlotte Haldane was first plunged into the fray in 1936 when Ronald Haldane, her son by a previous marriage, volunteered to fight in Spain. Haldane joined the Communist Party in 1937 (although she was asked to keep her membership a secret because it was believed she could do more effective work "from outside"), became honorary secretary of the Dependents Aid Committee, and served as Comintern organizer and receptionist of recruits in Paris. Her husband, scientist J. B. S. Haldane, also worked for the Party as a "crypto-Communist" and openly identified himself as a member in 1942. He visited Spain in the winter of 1936–37 to advise the Spanish government on the question of gas defense, toured the front in the spring of 1937, and visited again in the winter of 1937–38 (Neal Wood, *Communism and the British Intellectuals* [New York: Columbia University Press, 1959], 54–56). See also Charlotte Haldane, *The Truth Will Out* (New York: Vanguard, 1950), 266; Henry Pelling, *The British Communist Party: A Historical Profile* (London: A. and C. Black, 1958), 92; interview with Herbert Marshall, Sept. 20–21, 1974. On the *Daily Worker* and its influence, see Jupp, *The Radical Left in Britain,* 128. The principal London agent for the Communist Party was R. W. Robson, formerly the London district organizer. On Minor and Browder, see Peter N. Carroll, *The Odyssey of the American Lincoln Brigade* (Stanford:

Stanford University Press, 1994), 135–36, and Fraser M. Ottanelli, *The Communist Party of the United States* (New Brunswick, N.J.: Rutgers University Press, 1991), 14–15.

12. Interviews with Herbert Marshall (Sept. 20–21, 1974), Revels Cayton (July 16, 1980), Doxie Wilkerson (Mar. 9, 1977), and Joe Andrews (Nov. 13–20, 1974).

13. ER Diary, Jan. 23, 1938, Robeson Collections (PR Jr.).

14. Haldane, *Truth Will Out*, 128.

15. ER Diary, Jan. 25, 1938, Robeson Collections (PR Jr.).

16. Charlotte Haldane, *Daily Worker* (London), Feb. 15 and 16, 1938; Peter Wyden, *The Passionate War: The Narrative History of the Spanish Civil War, 1936–1939* (New York: Simon and Schuster, 1983), 433–34.

17. Haldane, *Truth Will Out*, 128.

18. ER Diary, Jan. 26, 1938, Robeson Collections (PR Jr.).

19. Haldane, *Truth Will Out*, 128.

20. ER Diary, Jan. 1938, Robeson Collections (PR Jr.); Haldane, *Truth Will Out*, 128.

21. Charlotte Haldane in the *Daily Worker* (London), Feb. 16, 1938.

22. Collum, *African Americans in the Spanish Civil War*, 18–19; *Daily Worker* (London), Mar. 2, 6, 22, and 27, 1937, and Nov. 12, 17, and 24, 1938.

23. Langston Hughes, *I Wonder as I Wander* (New York: Hill and Wang, 1956), 354. Hughes wrote extensively of Milton Herndon, the younger brother of Angelo Herndon who in 1932 had been charged with insurrection when he tried to fight for black rights in Atlanta. Angelo Herndon was defended by the Communist Ben Davis; Milton Herndon was killed in Spain.

24. ER Diary, Jan. 1938, Robeson Collections (PR Jr.); Morgan qtd. in Collum, *African Americans in the Spanish Civil War*, 32. Collum, however, makes the point that because Spaniards treated American blacks well did not mean that they were free of racial prejudice. The respect conferred on American blacks was due largely to their status as volunteers. Spanish Loyalists had utter contempt for the Moroccans fighting on Franco's side. This contempt had roots that stretched back a millennium to the age of "Moorish domination."

25. ER Diary, Jan. 1938, Robeson Collections (PR Jr.); see also *Pittsburgh Courier* (Louise Thompson), Oct. 9, 1937. Law served in the U.S. Army for six years but never advanced beyond the rank of private. See Arthur H. Landis, *The Abraham Lincoln Brigade* (New York: Citadel, 1967), 205–7; Steve Nelson, James Barrett, and Rob Ruck, *Steve Nelson: American Radical* (Pittsburgh: University of Pittsburgh Press, 1981), 216–18.

26. *Sunday Times* (Johannesburg), Mar. 3, 1938.

27. The *Daily Worker* (London) reports one broadcast in Madrid (Jan. 29, 1938); Essie records three over the course of two days — one on Jan. 26 at 10:00 p.m. from Madrid Central Station, a second on Jan. 27 for the "English Hour" at 9:40 p.m., and a third at 12:30 p.m. for the "American Hour" (ER Diary, Jan. 27–28, 1938, Robeson Collections [PR Jr.]).

28. Hughes, *I Wonder as I Wander*, 336.

29. PR qtd. in *Daily Worker*, Jan. 29, 1938.

30. Nancy Cunard for American Negro Press (ANP), *Black Dispatch*, Jan. 27, 1938; also PR interview with Cuban poet Nicolas Guillen. The Guillen interview was first published in the Cuban journal *Mediodia* and was later reprinted in translation by Katheryn Silver in *World Magazine*, July 24, 1976.

31. Andrews interview, Nov. 13–20, 1974.

32. Unnamed Paris paper, Feb. 1938.

33. PR qtd. in *Scotsman*, Feb. 4, 1938; *Daily News Chronicle*, Feb. 4, 1938.

34. *Bristol Evening Post*, Sept. 26, 1938; *Daily News Chronicle*, Dec. 23, 1938.

35. *Cambridge Daily News*, Dec. 1, 1938.

36. Larry Brown qtd. in Marie Seton, *Paul Robeson* (London: Dennis Dobson, 1958), 115.

37. *Daily Express*, Nov. 27, 1937; see also June 9, 1938.

38. PR qtd. in *Worthing Herald*, Sept. 23, 1938, and in M. H. Halton, "Negroes Free When All Men Emancipated," unnamed paper, June 1938. On labor unrest in Jamaica, see Richard Hart, "Labor Rebellions in the 1930s," in *Caribbean Freedom: Economy and Society from Emancipation to*

the Present, ed. Hilary Beckles and Verene Shepherd (Kingston, Jam.: Ian Randle Publishers, 1993), 370–76. Throughout the mid-thirties the British colonies of Guyana, St. Kitts, St. Vincent, Trinidad, Barbados, British Guiana, and Jamaica saw strikes among laborers on sugar, cocoa, coconut, and banana plantations who resented being treated as coolie laborers with cuts in wages and increased unemployment commonplace. In Jamaica, the largest of the islands, dissatisfaction erupted in violence among union dock workers and trash and street cleaners in May and June 1938.

39. *Evening News* (London), Apr. 4, 1938; see also Edwin Evans, *Daily Mail,* Apr. 4, 1938.

40. PR qtd. in Halton, "Negroes Free."

41. PR qtd. in *Reynold's Newspaper,* Oct. 10, 1937.

42. PR qtd. in Halton, "Negroes Free."

43. PR interview with Danvers Williams, unnamed newspaper.

44. *Daily Sketch* (London), Nov. 1, 1938.

45. Interview with Elliseva Sayers in *Answers* (London), Apr. 8, 1939; *Daily Sketch,* Nov. 1, 1938.

46. See Raphael Samuel, Ewan McCall, and Stuart Consgrove, *Theatre of the Left, 1880–1935: Workers' Theatre Movements in Britain and America* (London: Routledge and Kegan Paul, 1985), and Colin Chambers, *The Story of Unity Theatre* (New York: St. Martin's Press, 1989).

47. On the influence of German left-wing theater groups, see L. Hoffman-Ostwald, *Theatre as Weapon: Deutsches Arbei Theatre, 1918–1933* (Berlin: Henschelverlag, 1972).

48. Andre Van Gyseghem, "British Theatre in the Thirties: An Autobiographical Record," and Jon Clark, "Agitprop and Unity Theatre: Socialist Theatre in the Thirties," in *Culture and Crisis in Britain in the Thirties,* ed. Jon Clark, Margot Heinemann, David Margolies, and Carole Snee (London: Lawrence and Wishart, 1979), 209–40.

49. See Chambers, *Unity Theatre;* Pelling, *British Communist Party,* 81–82.

50. Although Unity secretary F. Roberts in 1938 vehemently denied that Unity was an organ for *any* political party, Herbert Marshall and Bram Bootman both said that Party members dominated Unity's ranks (Bram Bootman, unnamed paper, Aug. 19, 1938). Certainly, Unity received the wholehearted support of Communist groups and organizations. The *Daily Worker* gave the group's activities detailed coverage and James W. Ford, in a speech delivered on May 29, 1938, at the Tenth Annual Convention of the CPUSA praised Unity in general and Robeson in particular for his role in *Plant in the Sun* as well as for his contributions as an artist (James W. Ford, "Forging the Negro People's Sector of the Democratic Front," *Political Affairs* 17 [July 1938]: 615–23). See Chambers, *Unity Theatre;* interviews with Herbert Marshall (Sept. 20–21, 1974) and Bram Bootman (Nov. 10, 1974). On the Communist Party and artists in Britain, see Andy Croft, "Authors Take Sides: Writers and the Communist Party, 1920–56," in *Opening the Books: Essays on the Social and Cultural History of British Communism,* ed. Geoff Andrews, Nina Fishman, and Kevin Morgan (Boulder, Colo.: Pluto, 1995), 83–101.

51. The period's successes were light romantic comedies (Dodie Smith's *Autumn Crocus*), society comedies (Noel Coward's *Private Lives*), historical plays (*The Barretts of Wimpole Street*), and musicals (Coward's spectacular *Cavalcade*). See also "The Wandering Scot," *Edinburgh Evening News,* Aug. 27, 1938.

52. Herbert Marshall, from "Artistic Perspectives of the Unity Theatre Society of Great Britain," typed ms., 8.

53. Interview with Peter Noble, Oct. 30, 1974.

54. *Hampstead Express,* Oct. 18, 1937. For announcement, see also *Journals Guide* (London), Oct. 20, 1937; *Black Dispatch,* Oct. 29, 1937; *Reynold's Newspaper,* Oct. 10, 1937; *Daily Worker,* Nov. 4, 1937.

55. PR qtd. in *Daily News Chronicle,* Nov. 8, 1937.

56. PR qtd. in *Journals Guide,* Nov. 20, 1937.

57. *Daily News Chronicle,* Oct. 9, 1937; *Reynold's Newspaper,* Oct. 10, 1937.

58. *Reynold's Newspaper,* Oct. 10, 1937; also Rudolph Dunbar, *Black Dispatch,* Oct. 10, 1937.

59. *Journals Guide,* Oct. 20, 1937; *News Review,* June 9, 1938. See also Sidney Cole interview with PR, "Paul Robeson Tells Us Why," *Cine-Technician,* Sept.–Oct., 1938.

60. Noble interview, Oct. 29, 1974.

61. Bootman interview, Nov. 10, 1974.

62. Interview with Andre Van Gyseghem, Nov. 4, 1974. Unity's summer school sessions were held at A. S. Neill's Summerhill School in Leiston, Suffolk, and included dormitory facilities for up to seventy people. Lecturers included Herbert Marshall, John Allen, Maurice Brown, Alan Bush, Flora Robson, Michel St. Denis, John Fernald, Andre Van Gyseghem, S. I. Hsiung, and Paul Robeson (*Tribune* [London], Sept. 30, 1938).

63. Nearly 400 volunteers from London's various trade unions had transformed the old Methodist church into a technically modern, well-equipped theater capable of seating 330. Not only trade union volunteers but *all* Unity members, even those unskilled in the building trades like Joyce Herbert (daughter of author and member of Parliament A. P. Herbert), who was pictured by the *Sunday Dispatch* working far into the night after a long day of her own work, pitched in.

64. O'Casey conveyed the hope that Unity would "smash the myth that culture and the enjoyment of art are confined to what is sometimes called 'the better class.'"

65. In the United States the play carried off first prize in the American New Theatre League Competition and later won a competition judging the best plays from the British Isles (*New Review*, June 9, 1938; Bootman interview, Nov. 10, 1974).

66. *New Review*, June 9, 1938; *Reynold's Newspaper*, Oct. 31, 1937.

67. 1938 Unity Press Release, Bram Bootman Unity Theatre Scrapbook, Nov. 4, 1936–Dec. 30, 1938 (National Museum of Labour History, Manchester); see also Bram Bootman papers, personal collection.

68. Bootman interview, Nov. 10, 1974.

69. "Unity Theatre," a handwritten reminiscence by Mike O'Connell, ca. 1963.

70. Noble interview, Oct. 29, 1974.

71. Interview with Norman Bedow, Nov. 3, 1974.

72. Bootman interview, Nov. 10, 1974.

73. Ibid. An advertisement for Irwin Shaw's *Bury the Dead* in the same flyer made no mention of any specific actor.

74. *New Statesman and Nation*, June 25, 1938.

75. *Times* (London), June 15, 1938; J. K. Prothero, "The Drama," *Weekly Review* 27, no. 15 (June 23, 1938).

76. Fan qtd. in *New Statesman and Nation*, June 25, 1938.

77. Prothero, "The Drama"; *New Statesman and Nation*, June 25, 1938; E.P.M., *Daily News Chronicle*, June 15, 1938; *Reynold's Newspaper*, June 19, 1938.

78. Van Gyseghem interview, Nov. 4, 1974.

79. Other speakers included producer-director Maurice Browne, Luther Adler of New York's Group Theatre, and Kingsley Martin, editor of the *New Statesman and Nation*.

80. *Daily Worker*, July 16, 1938; *Daily News Chronicle*, July 16, 1938; *Daily Telegraph*, July 14, 1938.

81. Members of Unity's General Council included Harold Laski, Miles Malleson, Sean O'Casey, D. N. Pritt, KC, MP, Maurice Brown, Alan Bush, Lewis Casson, Sir Stafford Cripps, KC, MP, Michel St. Denis, Victor Gollancz, Tyrone Guthrie, Joseph Reeves, Paul Robeson, and G. R. Strauss, MP.

82. ER to Herbert Marshall, June 27, 1938. "I have been over the schedule, and find that we can, with difficulty play until July 8th" (qtd. in Ron Travis, "The Unity Theatre of Great Britain, 1936–1946: A Decade of Production" [Ph.D. diss., University of Southern Illinois, 1968], 84).

83. Unnamed paper, Aug. 19, 1938.

84. *Daily Worker*, May 25, 1936. See also Nina Fishman, *The British Communist Party and the Trade Unions, 1933–45* (London: Ashgate Publishing, 1995).

85. Will Paynter, *My Generation* (London: Allen and Unwin, 1972), 63, 78. Hywel Francis, "Welsh Miners and the Spanish Civil War," *Journal of Contemporary History* 5, no. 3 (1970): 170, 177–90, and *Miners against Fascism: Wales and the Spanish Civil War* (London: Lawrence and Wishart, 1984), 61–83, 249.

86. For example, local memorial meetings were held at Abercave, Aberdare, Ammanford,

Cardiff, Fforestfach, Mardy, Orgmore, Vale, Seven Sisters, Tonypandy, and Trealaw. See Francis, *Miners against Fascism,* 248–49.

87. Rich Ruda interview with David Francis, Mar. 14, 1975.

88. *Western Mail,* Dec. 8, 1938; Francis, *Miners against Fascism,* 249.

89. Hannen Swaffer wrote a stirring account of the services in the *Daily Herald,* Jan. 9, 1938; 2,762 British volunteers fought for Spain; 1,747 of these men were wounded, and 543 died.

90. On Jan. 9, 1939, the *Daily Herald* wrote: "The Church has proved itself to be an unreliable leader in political affairs. . . . the Catholic press cannot be believed when it talks about Spain."

91. Ibid. On Pollitt see Kevin Morgan, *Harry Pollitt* (Manchester: Manchester University Press, 1993); Harry Pollitt, *Serving My Time: An Apprenticeship to Politics* (London: Lawrence and Wishart, 1940).

92. *Daily Record,* Jan. 26, 1939. Others signing the letter to Roosevelt included Walter Damrosch, Jessica Dragonette, Lawrence Tibbett, Sigmund Spaeth, Ephrem Zimbalist, Yehudi Menuhin, and Rosina and Josef Lehevinne.

93. In attendance at the Society for Cultural Relations dinner were Victor Gollancz, Ivor Montague, Philip Noel Baker, Julian Huxley, J. M. Keynes, H. J. Laski, E. M. Forster, Kingsley Martin, Sir William Rothenstein, R. H. Tawney, Beatrice Webb, and Virginia Woolf, to name a few.

94. *Daily Express,* Apr. 3, 1939; *Observer,* Apr. 2, 1939; *Daily Telegraph,* Apr. 3, 1939.

95. *South Wales Evening Post,* Jan. 1, 1939; also reported in *Sheffield Telegraph,* Feb. 24, 1939.

96. Eugene Gordon interview with PR, *Sunday Worker,* June 17, 1939.

97. *Lancashire Daily Post,* Mar. 6, 1939; *Yorkshire Observer,* Jan. 12, 1939.

98. Unnamed paper, Mar. 13, 1939.

99. *Express and Star* (London), Jan. 23, 1939.

100. Unnamed paper, Mar. 20, 1939.

101. *Birmingham Gazette,* Mar. 7, 1939; *Journal* (Nottingham), Feb. 22, 1939.

102. *Aberdeen Express,* Jan. 18, 1939.

103. Ibid.; *Daily Mail,* Jan. 14, 1939.

104. *Stafford Sentinel,* Feb. 24, 1939; *Belfast Telegraph,* Mar. 28, 1939; *Midland Daily Telegraph,* Apr. 3, 1939.

105. *Cambridge Daily News,* Mar. 3, 1939.

106. *Stafford Sentinel,* Feb. 24, 1939.

107. *Birmingham Gazette,* Mar. 7, 1939.

18. GOING HOME

The first epigraph to this chapter can be found in Susan Robeson, *The Whole World in His Hands: A Pictorial Biography of Paul Robeson* (Secaucus, N.J.: Citadel, 1981), 248. (The quote also appears in "My Father Was a Slave," an interview with PR, *Forward,* June 11, 1938, and a variation of it in *News Review,* June 9, 1938.) The second quote can be found in *Express and Star,* Jan. 23, 1939.

1. ER to Robert Rockmore, qtd. in Anatol Schlosser, "Paul Robeson: His Career in the Theatre, in Motion Pictures, and on the Concert Stage" (Ph.D. diss., New York University, 1970), 38.

2. PR, *Here I Stand* (1958; reprint, Boston: Beacon Press, 1971), 54.

3. PR, "Here's My Story," *Freedom,* April 1951 (reprinted in *Paul Robeson Speaks: Writings, Speeches, Interviews, 1918–1974,* ed. Philip S. Foner [Secaucus, N.J.: Citadel, 1978], 270–72).

4. Hywel Francis, "Welsh Miners and the Spanish Civil War," *Journal of Contemporary History* 5, no. 3 (1970): 183; Julia Dorn, "Paul Robeson Told Me," *TAC* [Theatre Arts Committee] 1, no. 12 (1939): 23; M. H. Halton, "Negro Free When All Men Emancipated, Says Robeson," unnamed newspaper, 1938; PR, *Here I Stand,* 53–54.

5. *Amsterdam News,* May 20, 1939.

6. Robert Rockmore to Larry Brown, Feb. 21, 1938, Lawrence Brown Papers, Schomburg Collection, New York Public Library; NAACP Papers, Box 218, File Spingarn Medal. (Dr. Louis Wright won the Spingarn Medal in 1940.)

7. See, for example, *Daily Worker,* May 9, 15, 16, June 12, 15, 28, 29, July 12, and Aug 19, 1939.

8. Interview with Fred Schang, Oct. 25, 1978. In addition to Robeson, Schang also managed such artists as tenor Enrico Caruso and violinist David Oistrakh. See *New York Times,* Aug. 29, 1990.

9. While in England, Robeson said nothing publicly about returning to America, but once he was on American soil, he all but announced his intended return. PR interviewed by Eugene Gordon, *Sunday Worker,* June 4, 1939 (reprinted in *Chicago Defender,* June 17, 1939).

10. Kelly Miller, *Amsterdam News,* Dec 18, 1929; PR qtd. in *Amsterdam News,* May 27, 1939, and *Chicago Defender,* May 27, 1939. See also *Pittsburgh Courier,* June 10, 1939.

11. On Robeson's earlier views see "Robeson's Amazing Attack on Americans," *Daily Express* (London), Aug. 3, 1933, and responses in *Amsterdam News,* Aug. 23 and Sept. 2, 1933, and various Robeson articles and interviews, including "The Culture of the Negro," *Spectator* (London), June 15, 1934, 916–17; "Negroes Don't Ape Whites," *Daily Herald* (London), Jan. 9, 1935, reprinted as "I Don't Want to Be White" in *Chicago Defender,* Jan. 26, 1935; and "Paul Robeson on the Negro Race," *Jamaica Gleaner* (British West Indies), July 17, 1935. PR interviewed by Julia Dorn, "Paul Robeson Told Me."

12. PR interviewed by Gordon, *Sunday Worker,* June 4, 1939. See also the *Chicago Defender,* June 17, 1939.

13. *New York Daily News,* June 20, 1939.

14. Sidney B. Whipple, *New York World Telegram,* June 22, 1939; Vernon Rice, *New York Post,* June 20, 1939.

15. Walter White to PR, May 13, 1939, and ER (from London) to White, May 31, 1939, NAACP Papers, File May–Dec. 1939, Box C-221. Schang interview, Oct. 25, 1978. Other black artists White contacted were Marian Anderson and Hubert Delaney.

16. M. S. Novik to White, June 19, 1939; White to Novik, June 20, 1939, NAACP Papers, File 1939, Box C-222.

17. Fania Marinoff to Carl Van Vechten, Aug. 3, 1939, Carl Van Vechten Papers, New York Public Library; Van Vechten to Marinoff, Aug. 4, 1939, in *Letters of Carl Van Vechten,* ed. Bruce Kellner (New Haven: Yale University Press, 1987), 167–68; ER to Van Vechten, Aug. 19, 1939, Yale University; Van Vechten to Marinoff, Aug. 29, 1939, in Kellner, *Letters,* 167–68.

18. Interviews with Helen Rosen, Feb. 9, 1981; William Schatzkammer, Sept. 20, 1975; Fredda Brilliant, Feb. 14, 1975; and Antonio Salemme, Sept. 7, 1976.

19. See Mark Naison, *Communists in Harlem during the Depression* (New York: Grove Press, 1983), and Mark Solomon, *The Cry Was Unity: Communists and African Americans, 1917–1936* (Jackson: University Press of Mississippi, 1998). On blacks in the Communist Party, see also Harold Cruse, *The Crisis of the Negro Intellectual* (New York: Morrow, 1967); Philip S. Foner and James S. Allen, eds., *American Communism and Black Americans: A Documentary History, 1919–1929* (Philadelphia: Temple University Press, 1987); Philip S. Foner and Herbert Shapiro, eds., *American Communism and Black Americans: A Documentary History, 1930–34* (Philadelphia: Temple University Press, 1991); Earl Ofari Hutchinson, *Blacks and Reds: Race and Class in Conflict, 1919–1990* (East Lansing: Michigan State University Press, 1995); and Theodore Kornweibel Jr., *Seeing Red: Federal Campaigns against Black Militancy, 1919–1925* (Bloomington: Indiana University Press, 1998).

20. Naison, *Communists in Harlem,* 31–37; Solomon, *Cry Was Unity,* 96–97.

21. The trial began and finished with astonishing speed, opening on April 6, 1931, and ending with a guilty verdict on April 9. On April 10 the ILD attorney Allen Taub and organizer Douglas McKenzie announced that the ILD had been retained by the defendants and would file an appeal for a new trial. The Supreme Court overturned the Scottsboro convictions in November 1932, ordering new trials on the grounds that the defendants had not received adequate counsel. See Dan T. Carter, *Scottsboro: A Tragedy of the American South* (1969; reprint, Baton Rouge: Louisiana State University Press, 1979); Solomon, *Cry Was Unity;* Naison, *Communists in Harlem;* Charles H. Martin, "The International Labor Defense and Black America," *Labor History* 26 (Spring 1985); and Hugh T. Murray Jr. "The NAACP versus the Communist Party: The Scottsboro Rape Case, 1931–1932," *Phylon* 28 (1967).

22. PR, "Here's My Story," reprinted in Foner, *Paul Robeson Speaks,* 283; PR interview with Julia Dorn, "I Breathe Freely," *New Theatre,* July 1935, 5.

23. Solomon, *Cry Was Unity,* 113–14; Benjamin J. Davis, *Communist Councilman from Harlem: Autobiographical Notes Written in a Federal Penitentiary* (New York: International Publishers, 1969), 53–100.

24. Davis, *Communist Councilman from Harlem,* 25, 27, 45.

25. Naison, *Communists in Harlem,* 60–61, and Solomon, *Cry Was Unity,* 185–206.

26. *New York Age,* June 24 and July 8, 1939.

27. PR to ER, Western Union cablegram, July 14, 1939, Robeson Collections (PR Jr.).

28. *New York Age,* June 24 and July 8, 1939.

29. PR qtd. in *Daily Worker,* July 21, 1939; *Daily Worker,* June 12, 29, and July 21, 1939.

30. On Harlem theater during the Depression years, see Annette T. Rubenstein, "The Cultural World of the Communist Party: An Historical Overview," in *New Studies in the Politics and Culture of U.S. Communism,* ed. Michael E. Brown, Randy Martin, Frank Rosengarten, and George Snedeker (New York: Monthly Review Press, 1993), 248–60; Naison, *Communists in Harlem,* 204–9, 272–73.

31. On McClendon, see Darlene Clark Hine, ed., *Black Women in America: An Historical Encyclopedia,* vol. 2 (New York: Carlson Publishing, 1993), 765–66. On the Federal Theatre, see Hallie Flannagan, *Arena: The History of the Federal Theatre* (1940; reprint, New York: Arno Press, 1980), 62–63, 435.

32. Interview with Leonard de Paur, Mar. 12, 1998. On de Paur, see *Amsterdam News,* Feb. 25, 1989; Raymond Ericson, "Changing Lincoln Center's Image," *New York Times,* Oct. 10, 1971; and Elizabeth Hanly, "Leonard de Paur: President of the West Side Chamber of Commerce," *West Side TV Shopper,* Jan. 15–21, 1983, 17.

33. De Paur interview, Mar. 12, 1998.

34. *Amsterdam News* July 22, 1939; PR interview with Eugene Gordon, *Sunday Worker,* June 4, 1939.

35. PR interviewed by J. Danvers Williams, "Why Robeson Rebelled," *Film Weekly* (London), Oct. 8, 1938, reprinted in *Daily Record* (Chicago), Feb. 28, 1939; PR quoted in *Daily Worker* (London), June 9, 1938, and by Haemi Scheien in "Paul Robeson Wants to Becomes an Amateur," *Drama,* July 1938, 154. See also *Jewish Chronicle,* Nov. 4, 1938.

36. Ken Nelson interview with Fredda Brilliant and Herbert Marshall, Feb. 4, 1975.

37. Ibid.

38. Ibid.

39. Ibid.

40. Ibid.

41. Ibid.

42. Ibid.; ER to Pen Tennyson, July 13, 1939, Robeson Collections (PR Jr.).

43. The National Eisteddfod is an eight-day cultural festival—the largest popular festival of competitive music-making and poetry writing in Europe—which takes place alternately in North and South Wales. *Eisteddfod,* which means "sitting together" or "gathering," has roots dating back over 800 years and evolved from bardic tournaments in which apprentice poets and musicians competed against each other to win a seat of honor in the households of noblemen. Competition among various choirs was fierce, generating the kind of aggressiveness associated with athletic events. "Every valley had a chorus and we literally raided each other for either a bass or a tenor," said Clifford Banfield, a native. "We would promise the good ones anything. Our valley even tried one time to kidnap a tenor, but he wouldn't go" (interview with Clifford Banfield, Aug. 3, 1997).

44. Stephen Bourne, *Black in the British Frame: Black People in British Film and Television, 1896–1996* (London: Cassell, 1998), 34.

45. Historically, the unemployed who took part in Britain's hunger marches "depended completely on the money they could collect en route to buy food and often boots and overcoats" (Will Paynter, *My Generation* [London: Allen and Unwin, 1972], 8).

46. Ibid., 78. These figures are based on the study done by Hywel Francis, "Welsh Miners and the Spanish Civil War."

47. Nelson–Brilliant interview, Feb. 4, 1975.

48. H. V. Morton, *In Search of Wales* (New York: Dodd, Mead, 1932), 318.

49. Interview with Graham Bradley, Aug. 1, 1977.

50. Morton, *In Search of Wales,* 266; interview with Grantham Spear, Aug. 3, 1997.

51. Qtd. in Bourne, *Black in the British Frame,* 248.

52. *Jewish Chronicle,* Aug. 13, 1940; *Sunday Times,* Mar. 10, 1940; C. A. Lejeune, *Observer,* Mar. 10, 1940; *Yorkshire Observer,* Aug. 3, 1940.

53. Anthony Bower, "The Movies—'Proud Valley,'" *New Statesman and Nation* 19, no. 42 (Mar. 9, 1940): 306.

54. On censorship concerning documentary and dramatic presentations of Wales see Peter Stead, "Wales at the Movies," in *Wales, the Imagined Nation: Studies in Cultural and National Identity,* ed. Tony Curtis (Bridgend, Wales: Poetry Wales Press, 1986), 159–80.

55. Qtd. in Bourne, *Black in the British Frame,* 253.

56. The *Daily Worker* echoed this sentiment editorially: "The war is here. It is a war that CAN and MUST be won" (Sept. 4, 1939).

57. Ibid., Sept. 20, 1939.

58. Pollitt was sent to Wales; Campbell to Scotland. R. Palme Dutt, the Party's leading theoretician in Britain, and William Rust took over editing the *Daily Worker.* Pollitt remained outside the good graces of the Party until 1941 when Hitler invaded Russia.

59. Robert Graves and Alan Hodge, *The Long Week-End: A Social History of Great Britain, 1918– 1939,* 2nd ed. (New York: Norton, 1963), 454–55.

60. Victor Gollancz, ed., *The Betrayal of the Left* (London, 1941).

61. Ellen Wilkinson, Victor Gollancz, Sybil Thorndike, and Sir Stafford Cripps were a few of the Labourites who denounced the Soviet Union at this time.

62. PR, Notes, "Soviet Union Politics," 4-page manuscript, ca. 1940, Robeson Collections (PR Jr.).

63. Interview with Joe Andrews, Nov. 13–20, 1974; also interview with Herbert Marshall, Sept. 20–21, 1974.

64. *Amsterdam News,* Oct. 29, 1939.

65. PR interviewed by Ben Davis, *Daily Worker,* Oct. 26, 1939.

INDEX

criticism *cont.*
cert performance, 148; first Brown/PR concert tour (America), 170–71, 172, 173;
Gilpin's performance in *The Emperor Jones*,
91; *The Hairy Ape*, 246–47; *Jericho*, 371;
King Solomon's Mines, 353–54; *Plant in the
Sun*, 394–95; *Porgy*, 188; PR's concert tour
of Great Britain with Essie, 321; PR's first
concert tour of Russia, 362–63; PR at
Albert Hall, 399; PR at Carnegie Hall, 216–
17, 241; PR concert tour of the British Isles,
400; *The Proud Valley*, 417–18; revues in
England and, 195; *Sanders of the River*, 322–
23, 325, 326–27; second Brown/PR concert tour (America), 180, 182–83; *Show
Boat*, 190, 193–94; *Show Boat* film, 336;
Show Boat revival, 253–54; *Simon the Cyrenian*, 90; *Song of Freedom*, 349–50; *Taboo*,
103; *Toussaint L'Ouverture*, 342. *See also*
Celebrity Concert Series
Crowder, Henry, 254, 460n. 25
Cullen, Countee, 115, 141, 207, 250
culture: Eastern, PR and, 300; Western, PR
on, 295–96, 301, 329. *See also* African cul-
ture; society
Cunard, Nancy, 254–55, 374
Czechoslovakia, 395

Dabney, Ford, 136
Dadoo, Yusuf, 324
Dafora, Asadata, 406
Daily Eagle, 177, 216
Daily Express (London), 194, 195, 200, 211,
285, 323, 331, 387; PR on American blacks,
284; on the refusal of London hotels to
accommodate Abbott, 213
Daily Herald (London), 235, 353
Daily Mail (London), 211, 265
Daily Mirror (London), 248, 254, 322, 323
Daily News Chronicle, 377
Daily Sketch (London), 161, 193, 196, 251,
265
Daily Telegraph (London), 196, 211
Daily Worker (Communist), 309, 319, 382,
404, 419, 495n. 58; Paul Jr. and, 372
dance: the Charleston, 116; in *Sanders of the
River*, 321, 326; in *Taboo*, 442n. 3.
Dancer, Maurice, 253
"Daniel in the Lion's Den," 280
Dark Sands (film). *See Jericho*
Darnton, Charles, 103
Davenport, Robert, 56, 62
Davidson, Jo, 410
Davis, Benjamin, Jr., 367, 407, 409, 421

Davis, Burton, 177; on the Brown/PR Com-
edy Theater concert, 180
Davis, Charlie, 99
Davis, John P., 178
Davis, Joseph E., 367
Day, Edith, 189, 190, 205, 335
Dazey, Frank, 176
Dea, Lawrence, 99
Decline and Fall (Waugh), 263
"Deep River," 137, 156, 193, 209, 288, 289,
321, 414
Deeter, Jasper, 90
Delaney, Thornton, 281
De La Tour, H., 285
Delta Sigma Theta, 95
Demarest, William, 44, 47, 71
De Mille, William, 277
Democratic National Convention, 121
Dempsey, Jack, 110
Dempsey-Tunny fight, 177
Dennis, Eugene and Peggy, 361
Denny, Abraham P., 20
Depression, the: Communist Party and Jews in
Great Britain and, 374; Harlem during, 408;
Lafayette Theater's Tree of Hope and, 286
Detroit News, 171
Dett, Nathaniel, 137
Deutsches Theater, 223
Dewey, John, 115
Dickey, James Miller, 6, 7, 9
Dies, Martin, 411, 412
Digges, Dudley, 275, 281
Disher, William, 229, 265
Disher, Wilson M., 265
Dixie to Broadway (musical), 135
Dodge, Mabel, 155
Dorn, Julia, 333
Dougherty, Romeo, 179, 204, 282–83
Douglas, James, 184
Douglas, William O., 443n. 32
Douglass, Sarah Mapps, 11
"Dover to Dixie" (musical), 135, 195
"Down de Lovah's Lane," 147
Draper, Muriel, 153, 309
Drayton, Exodus, 99
Dreiser, Theodore, 154
Drinkwater, John, 91
Drury Lane Theatre, 189–94, 196, 198
Drysdale, Louis, 213, 460n. 23
Duberman, Martin, 94
Dublin, 290
Du Bois, W. E. B., 71–72, 79, 115, 178; in
defense of O'Neill's *All God's Chillun Got
Wings*, 120; as editor of *The Crisis*, 116

film *cont.*
478n. 10, 479n. 24, 479n. 25; *Show Boat*, 332, 333, 334–37; *Song of Freedom*, 343–44, 349–50; stereotypes in, 328, 350; *Toussaint L'Ouverture*, 341–42; *Within Our Gates*, 446n. 99. *See also* Eisenstein

Film Art, 302
Film Weekly, 322
Finland, 419, 420
Fire! (black journal), 178
Fire in the Flint (White), 141, 259
Firth, Raymond, 292
Fisher, Bud (Rudolph), 81, 82, 102–4, 142, 201, 438n. 8; on Harlem cabarets, 135
Fisher, Miki, 1, 260
Fisher, Saul, 1; on PR, 2–3
Fisk Jubilee Singers, 137, 417
Fitzgerald, Eleanor "Fitzy," 164
Fitzgerald, F. Scott, 154
Five-Year Plan (Stalin), 310, 338, 475n. 10
Fletcher, James, 16, 20–21, 24, 28, 39, 428n. 97
folk music, 171, 237, 288, 319, 321, 389, 401; PR and affinity among Russian, Hebrew, and black folk songs, 288, 303, 474n. 8
football: Akron Pros, 92–93, 95–97; bigotry of the Naval Academy team and, 435n. 74; blacks and, 64; in its infancy, Camp and, 436n. 119; in its infancy, colleges and, 46, 47, 63, 433n. 20; in its infancy, public outrage against, 46; Milwaukee Badgers, 108–10; number of black collegiate players (1889–1920), 433n. 20; Ooorang Indians, 109–10; Pollard as a scrub at Brown University, 51; PR at Somerville High School and, 35, 37; PR excluded from restaurants during travel with Rutgers team, 54; the racial and, 50–51; Rutgers v. Newport Naval Reserves, 65–66, 72; Rutgers v. Princeton University, 52–53; Rutgers v. various teams, 63–64, 72–73; Rutgers v. Washington and Lee University, 58–60; Rutgers v. West Virginia University, 61
Forbes, Maj. K., 150
Ford, James, 407
Ford, Wallace, 370
Foreman, Clark, 23
Forum, 301
Foster, Stephen, 99, 238, 288, 471n. 56
"Fourteenth Amendment, The" (PR's senior thesis), 75
France, 410; Communists in, 380, 382; declares war on Germany, 417; enters war against Germany, 419. *See also* Paris; Villefranche

Franco, Francisco, 372, 374; Catholic Church and, 398; Hughes on, 385
Frank, Leo, 55, 356
fraternities at Rutgers, 53, 55
Frazier's, 247
Freeman, Bee, 133
Friede, Donald, 176–77

Gambs, Alexandre, 303
Garden, Mary, 165
Gardner, Ethel, 421
Garland, Robert, 253
Garner, George, 205
Garrett, Budge, 108, 109
Garrett, Eleanor, 160
Garvey, Amy Ashwood, 341
Garvey, Marcus, 80, 325, 408
Gaston, Louis P., 44, 429n. 4
Gaul, Harvey, 171
Gay, Katherine, 143
Gee, Lottie, 99
Gentlewoman (London), 161
Germany, 223, 368, 419, 459n. 7; v. Jews, 357; militarism under Hitler, 306, 357, 374, 383, 395; nonaggression pact with the Soviet Union and, 417, 418; PR's plans to live in, 236. *See also* Berlin
Germany Today: Inside Germany, 358
Gershwin, George, 154
Gibbons, Margaret Potter, 36, 431n. 45
Gilman, Mildred, 141, 153, 158, 159, 160
Gilmore, Frank, 199
Gilpin, Charles, 90–91, 92, 93, 103, 112, 116, 118, 120, 121, 122, 125, 129, 136; Benchley and, 454n. 29; on the black audience of *The Emperor Jones*, 122; v. O'Neill, 116–17
Gish, Lillian, 221
Glover, T. A., 370
"Go Down Moses," 107, 146, 185, 288, 321
Godfrey, Peter, 341
Gold Michael, 117
Goldberg, Rube, 152
Goldie, Wyndham, 328
Golding, Louis, 413
Goldman, Emma, 164
Goldwyn, Samuel, 270, 275
Gollancz, Victor, 375, 376, 419
Gone With the Wind (film), 335, 418
Goode, Eslanda (PR's mother-in-law), 84, 85, 186, 188, 203, 214, 235, 305, 307, 345, 346, 360, 371, 403, 421, 439n. 30; accompanies Paul Jr. to the Soviet Union, 361

Goode, Frank (PR's brother-in-law), 84, 305, 307, 395
Goode, John (PR's father-in-law), 84–85
Goode, John, Jr. (PR's brother-in-law), 84, 305, 306, 307, 309, 316
Gordon, Eugene, 404
Gould, George, 113–14
Graham, Shirley (Du Bois), 36
Grant, William, 99
Great Britain: blacks in, 105–6; Communist Party in, 372, 375, 380, 382; declares war on Germany, 417; "the Empire," 302, 324, 325–26; enters war against Germany, 419; Spanish Civil War and, 365, 392; unemployment in, 373, 415, 465n. 46, 494n. 45. *See also* British, the; England; London; Wales
Green, William "Kid," 16–17
Greene, Lillian, 127
Green Pastures (play), 281
Greensboro Daily News, 119
Greenwich Village, 129, 154, 155, 156, 160, 174; sexual attitudes in, 158
Griffith, D. W., 45, 132
Gunn, Glen Dillard, 172

Haggard, H. Rider, 351, 352–53, 483n. 58
Hairy Ape, The (O'Neill play), 93, 244–49
Haldane, Charlotte, 382, 488n. 11
Haldane, Prof. J. B. S., 382, 392
Hall, Chatwood. *See* Smith, Homer
Hamill, Pete, 191
Hamilton, Cicely, 161
Hamlet (Shakespeare), 61
Hammerstein, Oscar, II, 188, 189, 334, 335
Hammond, John H., 308
Hammond, Percy, 127, 253
Hanau, Stella, 143
Handy, W. C., 116
Hann, William H., 99
Hanrey, Lawrence, 244
Hardwicke, Credic, 189, 190, 335, 353
Hardy, Betty. *See* Salemme, Betty Hardy
Hardy, Thomas, 61
Harlem, 78–79; black social circles, 153–54; Communists and fellow travelers in, 407–9; during the Depression, 408; Lafayette Theater's Tree of Hope, 286; Negro vogue in, 135; optimism of, 81; and PR, 108; public library, 115; radical literati of, 178; in ER's *Paul Robeson, Negro*, 230–31; St. Philips Episcopal Church, 83; Strivers' Row, 87–88; various clubs, 116; various musicians supporting Republican Spain, 384; Works Projects Admin., 410–12

Harlem Children's Aid Society, 258
Harlem Community Art Center, 411
Harlem Musician's Committee for Spanish Democracy, 384
Harlem Renaissance, 79, 117, 129, 135, 149, 151
Harlem Shadows (McKay), 116
Harmony Kings, 99–100, 138, 195, 204, 205, 215
Harper's Bazaar (London), 322
Harris, Frank, 165, 166, 167
Harrison, Richard, 281
Haston, Augusto "Gus," 106
Hathorn, Frank, 61
Hayes, George, 142–43
Hayes, Helen, 410
Hayes, Louise, 142–43
Hayes, Roland, 106, 136–37, 138, 139, 141, 151, 183, 185, 198, 211, 241; audience segregation and, 454n. 41; refuses the Spingarn Medal, 152–53
Hays office, 278
Heart of Darkness (Conrad), 477n. 1
Hebrews. *See* Jews
Henderson, Fletcher, 116
Henley, William Ernest, 99
Henschel, Sir George, 214
Hentoff, Nat, 191
Here I Stand (Robeson), 42, 147, 423n. 7
Herndon, Angelo, 409
Herndon, Milton, 489n. 23
Heyward, Dorothy, 188
Heyward, Du Bose, 188; *The Emperor Jones* and, 275, 276, 281
Higgins, Harold, 56, 82; on PR's disinterest in practicing law, 114
Hitler, Adolf, 209, 306, 365, 368, 374, 395, 419; v. Jews, 357; Olympics and (1936), 358; v. Republican Spain and the Soviet Union, 365
Holiday, Billy, 191, 277
Hollywood (motion-picture industry), 296, 326, 332
Holt, Harold, 212, 237, 288, 318
Holt, Nora, 201
Hooks, Ted, 83
Hoover, J. Edgar, 80
Horner, Arthur, 396, 415
House of Cinema Workers (Moscow), 316
House of Commons, 395
How Green Was My Valley (film), 417
Howard Players, 122
Howard University, 140
Hughes, Langston, 116, 129, 135, 141, 149,

Hughes, Langston *cont.*
153, 178, 201, 207, 359, 384, 407; on blacks in Harlem, 149; on Essie, 159; on Essie's biography of PR, 233; on Franco, 385; Soviet Union and, 305; on Stalin purge trials, 368; on the word "nigger," 178
Hume, Cyril, 177
Hunter, Alberta, 106, 185, 188, 189, 192, 205
Hurok, Sol, 223, 244
Hurst, Fannie, 177
Hurston, Zora Neale, 141, 178, 207
Hutchinson, Leslie, 205, 261
Huxley, Julian, 371
Hylan, John F. (mayor of New York), 125

"I Want to Be Ready," 251
"I've Got a Robe," 265
"If" (Kipling), 61–62
Imperial Hotel, Narragansett Pier, 40, 41
imperialism, 297, 302, 325, 479n. 26; v. fascism, 297; *Sanders of the River* and, 325. *See also* anti-imperialists
Incorporated Stage Society, 339
Independent Labour Party, 365, 380
India League, 299, 324
Institute for Coloured Youth, 11–12, 426n. 52
integration (audiences): in Atlanta, 454n. 41; in Kansas City, 181–82
International African Friends of Abyssinia, 341
International Brigade, 380, 396, 398, 415; British Battalion, 380, 398; Abraham Lincoln Battalion, 384–85; disbands in Britain, 398; disbands in Spain, 396; Welsh miners and, 415
International and Commercial Workers' Union (ICU), 318
International Defense League (ILD), 313, 408–9, 493n. 21
International Film Festival (Moscow), 310
internationalism, 397
Interracial Cooperation Assoc., 80
Intourist, 307
Irish Independent, 322
Irving, Ernest, 413
Ish-Kishor, Salumith, 357
Italy. *See* Mussolini

Jackman, Harold, 250
Jackson, Fay, 371
Jackson, Yolande Olive (Olivia), 252, 258, 260, 467n. 29, 468n. 32; PR's political awakening upon her attitude toward her Indian servants, 266; rejection of PR and, 262–63, 265, 266, 269

James, Cyril Lionel Robert, 319, 320, 324, 325, 339–40; on British colonialism and PR, 299, 365–66; on Kenyatta, 473n. 74; on PR and the Mountbatten scandal, 261
Jamison, J. L., 35
jazz: banned from German radio, 459n. 7; in Europe, 209; in Harlem, 116; as pernicious influence on German values, 209; PR's avoidance of, 201, 237, 264; in *Shuffle Along*, 99
Jenkins, Clarence ("Fat"), 83
Jericho (film), 345, 369–71
Jew Suss (play), 224
Jewish Chronicle, 331
Jewish Transcript, 358
Jewish Tribune, 357
Jews, 12, 144, 145, 356–58; Communist Party and during the Depression, 374; fraternities and, 53, 55; German Jewish refugees, 357; Jewish Theatre (Soviet Union), 311–12; in Nazi Germany, 357–58; Republican Spain and, 380; PR and, 58, 355, 356, 484n. 1; William Drew Robeson and, 31, 356; at Rutgers, 55; in Russia, 311, 314, 359; spirituals and, 144–45; theater in Germany and, 306; Unity Theatre and, 389–90
John Henry (play), 404
Johnson, Charles, 106
Johnson, Charles Spurgeon, 81, 116
Johnson, Hall, 99, 137, 280
Johnson, Jack, 49, 67, 111, 162, 175
Johnson, J. Rosamond, 137, 275
Johnson, James Weldon, 89, 103, 120, 122, 128, 137, 140, 144, 151, 153
Johnson, Manning, 407
Johnstone, Clarence (Tandy), 164, 204
Jolson, Al, 162, 180, 185
Jones, Alan, 334
Jones, Jack, 410
Jones, Robert Edmond, 90
Jordan, Howard, 185
Jordan, Philip, 398
"Joshua Fit de Battle of Jericho," 148, 400
Josten, Werner, 259
Journey's End (Sherriff play), 218
Joyce, James, 185

Kadalie, Clements, 318
Kahn, Otto H., 111, 118, 136, 161, 219, 356
Kamerny Theatre (Moscow), 309, 310
Kansas City, 241, 242
Kansas City Call, 181, 182, 217; v. Bacoté, 183
Kansas City Journal, 182
Kansas City Star, 181

208–9; marries PR, 94–95; v. McKay, 166, 167; meets PR, 84, 88; motherliness toward PR, 158–59, 160; move from apartment in St. John's Wood to house in Hampstead Heath, 207; Paul Jr. and, 249; on PR's enjoyment of London, 163; on PR's happiness in London, 164, 198; PR's social life in Greenwich Village and, 157; PR's social prominence in London and, 206; PR's success on stage and, 154; on PR and the Whites, 142; v. PR over money, 174–75; qualities as a companion to PR, 89; reconciliation with PR, 267–68; relationship with PR, 114–15, 174–75, 232–33; on *Sanders of the River*, 479n. 25; secures loan from Kahn, 161; separation from PR and, 247–48; stars in *Borderline*, 221; surgery, 105, 107; University of Illinois and, 86; in Villefranche, 165–67, 232; visits Spain with PR, 381–82; Wescott and, 232; Wescott on, 250

Robeson, Hattie (William's sister-in-law, wife of Benjamin Robeson), 23

Robeson, John (brother of William Robeson), 23

Robeson, Maria Louisa (Bustill, PR's mother), 10; birth, 11; death, 22–23; gives birth to PR, 18; health, 18, 22; marries William, 14; and physical characteristics of, 12; Quakers and, 14, 426n. 58

Robeson, Marian (Marguerite, sister of PR), 18, 22, 23, 28, 62

Robeson, Paul, Jr. (son of PR), 188, 203, 210, 234, 235, 240, 249, 276, 289, 306, 346, 348–49, 360, 364–65, 371, 420, 421, 469n. 15; birth, 185, 187; on Essie, 257; racism and, 346, 359–60; school in the Soviet Union and, 361, 362, 364, 372; trip to Africa,

Robeson, Paul Leroy
— ACTING: 79, 136; *All God's Chillun Got Wings*, 116, 125–26, 129, 130; *All God's Chillun Got Wings* (repertory), 269, 271–74; Andrews on, 225; *Basilik*, 328–29; *Big Fella*, 355; *Black Boy*, 175–76, 177–79; *Body and Soul*, 132, 133, 134; *Borderline*, 221–22; difficulty finding good roles, 284, 311–12, 312, 327, 337–38, 339, 343; *The Emperor Jones* (film), 269–70, 274–84; *The Emperor Jones* (play), 91, 116–17, 124–25, 130, 131, 161–62; *The Emperor Jones* (revival), 405–6; first adult performance (YWCA), 89–90; Gilpin's fame and, 93; *The Hairy Ape*, 244–49; *Jericho*, 345, 369–71; *King Solomon's Mines*, 351–55; Light as a director and, 123; Murphy on, 277; *My Song Goes Forth*, 350–

51; nervousness with roles, 225; *Othello*, 219–21, 223–27, 235–36; *Plant in the Sun*, 389, 393–95; *The Proud Valley*, 412, 413–15, 417–18; Provincetown Players and, 130; PR as an actor, 229, 272–73, 274, 279–80, 342, 395; PR's desire to do repertory theater, 267; PR's interest in Russian theater, 267, 311–12; PR's need for direction, 225; PR's refusal of stereotypical roles, 222, 336–37, 339, 391; *Roseanne*, 121–22; *Sanders of the River*, 293–94, 296–300, 322; *Sanders of the River*, displeasure with, 323–25, 327; at Somerville High School, 34; *Song of Freedom*, 343–44, 349–50; *Stevedore*, 329–31; *Taboo*, 100, 101, 102–3, 105; *Toussaint L'Ouverture*, 341–42; Van Gyseghem on, 395; *Voodoo*, 105, 107

— ATHLETICS: baseball, 35, 73–74; basketball, 57, 73, 74, 83; Calvin on, 74; Cayton on, 50; coaching the Lincoln University football team, 92–93; Eschenfelder on, 73–74; exclusion from playing Homecoming Day football game against Washington and Lee University, 59–60, 435n. 74; football, Somerville High School, 35, 37; football at Rutgers, 46, 47, 48–50, 51, 53, 54, 61, 63–66, 72–73, 76; football with the Akron Pros, 93, 95–97; football with the Milwaukee Badgers, 108–10; *New York Age* on, 83; *New York Sunday Tribune* on, 65–66; *New York Times* on, 65; *New York World* on, 61; track, 73, 74; Van Fleet on, 74; White on, 52

— CHARACTER: ambition, 203; anger, 1–2, 3, 25, 50, 218, 230, 275, 276, 277, 278, 279, 284, 287, 323, 324, 327, 376; apartness (loneliness), 45, 53, 54, 56, 61–62; charisma, 290, 377, 378, 399, 401; charm, 221, 289; 321, 341; class, 289, 388; compassion, 273, 399; with children and students, 148, 289–90, 307–10, 324–25, 394, 473n. 84, 478n. 5; courting approval of British upper classes, 162–63, 198, 220, 235–36, 263, 265, 267; dignity, 41, 196, 289, 324; depression, 263–65, 269, 406; determination, 45–46; disappearances, 249, 252, 259, 265; Fisher on the psychology of, 3; generosity with audiences, 172, 183, 221, 289, 384, 396, 400; humiliation and, 3, 38, 275; idealism, 315, 393–94; identification with Jews, 365, 388; identification with Russian serfs, 365; identification with working classes, 365, 387, 388, 391, 401, 403; image, concern over his, 234, 256, 260–61, 263–64; impatience with criticisms from American blacks, 242–243;

strelsy and, 38; nearly punches a doorman for refusing entrance, 279; Patterson on, 313; Pitt on, 54; racial freedom in England, 163, 198; in *Show Boat*, 205; PR and colonials, 299–300; PR's loyalty to the Soviet Union and, 309–10, 316–17, 319, 364, 365, 403, 420; PR minimizing racial insults, 151, 163; PR's social prominence in London and, 163–64; 205; PR on the color bar in England, 301; PR on the Spanish people, 366; recognizes that he is black, 265; restaurants in New York and, 176, 275, 277; reviews and, 171, 180; roles and stereotypes, 175; Rutgers graduation speech and, 76–77; social life and, 158, 407; success and, 46; third American concert tour and, 217–18; the upper classes and, 388; various speaking engagements, 299, 300; Wales and, 397, 403; White on, 218; Wittpenn on, 54
— SINGING: 466n. 1; 251, 381, 398–99; American eastern seaboard tour with Fisher, 81; autographs and, 196–97, 399–400; avoidance of jazz, 201, 237, 264; banned from performing, 2; for BBC, 162, 287; in *Black Boy*, 175; blues and, 199, 200, 466n. 1; Brown as mentor of, 140; cancels performance at Albert Hall, 250, 267; at Carnegie Hall, 216–17, 240–41; at church services, 56–57; as a citizen of the world, 402; classical and,182, 211, 236–37, 241, 243, 289; classical repertoire in concerts at the Savoy, 238; at Comedy Theater, 180; in comparison to Bledsoe in England, 244; concert tour of British industrial centers, 238; concert tours of British provinces, 316; concert tour of British seaside towns, 212; concert tours of Europe, 184–85, 208–10; concert tours of the British Isles, 288–91, 399–401; criticism of repertoire, 241; diction, 171, 196, 240, 289; disdain of revues, 198–99, 200–201; Drury Lane concerts, 193–94, 196, 203; first American concert tour, 169–73; second American concert tour, 179–84; third American concert tour, 216–18, 241–42; fourth American concert tour, 252; fifth American concert tour, 334; Boardman on PR studying lieder, 236–37; first concert with Brown, 143–44; first concert tour of Great Britain, 221; first concert tour of Russia, 362–64; foreign languages, 238; Stephen Foster songs, 238; German lieder and, 219, 236–37, 238, 284; in Harlem with Fisher, 83, 103–4; Hayes on, 236–37; for the Intl. Brig., 384, 385; joins the Harmony

Kings in *Shuffle Along*, 99–100; at the London Comedy Club, 398; meets Brown, 138; microphone technique and, 335; at Narragansett Pier, 58; at the Mother AME Zion Church, 410; at Narragansett, 58; for NBC, 258; *New York World* on, 143; in the Pharaoh's Chamber of the Pyramid of Gizeh, 371; in *Plantation Revue*, 111–12; plantation songs, 288–89; *Porgy*, 188; PR on, 388–89; in *The Proud Valley*, 417; recording and, 149, 335, 450n. 42, 476n. 23; first record releases, 173; repertoire at the Palladium, 265; repertoire in concert tour of Great Britain with Essie, 321; at the Royal Albert Hall, 210–11, 251, 381, 388, 398–99; Russian songs, 252, 303; at Rutgers, 54; in *Sanders of the River*, 327; Scandanavia, 316; *Show Boat*, 188–92; *Show Boat* film, 332, 335–37; *Show Boat* revival, 253; social life and, 141–43; at Somerville High School, 34–35; in Spain, 383; for the Spanish Refugee Relief Campaign, 410; on spirituals, 184, 237, 242–43; spirituals and, 143–44, 145–46; *Star* on, 162; various appearances (1924), 143; style, 146–48, 156, 169–70, 171, 190–92, 194, 211, 289, 335, 400, 401; various concerts in the cause of Republican Spain, 386–87; voice and, 170, 171, 173–74, 185, 199, 216; in *Voodoo*, 107; in Wales, 397, 398; women admirers and, 251
— SOCIAL LIFE: the Cunard and Mountbatten scandals and, 256, 260, 261; dancing in Harlem, 83; Eisenstein and, 314–16; friendship with Andrews and, 197–98; greeting party upon first visit to Moscow, 308; Haldane and, 392; Harlem public library and, 115; Hayes and, 142–43; Jackson and, 262–63, 265; James and, 339–42; Light on, 163, 208; Marshall and, 312–13; Moore and, 40; Narragansett Pier and, 41, 57–58; Neale and, 62–63, 435n. 82; Patterson and, 313; political commitments and, 407; Pollard and, 54, 57; posing for Salemme, 154, 156–57; Russian children and, 309–10, 311; at Rutgers, 53–54, 56; Salemme and, 407; social gatherings in Harlem, 154; social gatherings in London, 164, 196, 208; social prominence in London, 205–6; at Somerville High School, 38; Van Vechten and, 142, 406–7; White and, 141, 406; white women at Narragansett and, 58; women and, 156, 157–58, 160, 175, 197, 234, 248, 251, 252, 254
— TRAVEL: America (first concert tour),

Robeson, Paul Leroy *cont.*
169–73; America (second concert tour),
179–84; America (third concert tour), 184–
85, 216–18; America (fourth concert tour),
252; America (fifth concert tour), 334;
avoidance of southern portion of the United
States, 270, 271; Berlin, 222, 223, 306–7;
British Isles (concert tours), 288–91, 399–
401; Cairo to star in *Jericho*, 369–71; Europe
(concert tour), 208–10; first visit to
Moscow, 308; Great Britain (concert
tours), 221, 320; Leningrad, 316; first visit
to London to star in *Taboo*, 105; second visit
to London to star in *The Emperor Jones*, 161–
64; third visit to London to star in *Show
Boat*, 188–92; Paris, 164–65, 184–85, 260,
262; Soviet Union, 351, 361, 371; Spain
with Essie, 381–85; Switzerland to star in
Borderline, 221–22; Villefranche, 165
Robeson, Reeve (John Bunyan, brother of
PR), 18, 22, 23, 24–25, 28, 428–29n. 109
Robeson, Sabra (mother of William Drew
Robeson), 3, 5
Robeson, William Drew (father of PR), 17,
18, 23, 198, 356, 428n. 105; Africa and,
425n. 43; African Methodist Episcopal
Zions and, 25; ambition for children, 28;
and Bustill family, 23; children of, 18; death,
69; dismissal from Witherspoon pastorate,
18–21; escape from slavery, 4–5; faltering
of, 18; humiliation and, 3, 21, 26, 28; illness,
68; as an itinerant preacher, 22; Lincoln
University and, 5–10, 425n. 43; marries
Maria, 14; as an orator, 8–9, 33; and physical characteristics of, 12; and PR's disobe-
dience of, 27; PR's education and, 32, 33;
PR's exclusion from the Rutgers Homecoming Day football game and, 59; personal
characteristics of, 13, 17, 18, 21, 36; politics
of, 8, 13, 20; poverty of, 17, 21, 22; publicizing his children's accomplishments, 56;
racial slights and, 13, 31; respectability and,
9, 10, 13, 17, 26, 27–28; as a slave, 3, 164,
387–88; Welsh miners and, 416; and whites,
17, 30–31
Robinson, Bill, 410
Robinson, Robert, 313–14
Robson, Flora, 272, 273, 274, 298–99
Rockmore, Robert, 181, 244, 270–71, 333,
357, 402, 406, 468n. 3; Schang on audiences
v. politics and, 403–4
Rogers, Joel A., 122, 179, 185, 264, 282, 341,
404

Romany Marie's, 130
Romilly, Rita, 153
Roosevelt, Eleanor, 469n. 14
Roosevelt, Franklin, 398
Roosevelt, Theodore, 47
Roosevelt theater, 280–81, 283, 470n. 29
Rose, Ernestine, 115
Roseanne (play), 121, 122, 126
Rosenwald, Julius, 356
Ross, Harold, 153
Royal Albert Hall, The (London), 210–11,
250–51, 267, 379–80; benefit for Spanish
refugee children, 376, 277, 379–80, 398
Rudd, Wayland, 305
Run, Little Children! (musical), 244
Runnin' Wild (musical), 116, 135
Russell, Theresa, 133
Russia, Russians: bigotry and, 359; black
music in comparison to music of, 288, 474n.
8; Cayton on, 367–68; folksongs, 149, 288;
foreign artists and, 476n. 38; as a military
threat to the British, 475n. 10; PR's interest
in, 303, 371; PR's view of upon first visit,
307, 316–17; spirituals and, 362–63; theater, 267, 271, 304. *See also* Leningrad;
Moscow; Soviet Union
Rust, William, 382
Rutgers Alumni Quarterly, 67
Rutgers College: awards PR honorary masters
of arts degree, 258; football tradition of, 47;
fraternities, 52; glee club, 34, 54, 158; history, 44; Homecoming Weekend (1916),
58–60; racial etiquette at, 53; racism at, 49–
51, 53–54; PR and alumni, 199; PR, entry
and adjustment, 44; PR wins scholarship to,
41–42; skull and cap award, 74, 437n. 130.
See also football
Rutgers Targum, 74, 76

Sacco and Vanzetti, 152
Sagan, Leontine, 275
Salemme, Antonio, 114, 154–55, 156–57, 159,
160, 179, 191, 207, 235, 255, 407; on PR's
fright of drafts, 173
Salemme, Betty Hardy, 155
Salle Gaveau, 185
Sanders of the River (Korda film), 293–94,
296–300, 321–22, 365, 478n. 10, 479n. 24;
criticism of, 322–23, 325, 326–27; Essie on,
479n. 25; *Mickey Mouse* and, 478n. 10; PR's
displeasure with, 323–25; profit after production costs, 328
San Domingo, 340–41
Sanford, Foster, ("Sandy"), 47–48, 72; PR

songs *cont.*

The Proud Valley, 413–14, 417, 418; PR v. Sissle, 212; religious, 57; in *Sanders of the River*, 327; in *Shuffle Along*, 98, 99–100; spirituals in Russia and, 362–63; in *Voodoo*, 107; "Water Boy," 147; Welsh hymns and, 416–17. *See also* blues, the; minstrels; musicals; poems; recording; revues; spirituals

Songs of Innocence (Blake), 290

Songs of Negro Protest (Gellert/Siegmeister), 362

South, the, 45, 139, 140; Ku Klux Klan and, 80; PR's avoidance of, 270, 271, 275–76, 334; 481n. 51

South Africa, 318, 347, 477n. 1

South Wales, 396–97, 415, 416; National Eisteddfod, 416, 494n. 43

South Wales Evening Post, 399

South Wales Miners Federation, 397

Southern Syncopated Orchestra, 303

Soviet Communism: A New Civilization? (Webb), 359

Soviet National Minority Theatre, 311

Soviet Union, 42, 351, 361, 364–65, 371; American popular music and, 308; artistic freedom in, 312; artists in, 310–12, 338–39; blacks in, 304–6, 475n. 15; construction (1936), 361; economy, 361; and Ethiopia, 320; Essie and PR's first visit, 308; v. fascism, 319, 372, 374; film in, 312–13; minorities in v. the United States, 304, 311, 368; nonaggression pact with Nazi Germany and, 417, 418–19; racial tolerance in 359, 364, 365, 368, 384–85; Paul Jr. and, 361, 362, 364, 372; PR's loyalty to, 2, 318, 364, 365, 368, 403, 420, 421; PR and Russian children and, 309–10; theater in, 311. *See also* Leningrad; Moscow; Russia

Soviet Union Society for Cultural Relations with Foreign Countries (VOKS), 308

Spain, 485n. 31; Catholic Church and, 492n. 90; internationalism and, 397; Intl. Brig. disbands, 396; Loyalist v. Roosevelt, 398; PR and, 376–77; PR on, 366, 488n. 9; PR visits with Essie, 381–85; prejudice in, 489n. 24; Republican, 365, 386, 487n. 2; Republican, Jews and, 380; Republican, Mexican government and, 410; Republican, number of British volunteers, 492n. 89; Republican, relief organizations for, 375; Republican, Unity Theatre and, 392–92; Republican, various supporting black newspapers, 384; Republican v. Franco's

Nationalists (Spanish Civil War), 365, 372, 374, 376, 382, 403, 487n. 2

Spanish Children's Milk Fund, 384

Spanish Refugee Relief Campaign, 410

Special Committee to Investigate Un-American Activities, 411

Spender, Stephen, 376, 382

Spingarn, Arthur, 141

Spingarn, Joel, 141, 153

Spingarn Medal, 153

spirituals, 6, 57, 107, 144–45, 175, 399, 401, 449n. 24; All Soviet Broadcasting Committee and, 308; black audiences and, 170, 182–83, 210, 241–42; in *Black Boy*, 175; Brown and, 137, 138, 139–40; criticism of PR's reliance on, 241; Drury Lane concerts and, 193–94; Epstein on, 171; first Brown/PR concert performance and, 145–48; Gertrude Stein on, 165; at Lincoln, 6–7, 9; minstrels v. PR and, 169–70; "Ol' Man River," 190–92, 381; Parisian audiences and, 185; religiousness, 209; PR's repertoire in second concert at Albert Hall, 251; PR and, 142–43; PR on, 184, 237, 242–43; resources, 449n. 24; in revues, PR's objection to, 199–200, 201; slavery and, 144–45; as songs of protest, 362–65; Soviet Union and, 362–63; various black arrangers of, 137; Welsh hymns and, 416–17; whites and, 57

St. Christopher Club, 104

St. Christopher's basketball team, 83

St. Louis Blues (film), 275

St. Philip's Episcopal Church, 83

Stafford Sentinel, 400

Stagg, Amos Alonzo, 96

Stalin, Joseph V., 310, 319, 338, 364, 368; v. fascism, 319; Five-Year Plan, 310, 335; purges and, 362, 366–68

Star (London), 161, 162, 274; on PR's singing, 162

The Stars Look Down (film), 417

"Steal Away," 147, 173, 190, 193, 307, 321

Stein, Gertrude, 164–65

Stephen, Nan Bagby, 121

Stern, G. B., 165

Stevedore (Sklar play), 329; blacks in, 330; criticism, 331–32; stages for, 331

Stone, Harlan, 82, 104

Stone, Percy, 176

Straight, Mrs. Willard, 118

Strange, Michael, 185

strikes, 390; in British colonies, 490n. 38

Strivers Row, 87, 94

Stuckey, Sterling, 425n. 43

SHEILA TULLY BOYLE

received her education at Regis College and Boston College. She works as an editorial
manager for Houghton Mifflin Publishing Company in Boston and currently lives
with her husband, Thomas Boyle, in Malden, Massachusetts.

ANDREW BUNIE

is a Professor of History at Boston College and the author of *The Negro in Virginia
Politics: 1902–1967* (1967) and *Robert L. Vann of the Pittsburgh Courier: Politics and Black
Journalism* (1974). He is currently working with Francis (Mickey) Roache, former
Boston police commissioner, on Roache's autobiography.